TECHNICAL REPORT #23

MOTIVATION AND SECOND LANGUAGE ACQUISITION

edited by

ZOLTÁN DÖRNYEI & RICHARD SCHMIDT

SECOND LANGUAGE TEACHING & CURRICULUM CENTER
University of Hawai'i at Mānoa

The contents of this Technical Report were developed under a grant from the US Department of Education (CFDA 84.229, P229A990004). However, the contents do not necessarily represent the policy of the Department of Education, and one should not assume endorsement by the Federal Government.

ISBN 0–8248–2458–X

(∞)ᵀᴹ The paper used in this publication meets the minimum requirements of the American National Standard for Information Sciences–Permanence of Paper for Printed Library Materials.

ANSI Z39.48–1984

Book design by Deborah Masterson

Distributed by
University of Hawai'i Press
Order Department
2840 Kolowalu Street
Honolulu, HI 96822

ABOUT THE NATIONAL FOREIGN LANGUAGE RESOURCE CENTER

THE SECOND LANGUAGE TEACHING AND CURRICULUM CENTER of the University of Hawai'i is a unit of the College of Languages, Linguistics and Literature. Under a grant from the US Department of Education, the Center has since 1990 served as a National Foreign Language Resource Center (NFLRC). The general direction of the Resource Center is set by a national advisory board. The Center conducts research, develops materials, and trains language professionals with the goal of improving foreign language instruction in the United States. The Center publishes research reports and teaching materials; it also sponsors a summer intensive teacher training institute. For additional information about Center programs, contact:

Dr. Richard Schmidt, Director
National Foreign Language Resource Center
1859 East-West Road #106
University of Hawai'i
Honolulu, HI 96822

email: nflrc@hawaii.edu
web site: http://www.LLL.hawaii.edu/nflrc/

CONTENTS

PREFACE

This volume contains the largest-ever collection of studies on motivation in the second language (L2) field. All the papers in it are original studies, appearing in print for the first time. Some were presented in a state-of-the-art colloquium on L2 motivation at the annual meeting of the American Association for Applied Linguistics (Vancouver, 2000), whereas others were specifically commissioned for this collection. As editors, we are particularly pleased that so many researchers have accepted our invitation and contributed to the book, covering a comprehensive list of topics. Thus, as has been our original intention, the present volume offers a representative cross-section of current thinking on L2 motivation and outlines a number of exciting and potentially fruitful future research directions.

Without trying to give a systematic overview of the rich content of the 20 chapters, we would like to highlight some noteworthy aspects. To start with, we consider it a significant step in research on motivation in second and foreign language learning that traditional quantitative research methodologies are increasingly complemented by qualitative approaches. The qualitative studies in this book provide firm evidence that various interpretative approaches are very well suited to the investigation of motivational dynamics and motivational thinking and will hopefully inspire further research in this vein. On the other hand, as if to prove that quantitative techniques are not to be discarded either, this volume contains reports of some particularly large-scale investigations in locations as diverse as Hawai'i, Hungary, Israel, and Spain, involving nearly 10,000 participants. Other studies present data from another seven countries (Bahrain, Brazil, Canada, Egypt, Finland, Ireland, and Japan), and the target languages investigated are also numerous: Arabic, Chinese, English, Filipino, French, German, Hindi, Italian, Japanese, Russian, and Spanish. The participants range from children to adults, in second, foreign, and heritage language learning situations.

To give a taste of the richness of the various issues discussed in the chapters, let us mention a few topics that have received little attention before: the interrelationship between motivation and learning strategy use; motivational self-regulation and the role of learner autonomy; teacher motivation and its impact on student motivation; task motivation; the role of cognitive attributions; learning as mental foraging; and the willingness to communicate. We are also pleased that several chapters explicitly address methodological questions relevant to this area of research.

In sum, the colorful palette of topics and issues covered in this book indicates that L2 motivation research has reached maturity and that the motivational basis of second language acquisition is fertile ground for research. We sincerely hope that the studies in this book will successfully contribute to the renaissance of research on motivation observed during the past seven or eight years. Editing this book has been a real learning experience, and we are pleased to share this experience with a wider audience of readers.

Zoltán Dörnyei
School of English Studies
University of Nottingham

Richard Schmidt
Department of Second Language Studies and NFLRC
The University of Hawai'i at Mānoa

Robert C. Gardner
University of Western Ontario

INTEGRATIVE MOTIVATION AND SECOND LANGUAGE ACQUISITION

Author's note

Preparation of this manuscript was facilitated by a grant (410–99–0147) from the Social Sciences and Humanities Research Council of Canada. I would like to express my appreciation to Anne-Marie Masgoret, Ljiljana Mihic, and Vicki Galbraith for their assistance with its preparation. This manuscript was the basis of a presentation by the author at the annual meeting of the American Association of Applied Linguistics in March, 2000, in Vancouver, Canada.

INTRODUCTION

The concept of integrative motivation is considered by many researchers and scholars to be a factor involved in learning a second language. The term is used frequently in the literature, though close inspection will reveal that it has slightly different meanings to many different individuals. My intention today is to discuss the meaning of the term in the context of the socio-educational model of second language acquisition (Gardner, 1985a, 2000). I do not intend by this to indicate that this is the only meaningful definition, nor that other definitions are necessarily flawed. This concept is used in a number of theoretical models of the second language learning process (see, for example, Clément, 1980; Dörnyei, 1994; Schumann, 1978), while other models use elements conceptually very similar to it (e.g., MacIntyre, Clément, Dörnyei, & Noels, 1998). This is perfectly reasonable, but it is also the case that different interpretations can lead to difficulties in communication. I hope that by focussing attention on the concept of integrative motivation as it relates to the socio-educational model of second language acquisition (Gardner, 1985a, 2000), some ambiguity might be eliminated. As a consequence, I plan to review the historical roots of the socio-educational model and to identify the major features of the model and its associated research.

In this presentation, I hope to emphasize four major points, which can be summarized as follows:

1. Integrative motivation is a complex of attitudinal, goal-directed, and motivational variables.

Gardner, R. C. (2001). Integrative motivation and second language acquisition. In Z. Dörnyei & R. Schmidt (Eds.), *Motivation and second language acquisition* (Technical Report #23, pp. 1–19). Honolulu: University of Hawai'i, Second Language Teaching and Curriculum Center.

2. The concept of integrative motivation assumes that

    a. Second language acquisition refers to the development of near-native-like language skills, and this takes time, effort, and persistence.

    b. Such a level of language development requires identification with the second language community.

3. There is an important distinction between integrative motivation and an integrative orientation.

4. Theory should be accompanied by measuring instruments and research directed to testing the adequacy of the theory.

HISTORICAL ANTECEDENTS OF THE SOCIO-EDUCATIONAL MODEL

The concept of integrative motivation is associated with a social psychological interpretation of second language acquisition for a number of reasons, some of which are historical. In 1945, Arsenian devoted a section of his review article on bilingualism to "Social Psychology of Language and Bilingualism." In this section, he discussed factors such as the relation between language and acculturation, and between affect, intergroup relations and language learning. Later, Markwardt (1948) identified five motives that he felt were important for language learning. Three of them, he characterized as practical (i.e., assimilation of an ethnic minority, trade and commerce, and scientific utility), and two as non-utilitarian (self-cultural development and maintenance of ethnic identity of a minority group). Two other articles focussed attention on the role of self-identity and affect in second language learning. One was a case study by Nida (1956) of a missionary who was not able to learn the language of the group with which he was to work. According to Nida, this individual was the son of immigrants, and he had reacted against this background, developing an intense attachment to the English speaking culture of the USA. Nida saw this emotional reaction against anything foreign as the reason for this individual's inability to learn another language.

The second article was an essay on industrial relations. In their essay on "Human problems of U.S. enterprise in Latin America," Whyte and Holmberg (1956) noted that there were a number of problems facing businesses that wished to be successful in Latin America. One that is relevant to the present discussion was that of learning Spanish. They discussed four factors that they felt influenced second language learning. Three of them were *Contact* (with the local community), *Variety of Experience* (using the language), and *Ability* (i.e., language aptitude). The fourth was *Psychological Identification*, by which they meant the capacity for learners to perceive themselves like Latin Americans. In their view, Psychological Identification was perhaps the most important factor in learning the language even in this instrumental setting. They state, "If the employee learns the language simply as a tool to get the job done, then he has little incentive to go beyond 'job English.' If he views language as a means of establishing real bonds of communication with another people, then he has the psychological foundations for language mastery" (p. 15). Note here the distinction between integrative and instrumental orientations. There is often a distinction made between integrative and instrumental motives in second language learning, and it is interesting to find that one of the stronger arguments for an integrative orientation in language study was proposed in the context of industrial relations, which would be typically viewed as an instrumental context (i.e., be successful in business).

The socio-educational model of second language acquisition developed from this background, but the first empirical investigations associated with it can be traced to Lambert's (1955, 1956a, 1956b, 1956c) research on bilingual dominance and the development of bilingualism. In this research, he compared three samples of individuals on a number of measures of French-English bilinguality. One group comprised undergraduate students majoring in French, another group was made up of graduate students majoring in French, and the other consisted of French native speakers who had lived for a period of time in an English speaking environment. Lambert (1956c) found consistent patterns of differences among the groups on various measures of French proficiency and bilinguality, and concluded that the development of bilingualism involved passing through a number of barriers. The easiest was the vocabulary barrier, where individuals developed knowledge and use of the elements of the language. The toughest was the cultural barrier, where only very skilled language learners begin to use the language (in this case French) like native speakers. In his research, Lambert (1955) identified two graduate students who had tended to break through this latter barrier. Lambert noted that they were both very highly motivated to learn French, one because he had developed a very strong attachment to France and planned to move there, and another because of her job as a French teacher. Again, you might recognize the distinction between integrative and instrumental motivation that is now part of the literature. Note too, that both motivations presumably led to the development of bilingual skills.

The socio-educational model of second language acquisition grew out of this history. The first study to attempt to measure variables directly relevant to this approach was conducted by Gardner and Lambert (1959). That study focussed on anglophone grade 11 students in Montreal, Canada, studying French as a second language. A factor analysis of a set of variables assessing language aptitude (language learning ability), verbal ability, attitudes, motivation and oral/aural skill in French identified three factors, two of which shared variance in common with the measure of French proficiency. One was defined primarily by the measures of language aptitude and verbal ability, and was identified as *Language Aptitude*. The other was comprised of measures of attitudes toward French Canadians, motivation to learn French, and *Orientation* (in which individuals indicated the relative importance of different reasons, reflecting either integrative or instrumental orientations, for them personally to learn French). This factor was defined as *Motivation*, and was further described as "*characterized by a willingness to be like valued members of the language community* "(Gardner & Lambert, 1959, p. 271).

THE SOCIO-EDUCATIONAL MODEL OF SECOND LANGUAGE ACQUISITION

Following a series of studies, including those by Gardner and Lambert (1972), Gardner and Smythe (1975) proposed a model of second language acquisition that focussed on learning another language in school. Despite the fact that it focussed on the acquisition of the second language in formal (i.e., school) contexts, a basic premise underlying the use of the concept, integrative motivation, was that second language acquisition involves the development of bilingual skill in the language, and that this requires considerable time, effort, and persistence. Often, in our research, we relate the variables of interest to measures of achievement in the second language such as grades in a language class, scores on some objective measure of vocabulary knowledge, grammar, and/or aural comprehension, ratings of oral proficiency, or self-ratings of proficiency, but these are used simply to operationalize achievement in that study. In the socio-educational model, second language achievement is seen to refer to the development of near-native like proficiency, and the various measures used in our studies are just indicators of achievement along the way. Near-native-like proficiency implies a level of expertise, and research on the development of expert behaviour indicates that it requires approximately 10 years of consistent and persistent practice to develop such expertise (Ericsson, Krampe, & Tesch-Römer, 1993). Interestingly, these authors also point out that it takes about this much time to develop the language proficiency of an average adult.

In their model, Gardner and Smythe (1975) identified possible motivational characteristics in terms of four categories, Group Specific Attitudes, Course Related Characteristics, Motivational Indices, and Generalized Attitudes. Later, Gardner (1979) proposed a modification of this general model in which he distinguished between four segments, Social Milieu, Individual Differences, Second Language Acquisition Contexts, and Outcomes. He also presented a schematic model in which it was proposed that attitudes influence motivation, which in turn influences achievement. Furthermore, he proposed that achievement can be exhibited in both linguistic and non-linguistic outcomes, and that these in turn have an influence on attitudes. Thus, the model was seen as a dynamic one in which attitudes and motivation influenced language achievement, which in turn had an influence on subsequent attitudes and motivation. This model has undergone a number of changes since then (see, for example, Gardner, 1985a; Gardner & MacIntyre, 1993a; Gardner, 2000). The most recent version, adapted from Gardner (2000), is presented in Figure 1. This figure shows that two classes of variables, Integrativeness and Attitudes Toward the Learning Situation are two correlated variables that influence Motivation to learn a second language, and that Motivation and Language Aptitude have an influence on Language Achievement.

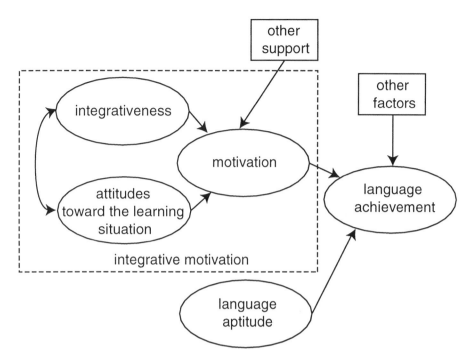

**Figure 1: Basic model of the role of aptitude and motivation
in second language learning**

The variable *Integrativeness* reflects a genuine interest in learning the second language in order to come closer to the other language community. At one level, this implies an openness to, and respect for other cultural groups and ways of life. In the extreme, this might involve complete identification with the community (and possibly even withdrawal from one's original group), but more commonly it might well involve integration within both communities. Since Integrativeness involves emotional identification with another cultural group, the socio-educational model posits that it will be reflected in an integrative orientation toward learning the second language, a favourable attitude toward the language community, and an openness to other groups in general (i.e., an absence of ethnocentrism). In short, the variable of Integrativeness is a complex of attitudes involving more than just the other language community. It is not simply a reason for studying the language.

The variable *Attitudes Toward the Learning Situation* involves attitudes toward any aspect of the situation in which the language is learned. In the school context, these attitudes could be directed toward the teacher, the course in general, one's classmates, the course materials, extra-curricular activities associated with the course, and so forth. This is not meant to imply that the individual necessarily thinks everything about the class is ideal. If the language teacher is ineffective or non-responsive, and so forth, or if the course is particularly dull or confused, and so forth, these factors will undoubtedly be reflected in the individuals attitudes toward the learning situation, but in the model it is recognized that, in any situation, some individuals will express more positive attitudes than others, and it is these differences in attitudes toward the learning situation that are the focus of the model.

The variable *Motivation* refers to the driving force in any situation. In the socio-educational model, motivation to learn the second language is viewed as comprising three elements. First, the motivated individual expends effort to learn the language. That is, there is a persistent and consistent attempt to learn the material, by doing homework, by seeking out opportunities to learn more, by doing extra work, and so forth. Second, the motivated individual wants to achieve the goal. Such an individual will express a strong desire to learn the language, and will strive to achieve success. Third, the motivated individual will enjoy the task of learning the language. Such an individual will say that it is fun, a challenge, and enjoyable, even though at times enthusiasm may be less than at other times. In the socio-educational model, all three elements, effort, desire, and positive affect, are seen as necessary to distinguish between individuals who are more motivated and those who are less motivated. Each element, by itself, is seen as insufficient to reflect motivation. Some students may display effort, even though they have no strong desire to succeed, and may not find the experience particularly enjoyable. Others may want to learn the language, but may have other things that detract from their effort. The point is the truly motivated individual displays effort, desire, and affect. Motivation is a complex concept.

The figure also shows that the three classes of variables, Integrativeness, Attitudes Toward the Learning Situation, and Motivation, form "Integrative Motivation." As conceived in the socio-educational model of second language acquisition, integrative motivation is a complex of attitudinal, goal-directed, and motivational attributes. That is, the integratively motivated individual is one who is motivated to learn the second language, has a desire or willingness to identify with the other language community, and tends to evaluate the learning situation positively. In the model, Integrativeness and Attitudes Toward the Learning Situation are seen as supports for motivation, but it is motivation that is responsible for achievement in the second language. Someone may demonstrate high levels of Integrativeness and/or very positive Attitudes Toward the Learning Situation, but if these are not linked with Motivation to learn the language, they will not be particularly highly related to achievement. Similarly, someone who exhibits high levels of Motivation that are not supported by high levels of Integrativeness and/or favourable Attitudes Toward the Learning Situation may not exhibit these high levels of motivation consistently. Integrative Motivation represents a complex of these three classes of variables.

The model is silent with respect to other attributes of the motivated individual, but clearly an integratively motivated individual, like any other motivated individual, exhibits a number of characteristics. In our research, we have focussed on only the defining attributes in the interest of parsimony. We believe that in our attempts to measures the elements of integrative motivation, we have defined the primary characteristics. Nonetheless, it is obvious that integratively motivated individuals have salient goals in addition to integration with the other community, that they have specific aspirations, that they make attributions concerning their successes and failures, and so forth. The question is, does considering these other aspects appreciably improve prediction of success in learning the second language? Tremblay and Gardner (1995) investigated the elements of the socio-educational model as well as a number of other indices of motivation, and attempted to integrate them into a structural equation model. Using structural equation modelling, they demonstrated that the other motivational variables could be integrated into the model, but that the basic structure of the model was maintained.

Figure 1 shows that there can be other supports for motivation not directly associated with integrative motivation. Thus, there may be instrumental factors contributing to motivation (cf. Dörnyei, 1994), and we could label this combination of instrumental factors and motivation as Instrumental Motivation. Or, there may be other factors such as a particularly stimulating teacher or course that promotes motivation. There is no reason to argue that motivation is driven only by integrative factors.

It is also shown in Figure 1 that other factors might have direct effects on Language Achievement. Thus, research has indicated that language learning strategies (Oxford, 1990), and/or language anxiety (Horwitz, Horwitz, & Cope, 1986; MacIntyre & Gardner, 1989) and/or self confidence with the language (Clément, 1980) influence language achievement, and it is possible that such factors could have a direct effect on language achievement, though they might also have indirect effects through motivation or language aptitude. The model does not attempt to show all the possible links or even all the possible variables, since the intent is to focus attention on the role of integrative motivation.

THE ATTITUDE/MOTIVATION TEST BATTERY

The Attitude/Motivation Test Battery (AMTB) was developed by Pat Smythe and me to assess what appeared to be the major affective factors involved in the learning of a second language. We conducted a number of studies in London, Ontario on students studying French as a second language in regular 30 to 50 minute-a-day programs. The purpose of this research was to develop scales that were internally consistent and valid (see, for example, Gardner & Smythe, 1975, 1981). Once these scales were perfected, we conducted a series of studies in various regions across Canada (see, for example, Gardner, Smythe, Clément, & Gliksman, 1976), and reliability and validity data from this research are presented in an unpublished technical report (Gardner, 1985b).

The AMTB was originally developed for use with English speaking Canadians studying French as a second language. In that form, it currently consists of 11 sub-tests that can be grouped into five categories. Three of the categories, Integrativeness, Attitudes Toward the Learning Situation, and Motivation have

---

been discussed and defined above. One of the remaining two is Instrumental Orientation, which refers to an interest in learning the language for pragmatic reasons that do not involve identification with the other language community. The other is Language Anxiety, which involves anxiety reactions when called upon to use the second language in classroom or non-classroom contexts.

There have been a number of forms of the AMTB over the years, and at least three published articles include the items as appendices. Two of these articles are Gliksman, Gardner, and Smythe (1982), and Gardner, Tremblay and Masgoret (1997) for items in English appropriate for students learning French in grades 7 to 11, and university, respectively. A third article (Clément, Smythe, & Gardner, 1976) presents items in French for francophone school students learning English.

Table 1 presents a listing of the constructs assessed in the AMTB, the subtests that define each construct, and the number of items typically used in each subtest. In addition, a sample Likert item is also presented for each subtest. Unless otherwise specified, the item was taken from a scale in which there were an equal number of positively or negatively worded items. These items were adapted from the study by Gardner, Tremblay, and Masgoret (1997) for all but two of the subtests. The two subtests assessing Attitudes Toward the Learning Situation made use of a semantic differential format in that study. In a current study, we have developed Likert items for these as well, and examples of these items are given instead.

Table 1: Constructs, scales, and sample items from the AMTB

Integrativeness

Integrative orientation (4 positively keyed items)
> sample: Studying French can be important to me because it will allow me to participate more freely in the activities of French Canadians.

Interest in foreign languages (10 items)
> sample: If I planned to stay in another country, I would make a great effort to learn the language even though I could get along in English.

Attitudes toward French Canadians (10 items)
> sample: If Canada should lose the French culture of Quebec, it would indeed be a great loss.

Attitudes toward the learning situation

Evaluation of the French teacher (10 items)
> sample: I really like my French teacher.

Evaluation of the French course (10 items)
> sample: If I knew that more advanced French classes would be like the one I'm in this year, I would definitely take more in the future.

Motivation

Motivational intensity (10 items)
> sample: I keep up to date with French by working on it almost every day.

Desire to learn French (10 items)
> sample: I want to learn French so well that it will become second nature to me.

Attitudes toward learning French (10 items)
> sample: I really enjoy learning French.

Instrumental orientation

Instrumental orientation (4 positively keyed items)
> sample: Studying French can be important for me because I think it will someday be useful in getting a good job.

Language anxiety

French class anxiety (10 items)
> sample: It embarrasses me to volunteer answers in our French class.

French use anxiety (10 items)
> sample: I would get nervous if I had to speak French to someone in a store.

RESEARCH USING THE AMTB

In our research, we have made use of the AMTB, or in some contexts, parts of it, to investigate a number of issues associated with the notion of Integrative Motivation in second language acquisition. Table 2 presents a summary of the topics investigated along with an indication of one relevant publication (in chronological order) for each.

As can be seen in Table 2, many different issues have been investigated using the AMTB. Some studies investigate how scores on this test correlate with measures of second language achievement, some have made use of structural equation modelling to test specific pathways like those indicated in Figure 1, some have focussed on criteria other than achievement in the other language, such as "Continuing or dropping out of the language class the following year." Research on the role of integrative motivation in second language acquisition has considered many issues and, in all instances, integrative motivation has been shown to be implicated.

Table 2: Areas of research involving integrative motivation

topic	representative publication
Language drop outs	Clément, Smythe, & Gardner (1978)
Achievement in intensive immersion programs	Gardner, Smythe, & Clément (1979)
Factor analytic studies	Gardner & Smythe (1981)
Bicultural excursion programs	Desrochers & Gardner (1981)
Language classroom behaviour	Gliksman, Gardner, & Smythe (1982)
Second language attrition	Gardner, Lalonde, Moorcroft, & Evers (1987)
Laboratory studies	Gardner & MacIntyre (1991)
Multi-trait/multi-method studies	Gardner & MacIntyre (1993b)
Other motivational attributes	Tremblay & Gardner (1995)
Trait vs. state motivation	Tremblay, Goldberg, & Gardner (1995)
Structural equation models	Gardner, Tremblay, & Masgoret (1997)
Acculturation	Masgoret & Gardner (1999)
Home background variables	Gardner, Masgoret, & Tremblay (1999)

In some of our studies, we have focussed on scores on the individual subtests, while in others we have used aggregates of these scores, depending on the purpose. There are a number of aggregates that can be formed. For example, aggregates can be computed to provide assessments of the basic components of the model, that is, Integrativeness, Attitudes Toward the Learning Situation, Motivation, and Language Anxiety. Thus, a Motivation score would be computed by summing the scores on Motivational Intensity plus Desire to Learn French plus Attitudes Toward Learning French. Studies by Lalonde and Gardner (1985) and Gardner and MacIntyre (1993b) used this approach to investigate the correlations of the basic components with measures of second language achievement. It is also possible to compute an Integrative Motive Score in which we aggregate the scores on Integrativeness, Attitudes Toward the Learning Situation, and Motivation. Gardner and MacIntyre (1993b) used this to show the relation of Integrative Motivation to measures of proficiency in the second language. And sometimes we have computed an Attitude/Motivation Index (AMI) with one number summarizing behaviour on all 11 tests (e.g., Gardner, 1980). This score is comprised of the Integrative Motivation Score plus Instrumental Orientation minus Language Anxiety. AMI is thus conceived of as a resultant motivation score where the debilitating effects of anxiety are removed. The availability of the Attitude/Motivation Test Battery thus permits us to investigate different questions that relate to the socio-educational model of second language acquisition. These questions are represented in the various articles referred to in Table 2.

Much of this research has been conducted in Canada, and often it involves French as a second language. Recently, there has been a tendency for researchers to distinguish between second and foreign languages and to propose that the dynamics involved in learning these two different types of language may be quite different (see, for example, Oxford, 1996). Often, it is claimed that a language is a second language for an individual if it is readily available in that individual's environment, and the individual has many opportunities to hear, see, and use it. Similarly, it is proposed that a language is a foreign one for the individual if it is the language of a group that is not in close contact with that individual, so that there is little opportunity to meet with members of that language group, or to experience the language first hand. Although this is a very meaningful hypothesis, and it is undoubtedly the case that the social context can well influence the dynamics of learning a second language (cf. Clement & Gardner, in press), care must be taken in classifying studies as involving second or foreign languages as characterized above. For example, most of our studies are described as involving second language learning. This is because most of our research involves Canadians learning either French or English, and both French and English are official languages in Canada. It is not the case, however, that French or English is necessarily readily available in individuals' environments, as is evident by the material presented in Table 3.

Table 3: Population by knowledge of official language in Canada, 1996 census

region	population	percentage English only	percentage French only	percentage English and French
Canada	28,528,125	67.07	14.30	16.97
Newfoundland	547,160	95.99	.03	3.89
Prince Edward Island	132,855	88.88	.13	10.97
Nova Scotia	899,970	90.37	.15	9.33
New Brunswick	729,625	57.29	10.06	32.59
Quebec	7,045,085	5.09	56.09	37.77
Ontario	10,642,790	85.66	.44	11.60
Manitoba	1,100,290	89.41	.14	9.37
Saskatchewan	976,615	94.26	.04	5.20
Alberta	2,669,195	91.98	.06	6.69
British Columbia	3,689,755	90.58	.05	6.74
Yukon Territory	30,650	89.20	.16	10.47
Northwest Territories	64,125	87.14	.07	6.29

Table 3 presents information about knowledge of the two official languages, French and English, in Canada and by province and territory. This information is based on the most recent census in 1996 (Statistics Canada, n.d.). As can be seen, of the total population of 28,528,125 individuals, 67% know English only, 14% know

French only, and 17% know English and French. Phrased slightly differently, 84% (67 + 17) of the population knows English, and 31% (14 + 17) knows French. In this light, one might meaningfully characterize Canada as bilingual, albeit dominantly English.

The picture changes somewhat when attention is directed toward the 10 provinces and two territories. In 10 of these regions, more than 85% of the respective populations know English only, and less than .5% know French only. Moreover, less than 12% in each of the 10 regions report a knowledge of French and English. Thus, 10 of the 12 regions of Canada can hardly be characterized as bilingual in the sense that they provide ample opportunities for individuals to hear and practice their French.

In the other two regions, the percentages of the population that know English only are much lower (57% in New Brunswick and 5% in Quebec), and the percentage that know French only is much higher (10% and 56%, respectively). Moreover, the percentage that know both English and French are 33% and 38%, respectively. These two regions then could be characterized as bilingual communities, and it is clear that opportunities exist to experience both languages.

This distinction is important when considering research conducted in Canada. Since Canada is officially a bilingual (French/English) country, either of the two languages is by definition a second language, even though many regions in Canada cannot be characterized as bilingual communities. Thus, if we were to use the defining characteristics of availability to distinguish between second and foreign language learning, many of the studies referred to in Table 2 would have to be classified as involving foreign language learning — which would not be appropriate given the official bilingual status of these two languages in Canada.

One point that has been emphasized in our research is that the two variables, Integrativeness and Attitudes Toward the Learning Situation are considered to be supports of Motivation, but that Motivation is seen to be the major determinant of Language Achievement. This doesn't mean that scores on the measures of Integrativeness and Attitudes Toward the Learning Situation will not correlate with Language Achievement. They might very well do so. It is expected, however, that scores on Motivation will correlate more highly with indices of Language Achievement. The following figure summarizes data obtained from our cross Canada investigation. These data were derived from an article by Lalonde and Gardner (1985). The results are presented here to show how the three components relate to three different measures associated with learning a second language, Behavioural Intention to Continue French Study, Grades in French, and scores on Objective measures of achievement in French. That study presented the correlations for 24 samples of students ranging in sample size from 96 to 226, for students in grades 7 to 11. Of the 216 correlations calculated, 176 (81%) were significant at the .05 level. Figure 2 presents the mean correlations for each attribute for each of the three criteria.

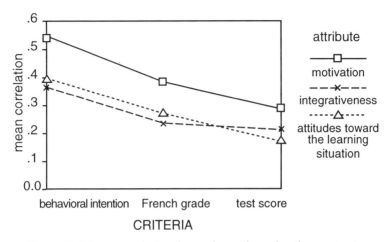

Figure 2: Mean correlation for each attribute for three criteria

As can be seen in Figure 2, the correlations tend to be largest for all three attributes when the criterion is the Behavioral Intention to Study French again the following year, though it is clear that the mean correlation is larger for Motivation than for either Integrativenenss or Attitudes Toward the Learning Situation. The next highest correlations involve the criterion of Grades in French, and again the correlations are higher for Motivation than for either Integrativeness or Attitudes Toward the Learning Situation. A similar pattern holds for the correlations involving the objective tests of French Achievement. Thus, for these samples from various regions across Canada, Motivation is clearly the superior predictor of any of the three criteria, while both Integrativenenss and Attitudes Toward the Learning Situation are similar, but clearly lower correlates. Such results confirm the generalization that Motivation is the primary factor, among these three, accounting for achievement in the second language.

INTEGRATIVE MOTIVATION VS. INTEGRATIVE ORIENTATION

It appears as though some researchers assess orientations or reasons for studying a second language, and equate these with motivation. As I have tried to show in the preceding, however, the operative variable is motivation, not orientation. Also, as indicated in the introduction, the notions of integrative and instrumental approaches to language study can be traced back to Lambert (1955) and Whyte and Holmberg (1956). The first study to attempt to assess these orientations directly was conducted by Gardner and Lambert (1959). That study made use of the Orientation Index, which is reproduced in Table 4.

Table 4: Measures of orientation

The orientation index

Following is a statement with four possible answers given. You are asked to read the statement and then rank the alternatives from "1" to "4" as they refer to you. Mark "1", the alternative most applicable to your case, "2", the next most applicable, and so on.

It may be that you have some reason which has not been included among the alternatives. Item "e" is, therefore, left blank to allow you to include your own personal reason. Insert your reason in the space provided and include it anywhere in the ranking that you think it belongs. If two alternatives appear to be equal, give them the same ranking.

I am studying French because

_____ a. I think it will someday be useful in getting a good job.
_____ b. I think it will help me to better understand the French-Canadian people and their way of life.
_____ c. It will allow me to meet and converse with more and varied people.
_____ d. A knowledge of two languages will make me a better educated person.
_____ e. Any other personal reason.

Sample degree of orientation items

Integrative orientation
sample: Studying French is important because it will allow me to gain good friends more easily among French Canadians.
Instrumental orientation
sample: Studying French can be important to me because I think it will someday be useful in getting a good job.

The Orientation Index presented students with four possible reasons for studying French, and invited them to rank them from 1 to 4 in terms of their personal relevance to them. Two of the reasons were classified as integrative, and two as instrumental. The students were also given the opportunity to write in a reason if they felt it was not covered by one of the four given, and to include it in their ranking. Such reasons were also classified by the researchers as integrative or instrumental. For the purposes of the data analysis, students were classified as either integrative or instrumental based on the item they ranked as most appropriate to them personally.

This measurement decision was unfortunate because it gave the impression that individuals could be classified as either integratively or instrumentally oriented in their study of the second language. In the Gardner and Lambert (1959) study, individuals who were classified as integratively orientated obtained higher scores on the measure of French proficiency than students classified as instrumentally oriented, leading to the conclusion in that study that integratively oriented students were more successful in learning the second language than students who were instrumentally oriented. That study also demonstrated, however, that in comparison with the instrumentally oriented students, those who were integratively oriented were also more motivated to learn French and also had more favourable attitudes toward French Canadians. That is, even in this study, it was demonstrated, as above, that it wasn't just the orientation responsible for the heightened level of achievement but the motivation as well.

In subsequent studies (e.g., Gardner & Lambert, 1972; Gardner & Smythe, 1975), we attempted to assess degree of integrative and instrumental orientations using items like those shown in Table 1. In these items, individuals rated on a seven point scale how strongly they agreed or disagreed with each one. In the different studies, we noted two things. First, generally speaking, scores on Integrative Orientation tended to correlate significantly, and appreciably with scores on Instrumental Orientation. And this is to be expected. It is certainly reasonable to expect that individuals who thought that integrative reasons were applicable for learning French would also endorse instrumental reasons for learning French. Or, alternatively expressed, individuals who felt that it was not important to learn French for instrumental reasons would quite probably feel the same about integrative reasons. The high positive correlations between the two classes of reasons simply indicate that neither class of reasons is mutually independent. The second thing we noted was that often these measures related to the measures of motivation to learn French (i.e., Motivational Intensity, Desire to Learn French, and/or Attitudes Toward Learning French), and sometimes neither was that related to the Orientation Index. Ultimately, in our research, I omitted the Orientation Index as a measure, and instead opted for the measures of Integrative and Instrumental Orientation. The two items shown in Table 4 are from Gardner, Tremblay, and Masgoret (1997).

SUMMARY AND CONCLUSIONS

The purpose of this presentation was to discuss the concept of integrative motivation as it has been investigated in the context of the socio-educational model of second language acquisition, and assessed by means of the Attitude/Motivation Test Battery (AMTB). I attempted to achieve this goal by considering five topics. First, I reviewed the historical antecedents of the Socio-Educational Model, showing where the basic concepts originated. Second, I presented the fundamentals of the Socio-Educational Model and showed how the concepts are currently viewed to be interrelated. Third, I reviewed the nature and contents of the Attitude/Motivation Test Battery, discussing some modifications that have been made over the years. Fourth, I mentioned 13 research topics that have been addressed using the AMTB, and described various ways in which the scales from the AMTB can be aggregated to form scores measuring constructs associated with the model. In this context, I raised the issue of second-language versus foreign-language acquisition and showed how the distinction is sometimes more imaginary than real. Fifth, I discussed the distinction between Integrative Motivation and Integrative Orientation, and attempted to resolve an issue that still pervades much of this literature. I recommended that researchers focus attention on motivation rather than on orientations. There is very little evidence, even in our own research, to suggest that orientations are directly associated with success in learning a second language. Orientations are simply classifications of reasons that can be given for studying a language, and there is little reason to believe that the reasons, in and of themselves, are directly related to success. As I have attempted to show here, motivation is a complex phenomenon, and though the reasons or the goals are part of it, it is the motivation that is responsible for the success.

REFERENCES

Arsenian, S. (1945). Bilingualism in the post-war world. *Psychological Bulletin, 42,* 65–86.

Clément, R. (1980). Ethnicity, contact and communicative competence in a second language. In H. Giles, W. P. Robinson, & P. M. Smith (Eds.), *Language: Social psychological perspectives* (pp. 147–159). Oxford, UK: Pergamon Press.

Clément, R., & Gardner, R. C. (in press). Second language mastery. In H. Giles & W. P. Robinson (Eds.), *Handbook of language and social psychology*. London: Wiley.

Clément, R., Smythe, P. C., & Gardner, R. C. (1976). Echelles d'attitudes et de motivation reliees a l'aprentissage de l'anglais, langue seconde [Attitude and motivation scales related to the learning of English as a second language]. *Canadian Modern Language Review, 33,* 5–26.

Clément, R., Smythe, P. C., & Gardner, R. C. (1978). Persistence in second language study: Motivational considerations. *Canadian Modern Language Review, 34,* 688–694.

Desrochers, A., & Gardner, R. C. (1981). *Second-language acquisition: An investigation of a bicultural excursion experience.* Quebec, Canada: International Centre for Research on Bilingualism.

Dörnyei, Z. (1994). Motivation and motivating in the foreign language classroom. *The Modern Language Journal, 78,* 273–284.

Ericsson, K. A., Krampe, R. T., & Tesch-Römer, C. (1993). The role of deliberate practice in the acquisition of expert performance. *Psychological Review, 100,* 363–406.

Gardner, R. C. (1979). Social psychological aspects of second language acquisition. In H. Giles & R. St. Clair (Eds.), *Language and social psychology* (pp. 193–220). Oxford, UK: Basil Blackwell.

Gardner, R. C. (1980). On the validity of affective variables in second language acquisition: Conceptual, contextual, and statistical considerations. *Language Learning, 30,* 255–270.

Gardner, R. C. (1985a). *Social psychology and second language learning: The role of attitudes and motivation.* London: Edward Arnold Publishers.

Gardner, R. C. (1985b). *The Attitude/Motivation Test Battery: Technical report.* London, Ontario, Canada: Department of Psychology, The University of Western Ontario.

Gardner, R. C. (2000). Correlation, causation, motivation and second language acquisition. *Canadian Psychology, 41,* 1–24.

Gardner, R. C., Lalonde, R. N., Moorcroft, R., & Evers, F. T. (1987). Second language attrition: The role of motivation and use. *Journal of Language and Social Psychology, 6,* 29–47.

Gardner, R. C., & Lambert, W. E. (1959). Motivational variables in second language acquisition. *Canadian Journal of Psychology, 13,* 266–272.

Gardner, R. C., & Lambert, W. E. (1972). *Attitudes and motivation in second-language learning.* Rowley, MA: Newbury House.

Gardner, R. C., & MacIntyre, P. D. (1991). An instrumental motivation in language study: Who says it isn't effective? *Studies in Second Language Acquisition, 13,* 57–72.

Gardner, R. C., & MacIntyre, P. D. (1993a). A student's contributions to second language learning. Part II: Affective variables. *Language Teaching, 26,* 1–11.

Gardner, R. C., & MacIntyre, P. D. (1993b). On the measurement of affective variables in second language learning. *Language Learning, 43,* 157–194.

Gardner, R. C., Masgoret, A.-M., & Tremblay, P. F. (1999). Home background characteristics and second language learning. *Journal of Language and Social Psychology, 18,* 419–437.

Gardner, R. C., & Smythe, P. C. (1975). Motivation and second-language acquisition. *The Canadian Modern Language Review, 31,* 218–230.

Gardner, R. C., & Smythe, P. C. (1981). On the development of the Attitude/Motivation Test Battery. *The Canadian Modern Language Review, 37,* 510–525.

Gardner, R. C., Smythe, P. C., & Clément, R. (1979). Intensive second language study in a bicultural milieu: An investigation of attitudes, motivation and language proficiency. *Language Learning, 29,* 305–320.

Gardner, R. C., Smythe, P. C., Clément, R., & Gliksman, L. (1976). Second language learning: A social psychological perspective. *Canadian Modern Language Review, 32,* 198–213.

Gardner, R. C., Tremblay, P. F., & Masgoret, A.-M. (1997). Towards a full model of second language learning: An empirical investigation. *Modern Language Journal, 81,* 344–362.

Gliksman, L., Gardner, R. C., & Smythe, P. C. (1982). The role of the integrative motive on students' participation in the French classroom. *Canadian Modern Language Review, 38,* 625–647.

Horwitz, E. K., Horwitz, M. B., & Cope, J. (1986). Foreign language classroom anxiety. *Modern Language Journal, 70*, 125–132.

Lalonde, R. N., & Gardner, R. C. (1985). On the predictive validity of the Attitude/Motivation Test Battery. *Journal of Multilingual and Multicultural Development, 6*, 403–412.

Lambert, W. E. (1955). Measurement of the linguistic dominance of bilinguals. *Journal of Abnormal and Social Psychology, 50*, 197–200.

Lambert, W. E. (1956a). Developmental aspects of second-language acquisition: I. Associational fluency, stimulus provocativeness, and word-order influence. *The Journal of Social Psychology, 43*, 83–89.

Lambert, W. E. (1956b). Developmental aspects of second-language acquisition: II. Associational stereotypy, associational form, vocabulary commonness, and pronunciation. *The Journal of Social Psychology, 43*, 91–98.

Lambert, W. E. (1956c). Developmental aspects of second-language acquisition: III. A description of developmental changes. *The Journal of Social Psychology, 43*, 99–104.

MacIntyre, P., & Gardner, R. C. (1989). Anxiety and second language learning: Toward a theoretical clarification. *Language Learning, 39*, 251–275.

MacIntyre, P. D., Clément, R., Dörnyei, Z., & Noels, K. A. (1998). Conceptualizing willingness to communicate in a L2: A situational model of L2 confidence and affiliation. *Modern Language Journal, 82*, 545–562.

Markwardt, A. H. (1948). Motives for the study of modern languages. *Language Learning, 1*, 1–11 (Reprinted in *Language Learning, 38*, (1988), 159–169.

Masgoret, A.-M., & Gardner, R. C. (1999). A causal model of Spanish immigrant adaptation in Canada. *Journal of Multilingual and Multicultural Development, 20*, 216–236.

Nida, E. A. (1956). Motivation in second language learning. *Language Learning, 7*, 11–16

Oxford, R. (1990). *Language learning strategies: What every teacher should know.* New York: Newbury House.

Oxford, R. L. (1996). New pathways of language learning motivation. In Oxford, R. L. (Ed.), *Language learning motivation: Pathways to the new century* (Technical Report #11; pp. 1–8). Honolulu: University of Hawai'i, Second Language Teaching & Curriculum Center.

Schumann, J. H. (1978). The acculturation model for second language acquisition. In Gingras, R. C. (Ed.), *Second language acquisition and foreign language teaching* (pp. 27–50). Arlington, VA: Centre for Applied Linguistics.

Statistics Canada (n.d.). Population by knowledge of official language, 1996 Census, Canada, the provinces and territories. URL http://www.statcan.ca:80/english/Pgdb/People/Population/demo19.html

Tremblay, P. F., & Gardner, R. C. (1995). Expanding the motivation construct in language learning. *Modern Language Journal, 79*, 505–518.

Tremblay, P. F., Goldberg, M. P., & Gardner, R. C. (1995). Trait and state motivation and the acquisition of Hebrew vocabulary. *Canadian Journal of Behavioural Science, 27*, 356–370.

Whyte, W. F., & Holmberg, A. R. (1956). Human problems of U.S. enterprise in Latin America. *Human Organization, 15*, 1–40.

John H. Schumann
University of California at Los Angeles

LEARNING AS FORAGING

Author's note

I want to thank the members of the Higher Cognitive Function Affinity Group and the Behavior, Evolution and Culture Group at UCLA for their comments on earlier drafts of this paper. I also want to thank David Kemmerer, Donald Favareau, and Hans Miller.

Abstract

This paper suggests that learning is a form of foraging. It argues that both activities involve 1) the same neurobiological mechanisms for transforming motivation into action, 2) the same dopaminergic responses to stimulus appraisals, and 3) the same kinds of decision making.

INTRODUCTION

This paper provides a biological and evolutionary perspective on learning, with special reference to post-critical period second language acquisition (SLA). Neurobiology, evolutionary biology, and evolutionary psychology have become important sciences in the study of human behavior. A biological focus allows us to propose possible mechanisms for SLA; an evolutionary focus provides suggestions for phylogenetically antecedent behaviors upon which learning, in general — and SLA, in particular — may be built. Because evolution is conservative, one process is frequently adapted to another purpose (in birds, for example, feathers used for warmth were adapted for flight). In the formulation offered here, learning is seen as a form of foraging. Just as organisms forage for food, humans may forage for information, knowledge, and skill.

In foraging for food, signals indicating reduced glucose levels cause an animal's nervous system to generate an incentive motive to acquire food. That motive is then translated into motor activity whereby the animal moves through its environment in search of food. The desire to acquire certain knowledge or skill similarly constitutes an incentive motive that a learner must translate into activity in order to acquire the desired information or skill. In other words, a learner must *do* things in order to learn. Here we will adopt a notion with a long history in neurobiology, that is, the notion that cognition is an adaptation of motor systems (Calvin, 1996). This view of cognition may prove particularly true of motor activity that is undertaken with the goal of learning something. Thus, motor activity is an essential part of cognition in learning.

Schumann, J. (2001). Learning as foraging. In Z. Dörnyei & R. Schmidt (Eds.), *Motivation and second language acquisition* (Technical Report #23, pp. 21–28). Honolulu: University of Hawai'i, Second Language Teaching and Curriculum Center.

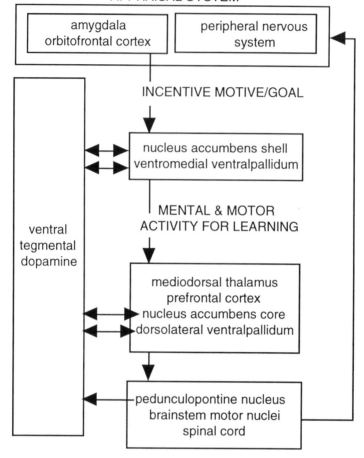

APPRAISAL SYSTEM

Figure 1: The neural system for transforming incentive motivation into mental and motor activity

THE NEURAL SUBSTRATE FOR
TRANSLATING AN INCENTIVE MOTIVE INTO ACTION

Figure 1 depicts the neural system involved in the transformation of motivation into action. The crucial impetus for foraging behavior is the generation of an incentive motive or goal. The circuits in the brain involved in incentive motivation seem to reside in the amygdala of the temporal lobes, the orbitofrontal cortex of the prefrontal area, and in the connections of these areas to a) the peripheral nervous system, b) the nucleus accumbens shell, and c) the ventromedial ventralpallidum of the basal ganglia. In addition, the nucleus accumbens shell and the ventromedial ventralpallidum are innervated by dopamine from the ventral tegmentum (Depue &

Collins, 1999; Deutch, Bourdelais, & Zahm, 1993; Heimer, Alheid, & Zahm, 1993; Kalivas, Churchill, & Klitenick, 1993; Mogenson, Brudzynski, Wu, Yang, & Yim, 1993; Schumann, 1997, in press).

The amygdala and the orbitofrontal cortex are also involved in the appraisal of the motivational significance of incentive stimuli related to the forager's goal. These stimuli are appraised according to whether they are novel or pleasant, whether they facilitate the achievement of the goal, whether they are within the forager's coping ability, and, in higher organisms, whether they are enhancing of the forager's self and social image (Scherer, 1984; Schumann, 1997, in press).

The role of dopamine in this circuit is to exert modulating facilitation on the organism's incentive motivation, based on the organism's appraisal of environmental stimuli relevant to achieving its goal (Depue & Collins, 1999). The incentive motive seems to be generated mainly in the amygdala and orbitofrontal cortex on the basis of a positive appraisal of the goal (e.g., to learn or to feed) and is maintained via the ventral tegmentum — nucleus accumbens shell — ventromedial ventralpallidal loop. (Depue & Collins, 1999; Kalivas et al., 1993; Schumann, 1997, in press).

From this circuit in which goals are generated, maintained, and modulated, motivation must be translated into mental and motor behavior designed to achieve such goals. This process is subserved by projections from the ventromedial ventralpallidum to the mediodorsal thalamus, and from there to area 32 of the prelimbic prefrontal cortex. The circuit then projects back to the core segment of the nucleus accumbens and the dorsolateral ventralpallidum. From there, the circuit connects to the pedunculopontine nucleus, the brainstem motor nuclei, and the spinal cord (Deutch et al., 1993; Heimer et al., 1993; Kalivas et al., 1993; Mogenson et al., 1993; Schumann, in press; Skinner & Garcia-Rill, 1993). This system transforms the incentive motive into goal-directed motor and mental foraging activity (Montague, Dayan, Pearson, & Sejnowski, 1995; Schumann, in press; Robbins & Everitt, 1996).

What I've suggested so far is that learning and foraging may share the same neural mechanisms because both processes involve translating an incentive motive or goal into relevant motor activity in order to achieve said goal. In addition, both processes are guided by dopamine which serves a) to signal stimuli that are predictive of reward — here, the achievement of one's goal (Schultz, 1997); b) to focus attention on those stimuli (Fellous, 1999); and c) to maintain goal-directed behavior by providing "go" signals (Rolls, 1999). Finally, the dopamine response results from stimulus appraisals that evaluate the stimuli according to whether they are novel, pleasant, and compatible with the individual's goals, coping potential, and self and social image. For a detailed account of motivation in action at the psychological level, see Dörnyei and Ottó (1998). The neural system depicted in Figure 1 is proposed to subserve the transformation of motivation into motor and mental action. Among neurobiologists, research designed to further explicate this mechanism continues. As new information is discovered, the model presented in this paper will be modified accordingly. An important development for the future is to provide an understanding of how the brain encodes the information that it encounters during the foraging process. Thus while the current model deals with the neurobiology underlying the learner's effort to locate and engage target language input, the biology subserving input processing and central processing (Skehan, 1998) will be dealt with in subsequent work. A very preliminary proposal in this regard is presented in Figure 5 and related text in Schumann (in press).

The following section will focus on the similarities in decisions that both foragers and learners have to make.

FORAGING FOR FOOD

Foraging can be defined as the "tactics used to obtain nonproduced food stuffs" (Winterhalder, 1981a, p. 16). Stephens and Krebs (1986) divide the foraging process into three stages: search, encounter, and decide. The forager moves through the environment looking for an area containing food sources. As he encounters stimuli predictive of reward, dopamine responses are activated (Schultz, 1997) as a signal to continue the search (Rolls, 1999). The forager must recognize a potential reward patch when it is encountered, and then he must make a series of decisions (Stephens & Krebs, 1986). The following decision structure for foraging is based on discussions of the foraging process in Winterhalder (1981a), Winterhalder (1981b), and Stephens & Krebs (1986). The general decision to be made is whether or not the foraging effort generates adequate energy accrual in relation to energy use. This assessment is ongoing.

Another decision involves assessments of the richness of the food source. In addition, appraisals are made of the desirability of food in the patch, for example, from the food available, what items should be chosen. The forager also must decide how long to remain at the foraging task. Within a patch, he must decide how long a particular strategy (e.g., shaking trees, climbing trees, gathering windfalls) should be employed before switching to a different method, and he must calculate whether or not the activity alters the patch such that a different strategy must be introduced. His decision about whether to continue with a particular strategy will be affected by the perception of his ability to perform the task effectively. He must also make decisions about whether or not to switch to an alternative food source within the patch or whether to leave the patch and to locate another. The forager also has to assess potential sources of toxicity in the patch as well as dangers from predators. Finally, the forager will have to operate under constraints related to the distance of the patch from where he lives and the competition between foraging time and the demands of other tasks (such as tool manufacture, hunting, social obligations, and recreation).

FORAGING FOR KNOWLEDGE OR SKILL

A learner generates an incentive motive to acquire some particular knowledge or skill and must search the environment to locate sources of relevant information. Someone whose goal it is to acquire a second language must locate an environment where the L2 is used, a class where it is taught, or materials in which it is contained (books, tapes, etc.). Such environments could constitute a single patch containing alternate information sources or could be considered three different kinds of patches. Like the forager, as the learner acts on the information sources in the patch, she must assess whether or not the effort expended generates an adequate rate of learning. In the array of information sources available, the learner makes appraisals of which sources and activities provide the most information, most efficiently and effectively. Thus, the learner must decide whether to remain at a particular task or activity or whether to move on to another. Since learning is cumulative, the time span for making such decisions may be longer than those related to food foraging activities.

Let's consider a language class as a foraging patch. The learner will have to locate a "class patch" and will ultimately have to decide how long to remain in that patch. This decision may be influenced by the academic requirements of an educational institution, but let's examine the case in which the learner is acquiring the language without such constraints. This learner will assess the class activities with respect to her perception of the amount of learning achieved for the effort expended. As part of this process, the learner appraises the activities in the class (i.e., the incentive stimuli) with respect to their novelty, coping challenges, and their impact on her self image. Are they so novel as to be threatening, or are they so routine as to be boring, or are they someplace in between? The learner also has to evaluate whether the level of the class is appropriate to her coping ability. She will also assess the learning activities with respect to their compatibility with her self and social image. Does she find the activities enhancing or diminishing of her self-esteem? We can speculate that these assessments are mediated via dopamine signals which respond to stimuli (activities) which are predictive of reward and which also indicate whether or not such stimuli are worthy of continued attention and effort. Thus, the learner has to make decisions about which information sources in the patch merit continued engagement. Should she focus attention and effort on interaction with the teacher and classmates, or on explanations in the text, exercises in the class material, and assigned homework activities, or on language laboratory and other technology-based activities? Thus, within the foraging space defined by the language class, the learner has to find activities that are sufficiently rewarding. Otherwise, she'll leave the patch and attempt to find a better one (another class or some sort of self-study), or perhaps she might abandon the goal altogether.

Like a food forager, the learner operates under some general constraints. Both must make decisions about distance. For example, a learner may have to choose between studying in her room or taking the time to go to the language laboratory to exploit the information sources there. Similarly, but on a larger scale, a learner may have to decide whether to travel to the country where the target language is spoken (say, for a summer) or instead to take an intensive course in the language at a local educational institution. Learners, like foragers, also have to deal with competition between time necessary for language learning activities and demands made by other learning goals, work requirements, and family commitments.

An additional evolutionary consideration to make with respect to the model involves foraging differences between wild and domestic animals. The foraging decisions for cows and sheep are made by farmers or herders. The animals graze in foraging spaces defined by their human caretakers. Learners in educational institutions are in an analogous situation. Here, foraging space is progressively defined by the requirements of the institution as a whole, the particular academic department, and the individual teacher. The advantages and disadvantages of both situations are similar. The herder and the teacher can provide efficient access to food and knowledge sources. In learning, an autodidact might make less optimal decisions about where to place his or her effort (Favareau, 1999).

On the other hand, particularly with respect to human foraging for knowledge and skill, teacher or institution-defined foraging activities may at times be incompatible with learner goals and abilities (i.e., with the learner's incentive motives and coping potential). For example, the learner may want to develop oral skills, and the class may only provide instruction in reading and writing. Or the learner may find that the pace at which the material is presented in the class is beyond his coping ability. Under such conditions, the learner might search for alternate foraging space or abandon his or her goal.

SUMMARY

1. Both learning and foraging involve the generation of an incentive motive or goal and the transformation of that motivation into motor and cognitive activity to achieve the goal. The neural mechanisms subserving these processes may be largely identical.

2. The trajectories in both cases are guided by the dopaminergic system that responds to incentive stimuli that are predictive of reward, such that attention is paid to the relevant stimuli and goal-directed behavior is maintained.

3. In both cases, the incentive stimuli are evaluated by the brain's stimulus appraisal system, and — especially in the case of foraging for knowledge and skill — positive appraisals tend to lead to eventual proficiency or expertise, while negative appraisals can lead to abandonment of the learning activity before the process is completed. Such curtailment results in variable proficiency across learners.

4. Finally, in both types of foraging — for food and for knowledge and skill — motor and cognitive activity is driven by affect governed by the brain's reward system.

REFERENCES

Calvin, W. (1996). *How brains think*. New York: Basic Books.

Depue, R. A., & Collins, P. F. (1999). Neurobiology of the structure of personality: Dopamine, facilitation of incentive motivation, and extraversion. *Behavioral and Brain Sciences, 22*, 491–569.

Deutch, A. Y., Bourdelais, A. J., & Zahm, D. S. (1993). The nucleus accumbens core and shell: Accumbal compartments and their functional attributes. In P. W. Kalivas & C. D. Barnes (Eds.), *Limbic motor circuits and neuropsychiatry* (pp. 45–88). Boca Raton, FL: CRC Press.

Dörnyei, Z., & Ottó, I. (1998). Motivation in action: A process model of L2 motivation. *Working Papers on Applied Linguistics, 4*, 43–69 (Thames Valley University, London).

Favareau, D. (1999). Stimulus appraisal in the wild. Unpublished manuscript, Masters Program in Applied Linguistics, University of California, Los Angeles.

Fellous, J. M. (1999). Neuromodulatory basis of emotion. *The Neuroscientist, 5*, 283–293.

Heimer, L., Alheid, G. F., & Zahm, D. S. (1993). The basal forebrain organization: An anatomical framework for motor aspects of drive and motivation. In P. W Kalivas & C. D. Barnes (Eds.), *Limbic motor circuits and neuropsychiatry* (pp. 1–43). Boca Raton, FL: CRC Press.

Kalivas, P. W., Churchill, L., & Klitenick, M. A. (1993). The circuitry mediating the translation of motivational stimuli into adaptive motor responses. In P. W. Kalivas & C. D. Barnes (Eds.), *Limbic motor circuits and neuropsychiatry* (pp. 237–287). Boca Raton, FL: CRC Press.

Mogenson, G. J., Brudzynski, S. M., Wu, M., Yang, C. R., & Yim, C. C. Y. (1993). From motivation to action: A review of dopaminergic regulation of limbic→ nucleus accumbens→ventral pallidum→pedunculopontine nucleus circuitries involved in limbic-motor integration. In P. W. Kalivas & C. D. Barnes (Eds.), *Limbic motor circuits and neuropsychiatry* (pp. 193–236). Boca Raton, FL: CRC Press.

Montague, P. R., Dayan, P., Pearson, C., & Sejnowski, T. J. (1995). Bee foraging in uncertain environments using predictive Hebbian learning. *Nature, 337*, 725–728.

Robbins, T. W., & Everitt, B. J. (1996). Neurobehavioral mechanisms of reward and motivation. *Current Opinion in Neurobiology, 6*, 228–236.

Rolls, E. T. (1999). *The brain and emotion*. Oxford, UK: Oxford University Press.

Scherer, K. R. (1984). Emotion as a multicomponent process: A model and some cross-culture data. In P. Shaver (Ed.), *Review of personality and social psychology: Vol. 5, Emotions, relationships and health* (pp. 37–63). Beverly Hills, CA: Sage.

Schultz, W. (1997). Dopamine neurons and their role in reward mechanisms. *Current Opinion in Neurobiology, 7*, 191–197.

Schumann, J. H. (1997). *The neurobiology of affect in language*. Boston: Blackwell. (Also published by the journal, *Language Learning*, as a supplement to volume 48, 1997).

Schumann, J. H. (in press). Biology, biography and bilingualism: A neurobiological perspective on variable success in second language acquisition. In R. Franceschini (Ed.), *Sprachbiographien-linguistic biographies: Leben mit meheren Sprachen* [Linguistic biographies: Living with multiple languages]. Tübingen, Germany: Stauffenberg Verlag.

Skehan, P. (1998). *A cognitive approach to language learning*. Oxford, UK: Oxford University Press.

Skinner, R. D., & Garcia-Rill, E. (1993). Mesolimbic interactions with mesopontine modulation of locomotion. In P. W. Kalivas & C. D. Barnes (Eds.), *Limbic motor circuits and neuropsychiatry* (pp. 155–191). Boca Raton, FL: CRC Press.

Stephens, D. W., & Krebs, J. R. (1986). *Foraging theory*. Princeton, NJ: Princeton University Press.

Winterhalder, B. (1981a). Optimal foraging strategies and hunter-gatherer research in anthropology: Theory and models. In B. Winterhalder & E. A. Smith (Eds.), *Hunter-gatherer foraging strategies* (pp. 13–35). Chicago: University of Chicago Press.

Winterhalder, B. (1981b). Foraging strategies in the boreal forest: An analysis of Cree hunting and gathering. In B. Winterhalder & E. A. Smith (Eds.), *Hunter-gatherer foraging strategies* (pp. 66–98). Chicago: University of Chicago Press.

Kyösti Julkunen
University of Joensuu, Finland

SITUATION- AND TASK-SPECIFIC MOTIVATION IN FOREIGN LANGUAGE LEARNING

INTRODUCTION

The purpose of this paper is to define motivation in the classroom context and to outline a motivation model that attempts to capture situation-specific motivation. The model also makes it possible to study the relationship between general motivational orientation and situation- and/or task-specific motivation. Then, as an application of the model to foreign language (FL) learning, a study carried out in the comprehensive schools in Joensuu, Finland, is briefly described and some research results presented. Further, literature is surveyed on task motivation, and a variety of task types that could be used in further research are introduced. Finally, implications for research on learning tasks/activities and learning materials are discussed.

MOTIVATION IN THE CLASSROOM

Foreign language learning motivation has mainly been studied as a trait, as part of students' personality. Students may be integratively, instrumentally, or even cognitively oriented towards language study. Less research has been done in the actual learning situation, although it would be reasonable to assume that students' motivation and attitudes can best be affected in the classroom. The learning process can be made enjoyable. Learning activities, instructional materials, and even individual tasks can motivate students (Dörnyei, 1994; Ellis, 1985; Julkunen, 1989, 1993, 1997). Teaching and learning can be experienced either as motivating or demotivating. This is particularly important because teaching is the component that can easiest be modified.

In the classroom context, motivation can be seen as a continuous interaction process between the learner and the environment. It can be conceptualized either as an impulse arising from the organism or as an attraction arising from an object outside the individual (Nuttin, 1985, p. 15). Motivation does not only affect the selection and conceptualization of a specific goal in the beginning of an activity. Its main role is in controlling and directing an activity. In directing and coordinating various operations towards an object or goal, motivation transforms a number of separate reactions into significant action. Learners build object-directed means-end structures, such as tasks, plans, projects, intentions, and interests (Klausmeier, 1979; Nuttin, 1976; see also Crookes & Schmidt, 1991). Pintrich and Schunk (1996)

Julkunen, K. (2001). Situation- and task-specific motivation in foreign language learning. In Z. Dörnyei & R. Schmidt (Eds.), *Motivation and second language acquisition* (Technical Report #23, pp. 29–41). Honolulu: University of Hawai'i, Second Language Teaching and Curriculum Center.

emphasize the same process character of motivation in their definition: "Motivation is a process whereby goal-directed activity is instigated and sustained" (p. 4). As for research, the above implies that learning motivation should be studied in the actual learning situation and data should be collected before, during, and after learning tasks or activities.

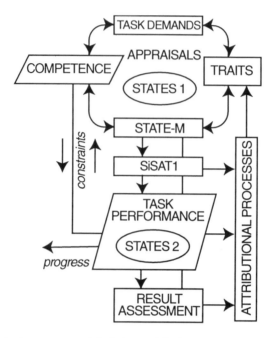

Figure 1: Model of motivation (slightly modified after Boekaerts, 1988, p. 271)

SITUATION-SPECIFIC MOTIVATION

In the classroom, FL learning takes place in situations that vary in their motivational effects. As for research, an appropriate classification of situations is needed. For instance, cooperative, competitive, and individualistic situations have been found to affect motivation differently (e.g., Johnson & Johnson, 1985; Julkunen, 1989; Slavin, 1990; Stipek, 1996). Situation specific motivation refers to the motivational state in a given situation. According to Boekaerts (1987a, 1987b) the learner's general motivational orientation, *motivation as a trait* (TRAITS), and his/her situation specific motivation, *motivation as a state* (STATE–M), interact and produce the *situation-specific action tendency* (SiSAT), which denotes the learner's readiness to devote his/her personal resources, that is, time, energy, competence, and so forth, to completing a task (c.f. Keller, 1983; Maehr, 1984). The content of situation specific action tendency is mainly determined by *appraisal processes* (APPRAISALS). Appraisal processes categorize encounters, tasks, and so forth with respect to their significance to an individual's well-being (see Figure 1.)

Although the above appraisal processes are primarily associated with stressful encounters where an individual's well-being is threatened, Boekaerts (1987b) assumes that the framework can be applied to learning situations as well. In fact, foreign language learning offers threatening and anxiety-provoking situations, especially to low-achieving students. In the classroom context, the appraisal processes are biased; that is, each learner has had different learning experiences and has learnt to classify learning situations, tasks, activities, content areas, and even school subjects in different ways. High and low achievers have their characteristic appraisals, and there are also age-related differences (Boekaerts, 1987b; Julkunen, 1989; cf. also Maehr, 1984). Further, boys and girls tend to interpret tasks in different ways (Julkunen, 1994). Finally, students' situational and task preferences are affected by cultural factors (Schmidt, Boraie, & Kassabgy 1996).

As stated above, the student's general motivational orientation, that is, instrumental, integrative, and cognitive ones in FL learning (e.g., Gardner, 1985; Laine, 1978), and state motivation are expected to interact and produce the situation specific action tendency (SiSAT). In addition to the three orientations, several other dispositional characteristics or traits (TRAITS) can here be considered, including intrinsic versus extrinsic motivation, FL self-concept, attributional styles, trait anxiety, situational preferences (individualistic, competitive, cooperative), task preferences, and so forth (Julkunen, 1989). State motivation (STATE–M), in turn, is affected by the learner's cognitive abilities (COMPETENCE), task demands (TASK DEMANDS) as perceived and conceptualized by the learner, and his/her emotional states before task performance (STATES1). The emotions may include anxiety, gladness, distress, sadness, anger, satisfaction, and so forth. As a result, the learner has a notion of the attractiveness, difficulty level, personal significance, own competence in relation to the task, and his/her eagerness to participate in the activity (SiSAT1). Emotions are also involved in the task performance (STATES2). After task performance, the learner assesses his or her performance (RESULT ASSESSMENT), and then attributes success or failure to ability, luck, task difficulty, effort, task attraction, and the feeling during task completion (ATTRIBUTIONAL PROCESSES; Boekaerts, 1987a, 1987b). Competence sets constraints on task performance, while appraisals regulate the effort expenditure and choice of appropriate strategies. Performing tasks leads to increased knowledge and skills, that is, competence. Result assessment and attributional processes change the belief system, that is, traits, of students (Boekaerts, 1988).

Boekaerts's model was applied to the foreign language learning context in a Finnish study (Julkunen, 1989, 1990) where 593 comprehensive school students (aged 12 and 14) performed open (e.g., "Categories") and closed (e.g., "Three of a kind") vocabulary tasks, as part of regular English lessons, in three different situations: individualistic (working alone), cooperative (working in pairs or groups of three), and competitive. The competitive character of the situation was stressed in the instructions given by the teacher. In the closed task, the students were given a sheet of paper with 48 words arranged in three columns. The students had to take one word from each column to form groups of three words. The groups of three had to have something in common, such as three colors ("yellow," "blue," "red"). The words had been chosen so that there was one logical solution. The open task sheet consisted of two titled columns, for example, "Traffic" and "Adjectives describing people." Each column was divided into eight boxes marked with a letter. The students had to write down as many words as they could in each box, for example, words beginning with B and denoting traffic ("bus," "bridge," "bike," etc.). The words in the closed tasks and the topics in the open tasks were based on the national syllabus and the textbooks used in the schools.

Students' state motivation was measured, using a short on-line questionnaire before and after each task. The pre-task questionnaire focused on students' learning intention (state motivation) and on how motivated they were to do the task (situation-specific action tendency, SiSAT 1). The post-task questionnaire measured the realized intention: how motivated they had actually been while doing the task (SiSAT2). The change in the situation-specific action tendency is assumed to measure the impact of tasks and situations on students' motivation. The students were divided into low- and high-achievers, according to their school marks in English. The results demonstrated that in the individualistic situation high-achievers' responses were more positive, particularly in the closed task. In the cooperative situation all changes were positive. The competitive situation offered a similar pattern as the individualistic one. The cooperative situation was experienced as the most motivating in both groups, regardless of task type.

The study as a whole stressed the importance of classroom, situation, and task levels for learning motivation. The cooperative learning situation proved to be the best for both low- and high-achievers. The similar response pattern in individualistic and competitive situations was not surprising because students worked individually in both situations, and the competitive nature was created only through instructions. As for the task type, open tasks seemed to be more motivating than closed ones. This may result from the fact that the competence of the pair or group could be used in task completion. Further, getting feedback, for example, how to decide on success or failure in tasks, was no problem in a cooperative situation because the group could provide the feedback. In the other two situations, it was difficult for students to assess their performance in open tasks because they did not immediately see how well they had done.

As one of the purposes of the study was to investigate the relationship between traits and the situation- and task-specific motivation, traits were measured using a background questionnaire administered on a separate occasion. The questionnaire included integrative, instrumental, and cognitive orientations, intrinsic and extrinsic motivation, English language self-concept, attributional styles, and situational preferences.

On the whole, the motivation model developed by Boekaerts seems to function well in studying the relationship between general motivational orientation and situation or task specific motivation, motivation as a state. It also provides an appropriate framework for research on learning materials and activities, for example, for comparing the affective effects of different learning situations (e.g., individualistic, cooperative, competitive) and different tasks (e.g., open vs. closed; Julkunen, 1989). Boekaerts (1991, 1993a, 1993b, 1996) has further developed the model by deleting the attributional processes and by dividing the outcome of appraisal processes (situation-specific action tendency or learning intention) into two alternatives: learning versus coping intention, which would then result in learning or coping modes respectively. The new model also implies that the learner may change the mode during task completion, which gives a better description of the learning process but also sets demands for data collection method.

TASK MOTIVATION

Learning tasks and activities decisively influence how and what students learn from instruction; they organize student experience (Bennett, 1987; Brophy & Alleman, 1991; Doyle, 1983; Winne, 1987). Different tasks affect motivation and learning in different ways. Consequently, the study of instruction has to pay attention to learning tasks and activities, that is, to what the learner has to do in the classroom. In addition, tasks have an important role to play in examinations. Interestingly, task type, response mode, and format have produced gender differences in examination results; for example, some tasks favor girls and some favor boys (Gipps & Murphy, 1994).

When task characteristics are the focus of attention in motivation, the term *task motivation* can be used. Gagné (1985, p. 307) views task motivation as one of the major types of motivation (the others being incentive and achievement motivation). Referring to Ausubel (1968), he notes that the motives are intrinsic to the task, and the completion of the task satisfies the underlying motive. Task motivation refers to the characteristics of the task, to task design. Maehr (1984) points out that certain tasks are more interesting, more attractive, and more motivating than others. Tasks that include an optimal amount of uncertainty and unpredictability attract the learner. Language games are a case in point.

In line with the model above, Marzano (1991) writes that an individual's motivation for and success at a given task are, at least partially, a function of the attitudes and beliefs he/she has relative to such factors as control over the task, the perceived value of the task, and perceived competence for the task. Task motivation depends partly on general motivation and partly on the unique way the student perceives the task (Boekaerts, 1993a).

Keller (1983, 1994) has formulated four determinants of motivation that affect an individual's (student's) choices of goals and tasks and the degree of effort he/she will exert in learning: interest (attention), relevance, expectancy (confidence), and outcomes (satisfaction). Interest means that the learner's curiosity is aroused and sustained throughout the task, activity, course, and so forth. Relevance is essential for the learner's sustained motivation. The learner has to perceive that important personal needs are being met by the learning task. He/she can achieve personal goals by studying. Expectancy refers to locus of control, expectation of success/failure, and attributions. The learner has to perceive that he/she has a chance to succeed, to think that he/she controls his/her own learning, and to attribute success/failure to effort. Finally, the learner should feel, preferably intrinsically, satisfied with the outcomes of learning. As can be seen, Keller's determinants of motivation have a lot in common with Boekaert's model presented above.

Csikszentmihalyi (1991, p. 49) has listed eight components that are characteristic of an activity (or a task) providing enjoyment. First, we must have a chance of completing the task. Second, we must have an opportunity to concentrate on the activity. Third and fourth, the task has a clear goal and immediate feedback is provided. Fifth, we are deeply but effortlessly involved in the task and forget the worries and frustrations of everyday life. Sixth, we have a sense of control over our actions. Seventh, concern for the self disappears when we are engaged in the activity. Finally, sense of time is altered; we simply forget about time. Again, play and games include many of the above components. To be realistic, it may be difficult to provide tasks that satisfy all or most of the above criteria. But it is worth trying. Some of the points presented by Csikszentmihalyi apply to the learning situation while others may be felt when performing a well-mastered activity. According to Brophy and Alleman (1991), "Other things being equal, activities that students are likely to enjoy (or at least find meaningful and worthwhile) are preferable to activities that students are not likely to enjoy" (p. 18).

Instruction, tasks,a and courses have a motivational structure. Erickson and Shultz (1992) suggest that the overall academic task structure that the student faces in the classroom consists of social participation task structure and a subject matter task structure. In planning instruction and in designing tasks, activities, and learning materials, both content and format should be taken into account because they are independent of each other. The same content can be taught in a more or less interesting way. Further, the format or structure may be simple, but the content is cognitively demanding or vice versa (Good & Brophy, 1990). For instance, the guessing game "20 Questions" has a simple format, but it can be cognitively very demanding. The distinction between form and content is equally important for research into instructional materials and classroom learning.

TASK TYPES

A task is something the student has to do: a question asked by the teacher or an exercise to be completed, a problem to be solved, an activity to be performed, and so forth. In communicative language teaching Nunan's (1988) definition sounds reasonable. A communicative task is "a piece of classroom work which involves learners in comprehending, manipulating, producing or interacting in the target language while their attention is principally focused on meaning rather than form" (p. 18).

In order to study the cognitive and affective effects of academic tasks, a classification has to be developed. Task categories can be based on the cognitive operations that are involved in doing the task, for example, memory tasks, procedural or routine tasks, and comprehension or understanding tasks. In memory tasks, the student is supposed to recognize or reproduce previously encountered information. Procedural or routine tasks require that the student applies a standardized and predictable formula or algorithm to produce an answer or to solve a problem. In comprehension or understanding tasks the student is expected to (a) recognize transformed versions of previously encountered information, (b) apply procedures to new problems, or (c) draw inferences from previously encountered information or procedures. Finally, in opinion tasks students have to express preferences for something (Doyle, 1983, 1992).

In the language classroom, students frequently work in pairs or in groups, which means that task classifications have to be developed for group learning. McGrath (1984), drawing on previous research, has compiled a classification for small group work, based on processes that are involved in group activities. The system consists of four major categories, with two subcategories for each:

Generate	planning tasks and creative tasks (e.g., brainstorming)
Choose	intellective tasks (solving problems that have a correct answer) and decision-making tasks (arriving at consensus is required)
Negotiate	cognitive conflict tasks (viewpoint conflict is to be solved) and mixed motive tasks (negotiations/bargaining/coalition forming)
Execute	contests/battles/competitive tasks and performance/psychomotor tasks.

Nation's (1990) focus in task classification is on how tasks help the learner to cover the gap between his/her present knowledge and the requirements of the task. The way learners are helped to cope with the tasks will have a major effect on the kind of learning that occurs. He divides tasks into four categories: experience, shared, guided, and independent tasks. Experience tasks try to narrow the gap by using or developing learner's previous experience and prior knowledge. Graded readers (simplification), predicting what is to follow, interpreting titles, and pre-teaching vocabulary are examples of this type. Shared tasks endeavor to get learners to help each other to cross the gap. A group or a team can solve more difficult tasks than an individual student. Guidance tasks try to bridge the gap by providing support and guidance, instructions, or the teacher's help. Independent tasks leave the learner to work on his or her own, to rely on his or her own resources. In order to succeed, students have to know how to study and use appropriate learning strategies. Nation's classification is related to the social participation task structure (Erickson & Shultz, 1992) mentioned above.

Long (1990) rightly suggests that we have to identify tasks that promote language learning. Tasks have to encourage negotiation work, stimulating learners and the teacher to reformulate their ideas and utterances. Tasks make learners use their potential, to operate at the outer limits of their current abilities. He analyses one-way versus two-way tasks. The latter refers to tasks that include exchange of information. They require negotiation of meaning and have been demonstrated to be more effective, in terms of learning, than one-way tasks. Further, Long (1990) divides tasks into open and closed tasks. In the former type, the learners know that there is no predetermined right solution while the latter requires that the learners should end up with a single correct answer. Closed tasks produce more negotiation work and more useful negotiation than open tasks. Free conversation is notoriously ineffective. As can be seen, Long mainly refers to oral tasks.

Oostdam and Rijlaarsdam (1995) have developed a comprehensive system for analysing language exercises, including mode of communication, domain of learning, language learning and language processing strategy, learning goal, metacognitive control, and type of activity. The most interesting feature is, however, the main division of tasks into language learning and language processing tasks. The learning and processing tasks, 19 types altogether, are grouped under receptive/productive, receptive, and productive skills. The focus on communication and learning strategies is interesting. It might prove useful for research and materials design purposes, though it seems to be too detailed as far as motivation is concerned.

In terms of motivation, a quite general and comprehensive classification could be developed. One alternative could be a division of tasks into *open* and *closed* ones. In a closed task a precise, single right answer can be defined in advance, whereas in an open task there is no single right answer but each student may produce a unique response within his/her competence (Barnes, 1975; Doyle, 1983; Julkunen 1989, 1990; Kauchak & Eggen, 1989).

The above two task types (open and closed) have been found to affect motivation in different ways. A closed task is high in risk, especially for less able students, since failure is easily detectable. Open tasks are low in risk because several right answers are available. However, it is difficult for the student to establish criteria for success/failure in an open task (cf. Doyle, 1983). Moreover, highly anxious students should benefit from structured (closed) tasks demanding little processing capacity (Tobias, 1986). Finally open tasks are more flexible in that they allow the student to use his/her whole competence in performing the task. For instance, in vocabulary tasks the student may resort to the words learnt or acquired outside school (Julkunen, 1990).

Finally, van Lier (1988) points out that the sequence of tasks is important for motivation. The materials designer and the teacher should provide students with chains of tasks, one task leading to another. Nuttin (1976) referred to these kinds of tasks as open ones. This implies that instruction should make use of projects and other tasks that take a longer time to complete. On the other hand, longer tasks may be broken down to smaller units to make them more motivating for students (Stipek, 1996).

CONCLUSIONS

Boekaert's conceptual model provides a feasible framework for studying the relationship between students' general motivational orientations and their situation- or task-specific motivation. It can also be applied to investigating the affective characteristics of different types of learning situations and tasks/activities. Keller's determinants of motivation may be used in evaluating tasks, activities, learning materials, and even courses (Julkunen, 1998).

As for the development of theories on FL learning motivation, a working combination of general and subject specific theories can and should be used. One obvious reason for this is the fact that there seems to be a time lag between general psychological research and its eventual subject (FL) specific applications. Further, when foreign languages are studied in schools, they are part of the curriculum, and general learning motivation theories seem to work well in the classroom context. Finally, more attention should be paid to the learning situation, because what goes on in the classroom has a decisive role to play in FL learning.

In studying tasks, whether analyzing instruction materials or measuring students' response to them in the classroom, appropriate classification of tasks has to be developed. The classifications outlined above (cognitive operations, group processes, teaching related, and strategy oriented) could all serve the purpose. On the whole, the classification has to be kept at a general level. If too many variables are included, the system becomes too complicated to produce any applicable results. The division of tasks into open and closed ones has so far proved to be productive. Further, the emphasis or focus of research will influence the choice of task classification.

Task level motivation should ideally be studied in three stages: the initial stage, the actual performance stage, and the evaluation stage (Boekaerts, 1988; Julkunen, 1989; Nuttin, 1985; Winne, 1987). The research design should also include the interaction of task types and learning situations. Further, student characteristics have to be considered, for example, anxiety, high- and low-achievers, attributional styles, cognitive and learning styles, learning strategies, age, and gender. Finally, the relationship between students' affective response and academic achievement has to be studied.

The methods that could be applied in investigating situational or task motivation include short on-line questionnaires administered before and after task performance (e.g., Boekaerts, 1988; Julkunen, 1989), classroom observations, stimulated recall, interviews, think-aloud protocol, or diaries related to homework.

REFERENCES

Ausubel, D. P. (1968). *Educational psychology; A cognitive view*. New York: Holt, Rinehart, & Winston.

Barnes, D. (1975). Language in the secondary school classroom. In D. Barnes, J. Britton, & H. Rosen (Eds.), *Language, the learner and the school* (pp. 9–77). Harmondsworth, UK: Penguin.

Bennet, S. N. (1987). Recent research on teaching-learning process in classroom settings. In E. DeCorte, H. Lodewijks, R. Parmentier, & P. Span (Eds.), *Learning and instruction: European research in an international context*, Volume 1 (pp. 201–216). Oxford, UK: Pergamon.

Boekaerts, M. (1987a). Die Effekte von state- und traitmotivationaler Orientierung auf das Lernergebnis [The effect of state and trait motivational orientations on learning outcomes]. *Zeitschrift für Pädagogische Psychologie, 1987*(1), 29–43.

Boekaerts, M. (1987b). Individual differences in the appraisal of learning tasks: An integrative view on emotion and cognition. *Communication and Cognition, 20*, 207–224.

Boekaerts, M. (1988). Motivated learning: Bias in appraisals. *International Journal of Educational Research, 12*, 267–280.

Boekaerts, M. (1991) Subjective competence, appraisals and self-assessment. *Learning and Instruction, 1*, 1–17.

Boekaerts, M. (1993a). Task motivation and mathematics achievement in actual task situations. *Learning and Instruction, 3*, 133–150.

Boekaerts, M. (1993b). Being concerned with well-being and with learning. *Educational Psychologist, 28*, 149–167.

Boekaerts, M. (1996). Personality and psychology of learning. *European Journal of Personality, 10*, 377–404.

Brophy, J., & Alleman, J. (1991). Activities as instructional tools: A framework for analysis and evaluation. *Educational Researcher, 20*, 9–23.

Csikszentmihalyi, M. (1991). *Flow: The psychology of optimal experience*. New York: Harper Perennial.

Crookes, G., & Schmidt, R. W. (1991). Motivation: Reopening the research agenda. *Language Learning, 41*, 469–512.

Dörnyei, Z. (1994). Motivation and motivating in the foreign language classroom. *The Modern Language Journal, 78*, 273–284.

Doyle, W. (1983). Academic work. *Review of Educational Research, 53*, 159–199.

Doyle, W. (1992) Curriculum and pedagogy. In P. W. Jackson (Ed.), *Handbook of research on curriculum* (pp. 486–516). New York: Macmillan.

Ellis, R. (1985). *Understanding second language acquisition*. Oxford, UK: Oxford University Press.

Erickson, F., & Shultz, J. (1992). Students' experience of the curriculum. In P. W. Jackson (Ed.), *Handbook of research on curriculum*. (pp. 465–485). New York: Macmillan.

Gagné, R. M. (1985). *The conditions of learning and theory of instruction*. New York: Holt, Rinehart, & Winston.

Gardner, R. C. (1985). *Social psychology and second language learning: The role of attitudes and motivation*. Bungay, Suffolk, UK: Edward Arnold.

Gipps, C., & Murphy, P. (1994). *A fair test? Assessment, achievement and equity*. Buckingham, UK: Open University Press.

Good, T. L., & Brophy, J. E. (1990). *Educational psychology: A realistic approach*. New York: Longman.

Johnson, D. W., & Johnson, R. T. (1985). Motivational processes in cooperative, competitive and individualistic learning situations. In C. Ames & R. Ames (Eds.), *Research on motivation in education*, Vol. 2: *The classroom milieu* (pp. 249–286). Orlando, FL: Academic Press.

Julkunen, K. (1989). *Situation- and task-specific motivation in foreign-language learning and teaching* (Publications in Education No.6). Joensuu, Finland: University of Joensuu.

Julkunen, K. (1990). Open and closed vocabulary tasks in foreign language learning. In J. Tommola (Ed.), *Foreign language comprehension and production* (Publications of AFinLA 48, pp. 7–25). Turku, Finland: AFinLA.

Julkunen, K. (1993). On foreign language learning motivation in the classroom. In S. Tella (Ed.), *Kielestä mieltä-mielekästä kieltä* [Meaningful language learning] (Research Report No. 118, pp. 70–78). Helsinki, Finland: University of Helsinki, Department of Teacher Education.

Julkunen, K. (1994). Gender differences in students' situation- and task-specific foreign language learning motivation. In S. Tella (Ed.), *Näytön paikka. Opetuksen kulttuurin arviointi* [Evaluating the culture of teaching] (Research Report No. 129), pp. 171–180). Helsinki, Finland: University of Helsinki, Department of Teacher Education.

Julkunen, K. (1997). Tasks, motivation, and learning in foreign languages. In S. Tella (Ed.) *Media nykypäivän koulutuksessa: Osa II* [The media in present-day education, Part 2] (Research Report No. 179, pp. 83–92). Helsinki, Finland: University of Helsinki, Department of Teacher Education.

Julkunen, K. (1998). *Foreign language learning: Students' learning strategies and learning experiences*. (Research Reports of the Faculty of Education No. 73). Joensuu, Finland: University of Joensuu.

Kauchak, D. P., & Eggen, P. D. (1989). *Learning and teaching*. Needham Heights, MA: Allyn & Bacon.

Keller, J. M. (1983). Motivational design of instruction. In C. M. Reigeluth (Ed.), *Insructional design theories and models* (pp. 386–433). Hillsdale, NJ: Erlbaum.

Keller, J. M. (1994). Motivation in instructional design. In T. Husén & T. N. Postlethwaite (Eds.), *The international encyclopedia of education*, Vol. 7 (2nd ed., pp. 3943–3947). Oxford, UK: Pergamon.

Klausmeier, H. J. (1979). Introduction. In H. J. Klausmeier & Associates (Eds.), *Cognitive learning and development: Information-processing and Piagetian perspective* (pp. 1–27). Cambridge, MA: Ballinger.

Laine, E. (1978). *Foreign language learning motivation in Finland II* (Publications of AfinLA 21). Turku, Finland: AfinLA.

Long, M. H. (1990). Task, group, and task-group interactions. In S. Anivan (Ed.), *Language teaching methodology for the nineties* (Anthology Series 24, pp. 1–50). Singapore: RELC.

Maehr, M. L. (1984). Meaning and motivation: Toward a theory of personal investment. In R. E. Ames & C. Ames (Eds.), *Research on motivation, Vol.1: Student motivation* (pp. 115–144). Orlando, FL: Academic Press.

Marzano, R. J. (1991). Language, the language arts, and thinking. In J. Flood, J. M. Jensen, D. Lapp, & J. R. Squire (Eds.), *Handbook of research on teaching the English language arts* (pp. 559–586). New York: Macmillan.

McGrath, J. E. (1984). *Groups: Interaction and performance*. Englewood Cliffs, NJ: Prentice Hall.

Nation, P. (1990). A system of tasks for language learning. In S. Anivan (Ed.), *Language teaching methodology for the nineties* (Anthology Series 24, pp. 15–63). Singapore: RELC.

Nunan, D. (1988). Principles of communicative task design. In B. K. Das (Ed.), *Materials for language learning and teaching* (Anthology Series 22, pp. 16–29). Singapore: RELC.

Nuttin, J. R. (1976). Motivation and reward in human learning: A cognitive approach. In W. K. Estes (Ed.), *Handbook of learning and cognitive processes, Vol. 3: Approaches to human learning and motivation* (pp. 247–281). Hillsdale, NJ: Erlbaum.

Nuttin, J. R. (1985). *Théorie de la motivation humaine* [Theory of human motivation] (2nd ed.). Paris: Presses Universitaires de France.

Oostdam, R., & Rijlaarsdam, G. (1995). *Towards strategic language learning*. Amsterdam: Amsterdam University Press.

Pintrich, P. R., & Schunk, D. H. (1996). *Motivation in education: Theory, research, and applications*. Englewood Cliffs, NJ: Prentice Hall.

Schmidt, R., Boraie, D., & Kassabgy, O. (1996). Foreign language motivation: Internal structure and external connections. In R. L. Oxford (Ed.), *Language learning motivation: Pathways to the new century* (Technical Report #11, pp. 14–87). Honolulu: The University of Hawai'i, Second Language Teaching & Curriculum Center.

Slavin, R. E. (1990). Cooperative learning: Engineering social psychology in the classroom. In R. S. Feldman (Ed.), *The social psychology of education: Current research and theory* (pp. 153–171). Cambridge, UK: Cambridge University Press.

Stipek, D. J. (1996). Motivation and instruction. In D. C. Berliner & R. C. Calfee (Eds.), *Handbook of educational psychology* (pp. 85–113). New York: Macmillan.

Tobias, S. (1986). Anxiety and cognitive processing of instruction. In R. Schwarzer (Ed.), *Self-related cognitions in anxiety and motivation* (pp. 35–54). Hillsdale, NJ: Erlbaum.

van Lier, L. (1988). *The classroom and the language learner*. London: Longman.

Winne, P. H. (1987). Students' cognitive processes. In M. J. Dunkin (Ed.), *The international encyclopedia of teaching and teacher education* (pp. 496–509). Oxford, UK: Pergamon.

Kimberly A. Noels
University of Alberta

NEW ORIENTATIONS IN LANGUAGE LEARNING MOTIVATION: TOWARDS A MODEL OF INTRINSIC, EXTRINSIC, AND INTEGRATIVE ORIENTATIONS AND MOTIVATION

Author's note

This paper was supported financially by a research grant from the Social Sciences and Humanities Research Council of Canada. The author is grateful to Jennifer Chu for her efficient clerical and research assistance while this chapter was being written.

INTRODUCTION

During the 1990s, there was a resurgence of interest in issues concerning motivation in second language (L2) learners, involving much discussion and debate about the nature of L2 motivation (e.g., Dörnyei, 1994a, 1994b; Gardner & Tremblay, 1994; Oxford, 1994; Oxford & Shearin, 1994). Several scholars advocated a shift to consider a variety of motivational constructs in addition to those already the focus of research attention (e.g., Clément, Dörnyei, & Noels, 1994; Crookes & Schmidt, 1991; Dörnyei, 1990; Tremblay & Gardner, 1995; Wen, 1997). The purpose of this chapter is to outline one such formulation, developed by Noels and her colleagues (e.g., Noels, Pelletier, Clément, & Vallerand, 2000), which attempts to broaden the range of motivational constructs studied through a close consideration of L2 orientations. It is argued that by combining the constructs of intrinsic and extrinsic motivation described in Deci and Ryan's (1985) self-determination theory with intergroup constructs discussed by Gardner (e.g., 1985), Clément (e.g., 1980), and others, a more complete understanding of the development of particular orientations and their role in language learning motivation can be achieved.

ORIENTATIONS AND MOTIVATION

Following Gardner's (1985, p. 10) definition, L2 motivation can be described as a complex of constructs, involving "the combination of effort plus desire to achieve the goal of learning the language plus favorable attitudes toward learning the language." It is thus convenient to think of the goal of language learning as providing an orientation for the amount of desire and energy expended, and these aspects are associated with more or less positive affect. Two orientations (i.e., classes of reasons for learning the L2) have received the most empirical attention. The first

Noels, K. (2001). New orientations in language learning motivation: Towards a model of intrinsic, extrinsic, and integrative orientations and motivation. In Z. Dörnyei & R. Schmidt (Eds.), *Motivation and second language acquisition* (Technical Report #23, pp. 43–68). Honolulu: University of Hawai'i, Second Language Teaching and Curriculum Center.

was the integrative orientation, which referred to the desire to learn a language in order to interact with, and perhaps to identify with, members of the L2 community. The instrumental orientation described reasons for L2 learning that reflect practical goals, such as a attaining an academic goal or job advancement. In their early work, Gardner and Lambert (1959, 1972) suggested that because it was related to positive attitudes towards the L2 community, the integrative orientation would be a better predictor of eventual proficiency than the instrumental orientation.

Research over the past forty years suggests that there are at least two limitations to this hypothesis. First, the relative predictive power of each orientation was found to be inconsistent (for review see Au, 1988). Although some studies indicated that the integrative orientation was a good predictor of L2 variables (e.g., Gardner & Lambert, 1959), others found that the instrumental orientation was an equivalent or a better predictor than the integrative orientation (e.g., Chihara & Oller, 1978; Gardner & Lambert, 1972; Lukmani, 1972; Oller, Hudson, & Liu, 1977). It has more recently been argued (cf. Gardner, 1985) that these two orientations are not mutually exclusive, and that both orientations could sustain effort. Not only might both orientations support effort, the integrative orientation may not be relevant to many learners. In a study of learners in different contexts, Clément and Kruidenier (1983; Kruidenier & Clément, 1986) found that the integrative orientation was only evident in particular contexts and that four other orientations, including the instrumental orientation, had cross-contextual relevance. This study thus brings into question the universal necessity of the integrative orientation as a determinant of other motivational and proficiency variables, and raises the theoretical question of what psychological mechanism explains any differential predictive power that the two orientations might have.

A second, related concern is that there may be additional orientations besides the integrative and instrumental orientations, a point Gardner and Lambert have argued since their early studies (1959, 1972). For instance, people may wish to learn an L2 in order to be intellectually stimulated, to show off to friends, because of a fascination with aspects of the language (Oxford & Shearin, 1994), because of a need for achievement and stimulation (Dörnyei, 1990), interest and curiosity (Crookes & Schmidt, 1991), or a desire for assimilation (Graham, 1985). Many other orientations have been described empirically, including travel, friendship, and knowledge orientations (Clément & Kruidenier, 1983), identification-influence (Noels & Clément, 1989), prestige-influence (Moïse, Clément, & Noels, 1990), career and school instrumental (Belmechri & Hummel, 1998; see also Samimy & Tabuse, 1992), media usage (Clément, et al., 1994), national security (Kraemer, 1993), as well as combinations of these (e.g., "instrumental-knowledge" found by Clément et al., 1994). A limitation of these studies is that there has been little attempt to systematically organize the various orientations in such a way as to indicate the psychological mechanism by which a given orientation sustains effort, desire and positive affect over the long term (but see Dörnyei, 1990; Ramage, 1990; Tremblay & Gardner, 1995).

ORIENTATIONS AND SELF-DETERMINATION THEORY

In an attempt to resolve some of these issues, we are conducting a program of research to examine L2 orientations in light of Deci and Ryan's (1985) self-determination theory, which suggests that orientations can be divided broadly into three categories, including intrinsic and extrinsic orientations and amotivation (e.g., Noels, in press; Noels et al., 2000; Noels, Clément, & Pelletier, 1999, in press). Ryan's (1995) discussion of intrinsic and extrinsic motivation suggests that it is reasonable to think of these constructs as orientations. Consistent with Gardner's (1985) definition of orientations, Ryan states that the subtypes of motivation reflect the motivational "orientation" but not necessarily the level or amount of motivation. He notes that a person acting for an external reward may be as energized and effortful as one who is acting for more self-determined reasons. The difference between the types of motivation lies in the different attitudes espoused and the likelihood of engagement in the activity in the long run.

INTRINSIC ORIENTATIONS

Intrinsic orientations refer to reasons for L2 learning that are derived from one's inherent pleasure and interest in the activity; the activity is undertaken because of the spontaneous satisfaction that is associated with it. Deci and Ryan (1985, 1995; Ryan & Deci, 2000) maintain that these feelings of enjoyment come from developing a sense of competence over a voluntarily chosen activity. At least three related subtypes of intrinsic orientations have been identified (Vallerand, 1997; Vallerand, Blais, Brière, & Pelletier, 1989; Vallerand, Pelletier, Blais, Brière, Senécal, & Valliires, 1992, 1993). *Intrinsic-Knowledge* refers to the feelings of pleasure that come from developing knowledge and satisfying one's curiosity about a topic area. For instance, a student with such an orientation may look up obscure foreign words just for curiosity's sake, not because of some immediate necessity. *Intrinsic-Accomplishment* refers to the enjoyable sensations that are associated with surpassing oneself and mastering a difficult task The emphasis is on the process of achievement and not the end result. This orientation might describe the satisfaction associated with successfully attaining fluency with a difficult grammatical construction. *Intrinsic-Stimulation* refers to the simple enjoyment of the aesthetics of the experience. This type of intrinsic motivation is characterized by a sense of "flow" (Csikszentmihalyi, 1975). In the language learning context, this orientation might be characterized by the student who delights in the sounds, melody, and rhythm of a piece of prose or poetry in the foreign language. The pleasurable feelings that are central to each of these subtypes are very apparent in the comments of Anglo-American students involved in Spanish language classes presented in Table 1.

Table 1: Selected quotations from students learning Spanish at a California university in response to the question "Why are you learning Spanish?": Intrinsic orientation

"The exciting ability to become bilingual."

"Challenging myself to learn a tongue which is not native to me."

"The ability to communicate in another language is a good feeling. Communication is a big part of life as it is, but with 2 languages it is that much larger."

"I enjoy the language, I am good at it, and I want to become fluent in speaking Spanish"

"Because Spanish is fun to me."

"I studied it in Spain for about two months and I loved it."

EXTRINSIC ORIENTATIONS

Not all activities are sufficiently novel, challenging, or aesthetically pleasing to be intrinsically motivating (Ryan & Deci, 2000). Extrinsic orientations refer to reasons that are instrumental to some consequence apart from inherent interest in the activity. Several types of extrinsic orientations have been identified, and they vary in the extent to which they have been internalized and integrated into the person's self-concept (Grolnick, Deci, & Ryan, 1997). For instance, both the student learning a language because it is a requirement of a degree program and the student learning a language because she feels it will help her to develop her talents in her chosen career are learning the language because it is instrumental to achieving an end other than enjoyment of the activity per se. These two students differ, however, in the extent to which the activity involves personal choice and a sense of personal relevance. The range of extrinsic orientations is evident in the students' comments presented in Table 2.

The least self-determined type of extrinsic orientation is *External Regulation*. Students who are externally regulated are learning the L2 because of some contingency in the environment, such as the possibility of attaining a reward, because of a course requirement, or in order to avoid losing a job. The learner's behavior is in effect regulated by some external source. The comments of the students in Table 2 illustrate how some students only take a L2 to achieve goals such as course credit or to attain tangible, necessary goals.

Table 2: Selected quotations from students learning Spanish at a California university in response to the question "Why are you learning Spanish?": Extrinsic orientations and amotivation

Integrated regulation

"Knowing another language, being bilingual or tri-lingual makes me feel educated. I associate a person who can speak many languages with intelligence and very aware [sic] of the world around him/her (cultured)."

Identified regulation

"I'd like to work with youth, possibly in school (public or private) setting, I may stay in CA, and Spanish is a useful tool to be able to use as a teacher and/or counselor."

"As a grad student in linguistics, I may have an opportunity to do research in Mexico or Bolivia studying indigenous languages. Spanish would be the contact language."

"…[to] be able to learn Spanish so that if I decide to take my Math major into the teaching area that I will be better adept to help the students w/ Spanish as their first language…"

Introjected regulation

"I'm tired of people automatically speaking to me in Spanish and I always have to tell them that I don't know it that well. It embarrasses me and sometimes it embarrasses them as well. I am/was so frustrated that I was willing to take the Spanish class w/o any credits. I planned to go to class as long as there was always an empty seat."

"…because there is an odd kind of respect given to a blond, blue eyed person speaking comprehensive Spanish. I like to be able to pass the tests the Spanish-speaking people give me, surprise them."

External regulation

"The only reason that I'm taking Spanish is because I have to get the "GE" [general education] requirement filled."

"To be able to communicate in the basics in a Spanish-speaking country. To buy things, eat, get directions and not get ripped off or taken advantage of."

"Get a job, GE [general education] requirements, Mom wants me to."

Amotivation

"The school is making me. I don't know why. I'm a Bio major and I want to be an astronaut. This isn't fair. I didn't like Spanish in high school and I don't like it now. If I wanted to learn another language, I would do it without tests, quizzes, and "language labs." With every fiber of my being, I wish I didn't have to take this class."

"I was going [to] be an English Major along with Communications, but I am not any more because I hate Spanish!"

Introjected regulation is somewhat more internalized. The student has adopted contingencies and now self-imposes pressures or rewards. This orientation is nonetheless extrinsic in the sense that the student is not performing the behaviour because it is inherently enjoyable. Rather, such a person, who is often motivated to demonstrate their ability or avoid failure in order to regulate their feelings of self-worth (Deci, Egharari, Patrick, & Leone, 1994), performs a task because of some internally governed system of rewards and punishments. The two quotes in Table 2 illustrate introjected regulation in terms of avoiding feelings of embarrassment and the desire to "show off" in order to gain respect from others.

Identified regulation is more self-determined. At this point a student chooses to engage in an activity because its value is recognized to be important for some aspect of the self. As illustrated in Table 2, a student with an identified regulation orientation might desire to learn the L2 because it is useful in order to achieve another important goal. For instance, for some students, becoming a good teacher, scholar, or counsellor (which they presumably value) may be enhanced by developing skills in the L2. This is somewhat different than external regulation, in that attaining the goal is important not because of some externally imposed requirement, but because that goal has self-determined importance.

Integrated regulation is the most self-determined of the extrinsic orientations. "Integrated regulation occurs when identified regulations are fully assimilated to the self, which means they have been evaluated and brought into congruence with one's other values and needs" (Ryan & Deci, 2000, p. 73). In some ways, it is similar to intrinsic motivation because it is fully governed by the self. Unlike intrinsic motivation, however, the activity is not done because of enjoyment in it but because it is viewed as an aspect of self-concept. An example of this type of orientation is the student who considers herself to be a "universal person," capable of traveling freely across cultural boundaries and thus sees competence in one or more L2s as an inherent part of that self-concept (see Table 2). This orientation should not be confused with Gardner's integrative orientation. Integrated regulation means that the activity is chosen because it is coherent with other aspects of the self. The integrative orientation refers to the desire to interact and identify with members of the L2 community. Thus the former orientation does not have the same intergroup connotation that the latter orientation has. It should also be noted that integrated regulation has not been studied widely in the L2 context, nor in the general educational context, because it is generally assumed to be evident only in people who are advanced in the activity. Most of the research to date has focused on novice learners or children, who have not yet had an opportunity to completely integrate the activity into their self-concept.

Amotivation. A third category of motivational constructs is Amotivation. Amotivation can be seen as the opposite of the other types of orientations, particularly the intrinsic subtypes. Students who are amotivated feel that what happens to them is independent of how they behave. Such an experience is suggested to be similar to "learned helplessness" (Abramson, Seligman, & Teasdale, 1978; Seligman, 1975). These people tend not to value the activity, do not feel competent, and do not expect it will necessarily lead to a desired outcome (Ryan & Deci, 2000). When there is no clear relation between their behaviour and an outcome, they tend to disengage from the activity and, without a clear, personal reason for continuing, students might passively go through the motions if necessary, but would likely quit the activity as soon as it is feasible. If this situation is traumatic and of a long duration, feelings of perpetual anxiety and eventually depression and apathy may occur. This disengagement is illustrated by the comments of two students who clearly dislike their Spanish class and wish for it to be over (see Table 2).

The intrinsic and extrinsic orientations and amotivation lie on a continuum of self-determination, from amotivation, through external, introjected, identified and integrated regulation, to intrinsic motivation (the three subtypes of intrinsic motivation are not hypothesized to vary in terms of self-determination; see Figure 1). They are, therefore, expected to be correlated to greater or lesser degree, and amotivation is expected to be negatively correlated to the other types, to a greater or lesser extent. Our research generally supports this continuum. For instance, Noels et al. (in press; see also Noels, in press) found that, generally, orientations that were theoretically closer together on the self-determination continuum were more highly correlated than those further apart conceptually. Amotivation was moderately negatively related to the less self-determined forms of regulation and more strongly negatively related to the more self-determined forms. The practical implication of a continuum of orientations is that the orientations are not necessarily exclusive. If a learner is high in, for example, identified regulation, it might be expected that she will also show moderate levels of the orientations adjacent on the continuum. Hence, learners are not driven solely by one goal or another but rather may endorse several reasons for learning a language, although some are expected to be more important than others.

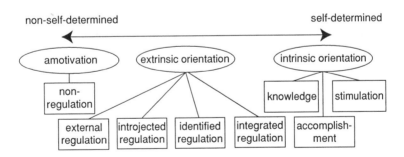

Figure 1: Orientation subtypes along the self-determination continuum (adapted from Ryan & Deci, 2000)

THE RELATIONS BETWEEN INTRINSIC AND EXTRINSIC ORIENTATIONS AND RELEVANT LANGUAGE LEARNING VARIABLES

Scholarly interest in the intrinsic orientation for L2 learning has grown over the past decade (e.g., Brown, 1990, 1994; Dörnyei, 1990, 1994a, 1994b, 1998; Julkunen, 1989), and several researchers have empirically examined the relations between this orientation and a variety of affective, behavioral, and cognitive variables. For instance, intrinsic motivation has been associated with lower anxiety, more positive attitudes towards language learning, and increased feelings of self-efficacy in language learning (Ehrman, 1996; Schmidt, Boraie, & Kassabgy, 1996). It has also been linked with behavioral variables, including language use, language learning strategy preferences, persistence and motivational intensity (Ramage, 1990). As well, it has been associated with cognitive variables, such as grammatical sensitivity, speaking and reading proficiency, and teacher ratings of competence (e.g., Ehrman, 1996; Noels, Clément, & Pelletier, 1999, in press; Tachibana, Matsukawa, & Zhong, 1996)

Looking specifically at the orientations described by self-determination theory, there is some support for the differential predictive power of the subtypes of orientations. Several studies show positive correlations between the intrinsic orientation and identified regulation and various outcome variables, such as motivational intensity and persistence (e.g., Noels, Clément, & Pelletier, 1999; Noels, 1999), positive attitudes towards language learning (e.g., Noels, in press), and competence in the L2 (Noels, in press; Noels et al., in press). As with the results described above, these findings suggest that those people who have an intrinsic or self-determined orientation are likely to feel positively about the activity and put in more effort over a longer period of time. In contrast, the correlations between less self-determined forms and these variables are generally lower or nonsignificant. This pattern suggests that having internal or external pressures does not reliably predict effort, persistence and attitude (Noels, in press; Noels et al., in press). Rather, it might be expected that such people will be involved in the activity as long as that contingency is present but less involved if it is withdrawn. Lastly, amotivation is consistently negatively correlated with motivational intensity, persistence, and positive attitude. Thus, having a reason of any kind is better than amotivation for ensuring that students are at least neutral regarding their L2 studies; having an intrinsic or self-determined orientation, however, is particularly helpful in the long run.

THE RELATIONS BETWEEN INTRINSIC, EXTRINSIC, AND INTEGRATIVE ORIENTATIONS

Although this paradigm may be useful for describing some L2 orientations, it is not intended to replace the notion of an integrative orientation. Indeed, the importance of the integrative orientation for some students is illustrated by the comments in Table 3. Rather, this framework should complement those in which intergroup orientations figure prominently. While the integrative orientation may be relevant for some learners, the exact manner by which the intrinsic/extrinsic and integrative/instrumental orientations relate to each other has received rather little attention. Some scholars claim that the integrative and instrumental orientations are synonymous with intrinsic and extrinsic orientations, respectively. For instance, Soh (1987) suggests that, like the integrative orientation, intrinsic motivation is defined by reasons that are more directed to the language and its culture for their own value; for example, language learning is viewed less as a means to an end than as an end in itself. On the other hand, like the instrumental orientation, extrinsic motivation refers to reasons for learning a language which are extraneous to that activity (e.g., Jakobovitz, 1970; Kelly, 1969; see also Dickinson, 1995); language learning helps one to achieve a distinctly different goal. Gardner (1985; Gardner & Tremblay, 1994; see also Stevick, 1976) maintains that these two sets of orientations are not parallel constructs. He suggests that both the integrative and instrumental orientations are extrinsic in that the language is acquired to achieve goals (i.e., intergroup engagement and tangible rewards, respectively) that are distinct from pleasure in the activity per se. It might also be argued, however, that the integrative orientation is similar to intrinsic motivation in that it refers to positive attitudes towards the activity and the learning process.

Table 3: Selected quotations from Anglo-American university students learning Spanish in response to the question "Why are you learning Spanish?": Integrative orientation

"I have a great affinity for Latino America and its various rich cultures. Learning Spanish will enable me to better absorb the culture. I genuinely like the language. It has been estimated that by the year 2025 at least 50–60% of California's population will be Latino. That's a lot of people! I wanna be able to communicate with them. It will become more and more necessary to know Spanish"

"(Honestly!) My friend that I feel that I will marry speaks Spanish because her mother is a native from Mexico. Speaking the language will allow me to assimilate easier into the family."

"To be able to speak with my boyfriend's family. To make friends in Latino communities."

"My boyfriend's family only speaks Spanish, and I want to get to know them better."

"Both of my parents are fluent in Spanish. Everyone on my dad's side of the family only speaks Spanish. I would like to be able to converse with them. Also, last summer I was in Ecuador and made many friends. However our communication was sometimes hindered [because] of my Spanish knowledge (they only spoke Spanish). When I return to Ecuador to visit my friends and Guatemala to visit my family in the summer, I would like to be able to converse [with] them."

continued…

Table 3: Selected quotations from Anglo-American university students learning Spanish in response to the question "Why are you learning Spanish?": Integrative orientation (cont.)

"Because I live in [California] and I would like to be able to communicate [with] the other half of [California's] community."

"The Spanish culture is so wonderful it appeals to me. It is everything that the culture I am used to isn't."

"I love being able to communicate with people who speak another language. I love the Spanish culture and the language is beautiful."

"I want to be able to communicate with as many people as possible. I find I have a lot of interest in other cultures, I respect my own culture, but wish to participate in as many diverse cultures as possible. My hope is a better connection for understanding others, but I don't have expectations of how they will respond."

"Basically I am studying Spanish [because] I have been interested in the language. I am very interested in the Latino/Mexican culture and beliefs. By learning the language, I hope to understand the culture and popular beliefs even better. I hope to teach my children the language and culture as well. I also hope to work with the latino community in some way, and by understanding the language and culture I can serve them better."

We have addressed this question empirically on several occasions. In one study (Noels et al., in press), correlations between the intrinsic and extrinsic orientations and the four orientations identified by Clément and Kruidenier (1983), including the instrumental, travel, knowledge, and friendship orientations, showed a strong link between the instrumental orientation and external regulation. The instrumental orientation was only modestly related to the other orientations. The three other orientations were most highly correlated with the intrinsic and identified regulation orientations. In particular, Clément and Kruidenier's Knowledge orientation was strongly correlated with the *Intrinsic-Knowledge* orientation.

In another examination of the link between the instrumental orientation and the intrinsic/extrinsic orientations (Noels, 1999), Gardner's (1985) index of the instrumental orientation was used. It was shown to be equally correlated with external regulation and with the more self-determined orientations (i.e., identified regulation and intrinsic motivation). One reason for the difference between the two studies may lie in the different operational definitions of the instrumental orientation. While Clément and Kruidenier's measure focuses on academic and career advancement, Gardner's measure assesses not only career goals but also the desire to develop knowledge and to gain respect from others. These different items may be tapping other forms of extrinsic orientations, and/or possibly intrinsic motivation (especially *Intrinsic Motivation — Knowledge*). Given the similarity in the conceptual definitions of external regulation and the instrumental orientation, it would seem reasonable to suggest that they represent the same construct, although the measurement instrument may require some refinement to ensure construct validity.

In examinations of the relation between the integrative orientation and the extrinsic/intrinsic orientations (e.g., Noels, 1999, in press; Noels et al., in press), we found that the integrative orientation is most strongly associated with the more self-determined forms of motivation (i.e., identified regulation and intrinsic motivation), although it does have modest correlations with the less self-determined orientations. It would thus appear that those students who are learning a language because they enjoy it are also learning the language because it may afford them an opportunity to interact with that language community.

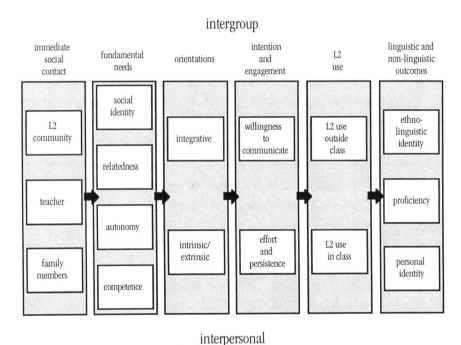

Figure 2: Heuristic model of the motivational process

This is not to suggest that the more self-determined orientations are conceptually the same as the integrative orientation. Indeed, the integrative orientation refers to social identity issues that are addressed by neither the intrinsic orientation nor identified regulation. Other research suggests that although some intrinsic and extrinsic orientations and the integrative orientation may be associated with variables such as motivational intensity and the intention to pursue studies in the

L2, the intrinsic orientation is more strongly linked with attitudes towards L2 learning than the integrative orientation, and the integrative orientation is a better statistical predictor of various intergroup contact and ethnolinguistic identity variables than the intrinsic/extrinsic orientations (Noels, in press). It is argued that these two orientations represent two separate motivational substrates, one pertaining to the intergroup situation and the other to the immediate learning situation (cf. MacIntyre, Clément, Dörnyei, & Noels, 1998; see Figure 2). Future research must determine how these systems interact in learners from different contexts.

FACILITATING INTRINSIC MOTIVATION: THE ROLE OF SIGNIFICANT OTHERS

Given that the intrinsic/extrinsic motivational substrate differentially predicts various language learning outcomes, how can an intrinsic orientation be promoted? The answer to this question rests on the fundamental assumption of self-determination theory that human beings have certain psychological needs, and fulfillment of these needs is necessary for individuals to behave in a self-motivated manner (Deci & Ryan, 1985; Ryan & Deci, 2000). Three inherent psychological needs are postulated. The first of these is autonomy (cf. de Charms, 1968; Deci, 1975), which refers to the need "to have one's behavior emanate from the self, for example, to feel volitional and self-determined" (Ryan & Solky, 1996, p. 251). Thus, human beings need to feel agentic, not as if they were the pawn of external forces. The centrality of this need is emphasized by the fact that it is the basis for the self-determination continuum described above. A second is a sense of competence (cf. Harter, 1978; White, 1963), for example, the feeling that one is effective in dealing with the environment (Ryan, Deci, & Grolnick, 1995). Individuals are motivated to develop their competencies by seeking out and overcoming challenges, in part because being competent can strengthen their control over their own behaviour. The third is relatedness (cf. Baumeister & Leary, 1995; Reis, 1994), which reflects the "propensity to be securely connected to and esteemed by others and to belong to a larger social whole" (Ryan & Solky, 1996, p. 251). As illustrated by research on attachment theory (e.g., Ainsworth, 1989; Ainsworth, Blehar, Waters, & Wall, 1978), the willingness to explore unfamiliar environments depends upon sense of security and trust in relationships with relevant others. These three needs are argued to be critical for fostering human beings' potential for growth and integration of the self.

To foster such development, these needs must be nurtured by contextual supports. If circumstances thwart these basic psychological needs, a person's self-motivation is undermined. Each of the needs is supported through different kinds of feedback from relevant others (Ryan et al., 1995). To enhance a sense of autonomy, individuals in the learner's social world must provide autonomy-supportive feedback. These significant others must encourage learners to be self-initiating, provide them with choices about learning, allow them to solve problems independently, and avoid asserting authority and control over them. The use of threats, deadlines, directives, imposed goals, or even imposed rewards, is likely to lower motivation (cf. Deci, 1975; Deci, Koestner, & Ryan, 1999; but see Cameron & Pierce, 1994; Eisenberger & Cameron, 1996).

To help develop a sense of competence, relevant others must provide informative feedback. It is essential that they structure the environment in such a way that the learner is clearly guided through the learning process. This is accomplished by providing a rationale for requested activities and by giving feedback that helps learners to determine why they performed as they did and how they could improve in future attempts. This should be done in a positive manner, by providing praise for achievements, making constructive suggestions for improvement, and not negatively criticizing shortcomings. To support a sense of relatedness, relevant others should be implicated in the learner's progress. This involvement includes supplying time, resources and attention to the learner, especially in a manner that encourages a sense that one is accepted and valued.

FUNDAMENTAL NEEDS AND THE COMMUNICATION STYLE OF RELEVANT OTHERS IN THE L2 CONTEXT

A variety of people in the L2 learner's social world can influence her self-perceptions of autonomy, competence, and relatedness. For the purposes of the present discussion, the role of teachers, family members, and members of the L2 community is considered, although other people may also play a part, including peers, employers, administrators, and so on (cf. Liskin-Gasparro, 1998; MacIntyre & Clément, 1998).

Teachers. It is reasonable to think that, as the person most directly implicated in L2 instruction, the language teacher has considerable influence on a L2 learners' motivation. Considerable research has looked at teachers' behaviours (or more often students' perceptions of their teachers' behaviours) and their link with students' behaviour. In most studies, teacher evaluation measures ask students to rate how positively they perceived their instructor in general terms, and the results suggest that these perceptions are related to L2 proficiency. In his review of 30 studies, Gardner points out (1985, p. 50) that the mean correlation between the evaluation of the teacher and grades across 30 studies is +.182. Although it is statistically significant, it must be acknowledged that this correlation is nonetheless low. It is conceivable that this association would be enhanced by including potential mediating variables, such as effort, although Vijchulata and Lee (1985) found no significant relation between general perceptions of teacher encouragement and motivational intensity.

Recently, we looked more directly at the particular aspects of communication style that are suggested by self-determination theory to facilitate motivation. Perceptions of the teacher as providing feedback about how to improve competence in a positive and autonomy-supportive (i.e., not controlling) style were associated with increased intrinsic motivation (Noels, Clément, et al., 1999). Elsewhere, it was demonstrated that perceptions of the teacher as providing informative feedback in a non-controlling manner are more important for self-perceptions of competence and autonomy than simply whether the teacher is perceived positively or negatively (Noels, in press). It must be noted that, like the correlations with general perceptions, the correlations between teacher perception and self-perception variables are not high. One possible explanation for this low correlation is that other people also influence learners' motivational intensity and ultimately L2 proficiency.

Family members. Other individuals who may foster or undermine students' L2 motivation are family members, particularly parents (e.g., Feenstra, 1969; Gardner, 1968; Koizumi & Matsuo, 1993; Sung & Padilla, 1998). Gardner (1985) suggests that, to the degree that parents are implicated in their offspring's attitude development, parents will also affect their child's language learning. He further argues that parents can actively and passively affect attitudes in two ways, by influencing general beliefs about language learning and the L2 community and attitudes towards the specific language course. He emphasizes that parental support is not directly related to achievement in the L2 but related to the willingness to persist at language study. In support of this position, Vijchulata and Lee (1985) found a positive relation between parental encouragement and students' motivational intensity in their sample of 1000 Malaysian university students learning English. Elsewhere, Gardner, Masgoret, and Tremblay (1999) found that retrospective accounts of parental encouragement predicted students' motivational intensity and attitudes towards the learning situation (both retrospective measures) but did not directly predict their current levels of motivation or attitudes. These findings suggest that parental encouragement contributes to the development of motivational intensity especially in the early years, which in turn is predictive of motivation as an adult.

Although parents may have the strongest familial influence, particularly when the learner is young, other family members may also affect motivation. For instance, spouses and romantic partners who come from other language communities may encourage (or discourage) the acquisition of their language. Grandparents who speak a language other than the language of the local community may support their grandchildren's attempts to learn the ancestral language. As well, anecdotal accounts (e.g., Noels, Adrian-Taylor, & Johns, 1999) suggest that siblings who speak the family's heritage language may foster younger siblings' L2 motivation. Thus, familial influences on motivation are not restricted to parents, but, depending on the background and life experience of the learner, other members may also play important roles in supporting motivation.

Members of the L2 community. Consistent with the intergroup perspective evident in many models of L2 motivation, several scholars have examined how support from the L2 community facilitates learners' motivation. For example, Genesee, Rogers, and Holobow (1983) argued that achievement and use depend upon the motivational support that the learner expects from the target language group. They asked English-speaking Canadian students why they were learning French and why they perceived French-speaking Canadians wanted them to learn French.

Perceptions of support from the French community predicted proficiency, use, and social affiliation measures over and above the students' own orientation.

In his socio-contextual model of L2 motivation, Clément (1980, 1986) addresses the intergroup communication climate more directly. He maintains that the quality and frequency of contact with members of the L2 group will influence self-confidence, motivation, and ultimately language proficiency. Elsewhere, Spada (1985, 1986) looked at aspects of contact and found that differences in amount and type of contact (e.g., interpersonal vs. media) were related to proficiency on some measures. Landry and Allard (1992; see also Allard & Landry, 1992) argue that the individual's network of linguistic contacts is an important predictor of aptitude/competence, cognitive-affective disposition, and ultimately language behaviour. This network includes interpersonal contacts (assessed usually in terms of the relative number of L1 to L2 speakers), access to media sources, and educational ambiance. This consideration of interpersonal contact generally focuses on the quantity of contact (but see Landry & Allard, 1992, for inclusion of other factors such as stability and quality of contacts). Research by Labrie and Clément (1986) suggests, however, that the quality or pleasantness of contact is of greater importance than the frequency of contact for developing the motivational process of self-confidence.

There has been some work that goes beyond general assessments of quality of contact to look at the specific aspects of the intergroup communication climate that facilitate L2 proficiency. Based on Giles and Byrne's (1982) intergroup model of L2 motivation, Leets and Giles (1995) argued that, depending on whether individuals construe the encounter as "interpersonal" (i.e., dependent on the individuals' personal characteristics) or as "intergroup" (i.e., based on perceptions of the other as a representative of a particular social category or group), individuals react differently towards members of the L2 community. It is assumed that individuals need to maintain a positive and distinct group identity in order to affirm their self-esteem. In intergroup encounters, they are therefore motivated to interact with the target language group in a way that ensures a positive social identity. When intergroup cognitions support a strong sense of ingroup loyalty and injustice, communicative climates are characterized by strong ingroup networks and negatively-valenced interactions with outgroup members. Such a communication climate would have negative implications for the development of L2 proficiency. In contrast, when cognitions entail less concern about ingroup loyalty and injustice, second language proficiency is likely to develop.

In addition to intergroup factors and social identity concerns, communication with the L2 community can be characterized by its autonomy-supportiveness, informative feedback and relatedness-enhancing involvement. In an initial examination of this issue, Noels and Rollin (1998) found that perceptions of control from the Spanish community tended to make Anglo-American university students feel greater introjected and external regulation, although these feelings were not associated with intrinsic motivation. Perceptions of positive feedback were associated most strongly with the intrinsic orientation, less strongly with the extrinsic orientations, and negatively with amotivation. Elsewhere, Noels (1999) found some support for this possibility, and further suggested that these support variables are more strongly related to the various motivational subtypes in heritage language learners than in modern language students of German.

In sum, then, some initial evidence suggests that different people can facilitate learners' motivation, including instructors, family members, and members of the language community. More research with each of these groups of people is necessary to understand how they support the learners' autonomy, provides information that can help improve the learners' competence, and make the learner feel that they are connected to relevant others. In addition, it should not be forgotten that social identity concerns are often pressing in many intergroup settings, and hence attaining a positive group identity may also be an important issue for language students. Thus, aspects of communication that relate to social identity needs should also be considered. As indicated in Figure 2, then, at least four fundamental needs are relevant to the language learning context, and each of these needs can be more or less nourished by relevant others in the social environment.

It is moreover conceivable that different people influence different fundamental needs in different ways. For example, it is reasonable to think that interactions with members of the L2 community, and perhaps the language teacher (if the teacher is a member of that community) are more relevant to social identity concerns than interactions with family members and/or peers. Because teachers generally set contingencies for developing language competence, issues of autonomy may be more important with instructors than with other groups who have less ability to directly control the student. Family members who are not fluent in the L2 may be able to provide little informative feedback but be quite capable of providing a sense of connectedness. In line with these speculations, we are currently conducting research to determine whether different people influence learners' motivation through different routes (i.e., through different fundamental needs; see Noels, 1999; Noels, Adrian-Taylor, et al., 1999).

THE LANGUAGE LEARNING CONTEXT

Implicit in the above discussion is the notion that aspects of the learning context have an impact on motivation (cf. Clément & Gardner, in press; Gardner & Clément, 1990). Clément and Kruidenier (1983) articulated several aspects of context that can affect the emergence and predictive power of orientations. The first factor is the opportunity for immediate contact with members of the target language community. Their research indicated that in unicultural settings there was a greater tendency for individuals to be interested in the L2 for sociocultural reasons, though not necessarily for friendship reasons. On the other hand, a Familiarity-Involvement factor, which included the notions of integration and identification, was relevant for learners who were at least minimally acquainted with members of the language group. The integrative orientation was only found among individuals in a multicultural setting who were learning a nondominant language. This suggests that a solid confidence in one's own group's position is necessary, as well as immediate access to the target language group, to support an integrative orientation. Elsewhere, Gardner and Lambert (1972) suggest that an instrumental orientation may be particularly useful when there is "an urgency about mastering a second language" (p. 141), such as when learning English in North America. Thus, the availability of members of the L2 group in the immediate environment would seem to influence the emergence and importance of different orientations.

The second related aspect is the relative dominance or nondominance of the language learner's ethnolinguistic group in comparison to that of the target group. Clément and Kruidenier argue that the relative ethnolinguistic vitality (Giles, Bourhis, & Taylor, 1977) of the ethnic group of the learner and that of the target language group influence patterns of orientations. For instance, they found that dominant groups reported learning the language to gain prestige and respect from the nondominant group or in order to maintain the relative status. As noted above, Giles and Byrne (1982) argue that perceived ethnolinguistic vitality and other intergroup cognitions (e.g., strength of cultural identification, perceptions of alternatives to the existing group situation, perceived ethnolinguistic vitality, perceived permeability between language group boundaries, and multiple group memberships) predict the strength of the integrative orientation. In examining various structural equation models of the intergroup model into which the integrative orientation was incorporated, Hall and Gudykunst (1987) found some support for a model in which intergroup cognitions, including the ingroup vitality, predicted feelings of integrativeness, which in turn predicted perceived nonlinguistic outcomes, which were correlated with perceived linguistic outcomes. Although an alternative model suggested that the causal sequence was more complicated in that some of the intergroup cognitions had direct effects on the linguistic and nonlinguistic outcomes, it is feasible to suggest that intergroup cognitions, including vitality, are related to feelings of integrativeness.

A third aspect of context is the ethnolinguistic background of the learner (Noels & Clément, 1989). In some cases, individuals desire to learn an ancestral language which is not the language of the dominant society (Cummins, 1998; Cummins & Danesi, 1990). Most of the research on the orientations of heritage language learners has focussed on the integrative and instrumental orientations (e.g., Feuerverger, 1989, 1991). This research has yielded somewhat contradictory results regarding the relative predictive power of these two orientations. For example, Teitelbaum, Edwards, and Hudson (1975) found that Spanish students who wished to use their new language skills in employment in the local Spanish community had lower Spanish proficiency than those who were learning Spanish for other reasons. Anisfeld and Lambert (1961) found that Jewish learners of Hebrew acquired greater competence if they were instrumentally oriented. The researchers suggested that the "instrumental" orientation of gaining employment possibly reflected a desire to integrate into the target language group's labour force, and by extension, into the group's culture. Elsewhere, Noels and Clément (1989) found that heritage language students in German university classes had a stronger orientation to learn the language in order to identify with and to have influence on the German community than did learners without such a background. This orientation was, however, negatively associated with motivation and German proficiency indices.

This research indicating contextual influences on the emergence and importance of orientations suggests that the integrative, intrinsic and extrinsic orientations may be more or less relevant depending upon the context. Some recent research (Noels, 1999) examined the orientations of university students of German who either had, or did not have, a heritage language background. The results indicated that heritage language learners had higher levels of identified regulation, but showed no difference from their nonheritage counterparts on the other extrinsic, intrinsic and integrative orientations. This is consistent with the idea that heritage learners feel that learning the language is important because it is personally relevant to their goals. Elsewhere, Noels, Adrian-Taylor and Johns (1999) found that, whereas English as a Second Language (ESL) students reported an external regulation orientation more often than heritage and nonheritage (i.e., modern language) students when describing their reasons for learning a language, integrated regulation and the integrative orientation were mentioned more often by heritage learners than by the other two groups. These results are consistent with the idea that different contexts sustain different orientations: where there is an "urgency" about learning, the focus may be on achieving immediate instrumental goals (as in the case of ESL learners), and where there is a strong familial influence there may be a heavier emphasis on issues of personal and social identity.

CONCLUSION: TOWARDS AN INTEGRATED MODEL

Figure 2 presents a theoretical framework which provides a heuristic for understanding how the various sets of constructs might be related. The model broadly divides motivational propensities into intergroup (the upper half of the model) and interpersonal (the lower half of the model) processes. These are not seen as exclusive categories but as a continuum along which some issues may be more or less relevant depending upon the context (cf. Turner, Hogg, Oakes, Reicher, & Wetherell, 1987). On the far right side, the individuals in the immediate context can nurture or frustrate learners' fundamental needs. Four fundamental needs are specified, following previous formulations of L2 motivation and self-determination theory. The more "intergroup" of these needs is a positive social identity. Somewhat less "intergroup" are the issues of relatedness, autonomy, and competence, although these may also be "intergroup" if they relate to interactions with other individuals from the L2 community on that level. To the extent that relevant others communicate with the learner in a way that supports the learner's autonomy provides positive and informative feedback for developing learner's competence, demonstrates their commitment to and acceptance of the learner by being involved in the learner's progress, and supports the learner's social identity, these fundamental needs should be met.

To the extent that autonomy, competence, and relatedness needs are fostered, a more self-determined orientation should develop. It is also expected that the provision of positive social identity support should encourage an integrative orientation, whereby the learner is interested in identification, influence, and interaction with the target language community. These different orientations are suggested to differentially predict how engaged the learner is in the L2 learning process, including effort (i.e., motivational intensity), persistence in L2 learning, and willingness to communicate with the L2 community (cf. MacIntyre et al., 1998). A related set of behavioural variables is language use, both inside and outside the formal classroom setting. Finally, language use is expected to have ramifications for L2 proficiency. As well, it might be expected that L2 proficiency has significance for ethnolinguistic identity (cf. Clément, 1980; Lambert, 1978) and also for personal identity concerns, such as personal self-esteem and the development of a sense of oneself as a good language learner.

Although these sets of variables are expected to be implicated in the motivational process of all language learners, as noted above, the relative emphasis on intergroup or interpersonal concerns is expected to be influenced by the contextual factors described above. For instance, for those people who have the opportunity for contact with the L2 group, and especially those who come from a relatively low vitality group and are learning a dominant language, interactions with the L2 community, social identity concerns, the integrative orientation, and L2 use in informal contexts may be particularly important. In contrast, those who have little contact and have high group vitality may evidence less concern about these issues. An example of such people is the member of a group with high relative vitality learning a nondominant language (i.e., a foreign language student). Another example might be international/ESL students who expect to return to their original culture and thus have limited interaction with the target language community beyond that necessary to successfully complete their program. Finally, both motivational aspects may be very relevant to heritage language students, who are learning a language which is not their dominant languageß but which is also an important part of their personal life.

In many respects, this model does not differ dramatically from the predominant models in the field (cf. Clément & Gardner, in press). Many of the constructs included and the predictions made are consistent with other models; the difference lies in the interpretation of those relations. Like Gardner's (1985) model, the model presented here emphasizes the important role that the social milieu has for learners' motivation, which in turn relates to the learner's experience in different contexts, and ultimately linguistic and nonlinguistic outcomes. Like Clément's (1980) model, aspects of the language learning context are suggested to have differential influences on the motivational processes. Like Giles and Byrne's (1982) model, it is emphasized that intergroup processes are relevant to language learning, particularly in certain contexts. The primary contribution of this approach lies in that it figuratively takes a magnifying glass to look more closely at the nature of orientations, how they are affected by significant others in different contexts, and how they may be differentially related to L2 variables. The result is that many issues important to language learning, such as anxiety, aptitude, and personality characteristics, are not yet incorporated into the model. Nonetheless, such an approach is useful because it provides a systematic framework for organizing orientations in a comprehensive fashion and also suggests the psychological mechanisms by which motivation may be enhanced or frustrated in different contexts. In turn, these principles provide suggestions for facilitating learner motivations, which may have considerable applied value in the language classroom and beyond. To date, our studies have provided some empirical support for aspects of this model; we expect that our current and future research will provide further insight into how the two motivational substrates work together, taking into consideration the various people who affect learners' motivation, and the diverse contexts in which language learning occurs.

REFERENCES

Abramson, L. Y., Seligman, M. E. P., & Teasdale, J. D. (1978). Learned helplessness in humans: Critique and reformulation. *Journal of Abnormal Psychology, 87,* 49–74.

Ainsworth, M. D. S. (1989). Attachments beyond infancy. *American Psychologist, 44,* 709–716.

Ainsworth, M. D. S., Blehar, M. C., Waters, E., & Wall, S. (1978). *Patterns of attachment.* Hillsdale, NJ: Erlbaum.

Allard, R., & Landry, R. (1992). Ethnolinguistic vitality beliefs and language maintenance and loss. In W. Fase, K. Jaspaert, & S. Kroon (Eds.), *Maintenance and loss of minority languages* (pp. 171–195). Amsterdam: Benjamins.

Anisfeld, M., & Lambert, W. E. (1961). Social and psychological variables in learning Hebrew. *Journal of Abnormal and Social Psychology, 63,* 524–529.

Au, S. Y. (1988). A critical appraisal of Gardner's social psychological theory of second-language learning. *Language Learning, 38,* 75–100.

Baumeister, R., & Leary, M. R. (1995). The need to belong: Desire for interpersonal attachments as a fundamental human motivation. *Psychological Bulletin, 117,* 497–529.

Belmechi, F., & Hummel, K. (1998). Orientations and motivation in the acquisition of English as a second language among high school students in Québec City. *Language Learning, 48,* 219–244.

Brown, H. D. (1990). M & Ms for the language classrooms? Another look at motivation. In J. E. Alatis (Ed.), *Georgetown University Round Table on Language and Linguistics* (pp. 383–393). Washington, DC: Georgetown University Press.

Brown, H. D. (1994). *Teaching by principles.* Englewood Cliffs, NJ: Prentice Hall.

Cameron, J., & Pierce, W. D. (1994). Reinforcement, reward, and intrinsic motivation: A meta-analysis. *Review of Educational Research, 64,* 363–423.

Chihara, T., & Oller, J. W. (1978). Attitudes and attained proficiency in EFL: A sociolinguistic study of adult Japanese speakers. *Language Learning, 28,* 55–68.

Clément, R. (1980). Ethnicity, contact and communicative competence in a second language. In H. Giles, W. P. Robinson, & P. M. Smith (Eds.), *Language: Social psychological perspectives* (pp. 147–154). Oxford, UK: Pergamon.

Clément, R. (1986). Second language proficiency and acculturation: An investigation of the effects of language status and individual characteristics. *Journal of Language and Social Psychology, 5,* 290.

Clément, R., & Gardner, R. C. (in press). Second language mastery. In H. Giles & W. P. Robinson (Eds.), *The new handbook of language and social psychology* (2nd ed.). London: John Wiley.

Clément, R., Dörnyei, Z., & Noels, K. A. (1994). Motivation, self-confidence and group cohesion in the foreign language classroom. *Language Learning, 44,* 417–448.

Clément, R., & Kruidenier, B. G. (1983). Orientations in second language acquisition: I. The effects of ethnicity, milieu and target language on their emergence. *Language Learning, 33,* 272–291.

Crookes, G., & Schmidt, R. W. (1991). Motivation: Reopening the research agenda. *Language Learning, 41,* 469–512.

Csikszentmihalyi, M. (1975). *Beyond boredom and anxiety.* San Francisco: Jossey-Bass.

Cummins, J. (1998). *Empowering minority students.* Sacramento: California Association for Bilingual Education.

Cummins, J., & Danesi, D. (1990). *Heritage languages: The development and denial of Canada's linguistic resources.* Toronto, Canada: Our Schools/Our Selves Education Foundation.

de Charms, R. (1968). *Personal causation: The internal affective determinants of behavior.* New York: Academic Press.

Deci, E. L. (1975). *Intrinsic motivation.* New York: Plenum.

Deci, E. L., Eghrari, H., Patrick, B. C., & Leone, D. R. (1994). Facilitating internalization: The self-determination theory perspective. *Journal of Personality, 62,* 119–142.

Deci, E. L., Koestner, R., & Ryan, R. M. (1999). A meta-analytic review of experiments examining the effects of extrinsic rewards on intrinsic motivation. *Psychological Bulletin, 125,* 627–668.

Deci, E. L., & Ryan, R. M. (1985). *Intrinsic motivation and self-determination in human behavior.* New York: Plenum.

Deci, E. L., & Ryan, R. M. (1995). Human autonomy: The basis for true self-esteem. In M. H. Kernis (Ed.), *Efficacy, agency and self-esteem* (pp. 31–48). New York: Plenum.

Dickinson, L. (1995). Autonomy and motivation: A literature review. *System, 23,* 165–174.

Dörnyei, Z. (1990). Conceptualizing motivation in foreign-language learning. *Language Learning, 40,* 45–78.

Dörnyei, Z. (1994a). Motivation and motivating in the foreign language classroom. *Modern Language Journal, 78,* 273–284.

Dörnyei, Z. (1994b). Understanding L2 motivation: On with the challenge. *Modern Language Journal, 78,* 515–523.

Dörnyei, Z. (1998). Motivation in second and foreign language learning. *Language Teaching, 31,* 117–135.

Ehrman, M. E. (1996). An exploration of adult language learner motivation, self-efficacy and anxiety. In R. L. Oxford (Ed.), *Language learning motivation: Pathways to the new century* (Technical Report #11) (pp. 81–103). Honolulu: University of Hawai'i, Second Language Teaching & Curriculum Center.

Eisenberger, R., & Cameron, J. (1996). Detrimental effects of reward: Reality or myth? *American Psychologist, 51,* 1153–1166.

Feenstra, H. J. (1969). Parent and teacher attitudes: Their role in second-language acquisition. *Canadian Modern Language Review, 26,* 5–13.

Feuerverger, G. (1989). Ethnolinguistic vitality of Italo-Canadian students in integrated and non-integrated heritage language programs in Toronto. *Canadian Modern Language Review, 46,* 50–72.

Feuerverger, G. (1991). University students' perceptions of heritage language learning and ethnic identity maintenance. *Canadian Modern Language Review, 47,* 660–677.

Gardner, R. C. (1968). Attitudes and motivation: Their role in second-language acquisition. *TESOL Quarterly, 2,* 141–150.

Gardner, R. C. (1985). *Social psychology and second language learning.* London: Edward Arnold.

Gardner, R. C., & Clément, R. (1990). Social psychological perspectives on second language acquisition. In H. Giles & W. P. Robinson (Eds.), *Handbook of language and social psychology* (pp. 495–517). Chichester, UK: John Wiley & Sons.

Gardner, R. C., & Lambert, W. E. (1959). Motivational variables in second-language acquisition. *Canadian Journal of Psychology, 13,* 266–272.

Gardner, R. C., & Lambert, W. E. (1972). *Attitudes and motivation in second language learning.* Rowley: Newbury House.

Gardner, R. C., Masgoret, A. M., & Tremblay, P. F. (1999). Home background characteristics of second language learning. *Journal of Language and Social Psychology, 18,* 419–437.

Gardner, R. C., & Tremblay, P. F. (1994). On motivation, research agendas, and theoretical frameworks. *Modern Language Journal, 78,* 359–368.

Genesee, F., Rogers, P., & Holobow, N. (1983). The social psychology of second language learning: Another point of view. *Language Learning, 33,* 209–244.

Giles, H., Bourhis, R. Y., & Taylor, D. M. (1977). Towards a theory of language in ethnic group relations. In H. Giles (Ed.), *Language, ethnicity and intergroup relations* (pp. 307–48). New York: Academic Press.

Giles, H., & Byrne, J. L. (1982). An intergroup approach to second language acquisition. *Journal of Multilingual and Multicultural Development, 1*, 17–40.

Graham, C. R. (1985). Beyond integrative motivation: The development and influence of assimilative motivation. In P. Larson, E. L. Judd, & D. S. Messerschmidt (Eds.), *On TESOL '84: A brave new world for TESOL* (pp. 75–87). Washington, DC: TESOL.

Grolnick, W. S., Deci, E. L., & Ryan, R. M. (1997). Internalization within the family: The self-determination theory perspective. In J. E. Grusec & L. Kyczynski (Eds.), *Parenting and children's internalization of values: A handbook of contemporary theory* (pp. 135–161). New York: John Wiley.

Hall, B. J., & Gudykunst, W. B. (1987). The intergroup theory of second language ability. *Journal of Language and Social Psychology, 5*, 291–301.

Harter, S. (1978). Effectance motivation reconsidered: Toward a developmental model. *Human Development, 21*, 36–64.

Jakobovitz, L. A. (1970). *Foreign language learning: A psycholinguistic analysis of the issues*. Rowley, MA: Newbury House.

Julkenen, K. (1989). *Situation- and task-specific motivation in foreign-language learning and teaching*. Joensuu, Finland: University of Joensuu.

Kelly, L. G. (1969). *Description and measurement of bilingualism: An international seminar*. University of Moncton, June 6–14, 1967. Toronto, Canada: University of Toronto Press/Canadian National Commission for UNESCO.

Koizumi, R., & Matsuo, K. (1993). A longitudinal study of attitudes and motivation in learning English among Japanese seventh-grade students. *Japanese Psychological Research, 35*, 1–11.

Kraemer, R. (1993). Social psychological factors related to the study of Arabic among Israeli high school students: A test of Gardner's socioeducational model. *Studies in Second Language Acquisition, 15*, 83–106.

Kruidenier, B. G., & Clément, R. (1986). *The effect of context on the composition and role of orientations in second language acquisition*. Québec: Laval University, International Center for Research on Bilingualism (ERIC Document Reproduction Service No. ED 347 790).

Labrie, N., & Clément, R. (1986). Ethnolinguistic vitality, self-confidence and second language proficiency: An investigation. *Journal of Multilingual and Multicultural Development, 7*, 269–282.

Lambert, W. E. (1978). Cognitive and socio-cultural consequences of bilingualism. *The Canadian Modern Language Review, 34*, 537–547.

Landry, R., & Allard, R. (1992). Ethnolinguistic vitality and the bilingual development of minority and majority group students. In W. Fase, K. Jaspaert, & S. Kroon (Eds.), *Maintenance and loss of minority languages* (pp. 223–251). Amsterdam: John Benjamins.

Leets, L., & Giles, H. (1995). Dimensions of minority language survival/non-survival: Intergroup cognitions and communication climates. In W. Fase, K.

Jaspaert, & S. Kroon (Eds.), *The state of minority languages* (pp. 37–71). Lisse: Swets & Zeitlinger.

Liskin-Gasparro, J. E. (1998). Linguistic development in an immersion context: How advanced learners of Spanish perceive SLA. *Modern Language Journal, 82,* 159–175.

Lukmani, Y. (1972). Motivation to learn and language proficiency. *Language Learning, 22,* 261–274.

MacIntyre, P. D., & Clément, R. (1998, May). *Willingness to communicate and language learning orientations of immersion students.* Paper presented at the meeting of the Canadian Psychological Association, Edmonton, Canada.

MacIntyre, P. D., Clément, R., Dörnyei, Z., & Noels, K. A. (1998). Conceptualizing willingness to communicate in a L2: A situational model of L2 confidence and affiliation. *Modern Language Journal, 82,* 545–562.

Moïse, L. C., Clément, R., & Noels, K. A. (1990). Aspects motivationnels de l'apprentissage de l'espagnol au niveau universitaire [Motivational aspects of learning Spanish at the university level]. *Canadian Modern Language Review, 46,* 689–705.

Noels, K. A. (in press). Learning Spanish as a second language: Learners' orientations and perceptions of teachers' communicative style. *Language Learning, 51.*

Noels, K. A. (1999, May). Intrinsic, extrinsic and integrative orientations for learning German: An examination of the role of others in supporting learners' motivation. In K. A. Noels & R. Clément (Chairs), *Language and social psychology: Current directions in Canadian research,* Symposium conducted at the meeting of the Canadian Psychological Association, Halifax, NS, Canada.

Noels, K. A., Adrian-Taylor, S., & Johns, K. (1999, November). *Motivation for language learning and communication style of significant others: An examination of learners in three contexts.* Paper presented at the meeting of the National Communication Association, Chicago, IL.

Noels, K. A., & Clément, R. (1989). Orientations to learning German: The effect of language heritage on second language acquisition. *The Canadian Modern Language Review, 45,* 245–257.

Noels, K. A., Clément, R., & Pelletier, L. G. (in press). Intrinsic, extrinsic and integrative orientations of French Canadian learners of English. *Canadian Modern Language Review.*

Noels, K. A., Clément, R., & Pelletier, L. G. (1999). Perceptions of teacher communicative style and students' intrinsic and extrinsic motivation. *Modern Language Journal, 83,* 23–34.

Noels, K. A., Pelletier, L. G., Clément, R., & Vallerand, R. J. (2000). Why are you learning a second language? Motivational orientations and self-determination theory. *Language Learning, 50,* 57–85.

Noels, K. A., & Rollin, E. (1998, August). *Communicating in a second language: The importance of support from the Latino community for Anglo-Americans' motivation to learn Spanish*. Paper presented at the meeting of the International Association of Cross-Cultural Psychology, Bellingham, WA.

Oller, J. W., Hudson, A. J., & Liu, P. F. (1977). Attitudes and attained proficiency in ESL: A sociolinguistic study of native speakers of Chinese in the United States. *Language Learning, 27*, 1–26.

Oxford, R. (1994). Where are we regarding language learning motivation? *Modern Language Journal, 78*, 512–514.

Oxford, R., & Shearin, J. (1994). Language learning motivation: Expanding the theoretical framework. *Modern Language Journal, 78*, 12–28.

Ramage, K. (1990). Motivational factors and persistence in foreign language study. *Language Learning, 40*, 189–219.

Reis, H. T. (1994). Domains of experience: Investigating relationship processes from three perspectives. In R. Erber & R. Gilmour (Eds.), *Theoretical frameworks for personal relationships* (pp. 87–110). Hillsdale, NJ: Erlbaum.

Ryan, R. M. (1995). Psychological needs and the facilitation of integrative processes. *Journal of Personality, 63*, 397–427.

Ryan, R. M., & Deci, E. L. (2000). Self-determination theory and the facilitation of intrinsic motivation, social development, and well-being. *American Psychologist, 55*, 68–78.

Ryan, R. M., Deci, E. L., & Grolnick, W. S. (1995). Autonomy, relatedness, and the self: Their relation to development and psychopathology. In D. Cicchetti & D. J. Cohen (Eds.), *Developmental psychopathology: Vol.1. Theory and methods* (pp. 618–655). New York: Wiley.

Ryan, R. M., & Solky, J. A. (1996). What is supportive about social support? In G. R. Pierce, B. R. Sarason, & I. G. Sarason (Eds.), *Handbook of social support and the family* (pp. 249–267). New York: Plenum Press.

Samimy, K. K., & Tabuse, M. (1992). Affective variables and a less commonly taught language: A study in beginning Japanese classes. *Language Learning, 42*, 377–398.

Schmidt, R., Boraie, D., & Kassabgy, O. (1996). Foreign language motivation: Internal structure and external connections. In R. L. Oxford (Ed.), *Language learning motivation: Pathways to the new century* (Technical Report #11) (pp. 14–87). Honolulu: University of Hawai'i, Second Language Teaching & Curriculum Center.

Seligman, M. E. P. (1975). *Helplessness: On depression, development, and death*. San Francisco: Freeman.

Skehan, P. (1991). Individual differences in second language learning. *Studies in Second Language Acquisition, 13*, 275–298.

Soh, K. C. (1987). Language use: A missing link. *Journal of Multilingual and Multicultural Development, 8*, 443–449.

Spada, N. M. (1985). Effects of informal contact on classroom learners' L2 proficiency: A review of five studies. *TESL Canadian Journal, 2*, 51–62.

Spada, N. M. (1986). The interaction between type of contact and type of instruction: Some effects on the L2 proficiency of adult learners. *Studies in Second Language Acquisition, 8,* 181–199.

Stevick, E. W. (1976). *Meaning, memory, and method: Some psychological perspectives on language learning.* Rowley, MA: Newbury House.

Sung, H., & Padilla, A. M. (1998). Student motivation, parental attitudes, and involvement in the learning of Asian languages in elementary and secondary schools. *Modern Language Journal, 82,* 205–216.

Tachibana, Y., Matsukawa, R., & Zhong, Q. X. (1996). Attitudes and motivation for learning English: A cross-national comparison of Japanese and Chinese high school students. *Psychological Reports, 79,* 691–700.

Teitelbaum, H., Edwards, A., & Hudson, A. (1975). Ethnic attitudes and the acquisition of Spanish as a second language. *Language Learning, 25,* 255–266.

Tremblay, P. F., & Gardner, R. C. (1995). Expanding the motivation construct in language learning. *Modern Language Journal, 79,* 505–520.

Turner, J. C., Hogg, M. A., Oakes, P. J., Reicher, S. D., & Wetherell, M. S. (1987). *Rediscovering the social group: A self-categorization theory.* Oxford, UK: Basil Blackwell.

Vallerand, R. J. (1997). Toward a hierarchical model of intrinsic and extrinsic motivation. In M. P. Zanna (Ed.), *Advances in experimental social psychology* (pp. 271–360) New York: Academic Press.

Vallerand, R. J., Blais, M. R., Brière, N. M., & Pelletier, L. G. (1989). Construction et validation de l'Échelle de motivation en education (EME). [Construction and validation of the Motivation toward Education Scale]. *Canadian Journal of Behavioural Science, 21,* 349.

Vallerand, R. J., Pelletier, L. G., Blais, M. R., Brière, N. M., Senécal, C., & Valliires, E. F. (1992). The academic motivation scale: A measure of intrinsic, extrinsic, and amotivation in education. *Educational and Psychological Measurement, 52,* 1003–1017.

Vallerand, R. J., Pelletier, L. G., Blais, M. R., Brière, N. M., Senécal, C., & Valliires, E. F. (1993). On the assessment of intrinsic, extrinsic and amotivation in education: Evidence on the concurrent and construct validity of the Academic Motivation Scale. *Educational and Psychological Measurement, 53,* 159–172.

Vijchulata, B., & Lee, G. S. (1985). A survey of students' motivation for learning English. *RELC Journal, 16,* 68–81.

Wen, X. (1997). Motivation and language learning with students of Chinese. *Foreign Language Annals, 30,* 235–251.

White, R. W. (1963). *Ego and reality in psychoanalytic theory.* New York: International Universities Press.

Mary McGroarty
University of Northern Arizona

SITUATING SECOND LANGUAGE MOTIVATION

Author's note

This paper is a much expanded version of remarks presented as a discussant at the Motivation and Second Language Acquisition colloquium at the American Association for Applied Linguistics conference in Vancouver, March 2000 (which included papers by Dörnyei & Clément; Gardner; Inbar, Donitsa-Schmidt, & Shohamy; MacIntyre, MacMaster, & Baker; Schmidt & Watanabe; Schumann; Williams, Burden, & Al-Baharna — all in this volume). I would like to express particular gratitude to Zoltán Dörnyei for organizing the colloquium and thank the other presenters for creating the opportunity for me to reexamine my perspective on L2 motivation by reflecting on the significance of their impressive and varied work.

INTRODUCTION

The question of why people learn or fail to learn second languages effectively has attracted attention from several scholarly quarters over the past decades and will surely continue to do so. The topic has tremendous theoretical import because of its relevance to models of learning processes and powerful practical consequences because of its implications for learning and instruction. In this discussion, I want to situate the study of second language (hereafter L2) motivation within concomitant developments in the fields of educational psychology and L2 learning. Contextualizing the study of L2 motivation amidst some of the developments in cognitive and social psychology as a whole contributes to renewed appreciation of the complexity and particularity of the factors affecting L2 learning. Taken together, the seven papers in the AAAL colloquium illustrate the breadth of concerns and suggest some of the directions for productive theorizing and research. I have added some additional examples from contemporary research to corroborate and complement some of the points made in the articles discussed. Many such examples are drawn from research on L2 learning in bilingual or multilingual settings. Hakuta and McLaughlin (1996) observe (accurately, I believe) that issues related to bilingualism are often regarded as derivative by mainstream psychology. However, I concur with Woolard (1999) that applied linguistics "should place bilingual and multilingual speakers and communities at its center, as prototypes rather than exceptions" (p. 4) in considering pedagogical issues as well as the sociolinguistic matters Woolard discusses. Many of the pedagogical questions related to L2 motivation in bilingual communities provide particularly apt examples of the multiple contributors to relative success or failure in L2 learning.

I have argued elsewhere (McGroarty, 1998) that one of the major theoretical frontiers for applied linguistics is the need to integrate constructivist forms of

McGroarty, M. (2001). Situating second language motivation. In Z. Dörnyei & R. Schmidt (Eds.), *Motivation and second language acquisition* (Technical Report #23, pp. 69–91). Honolulu: University of Hawai'i, Second Language Teaching and Curriculum Center.

scholarship with other approaches to problem definition and analysis, emphasizing the confluence of personal, social, and situational factors in language learning. I continue that line of argument here and use it to explore current work on L2 motivation. The seven papers presented at the AAAL 2000 colloquium on motivation and second language acquisition reflect major trends in the study of motivation generally by providing new information on the personal, social, and situational aspects of L2 motivation. In particular, they help to identify social and situational factors neglected in past research. Some of this neglect derives from the overemphasis on the cognitive in formulations of motivation (see Danziger, 1997, for an enlightening discussion of historical grounding of psychological categories, including motivation, in North American psychology;[1] and Dörnyei, in press, for a cogent presentation of contemporary developments in second language motivation). Psychological models of behavior dating from the last century ascribed equal emphasis to cognitive, affective, and conative[2] dimensions, as Snow, Corno, and Jackson (1996) note in a recent review. Even these dimensions are "somewhat arbitrary," as Snow (1989) remarks, for they are interrelated and dynamic: "Achievements become aptitudes for further learning, and knowledge, skill, strategy, regulation, and motivation intermingle; all have both cognitive and conative aspects" (p. 8). Hence educational psychology, like the psychology of L2 learning, is once again striving for a more holistic explanation for learning on a theoretical level.

---

[1] The historicity of psychological categories includes their cultural nexus. In that connection, it is fortuitous (but most relevant to this chapter) that the topic of motivation constitutes Danziger's initial extended example of cross-cultural variation in the conceptualization of fundamental psychological categories. He recounts that, while teaching at an Indonesian university for two years, he tried to plan a joint seminar with an Indonesian colleague in psychology; he suggested they might both discuss motivation, but found to his consternation that "the phenomena that I quite spontaneously grouped together as 'motivational' seemed to him to be no more than a heterogeneous collection of things that had nothing interesting in common" (1997, p. 1). Ultimately, he and his Indonesian colleague could find no mutually acceptable topics that they agreed could be addressed within the framework of psychology as each understood it, and no joint seminar ever occurred. This is but one example of the cultural specificity of categories often presumed to have universal relevance. The cultural appropriateness of any psychological category deserves particularly close scrutiny when used to justify any kind of intervention, including education, in settings to which it is imported.

[2] "Conation" is defined in this discussion, following Snow, Corno, and Jackson (1996), as "the tendency to take and maintain purposive action or direction toward goals" (p. 264). It is further comprised of motivation, the complex of attitudinal predispositions toward choices available in the environment, and volition, the set of decision processes and actions used to execute one's wishes or goals; together these form a "commitment pathway" linking deliberation with implementation (p. 264). The term was used in the late 19th century to denote "an assumed active principle in consciousness," notes Danziger (1997), but "suffered from the company it kept" (p. 114) because it was invented by philosophers and philosophical psychologists for whom evidence was largely introspective. Both the construct and its associated research method were much distrusted by North American psychologists, who preferred to speak of "motivation" of people's wishes and wants as objects that could be investigated and manipulated in the external world for practical purposes such as increasing consumer demand, improving personnel selection, and adapting educational programs.

The search for more holistic explanations also warrants new research approaches and analytical tools. As in other branches of psychology, studies of L2 motivation require additional methods to supplement the usual mode of data gathering and analysis, namely, the administration of surveys or questionnaires to individuals followed by statistical aggregation and manipulation of results. There are historical and disciplinary reasons for the predominance of this paradigm. Early on, North American psychology developed strong reliance on quantitative methods in order to distinguish itself as an objective, "scientific" pursuit, in contrast to European allegiance to methods such as introspection and case studies (Danizger, 1997). Quantitative, statistical methods have been typical of most work done in educational psychology, where individual differences have usually been identified and explored based on individuals' responses to various forms of questionnaires. Responses are then subjected to various types of correlational analysis and related techniques such as factor analysis, as Snow, Corno, and Jackson (1996) report; thus research in educational psychology has generally relied on statistical combinations or derivations of quantitative variables, in contrast to the concurrent use of projective techniques and clinical inference employed in other areas of psychology (p. 249). Research on L2 motivation has generally followed other branches of educational psychology in the dominance of the cognitive dimension and the predilection for quantitative and statistical methods found in the larger field of educational psychology, and many of the papers in the AAAL colloquium reflect these trends.[3] I address issues of additional research methods and approaches as they bear on some of future directions for L2 motivational research mainly in the latter half of this chapter. First, though, a recap of the colloquium papers as they touch on issues of the personal, social, and situational influences on L2 learning.

CONNECTING THE PERSONAL AND THE SOCIAL

The use of large-scale statistical approaches has offered foundational insights into reasons individuals might choose to study language. Certainly, Gardner's work (this

---

[3] It is enlightening that two quite current treatments of motivation, one aimed at educators generally (Blumenfeld & Marx, 1997) and one directed specifically at second language teachers (Williams & Burden, 1997) persist in ascribing a dominant role in motivation to cognitive factors, despite accumulating theory and empirical evidence that cognition is not all-encompassing and ought not to be considered the most influential or even the primary factor in either developing or sustaining motivation in classrooms (Snow, Corno, & Jackson, 1996) or, for that matter, elsewhere. It seems that academic psychology's allegiance to cognitive approaches, and the presumed prestige they entail, cannot easily be displaced in professional discourse by competing paradigms, as Danziger (1997) would attest. Indeed, in describing their "cognitive" model of motivation, Williams and Burden (1997) remark, "we are also acutely aware of the dangers involved in taking an entirely cognitive perspective, since this would be at odds with our emphasis upon the whole person, the importance of social interaction, and the influence of the context" (p. 141). The list of factors affecting motivation and the teacher guidelines they supply go well beyond the cognitive, as do the pedagogical guidelines suggested by Blumenfeld and Marx. It is hard to escape the conclusion that the writers here have struck an uneasy compromise between their sense of what counts in academic discussions and what matters for teachers in classrooms; to their credit, both sets of authors provide suggestions that are not limited to typical cognitive concerns for their practitioner audiences.

volume) on components of the integrative motive have helped us better understand that attitudes affect choices of language to study and behaviors directed at success. It is gratifying to clarify some misunderstandings, such as the presumptive superiority of integrative to instrumental orientations, apparently an overinterpretation of the rank order of two factors emerging in one of the early investigations, and useful to reiterate that both orientations are associated with success (see also Spolsky, 2000). Gardner's current conceptualization of an L2 aptitude that represents a combination of sociocognitive factors — the salience of a language in a particular environment, along with evaluations of the people who speak it — and learning preferences, which arise from, and in turn, shape, behavioral choices related to mode and frequency of second language study prefigures some of the suggestions I shall make regarding instructionally relevant research. Nonetheless, the appropriateness of the model implied in this approach poses some difficulties, as Dörnyei (in press) remarks, because of the premise that students have enough information about the target language group to have developed a relevant attitudinal set. In some foreign language settings, first-hand information about speakers of the target language is difficult to come by; learners may then depend on preconceptions or stereotypes. The large number of factors posited in this approach attenuates such concerns, in part; the multiple component scales included in the questionnaires also tap other relevant constructs such as perceived usefulness of the language and attitudes toward the language classroom. Most importantly, this model allows for systematic assessment of overall motivational intensity comprised of several possible factors, and thus allows for identification of multiple contributors to success in instructed L2 acquisition.

The link between individual and social influences is also foregrounded in Schmidt's research (Schmidt & Watanabe, this volume) on the motivational and attitudinal characteristics of university L2 students. Among other pertinent issues, this work raises the question of whether and how attitudes toward one's ancestral language could contribute to the integrative motive, or to motivational intensity generally, as in the case of Japanese background learners of Japanese as an L2 in Hawai'i. Such questions simultaneously invoke the personal significance and the contemporary social relevance of a particular language; one might study Japanese in Hawai'i not only to connect with part of one's family background and history but also to be able to deal with contemporary Japanese visitors, tourists, or businesspeople. It is not merely possible but even likely that such influences are not mutually exclusive. These findings demonstrate that individual motivation can simultaneously reflect group membership and contemporary social conditions.

Further research that illuminates such connections for a variety of ethnolinguistic groups in a variety of settings would be enormously valuable. Its value would be much enhanced by the addition of qualitative information on individual differences and longitudinal information on changes in motivational profiles over time. Additional qualitative follow-up of selected subgroups of L2 learners would help to distinguish the relative importance of family background and perceived usefulness as rationales for L2 study and/or L1 maintenance; longitudinal data would help to illuminate how change in individual circumstances affects language outcomes.

Zentella's (1997) thoughtful discussion of the dynamic relationship and some of the trade-offs between acquisition and use of English versus Spanish in a group of young New York Puerto Rican women suggests some of the ways the personal-social connection could be explored.

Another area reflecting the salience of social connections to L2 motivation is the degree to which students sense that valued others (parents and friends) support their efforts at L2 mastery. This perception is part of the attributional framework surrounding efforts to learn a second language. Many contemporary attribution theories (see MacIntyre, MacMaster, & Baker, this volume, for a description of some of them) place primary emphasis on the attributions that reflect judgments made by the individual self. Typically, in many psychological models of individual functioning, factors related to the opinions of others have been viewed as representing a distinctly secondary path of influence on learning, less consequential than concepts that relate to the individual learner's self. But is this justified either developmentally or cross-culturally? From a developmental perspective, it is quite natural that students should be sensitive to opinions of parents and teachers, surely one of the reasons that Gardner's socio-educational model included a role for the opinions of parents regarding language study. It is not surprising that the Bahraini secondary school students studied by Williams, Burden and Al-Baharna (this volume) rated opinions of parents and teachers as highly consequential in motivating students positively for language study.

The assumption that individual drives and motives outrank those ascribed to valued others also demands reexamination in light of recent cross-cultural work in psychology (e.g., Portes, 1996; Rueda & Moll, 1994; Segall, Dasen, Berry, & Poortinga, 1999) and anthropology (e.g., D'Andrade, 1992). This body of scholarship outlines the culturally mediated construction and directive force of motives for a wide range of choices and actions; so considered, an individual's reasons for doing (or not doing) anything are shaped and channeled by the cultural framework of beliefs and practices shared with significant others. Hence, behavioral choices regarding whether or not to study language, which language to study, and what kind of effort to make in studying language will be related to a host of other culturally as well as situationally anchored conditions. In this vein, current scholarship suggests that a more profound understanding of L2 motivation might emerge from the use of projective measures in addition to questionnaires. A stellar example of such research is the work of the Suárez-Orozcos (1995, chapter 5) on achievement motivation in four groups of adolescents: Mexican, first- and second-generation Mexican immigrants to the US, and non-Latino teens. They administered a widely used projective measure, the Thematic Apperception Test (TAT) to all four groups and found that, contrary to past stereotypes, the Mexican group showed the greatest need for self-initiated achievement. Moreover, and more pertinent to the present discussion, for the Mexican adolescents as for all the Latino groups, achievement as described in informants' accounts was invariably justified by the need to help family and community members rather than to attain personal independence, the justification most widely provided by non-Latino teens. Such findings argue that the connection between the personal and the social is strongly mediated by superordinate cultural patterns. Though there is certainly variation in such patterns, and though cultures are all, to some degree, dynamic, so that even superordinate patterns change, this approach to research suggests that studies of L2 motivation are incomplete to the degree that they do not gather information on broader cultural patterns that might affect L2 learning.

REFLECTING THE SOCIAL CONTEXT OF L2 STUDY

That students' motivation for L2 study both reflects and responds to changing social conditions is another central theme documented in several of these papers. Dörnyei and Clément (this volume) provide a fascinating glimpse of language choices made by Hungarian adolescents in a time of social change. When alternatives are available, the choice of language studied indexes many aspects of motivation, with social attitudes towards speakers of the target language and its perceived usefulness playing central but not exclusive roles. Attitudes towards speakers are bound up with attitudes towards a host of other factors such as likelihood and frequency of contact, historical connections and relationships between peoples, and relationship of language study to other valued social outcomes such as completion of formal schooling, university entrance, perceived occupational relevance, and so forth. The choices made by Hungarian youth reflect, thus, not only the unsurprising rejection of the once-required study of Russian (despite continued geographic proximity to Russian language areas) but also the attraction of English as a vehicle for personal growth and cosmopolitan contact. To some extent, it appears that English may have usurped the historic role of German as vehicle for advancement for Hungarian speakers. The differential preference patterns of young men versus young women invite further scrutiny as well, particularly given the relevance of language knowledge and loyalties elsewhere along the Hungarian-German language border. One might wish for some current comparative data from Oberwart, the village studied by Gal (1979), where even members of the Hungarian mother tongue community favored the study of German to provide greater opportunities for their children, who were increasingly required to make a living by wage work rather than by the agricultural pursuits that had sustained their parents and grandparents. Choice of language to study within an educational system is, hence, one piece of evidence for possible changes in social attitudes, which are themselves dynamic. Furthermore, such choices may lead to changes in patterns of linguistic interactions which shape and express social relations: in the future, will educated Hungarians and Germans speak to each other in English rather than German? Such diachronic questions are admittedly beyond the Dörnyei and Clément research. Their work on motivational profiles would be usefully supplemented by additional qualitative, ethnographic, and longitudinal reports of languages not only studied but eventually used by these young people.

Contemporary descriptions of L2 motivation (Dörnyei, in press) suggest that self and social context are mutually influential. All selves are socially situated, including the selves of language learners. The research on the teaching of Arabic to Hebrew speakers in Tel Aviv reported by Inbar, Donitsa-Schmidt, and Shohamy (this volume) presents another instance of the interplay between individual and social factors at a time of social change in a situation marked by decades, if not centuries, of close proximity and historic conflicts. To the personal-social dimensions of L2 motivation, the Israeli research adds explicit examination of the pedagogical context, thus bringing us to consider situational influences on motivation.

RESPONDING TO THE CLASSROOM SITUATION

The nature and quality of language instruction affect motivation. The Israeli research (Inbar, Donitsa-Schmidt, & Shohamy, this volume) demonstrates that, even when relations between language groups are marked by tension and lack of unanimity at the level of policy, second language learners are sensitive to the quality of the teaching of the "Other's" language. Their research on the attitudes of Hebrew-speaking students in Tel Aviv to Arabic instruction reminds L2 researchers (and reassures L2 teachers) that, in general, students recognize and respond positively to good quality instructional efforts. Whether or not L2 study in such contexts affects social harmony is a question worth asking and answering specifically in a variety of contact settings,[4] though beyond this chapter. More relevant to this discussion is the salience of L2 instructional quality, even in situations where there is tension between learners and the target language community, an issue that brings motivational concerns closer to instructional processes. These findings corroborate other recent Israeli research indicating that students give high priority to classroom-relevant aspects of L2 instruction (i.e., teacher command of the L2, teacher ability to organize instruction clearly, teacher propensity to treat students fairly) even when languages are taught largely by non-native speakers (Brosh, 1996). Clearly, situational factors reflecting the classroom realities of L2 students and teachers affect students' motivation in L2 instruction.

To any classroom, learners bring a sense of themselves as students and a set of expectations derived, in part, from all their past history of school learning. The role of learning expectations and preferences and their contributions to attributions of success in the L2 is highlighted in the MacIntyre, MacMaster, and Baker (this

---

[4] This is one variant of the argument that second language study produces individuals who are more open-minded than those without similar experiences, an argument often raised by proponents of second language study despite lack of unequivocal empirical support (see discussion in Robinson, 1997, among other sources). Perhaps what deserves comment is not the lack of empirical support but the assumption that required study of any subject will imbue learners with not only useful skills but also with necessarily positive attitudes toward the subject, an unjustified leap of faith for any instructional area. The case of attitudes related to second language study is further complicated by issues of relative proximity and political and social relationships across groups that use different languages as well as the fact that most language groups demonstrate considerable internal diversity in class structure, belief systems, and openness to interactions with outsiders or even younger community members who do not know their language well. Given individual differences across students of second languages, variety of teaching methods and materials (not to mention teacher preparation), and the internal diversity of most language communities, then, expectations of uniformly positive attitudinal outcomes from L2 instruction are not automatically warranted.

volume) research. In drawing on contemporary frameworks emphasizing the scope for action and control of action, notably Pintrich's expectancy value theory and Kuhl's action control model, this research approach applies to L2 learning an analytical framework found useful in the general study of individual differences in motivation (Snow, Corno, & Jackson, 1996). Further, it adds a dimension of self-efficacy (Bandura, 1997) to existing considerations of second language study, and also implicates the learners' sense of their own social image of themselves, an aspect of motivation included, though in much different fashion, in Schumann's (this volume) formulation. This line of investigation makes the crucial point that, whenever L2 learning takes place in school, L2 motivation must be identified and assessed in conjunction with general academic motivation. In such circumstances, L2 learning co-occurs with the student's general educational experience, so investigators should gather and analyze information on overall academic motivation either with separate instruments or through methods designed to tap the intersection of L2 and general motivation.

Such an approach honors the complexity of the many possible degrees of reciprocity and interrelationships between student motivation and educational situations. In educational institutions, as in other settings, situational influences on motivation are not always positive. Situational factors can affect academic and attitudinal outcomes in many directions, as studies of marginalized groups where students have developed identities of resistance or opposition to the dominant culture (e.g., Ogbu, 1991; Peshkin, 1997) have indicated.[5] In this regard, too, it is valuable to gather qualitative and longitudinal data to probe the perspectives of students, teachers, and parents in any setting of interest, to be aware that public statements regarding the value of education can coexist with profound ambivalence about educational

---

[5]   A detailed exploration of the concept of resistance as it affects a learner's educational career, including the dimensions of both formal language instruction and informal language acquisition, is beyond the scope of this chapter. Nonetheless, considerations of the individual and collective school experience of language minority communities raises a vital point: Most (but not all) early academic theorizing regarding L2 motivation has been initially constructed based on social situations where members of dominant language groups sought to acquire another language through formal instruction. Such learners face different personal and social contexts from members of non-dominant groups. Often, though again not always, they have comparatively little contact with the native speakers of the language they seek to learn. Often, though not always, they are enrolled in educational programs in which instruction and assessment are specially tailored for them, so that the situations in which they compete with native speakers in academic areas are comparatively rare. Learners from non-dominant groups whose education takes place perforce in their non-native language along with native speakers of that language (the so-called submersion model) face different educational demands. While the distinction between members of dominant and non-dominant groups is often clearer in the abstract than in actual situations, and there are emergent program models (e.g., what is now termed in the US *dual immersion*, or *developmental bilingual education*) that seek to teach members of two different native speaker communities together, it is still generally true that learners from dominant and non-dominant social groups experience different types of L2 education programs, formal and informal. Thus differences in personal and social circumstances co-occur with important differences in situational aspects of L2 learning in classrooms and of formal education generally. Comprehensive models of L2 motivation need to be able to describe the experiences of both sorts of learners.

requirements and processes and the consequent importance of devoting effort to instructional tasks. School and classroom environments are not necessarily either neutral or uniformly supportive of L2 mastery, even when a second language is the explicit focus of instruction.

What makes life in classrooms worthwhile for participants? Such a question lies at the heart of all formal education (Csikszentmihalyi, 1997). Schumann's chapter (this volume), one of the more speculative treatments of L2 motivation, suggests that some aspects of motivation and volition are usefully conceived by analogy to a foraging patch, an environment so important to our biological forebears that it has left an evolutionary mark on human neural organization. To what extent does it make sense to view a language learning classroom as a "good foraging patch"? Schumann suggests that some predispositions for learning are hardwired, and that understanding more about the neural and cognitive processes involved in translating a goal into motor activity will help us better understand how learning occurs. Minimally, he suggests, individuals show differing levels of need for novelty, levels of coping ability, and conceptualizations of actions compatible with their self-image as learners; the implication is that successful L2 instruction must take these into account. Even if the analogy seems farfetched, both the comparison and some of its attendant implications mirror pertinent developments in the conceptualization of effective learning environments, the area most in need of greater specification in understanding L2 motivation.

FORGING MISSING LINKS: INVESTIGATING THE MOTIVATIONAL POWER OF SITUATIONS

Dörnyei (in press) explains that "motivation as a psychological construct lies between the personal and social dimensions" and thus demands an analytical framework synthesizing these; he sees developments in sociocultural approaches to motivation as major relevant contributions in recent work. To this analysis I would add that, insofar as a framework for the study of motivation is intended to bear on theories of L2 learning or guide pedagogical decisions, it must also provide ways to identify and assess motivationally-relevant aspects of L2 instruction to a far greater degree than is now usually done. Without such research foci, investigation of L2 motivation becomes an intellectual enterprise worthwhile in its own terms but removed from the major site of planned L2 acquisition, the classroom. While current models of L2 motivation are indeed useful in understanding general outlines and individual differences across various language learning contexts, they do not (and cannot) provide support for a comprehensive L2 learning theory or guidance for concrete pedagogical alternatives aside from some general precepts regarding provision of varied, well-organized instruction delivered with due consideration to students' language levels and affective states. Though many of the articles include data gathered from the occupants of classrooms, only a few chapters tap the participants' perceptions of classroom activities, and none examines classroom activities or processes directly. In the balance of the chapter, I review some current developments in educational psychology, cognitive science, applied linguistics (particularly sociocultural theory and research as applied to L2 issues), and applied pedagogical work on educational innovations to point out the still-missing links between the much-expanded understanding of individual differences in L2 motivation to which many chapters contribute welcome new data and the areas requiring further specification to bridge the gap between individual L2 motivation and an adequate theory of L2 instruction. For further insights into possible links between L2 learning and actual instructional techniques, it is necessary to revisit past paradigms in educational psychology and go outside the bounds of quantitative educational psychology to identify research topics and methods of potential relevance. In this discussion, I am explicitly *not* concerned with those who acquire L2s informally, without participation in formal instruction, though some of the following guidelines may well apply to uninstructed learners. While it is essential that adequate theories of L2 motivation capture the experiences of all learners, instructed and uninstructed, successful and less successful, I contend that the most productive directions for future work on L2 motivation as related to instructed learners will come from research that examines aspects of instruction directly.

REVIVING AND REFINING ATI STUDIES

The renewed attention to the connections between personal and social dimensions of language study amply demonstrated by many chapters here argues for renewed use of an investigative paradigm not often applied to L2 learning, the Aptitude-Treatment Interaction (ATI) approach (Cronbach & Snow, 1977). In ATI work, a particularly relevant student attribute, or aptitude, is defined, measured, and assessed in conjunction with a particular instructional intervention, or treatment. Assuming appropriate measures of both aptitude and treatment, analysis permits identification of the ways in which the aptitude interacts with the treatment, such that student outcomes may vary systematically according to aptitudinal profiles. In ATI studies, the interaction effects — ascribed to error in most conventional statistical analyses — become interpretable based on the accuracy and situational appropriateness of the aptitude measure employed. When aptitudes and treatments are both carefully defined, and systematically monitored and assessed, observed interactions between them on outcome measures of interest (i.e., for our purposes, some aspect of L2 learning) can be interpreted to illuminate their pedagogical relevance.

An early instance of language-related ATI research is Tang's (1971/1972) investigation of the learning of English by Cantonese-speaking children aged 7 to 13, all relatively recent (average length of US residence was 10 months) immigrants from Hong Kong. She assessed the children's attitudes towards their native Chinese dialect (Cantonese) and English through matched-guise instruments; thus attitudes towards Chinese and attitudes toward English were the relevant aptitudes. She then split the entire sample into two equivalent groups of small classes, and had both groups instructed in science concepts by the same teacher who used two different methods, or treatments, one requiring translation of science concepts into Cantonese along with English and one using only English. The translation and non-translation groups were then compared on their mastery of science concepts on a science-related reading test in English, the criterion measure. Findings showed a significant interaction between method of instruction used and attitudes of the learners towards the two languages: When the instructional method used native-language translation, as it did for half the classes tested, English science reading scores had a significant positive correlation with positive attitudes towards Chinese, whereas when instruction used only English, there was a significant positive correlation between English science reading ability and attitudes toward English and a significant negative correlation with attitudes towards Chinese. Thus attitudes towards both of the languages used during instruction were associated with differential student outcomes, suggesting that, from a student perspective, the value of native language instruction is mediated by student attitudes toward the L1 and L2. This provocative finding has considerable potential relevance for bilingual instruction in many settings and invites replication with other language groups and in other subject areas.

Findings from ATI research are not always so straightforward. Even the developers of the ATI model cautioned against its use to establish invariant models of learning, emphasizing that "ATI cannot be pinned down as generalizations" (Cronbach & Snow, 1977, p. 494). They advised that ATI research should instead be used to build up a body of pedagogically relevant knowledge about the probabilities of various types of learner X treatment interactions in identifiable circumstances. They further noted the need to distinguish between interactions based on general intellectual abilities and those based on specialized abilities, such as spatial or mathematical reasoning, prior learning experiences in the same subject, or memory capacity, relevant to a particular content area or outcome measure. Because most ATI-related research had been done on a relatively short-term basis with well-defined skill areas such as the learning of mathematical concepts or computational algorithms, concepts or procedures in science classes, and structural aspects of foreign language learning, they pointed out that all such constraints limited its utility as a source of guidance in everyday instructional contexts.

Later critiques of the ATI approach (e.g., Driscoll, 1987) echoed these cautions and added to them other observations regarding, for example, the difficulty of specifying which aptitudes might be relevant to a given instructional situation and the near impossibility of locating instructional interventions that embody a single, consistent approach, among others.

However, subsequent scholarship in educational psychology and other fields suggests that these potential shortcomings can be remedied fairly easily, and remedied in ways that would enhance the potential of ATI work to illuminate relevant aspects of L2 learning and teaching. In the first place, the concept of aptitude, treated for many years, erroneously, as unitary and more or less equivalent to intelligence (particularly in North American discourse and practice) has been revived and expanded to include concurrent dimensions of affect and conation, very much in line with its historic meaning (Snow, 1992); aptitudes are now seen as "a complex of properties, qualities, states, or conditions of persons (not just a traitlike cognitive unity) that enable profitable learning or development under specified situational constraints" (Snow, 1992, p. 8). In the nearly quarter century since the ATI approach was first propounded, there have been several important sources of more precise information on aptitudes relevant to L2 learning. These include descriptive portraits of effective learners that provide learners' detailed accounts of their own favorite learning techniques (e.g., Stevick, 1989); ethnographic descriptions of programs promoting success for language minority students by, among other means, incorporating constant and explicit attention to students' affective states (Abi-Nader, 1990; Hornberger & Micheau, 1993); and additional formal psychometric explorations of components of L2 aptitude (e.g., Parry & Stansfield, 1990). Findings from some of the studies included in other chapters in this volume also suggest constructs that might reasonably be incorporated into an expanded definition of L2 aptitude relevant to a particular student sample. Such widely varied investigations yield a much greater body of descriptive research to assist in generating expanded definitions of L2 learning aptitudes for investigation in specific instructional situations.

The second main objection to ATI research, that is, the difficulty of ensuring the conceptual or functional coherence and distinctiveness of any instructional treatment, or method, can readily be addressed if investigators recognize it as an issue. Advances in technology and openness to a wider range of methodologies in educational research both provide ways to document the nature of instructional methods. The increasing availability and relatively low cost of video and audio recording have made it possible to collect reasonable samples of classroom activity and various types of student and/or teacher think-aloud or other process-oriented protocols. (The collection of such data, though, constitutes only part of the necessary information here; equally crucial is the analytical system used to identify and analyze events recorded and the research time needed to conduct such analysis.) An increasing openness to a range of approaches to classroom and school observation, including ethnographic and qualitative work, participant interviews, and examination of student work samples, now enable investigators to draw on an array of alternative and complementary approaches if they wish to gather information on the activities of actual teachers and students interacting in classrooms and schools. Ensuring (or, minimally, monitoring) fidelity of treatment or adherence to any instructional method in ATI research is certainly feasible in principle, if expensive to implement.

While the ATI paradigm no longer promises to establish "all the answers" as was (naively) hoped in the late 1970s, it can still provide useful, context-specific information of theoretical as well as practical value. The insight that students may respond differentially to instructional programs based at least in part on relevant aptitudes, with aptitudes now defined in a comprehensive and multi-faceted fashion, following Snow (1992), merits continuing investigation across the full range of school contexts in which students acquire L2s through instruction.

CREATING DIVERSIFIED LEARNING ENVIRONMENTS

Research on expanded definitions and explorations of aptitudes and treatments represents but one avenue of potential utility in future investigations of L2 motivation. Another body of literature with nascent but suggestive relevance to L2 learning grows from current research, still largely descriptive and exploratory, on innovative learning environments such as children's museums, after-school enrichment clubs, and classrooms designed for innovative instruction in math, science, or literacy (Schauble & Glaser, 1996). At the outset, some mismatches in level and setting that argue against direct applicability to L2 instruction should be noted. To date, such research has been conducted mainly with students at the elementary or middle school levels; moreover, much of it focuses explicitly on informal learning environments outside the confines of traditional classrooms. Nevertheless, it bears examination because of the expanded definitions of the goals and means of instruction suggested. It is the sense of expanded instructional goals and varied means of achieving them that speak to all educators and have, I think, potential for establishing an expanded concept of L2 motivation. Research on innovative and informal learning environments raises pedagogically relevant questions about whether and how classrooms can provide students with a menu of relevant activities to support L2 acquisition.

Learning in informal environments tends to be marked by several features differing from conventional grade- or level-segregated classrooms. It is usually voluntary; responsive to a broader agenda such as personal or group development; tied to developing successful social interactions with a wide variety of others, including age peers, younger children, and adults; and more supportive of individual differences, attesting that "the path of learning in these contexts will vary substantially from individual to individual" (Schauble, Beane, Coates, Martin, & Sterling, 1996, p. 8). Attention to individualization is a characteristic of some other approaches to education, including the Montessori approach. Discussing Montessori classrooms, Csikszentmihalyi notes that they offer "enough interesting, useful, growth-producing material to catch the child's attention so that we can allow that freedom and choice because...the outcome is going to be productive whatever the child does in that setting" (1997, p. 28); he associates such conditions with higher probability of becoming engaged enough in an activity to achieve the "flow" experience, which is marked by clear goals, immediate feedback, challenges that match available skill levels, ability to focus and avoid distractions, having a large degree of control over the situation, and not being made to be self-conscious (Csikszentmihalyi, 1997, p. 8). Educational psychologists working with mainstream school subjects have also noted that the tasks occupying the majority of student time in classrooms strongly shape the levels of student engagement shown, observing that "Meaning, challenge, variety, and choice are important dimensions of tasks on which students work" (Blumenfeld & Marx, 1997, p. 96).

Creation of such conditions to support learning poses enormous challenges for all educational areas, not only for L2 education. The hallmark characteristics — variety, choice, control, opportunity for immediate feedback — contrast sharply with most school curricula, including those typical of L2 instruction, which usually specify not only goals but also the means, including prescribed methods and materials, used to achieve them. To the degree that L2 instruction must follow a relatively small set of pre-specified directives regarding classroom materials, activities and forms of testing based either on teacher or student expectations or policies from other authorities such as ministries of education, university entrance exam boards, or large commercial testing companies, there is relatively less scope for the variety and personalization that can attract and sustain engagement in L2 learning tasks. The reduced scope for personalization and individualization then places greater responsibility on the teacher to devise a variety of learning tasks to see that students can make progress in L2 learning.

Note that such a view of motivation shifts the primary object of investigation somewhat. It implies moving away from identification of individual differences in the motivational profiles of students in a class and towards identification of the varieties of motivating activity available in the instructional environment. The relative motivational power of the classroom and the motivational value of the tasks and activities students are asked to complete are paramount. Because not all students would, presumably, find the same types of activity interesting, engaging, and productive, individual differences would still show up in the range of activities identified, but now it is the characteristics of the learning activities themselves that come into focus. As yet, few L2 researchers have taken this fundamental issue seriously, although it is a major concern of practicing educators.

Questions about the motivational power of various possible learning activities pose particular challenges for L2 instruction, notably but not only at beginning levels of proficiency. By definition, L2 students have little proficiency in the language and must thus somehow manage to acquire a sufficient base in the language — its grammatical structures, vocabulary, knowledge of necessary functions and discourse conventions, awareness of relevant sociolinguistic patterns — to allow them to carry out engaging tasks. In L2s classrooms, students have to find a way to "get far enough to like it" (Hornberger & Micheau, 1993)[6] so that L2 use supports a variety of interesting activities which, in turn, promote further L2 mastery. In this respect, L2 instructors must consider an explicitly linguistic dimension to other elements of designing instructional tasks and activities that manifest variety, choice, and control. It is no accident that much of the most enlightening or instructionally relevant research on tasks affecting L2 learning has been conducted either in

---

[6] The researchers cite this phrase from one of their participants, the coordinator of a bilingual enrichment program, who used it to describe her own professional development; she had managed to get through an initial period of uncertainty and opposition to the new program, and observed that she was at last "getting far enough to like it." While the article does not specifically relate the quote to language learning, it aptly captures one of the principal goals of L2 instruction (and instruction in other areas, for that matter), namely getting to a stage of proficiency or skill that is personally rewarding. Thus, while I have appropriated the quote to apply it to language learning, doing so is consistent with the metaphorical extension offered by Hornberger and Micheau (1993) in their description of the nature and quality of the accomplishments and challenges of the program they observed.

immersion or bilingual programs.[7] Both types of programs must address all curricular areas; thus their instructional responsibilities are greater, but so is the range of subjects which can (and, depending on student circumstances, must) become a potential means of further L2 learning. As interest in task- and content-based L2 instruction grows, it is natural to ask about appropriate sources for learning tasks and content. In most formal instructional settings, the required school curriculum offers possibilities greater than a structurally based language curriculum, and so furnishes a reasonable point of departure.

In many L2 instructional contexts, calls for even a modicum of instructional variety and student choice and control of tasks are quite daunting, particularly in settings where curricula, syllabus design, materials, methods, and forms of assessment are preordained and teachers have little or no scope to alter them (or when teachers have such an unsteady grasp of the L2 themselves that they feel lost without a detailed instructional script). Yet the difficulty of replicating all such conditions does not obviate the need to explore their applicability to L2 instruction and acquisition.

SHAPING L2 LEARNERS' SOCIAL INTERACTIONS

Documentation of tasks and activities that promote and support learning must include the social relations that surround the classroom and the social and interactional patterns within it; social relations and learner interactions can support, constrain, or inhibit learning. Teachers have long noted that classes, even in the same subject at the same level, can differ greatly from one another in overall tone. Such differences are sometimes ascribed to temporal constraints (teaching the first period of the day or the slots before or after lunch breaks being notoriously difficult), sometimes to actual physical conditions in classroom life (Shamim, 1996, reports the poignant case of "girls in front" in extremely large English classes in Pakistan developing identities as successful learners, while "girls in back" were seen by teachers and themselves as less motivated, less interested, and less likely to do well — this in crowded classrooms where neither teachers nor students had much physical mobility), but oftentimes the source of differences between otherwise similar student groups appear inexplicable although palpably present. Teachers, including L2 teachers, regularly speak of "unmotivated classes." Current investigations of psychology in organizations confirms their intuitions in

---

[7] I am well aware that there is enormous internal variation in programs designated either "immersion" (Johnson & Swain, 1997) or "bilingual" (Baker, 1996; Freeman, 1998; Ramirez, 1992), and that many contextual factors determine program choice (Genesee, 1999). Because (in theory) full immersion and bilingual programs must address all curricular areas, they have more instructional time available. Because both types of program, broadly speaking, demand that language become a medium as well as an object of instruction, they offer relatively greater scope for a variety of learning tasks. While it is important to have an accurate sense of program conditions, it is still quite possible that some of the learning activities and tasks developed in immersion or bilingual education contexts could be used in other types of L2 programs, given appropriate conditions and instructional support.

demonstrating that "the average level of motivation [is] a key group resource" (Siebold, 1994, p. 173); organizations such as the military and large corporations take the creation and maintenance of highly motivated groups or teams as one of the major challenges of leadership. It is also one of the major challenges of pedagogy, though not often recognized as such.

Theoretical developments in the genesis of learning, considered at a conceptual level, and the study of educational innovations suggest that the awareness of groups as being different from collections of individuals and having their own distinct processes and mores will begin to open up new avenues of insight in education generally and in L2 work specifically. Cognitive science now seeks to incorporate the temporally, physically, and socially grounded nature of experience more effectively in its theoretical apparatus (Clark, 1997). The social relations prevailing in any environment frame and channel the activities occurring therein. Discussing the origin of advanced cognition, Clark explains that human brains are meant to "make us masters at structuring our physical and social worlds" to support activities we wish to pursue, and that "it is the human brain *plus* these chunks of external scaffolding that finally constitutes the smart, rational inference engine we call mind" (1997, p. 180). The external scaffolding includes social relations and interaction patterns; educational theorists and L2 instructors must consequently ask what kinds of social relations can scaffold and promote (or, conversely, inhibit) motivation for the students with whom they work (Drillings & O'Neil, 1994). On a theoretical plane, much important work is now done within the context of sociocultural theory. Investigators working under this general rubric (e.g., Granott, 1998) have begun to document the kinds of verbal exchanges that occur as small groups of learners try to explain novel observations and processes to each other. Carried out in an engineering lab where graduate student participants tried to induce the constraints on the movement patterns of robots, such descriptive work suggests that learners can create together a joint discourse that all involved find to be genuinely instructional.

Within L2 scholarship, there is also considerable interest in using sociocultural theory to explore and explain L2 learning (Lantolf, 2000). Like the cognitive theory work described by Granott, many such studies highlight the importance of collectively-constructed discourse as a means of L2 learning. Similar findings come from research on the way two learners doing a picture-based jigsaw story-reconstruction task assist each other's language development (Swain & Lapkin, 1998). Thus far, studies in following this paradigm have provided intriguing descriptions based on the learning processes observed in selected small groups of high ability learners. L2 researchers have provided evidence that students can indeed assist each other's target language performance, but such assistance does not always lead to either content accuracy or linguistic correctness. It is, rather, an opportunity for additional language use that may or may not contribute to mastery of content or growth in linguistic proficiency or, to the point of this chapter, growth and maintenance of motivation for the subject in question. Furthermore, and a point of considerable challenge to typical forms of assessment, it is quite likely that different pairs of students will construe and execute tasks differently, thus necessitating pair-specific assessments to reflect their language learning accurately (Swain, 1995). Still needed, as the researchers note, are descriptions of learners with a variety of levels of knowledge, task familiarity, familiarity with each other, and L2 proficiency doing these tasks and others (Swain & Lapkin, 1998). I suggest that the social relations surrounding and governing learner interactions must also be studied if their impact on L2 motivation is to be fully understood.

Despite evidence that social units larger than the individual can be legitimate foci of educational investigation, there is great uncertainty about whether and how to use group configurations during actual classroom instruction. Nowhere is this clearer than in the literature related to implementation of cooperative learning, an approach that has elicited considerable interest for its potential to provide academically relevant L2 development and an arena for acquisition of academically relevant social skills. Indeed, researchers committed to the development of cooperative approaches emphasize the need to pre-train learners in appropriate social skills prior to attempting group work (Cohen, 1994; Shulman, Lotan, & Whitcomb, 1998). Some observations pertinent to an expanded view of L2 motivation come from a year-long, ethnographic study of the implementation of a cooperative approach across a variety of subjects in linguistically heterogeneous upper elementary classes (grades 4–6) in the US (Jacob, 1999). Teachers had been attracted to the use of cooperative learning because of its potential to provide students with peer support for academic and social skill development, including a motivational environment that would, teachers hoped, sustain student engagement. As the year went on, investigators found, teachers' relative focus on and commitment to aspects of academic and social growth changed in response to their experience with cooperative instruction. Closer observation of the interactions of students showed that cooperative approaches often afforded L2 learners considerable opportunities to develop academic English, but, aside from overt assistance with decoding, relatively infrequent opportunities for other, more challenging forms of language development. Investigators observed that "local contextual features [such as] students' definitions of the task, features of the task, and participant structures" appeared to affect the outcomes observed (Jacob, Rottenberg, Patrick, & Wheeler, 1996, p. 274). Particularly important from a motivational standpoint was the delicate interplay between group dynamics and level of task challenge: when group cohesiveness broke down somewhat and tasks became more difficult, students were less likely to help each other, suggesting a sort of dynamic equilibrium between need to attend to social relationships and need to complete academic tasks. Such an equilibrium would explain some of the connections between task types, group configurations, and the motivational power of the learning environment. The investigators' rendition of a "mixed picture of positive opportunities and lost potential" argues for careful exploration and documentation of the contextual specificity of cognitive, affective, and conative dimensions of cooperative experience. All vary by task; all are channeled, in part, by the social interactions that comprise instruction; and all affect learning outcomes with respect to subject mastery and L2 acquisition. Further, expanding the focus of L2 motivational work to include the variety, nature, and effects of various group configurations on task interpretation and completion poses complexities for researchers, but such complexities are precisely those that face educators who want to know when, where, and how interactions can support L2 learning.

A methodological note: it is germane that much of the research cited in this section is qualitative and ethnographic in nature. Ethnographic techniques add an element of temporality to educational research that is doubly important for the study of motivation. All academic studies of motivation now distinguish between the incentives to begin an action and the incentives related to making continued effort (see, for example, Blumenfeld & Marx, 1997; Snow, Corno, & Jackson, 1996, for discussion of educational motivation generally, and Dörnyei, in press, for applications of this difference to the study of L2 motivation). The motivational tenor of any classroom, including its constitutive social relations, can probably only be gauged over time. It is likely that the motivational level of a social unit, whether an entire classroom or a small group or pair working within the class, waxes and wanes somewhat depending on both the variety of activities and tasks occurring (the situational dimensions described in the previous section) and on the social interactions framing the activity.

CONCLUDING THOUGHTS ON L2 MOTIVATION: THE INSTRUCTIONAL CHARGE

To be relevant to L2 instruction, motivational research must broaden its investigative focus on the individual learner. For the last 50 years, motivational research has largely relied on statistical aggregation of results from individual learner surveys or questionnaires to derive factors associated with success in L2 learning. Existing research on L2 motivation, like much research in educational psychology, has begun to rediscover the multiple and mutually influential connections between individuals and their many social contexts, contexts that can play a facilitative, neutral, or inhibitory role with respect to further learning, including L2 learning. This work has contributed to a better understanding of the multi-faceted nature of motivation across groups, but it has not generally included attention to particular individual meanings or detailed assessment of participants' interpretations of instructional tasks, school or classroom environments, or social groups within the classroom; hence its applicability to L2 learning theory and instructional applications is limited. In the last decade, some of these limitations have been surmounted by developments within and outside the bounds of traditional L2 motivational research. Many of the studies included in this volume link L2 learning with contemporary social and situational factors, including theories related to perceptions of classroom experience. Within educational psychology, rediscovery and redefinition of an expanded construct of aptitude suggests further investigation of the many aspects of aptitude affecting L2 learning as indicated by interactions with certain instructional methods in specific contexts. Other current research, much of it done with bilinguals, from several streams of social science substantiates a mandate to view L2 learners as, simultaneously, individuals with sets of varied aptitudes and members of cultural groups with characteristic orientations and interpretations of the need for and value of L2 learning as it relates to other meaningful goals. The sociocultural approach suggests that all learning is situated in particular physical and social environments; applying this insight to L2 learning, we must then ask how learners and teachers in different educational environments design, carry out (or avoid or subvert), and evaluate and interpret the tasks, activities, group processes, social relationships, and reward structures available to them. Current work in educational psychology, cognitive science, and L2 theory suggest it is the interplay between these areas that affects progress in instructed L2 learning. Finally, contemporary advances in cognitive science and sociocultural theory as well as applied study of educational innovations suggest a radical expansion of the construct of motivation; they imply that motivation is an attribute not only of individuals, but also of particular school and classroom environments, of varied learning tasks and activities, and of various social groups and processes, each of which can have motivational force. Further research on these very context-specific aspects of motivation demands the addition of qualitative and ethnographic approaches to available quantitative techniques. All these trends represent promising directions in the quest to position the study of pedagogically-relevant L2 motivation not only within the heads of learners but also within the classrooms, learning tasks, and social processes wherein L2 instruction is delivered and experienced.

REFERENCES

Abi-Nader, J. (1990). "A house for my mother": Motivating Hispanic high school students. *Anthropology and Education Quarterly, 21,* 41–58.

Baker, C. (1996). *Foundations of bilingual education and bilingualism,* 2nd. ed. Clevedon, UK: Multilingual Matters.

Bandura, A. (1997). *Self-efficacy: The exercise of control.* New York: W. H. Freeman.

Blumenfeld, P., & Marx, R. (1997). Motivation and cognition. In H. J. Walberg & G. D. Haertel (Eds.), *Psychology and educational practice* (pp. 79–106). Berkeley, CA: McCutchan Publishing.

Brosh, H. (1996). Perceived characteristics of the effective second language teacher. *Foreign Language Annals, 29,* 125–138.

Clark, A. (1997). *Being there: Putting brain, body, and world together again.* Cambridge, MA: The MIT Press.

Cohen, E. G. (1994). *Designing groupwork: Strategies for the heterogeneous classroom,* 2nd ed. New York: Teachers College Press.

Cronbach, L., & Snow, R. E. (1977). *Aptitudes and instructional methods: A handbook for research on interactions.* New York: Irvington Publishers.

Csikszentmihalyi, M. (1997). Flow and education. *The NAMTA [North American Montessori Teachers' Association] Journal, 22*(2), 3–35.

D'Andrade, R. (1992). Schemas and motivation. In R. G. D'Andrade & C. Strauss (Eds.), *Human motives and cultural models* (pp. 23–44). Cambridge, UK: Cambridge University Press.

Danziger, E. (1997). *Naming the mind: How psychology found its language*. London: Sage.

Dörnyei, Z. (in press). Motivation. In J. Verschueren, J-O. Ostmann, J. Blommaert, & C. Bulcaen (Eds.), *Handbook of pragmatics*. Amsterdam: John Benjamins.

Dörnyei, Z., & Clément, R. (2001). Motivational characteristics of learning different target languages: Results of a nationwide survey. In Z. Dörnyei & R. Schmidt (Eds.), *Motivation and second language acquisition* (Technical Report #23, pp. 399–432). Honolulu: University of Hawai'i, Second Language Teaching and Curriculum Center.

Drillings, M, & O'Neil, H. F. (1994). Introduction. In H. F. O'Neil, Jr., & M. Drillings (Eds.), *Motivation: Theory and research* (pp. 1–9). Hillsdale, NJ: Lawrence Erlbaum.

Driscoll, M. (1987, February). *Aptitude-treatment interaction research revisited*. Paper presented at the Annual Convention of the Association for Educational Communications and Technology, Atlanta, GA. [ED 285 532].

Freeman, R. (1998). *Bilingual education and social change*. Clevedon, UK: Multilingual Matters.

Gal, S. (1979). *Language shift: Social determinants of linguistic change in bilingual Austria*. New York: Academic Press.

Gardner, R. C. (2001). Integrative motivation and second language acquisition. In Z. Dörnyei & R. Schmidt (Eds.), *Motivation and second language acquisition* (Technical Report #23, pp. 1–19). Honolulu: University of Hawai'i, Second Language Teaching and Curriculum Center.

Genesee, F. (Ed.). (1999). *Program alternatives for linguistically diverse students*. Washington, DC: Center for Research on Education, Diversity, and Excellence/Center for Applied Linguistics.

Granott, N. (1998). Unit of analysis in transit: From the individual's knowledge to the ensemble process. *Mind, Culture, and Activity, 5*, 42–66.

Hakuta, K., & McLaughlin, B. (1996). Bilingualism and second language learning: Seven tensions that define the research. In D. Berliner & R. Calfee (Eds.), *Handbook of educational psychology* (pp. 603–621). New York: Macmillan.

Hornberger, N., & Micheau, C. (1993). "Getting far enough to like it": Biliteracy in the middle school. *Peabody Journal of Education, 69*(1), 30–53.

Inbar, O., Donitsa-Schmidt, S., & Shohamy, E. (2001). Students' motivation as a function of language learning: The teaching of Arabic in Israel. In Z. Dörnyei & R. Schmidt (Eds.), *Motivation and second language acquisition* (Technical Report #23, pp. 297–311). Honolulu: University of Hawai'i, Second Language Teaching and Curriculum Center.

Jacob, E. (1999). *Cooperative learning: An educational innovation in everyday classrooms*. Albany, NY: State University of New York Press.

Jacob, E., Rottenberg, L. Patrick, S., & Wheeler, E. (1996). Cooperative learning: Context and opportunity for acquiring academic English. *TESOL Quarterly, 30*, 253–280.

Johnson, R., & Swain, M. (Eds.). (1997). *Immersion education: International perspectives*. Cambridge, UK: Cambridge University Press.

Lantolf, J. P. (Ed.). (2000). *Sociocultural theory and second language learning*. Oxford, UK: Oxford University Press.

MacIntyre, P. D., MacMaster, K., & Baker, S. C. (2001). The convergence of multiple models of motivation for second language acquisition: Gardner, Pintrich, Kuhl, and McCroskey. In Z. Dörnyei & R. Schmidt (Eds.), *Motivation and second language acquisition* (Technical Report #23, pp. 461–492). Honolulu: University of Hawai'i, Second Language Teaching and Curriculum Center.

McGroarty, M. (1998). Constructive and constructivist challenges for applied linguistics. *Language Learning, 48,* 591–622.

Ogbu, J. (1991). Immigrant and involuntary minorities in comparative perspective. In M. Gibson & J. Ogbu (Eds.), *Minority status and schooling: A comparative study of immigrant and involuntary minorities* (pp. 3–33). New York: Garland Publishing.

Parry, T., & Stansfield, C. (Eds.). (1990). *Language aptitude reconsidered*. Englewood Cliffs, NJ: Center for Applied Linguistics/Prentice Hall Regents.

Peshkin, A. (1997). *Places of memory: Whiteman's schools and native American communities*. Mahwah, NJ: Lawrence Erlbaum.

Portes, P. R. (1996). Ethnicity and culture in educational psychology. In D. C. Berliner & R. C. Calfee (Eds.), *Handbook of educational psychology* (pp. 331–357). New York: Macmillan.

Ramirez, J. D. (1992). Executive summary of Final Report: Longitudinal study of structured English immersion strategy, early-exit, and late-exit transitional bilingual programs for language-minority children. *Bilingual Research Journal, 16*(1/2), 1–62.

Robinson, G. L. (1997). The magic-carpet-ride-to-another-culture syndrome: An international perspective. In P. Heusinkveld (Ed.), *Pathways to culture* (pp. 75–95). Yarmouth, ME: Intercultural Press.

Rueda, R., & Moll, L. (1994). A sociocultural perspective on motivation. In H. F. O'Neil & M. Drillings (Eds.), *Motivation: Theory and research* (pp. 117–137). Hillsdale, NJ: Lawrence Erlbaum.

Schauble, L., Beane, D. B., Coates, G. D., Martin, L. W., & Sterling, P. V. (1996). Outside the classroom walls: Learning in informal environments. In L. Schauble & R. Glaser (Eds.), *Innovations in learning* (pp. 5–24). Mahwah, NJ: Lawrence Erlbaum.

Schauble, L., & Glaser, R. (Eds.). (1996). *Innovations in learning: New environments for education*. Mahwah, NJ: Lawrence Erlbaum.

Schmidt, R., & Watanabe, Y. (2001). Motivation, strategy use, and pedagogical preferences in foreign language learning. In Z. Dörnyei & R. Schmidt (Eds.), *Motivation and second language acquisition* (Technical Report #23, pp. 313–359). Honolulu: University of Hawai'i, Second Language Teaching and Curriculum Center.

Schumann, J. (2001). Learning as foraging. In Z. Dörnyei & R. Schmidt (Eds.), *Motivation and second language acquisition* (Technical Report #23, pp. 21–28). Honolulu: University of Hawai'i, Second Language Teaching and Curriculum Center.

Segall, M. H., Dasen, P. R., Berry, J. W., & Poortinga, Y. H. (1999). *Human behavior in global perspective* (2nd ed.). Boston: Allyn & Bacon.

Shamim, F. (1996). In and out of the action zone: Location as a feature of interaction in large ESL classes in Pakistan. In K. M. Bailey & D. Nunan (Eds.), *Voices from the language classroom: Qualitative research in second language education* (pp. 123–144). Cambridge, UK: Cambridge University Press.

Shulman, J., Lotan, R., & Whitcomb, J. (Eds.). (1998). *Groupwork in diverse classrooms: A casebook for educators.* New York: Teachers College Press.

Siebold, G. L. (1994). The relation between soldier motivation, leadership, and small unit performance. In H. F. O'Neil & M. Drillings (Eds.), *Motivation: Theory and research* (pp. 171–190). Hillsdale, NJ: Lawrence Erlbaum.

Snow, R. E. (1989). Toward assessment of cognitive and conative structures in learning. *Educational Researcher, 18*(9), 8–14.

Snow, R. E. (1992). Aptitude theory: Yesterday, today, and tomorrow. *Educational Psychologist, 27,* 5–32.

Snow, R. E., Corno, L., & Jackson, D. (1996). Individual differences in affective and conative functions. In D. C. Berliner & R. C. Calfee (Eds.), *Handbook of educational psychology* (pp. 243–310). New York: Macmillan.

Spolsky, B. (2000). Language motivation revisited. *Applied Linguistics, 21,* 157–169.

Stevick, E. (1989). *Success with foreign languages: Seven who achieved it and what worked for them.* New York: Prentice Hall.

Suárez-Orozco, C., & Suárez-Orozco, M. (1995). *Transformations: Migration, family life, and achievement motivation among Latino adolescents.* Stanford, CA: Stanford University Press.

Swain, M. (1995). Three functions of output in second language learning. In G. Cook & B. Seidlhofer (Eds.), *Principle and practice in applied linguistics* (pp. 125–144). Oxford, UK: Oxford University Press.

Swain, M., & Lapkin, S. (1998). Interaction and second language learning: Two adolescent French immersion students working together. *Modern Language Journal, 82,* 320–337.

Tang, B. S. T. (1972). A psycholinguistic study of the relationships between children's ethnic-linguistic attitudes and the effectiveness of methods used in second-language reading instruction. (Doctoral dissertation, Stanford University, 1971). *Dissertation Abstracts International, 32*–10A, 5624.

Williams, M., & Burden, R. L. (1997). *Psychology for language teachers: A social constructivist approach.* Cambridge, UK: Cambridge University Press.

Williams, M., Burden, R.L., & Al-Baharna, S. (2001). Making sense of success and failure: The role of the individual in motivation theory. In Z. Dörnyei & R. Schmidt (Eds.), *Motivation and second language acquisition* (Technical Report

#23, pp. 171–184). Honolulu: University of Hawai'i, Second Language Teaching and Curriculum Center.

Woolard, K. A. (1999). Simultaneity and bivalency as strategies in bilingualism. *Journal of Linguistic Anthropology*, 8(1), 3–29.

Zentella, A. C. (1997). *Growing up bilingual: Puerto Rican children in New York.* Malden, MA: Blackwell Publishers.

Ema Ushioda
Trinity College Dublin, Ireland

LANGUAGE LEARNING AT UNIVERSITY: EXPLORING THE ROLE OF MOTIVATIONAL THINKING

Abstract

This chapter discusses how we may usefully complement the dominant quantitative tradition of research on language learning motivation with a more qualitative approach, wherein the empirical focus is on the qualitative content of language learners' motivational thinking. It reports on a small-scale study conducted among university-level learners of French in Ireland. Using open-ended and semi-structured interview techniques, the study aimed to explore (a) learners' own working conceptions of their motivation, and (b) their perspectives in relation to aspects of motivational evolution and experience over time. Analyzing the findings, the chapter discusses the role of varying temporal frames of reference in shaping motivational thinking, and identifies a number of patterns of thinking that seem effective in sustaining engagement in language learning. The chapter concludes by suggesting that the study of motivational thinking might best be pursued in the context of research on learner autonomy.

INTRODUCTION

In this chapter, I report on a small-scale empirical investigation of language learning motivation (Ushioda, 1996a). The study was conceived in 1991, prompted by a concern for theoretical expansion and alternative empirical exploration at a time when research interest in this topic seemed to be waning. It was in December of that year that Crookes and Schmidt (1991) launched their call for a new research agenda, beginning their seminal article with the comment that motivation "is not currently the subject of extensive investigation in applied linguistics" (p. 469).

Since then, of course, the climate of research interest in language learning motivation has changed quite dramatically, thanks in no small part to Crookes and Schmidt's provocative critique of traditional theory and rousing call for a new research agenda. It was the year 1994 that witnessed the principal response to this call, through a resurgence of discussion and debate in a series of articles published in *The Modern Language Journal* (Dörnyei, 1994a, 1994b; Gardner & Tremblay, 1994a, 1994b; Oxford, 1994; Oxford & Shearin, 1994). Motivation is once again a thriving issue in SLA research, as attested by the publication of this second volume dedicated to the subject, following on the heels of the earlier volume drawing together fresh perspectives from several quarters (Oxford, 1996), and by the current wealth of discussion and empirical research in different parts of the globe reviewed

Ushioda, E. (2001). Language learning at university: Exploring the role of motivational thinking. In Z. Dörnyei & R. Schmidt (Eds.), *Motivation and second language acquisition* (Technical Report #23, pp. 93–125). Honolulu: University of Hawai'i, Second Language Teaching and Curriculum Center.

by Dörnyei (1998) in his recent state-of-the-art survey article (see also Dörnyei, 2000).

Much of the renewed debate has been fueled by the kinds of questions raised by Crookes and Schmidt (1991), that is, questions about expanding the long dominant social-psychological conceptual framework, adopting new theoretical approaches and setting up new research agendas. It was a similar quest for an alternative perspective on language learning motivation that prompted my own research study in 1991. In brief, my study sought to complement the largely quantitative tradition of research on language learning motivation with a more qualitative ethnographic approach. To this end, the investigation chose to set aside the traditional view of motivation as a measurable affective variable implicated in second or foreign language (L2) achievement, in favor of a focus on the qualitative content of language learners' motivational thinking: specifically, (a) their own working conceptions of the factors shaping their motivation, and (b) their perspectives on aspects of motivational experience over time. Learner cognitions thus constituted both object and vehicle of empirical investigation.

Discussing the findings of this qualitative empirical study, the chapter does not seek to undermine the wealth of literature on language learning motivation that has evolved in the quantitative research paradigm or to generalize on the basis of what is a very small-scale and focused investigation. Rather, it seeks to present an alternative way of conceptualizing and exploring motivation, not as measurable cause or product of particular learning experiences and outcomes, but as an ongoing complex of processes shaping and sustaining learner involvement in learning.

THEORETICAL BACKGROUND

The quantitative research paradigm

Research on language learning motivation has evolved substantially since the major studies pioneered by Gardner and Lambert in the late 1950s and early 1960s and published in their seminal collective report in 1972. A great deal has been discussed and investigated, and much water has flowed under the bridge. For some three decades, the evolution of research on this subject was strongly shaped by social-psychological theories of language learning. Motivation was consistently conceived in the context of a cluster of social-psychological and attitudinal variables implicated in second language learning achievement. Thus Skehan, writing in 1989, suggested that almost all L2 motivation literature was in effect a kind of commentary on the social-psychological agenda established by Gardner (Skehan, 1989, p. 61). More recently, as we have noted, the evolution has been marked by a significant broadening of this conceptual framework and the exploration of new and different motivational dimensions drawn in particular from theories of motivation in educational research and the psychology of learning (for a recent comprehensive review, see in particular Dörnyei, 1998).

Yet, to some extent, it seems that the study of language learning motivation remains constrained by the original research question that first launched Gardner and Lambert (1972) on their empirical quest. It is worth reminding ourselves of this question: "How is it that some people can learn a second or foreign language so easily and do so well while others, given what seem to be the same opportunities to learn, find it almost impossible?" (p. 130). Believing that cognitive factors such as ability or aptitude did not provide a sufficient explanation, Gardner and Lambert turned their attention to the role of motivation. Research interest in motivation was thus kindled by speculations about its causal role in promoting language achievement.

Over the years, of course, the research instruments and methods of data analysis have become increasingly sophisticated, and the theoretical components of motivation have been refined and continue to be re-analyzed. Indeed, the current thrust is towards expanding the set of components that traditionally define this construct (see, for example, Dörnyei, 1994a, 1996, 1998; Schmidt, Boraie, & Kassabgy, 1996; Tremblay & Gardner, 1995; Williams & Burden, 1997). In addition, there has been much debate as to the direction of the relationship between motivation and achievement, and speculation too about relationships between motivation and other aspects of language learning behavior, such as classroom participation, persistence at learning, and use of strategies (e.g., Gardner & MacIntyre, 1992, 1993; Gardner, Tremblay, & Masgoret, 1997; Gliksman, Gardner, & Smythe, 1982; Ramage, 1990; Schmidt, Boraie, & Kassabgy, 1996).

In essence, nevertheless, Gardner and Lambert's original research question still shapes the way in which motivation is conceived and investigated: namely, as a measurable individual difference variable implicated in second language learning. Researchers continually strive to define and classify its components, to measure its relationship with achievement or other variables, and to analyze its role in theoretical models of the language learning process. The study of language learning motivation has thus evolved and continues to evolve in a largely quantitative research paradigm. This research paradigm is typified by a methodology reflecting a concept of motivation in terms of measurable components and yielding snapshot motivational indices for entry into statistical analyses with other variable indices. The components of the motivational construct and the range of relationships investigated may have evolved substantially over the years, yet the empirical focus in this research paradigm continues to center on the role of motivation as measurable cause or product of particular learning experiences and outcomes.

A qualitative approach to the study of motivation

There is clearly scope for a more qualitative approach to the study of language learning motivation, to complement this long-standing quantitative tradition of research (Ushioda, 1994). As Larsen-Freeman and Long (1991, pp. 10–24) suggest, the two types of approaches should not be regarded as being mutually exclusive, since a descriptive qualitative approach will nevertheless entail some degree of coding and quantification of data. The difference is rather one of scale, focus, and purpose. As Larsen-Freeman and Long add, the twin perspectives should thus be viewed as complementary rather than competing paradigms, and SLA research might usefully benefit from a combination of both approaches to the major theoretical issues.

Of course, qualitative methods have been used to a certain degree in studies of language learning motivation, but usually only in the preliminary stages of developing and piloting research instruments. Ramage (1990), for example, is unconvinced by the generalizability of the concepts of integrative and instrumental motivations and pilots a qualitative open-ended method of identifying language learners' motivations. On the basis of her qualitative data, she then develops new Likert-type scales for subsequent quantitative analysis of relationships between strength of motivations and students' persistence at or withdrawal from language learning.

A qualitative research approach, however, is not simply a question of methodology. It is defined by the nature of its theoretical focus and empirical purpose. The value of the approach lies in its potential to cast a different light on the phenomena under investigation and to raise a different set of issues. Where the study of language learning motivation is concerned, the issue is not whether qualitative research methods may yield data to support or undermine traditional and current theoretical approaches in the quantitative paradigm. The purpose is rather to analyze and explore aspects of motivation that are not easily accommodated within the dominant research paradigm. In essence, a qualitative approach is underpinned by a fundamentally different concept of motivation itself.

In this respect, Ames (1986, pp. 235–238) provides a useful distinction between quantitative and qualitative concepts of learning motivation in the classroom. As a quantitative variable, motivation may be equated with a conceptualization of measurable activity that involves energy and persistence, such as how much effort students put into their learning, how long they persevere at a task, how active they are, or how strong their level of arousal for learning seems to be. This view of motivation seems readily familiar to us as the concept that has prevailed in research on language learning motivation, a variable traditionally defined in terms of three principal components: "effort expended to achieve the goal, desire to achieve the goal and attitudes toward the activity involved in achieving the goal" (Gardner, 1985, p. 51).

As a qualitative variable, on the other hand, motivation may be defined not in terms of observable and measurable activity, but rather in terms of what patterns of thinking and belief underlie such activity and shape students' engagement in the learning process. For example, students may evaluate learning goals differently, some seeing learning as a means of gaining ability and others seeing it as a means of demonstrating ability. Similarly, they may evaluate their achievements in different ways, some deriving satisfaction from doing better than fellow students and others from experiencing growth in knowledge or understanding. As Ames (1986, pp. 236–237) suggests, within a quantitative perspective, goal-directed activity is translated into "time-on-task (academic engaged time)," resulting in the depiction of students being "highly motivated" or "not motivated." Within a qualitative perspective, on the other hand, goal-directed activity refers to the content of students' thoughts. The focus of interest is not on whether the more motivated students prove to be the more successful, but on how students differ in the way they value and interpret goals and how such differences in motivational thinking may affect their involvement in learning.

Subjective goal structures represent just one potential dimension of students' motivational thinking. As a qualitative concept, motivation may be viewed as a whole complex of cognitive-mediational processes, whereby how students think, what they believe, and how they interpret relevant experience, will determine the choice, level, and quality of their involvement in learning (Pintrich & Schunk, 1996). Ultimately, of course, research interest in the qualitative content of students' motivational thinking is shaped by a concern to define and foster those patterns of thinking that underpin what we might describe as positive or effective motivation (McCombs, 1994). Viewed in this light, after all, positive motivation is more than the demonstration of effortful activity or time spent on a task. It is reflected in how students think about themselves, the task, and their performance (Ames, 1986, p. 236). Thus, effectiveness of the learner "must be examined in relation to those beliefs, perceptions, interpretations, and expectations that enable learners to become involved, independent and confident in their own learning" (p. 238).

Such, then, is the basic research agenda underlying the study of motivation to be reported in this chapter: to explore the qualitative content of language learners' motivational thinking, with a view to identifying thought patterns and belief structures that seem effective in sustaining and optimizing involvement in learning.

THE STUDY

SUBJECTS

Practical considerations favored a project on a small scale, given the open-ended qualitative type of data to be elicited. A sample size of 20 was chosen for the investigation. Twenty was considered the upper limit for the provision of a manageable body of data for the purposes of detailed descriptive and content analysis. At the same time, the number was sufficiently large to allow for the necessary coding and quantification of data, the tracing of common underlying patterns and cross-comparisons between learners, and the application of some basic statistical procedures.

The learners were students at Trinity College Dublin, Ireland, taking French (L2) as part of their undergraduate degree program. The students had been learning French at secondary school for 5–6 years and had opted to pursue their study of the language further at university. It was hoped that this sample of self-selected and by definition motivated language learners might offer insight into the range of factors perceived to shape and sustain involvement in language learning.

At the university, students take French studies as part of a combined degree program with one or more subjects of study. All students taking French follow a broadly similar course of study in terms of language syllabus, level, and teaching approach. These courses are all run by the Department of French. However, students combining French with another arts or humanities subject (e.g., Spanish, German, History, etc.) have a substantial literature component in their course of study, which is not shared by those combining French with, for example, Computer Science. Degree programs are generally four years in duration, although some students opt to study French for three years only and major in their other degree subject in their fourth year.

For the purposes of this qualitative study, it was felt that the lack of uniformity across students' French course programs and academic subject combinations was not problematic. This was not, after all, a research experiment to investigate relationships between indices of motivation and indices of achievement, whereby it would have been necessary to control language learning experience and exposure in the overall research design. Variety in experience was indeed to be welcomed, since it increased the potential range of motivational perspectives to be yielded by a small learner sample. Similar reasons justified the use of a sample of learners who were not all in the same year of study. When the research project began in December 1991, 10 of the students were in their first year at university and 10 in their second year.

METHODOLOGY: DATA ELICITATION

The elicitation of motivational data was conducted in two stages, separated by 15–16 months. In the first round (December 1991), the purpose was simply to explore subjects' own working conceptions of the factors motivating them to learn French. In the follow-up round (March–April 1993), the purpose was to analyze their thinking in relation to aspects of motivational evolution and experience over time.

For the first round, it was clear that how language learners perceived their motivation could only emerge if they were given free rein to externalize their thinking with as little directional control as possible. It was particularly important that the research subjects should not be initially primed with motivational concepts and ideas (e.g., goals, aims, attitudes, successful learning experiences, etc.) that might influence what they said or the order in which they said things. Naturally, introspective methods that are as open-ended and minimally structured as possible bring with them the danger that the quality and quantity of elicited data may vary considerably from learner to learner. At the same time, however, variation in motivational clarity and awareness, as reflected in the quality and range of thinking verbalized, was itself of fundamental relevance to the research focus. Learner cognitions constituted both object and vehicle of the empirical investigation.

A very loosely structured interview technique was thus used to explore subjects' working conceptions of motivation. Each interview was conducted in English (L1) and began with initial warm-up pleasantries and a brief explanation of the general context and purpose of the session. This was done both to inform the subject of the kind of introspective data that was being sought and to emphasize that the data would be used for research purposes only, rather than for purposes of institutional records or students' academic assessment. On the understanding that personal identities would not be revealed in any project report, the subject was invited to talk freely in a relaxed and informal manner. It should be added that at the time of the first and second round interviews, the interviewer (myself) was a full-time doctoral student who was not attached to the Department of French and who had no contact with the subjects outside the context of the research project. The face-threatening potential of the interview situation as perceived by the subjects was thus minimal. Moreover, a generally co-operative frame of mind was readily encouraged through the payment of a small sum of money (£5) to each subject in return for participating in the interview.

The interview proper began on the basis of asking each subject to explain her motivation for learning French. The content and structure of the interview were thus largely dictated by the subject's own personal conception of what language learning motivation meant and by her identification of the factors that shaped her perceived motivational rationale. The course of the interview was mediated by occasional prompting by the researcher to encourage the subject to keep going or to expand upon points just mentioned. Once the momentum of the opening self-report account was perceived to slacken, the prompting became more structured as the subject was asked to consider possibly overlooked motivational perspectives and gauge their relevance. Each interview lasted about 15–20 minutes and was recorded on audiotape.

For the follow-up data elicitation, a more structured interview technique was used, since the aim was to explore subjects' thinking in relation to specific kinds of motivational experience and evolution over time. The interview questions were nevertheless couched in open-ended terms, encouraging subjects to describe events from their own point of view. The questions focused on motivation as a dynamic phenomenon in relation to four aspects:

Motivational evolution over time

- How would you describe your present state of motivation for learning French, and have you experienced any motivational changes over the past year?

- Have you any further ideas or experienced any changes in your ideas about future career plans? If so, do you think these have had any impact on the way you feel about studying French?

- Has anything happened in your personal life that has influenced the way you feel about your studies?

- Have you on the whole enjoyed or not enjoyed studying French at Trinity College, and how do you think your experience has affected your motivation?

- How do you now view your decision to study French at Trinity College? Was it the right or wrong decision and why?

Motivational perspectives on L2 development over time

- How motivationally important to you is "success" or "doing well" in French, and what kinds of criteria are most meaningful to you in evaluating your ability, success, or progress?

- To what in particular do you attribute your success or progress in French, or lack of success or progress, depending on how you think things are going?

Factors negatively affecting L2 motivation

- Are there any French-related tasks, conditions, or situations where you feel your motivation is low, and if so, why do you think this might be so?

Motivational strategies

- How do you manage to stay well-motivated? Do you have any strategies for dealing with, controlling, or maximizing your motivation during your course of study? Or do you not need to? Or do you believe that you cannot exercise conscious control over your motivational state?

Fourteen subjects out of the original sample of 20 took part in the follow-up interviews. The remaining subjects were unavailable for interview, either because they were abroad in France for the academic year or because they had withdrawn from their course of study through illness or reasons unknown. The subjects who took part were once again informed of the research purpose of the interview and assured that personal data would remain confidential. The interviews were taperecorded as before and lasted about 15–20 minutes each.

The study did not incorporate the specific pre- or post-testing of L2 proficiency within the subject sample. As already indicated, the research focus was on the qualitative content of learners' motivational thinking, rather than on the identification of motivational components found to co-vary with achievement or other variables (as has been the approach in the dominant research tradition). This did not mean, however, that subjects' L2 performance and proficiency levels were irrelevant to the research purpose. In effect, an important aim was to explore the *perceived* role of L2 success or proficiency in shaping motivational thinking. The indices of L2 achievement appropriate to the research design were thus specifically those indicators identified by subjects themselves as motivationally relevant (regardless of their validity, reliability or uniformity as test measures). These included post-primary and university examination results in French.

This study of motivation was itself set in the context of a wider multifaceted research project at Trinity College, known as the TCD Modern Languages Research Project (MLRP; see Singleton, 1990). The MLRP was launched in October 1988, with the aim of surveying different aspects of the L2 development of university learners, such as L2 lexical development and processing, cross-linguistic influence, problem-solving strategies, and motivation. The project entailed regular elicitation of L2 data and introspective data of various kinds. Its collaborative framework enabled participating researchers to pool resources and findings through a cumulative and collective database of learner data. With respect to the study on motivation, it was thus possible to refer to this central database for information on comparable samples of French language data elicited from the particular learners under investigation. Such information offered a means of making cross-comparisons between learners in terms of their relative levels of L2 proficiency, as well as exploring whether their subjective perceptions of success or ability were a good reflection of their L2 proficiency. It should be emphasized that the L2 data provided comparable samples of L2 proficiency only, rather than reliable measures of the L2 outcomes of the learning process. The students were not, after all, following the same course of study, since this aspect of the research design was deliberately not controlled.

In the MLRP, the instrument used to sample learners' L2 proficiency at periodic intervals was the C-test (Singleton, 1990, pp. 4–6). The C-test is a modification of the cloze procedure in which parts of words (specifically, the second half of every second word) rather than whole words are deleted. It has been argued that the C-test thereby offers a more general measure of underlying language proficiency which is not biased towards particular structural features or linguistic units (Spolsky, 1989, pp. 75–76). In this study of motivation, scores for the whole learner sample on two French C-tests were obtained. These tests were administered a couple of weeks before the first round interviews in December 1991.

DATA ANALYSIS

ANALYSIS OF FIRST ROUND INTERVIEW DATA

A detailed content analysis was made of the set of transcribed interviews from the first round. It seemed reasonable to intuit that subjects would explain their motivation in terms of what they perceived to be the most salient or important factors and that these would emerge in the early part of the interview, before more structured prompting became necessary. The priority features in subjects' opening self-report accounts were thus jotted down (e.g., enjoyed French at school, wants to live in France, finds learning French easy). The collective set of priority features was then examined in an attempt to trace common dimensions. The dimensions readily observable in the data related to the kinds of emotions or attitudes verbalized (enjoyment, love/liking, pride, satisfaction, etc.); the objects of affect identified (French language, language learning, speaking French, French-speaking people, etc.); the sources of influence attributed (internal factors, personal experience, external influences, etc.); and the direction of temporal reference expressed (past experience of learning or using French, ongoing process of learning or using French, future hopes and plans).

Further analysis suggested that these dimensions could be defined through a number of distinctions or contrasts. In relation to future temporal reference, for example, there seemed to be a distinction between language-extrinsic goals (e.g., personal career plans) and language-intrinsic goals (e.g., the aspiration to achieve fluency in French or to acquire a good French accent). A similar kind of distinction could be drawn between motivation ascribed to language-learning experience (in the classroom) and language-related experience (in a French-speaking environment). With respect to what might be classified as intrinsic types of motivation, there seemed to be differences in how subjects verbalized their feelings. These were identified as enjoyment or liking (e.g., love of the language, enjoyment of learning or speaking French), academic interest (e.g., in French literature or French culture), and personal satisfaction (e.g., of being able to communicate successfully in French or of possessing French language skills).

Through this process of discrimination and qualitative analysis, eight descriptive dimensions emerged, according to which all the priority features identified could be classified:

(a) Academic interest

(b) Language-related enjoyment/liking

(c) Desired levels of L2 competence

(d) Personal goals

(e) Positive learning history

(f) Personal satisfaction

(g) Feelings about French-speaking countries or people

(h) External pressures/incentives

Inevitably, there is a sense in which the choice of motivational dimensions may be thought as somewhat arbitrary, and it is certainly likely that numerous approaches to analyzing the data are possible. However, it is not of course claimed that the dimensions identified are defined by hard and fast distinctions. They are necessarily descriptive and schematic in status and do not offer an explanation of the data such as, for example, the patterns identified through a factor analytic reduction of quantitative data may provide. The dimensions serve rather to put some kind of collective shape on the introspective data, in order to facilitate the qualitative description of learners' working conceptions of motivation.

Furthermore, examination of the latter sections of subjects' interview transcripts seemed to confirm that a meaningful and appropriate set of descriptive dimensions had been established through the initial content analysis. The global picture was not significantly changed upon analysis of the remaining data, since no distinctive new groupings or patterns emerged. Table 1 summarizes the range of motivational features identified and classified.

Table 1: Classification of motivational features identified in first round interviews

(a) Academic interest		(b) Language-related enjoyment/liking	
language and languages	(1)	learning French	(7)
French language	(4)	learning languages	(4)
aspects of French language	(1)	French language	(13)
France	(3)	sound of French language	(7)
French people	(3)	speaking French	(2)
French culture	(4)	speaking languages	(1)
French literature	(11)	being able to communicate with French speakers	(2)
other Francophone literature	(1)	being able to communicate with foreign language speakers	(1)
(c) Desired levels of L2 competence		**(d) Personal goals**	
maximum all-round fluency	(4)	live in France/Francophone country long-term	(2)
maximum spoken fluency	(7)	live in France/Francophone country short-term	(14)
effective communicative ability	(1)	live abroad long-term	(1)
competence in business/ technical domain	(2)	live abroad short-term	(5)
competence to teach French	(1)	travel abroad	(3)
improve speaking skills	(1)	pursue French studies further	(1)
improve writing skills	(2)	definite career plans using French	(4)
become bilingual	(2)	possible career plans using French	(3)
ability to express oneself fully	(2)	regard French as potentially useful asset	(10)
get a good French accent	(2)	sense importance of European dimension	(3)
overcome frustration of communication limitations	(3)	life ambition for personal achievement	(1)
desire not to forget French	(1)		

continued…

Table 1: Classification of motivational features identified in
first round interviews
(cont.)

(e) Positive learning history		(f) Personal satisfaction	
good French language ability	(8)	sense of satisfaction in communicative success	(3)
ease of learning French	(7)	pride in French academic achievement	(2)
facility for language learning	(6)	sense of superiority in being able to speak French	(2)
good academic record in French	(6)	satisfaction from challenge of mastering French	(1)
sense of waste if discontinued French studies	(1)	sense of satisfaction in being able to blend in with French speakers	(1)
making steady progress in French from childhood	(1)		
positive childhood experience learning French	(4)		
(g) Feelings about French-speaking countries or people		**(h) External pressures/incentives**	
positive experience of contact with French speakers	(8)	degree award	(1)
personal ties with French speakers	(3)	getting a good degree	(5)
		examination pressure	(4)
positive experience of being in France/Francophone country	(12)	getting good grades	(11)
		coursework demands	(3)
attraction to France	(5)	class competitive standards	(5)
romantic image of France	(2)	learning atmosphere	(7)
attraction to French lifestyle	(1)	teacher stimulation	(1)
		course content stimulation	(7)
		learning materials	(1)
		parental encouragement	(4)
		family precedent of learning French	(3)
		pressure of others' expectations of continued success	(1)

Note: Figures in parentheses indicate number of learners who mentioned this
motivational feature.

On the individual level, some modifications and additions were made to subjects'
motivational profiles, based on the perceptions and responses offered in the later
stages of the interviews. For example, subjects who had originally made no mention
of personal goals or career plans were subsequently prompted to consider their
relevance in relation to the motivational factors they had already identified. It was
important that any attempt to schematize subjects' working conceptions of

motivation should somehow reflect the differing levels of priority attributed to the various factors cited. The simplest solution was to build a rough hierarchical configuration, with the dominant factors at the top, and the least important factors at the bottom, and others ranked in between. Table 2 illustrates the schematic hierarchy of motivational factors cited by Learner 6 in the sample.

Table 2: Sample motivational profile (Learner 6)

Motivation I (primary emphasis)	(e) **Positive learning history** ease of learning French good academic record in French (f) **Personal satisfaction** pride in French academic achievement
Motivation II (secondary emphasis)	(d) **Personal goals** definite career plans using French live abroad short-term (c) **Desired levels of L2 competence** effective communicative ability competence to teach French (b) **Language-related enjoyment/liking** French language sound of French language
Motivation III	(h) **External pressures/incentives** degree award learning atmosphere getting good grades
Motivation IV	(a) **Academic interest** French culture
Motivation V	(g) **Feelings about French-speaking countries or people** positive experience of being in Francophone country

RESULTS OF FIRST ROUND DATA ANALYSIS

In general, motivational factors attributed primary or secondary emphasis were those which had emerged in the initial flow of each subject's self-report account before much prompting became necessary and which were often reiterated during the course of the interview. These dominant features might thus be said to provide the principal defining rationale of each subject's perceived motivation. Of particular interest to the analysis was to examine what kinds of motivational features tended to fulfill this defining role. Table 3 indicates the number of subject profiles in which each motivational dimension was given primary or secondary emphasis.

Table 3: Predominant motivation dimensions

motivational dimension	number of profiles in which the dimension is given primary or secondary emphasis
(a) Academic interest	9
(b) Language-related enjoyment/liking	16
(c) Desired levels of L2 competence	11
(d) Personal goals	11
(e) Positive learning history	16
(f) Personal satisfaction	6
(g) Feelings about French-speaking countries or people	7
(h) External pressures/incentives	2

Table 3 indicates that four motivational dimensions in particular tended to be emphasized. Subjects most commonly accounted for their motivation to learn French in terms of Language-Related Enjoyment/Liking (b) and the impact of a Positive Learning History (e). These dimensions were each emphasized in 16 of the 20 subject profiles. Learners who highlighted enjoyment aspects typically talked about loving French, or of loving the way it sounds, or of enjoying speaking the language. Those who stressed the motivational impetus of a positive learning history typically made statements such as "you keep up something you're good at" or "I always found learning languages very easy at school."

Eleven subjects gave motivational emphasis to particular Personal Goals (d) relating to future use of the language. This figure was rather lower than expected, since it seemed reasonable to imagine that personal and vocational goals should have functioned as major motivational determinants among students in third-level education. Yet only slightly more than half the sample gave priority to this motivational dimension. True enough, personal goals of one kind or another did feature in the remaining subject profiles lower down the scale. Indeed, the most commonly cited motivational variable across the whole data set was the goal "live in France/Francophone country short-term," mentioned by 14 subjects. It was evident, nevertheless, that subjects did not necessarily think of their motivation as being principally defined by such goals but shaped instead by factors intrinsic to the process and experience of learning the language.

Eleven subjects did give motivational emphasis to language-intrinsic goals, or Desired Levels of L2 Competence (c) but not always with reference to specific vocational applications. Subjects talked, for example, about wanting to be as fluent as possible, to get a perfect French accent or to be able to express themselves fully in French.

In short, subjects' working conceptions of motivation seemed to be shaped by different temporal frames of reference, with the majority ascribing their motivation predominantly to the impact of language learning experience to date and individuals varying in the degree of importance they ascribed to long-term future motivational perspectives. This pattern was reflected also in the four other motivational dimensions that featured less prominently in subjects' profiles. All four dimensions were characterized by a focus on aspects of ongoing experience or past experience, whether in terms of intrinsic Academic Interest (a), such as interest in French literature or France; deriving Personal Satisfaction (f) from flaunting one's L2 skills or communicating successfully in the target language; positive Feelings About French-speaking Countries/People (g) stemming from particular personal experiences and encounters in the past; or the stimulation provided by External Incentives/Pressures (h) in the immediate learning environment from teachers, peers, parents, course content, and so on. This final dimension did of course incorporate some short-term goal incentives, such as getting a good degree or good grades. On the whole, however, this was not an aspect that was prioritized by subjects when explaining their motivation.

Thus, while learning a foreign language may be perceived as an essentially goal-directed activity, subjects' own working conceptions of their motivation for language learning were not necessarily defined in teleological terms in relation to specific goals, future purposes, or applications. A far more pervasive feature of their reported motivation was the shaping power of language-learning and language-related experience to date. Recourse was made to the MLRP database to explore to what extent attributions of motivation to positive learning experiences indeed reflected a successful history of learning French and to what extent they might also reflect relative levels of L2 proficiency within the sample. Subjects' grade averages in post-primary public examinations in French were obtained, as well as their average scores in two French C-tests. Since the same C-tests were administered to both first and second year undergraduates in the sample, the scores were standardized within each year group to compensate for differences in language level and the effects of training. The standardized scores employed were the z-scores, computed as the deviation of each value from the mean value within each particular year group, and expressed as a multiple of the standard deviation.

Spearman rank correlation coefficients were then calculated between each of the two French language measures and the respective degrees of emphasis attributed to the various motivational dimensions in subjects' profiles. To this end, the hierarchical structure of each subject's motivational profile offered a simple five-point ordinal scale reflecting levels of emphasis attributed to each motivational dimension (see Table 2 above). For each of the eight motivational dimensions, the set of 20 ratings on this five-point ordinal scale was ranked in order of magnitude, with the appropriate mean ranking assigned to tied values. Subjects' post-primary grade averages and C-test averages were similarly ranked, and the resulting sets of rank scores were used for the calculation of Spearman correlation coefficients.

Table 4 presents the matrix of Spearman rank correlations obtained. The table confirms a positive association of 0.59 (significant at the 1% level) between motivation attributed to a Positive Learning History (e) and subjects' post-primary French grades, indicating that such motivational emphasis was indeed well-founded in terms of a documented record of French achievement at school. A further positive association of 0.46 (significant at the 5% level) between the same motivational dimension and the C-test average suggests too that motivational perceptions of L2 ability (i.e., of being good at French) were a fair reflection of relative levels of L2 proficiency in the sample. Put another way, it seemed reasonable to infer from this that the more proficient subjects in the sample attributed greater motivational importance to perceptions of L2 ability and a positive learning history.

Table 4: Matrix of Spearman rank correlations between motivational dimensions and post-primary grade average in French/C-test Average

motivational dimension	post-primary grade average	C-test average
(a) Academic interest	−0.01	0.22
(b) Language-related enjoyment/liking	0.23	0.02
(c) Desired levels of L2 competence	0.45*	0.14
(d) Personal goals	−0.55*	−0.61**
(e) Positive learning history	0.59**	0.46*
(f) Personal satisfaction	0.07	0.27
(g) Feelings about French-speaking countries or people	0.23	−0.10
(h) External pressures/incentives	−0.01	−0.14

*   significant at 5% level (N=20)

** significant at 1% level (N=20)

Interestingly, moreover, the analysis indicated that the more successful subjects not only tended to attribute greater motivational importance to a positive learning history, but also tended to attribute less motivational importance to long-term personal and vocational goals. A negative correlation of −0.55 (significant at the 5% level) was obtained between post-primary French grade average and motivational importance ascribed to Personal Goals (d). By implication, the inverse association suggested that the subjects in the sample with less illustrious learning histories tended to define their motivation principally in terms of particular personal goals or career plans. This inverse association similarly emerged in the negative correlation of −0.61 (significant at the 1% level) between the same motivational dimension and subjects' relative L2 proficiency levels as sampled in the C-test measure.

The correlational analysis, however, pointed to a different pattern of association between subjects' learning histories and motivational emphasis attributed to language-*intrinsic* goals. A history of successful language learning (as reflected in post-primary grades) was found to be *positively* associated with motivation to attain Desired Levels of L2 Competence (c), as indicated by the correlation of 0.45 obtained (significant at the 5% level). It seemed that learners who were already relatively successful tended to feel intrinsically motivated by the aim of achieving a high level of L2 fluency or competence, largely irrespective of any specific personal goals or vocational ambitions (for a similar finding, see Ramage, 1990).

These findings indicated that the temporal frame of reference shaping learners' motivational thinking was not reducible to a simple past-future polarity, since subjects' working conceptions of motivation clearly embraced both temporal perspectives. It was equally clear, however, that subjects varied qualitatively in the perspectives they emphasized, and that these differences in their thinking seemed to stem from the quality of their language learning experience to date. Those who had very positive language learning experiences tended to emphasize intrinsic motivational factors relating to perceptions of L2 ability and the personal desire to master the language and achieve a high level of L2 competence. This configuration of perceived competence and the desire for mastery and skill development represent almost classical characteristics of intrinsic learning motivation (see, for example, Deci, 1980, 1996; Lepper & Greene, 1978; Maehr, 1984). On the other hand, it seemed that those with less positive language learning experiences to date were able to compensate motivationally by focusing on particular goals and incentives channeling their desire to learn the language. Certainly, the less successful learners in the sample could not be classified as being less motivated. Rather, they expressed their motivation in a qualitatively different kind of way.

In short, these findings suggested that *effective motivational thinking* might entail filtering experience and focusing on the positive elements or on positive incentives, while de-emphasizing the negative. Further attributional patterns reflecting this kind of positive motivational thinking emerged in the analysis of the follow-up interview data.

ANALYSIS OF FOLLOW-UP INTERVIEW DATA

The follow-up interview was concerned with exploring subjects' thinking in relation to aspects of motivational evolution and experience over time. The interview questions focused on four aspects of motivation as a dynamic phenomenon:

1. Motivational evolution over time

2. Motivational perspectives on L2 development over time

3. Factors negatively affecting L2 motivation

4. Motivational strategies

For each of these four aspects, subjects' responses to the open-ended questions posed were summarized in note form (e.g., change to exam-oriented motivation, positive experience in France over the summer). The noted features for all the subjects were then compared and common underlying patterns traced in the data.

Motivational evolution over time: Global and qualitative changes

Subjects' reflections on motivational evolution over time indicated that changes in motivation were perceived both in global terms (i.e., changes in overall strength of motivation) and in more qualitative terms. Global changes in motivation were all attributed to particular language-learning or language-related experiences:

Changes in degree of motivation
- Stronger motivation through coursework/exams
- Stronger motivation from personal relationship with L2 speaker
- Stronger motivation because of less anxiety over L2 grammar
- Stronger motivation because of L2 improvement after summer in France
- Stronger motivation to work harder following exam failure
- Weaker motivation through coursework dissatisfaction

Although the direction of motivational change was generally predictable (i.e., stronger motivation was associated with positive L2 experiences or outcomes), one subject described how failing her first year French examinations served to intensify rather than diminish her motivation. This was easily explained when taken in the context of a related major development in her motivation — the overriding incentive of spending the following academic year in France, pending success in the forthcoming set of examinations. Motivation to work extra hard to pass these examinations was all the more intensified in the light of failure the previous year.

Qualitative developments of this kind in certain aspects of motivation (e.g., intervention of short-term incentives, growth of intrinsic motivation, discovery of new interests) emerged as a common feature of subjects' reflections:

Qualitative developments
- Development of intrinsic motivation through positive L2 experience in France
- Positive feelings about France from personal experience
- Appreciation of instrumental value of L2 skill through work experience
- Interest in language pedagogy with definition of career goal
- Pride from association with well-respected academic staff
- Dominance of exam-oriented motivation at the expense of intrinsic motivation
- Negative feelings about French people from personal experience

Overriding short-term incentives
- High motivation from immediate exam pressure
- High motivation to pass exams for reward of spending year in France

Clearer definition of L2-related personal goals
- Pursue postgraduate studies in L2
- Enter teaching profession
- Integrate L2 into professional career

Patterns of motivational change were determined not only by the reinforcing or negative effects of L2-learning and L2-related experience, but also by the development in clarity or priority of particular goals or future perspectives which qualitatively modified the learner's original motivation. Learner 10, for example, had originally defined her motivation predominantly with reference to a very positive learning history, intrinsic enjoyment, and positive experiences in France. In the follow-up interview, she spoke about the potential instrumental value of her French skills following some work experience over the summer and talked about the career perspectives that now seemed to be shaping her motivation more. It seemed that motivational change could thus entail changes in the temporal frame of reference shaping subjects' thinking. In particular, the follow-up data pointed to the *evolving* nature of goal-orientation in learners' motivational experience.

Motivational evolution, however, was determined not only by factors within the L2-learning and L2-related context, but also by other elements of individual experience which competed for attention and priority within the learner's overall hierarchy of personal needs and motives:

Other priorities now affecting L2 motivation
- Development of stronger motivation for other subject of study
- Motivated by career prospects for other subject of study
- Motivated by better academic success potential in other subject of study
- L2 motivation restrained by immediate study pressures of other subject of study

Personal crises which have affected L2 motivation
- Temporary loss of motivation during period of depression
- Temporary loss of motivation following parental bereavement
- Disruption of motivation with parental separation
- Disruption of motivation with family emigration to US

These patterns of interaction with other factors in their experience were clearly a significant aspect of how subjects perceived their motivational evolution, though this relative perspective has perhaps received little attention so far in existing studies of language learning motivation. For a number of subjects, such patterns of interaction seemed instrumental in helping to define, shape, or modify the developing goal structure of their motivation for learning French, as they weighed the potential pros and cons of making particular choices and pursuing different vocational directions.

Motivational perspectives on L2 development over time

The rest of the follow-up interview probed subjects' thinking in relation to three specific kinds of motivational experience: motivational perceptions of L2 success or progress over time, the experience of demotivation, and the potential for remotivation or self-motivation.

Subjects who had given particular motivational emphasis to a positive learning history and perceptions of L2 ability in their original interviews generally confirmed the consistency of this important motivational pattern. They talked about gaining personal satisfaction from doing well or of feeling disappointed or ashamed if they did not experience success and progress. Most identified academic evaluative criteria (French grades, peer-group competitive standards) as relevant indicators of their L2 success and progress, although a few also mentioned language-intrinsic criteria (level of fluency, eradication of error). Learner 9 did not attribute motivational emphasis to L2 academic success but stressed instead the ability to put his knowledge of French to practical communicative use as a personally important criterion for self-evaluation. This pattern was consistent with his original reported motivation, when he had emphasized experiences of language use (personal satisfaction in achieving communicative success and being able to blend in with French speakers), rather than perceptions of a positive *learning* history.

Motivational importance of doing well in L2
- L2 academic success not especially important
- Doing average is good enough
- Like to know how one is doing
- Like to do well but more motivated toward other subject
- Quite important to do well
- Important for personal satisfaction of proving to oneself
- Important to do well/disappointed otherwise
- Ashamed if did not do well in subject loved so much
- Always done well anyway

Criteria for evaluating L2 success/development
Academic evaluative criteria
  - Passing exams
  - Exam performance

- Regular grades obtained
- Comparing grades with other students' grades
- Comparing grades with past grades
- Maintaining grade standard set in first year
- Verbal feedback from teachers
- With reference to competitive standards of other students

L2 intrinsic criteria
- Improvement in written work
- Improvement in L2 communication/understanding
- Eradication of mistakes in spoken L2
- Gain in mastery from time and effort
- Being able to put L2 knowledge to practical use
- With reference to future ideal of maximum spoken fluency

Three subjects did not seem to attach motivational importance to doing well in French. This pattern of thinking could partly be interpreted as a form of positive rationalization, since all three had in fact failed their summer examinations in French at the end of their first year and had been obliged to sit supplemental examinations in September. Rather than dwell on their L2 learning experience and performance levels, two of the subjects chose to focus instead on the main incentive channeling their motivation (spending the following academic year in France). Once again, this process of filtering language learning experience and de-emphasizing its negative elements while focusing on incentives seemed to illustrate a form of effective motivational thinking that clearly helped to sustain these subjects' engagement in learning, despite the setbacks encountered.

Moreover, this positive motivational thinking was supported by a firm belief that success in learning French was personally attainable through effort, hard work, and the opportunity to spend time in a French-speaking environment. All three subjects attributed success in language learning to such factors, rather than to ability factors, thereby maintaining the all-important motivational belief in their own potential for making substantial progress. Learner 18, for example, acknowledged that she was "not that hot on languages" and "better at more mathematical things" yet attributed her apparent lack of success with spoken French in particular to the fact that she had never spent any significant amount of time in France. This belief structure largely accounted for her strong desire to go on study experience there the following year.

Subjects who perceived themselves to be relatively successful also demonstrated patterns of positive motivational thinking when analyzing the causes of their success. In general, these patterns entailed enhancing their perceptions of ability and their self-concept by attributing success in French to internal attributes (personal ability, effort, love of the language, interest, a perfectionist approach, etc.)

and to harnessing opportunities arising from personal experience (time spent in France, learning French as a child, having a French girlfriend, etc.). The range of contributory external causes seemed much less prominent in subjects' thinking, limited to the quality or motivating influence of the teachers (mentioned by five subjects) or the competitive atmosphere generated by peer group standards (mentioned by one subject).

Attributed causes of L2 success/development
- *Internal factors*
  - Personal ability
  - Effort/hard work
  - Love of L2
  - Love of studying L2
  - Being a perfectionist/attentive to all input
  - Better interest in L2 study than before

Personal circumstances/experience
- Cumulative time spent in France including school experience
- Length of time speaking L2 since childhood
- Having to communicate in L2 while working in France in summer
- One-time personal relationship with L2 speaker
- Identifying with childhood days at L2-speaking school
- Being able to spend more time on L2 than at school

External factors
- Good teachers
- Enjoyment of class with particular teacher motivating hard work
- Competitive class standards motivating hard work

Factors negatively affecting L2 motivation

In sharp contrast, subjects' perceptions of demotivating experiences revealed an overwhelming predominance of external factors associated with the learning environment. Only one subject identified an internal attribute leading to demotivation — the pressure of setting himself standards which were too high. With this exception, all the factors perceived by subjects to have a negative effect on motivation seemed to relate to the institutionalized language learning experience:

L2 classes with native speakers
- Undercurrent of private jokes alienating teacher
- Atmosphere too casual

- Too many classes
- Classes too large
- Boring waste of time listening to artificial prepared speeches
- Difficulty speaking on uninteresting topics in contrived atmosphere

L2 coursework/methods
- Particular course of lectures
- Studying literature
- Opportunities for student interaction limited in some tutorials
- Dull teaching methods in particular grammar class
- Learning grammatical rules
- Emphasis on learning facts and figures in particular course
- Writing L2 passages on set topics of little relevance
- Role-play tasks in L2
- Time-consuming L2 tasks requiring effort of looking things up
- Hypercritical low marking from particular teacher
- Gap between coursework studied and exam questions

Institutional policies/attitudes
- Too many lectures in English rather than L2
- Lack of oral L2 use/practice
- Department's failure to meet student needs/expectations
- Lack of individual attention with too many students
- Resentment from being unable to change course option
- Department's inflexible attitude over work submission deadlines
- Lack of teacher concern about student motivation/progress

Personal factors
- Pressure of setting standards too high for oneself

Taken collectively, the subjects' responses seemed to express a strongly critical evaluation of their courses of study and the Department of French as a whole. On the level of individual responses, however the criticisms were quite selective and specific rather than across-the-board and were no doubt typical of university students' negative evaluations of their course of study in any discipline. As a research finding, on the other hand, the general uniformity of subjects' responses was quite revealing. After all, the subjects had not been asked to evaluate their course of study but to nominate tasks, conditions, or situations in their L2-related experience which they perceived to be demotivating.

To this end, laying the blame on external circumstances may be a way of limiting the damage and protecting one's own underlying motivation. Only three subjects identified a noticeable loss of motivation as a result of coursework dissatisfaction. The majority seemed to be able to dissociate the demotivating experiences of institutionalized learning from their own personal underlying motivation for wanting to learn French. Learner 8, for example, expressed considerable disillusionment with her course of study, yet seemed to retain her strong intrinsically motivating love of the language: "whatever I think about the French Department...my motivation...my love of French you know is still as it was."

Another subject explicitly differentiated motivation inside the classroom from personal motivation outside the classroom:

> It would be very hard to be motivated in class because classes aren't exactly always stimulating. The only time you really get motivated when you're learning a language is when you're out there speaking to a French person and you realize its true worth. Or when you're reading a book which isn't related to the course and you say — God, I've taken more in than I ever would have, so this course is really good. But within the course you can't really be motivated.

Motivational strategies

In this respect, belief in a personal capacity to generate one's own motivating experiences emerged as a major feature of subjects' effective motivational thinking. In response to the final open-ended question about self-motivational strategies, subjects identified a number of ways in which they attempted to revive or optimize their motivation in the face of negative experiences or setbacks:

Focus on incentives/pressures
- Think about reward of spending year in France pending exam success
- Think about exams coming up
- Look forward to summer trip to US following exams
- Think of dread of failure
- Thrive on assessment pressures/deadlines which have to be met
- Dread guilt of wasting parents' money

Focus on L2 study
- Psyche oneself up to get work done well before deadlines
- Set oneself L2 task to achieve
- Keep active through regular written/research work
- Try to study for a few hours

Seek temporary relief from L2 study
- Tend to avoid tasks disliked

- Take a break from L2 study
- Indulge in non-L2-related social activities
- Have regular outside interests to provide other motivation
- Try to talk to L2 speaker
- Indulge in enjoyable L2 activity unrelated to coursework (L2 film, TV, news, radio, music, newspaper, eavesdropping on tourists)

Talk over motivational problems
- Talk to other students about how they feel
- Remind oneself of reasons/liking for L2 study
- Talk to/encourage oneself

Most commonly, subjects seemed to rely on mobilizing their intrinsic motivational resources by engaging themselves in target language activity in a personally meaningful and relevant way, free from the controlling directives of the formal learning context; or in the words of one student, "rediscovering your enjoyment as it were by doing something you know you like doing" as a way of "getting your motivation on line again." Rediscovering their enjoyment might entail watching a French film or some French satellite television or in the case of one student, eavesdropping on French-speaking tourists in the shops for a bit of fun.

DISCUSSION

TEMPORAL PERSPECTIVES SHAPING MOTIVATIONAL THINKING

One of the most important features to emerge from the analysis of subjects' reported motivation was the varying temporal frame of reference shaping their thinking. We can classify all the factors in each language learner's motivational configuration as either *causal* (deriving from the continuum of L2-learning and L2-related experience to date) or *teleological* (directed towards short-term or long-term goals and future perspectives). The notion of a temporal frame of reference also integrates the phenomenon of motivational evolution over time, which seems central to the learner's experience of, and thus conception of, language learning motivation. The findings here suggest, for example, that goal-orientation may not necessarily be perceived by language learners to be the defining rationale of their motivation but a potentially evolving dimension which needs time to develop and assume motivational importance and clarity.

This is not to deny that many who engage in the business of tackling a foreign language are motivated by a well-defined set of goals, relating perhaps to specific vocational plans or job requirements. However, Dörnyei (1996, p. 76) makes the valid point that job-related motives are unlikely to be a relevant concern among school pupils learning foreign languages. Even for students in third-level education, moreover, it seems that these career perspectives may take considerable time to crystallize and provide a definitive goal structure to their motivation. In the meantime, the motivational mainspring guiding the choices they make and sustaining their engagement in language learning may well be the cumulative impact of language-learning and language-related experience to date. In other words, they may feel motivated to pursue language study because they perceive that this is what they are good at, or what they like best, and where therefore their future potential must lie.

Learners' evolving motivational experience may also entail the development of more short-term goals and incentives, such as the intervention of examination pressures or of rewards contingent upon success in examinations. By the same token, positive L2-learning or L2-related experiences may trigger the development of intrinsic motivational processes in learners who are predominantly goal-directed in their motivation.

Figure 1 offers a schematic representation of how learner conceptions of motivation might thus be defined within a theoretical framework of varying temporal perspectives. As shown, the motivational rationale of *learner A* is dominated by the positive impact of language-learning and language-related experience to date, while goal-directed patterns of thinking play a minor role only. In contrast, the motivational thought structure of *learner B* is shown as predominantly goal-directed. This motivational thought structure could indeed represent a potential later stage in the evolution of *learner A*'s own rationale, as personal goals develop and assume greater importance.

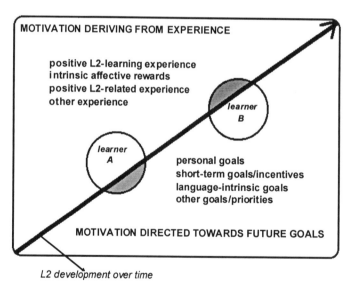

Figure 1: Learner conceptions of motivation: A theoretical framework

Although, like any schematic model, the diagram is a simplification of the complex motivational processes at work, it seems to provide a visually useful representation of an important conceptual distinction — namely, the distinction between the goal-directed progression of L2 development, represented by the arrow, and the configuration of past experience, current experience, and future perspectives defining learner motivation, represented by each circle and its position in the framework. The diagram thus attempts to decouple the concept of motivation as a multidimensional and multidirectional phenomenon from the concept of language learning as a goal-directed phenomenon. Furthermore, included within this schematized framework is interaction with patterns of experience and motivational priorities which lie outside the realm of L2-learning, since these are perceived also to have important repercussions for language learning motivation (for further discussion, see Ushioda, 1998).

PATTERNS OF EFFECTIVE MOTIVATIONAL THINKING

In relation to these varying temporal perspectives, the self-report evidence in this study suggests that differences in learning achievement and in quality of learning experience may entail important qualitative differences in how learners define their motivation. Successful language learners may tend to emphasize the motivational impetus of a positive learning history, while those with less illustrious learning histories may tend to emphasize instead the goals and incentives channeling their motivation.

In itself, of course, the finding that successful learners feel motivated by success is hardly remarkable, since few of us would quibble with the notion that motivation and successful learning go hand in hand. Motivation has traditionally been viewed as a cause or product of language learning success or more typically these days, cast in a dynamic cyclical relationship with positive learning experience and achievement outcomes (see, for example, Gardner & MacIntyre, 1992, 1993). However, the downside to viewing motivation in a simple cause-and-effect relationship with success is that it has rather damaging implications for the poorly motivated unsuccessful language learner, seemingly trapped in a vicious circle of negative learning experiences and negative motivation.

If, on the other hand, we regard the relationship between learning experience and motivation to be mediated by what the learner chooses to think and believe, the potential exists for breaking this vicious circle and generating positive motivation out of or in spite of negative experiences. This potential is realized by the subjects in the study with less positive learning histories to reflect upon, who are nevertheless motivated because they regard their motivation to be defined in terms of particular goals and incentives channeling their efforts to learn the language. The impact of learning experience on motivation is thus mediated by selective patterns of thinking and belief that focus the learners' attention on the positive rather than the negative. Such cognitive-mediational patterns are further illustrated in the follow-up interviews by the three learners who failed their French examinations the previous year. When prompted to consider the motivational importance of doing well in

French, none was inclined to dwell on this aspect of their experience as especially relevant, while two highlighted instead the motivational incentive of spending the forthcoming year in France.

These patterns suggest that effective motivational thinking may be a question of maintaining a positive motivational thought structure by focusing on the positive elements of experience or on positive incentives, while de-emphasizing the negative elements of experience. In this respect, it should be noted that *effectiveness* in this context does not imply that such motivation can or should be measured in terms of its impact on L2 achievement outcomes, as has been the traditional research focus in the study of language learning motivation. The effectiveness of motivational thinking is reflected instead in its capacity to sustain involvement in language learning through all the vicissitudes that learning experience over time inevitably brings.

It is not only, however, in patterns of temporal reference that effective motivational thinking is evident. The process of filtering experience and maintaining a positive belief structure seems to hinge in particular on sustaining a positive self-concept of personal ability or potential and on affirming a sense of motivational autonomy in the face of negative affective experiences. Four attributional patterns emerged from the follow-up data analysis reflecting this underlying belief structure:

- enhancing one's self-concept by attributing positive L2 outcomes and achievement to a belief in personal ability or personal qualities (e.g., hard work, effort, a perfectionist approach);

- maintaining motivation through a belief in personal potential by attributing negative L2 outcomes or lack of success to temporary shortcomings that might be changed (e.g., lack of effort, lack of opportunity to spend time in an L2 environment);

- dissociating demotivating experiences from one's own underlying motivation for wanting to learn the L2 by attributing such negative affective experiences to the demerits of the institutionalized learning context (e.g., teaching methods, coursework pressures);

- believing in a capacity for self-motivation through personal resourcefulness and initiative in the face of the demotivating experiences of institutionalized learning (e.g., setting oneself goals, engaging in intrinsically motivating target language activity).

In essence, these patterns of thinking seem to illustrate ways in which learners can take control of their affective learning experience. Capitalizing on their successes and achievements by attributing them to personal factors, learners can maximize their own subjective rewards and enhance their view of themselves, in particular, their perceptions of their own ability or their capacity for successful learning. By the same token, when faced with setbacks in their learning progress, they can minimize the motivational damage and sustain their belief in their own personal potential, by attributing such setbacks to particular shortcomings that can be worked on and overcome. In this way, they do not succumb to the debilitating belief that they are simply no good at language learning. These positive patterns of thinking in relation to learning and performance outcomes offer a classic illustration of the important functional role of causal attributional processes, as highlighted in the literature on attributional theories of motivation in education (see, for example, Weiner, 1984). In the present context of research on language learning motivation, these cognitive-mediational patterns serve once again to question the notion that success/failure and motivation are bound together in a one-to-one cause-and-effect relationship and illustrate the potential for learners themselves to take control of their affective learning experience by reflecting on performance outcomes in the most positive terms (for more detailed discussion, see Ushioda, 1996b, 1997).

Of course, language learners' affective learning experience relates not only to the subjective rewards and repercussions associated with performance outcomes and achievements. Taking control of their affective learning experience also requires learners to cope with the periods of tedium, frustration, stagnation, pressure, and so on that are an inevitable part of the long and often arduous process of learning a foreign language. Here, too, it seems that learners' belief structure can play a crucial role in limiting the motivational damage and sustaining involvement in learning. Once learners start blaming themselves for the loss of interest and negative affect they are experiencing, they run the risk of believing that they are simply no longer motivated or able to motivate themselves. On the other hand, if they mentally project the responsibility for their demotivation onto external causes (e.g., the conditions of institutionalized language learning), they may be able to dissociate the negative affect they are currently experiencing from their own enduring motivation for wanting to learn the language.

The process of affirming this sense of motivational autonomy becomes the process of self-motivation, as learners consciously reflect on their reasons for learning, remind themselves of their goals, set themselves targets, rediscover their enjoyment, and renew that vital sense of personal involvement in their language learning. In this respect, the self-report evidence from this study seems to underline the importance of target language *use* as a means of reviving flagging spirits and putting learners in touch with their motivation again, when the negative conditions of formal language learning experience take their toll.

CONCLUSION

Defined in this way as a complex of processes shaping and sustaining learner involvement in learning, the concept of language learning motivation presented in this chapter departs significantly from the traditional concept that has evolved in the quantitative research paradigm. Although much of the current renewed debate calls for the exploration of cognitive motivational dimensions (e.g., Dörnyei, 1994a, p. 273; Schmidt & Savage, 1994, p. 3), this chapter perhaps goes further than most in proposing that we re-cast the concept of motivation — traditionally an affective variable — in the cognitive domain of learner experience, whereby the role of affect is mediated by the learner's thought processes and belief structures. Motivation is thus viewed not simply as cause or product of particular learning experiences, but as process — in effect, the ongoing process of how the learner thinks about and interprets events in relevant L2-learning and L2-related experience and how such cognitions and beliefs then shape subsequent involvement in learning. Recent developments in research on L2 motivation suggest that there is plenty of scope for such a focus on motivational process and evolution over time (see in particular Dörnyei, 1998; Dörnyei & Ottó, 1998). This chapter has attempted to highlight the value of a qualitative research approach to the exploration of such dynamic phenomena. It has sought to examine how motivated language learners think about their motivation and what patterns of motivational thinking seem effective in enabling them to take control of their affective learning experience and to sustain their involvement in language learning.

Ultimately, of course, the perspective presented in this chapter invites us to integrate the study of language learning motivation with research on learner autonomy. Where autonomy implies taking responsibility for one's learning in all its aspects (Holec, 1981, p. 3), effective motivational thinking implies managing its affective dimension in order to optimize and sustain one's involvement in learning (Ushioda, 1996b, 1997). The interaction between motivation and autonomy has received considerable attention in the literature on educational psychology (see, for example, the collection of papers in Boggiano & Pittman, 1992; also Rueda & Moll, 1994). The concept of intrinsic motivation in particular has been closely associated with the fundamental human capacity and need for personal autonomy (Deci, 1996; Van Lier, 1996), while the notion of self-motivation is inextricably linked with processes of self-regulation and autonomy (McCombs, 1994). Viewed from this perspective, as Deci succinctly suggests (1996, p. 10), the agenda for teachers (and researchers) is not "how can people motivate others?" but "how can people create the conditions within which others will motivate themselves?" Such an agenda would seem to yield considerable scope for further qualitative research on language learning motivation. This might include, for example, exploring optimum kinds of autonomy-supportive learning environments, identifying pedagogical approaches that nurture intrinsic language learning motivation, and examining the role of feedback and teacher-learner interaction in promoting effective motivational thinking and self-regulated learning (for further discussion, see Ushioda, 1996b).

REFERENCES

Ames, C. (1986). Effective motivation: The contribution of the learning environment. In R. Feldman (Ed.), *The social psychology of education: Current research and theory* (pp. 235–256). Cambridge, UK: Cambridge University Press.

Boggiano, A. K., & Pittman, T. S. (Eds.). (1992). *Achievement and motivation: A social-development perspective*. Cambridge, UK: Cambridge University Press.

Crookes, G., & Schmidt, R. (1991). Motivation: Reopening the research agenda. *Language Learning, 41*, 469–512.

Deci, E. L. (1980). *The psychology of self-determination.* Lexington, MA: D. C. Heath & Co.

Deci, E. L. (with Flaste, R.) (1996). *Why we do what we do: Understanding self-motivation.* New York: Penguin.

Dörnyei, Z. (1994a). Motivation and motivating in the foreign language classroom. *Modern Language Journal, 78*, 273–284.

Dörnyei, Z. (1994b). Understanding L2 motivation: On with the challenge! *Modern Language Journal, 78*, 515–523.

Dörnyei, Z. (1996). Moving language learning motivation to a larger platform for theory and practice. In R. L. Oxford (Ed.), *Language learning motivation: Pathways to the new century* (Technical Report No. 11, pp. 71–80). Honolulu: University of Hawai'i, Second Language Teaching & Curriculum Center.

Dörnyei, Z. (1998). Motivation in second and foreign language learning. *Language Teaching, 31*, 117–135.

Dörnyei, Z. (2000). *Teaching and researching motivation.* Harlow, UK: Addison Wesley Longman.

Dörnyei, Z., & Ottó, I. (1998). Motivation in action: A process model of L2 motivation. *Working Papers in Applied Linguistics, 4*, 43–69. London: Thames Valley University.

Gardner, R. C. (1985). *Social psychology and second language learning: The role of attitudes and motivation.* London: Edward Arnold.

Gardner, R. C., & Lambert, W. E. (1972). *Attitudes and motivation in second language learning.* Rowley, MA: Newbury House.

Gardner, R. C., & MacIntyre, P. D. (1992). A student's contributions to second language learning. Part I: Cognitive variables. *Language Teaching, 25*, 211–220.

Gardner, R. C., & MacIntyre, P. D. (1993). A student's contributions to second-language learning. Part II: Affective variables. *Language Teaching, 26*, 1–11.

Gardner, R. C., & Tremblay, P. F. (1994a). On motivation, research agendas and theoretical frameworks. *Modern Language Journal, 78*, 359–368.

Gardner, R. C., & Tremblay, P. F. (1994b). On motivation: Measurement and conceptual considerations. *Modern Language Journal, 78*, 524–527.

Gardner, R. C., Tremblay, P. F., & Masgoret, A-M. (1997). Towards a full model of second language learning: An empirical investigation. *Modern Language Journal, 81*, 344–362.

Gliksman, L., Gardner, R. C., & Smythe, P. C. (1982). The role of the integrative motive on students' participation in the French classroom. *Canadian Modern Language Review, 38*, 625–647.

Holec, H. (1981). *Autonomy in foreign language learning.* Oxford, UK: Pergamon.

Larsen-Freeman, D., & Long, M. H. (1991). *An introduction to second language acquisition research.* New York: Longman.

Lepper, M. R., & Greene, D. (1978). *The hidden costs of reward: New perspectives on the psychology of human motivation*. Hillsdale, NJ: Erlbaum.

Maehr, M. L. (1984). Meaning and motivation: Toward a theory of personal investment. In R. E. Ames & C. E. Ames (Eds.), *Research on motivation in education: Vol. 1* (pp. 115–144). Orlando, FL: Academic Press.

McCombs, B. L. (1994). Strategies for assessing and enhancing motivation: Keys to promoting self-regulated learning and performance. In H. F. O'Neil, Jr., & M. Drillings (Eds.), *Motivation: Theory and research* (pp. 49–69). Hillsdale, NJ: Erlbaum.

Oxford, R. L. (1994). Where are we regarding language learning motivation? *Modern Language Journal, 78*, 512–514.

Oxford, R. L. (Ed.). (1996). *Language learning motivation: Pathways to the new century* (Technical Report No. 11). Honolulu: University of Hawai'i, Second Language Teaching & Curriculum Center.

Oxford, R. L., & Shearin, J. (1994). Language learning motivation: Expanding the theoretical framework. *Modern Language Journal, 78*, 12–28.

Pintrich, P. L., & Schunk, D. H. (1996). *Motivation in education: Theory, research, and applications*. Englewood Cliffs, NJ: Erlbaum.

Ramage, K. (1990). Motivational factors and persistence in foreign language study. *Language Learning, 30*, 189–219.

Rueda, R., & Moll, L. C. (1994). A sociocultural perspective on motivation. In H. F. O'Neil, Jr., & M. Drillings (Eds.), *Motivation: Theory and research* (pp. 117–137). Hillsdale, NJ: Erlbaum.

Schmidt, R., Boraie, D., & Kassabgy, O. (1996). Foreign language motivation: Internal structure and external connections. In R. L. Oxford (Ed.), *Language learning motivation: Pathways to the new century* (Technical Report No. 11, pp. 9–70). Honolulu: University of Hawai'i, Second Language Teaching & Curriculum Center.

Schmidt, R., & Savage, W. (1994). Challenge, skill and motivation. *University of Hawai'i Working Papers in ESL, 12*(2), 1–25. Honolulu: University of Hawai'i, Department of English as a Second Language.

Singleton, D. (1990). *The TCD modern languages research project: Objectives, instruments and preliminary results* (CLCS Occasional Paper No. 26). Dublin, Ireland: Trinity College, Centre for Language and Communication Studies.

Skehan, P. (1989). *Individual differences in second-language learning*. London: Edward Arnold.

Spolsky, B. (1989). *Conditions for second language learning*. Oxford, UK: Oxford University Press.

Tremblay, P. F., & Gardner, R. C. (1995). Expanding the motivation construct in language learning. *Modern Language Journal, 79*, 505–520.

Ushioda, E. (1994). L2 motivation as a qualitative construct. *Teanga, 14*, 76–84.

Ushioda, E. (1996a). *Language learners' motivational thinking: A qualitative study.* Unpublished doctoral dissertation, University of Dublin, Trinity College, Dublin.

Ushioda, E. (1996b). *Learner autonomy 5: The role of motivation.* Dublin: Authentik.

Ushioda, E. (1997). The role of motivational thinking in autonomous language learning. In D. Little & B. Voss (Eds.), *Language centres: Planning for the new millennium* (pp. 38–50). Plymouth, UK: Cercles.

Ushioda, E. (1998). Effective motivational thinking: A cognitive theoretical approach to the study of language learning motivation. In A. Alcón & V. Codina (Eds.), *Current issues in English language methodology* (pp. 77–89). Castelló de la Plana, Spain: Publicacions de la Universitat Jaume I.

Van Lier, L. (1996). *Interaction in the language curriculum: Awareness, autonomy and authenticity.* London: Longman.

Weiner, B. (1984). Principles for a theory of student motivation and their application within an attributional framework. In R. E. Ames & C. E. Ames (Eds.), *Research on motivation in education: Vol.1* (pp. 15–38). Orlando, FL: Academic Press.

Williams, M., & Burden, R. (1997). *Psychology for language teachers.* Cambridge, UK: Cambridge University Press.

Zafar Syed
Military Language Institute, Abu Dhabi, UAE

NOTIONS OF SELF IN FOREIGN LANGUAGE LEARNING: A QUALITATIVE ANALYSIS

Author's note

This research was supported in part by the National Foreign Language Resource Center and the Center for Second Language Research at the University of Hawai'i at Mānoa.

INTRODUCTION

There has been renewed interest in exploring learner motivation and why people learn languages. Traditionally this area of our field has been dominated by the seminal work of Gardner and Lambert (1972) and the resulting constructs of integrative and instrumental motivation. Increasingly, however, there is growing concern that sociocultural and psychosocial factors have not been given due attention in motivational studies, so much so that there has been a call for a re-examination of the prevailing research agenda (Crookes & Schmidt, 1991). Scholars have pointed out that there are cultural, psychological, and social variables in SLA that have not been properly addressed (Lantolf & Pavlenko, 1995; Norton Pierce, 1995; Ochs, 1993; Trueba, 1988) and that prevailing definitions and constructs (motivation, self, identity) in currency today are ethnocentric and vary across cultures (Castenell, 1984; Church & Katigbak, 1992; Duda & Allison, 1989; Markus & Kitayama, 1991; Norton Pierce, 1995). In short, there are many reasons why people learn languages, and these reasons are often related to one's social, ethnic, and cultural place in the community at large. How we measure or document learner motivation has also been under discussion. Crookes and Schmidt (1991) highlight the need for more qualitative exploration of these issues. As a qualitative variable, "motivation may be defined not in terms of observable and measurable activity, but rather in terms of what patterns of thinking and belief underlie such activity and shape students' engagement in the learning process" (Ushioda, this volume).

In this chapter, I seek to address learner motivation through a qualitative description of these "patterns of thinking and belief" stemming from a semester long study. The focus will be on how heritage language learners' notions of self are (re)defined as they struggle to find their voice and place in society. I begin by sketching a conceptual framework that identifies salient issues in this area leading to a description of the participants, setting, and study design. This is followed by a detailed exploration of the findings as they relate to the study of motivation, language education, and minority students.

Syed, Z. (2001). Notions of self in foreign language learning: A qualitative analysis. In Z. Dörnyei & R. Schmidt (Eds.), *Motivation and second language acquisition* (Technical Report #23, pp. 127–148). Honolulu: University of Hawai'i, Second Language Teaching and Curriculum Center.

CONCEPTUAL FRAMEWORK

MOTIVATION, CULTURE, AND CONTEXT

The study of motivation has been dominated (and directed) by categories like integrative, instrumental, intrinsic, and extrinsic. Recently, scholars have argued that while these constructs are useful, they do not give a complete picture. They suggest that there are several reasons why people study languages beyond these static and linear classifications (Clément & Kruidenier, 1983; Dörnyei, 1994; Oxford & Shearin, 1994). There is a growing sense in the field that cultural, social, and contextual factors need to be considered if we are to get a clearer impression of motivation. Several studies have highlighted how the ethnocentric assumptions and approaches in motivational studies simply do not account for cultural and social variations (Duda & Allison, 1989; Maehr & Braskamp, 1986; Markus & Kitayama, 1991; Svanes, 1987). These studies illustrate several important points: (a) that there are multiple motives operating in a given setting and these variations have different meaning and value across cultures; (b) that success, or failure, may not always be equated with objective competitive outcomes; (c) that there are several epistemological concerns with the Western notion of achievement; and (d) that there can be culturally based differences in expectations, competence, and interaction patterns within an academic setting. What motivates people to do something is a result of their cultural understanding of that situation and their culturally-based choice of action.

Similarly, contextual factors need to be addressed and their impact on motivation identified. Trueba (1988) offers a strong argument for linking the context and process of events in the home, school, and community to an individual's learning and academic achievement. He cites Vygotskian (and neo-Vygotskian) perspectives in viewing intellectual development as a socially- and culturally-based exercise. How and what we learn is determined by the social structures surrounding us and the learning context. Unfortunately, however, this connection, or paradigm, is only now being explored by linguists and SLA theorists (Lantolf & Pavlenko, 1995; Norton Pierce, 1995; Ochs, 1993). It is difficult to rule contextual factors out of any analysis of human behavior or source of behavior. It is precisely in how a person defines the situation for herself within a given sociocultural context that determines her personal investment in that situation (Maehr & Braskamp, 1986).

How motivation is measured and interpreted should reflect the influence culture and context have on this subject. That is to say, motivation needs to be examined from the point of view of those involved rather than from pre-conceived domains (i.e., researcher's bias or existing theoretical constructs). This need for a holistic and emic perspective demands a qualitative approach.

SELF-CONCEPT AND IDENTITY

At the heart of any motivation study is the individual under study, and central to any individual is their perception of self (Rogers, 1947). How we see ourselves, how others see us, will dictate to varying degrees our motives, actions, and involvement. Development of the self and self-concept have been positively linked with academic achievement (Combs & Snygg, 1959; Purkey, 1970). This connection has more recently been made by studies on immigrant populations in North America and England (Ghuman, 1991; Henze & Vanett, 1993; Hoffman, 1989; Phelan, Davidson, & Cao, 1991; Stopes-Roe & Cochrane, 1990). Four important issues with respect to self-concept are worth considering here: (a) that self-concept is socially constructed (Markus & Kitayama, 1991; Purkey, 1970; Rogers, 1947); (b) that the self is defined and understood differently across cultures (Markus & Kitayama, 1991); (c) that given a supportive environment/context, there is a tendency in each individual towards self-actualization and growth (Purkey & Schmidt, 1987; Weedon 1987, as cited in Norton Pierce, 1995; Fleming, 1985); and (d) that this process is dynamic, diverse, and developmental (Csikszentmihalyi & Larson, 1984; Norton Pierce, 1995). Studies in adolescent and ego development have shown how this process is heightened during the adolescent years (Csikszentmihalyi & Larson, 1984; Hauser, Powers, & Noam, 1991). It is during this time that "young people go through great emotional, cognitive, and social transformations. Out of these changes emerges a pattern of thought and volition that defines the self...when successfully achieved it is a stable feeling of confidence that one knows who one is" (Csikszentmihalyi & Larson, 1984, p. 8). Furthermore, it is suggested that "without a cohesive sense of self, life passes by without pattern or purpose" (Csikszentmihalyi & Larson, p. 8). Knowing who you are, how others see you, and how you fit into your environment are important issues for us as we negotiate our place in society.

Just as self-concept is socially constructed, so is the notion of identity. The literature distinguishes between several different types of identities (social, personal, racial, heritage, etc.). For the purposes of this study, I would like to focus on social and heritage identity. *Social identity* can be defined as "a range of social personae, including social statuses, roles, positions, relationships, and institutional and other relevant community identities one may attempt to claim or assign in the course of social life" (Ochs, 1993, p. 288). Any given individual will have a number of social identities that operate in different social domains and are contextually triggered. Studies in this area have highlighted the importance of others in how we see ourselves (Helms, 1990; Norton Pierce, 1995; Ochs, 1993). I use the term *heritage identity* as a cover term to include those attributes of the self that are linked with one's race, language, religion, and ethnicity. Heritage identity, thus, is ascribed, although there is some personal volition with respect to religion. That is to say, it is possible for an individual to select membership into a religious group. It must be said that there are clearly areas of overlap when talking about social and heritage identity. One's social position, role, or persona will invariably depend on one's race, cultural values, language ability, and ethnicity. Conversely, how one values and defines their heritage identity will be influenced by prevailing social practices. As Norton Pierce (1997) points out, these two constructs have more in common than previously postulated.

Identity development studies have drawn upon the work of Erik Erikson (1968, 1980) in explaining the nexus between social ascription and psychological processing. Using Erikson's stages of psychosocial development, Marcia (1980) identified 4 identity stages operating in college students (aged 18–25):

identity diffusion	The individual is highly impressionable and changes opinions; s/he is not committed to any one system. There is no strong sense of identity or identity crisis at this stage.
foreclosed status	The individual has made commitments to a set of values based on other people's (parents, peers) decisions.
moratorium status	The individual is actively searching for solutions and their identity. This is a prerequisite stage for identity achievement.
identity achieved status	The individual has resolved identity crisis. They start to feel "in harmony with themselves, accept their capabilities, limitations and opportunities." (Muss, 1988, p. 74).

There is a sense in this development of moving from the influences of the family, to peers, and eventually to one's own sense of the world. As young adults, these individuals are seemingly coming to grips with their place in their given environment. They are beginning to define for themselves who they are in relation to those around them (Erikson, 1980). It is important to note that the prevailing environmental conditions (whether supportive or marginalizing) will influence just what kind of identity is achieved (Erikson, 1980; Fleming, 1985; Helms, 1990; Marcia, 1980).

Environmental/social conditions highlight specific concerns with respect to how minorities negotiate identity. Individuals who come from ethnic minorities not only have to go through the types of adjustment Erikson talks about but have to face additional challenges stemming from the fact that they are visibly different. Such individuals also have to deal with appearance, accent, cultural values, prejudice, discrimination, and cultural border crossing (Cummins, 1986; Ghuman, 1991; Henze & Vanett, 1993; Hoffman, 1989; Lucas, Henze, & Donato, 1990; Phelan, et al., 1991; Stopes-Roe & Cochrane, 1990). Being different (racially, ethnically, culturally, religiously) exercises a cost on such individuals that needs to be accounted for on a daily basis. At the same time, ethnic minorities are said to undergo *enculturation* in their own ethnic culture. As a result, their identities, or sense of self, are continually challenged from within and without. For those caught in this process, it means membership in at least two worlds. Not surprisingly in a number of studies on Asian students, the participants identified themselves as bi-cultural (Berry, Kim, Power, Young, & Bujaki, 1989; Ghuman, 1991; Stopes-Roe & Cochrane, 1990). This polycultural identity is a difficult undertaking. There is always the danger that in opening the door to accommodate one culture, the individual ends up stranded between two doors unable to fully get into either one

(Henze & Vanett, 1993; Hoffman, 1989).[1] It has been argued that those individuals who identify strongly with their heritage culture are more likely to use that identification to enhance their sense of self (Lalonde, Taylor, & Moghaddam, 1992). Clearly, minority students have unique challenges in the process of self actualization and identity negotiation.

FOREIGN LANGUAGES, EDUCATION, AND MINORITIES

There is a well-established historical pattern of institutional discrimination of language minorities (Bankston & Zhou, 1995; Ortega, 1999; Popkewitz, 1987). Language policies have continually devalued foreign language use and promoted English monolingualism in school (Crawford, 1992; García, 1992). The present English Only Movement is an extension of such deeply rooted biases in American society. With the continual increase in the ethnic student population, there is a greater demand for addressing the heritage language and cultural needs of these students. Research in the social sciences has not only identified the challenges such students face (Berry, 1992; Berry, et al., 1989; Ward & Kennedy, 1994), but also how heritage language maintenance and a more positive ethnic identity can have an impact on academic success and socio-psychological well being (Brisk, 1991; Cummins, 1986; Davis, 1999; Hoffman, 1989; Lalonde, et al., 1992; Lucas, et al., 1990; Phelan, et al., 1991). Traditionally, university level language courses are primarily designed for foreign language learners; heritage language learners often have specific needs that dictate new solutions (Gambhir, 1992). For example, Gambhir (1992) discusses how learning script is the "most important skill" (p. 16) for such learners in developing self-esteem and allowing them to communicate with their extended families. He also suggests that heritage language teachers need to accommodate regional/colloquial influences and usage without labeling it as wrong. The purpose of education in this sense must be "to help all individuals understand their race and culture, including language and socialization experiences, had value, and could and should exist on a coequal basis with mainstream American values and experiences" (Ramsey, Vold, & Williams, 1989, p. 9). Scholars have also argued that validating students' heritage identity (as it relates to language, culture, and race) is important in building a positive self-concept and academic success (Angle, 1978; Cummins, 1986; Davis, 1999).

SUMMARY

Given this theoretical framework, it becomes increasingly clear that motivational studies need to account for far more than surface level answers to motivational/attitudinal questionnaires. An individual's psychosocial and sociocultural history, development, and interaction play an important contributing role in motivation. Further, ethnic minority students present a unique case in that they undergo additional challenges (stemming from their heritage membership) in the process of education and socialization. Studies addressing the above issues need

---

[1]   Stonequests' "marginal man" (1964) highlights this scenario.

to incorporate an emic, qualitative perspective and go beyond surface level analysis to discover underlying concepts and rationale.

THE STUDY

CONTEXTUAL BACKGROUND

This interpretive qualitative exploration documents how foreign language learners (especially heritage language learners) notions of self impact their involvement, persistence, and learning of their foreign/heritage language. The data and analysis presented here documents a semester long study involving participants learning Hindi[2] in the foreign languages department at a large American university. The university offers a large number of language courses (up to 29 different languages in a given semester) including a number of less commonly taught languages. Successful completion of a second-level foreign language is required for all undergraduate students at the university. The language requirement was not an issue in this study, however, as the participants were either graduate or visiting students. Two Hindi classes were involved in the study: a first year and a second year course. Classes met three times a week for a total of 4 1/2 hours a week. The classes were unique in a number of ways. Both classes had only 6 students each. Given lower student enrollment in these courses, there was only one section of each class. Further, the individuals in a given class, if continuing, move as a group to the next level. That means that the class stays together as the students move from semester to semester and from first level (101/102) to second level (201/202). Students are placed into a level and class after an interview with the instructor; there are no other forms of assessment used for placement. Also, there is only one instructor for these classes. A student learning Hindi would therefore have the same instructor throughout the course of their language studies at the university and probably the same classmates. A text packet was provided by the instructor and added to during the course of the term. The instructor provided vocabulary, grammar aids, lyrics of popular Hindi songs, and useful phrases, as necessary or dictated by the course. The instructor for the course practiced a pedagogy which created a positive, supportive, and student-centered course, in the sense that the cultural and linguistic needs of the students were addressed.

Although the community at large is very multicultural and multilingual (with particular focus on Asian cultures and languages), there is a relatively small Hindi speaking population. On campus, there were some 35 native Hindi speaking students enrolled in various degree programs; at present there are no student organizations from this region. There are shops selling Indian food, handicrafts, music, videos, and so forth close to the university. There are a small number of

---

[2] Hindi was a logical choice in that as a native Urdu speaker, I am able to understand spoken Hindi. My cultural and linguistic background would be invaluable in analyzing the content and process of the class. Also, it was useful in arranging an exchange of service with the five students who actively participated in this study. I was able to offer them practice in speaking Hindi in exchange for their involvement with the study.

Hindi speaking families in the community at large, and occasionally there are social events (concerts, parties, celebrations) when they all come together. Apart from these resources, there are limited opportunities for students learning Hindi at the university to interact with Hindi speakers.

PARTICIPANTS

There were a total of 12 students in the two classes; half of these were learning Hindi as a heritage language. From these 12, 5 students agreed to be interviewed and volunteered to participate in the study; consequently, they are the focus of this study. These students were in the first-level class that had 2 other members.[3] Of these five individuals, two were learning Hindi as a foreign language and three as a heritage language; all of them were female, single, and in the range of 21–34 years old (see Appendix 1).

Anna[4] is an American from the Midwest and a classified graduate student in education. She lived and worked in Nepal for 1 1/2 years and feels that her Nepali "oral pronunciation, comprehension, and conversation is very good." Anna was exposed to Hindi during this time through movies, music, "fruit sellers and people who tried to speak to me." She has also traveled to Indonesia and India. Prior to learning Nepali she also studied Spanish. She often practices Hindi with her Nepali boyfriend.

Nancy is also an American graduate student; she is pursuing a degree with a focus on India. Nancy was exposed to Indian culture through books "my mother used to give me" and through Indian friends she has had throughout her life. She spent a semester in India studying Buddhism and got her first Hindi language learning experiences during this time. Her time in India was an "eye opening experience" which further propelled her interest in this part of the world. It was during this time that she learned the Hindi alphabet. Nancy has also studied Spanish in high school and in her undergraduate studies.

Suzy is a visiting unclassified graduate student, born and raised in Canada, who is on leave from her teaching assignment in California. Ethnically she is from Goa (a province in India) and part of a community that was greatly influenced (religiously and linguistically) by the Portuguese presence in that part of India.[5] Suzy has traveled to Mexico, the US, and India (once). She is an avid learner of languages and has studied no less than 8 different languages (French, Spanish, Italian, Japanese, Chinese, German, Tagalog, and Hindi). She studied French and Spanish in high school and previously took Hindi classes in night school as an adult.

---

[3]   Of the other 2 members, 1 could not participate in interviews because of time constraints, and the other, the only male, dropped out of the course 2 weeks into the semester.
[4]   All names are pseudonyms.
[5]   A large community of English speaking Catholics has existed in Goa. Visibly these individuals are very much "Indian," but for most of them Hindi is a second/foreign language. Suzy and her family speak English as a native language.

Huma is the only first generation immigrant in this group. She was born in India and migrated with her family at an early age. She grew up on the east coast and is a university exchange student. Huma studied Spanish in high school. Hindi is her first language, but she forgot most of it soon after coming to the US. She never learned to read or write Hindi prior to her enrollment in this class. Huma has had continued exposure to Hindi at home over the years and through her extended family. She has visited India only once after moving to the States.

Rani is another visiting student. She is on a year long sabbatical from her work as a journalist. She was born and raised in the Midwest and is a second-generation Indian American. Rani never learned Hindi though she was exposed to it at home. She studied French in high school and Spanish in college. Rani has visited India on a couple of occasions.

All five of these individuals come from very different backgrounds. Each student brought with her some previous experience or knowledge that helped her in the course of study. Anna's fluency with Nepali, Suzy's Hindi night classes, Huma and Rani's exposure to Hindi at home, and Nancy's life-long love of Indian culture gave each one a kind of "leg up" and a "jump start" in the process of learning Hindi.

METHODOLOGY

My focus in this study was to get at the underlying patterns of thinking and belief, beyond the surface level answers given on questionnaires, of why students engage in foreign/heritage language studies. Given this focus, and my conceptual framework, I employed a qualitative approach to data collection and analysis. Qualitative methods lend themselves well to the holistic and emic nature of such exploration. "The openness of qualitative inquiry allows the researcher to approach the inherent complexity of social interaction and to do justice to that complexity, to respect it in its own right. Qualitative researchers...assume that social interaction is complex and that they will uncover some of that complexity" (Glesne and Peshkin, 1992, p. 7). Three broad questions framed my research at the outset:

- What motivated students to undertake foreign/heritage language studies?

- How did learners manage their interest during their present course of study?

- What are some of the social influences surrounding their participation in these language classes?

It is important that these questions be examined from the point of view of those involved (the learners) rather than from pre-conceived domains (i.e., existing theoretical beliefs).

I collected data through classroom observation in both classes, interviews with the students and the teacher, informal get-togethers with students, and materials used in the classroom. On rare occasions, the instructor would involve me in the classroom discussion, but by and large, I was solely an observer. I kept detailed field notes of my observations. Interviews were scheduled periodically over the course of the semester with the participating students. I met with the instructor on a weekly basis to talk about learning and teaching of Hindi and in particular the two classes. Interviews were audio-taped and transcribed. As part of an exchange of services, I met with the students in out-of-class get-togethers as a way of practicing Hindi. In these gatherings we would watch a movie, listen to music, and talk about learning and using Hindi. There were other informal communication exchanges, some through e-mail, that served to provide illuminating insights into the lives of these individuals. Class hand-outs, texts, and student writing samples (in Hindi and English) also contributed to the analysis presented here.

Guided by the above three overriding questions, data were analyzed to get a sense of the important sociocultural and psychosocial forces at work. The following analysis represents four major themes identified in the data collected: (a) needs, desires, and expectations, (b) the nature of language instruction, (c) the search within, and (d) personal development or maturation.

FINDINGS

NEEDS, DESIRES AND EXPECTATIONS

Learning Hindi appears to be meeting certain needs and fulfilling longstanding desires, and for these reasons the participants are continually investing themselves in this process. When initially asked as to why they were learning Hindi, the participants mentioned a number of academic and personal reasons. Anna and Nancy were interested in learning Hindi because it is one of the major languages of the region that is their academic focus at present. Both are taking courses that focus on this region and feel that knowing the language gives them a better understanding of the culture, religion, and history of this area. But there's more to it than academic transference. As Nancy states, "It does help me in my other classes but I can't say it's just because I'm taking this religion class and I just love this religion class. There's so many other things tied into it that I can't separate them." There are also professional reasons for learning Hindi. They both believe that knowing Hindi will be of extreme importance as they hope to be working in some capacity in literacy/educational programs in this region. But what really ties it all together for them is a love and appreciation for the culture. As Nancy continues,

> It has just fascinated me, intrigued me, ever since high school. I took classes in high school [Buddhist philosophy], went to India for a semester. I want to go back and work there. I love the culture, it's very intriguing to me. It's beautiful.

They clearly identify with the culture and people in this part of the world.

> I like the family structure. Just people know where they are, who they are which is I think it is pretty amazing. Of course there are negative things that go with it, but that's with everything. And the fact that it is totally different from American

society. A lot of people think it's really bad or negative but it's not. It works …and it has worked for thousands of years.

It is worth noting that both of them have very personal interests tied in with their professional/academic ones. Both have been, or are currently involved, in relationships with people from this part of the world. In fact, they always made it clear on several occasions that, "I have academic and personal interests." For Nancy, the interest in Indian culture and language was initially sparked by her high school boyfriend. Both Nancy and Anna listen to Hindi music, eat and cook Indian food, communicate with friends in India, and have an appreciation for Indian fashion. Learning Hindi has immediacy in that it allows them access to a culture and people they identify with. It is a gateway into a community that is "foreign" to them as Anglo-Americans but one that they appreciate, increasingly understand, and see themselves fitting into.

For Rani, Huma, and Suzy, learning Hindi means being able to speak a language that others expect them to speak. These three individuals are visibly identifiable as Indian. As such, they documented numerous occasions where others simply assumed that they spoke Hindi. Rani recounts her experience in meeting some of her relatives in India:

> We were in India in 1992 and this was the first time I had gone there as an adult…My relatives were sort of saying, "Why is it that you don't know Hindi?…And I was well I just never learned it and my mother was starting to blame herself and I got upset about that.

Family members are not the only people expecting Hindi fluency. All three commented on how people they would meet on a daily basis would automatically assume that they were Hindi speakers based on their ethnicity and race. This is especially troublesome for Suzy who is a native English speaker. Yet, she always has to "explain herself" to others that "I am Canadian, Christian, and we speak English at home. They see my brown skin and assume that I can speak the language." Such pressures/expectations are part of the reason why these learners find themselves learning Hindi. Still, this is not the sole reason why Suzy is learning Hindi. As she recounts, "I think they [language courses] will help me professionally, socially, and for the rest of my life." As a teacher, she feels that she needs to know the culture and the lived experiences of her students. "I think to know a people you must know their language." Clearly, she is an exceptional learner who has studied and learned (to varying degrees) a number of languages. Similarly, Rani talked about how learning Hindi will help her professionally as a journalist.

Huma and Rani, not unlike other heritage language learners (Burnett & Syed, 1999), feel that they need to have some fluency in their heritage language. They feel "embarrassed" and "ashamed" that they are not able to communicate in Hindi:

> Well, it's kind of bad that I don't know it by now. I feel really bad that I don't know my own language…kind of embarrassed, ashamed of myself a little bit, sometimes defensive.

This need is based primarily in wanting to be able to communicate with family members. As Rani explains, "It's very important to me personally to know it…I want to understand my family and read and translate old family documents." Huma longingly suggests, "It would be great to be able to go back [to India] and converse fluently with my relatives. I think it would impress them and just make me feel a lot better." Being able to "connect" with family members is clearly important. Given that these learners live in a society which is quite different and distant from that of their extended families, language becomes the common thread. So much so that these heritage learners are beginning to see the importance of language as it relates to family not only for themselves but also for their children as the following comment from Huma suggests: "I want to make sure I learn it so when I have kids I can keep the language going."

Learning Hindi also allows these heritage learners a pathway into their heritage culture. Having lived outside this culture, geographically and socially speaking, they feel they do not have the kind of cultural expertise they should have or are expected to have. Whether it is learning about Hinduism, cooking, religious strife, or family structures, these learners feel that this course is giving them what they need:

> I don't know too much about it but I'm learning. Actually here I'm learning a lot about it. I just want to be knowledgeable about my culture.

Being knowledgeable here means knowing, in some detail, the history, doctrines, customs, and social practices of those in their heritage culture. Again, it is as much for their own personal satisfaction as it is to meet the expectations of others. In an informal discussion with Rani, I learned how important this can be:

> I think people sort of look at you and think you should know more about your language and your culture than you do now. When you're sitting with a group of people and they are talking about stuff related to you [as an Indian] and you realize that they have maybe more information or maybe an opinion and you are like I should know about that. Or sometimes they ask you about something you should know and you need to know so you can answer them or teach them about it.

These learners are viewed as representatives of their heritage culture; as such, they feel they need to be able to bring an insider's perspective to related issues and topics. Learning Hindi can play a vital role in this in that it gives them access to what the terminology is, how to pronounce things, or simply "how to say it in Hindi," as well as an insider's legitimacy that is expected with their heritage membership. It is interesting to note that language requirement (for academic or institutional purposes) was not a reason for learning Hindi for any of these learners.

LANGUAGE LEARNING AND BEYOND

Irrespective of what kind of motivation learners bring into the classroom, it will be tempered by the content and process of the class. Learners in this Hindi class unanimously agreed that the classroom environment almost always kept them interested in learning. The instructor was able to create this learning environment in a number of ways.

The first remark made by all participants was that the class was not as structured as other classes they have taken. It was a lot more relaxed and informal. When asked what they felt were the course requirements, none of the participants could collaborate on a single set of requirements. Some like Anna thought the requirements were to "do our homework and show up for class, take a test every so often and that seems to be about all." For Huma it was more like, "there's a lab that you're supposed to go to every week then you have the homework that we turn in…making sentences, fixing sentences." Others, like Nancy, saw the requirements as "quizzes, mid-term, and final." The instructor never gave students a formal set of course requirements or a breakdown of percentages for mid-terms, quizzes, or the final. This ambiguity however did not seem to bother or influence student involvement. They all agreed with Nancy's assessment:

> I think as far as he [the instructor] sees it there are different requirements for everyone. I don't mean that in a negative way, but I think he is accepting of the fact that different people are at different spaces.

Some used the lab regularly; others never used it. Also, there was no practice of checking to see if students had done their homework. Even on quizzes and the mid-term, the focus was not on marks, passing, grades, and so forth. "I think he wants you to understand what you're doing rather than get the correct answer." Nancy recounts an incident during a mid-term when as she was turning in her paper, the instructor commented, "You know better than this. Look at number 3, go fix it." The learners really appreciated this approach to language education. They perceived this as a sign of commitment on the part of the instructor on helping the students learn the language as opposed to pass the course. As Anna concluded, "[the class] is very relaxed. Not so much structured on the language itself but the use of the language."

All of the participants also felt that they had a share in the direction their class was taking. "I think the class directs what's going on, the students direct the class as opposed to the teacher directing it…It's a very American kind of interaction not a very Asian classroom, it's kind of weird." Three out of the five commented how learning an Asian language, from an Asian teacher, but doing it in a very non-traditional manner was an unusual but interesting experience. Students felt comfortable enough with the teacher-student relationship that they could suggest topics or activities. On a number of occasions the instructor incorporated student-generated ideas into the focus of a class. As Huma recollects:

What really impressed me was we showed an interest in movies and it was like "Here watch this," or he asked us what we liked and brought in a movie we suggested. And then the following week, we showed interest in music and so every Wednesday he lets us listen to music. I think it's nice he makes an effort to make sure we get whatever we want out of the class.

On the days they listened to music, they would look at the lyrics of the song and talk about different grammatical, interpersonal, and social attributes of the language. It was clearly observable that students appeared to be really invested in what they were doing in class on these occasions. Being able to talk about, learn about, and participate in the kinds of topics and activities that were important to them made the learning experience that much more richer:

> I like learning all about the cultural things. He doesn't just talk about the Hindi, he gets sidetracked but it's interesting…and so I just eat it up. I just love it when we talk about different things; we're learning so much more than language.

This was really important for all, not just the heritage learners. Anna and Nancy, as mentioned before, have a love for Indian culture and this kind of cultural exchange in the class also served their needs. Most of them commented on how learning about the cultural, historical, and social aspects was in a sense framing their understanding of Hindi. In short, they were "getting a total feel for it." Being able to direct the class also meant being able to go back and (re)learn something previously covered without feeling embarrassed or guilty.

> He doesn't mind if you ask something that you were supposed to learn like two weeks into the class. He'll go over it extensively, make sure you understand it. I really like the way he explains things. He gives you the perfect example so you know what he means.

The students felt quite happy with the progress they had made in the class. They liked the "small group" feel of the class and how "I don't feel the competitiveness" of a "regular class." They did not perceive the instructor as particularly tough or even demanding. All of them felt their needs were being addressed in a very personal way and that they were getting a lot out of the class. For some the progress was beyond expectation. Huma recalls how she felt less than a month into the class:

> It's amazing that now I can read and write. It didn't take that long. However he did it, it was very easy to develop it without even thinking about it too much. It just kind of happened. So in a couple of weeks I was able to read and write.

The participants recognized the fact that their respective Hindi backgrounds were serving them well in this class. So much so, that many felt that had they not had previous exposure and experience with Hindi, they "would have been lost because it's very confusing." Those who felt they could be doing better were quick to bring the focus back on their own motivation or industry as illustrated by the following quote from Anna:

> I wish I could be making a little bit more [progress] but that's all myself. If I was more motivated I probably could do a little bit more on my own.

Anna, Huma, and Rani all mentioned that though they were generally happy with the course and their progress, they would have liked more focus on spoken and written Hindi. They also commented on the turn taking in the class.

> He [the teacher] talks a lot...some people talk a lot ...I guess if I want to talk more I should just be more vocal. But sometimes I feel I don't get a chance to.

Rani also mentioned that there should be more student-student interaction. The instructor, in response, had set up a "conversation only" day. Even on this day, however, the turn taking was not equal, and a lot of the time the interaction was teacher-fronted or teacher-student generated. When I asked the participants about this they also seemed perplexed as to why this ended up in this manner. They did feel that they could approach the instructor to address this situation but none did.

This kind of class places a lot of the responsibility on the students to have a sense of what they need, to articulate that to the instructor, to do the necessary work, and to take an active part in the learning process. All of them at different times echoed Huma and Nancy's sentiments that "I need to do that [practice speaking] on my own," or "If I wanted more of that [vocabulary] I could always do more of it." The emphasis on the "I" stresses the learners' understanding that "you get out of it [language learning] what you put into it."

WHO AM I AND WHERE DO I BELONG?

For Huma, Rani, and Suzy, learning Hindi was clearly tied in with a search for identity. On one hand this search was about reclaiming what they feel they have lost, and on the other it was about finding out where and how they fit into their present sociocultural community. Both Huma and Rani had been exposed to Hindi at home. Their parents, and visiting relatives, used it and it was always around them. As Huma explained:

> I used to speak Hindi, then I forgot it...In the beginning my parents said I was so eager to learn English when I first came here that I actually refused to speak Hindi...my parents talked to me in Hindi and I just talked back in English. When I came to college I really lost it. Because in high school I would hear it [at home] a lot.

Rani never learned Hindi as a child but she feels she "knew" about it:

> ...[T]he thinking was that they [parents] didn't want their children to grow up confused. So they decided not to teach us Hindi. I mean they spoke Hindi to each other and Hindi was around me always. They thought it would be easier for us to learn the language when we were older which had a lot of really bad consequences.

The bad consequences she talks about have a lot to do with feelings of having missed out on aspects of her identity in the process of growing up. These students wish they had learned Hindi earlier. They feel embarrassed that they still have not mastered it to some degree. Consequently, they are in the process of trying to reclaim their heritage membership. This is best exemplified by Rani as she recalls a particular incident during the course of the semester:

> It's been kind of a really emotional thing actually…the reason we watched the *Bobby* movie [as a group] was I saw it when I was 10 years old. I was in Maui one weekend…when the words from a song came into my mind…and I couldn't quite pronounce it but it kept bugging me…and I was afraid I'd get laughed at for butchering the Hindi. But he [the teacher] said, 'just say it'. So I said it and I was shocked after all these years I said it correctly…there's something really emotional about that…this happens all along.

Heritage membership, something that has been tugging at them for some time, is now being realized and exercised through language study. It is very emotional, immediate, and personal for them. Suzy, Huma, and Rani also talked emotionally about their visits to India. It was a "shocking," "revealing," and an "eye opening" experience for them. For Huma and Rani, it was a way to explore and identify with their culture. As Huma explains, "I like the kind of values and things that my culture teaches. I like Hinduism in itself; I like what it teaches you. I'm proud of that…I wanted to learn more about it, to experience it…it makes me closer to my roots."

Their travels back to India, however, spotlighted another theme: trying to figure out where and how they fit into their sociocultural environments (in India and here in the States). As I mentioned earlier, others expect these learners to know Hindi and "act" like Indians. These heritage language learners are a visible minority in North America, but their attitude, thinking, and daily life reflects the norms for this part of the world. In India, as they found out, the people had a different understanding of who these learners were:

> At the same time it was like I felt completely lost because the whole time you're in America you're not American, you're Indian or black. The whole time you're in India you're not Indian, you're American. So it was like I don't know what I am.

This feeling of not belonging was unsettling for all three. Rani talked about how as a teen-ager she tried very hard to "fit in and be a part of the crowd" but with little success. After a long time she found herself turning to her culture "to try to understand more about who I am." As if negotiating membership in two worlds was not taxing enough, these learners feel that their North American patterns of thinking often conflict with the "traditional" modes of thinking and gender role expectations in the Indian community here in the States:

> Also, since I think I left my family when I was 18 and sort of struck off on my own to college…I don't feel like I'm part of the Indian community here [in the US.]. I

always feel like I'm on the wall you know: you're not one of them in India, you're not one of them, those Americans, and you're not one of us either.

Their marginal and fluid existence in the multiple worlds they inhabit appears to have initiated a resolve to solidify from within and discover who you are and find a place for yourself in your worlds. Learning the language and culture are steps in this direction.

GROWING OLDER, GROWING WISER

It became clear in the process of this study that some of these learners were involved in language education and this search for identity and place as a byproduct of their particular stage in personal development. That is to say, they had reached a point in their maturation process that "naturally" prompted them towards self-actualization. Prior to this stage, they were never "really motivated to practice" or learn Hindi. Their time and energy was occupied by other exigencies including "fitting in" or "growing up." Now that they have come to a station in life where they are away from home, on their own, charting their own lives, working, considering future roles, they find themselves in a larger and more global setting in which to claim a place. As Rani so clearly articulates,

> When I grew up I was in a very white-dominated Midwest conservative town and sort of fitting in and being part of the crowd was my main goal and it became clear to me that I wasn't succeeding in this goal...I went to Chicago to go to college and you know for the first time you're in this multicultural environment and suddenly you realize that those folks are actually not the real world. This is the real world and you can be a part of it...I was turning to my culture to understand more about who I was. I needed to see who this part of me was and understand it before I could sort of go on with my life and do things you're supposed to do.

As they get closer to their adult roles (independent person, career woman, wife, mother) and away from their parents, high-school friends, and cliques, they realize they need to define themselves for who they are without the pressure from peers to "fit in" — where fitting in means to assimilate and homogenize. As Huma explains:

> You know with other kids around and things, it was really intimidating. So that was like the main break [from Hindi]. But ever since high school you get into other things, the less time I spent with my parents the less time I was close to it [Hindi] so that's what really happened.

Though they are now away from home and their heritage language and culture (as experienced through their parents and family friends) is no longer a part of their daily routine, they find themselves more actively learning Hindi and trying to understand their culture. On a number of occasions Suzy, Huma, and Rani talked about how it "felt like the time" to do this. Their "personal" reasons for learning Hindi have a lot to do with this maturation process. Learning Hindi is then a part of an overriding course of personal development that sees them shaping an image for themselves that is identifiable and comfortable from within and without.

IMPLICATIONS AND CONCLUSIONS

Motivation, or the desire and investment, in learning a language is far more complex than the static constructs usually used to measure it. What prompts people to learn languages? What keeps them active towards this goal? One thing that is clear from the present study is that there are sociocultural and psychosocial factors operating at the individual level that can "motivate" individuals toward learning languages. Studies in learner motivation require a more detailed and descriptive analysis to flush out these crucial cognitive and perceptual patterns governing behavior. There are a number of underlying contextual and personal factors that have been highlighted here which need to be accounted for in developing a more complete understanding of learner motivation.

Firstly, social and familial expectations are an important consideration. Others' expectations of the participants in this study impacted their notions of self. More importantly these expectations were often from family and friends and therefore perceived as more immediate and legitimate. Part of the reason for learning Hindi, then, was an effort to meet these expectations. Tied into these expectations are several needs: the need to communicate and "connect" with family members, the need to fit into their sociocultural communities here in the States, the need to understand their culture and history, and the need to explain who they are as individuals. Given these perceived needs, the expectations become very justified — something that requires attention and solution. Secondly, the notion of forging an identity is also a contributing factor in learner motivation. As individuals who move in multiple worlds, these learners need to continually define who they are, where they fit in, and what role(s) they play. Heritage language plays a key role in establishing their membership and shaping their identity. Negotiating an identity often means going back to their roots, reclaiming heritage membership, and (re)learning the language. The resulting positive impact on self-concept and self-esteem cannot be overlooked. Another factor in this process is that of personal development and maturation. Search for identity and the parallel interest and participation in language education are often tied in with a specific life-stage and an over-all program of self-actualization. As these heritage learners moved outside the narrow scope of the nuclear family and the high-school cliques and into more multicultural and multilingual communities, there was a resulting move towards a more independent/adult life-style. It was a natural progression for them to begin to articulate a personal philosophy and belief system that collaborated with how they see themselves in this global community and also how others see them. Interest in language learning, which hitherto before was never viewed as important, is now initiated because it falls into this larger framework of natural development. Finally, gender roles, especially as viewed in the heritage community, can be important in this process and seemingly cut through the different factors presented here. Being a woman does place additional expectations, limitations, and responsibilities on learners. Pressures from family, religion, and heritage norms, combined with how American society views women of color, influence the issues presented here.

It is clear from the data that how foreign/heritage language is taught has a very immediate impact on learners' motivation and interest. The instructor in these Hindi courses was able to personalize the syllabus by addressing the specific needs of his students. By including culture in the content (music, food, religion, history) and process (listening to music, watching movies, having a cooking class) of the course and by incorporating learner suggestions and interests, he was able to provide exactly what the learners were eager to learn. His classes went beyond language and focused on language in the sociopolitical context and language in use. During our discussions it was clear that he understood the specific needs of the heritage learners in his classes. For example, by teaching them reading and writing (which in Hindi involves a very different script than these students are used to) from the outset, he made it possible for them to communicate with family through letters. Heritage language education in particular needs to validate the backgrounds and identities of heritage learners. Teachers need to know and appreciate the kind of identity issues most of these learners are going through. By acknowledging and validating his students' needs and backgrounds, the teacher enhanced student involvement and industry.

The heritage language learners in this study serve to highlight the kinds of tension and inner struggle associated with being a minority student in the US. The ongoing negotiation of identity, the difficult border crossings between cultures, and the need to fit into different, at times contradicting, worlds is a comprehensive and consuming process. It can lead to self-doubt and loneliness. Institutional support across the spectrum, but specifically in education, needs to account for this and services and programs made available to support these individuals.

REFERENCES

Angle, J. (1978). *Language maintenance, language shift, and occupational achievement in the United States.* San Francisco, CA: R & E Research Associates, Inc.

Bankston, C. L., & Zhou, M. (1995). Effects of minority-language literacy on the academic achievement of Vietnamese youths in New Orleans. *Sociology of Education,* 68, 1–17.

Berry, J. W. (1992). Acculturation and adaptation in a new society. *International migration,* 30, 69–86.

Berry, J. W., Kim, U., Power, S., Young, M., & Bujaki, M. (1989). Acculturation attitudes in plural societies. *Applied Psychology: An International Review,* 38, 185–206.

Brisk, M. E. (1991). Toward multilingual and multicultural mainstream education. *The Journal of Education,* 173(2), 114–129.

Burnett, A., & Syed, Z. (1999). Emerging identities and heritage language education. In K. A. Davis (Ed.), *Foreign language teaching and language minority education* (Technical Report #19, pp. 105–117). Honolulu: University of Hawai'i, Second Language Teaching & Curriculum Center.

Castanell, L. (1984). A cross-cultural look at achievement motivation research. *Journal of Negro Education, 53*, 435–443.

Church, A., & Katigbak, M. S. (1992). The cultural context of academic motives: A comparison of Filipino and American college students. *Journal of Cross-Cultural Psychology, 23*(1), 40–58.

Clément, R., & Kruidenier, B. G. (1983). Orientations in second language acquisition: I. The effects of ethnicity, milieu, and target language on their emergence. *Language Learning, 33*, 273–291.

Combs, A. W., & Snygg, D. (1959). *Individual behavior*. New York: Harper & Roe.

Crawford, J. (1992). *Hold your tongue: Bilingualism and the politics of 'English Only.'* Reading, MA: Addison-Wesley.

Crookes, G., & Schmidt, R. (1991). Motivation: Reopening the research agenda. *Language Learning, 41*, 469–512.

Csikszentmihalyi, M., & Larson, R. (1984). *Being adolescent: Conflict and growth in the teenage years*. New York: Basic Books Inc.

Cummins, J. (1986). Empowering minority students: A framework for intervention. *Harvard Educational Review, 56*, 18–36.

Davis, K. A. (Ed.). (1999). *Foreign language teaching and language minority education* (Technical Report #19). Honolulu: University of Hawai'i, Second Language Teaching & Curriculum Center.

Dörnyei, Z. (1994). Motivation and motivating in the foreign language classroom. *The Modern Language Journal, 78*, 273–284.

Duda, J. L., & Allison, M. T. (1989). The attributional theory of achievement motivation: Cross-cultural considerations. *International Journal of Intercultural Relations, 13*, 37–55.

Erickson, E. (1968). *Identity, youth, and crisis*. New York: Norton.

Erickson, E. (1980). *Identity and the life cycle*. New York: Norton.

Fleming, J. (1985). *Blacks in college*. San Francisco: Jossey-Bass.

Gambhir, S. K. (1992). Challenges of ethnic student enrollments. *NASILP Journal*, 13–19.

García, O. (1992). Societal multilingualism in a multicultural world in transition. In H. Byrnes (Ed.), *Languages for multicultural world in transition* (pp. 1–27). Lincolnwood, IL: NTC.

Gardner, R. C., & Lambert, W. E. (1972). *Attitudes and motivation in second language learning*. Rowley, MA: Newbury House.

Ghuman, P. A. S. (1991). Have they passed the cricket test? A qualitative study of Asian adolescents. *Journal of Multilingual and Multicultural Development, 12*(5), 327–346.

Glesne, C., & Peshkin, A. (1992). *Becoming qualitative researchers: An introduction*. NY: Longman.

Hauser, S. T., Powers, S. I., & Noam, G. G. (1991). *Adolescents and their families: Paths of ego development*. New York: The Free Press.

Helms, J. (1990). *Black and white racial identity*. New York: Greenwood Press.

Henze, R., & Vanett, L. (1993). To walk in two worlds — or more? Challenging a common metaphor of native education. *Anthropology and Education Quarterly, 24*(2), 116–134.

Hoffman, D. (1989). Language and culture acquisition among Iranian in the United States. *Anthropology and Education Quarterly, 20*(2), 118–132.

Lalonde, R. N., Taylor, D. M., & Moghaddam, F. M. (1992). The process of social identification for visible immigrant women in a multicultural context. *Journal of Cross-Cultural Psychology, 23*, 25–39.

Lantolf, J. P., & Pavlenko, A. (1995). Sociocultural theory and second language acquisition. *Annual Review of Applied Linguistics, 15*, 108–124.

Lucas, T., Henze, R., & Donato, R. (1990). Promoting the success of Latino language minority students: An exploratory study of six high schools. *Harvard Educational Review, 60*, 315–340.

Maehr, M. L., & Braskamp, L. A. (1986). *The motivation factor: A theory of personal investment*. Lexington, MA: Lexington Books.

Marcia, J. E. (1980). Identity and adolescence. In J. E. Adelson (Ed.), *Handbook of adolescent psychology*. New York: Wiley.

Markus, H. R., & Kitayama, S. (1991). Culture and the self: Implications for cognition, emotion, and motivation. *Psychological Review, 98*, 224–253.

Muss, R. (1988). *Theories of adolescence*. New York: Random House.

Norton Pierce, B. (1995). Social identity, investment, and language learning. *TESOL Quarterly, 29*, 9–31.

Norton Pierce, B. (1997). Language, identity, and ownership of English. *TESOL Quarterly, 31*, 409–429.

Ochs, E. (1993). Constructing social identity: A language socialization perspective. *Research on Language and Social Interaction, 26*(3), 287–306.

Ortega, L. (1999). Rethinking foreign language education: Political dimensions of the profession. In K. A. Davis (Ed.), *Foreign language teaching and language minority education* (Technical Report #19, pp. 21–39). Honolulu: University of Hawai'i, Second Language Teaching & Curriculum Center.

Oxford, R. L., & Shearin, J. (1994). Language learning motivation: Expanding the theoretical framework. *Modern Language Journal, 78*, 12–28.

Phelan, P., Davidson, A., & Cao, H. (1991). Students' multiple worlds. *Anthropology and Education Quarterly, 22*(3), 224–249.

Popkewitz, T. S. (1987). *The formation of school subjects*. Philadelphia: Falmer Press.

Purkey, W. (1970). *Self concept and school achievement*. Englewood Cliffs, NJ: Prentice-Hall.

Purkey, W., & Schmidt, J. (1987). *The inviting relationship: An expanded perspective for professional counseling*. Englewood, NJ: Prentice-Hall, Inc.

Ramsey, P. G., Vold, E. B., & Williams, L. R. (1989). *Multicultural education: A source book*. New York: Garland.

Rogers, C. R. (1947). Some observations on the organization of personality. *American Psychologist, 2*, 358–368.

Stonequist, E. V. (1961). *Marginal man: A study in personality and culture conflict*. New York: Russell & Russell.

Stopes-Roe, M., & Cochrane, R. (1990). *Citizens of this country: The Asian-British*. Clevedon, UK: Multilingual Matters Ltd.

Svanes, B. (1987). Motivation and cultural distance in second language acquisition. *Language Learning, 37*, 341–359.

Trueba, H. T. (1988). Culturally based explanations of minority students' academic achievement. *Anthropology and Education Quarterly, 19*(3), 270–287.

Ushioda, E. (2001). Language learning at university: Exploring the role of motivational thinking. In Z. Dörnyei & R. Schmidt (Eds.), *Motivation and second language acquisition* (Technical Report #23, pp. 93–125). Honolulu: University of Hawai'i, Second Language Teaching and Curriculum Center.

Ward, C., & Kennedy, A. (1994). Acculturation strategies, psychological adjustment, and sociocultural competence during cross-cultural transition. *International Journal of Intercultural Relations, 18*, 329–343.

Weedon, C. (1987). *Feminist practice and poststructuralist theory*. London: Blackwell.

APPENDIX 1: PARTICIPANT BIO-DATA

name	classification	country of origin	foreign travel & residence	other languages studied	initial exposure to Hindi
Anna (F)	graduate student (Educational Psychology)	USA	Indonesia, India, Nepal (18 months)	Spanish, Nepali	during visit to India
Nancy (F)	graduate student (Asian Studies)	USA	India	Spanish	through books on religion and high school friends
Suzy (H/F)	unclassified graduate student	Canada	India, Mexico, USA	French, Spanish, Japanese, Chinese, German	took night classes after high school graduation
Huma (H)	semester long exchange student	India (moved to USA)	India	Spanish	at home
Rani (H)	unclassified graduate student	USA	India	French, Spanish	at home

Key: H = Heritage language learner
F = Foreign language learner

Marianne Nikolov
University of Pécs, Hungary

A STUDY OF UNSUCCESSFUL LANGUAGE LEARNERS

Abstract

This qualitative study attempts to explore how levels of foreign language (FL) proficiency in adulthood have been influenced by attitudes, motivation, an early start, classroom experiences, teachers, materials, and other factors in the case of unsuccessful Hungarian learners of various foreign languages. Aptitude and motivation are assumed to be the best predictors of success in the long run, but there is not enough empirical evidence to describe how personality variables, classroom-related variables, and other factors interact in a foreign language context. The research questions aim to explore how different variables are related to success or failure in foreign language learning.

INTRODUCTION

This empirical study looks at how unsuccessful young Hungarian adult language learners who started to study a foreign language (FL) between the ages of 6 and 9 evaluate their own language learning experiences and development. Participants come from a new generation of early starters of English, German, and Russian in Hungary, as they were given the option of studying a language besides or instead of Russian. They were chosen for this study based on their own perception of FL proficiency.

Altogether 94 low-achieving young adults (ages 19–27) were interviewed. Qualitative analysis of these structured interviews provides insights into how early and later classroom contacts and life experiences with modern languages have formed learners' attitudes, motivation, and language development and to what extent teachers, methodology, the intensity and continuity of programmes, parental support, and the study of other languages have contributed to the language knowledge and self-perception of the participants.

Emerging patterns indicate that although the interviewees consider themselves unsuccessful, they have experimented with studying several languages and their attitudes towards knowing languages are positive. They tend to see persistence and hard work as the keys to success rather than aptitude, motivation, or an early start. Classroom processes seem to play an important role in long-term outcomes. The most problematic areas relate to classroom methodology in general, and assessment, focus on form, and rote-learning in particular.

BACKGROUND TO THE STUDY

A number of studies have looked at successful learners and the ways in which cognitive and affective variables contribute to their success (see Dörnyei, 1998;

Nikolov, M. (2001). A study of unsuccessful language learners. In Z. Dörnyei & R. Schmidt (Eds.), *Motivation and second language acquisition* (Technical Report #23, pp. 149–169). Honolulu: University of Hawai'i, Second Language Teaching and Curriculum Center.

Gardner & MacIntyre, 1992, 1993; Naiman, Fröhlich, Stern, & Todesco, 1996, for summaries). However, there seems to be a lack of case studies and longitudinal enquiries in foreign language contexts. This study attempts to look at learners' language learning experiences in retrospect through their own eyes.

The study was conducted in Hungary, where foreign language education became an extremely important area after the change of regime in 1989. Russian ceased to be compulsory overnight, and since then a smorgasbord of language programmes have been launched. Although only 12% of the population claim to be able to manage in a FL (Terestyéni, 1996), all stakeholders' attitudes are positive; state and private sector education can hardly keep up with demand (for details see Medgyes & Miklósy, in press; Nikolov, 1999a). During the early 1990's, Russian teachers were retrained to teach English and German, and early language programmes for 6–9-year-olds became common. However, statistical data on language achievement do not reflect high initial hopes. Although Hungarians' attitudes and motivations are favourable towards studying and knowing FLs, state education has been ineffective in meeting social demands. Therefore, we set out in this study to explore why young adults who have had a chance to study FLs other than Russian have failed to achieve even a basic level FL competence.

RESEARCH QUESTIONS

The questions to which we hope to find answers are the following:

1. How has the status of the target languages influenced participants' foreign language learning attitudes, motivation, and proficiency? How can their FL-specific attitudes be characterised?

2. How do unsuccessful adults perceive themselves as language learners and in what areas do they identify their strengths and weaknesses? What do they consider to be the most important features of successful language learners?

3. How have pleasant and unpleasant classroom experiences in state education contributed to learners' attitudes towards FL studies and their achievement?

4. What was the role of teachers in forming attitudes and motivation and in developing proficiency?

5. How did materials contribute to outcomes?

6. What was the role of private tutoring and language examinations?

7. When and how have participants needed to apply their language knowledge in real life situations?

8. In what ways did an early start contribute to the FL development of young adults and to what extent was continuity of programmes ensured? How do unsuccessful adults relate to early start programmes for their children?

METHOD

Altogether 94 young adults (48 males and 46 females) participated in the study from all over Hungary. Their ages ranged from 19 to 27 (the average was 23.4, and most were between the ages of 23 and 25). These young adults belong to the group of language learners who were in state education when the major changes in FL policy took place, so they had a chance to study a language of their choice. They were chosen according to the following three criteria:

1. They did not use any FLs in their jobs or major in them in their university studies.

2. They considered themselves unsuccessful language learners.

3. They were known to the interviewers from their primary school years (age 6–14) as relatively low achievers.

Of the 94 participants, 36 were university or college students (law, history, music, theology, human resources management, education, etc.); 13 were recent university or college graduates (e.g., teacher, lawyer, bookkeeper, librarian); 18 were physical workers (e.g., driver, hatmaker, mechanic, waiter, guard, nurse); and 27 belonged to a mixed category (e.g., self-employed in small businesses, administrative staff, unemployed). The vast majority graduated from secondary school, but as Table 1 illustrates, their educational backgrounds varied greatly.

Table 1: Participants' educational background

number of participants	highest level of education
1	primary school (8 years)
8	vocational school (3 years to train skilled workers)
52	secondary grammar school (4 years)
15	secondary vocational school (4 years)
11	college (3 or 4 years)
7	university (4 or 5 years)

Although this group of young adults is not a representative sample of the population, their experiences are hypothesised to be similar to those of other Hungarian FL learners of their age group and are therefore expected to provide meaningful insights into why so many learners in Hungary fail to achieve a sufficient level of competence.

INSTRUMENT AND DATA COLLECTION

Data for this qualitative study were collected in November 1999 by 24 English majors at the University of Pécs after an intensive training in the procedures, as part of the requirements of an advanced elective course in applied linguistics.

The instrument included a structured interview of eight questions about the participants' background and 31 questions about their language learning experiences. All interviews were tape-recorded and transcribed; the transcripts were checked against the tapes; and answers were categorised and analysed. The interviews ranged between 14 and 27 minutes in length, lasting 19 minutes on average.

Participants were informed that the study focused on the language learning experiences of young adults, but there was no mention of failure. All of them wondered if their experiences would be relevant, but consented to participate and were helpful and interested.

First, background data were gathered. This section also functioned as a warm-up task. The interview questions followed the chronological order of FL studies, progressing from primary and secondary school studies to adult FL learning experiences. The remainder of the interview included direct but more general questions about attitudes, motivation and aptitude, self-evaluation, and future plans.

RESULTS

LANGUAGES STUDIED

As we wanted to find out about the participants' language learning experiences, the initial questions concerned the languages they had learnt, when they started learning them, how intensive the courses were, and to what extent schools ensured continuity of FL study.

As Table 2 illustrates, the majority studied two or three foreign languages, on average 2.85. In primary school they tended to learn one or two: They either discontinued the study of Russian and started English or German instead or learnt two languages in their primary years. In secondary school most of them learnt two or three languages. Since only one language is compulsory in primary school and one or two are required in secondary school, on the whole, they studied more languages than they were obliged to.

Table 2: The number of foreign languages studied by 94 participants

number of FLS studied	no. of participants (N=94)	languages studied (number of participants)
1	5	Russian 3; German 1; English 1
2	31	Russian & German 10; Russian & English 13; German & English 6; Russian & French 2
3	37	mostly Russian, German, & English + Spanish 7; Latin 2
4	17	mostly Russian, German, & English + Romanian 2; Italian 2; Latin 7
5	3	mostly Russian, German, & English + Turkish, Greek, Portuguese, & Hebrew
7	1	mostly Russian, German, & English + Dutch & Hebrew

FREQUENCY OF FLS

With regard to the frequency of the foreign languages studied, most participants learnt Russian, but there were seven (among the youngest of our interviewees) who received no Russian instruction at all. Table 3 shows the rank order of languages. As far as English and German are concerned, these numbers are in line with recent statistical data on state education on the rate of students studying various languages (Halász & Lannert, 1998; Vágó, 1999), whereas the other languages seem to be more popular among our participants than in statistical reports. Most probably they studied some languages (other than Russian, English, and German) privately.

Table 3: The rank order of FLs participants studied

language	no. of participants (N=94)
Russian	87
English	71
German	59
French	11
Latin	9
Italian	9
Spanish	7
Romanian	2
Hebrew	2
Dutch, Turkish, Greek, Portuguese	1

STARTING FL STUDIES

Officially, Hungarian schools start teaching FLs in Grade 4 (age 9), but because of parental pressure, more and more schools have launched early start language programmes since the early 1990's. These tended to be so-called "specialised classes," with usually two to four classes a week. Among our 94 participants, 24 started learning a foreign language before the age of 9. Three started their FL studies in the kindergarten (one English, two German); 7 studied German, 2 Romanian, and 1 English from Grades 1 and 2; whereas in Grade 3, 9 started German, 6 Russian, 2 English, and 6 of them studied two FLs from Grade 3. Looking at the national statistics for the 1996/97 academic year, this rate is somewhat worse than the Hungarian average, as 41% of all third graders learn a FL (Halász & Lannert, 1998, p. 430).

As for the intensity of FL programmes, altogether 21 of the interviewees attended specialised classes in the primary years of their education (8 German; 7 Russian; 5 English; and 1 French). Twenty of them were labelled as unsuccessful, so they did not continue the language they had studied for over 5 years. In secondary school, 9 participants attended intensive language programmes, usually providing five weekly classes: 5 studied German and 4 English.

Concerning the transition from primary to secondary school, altogether 59 participants started English and German from scratch. They could not continue on the level they had achieved in the primary school, as secondary schools took children from a variety of schools and they could not ensure pre-intermediate level classes. On the other hand, 14 interviewees continued their study of Russian where continuity was ensured, 3 went on with German and 1 with French. Nine participants received no language instruction after the age of 14, because the curricula of three-year vocational schools exclude FL studies.

SELF-ASSESSMENT OF LANGUAGE PROFICIENCY

Interviewees were asked to assess their own language levels in adulthood in the languages they had learnt by reporting how much they understood of TV programmes, films, or instruction manuals and how they could manage a simple conversation. Thirty-four claimed that they understood nothing at all in any FL (typically using the expression "zero level"); 36 reported minimal understanding, for instance, they could remember some (mostly international) words, or catch some expressions; 20 said they could comprehend basic language and could, for example, introduce themselves. Four reported themselves able to follow some TV programmes, understand simple instruction manuals and magazine articles, and participate in a simple conversation. The ones who mentioned Russian all claimed to be absolutely unable to use it, while some useful knowledge was typically related to English and German, for example, "In English I remember nouns, like facial cream, and restaurant language as I used to work as a waiter, like...I know vegetables."

To get more detailed data on language levels, interviewees were asked to identify their strengths in different skill areas. Forty-two rated themselves good at reading (when further specified, reading aloud); 21 said their strength was writing; 19 mentioned listening comprehension; and 13 mentioned speaking, all of them adding, "with lots of mistakes." Grammar was mentioned by 5 participants: all of them exam certificate holders (including International Conference Certificates [ICC] and Latin exams). Translation as a strength was listed by the same 5 people, while another participant mentioned memorising words.

When asked to assess their own places in their classes, 40 ranked themselves among the better pupils (mostly in primary school), 35 in the middle range and 19 among the worst; 3 even flunked Russian courses. Some pointed out a trend they observed: with the passage of time their achievements declined gradually. Another trend they pointed out referred to differences in languages: Being among the lowest achievers in Russian did not mean the same in another language.

EXAMS

Besides self-assessment, we explored some objective measures of language proficiency. Interviewees were asked what language examination certificates they held. The replies reflect the contradictory situation in Hungary: A prestigious external "state language proficiency examination" is considered the only reliable certificate of language proficiency, while the official and free-of-charge school-leaving examination is not. When asked about language exams, participants did not even consider school-leaving exams. Therefore, the specific question "Any school-leaving exam?" was also added after they answered in the negative.

Altogether, 36 interviewees had no examination certificate at all; 41 passed a school-leaving exam (English 17; German 12; Russian 10; and Italian 2); 6 had an internal university language exam (English 3; Latin 2; German 1); 5 of them passed a basic-level oral state exam (all in English); 8 had an intermediate-level oral or oral and written certificate (5 in German; 2 in English; and 1 in French); and 1 reported passing an international ICC exam in both German and English.

LIKED AND DISLIKED LANGUAGE CLASSROOM ACTIVITIES

Seven questions enquired about classrooms activities. First, interviewees were to list what they enjoyed doing in language classes. The vast majority did list some activities. Conversations, role plays, and dialogues were mentioned by 27, for example, "we talked, did a story, what are the new words, what can we do with this...and the like." Reading aloud was liked by 14; language games and competitions, by 12; translation, by another 12. Four interviewees found pleasure in grammar tasks, for example, "I liked to analyse sentences, underline the subject, the predicate..." Writing was mentioned by 4. Writing dialogues, learning new words, and listening to music or a tape were each mentioned by two. Acting out was mentioned by two participants, both referring to the same particular Russian tale. One person mentioned taking tests as a liked activity.

Other types of well-liked classroom activities were listed by nine participants, some tongue in cheek: thinking, volunteering, keeping quiet, getting good grades, drawing, sleeping, and fooling around. Four said they never liked anything.

On the list of most hated classroom activities, oral and written tests were ranked first by 32 interviewees. One extract illustrates their points: "You had to face the board and recite the material so that the others cannot help you by prompting, it was really sadistic." Grammar was mentioned by 19, rote-learning of texts ("memorising the history of Lake Baikal") and translation by 9 each, repeating texts after the tape, and writing by 6 each, "opening one's mouth" by 2, and homework, sitting there, and "listening to others reporting to the teacher" by 1 each.

When asked to mention pleasant primary school classrooms experiences, 34 recalled games, among them some with a language focus: "personal pronouns were written on a big cube and we kept throwing it about;" "there were red, yellow, and blue cards with *on, ona, ono* (in Russian) and we had to raise them." Fifteen interviewees listed songs and rhymes, for example, "blue records from the Russian magazine *Kolobok.*"

The pleasant feeling of success was mentioned in 10 cases, for example, "I knew the plural of a word;" "the teacher told us a funny story, and only I understood it, then she said it again and everyone laughed;" "I could recite a poem in Russian;" "I conjugated through *mal'cik,* I loved conjugations;" "I could memorise *eraser* and the teacher was pleased;" "I was about to flunk the course and then I memorised a poem and passed." Enjoyable primary-school memories were related to storytelling for 7 participants (*"Terem teremok," "Snow White"*).

Two interviewees described funny classroom scenes: "this teacher would throw his bunch of keys on students' desk [as a way of disciplining them], and this pupil did not return it, and the teacher, a priest, ran after him in his cassock;" "the teacher walked around and pretended to be on a tram, and she touched each pupil's head, 'ching-ching,' asked *cto eto?* she was cute." Other special memories included a samovar in class, letter writing in German to Russia, guest teachers, guitar playing, watching videos, a geography class in German, and performing for parents.

Unpleasant experiences from primary school were also explored. Oral and written tests were most frequently mentioned (in 34 cases): "they always taught us some grammar and wanted to hear it back, like in a deathcamp;" "the teacher was unable to discipline us, so we wrote a test on words in every class."

Grammar practice was mentioned seven times, for example, "[when reading aloud] the teacher kept stopping me after every second word to check the suffix and then I got a mark 2, as my reading was not fluent." Corporal punishment was remembered in four interviews: "he walked around all the time and kept hitting everyone's head with his bunch of keys;" "she applied a special slap in the face while holding your sidelocks; but if you allowed her to do so, it was sooner over." In one particular case, a disillusioning primary-classroom experience was related:

> "Our teacher asked us to tell her when it was our birthday, and we would recite a text in German. It was my birthday on an open day [when parents were invited to observe classes], and I said to her that it was my birthday and this upset her routine

and she did not like the idea. We and parents could see it and it was extremely unpleasant, as we realised she did not really mean it."

As far as pleasant secondary-school classroom memories are concerned, 26 interviewees claimed that they never had any. Seventeen participants talked about the teacher's personality and inventive methodology: "the teacher kept talking Italian and we had to concentrate a lot to understand him, and it was exciting, I enjoyed that;" "the German teacher allowed us close, and we listened to songs by Marlene Dietrich;" "the teacher had great ideas, allowed us to use "te" [friendly terms] and these were cathartic experiences." Seven interviews included references to teachers' talks about trips abroad, and 4 mentioned memorable holidays and performances, for example, "it was Halloween, and the teacher told us stories about those customs."

Among the most unpleasant experiences from secondary school, oral and written tests were again ranked first (e.g., "oral reports, suffering all the time") and grammar drills second: "grammar practice from morning till night, we never dealt with words;" "language teaching was never about survival, but about speaking without errors all the time;" "*der, die, das,* and past tense all over again."

One particular question asked why, if ever, participants felt anxious in language classes. Oral tests were mentioned most frequently (37 times): "this tense and that tense, all swirling in your head, you have to conjugate, and in the end you don't say what you have to, as they all confuse your thinking;" "in Latin classes we got a mark one even after learning a lot." Thirteen interviews included references to worrying about making mistakes and being laughed at by peers, whereas 11 participants said they had no reason for anxiety as "I was hopeless." Seven feared that the teacher would humiliate them, and 7 others worried about not understanding something. One participant recalled a special situation when they had a native German girl in the group and she frustrated everyone by being too good. One person mentioned that he always worried about getting caught when using cribs.

TEACHING MATERIALS

Participants were asked to comment on the teaching materials used in primary and secondary schools. Only a few titles of coursebooks were recalled, most frequently UK published English books, among them *Streamline, Hotline, Project English* and *Headway* by 22 interviewees. The only German title was *Themen,* mentioned by 13 people, while two grammar practice books were also recalled. A Russian publication by Havronina was remembered by the author's name by 2 participants. Hungarian coursebooks were mostly recalled by either the author (Budai 3 times; Czobor-Horlai 2 times), or the main hero (Linda 6 times). Besides these, most frequently the colour of the cover was remembered or the main characters (Arthur, Oliver, Linda). Other books were labelled as "traditional," "good old communist schoolbooks," "you know, the one with a babyblue cover."

Among the attractive features the following were listed by one third of the interviewees: "colourful," "full of pictures," "funny caricatures," and "included some good texts." As for negative features, they were characterised as "dead boring" despite colours and pictures; "full of grammar to be rote learnt" and "texts to be memorised." As one interviewee put it, "I have never had a book with exercises to my taste." The over use of course materials was referred to by 3 participants, for example, "we always translated texts, then did the grammar exercises, and that was it." Five participants pointed out that they preferred books with grammar explanations in Hungarian.

LANGUAGE TEACHERS

Interviewees were asked to characterise their best and worst language teachers. The most highly appreciated attributes of teachers, "consistent" and "strict" were mentioned most frequently, followed by "knowledgeable," "patient and nice," "dynamic," "funny and young," "a good person with nice human features," and "someone who allows students close," for example:

> "We could really talk with this teacher, he taught us Austrian German and did not demand all articles; for two years we did not learn articles and later I had problems, but this teacher was not up the wall if you made a mistake."

Native teachers were appreciated for telling lots of stories, and students had to listen carefully to understand them. Non-natives were often praised as "a good human being" and for their impressive knowledge. About half of the good teachers remembered by the participants were teachers of Russian; they emerged as "consistent," "strict," "knowledgeable," and "nice." Eight participants said they had never had a good language teacher.

The complex role of teachers is reflected in the following opinion:

> "My German teacher was my best ever, though I disliked German. Everyone wanted to be like her. And an English teacher, who demonstrated everything and we also had to make ourselves understood with body language, just to avoid using Hungarian. He never corrected you and you could feel this would not be a mark one, and the whole group was making progress."

Another example illustrates what weird classroom experiences learners need to cope with:

> "This was a Piarist priest, he came in and he asked who knew Stabat Mater. Well, one boy raised his hand. Then, "Who knows Phil Collins?" then everyone [raised hands], and he fell flat on his back in his cassock, expressing his shock. But he was likeable, despite this."

As for the worst teachers, 12 interviewees complained that teachers "humiliated" and "hit" them, "shouted all the time;" "wanted to find mistakes only;" or "did not like us." Three participants mentioned alcohol addiction; two teachers were perceived as unpleasant as they "had a stinking mouth;" while some "spoke Hungarian all the time," and others "did not speak English properly." As for some native speakers, "we never understood a word" (although the statement "we never learnt anything" mentioned by 6 participants referred to both native and non-native teachers). Finally, several teachers were disliked for being old, too strict and boring, or because they "did not understand students."

EXTRACURRICULAR LEARNING ACTIVITIES

As private tuition is typical in Hungary, participants were asked where and how they studied foreign languages besides state education. Altogether 66 of them received private tutoring, about one third of them in two languages and 6 in three languages. About half of them had private teachers and the other half attended language schools. A few received private tuition parallel to the entire length of school instruction. All interviewees with state or school-leaving exams had extensive private tutoring, except for one man with a school-leaving exam in German, who attended a specialised class. One participant said, "my form teacher gave me private lessons for long years."

All of these extracurricular activities were sponsored by parents, who paid for course fees, books, school trips, teachers, and examinations. When asked how parents supported participants' language studies, they mentioned paying for course fees, buying books, and telling them how useful it would be to be able to speak a foreign language.

At the time of the interview, a third of the participants were either attending a course as part of their current studies at university or at a private language school. Three were studying on their own, and 7 were planning to take up courses in the future.

TRAVEL ABROAD AND USE OF LANGUAGES

Altogether, 83 participants had been abroad, while 11 had never left Hungary. Trips abroad typically involved short holidays of a week or two and shopping trips of a few days to Croatia, Austria, Greece, Italy, or Germany. One interviewee spent a year travelling around the world visiting England, Australia, Singapore, and so forth but had no language exam certificate. Participants typically used FLs for international communication, that is, not in target language contexts but German in Italy, and English in Croatia, Greece, or Germany. The most typical uses included shopping, asking the way, and buying ice-cream.

All participants pointed out that only minimal competence was necessary to manage these language tasks, and half of them lacked even that. They tended to rely on friends or used body language to overcome difficulties. One participant studied in France for a term, and another worked as an au pair in London, reporting that they managed well. Three participants worked in Italy and Germany for a few months, but they did not really need more than basic language knowledge.

ATTITUDES TOWARDS LANGUAGES AND CULTURES

Participants were asked which foreign language they liked best and why (not only from among the ones they studied). Some mentioned two or three, most named one, but not all gave reasons. Altogether only 3 respondents gave instrumental motives for liking a particular language, while others referred to intrinsic motives. English was mentioned by 38, typically without a reason, 1 of them specified American English, and 2 others added negative comments about English: "I would not say I like English but I prefer it to German;" and "English is not attractive, German is, as it is logical and learnable." A third participant also contrasted English and German: "I like the German language, it's a bit hard language, Italian is musical, and I also like [the] English [language], but I like [the] German [people]."

Three languages were liked for their music, rhythm, pronunciation, and "the sounding": Italian by 36, Spanish by 23, and French by 22 interviewees. German was chosen by 10 (2 mentioned that it was logical), Russian, Portuguese, and Hebrew by 2 each, and Japanese, Turkish, Finnish, and Arabic by 1 participant.

Interviewees were asked to name the country whose culture they found the most attractive and interesting. Both France and the UK were chosen by 11 people, with no special explanation except for English rock music by 2 respondents. Italy was chosen by 9, with reference to good food. Both Greece and Spain were named by 7, with special mention of pretty girls and football for the latter. Five interviewees mentioned Hungary, 4 India and Egypt, 3 the Far East and Israel, 2 Portugal and Germany (both referring to Bayer beer parties), while Brazil, the Czech Republic, Russia, Belgium, Holland, Bulgaria, Croatia (because of pilgrimages), and Mexico received 1 vote each.

Regarding the question of which language they consider the most useful, 88 interviewees answered English, but 5 learners of German added "sorry to say" [sajnos]. All 88 mentioned that English was a world language. One referred to computers and 1 said it was easy to learn. German was ranked most useful by 24 respondents, but only 5 of them only mentioned German, 19 adding English as well. The reasons for choosing German included "our neighbours," holidaymakers speaking it, international firms requiring it, and its role in the EU. Two participants chose French as the "language of culture," while Russian got one vote.

FEATURES OF SUCCESSFUL LANGUAGE LEARNERS

The interview included questions about what makes language learners successful. Participants listed what they considered to be necessary for someone to be good at FLs. Persistence, strong will, hard work, and patience were mentioned by 55, good aptitude and memory by 34, a good teacher by 19, motivation and enthusiasm by 12. Seven listed money; 6, "a bottom" [to sit on for a long time]. Five mentioned an experience in the host environment, while a good book, success, a good method, and an early start received one vote each. The most optimistic view was expressed as follows: "even if someone has no aptitude it is possible to learn a language to some extent."

When asked to self-assess their level of success as language learners, all 94 interviewees labelled themselves as "unsuccessful" or "not really successful." Eight of them considered themselves lazy and hopeless. Five added that they could still survive with the FL. As one of them put it, "I have been learning languages for long years but haven't got anywhere."

As for their self-assessed level of aptitude, 25 considered themselves to have good aptitude, 20 rated themselves as average, and 35 said they have low aptitude. In their interpretations aptitude is associated with having a good memory ("my memory is poor, I was not invented to speak multilanguages"), learning fast and easily, liking translation, the rapid memorisation of words, or coping with grammar easily. Several respondents pointed out that their aptitude varied for different target languages, while one disputed the existence of the construct: "aptitude does not exist, if you are interested in the language, you will learn it."

PLANS FOR THEIR CHILDREN

Finally, participants were to reflect upon when and what FLs they would want their (future) children to study. Ninety of them voted for "the sooner the better," half of them meaning the kindergarten, half between ages 6 and 8. Four emphasised that children should first develop their mother tongue, and 3 were definitely against an early start:

> "My own example makes me uncertain. At the age of 12–13 you can achieve in minutes what children pick up from age 6, I don't think it is worth it, but I would still send my kid to learn English."

> "It's no use, s/he tells a poem in German and is claimed to be a wonderchild...but although I hate English, I would want him/her to start with English."

> "It's a stupid idea to make them study from kindergarten; what they hammer in in the kindergarten and [primary] school, s/he will acquire in a year at age 14."

As for which language children should study, 92 of them wanted English, and 7 wanted German. Some participants who suggested two languages to be learnt in early childhood thought that they would decide upon the first FL and would allow their kids to choose a second FL: German, French, or Italian.

DISCUSSION

It is obvious from the interviews that the 94 participants in this study do not form a homogeneous group of unsuccessful learners. Rather, they could be placed along a continuum between the extreme poles of successful and unsuccessful. Participants who managed to study a term abroad, travel around the world for a year, or work as an au pair for an extended period must have used a FL every day for different purposes, and therefore their self-assessed failure is different from what other participants, closer to the negative extreme end, mean by their lack of success. They do not understand anything of TV programmes or illustrated texts like manuals and will not risk saying a word when shopping abroad. However, trends and patterns have emerged indicating some common features. In this section these will be explored with reference to the research questions, to be followed by a discussion of limitations and weaknesses of the study and some methodological implications.

1. How has the status of the target languages influenced participants' foreign language learning attitudes, motivation, and proficiency? How can their FL-specific attitudes be characterised?

The status and perceived usefulness of FLs have definitely influenced the interviewees' attitudes, motivation, and proficiency on what Dörnyei (1994) called the "language level." No participant reported any proficiency in Russian or a liking of the language and culture, and only one listed it as useful. A similar tendency characterises Romanian: 2 participants studied it from early childhood, but they did not mention the language or the culture either as useful or attractive. The reasons must be sociolinguistic and need further research. It seems that the languages of neighbouring countries and ethnic minorities in Hungary (with the exception of German) are perceived differently from other foreign languages.

Another important point relates to the 4 participants voting for Hungarian culture and emphasising the importance of learning the mother tongue first. These views reflect a re-emerging nationalist line in Hungarian public thinking and politics. (In a parallel study in progress, a surprisingly high rate of the responses by unemployed adults reflected similar ideas.)

As far as other FLs were concerned, we find a greater variety of responses. Interviewees demonstrated overwhelmingly positive attitudes towards foreign languages and cultures in general and English and German in particular. Interestingly, many more participants expressed enthusiasm towards languages and cultures other than English, but only a few had the opportunity to study their choices. One particular reason why respondents found foreign languages attractive relates to their sound qualities. Italian, Spanish, and French are perceived as pleasant because of their prosodic features. They were described as fast ("pörgös"=rolling) and dynamic, but no interviewees commented on whether they would expect them to be easier or more difficult to learn because of these characteristics.

As a general trend, it can be observed that many more participants identify intrinsically motivating features of Italian, Spanish, and French than have ever studied them. As for the cultural aspects of languages, more countries were chosen for the appreciation of their culture (20) than for their language (12), and there seems to be a strong relationship between previous language study and appreciation of the culture. All participants who had learnt French, Italian, Spanish, or Hebrew chose the culture of the country, whereas many more interviewees chose a language without learning experiences in these languages. Whether learners of French, Italian, Spanish, and Hebrew came to appreciate the target culture as a result of language study or started learning these languages because of their interest in the culture is not clear from the data (it may have worked both ways).

In terms of instrumental motives, the vast majority consider English to be the most useful language as a means of international communication. However, only 11 participants mentioned the target culture of the English language as attractive, and none specified the USA. These findings are in line with arguments on the limitations of the instrumental-integrative dichotomy in conceptualising motivation (Crookes & Schmidt, 1991; Dörnyei, 1994; Nikolov, 1999b; Williams & Burden 1997). On the other hand, it seems that although all participants claim that knowing a language is necessary and they are motivated instrumentally, this is not enough for them to maintain effort and develop proficiency over years.

An unexpected finding needs further exploration. Five learners of German commented negatively on English being more important than German. In other places in the interview, the same theme kept recurring, that somehow these 5 adults considered themselves losers, because they were denied the opportunity to study English. A similar tendency is heard informally from various schools. Good achievers are placed in English groups, the rest study German. More research is needed to explore this issue.

Unexpectedly, American English did not emerge as a preferred variety, in contrast with a representative study conducted in the mid-1990's among 14-year-old Hungarians. Dörnyei and Clément (this volume) found a strong preference for American English to British English among young students, which was hypothesised to reflect a strong influence of popular culture. As some of our participants (now aged 21) come from that age group and might have participated in that study as eighth formers, the explanation may be that by adulthood the influence of films, music, and fashion has faded, replaced by more pragmatic features, like usefulness.

2. How do unsuccessful adults perceive themselves as language learners and in what areas do they identify their strengths and weaknesses? What do they consider to be the most important features of successful language learners?

As for the self-assessment of the participants, the picture varies. Some tend to underestimate their abilities and achievements, while others sound realistic. On the whole, interviewees' answers need to be interpreted in the light of objective measures like examinations and results from other studies.

When looking at what factors participants consider crucial for success, most insist on persistence, will power, and hard work on the one hand, and aptitude, memory, and enthusiasm on the other. These are the internal factors they think they are lacking, as they have been unable to persist in working on their own language development. Most of the necessary conditions they list are internal to the learners, while among the external factors mentioned 19 concerned teachers and 5 learning in the host environment. In sum, they tend to blame themselves for failing to learn a FL. As for their self-assessed aptitude, they place themselves in three groups (high, intermediate, and low) of approximately similar sizes, and this contradicts the previous statement. It seems that they do not consider aptitude the best predictor of success. Persistence emerges as more important, but in forming and maintaining motivation, they fail to see the role of what Williams and Burden (1997) call "significant others," including parents, teachers, and peers.

Group-specific motivational components are traced in interviewees' classroom experiences. Some participants felt anxious about being ridiculed by their peers. In a few cases good classroom atmosphere was mentioned. On the whole, classroom dynamics have only vaguely emerged as a determining variable.

The vast majority of our informants have not developed confidence in using foreign languages for communicative purposes, and it is dubious how the areas in which most of them identify their strengths might help them to overcome difficulties in real language use situations. To illustrate the point, reading skills are important both as language skills and as a means of becoming autonomous learners, but interviewees tended to mean reading aloud when referring to good reading skills. This is in line with findings reported in a classroom observation project on disadvantaged secondary-school English classrooms (Nikolov, 1999c), where in 118 observed groups the most frequently used reading task was reading aloud, often combined with translation. Similarly, writing may refer to typical classroom activities and not usable writing skills: copying, filling in exercises, and translation (found to be the most frequent writing tasks in Nikolov, 1999c).

The few who felt speaking was their strength all added that they lacked accuracy. One of the emerging trends in this study relates to the teachers' (and as a reflection, the learners') attitudes towards errors, their error treatment practices, and the role of errors in assessment.

3. How have pleasant and unpleasant classroom experiences in state education contributed to learners' attitudes towards FL studies and their achievement?

Participants' negative classroom experiences most frequently concerned testing and specific types of tasks they did not find intrinsically motivating. These two factors seem to be responsible for the gradual demotivation and low achievement of most of the interviewees. These claims are further supported by the high frequency of oral and written tests among disliked classroom activities in all types of schools. Assessment practices also caused most of the anxiety experienced by interviewees. There is no way of telling to what extent attainment targets in those classes were realistic for most learners, but obviously the lack of success for our participants must have contributed to their decrease in motivation and achievement. A small-scale study of Hungarian children learning English and Russian throws further light on how assessment and children's motivation are related. Moncsek (1999) observed pupils studying both languages over a term and asked them and their teachers about their classroom experiences. Both teachers used appropriate playful activities, the only difference being that children did not get grades and were not tested in Russian classes. Most children showed more favourable attitudes towards learning Russian than English and volunteered more in Russian classes, though they claimed that English was more useful.

Another closely related trend concerns focus on form and rote-learning. While heated academic debates on communicative language teaching have explored these issues over the heads of teachers and learners during the last decades and the pendulum is now back to focus on form in the guise of awareness raising, it seems that explicit grammar teaching, drills, extensive use of translation as a means of making meaning, and a heavy emphasis on rote-learning have dominated most of the FL classrooms our participants attended in primary and secondary school, similarly to secondary classrooms observed in a previous study (Nikolov, 1999c). Although most participants preferred role-plays, dialogues, and playful activities, a few also enjoyed translation and grammar tasks. It seems that a happy balance was rarely struck, as about a third of the interviewees could not recall any pleasant memories from their secondary-school years.

4.   What was the role of teachers in forming attitudes and motivation and in developing proficiency?

Among the factors Dörnyei (1994) has labelled "teacher-specific motivational components," in this study, consistency and strictness, knowledge of the field, patience and being nice emerged as the most appreciated characteristics. Despite the fact that no participant claimed to like Russian or achieved any useful level in it, a number of teachers of Russian were highly appreciated, and as indicators of their methodological skills, lots of pleasant memories were recalled from Russian classes, mostly in the primary-school years. It seems that these teachers succeeded in getting students' attention (Schumann, 2000) but because of other interfering factors, failed to maintain it over the years.

Students highly appreciated when teachers were genuinely concerned with them, allowed them close, and understood their problems, but when this interest turned out to be faked, it had a lasting negative effect. Unenthusiastic teachers were harshly criticised. Quite a number of them emerged as bored and boring, picking on errors, and unprofessional in other ways. These negative features must be related to the typically high workload and low pay of teachers in Hungary. Classroom observations and interviews with teachers of English have revealed that most of them were overworked, underpaid, and quite disillusioned (Nikolov, 1999c). Scholarly discussions often concern students' attitudes and motivation, but they rarely touch upon the same areas of their teachers. It would be important to see the other side of the coin as well.

5.   How did materials contribute to outcomes?

Language teaching materials did not emerge as one of the most important variables in predicting success. On the contrary, some modern communicative coursebooks were said to be as useless as the traditional materials. Obviously, the way teachers apply materials is more important than what they use.

6. What was the role of private tutoring and language examinations?

Private tutoring emerged as an important complementary activity besides state education, and this is in line with other sources (Dörnyei, Nyilasi, & Clement, 1996; Gazsó, 1997), putting the rate in state education at 40%. The rate in our unrepresentative sample is higher, and this fact may indicate that low achievers get more private tuition. This is a clear indication of social criticism: Both parents and students are dissatisfied with the teaching of FLs. Unfortunately, despite extracurricular and school tuition, participants have been unable to achieve useful levels.

As far as certification of language levels is concerned, over half of the interviewees had some sort of language certificate. They perceived official school-leaving exams as not worth mentioning, while external proficiency exams were beyond most of them. This indicates the problem of state education failing to provide meaningful and achievable attainment targets and valid, prestigious examinations, and thus contributing to students' further demotivation (Fekete, Major, & Nikolov, 1999).

7. When and how have participants needed to apply their language knowledge in real life situations?

As for using FLs in real life tasks, most of the interviewees would have had opportunities to put their language knowledge to use while travelling, but they tended to avoid situations or managed tasks with basic skills. It is doubtful whether they can benefit from new job, travel, and study opportunities now that Hungary is about to integrate into the European Union.

8. In what ways did an early start contribute to the FL development of young adults and to what extent was continuity of programmes ensured? How do unsuccessful adults relate to early start programmes for their children?

All participants started FL studies at or before the age of 9, but an early start did not ensure success. As they studied not only Russian but other languages as well, it is hard to maintain that they failed to achieve good levels because of the status of the target language. Two thirds of the participants were treated as beginners at secondary school, because continuity of the programmes was not ensured. Twenty of them had to start another language, as they were considered unsuccessful in the language they had studied in primary school.

Another crucial problem also needs some elaboration. Pupils progressing at a different pace tend to be streamed after a year or two. Good achievers are placed in groups of intensive instruction (four or more classes a week), while groups of low achievers go on in two classes a week. These educational practices must also have contributed to the negative outcomes of FL study of the interviewees. However, the vast majority would want their children to start FLs as early as possible, and only four participants argued against early FL programmes because of their own negative experiences. This tendency is common. Early start FL programmes have mushroomed not only in Hungary but also all over the world because of parental pressure.

LIMITATIONS OF THE STUDY

The limitations and weaknesses of the study are manifold. First, the focus is negative. We explored the experiences of unsuccessful FL learners, hoping that the insights would be relevant for others as well. Second, two of the criteria for choosing participants were subjective, based on self-assessment, with no direct objective measures. As a result, the term "unsuccessful" has turned out to cover a range of cases. Third, data were collected by means of interviews only; the study involved no observation, assessment of actual performance, or interviews with teachers. Thus, triangulation was not possible. Fourth, data collection was cross-sectional, and insights into development over time were gained only through retrospective recall. Our data cannot tell how participants would have performed at different ages on FL tests and how their views have changed over time.

CONCLUSIONS

This qualitative study explored the FL learning experiences, attitudes, and motivations of unsuccessful young adults in the Hungarian socioeducational context where only 12% of the population claim to speak a FL. Interviewees came from the 88% who don't. The findings indicate that despite the presence of innovative approaches in teaching materials, most teachers follow a hidden structural syllabus. Participants found oral and written assessment practices with an insistence on accuracy and memorisation threatening, the focus on grammar drills and rote-learning of texts boring and useless. Negative classroom experiences must have strongly influenced interviewees' motivation and self-perception and have not supported their FL development. Pleasant early language classroom activities could not counterbalance for the lack of feeling successful in later years. Participants' performances and motivation have gradually decreased over the years.

Interviewees claimed no proficiency at all in Russian, the most frequently learnt FL, while some levels have been achieved in other FLs, most often English and German. These are the languages they considered the most useful, though they also mentioned other languages and cultures as attractive. Participants believed that besides persistence and hard work, motivation, enthusiasm, and aptitude ensure success and that most of them lacked the first two.

The implications of these findings are important. Students need syllabuses tailored to their aptitude, interests, and needs, implemented by caring teachers. Their initial interest and motivation need to be sustained from class to class over the years and subsequent language programmes need to build on one another. The answers of the interviewees have hopefully provided insights into which types of activities should be favoured and which should be more carefully designed and implemented.

More research is necessary to explore how foreign-language learners actually develop and maintain or lose their motivation over the years, and how teachers can better understand and support them. A lot seems to depend on classroom practices and on us, the language teachers.

REFERENCES

Crookes, G., & Schmidt, R. (1991). Motivation: Reopening the research agenda. *Language Learning, 41*, 469–512.

Dörnyei, Z. (1994). Motivation and motivating in the foreign language classroom. *Modern Language Journal, 78*, 273–284.

Dörnyei, Z. (1998). Motivation in second and foreign language learning. *Language Teaching, 31*, 117–135.

Dörnyei, Z., & Clément, R. (2001). Motivational characteristics of learning different target languages: Results of a nationwide survey. In Z. Dörnyei & R. Schmidt (Eds.), *Motivation and second language acquisition* (Technical Report #23, pp. 399–432). Honolulu: University of Hawai'i, Second Language Teaching and Curriculum Center.

Dörnyei, Z., Nyilasi, E., & Clément, R. (1996). Hungarian school children's motivation to learn foreign languages: A comparison of target languages. *Novelty, 3*(2), 6–16.

Fekete, H., Major, É., & Nikolov, M. (Eds.). (1999). *English language education in Hungary: A baseline study*. Budapest: The British Council.

Gardner, R. C., & MacIntyre, P. D. (1992). A student's contributions to second language learning. Part I: Cognitive variables. *Language Teaching, 25*, 211–220.

Gardner, R. C., & MacIntyre, P. D. (1993). A student's contributions to second-language learning. Part II: Affective variables. *Language Teaching, 26*, 1–11.

Gazsó, F. (1997). *A társadalmi folyamatok és az oktatási rendszer* [Social processes and the educational establishment]. Budapest: MTA Nemzeti Stratégiai Kutatások, BKE, Szociológiai Tanszék.

Halász, G., & Lannert, J. (1998). *Jelentés a magyar közoktatásról 1997* [A report on Hungarian state education 1997]. Budapest: OKI.

Medgyes, P., & Miklósy, K. (in press). *The language situation in Hungary*. Clevedon, UK: Multilingual Matters.

Moncsek, M. (1999). Motivation to learn English and Russian of 31 Hungarian children. Unpublished MEd thesis, Pécs, Janus Pannonius University.

Naiman, N., Fröhlich, M., Stern, H. H., & Todesco, A. (1996). *The good language learner*. Clevedon, UK: Multilingual Matters.

Nikolov, M. (1999a). The socio-educational and sociolinguistic context of the examination reform. In H. Fekete, É. Major, & M. Nikolov, (Eds.), *English language education in Hungary: A baseline study.* (pp. 7–20). Budapest: The British Council.

Nikolov, M. (1999b). 'Why do you learn English?' 'Because the teacher is short.' Hungarian children's foreign language learning motivation. *Language Teaching Research, 3*(1), 33–56.

Nikolov, M. (1999c). Classroom observation project. In H. Fekete, É. Major, & M. Nikolov, (Eds.), *English language education in Hungary: A baseline study.* (pp. 221–50). Budapest: The British Council.

Schumann, J. (2000, March). Evolutionary psychology: Getting students' attention. Paper given at TESOL Conference, Vancouver.

Terestyéni, T. (1996). Vizsgálat az idegennyelv-tudásról [A survey on foreign language knowledge]. *Modern Nyelvoktatás, 2*(3), 3–16.

Vágó, I. (1999). *Tartalmi változások a közoktatásban a 90-es években* [Content changes in state education in the '90's]. Budapest: OKKER.

Williams, M., & Burden, R. (1997). *Psychology for language teachers.* Cambridge, UK: Cambridge University Press.

Marion Williams
Robert L. Burden
Safiya Al-Baharna
University of Exeter

MAKING SENSE OF SUCCESS AND FAILURE: THE ROLE OF THE INDIVIDUAL IN MOTIVATION THEORY

INTRODUCTION

A traditional approach to the psychology of language learning has been to seek to identify significant features of individuals to help differentiate between them (Skehan, 1989). Such an approach has tended to lead to research of a positivist nature, usually involving large groups to whom various tests are administered, the results of which are subjected to some form of statistical analysis, usually of a correlational nature. Alternatively, such research may seek to make use of experimental or quasi-experimental designs in an attempt to discover whether people with one or another set of personal attributes learn a language more or less effectively.

Critics of research of this nature argue that it has a tendency to produce lists of variables (e.g., language aptitude, introversion-extroversion, field dependence-independence) which are assumed to contribute in a significant way to successful language learning. This tendency reflects a view of psychology as akin to the natural sciences and researchers as objective observers of the human condition which they seek to predict and control (Guba & Lincoln, 1994). It also presupposes a view of knowledge as objective and external to the knower.

An alternative perspective is offered by an approach in which psychological research is carried out within an interpretative paradigm. Here the psychologist begins from the position of a searcher after personal meaning, as an inquirer into the ways in which individuals seek to make sense of various situations in which they find themselves and why they act in the ways that they do. (Salmon, 1988). This is more in line with the constructivist views of Jean Piaget and ultimately with the socio-cultural theory of Lev Vygotsky (Kozulin, 1999). Rather than seeking to identify and isolate within-person variables, this approach takes a more holistic view of the human individual learner as a seeker after meaning and sees knowledge as subjective and related to the knower.

The implications for research are radically different. Within the interpretative paradigm, large scale correlational or experimental studies are eschewed for small-scale, personally orientated investigations of a case study or qualitative nature. Here

Williams, M., Burden, R. L., & Al-Baharna, S. (2001). Making sense of success and failure: The role of the individual in motivation theory. In Z. Dörnyei & R. Schmidt (Eds.), *Motivation and second language acquisition* (Technical Report #23, pp. 171–184). Honolulu: University of Hawai'i, Second Language Teaching and Curriculum Center.

the focus is on the ways in which people construe (i.e., make sense of) the tasks with which they are faced in life and the ways in which they draw upon their understandings in guiding their subsequent actions. Thus, we can see an increasing interest in an exploration of the ways in which individuals' thoughts and feelings about themselves as learners affect their approaches to and success in learning.

Within cognitive psychology, one major shift has been away from formal testing of intelligence and other attributes towards an in-depth exploration of aspects of self-perception. Here, even static measures of self-concept and self-esteem have been replaced by more dynamic approaches to understanding the development of a sense of learner identity, the growth of autonomy, and the development of a sense of agency (Candy, 1991). Interest in such concepts as self-efficacy (Bandura, 1997) is directly related to the belief that individuals are in a constant process of predicting how well they will perform on prospective tasks by reflecting upon their performances on similar tasks previously.

Within the field of language learning, a number of different models have been proposed to explain motivation (Dörnyei, 1994; Gardner, 1985). Most of these have sought to identify different factors involved in motivation, mainly by statistical means. We have argued, however, (Williams & Burden, 1997) that two important elements that are often missing from standard theories of motivation are these aspects of identity and agency and that each must be taken into account if we are to be able to provide a fully comprehensive theory of motivation. An approach to these aspects which is receiving increasing attention is that of attribution theory.

ATTRIBUTION THEORY

The earliest formal manifestation of attribution theory is generally considered to have been an aspect of the "naïve" psychology of Fritz Heider (1944, 1958), but its most influential exponent has been Bernard Weiner (1986) whose "statement of theory" has been the guiding light for much of the early work in this field. Basically, people attribute different causes, or causal attributions, to events in their lives which they use to explain why a particular outcome occurred. Attribution theory is concerned, therefore, with the causes people attribute to the perceived successes and failures in their lives. For example, do they see a failure as being due to a lack of effort, lack of ability, or as someone else's fault. These personal contributions will affect an individual's subsequent actions. They will also give rise to different affective and emotional reactions.

In his early writings, Weiner claimed that there were four main causes to which people attributed outcomes in situations involving achievement, mainly ability, effort, task difficulty, and luck. But more recent research has led to a considerable extension of the common causes to include such factors as intrinsic motivation, interest, teacher competence, and mood (Little, 1985; Weiner, 1992).

An important aspect of attribution theory is the notion of attributional dimensions (Russell, McAuley, & Tarico, 1987; Weiner, 1986). Originally, Weiner (1979) proposed two dimensions of causal attributions: *locus of causality* and *stability*. *Locus of causality* refers to the perceived location of a cause as internal or external to the learner, whereas *stability* represents the potential changeability of a cause over time, as shown in Table 1.

Table 1: Weiner's original model of attribution

dimensions and elements	locus of causality	
	internal	external
stable	ability	task difficulty
unstable	effort	luck

A further dimension, *controllability* was added later. This concerned the extent to which an event or outcome is under the control of the learner or participant. Thus, an eight-cell, three-dimensional attributional model to account for the causes of success and failure was constructed (Weiner, 1986), as shown in Table 2.

Table 2: Causes of success and failure, classified according to locus, stability, and controllability

	locus of causality			
	internal		external	
	stable	unstable	stable	unstable
controllable	typical effort	immediate effort	teacher bias	unusual help from others
uncontrollable	ability	mood	task difficulty	luck

Thus individuals' approaches to achievement or learning tasks can be understood in terms of a) whether they see the main causes of their successes and failures as stemming from themselves or others, b) whether they see the cause as a fixed attribute or open to change, and c) whether they view possible changes as lying within their control or that of others.

An extreme constructivist view might argue that there could be at least as many attributional causes as there are individuals. Other theorists have argued that different situations tend to yield different attributions. Lalljee and Abelson (1983), for example, maintain that

> Events can be explained in a variety of different ways and the content of the explanation for the different types of event is systematically different. Thus, for instance, in the domain of achievement behaviour, success and failure are frequently explained in terms of the actor's intelligence or effort or interest in the subject. With reference to other domains, other explanations are relevant, and the explanations of success or failure on an academic task may be very different from success or failure of a marriage. (p. 65)

In the academic domain, much of the research has been carried out in the area of sport or within laboratory settings, with very little in the field of language learning. One of the first studies reported in this area was that of Williams and Burden (1999), the result of which revealed a tendency amongst British secondary school pupils to demonstrate a growing sense of externality in the ways in which they identified how well they were progressing in learning a foreign language. Effort became increasingly identified as the main reason for success, together with help from others and a growing feeling of aptitude. By contrast, reasons cited for failure included distraction by others, difficulty of work, and poor teaching, as well as lack of concentration.

ATTRIBUTIONS AND CULTURE

An analysis of the possible variables contributing to success and failure attributions in educational settings has identified age, gender, general behaviour, family influence, teacher influence, and like or dislike of a subject area as being particularly relevant (Little, 1985; Vispoel & Austin, 1995).

One further, potentially powerful contributing factor, which has been comparatively under-researched, is the cultural dimension. The few reported studies tend to suggest that different ethnic, religious, and other cultural groups are likely to cite different attributions for success and failure. Fry and Ghosh (1980) found, for example, that while students in Western societies were most likely to attribute their successes to internal causes, Asian students frequently made external attributions for their success. At the same time, Asian students were more likely than their Western counterparts to attribute failure to internal causes such as lack of ability or lack of effort. Similar findings were obtained by Miller (1984) with respect to Indian high school students, and by Power and Wagner (1983) in their comparison of Hispanic and Anglo high school students. A more recent study by Kivilu and Rogers (1998) based in Kenyan high schools has suggested, however, that other cultural differences may exist, such as a lack of emphasis upon effort as an explanation for success or failure in African societies. This study is important also in identifying the potential influence of the socialisation processes in urban and rural areas in non-Western countries.

The limited amount of research into attributions that has been carried out thus far in non-Western countries, despite the growing awareness of the important influence of cultural background, leads to the conclusion that this is an area in need of considerable further investigation. Accordingly, the study to be presented here represents the first of a series of explorations into the effect of cultural factors upon various aspects of motivation. In this case, a preliminary investigation into attributions in learning English among Bahraini secondary school students will be described.

In addition, only a limited number of studies have examined the difference in perspective between students' attributions and those given by their teachers for their students' successes and failures (Bar-Tal & Guttmann, 1981; Karniol, 1987). An understanding of such differences might help teachers to gain a more accurate understanding of their students' self perceptions, which might in turn enable them to act in ways that facilitate their students' development and progress.

The study therefore further aims to explore the reasons given by students for their perceived successes and failures, and to compare these with reasons given by teachers for their students' successes and failures.

The research questions were:

1. What reasons are given by secondary students in Bahrain to explain their perceived successes and failures in learning English?

2. What reasons are given by these students' teachers to explain their students' successes and failures in English?

3. What cultural aspects are reflected in the teachers' and students' attributions?

METHOD

APPROACH

The previous study by Williams and Burden (1999) offered an alternative perspective to much previous attribution research in its interpretative, grounded theory approach to methodology and its focus upon the sense that children of different ages made of their successes and failures in learning a foreign language. Despite the inevitable small-scale nature of work of this kind, it was concluded that this approach provided potentially useful insights into this area. Further research of a similar nature was felt to be warranted and an interpretive approach was therefore employed in the current study.

SAMPLE AND INSTRUMENTATION

Data were collected using mainly qualitative methods. First, 29 secondary teachers were selected. These represented an opportunity sample, being teachers of English to whom one of the researchers had access. They were all qualified TEFL teachers with University degrees in TEFL. Ten held Master's degrees. All had a minimum of 10 years of teaching experience, and 24 were heads of English departments.

The teachers were given an open questionnaire (see Figure 1). This was designed to elicit attributions without pre-conceived categories using a Grounded Theory approach, thereby allowing the categories to emerge from the data.

When my students do well in English the main reasons are:
1.
2.
3.
4.
When they don't do well in English the main reasons are:
1.
2.
3.
4.

Figure 1: Teachers' questionnaire

The students consisted of 13 boys from three boys' secondary schools, and 12 girls from three girls' secondary schools, aged between 16 and 18. This again represented an opportunity sample. A mix of abilities was represented in the sample, although, according to their teachers, rather more fell into the lower ability range. Such a distribution is, however, acceptable, as attributions made by lower proficiency learners can be of particular interest. In addition, Weiner (1979) states that "failure-oriented" students tend to supply attributions more than "mastery-oriented" students do.

A semi-structured interview was used with the students. The interview schedule developed by Williams & Burden (1999) was translated into Arabic and piloted before a final version was developed (see Figure 2).

- How well do you think you are doing in English?
- Give me an example(s) of when you did well.
- What were the reasons you did well?
- Is doing well up to you or someone else?
- Do you ever not do well? Give me an example.
- What were the reasons?

Figure 2: Selection of items from students' interviews

The questionnaires were completed by the teachers at the beginning of a teachers' meeting. The purpose was explained and the teachers were informed that participation was voluntary. All of the teachers opted to complete the questionnaire.

The data were content analysed using a Grounded Theory approach (Strauss & Corbin, 1990), and the frequency of occurrence of each category was determined. Thus both qualitative and quantitative methods were employed within an interpretative paradigm.

The students were interviewed individually with their permission in their schools during school time. Each interview began with the researcher explaining the purpose of the interview and asking permission to record it. All the students agreed to be tape-recorded. The data were again content analysed and the frequency for each category recorded. Finally the attributions given by students and teachers were compared.

LIMITATIONS

The limitations of this study are obvious. Its nature is mainly exploratory. The sample is small, and the results are tentative and limited to the context of teaching English as a foreign language in Bahrain. However, it is our contention that the accumulation of findings from such small scale investigations in different cultural contexts may not only throw light on specific aspects of how the group under investigation learns but can also help us to develop well grounded theories about socio-cultural influences on learning.

RESULTS

ATTRIBUTIONS FOR SUCCESS

Teachers' perspective

The teachers' perceptions of causes of students' success are shown in Table 3 below.

Table 3: Attributions for success – teachers' perspectives (N=29)

attributions	frequency
teaching materials	23
teaching methods	21
student motivation	12
knowledge of the basics of English	10
positive attitude	9

continued...

Table 3: Attributions for success – teachers' perspectives (N=29) (cont.)

attributions	frequency
effort	8
support from family and teachers	5
comprehension	5
classroom environment	4
interest	4
ability	3
circumstances/ a good start	2
use of appropriate strategies	2
exposure to the language	2
practice	1
miscellaneous	6

It was striking that the teachers attributed their students' success mostly to adequate teaching materials and teaching methods. They also identified, but to a lesser extent, a number of student-related factors such as motivation, knowledge of the basics of English, positive attitude, effort, comprehension, interest, and ability. Teachers therefore appeared to attribute success mainly to their own efforts rather than those of their students, thus exhibiting ego-protective behaviour.

Students' perspective

The students' perceptions of causes for their own successes are shown in Table 4 below.

Table 4: Attributions for success – students' perspective (N=25)

attributions	frequency
practice	20
support from family and teachers	11
exposure to the language	7
positive attitude	7
use of appropriate strategies	5
circumstances/a good start	5
effort	4
teaching methods	3
interest	2
knowledge of the basics of English	1
miscellaneous	1

There was a marked difference between the students' perspectives and those of their teachers. The students identified sufficient practice as the main cause for their success. They also mentioned causes like support from family and teachers, their own positive attitude, exposure to the language, and effort as relatively less important but nonetheless significant causes for success. In contrast, practice and exposure to the language came at the bottom of the list of attributions for success made by the teachers. In addition, while the teachers ranked teaching methods as a major cause of success, the students did not view this as a significant cause for their success. There appeared, therefore, to be a marked mismatch between teachers' and students' views, with students attributing success largely to factors internal to them and teachers attributing their students' success mainly to factors external to them.

ATTRIBUTIONS FOR FAILURE

Teachers' perspective

The teachers' perceptions of causes for failure in their students are shown in Table 5 below.

Table 5: Attributions for failure – teachers' perspectives (N=29)

attributions	frequency
inadequate teaching materials	21
insufficient knowledge of the basics of English	14
students' personality	12
inadequate teaching methods	9
negative attitude	8
insufficient effort	8
lack of motivation	6
insufficient practice	6
social background	6
psychological factors	5
lack of interest	5
insufficient exposure to the language	4
inadequate strategies	4
lack of support from family	3
poor comprehension	2
examinations	2
classroom environment	2
lack of ability	1
absenteeism	1
miscellaneous	4

The teachers attributed failure mainly to inadequate teaching materials. However, it is important to note that the textbooks used were prescribed by the Ministry and were therefore the same for all students. Thus, teachers were not assigning blame to themselves.

They also cited student-related causes such as their insufficient knowledge of language basics, personality traits, negative attitudes, and insufficient effort. This finding concurs with Weiner's (1992) claim that good performance by students is usually ascribed to good teaching while lack of improvement is generally ascribed to student-related factors. However, although the results did tend to show ego-protective behaviour, it was notable that 9 of the teachers did mention inadequate teaching methods. It was interesting that while the teachers did not consider practice and exposure to the language to be significant causes for success, they identified lack of these as potential causes for failure.

Students' perspective

The students' perceptions of causes for failure are shown in Table 6 below.

Table 6: Attributions for failure – students' perspective (N=25)

attributions	frequency
inadequate teaching methods	8
lack of support from family and teachers	8
poor comprehension	7
negative attitude	6
insufficient practice	5
lack of interest	5
inadequate teaching materials	5
examinations	3
inadequate strategies	3
insufficient effort	3
absenteeism	3
circumstances/social background	2
lack of resources	2
psychological factors	2
personality	1
lack of ability	1
insufficient exposure to the language	1
miscellaneous	1

Again there are differences in perspective between the teachers and the students. The students identified inadequate teaching methods and lack of support from family and teacher as the main causes for failure, both external and uncontrollable factors. However, there are a number of internal causes cited, showing a fair degree of internality among the students.

The responses to these two questions, shown in Table 7 below, indicate that the students felt a desire to do well in English, as well as a liking for it.

Table 7: Students' attitude towards English

	yes	average	no
Do you like English?	16	7	2
Do you want to do well in English?	25		

In addition, most of them exhibited an internal locus of control (see Table 8).

Table 8: Locus of control

	up to me	up to someone else	up to me and someone else
Is doing well up to you or someone else?	19	2	4

Finally, Table 9 shows the students' reasons for wanting to do well in English. The majority were instrumentally motivated, particularly regarding obtaining a job and studying further.

Table 9: Reasons for wanting to do well in English

reason	frequency
to get a job	11
for travelling and visiting places	4
for dealing with non-Arabic speakers	4
it is used a lot in Bahrain	4
for studying at university	4
life requires knowledge of English	3
it is an important language	3
to survive in this world/needed for everything	3
to raise my GPA	3
to pass all the subjects	2
to do well at school	1
it helps me improve	1
it is the language of the future	1
for shopping	1
to express myself	1
to cope with things around me	1

DISCUSSION

This small-scale study has raised a number of fascinating questions about the differing nature of teachers' and students' perceptions of reasons for success and failure in learning English within a non-Western culture. In doing so, we would argue, it has performed an important function of research in opening up further avenues for exploration. Research of this nature can never provide *the* answers to major questions; at best it can serve only to generate worthwhile hypotheses which can be explored by further research. It is our contention that several such hypotheses have been generated.

Prominent within the attribution literature is the notion of a "self-serving bias," which postulates that individuals are motivated by a need to enhance their self-esteem and tend to do so by ascribing success to internal factors and failure to external ones (Arkin & Maruyama, 1979; Marsh, 1986; Whitley & Frieze, 1985). In this study we found that such ego-protective behaviour did indeed occur but was somewhat more predominant amongst teachers than amongst students.

What also became clear, however, was that the situation is significantly more complicated than previous studies have assumed. Although the teachers quite reasonably ascribed their students' success in learning English mainly to high quality teaching and teaching materials, they also acknowledged the importance of such factors as student motivation, positive attitudes, and effort. Of particular interest is the large spread of internal attributions for failure that was found amongst the students. This finding does appear to be in keeping with an Islamic culture. Within this Islamic culture, the perceived importance of support from family and friends is also particularly notable. Attitudes towards learning the English language are seen, moreover, as carrying even greater significance than the amount of effort expended.

When it came to reasons for wanting to do well in English, about which there was total positive consensus amongst the students, by far the majority of reasons given were instrumental, in sharp contrast to large scale studies carried out elsewhere and reported in this book. Further investigation of whether this may be a cultural artefact or just specific to this particular group would appear to be warranted.

One further interesting finding which emerged from even this limited sample is the far wider range of attributions drawn upon than was identified in Weiner's original categories. Here the notion of luck was never mentioned, and ability was cited very rarely by either students or teachers. This may again well be a particularly significant effect of cultural background. At the same time, such factors as classroom environment, circumstances, exposure to the language, interest, strategy use, attitude, and support from others can be added to the ever expanding list of possible attributions (see Little, 1985).

This paper has been built upon the premise that the sense that people make of their perceived successes and failures in learning a language will play a significant part in their continuing motivation to learn that language.

We would suggest that teachers need to be aware of the importance of developing in their students internal and controllable attributions. The motivational process is complex, multi-faceted, and dynamic, and any model of motivation must incorporate the different interacting variables that arise from the learners themselves, the teacher, the task, and the whole environment. One such model is presented in Williams & Burden (1997). For teachers, we believe that building on their learners' feelings of internality and control and believing in their learners' abilities to succeed will go a long way towards fostering motivated behaviour.

REFERENCES

Arkin, R., & Maruyama, G. (1979). Attributions, affect and college exam performance. *Journal of Educational Psychology, 71*, 85–93.

Bandura, A. R. (1997). *Self-efficacy: The exercise of control.* New York: Freeman.

Bar-Tal, D., & Guttmann, J. (1981). A comparison of pupils', teachers', and parents' attributions regarding pupils' achievement. *British Journal of Educational Psychology, 51*, 310–311.

Candy, P. C. (1991). *Self-direction for lifelong learning.* San Francisco: Jossey Bass.

Dörnyei, Z. (1994). Motivation and motivating in the foreign language classroom. *Modern Language Journal, 78*, 273–84.

Fry, P. S., & Ghosh, R. (1980). Attribution of success and failure: Comparisons of cultural differences between Asian and Caucasian children. *Journal of Cross-Cultural Psychology, II*, 343–346.

Gardner, R. C. (1985). *Social psychology and language learning: The role of attitudes and motivation.* London: Edward Arnold.

Guba, E. G., & Lincoln, Y. S. (1994). Competing paradigms in qualitative research. In N. K. Denzin & Y. S. Lincoln (Eds.), *Handbook of qualitative research* (pp. 105–117). London: Sage.

Heider, F. (1944). Social perception and phenomenal causality. *Psychological Review, 51*, 358–374.

Heider, F. (1958). *The psychology of interpersonal relations.* New York: Wiley.

Karniol, R. (1987). Not all failures are alike: Self-attributions and perception of teachers' attributions for failing tests in liked versus disliked subjects. *British Journal of Educational Psychology, 57*, 21–25.

Kozulin, A. (1999). *Psychological tools.* Cambridge, MA: Harvard University Press.

Kivilu, J. M., & Rogers, W. T. (1998). A multi-level analysis of cultural experience and gender influences on causal attributions to perceived performance in Mathematics. *British Journal of Educational Psychology, 68*, 25–37.

Lalljee, M., & Abelson, R. P. (1983). The organisation of expectations. In M. Hewstone (Ed.), *Attribution theory: Social and functional extensions* (pp. 65–80). Oxford, UK: Blackwell.

Little, A. (1985). The child's understanding of the causes of academic success and failure: A case study of British schoolchildren. *British Journal of Educational Psychology, 55*, 11–23.

Marsh, H. W. (1986). Self-serving effect in academic attributions: Its relation to academic achievement and self-concept. *Journal of Educational Psychology, 78,* 190–280.

Miller, J. G. (1984). Culture and the development of everyday social explanation. *Journal of Personality and Social Psychology, 46,* 961–978.

Power, S., & Wagner, M. J. (1983). Attributions for success and failure of Hispanic and Anglo high school students. *Journal of Instructional Psychology, 19,* 171–176.

Russell, D., McAuley, E., & Tarico, V. (1987). Measuring causal attributions for success and failure: A comparison of methodologies for assessing causal dimensions. *Journal of Personality and Social Psychology, 52,* 1248–1257.

Salmon, P. (1988) *Psychology for teachers: An alternative approach.* London: Hutchinson.

Skehan, P. (1989). *Individual differences in second language learning.* London: Arnold.

Strauss, A., & Corbin, J. (1990). *Basics of qualitative research.* London: Sage.

Vispoel, W. P., & Austin, J. R. (1995). Success and failure in junior high school: A critical incident approach to understanding students' attributional beliefs. *American Educational Research Journal, 32,* 377–412.

Weiner, B. (1979). A theory of motivation for some classroom experiences. *Journal of Educational Psychology, 71,* 3–25.

Weiner, B. (1986). *An attributional theory of motivation and emotion.* New York: Springer-Verlag.

Weiner, B. (1992). *Human motivation: Metaphors, themes and research.* Newbury Park, CA: Sage.

Whitley, B., & Frieze, I. (1985). Children's causal attributions for success and failure in achievement settings: A meta-analysis. *Journal of Educational Psychology, 77,* 608–616.

Williams, M., & Burden, R. L. (1997). *Psychology for language teachers: A social constructivist approach.* Cambridge, UK: Cambridge University Press.

Williams, M., & Burden, R. L. (1999). Students' developing conceptions of themselves as language learners. *Modern Language Journal, 83,* 193–201.

Stephen R. Jacques
University of Hawai'i at Mānoa

PREFERENCES FOR INSTRUCTIONAL ACTIVITIES AND MOTIVATION: A COMPARISON OF STUDENT AND TEACHER PERSPECTIVES

Author's note

I would like to thank Dick Schmidt for his endless patience, inspiration, and guidance in this research; J. D. Brown for his help with the analytic framework; Yuichi Watanabe for his help with the statistical computations; Profs. Ray Moody, Paul Chandler, and Rafael Gomez and the Department of Languages and Literatures of Europe and the Americas at the University of Hawai'i at Mānoa for their participation.

INTRODUCTION

Interest in the study of motivation in the second language learning context has blossomed in the past few years. Following a call to arms by Crookes and Schmidt (1991) to broaden the old definitional framework of motivation in language learning from a dichotomous integrative/instrumental paradigm to a more multi-faceted approach, numerous researchers such as Dörnyei (1994a, 1994b), Oxford and Shearin (1994), Gardner and Tremblay (1994), Tremblay and Gardner (1995), and Schmidt, Boraie, and Kassabgy (1996) have studied the issue on both empirical and theoretical bases. Drawing on concepts from general, industrial, educational, and cognitive developmental psychology, they have attempted to construct a more complete picture of the complicated subject of motivation.

The pioneering work of Gardner and Lambert (1959) established the integrative/instrumental dichotomy, positing that language was learned either because one wanted to interact with or integrate into the target group (integrative) or in order to get a better job, earn more money, or pass an examination (instrumental). Of the two, Gardner believed integrative motivation to be the more supportive of language learning. Gardner and Tremblay (1994) have recently argued that this is a false dichotomy perpetuated in second language literature despite their repeated clarifications and that this distinction exists only insofar as *orientation* is concerned (that is, a class of reasons for studying a language), not motivation. However, as Dörnyei has responded, "Even though Gardner never fails to point out that orientations other than integrative and instrumental do also exist, the fact that he never elaborated on those or included them in his motivation test does suggest a certain prioritization" (1994b, p. 520). Despite these concerns and a number of studies that have produced sometimes conflicting results (Crookes & Schmidt, 1991), Gardner's socioeducational model has persevered, in no small part due to the

Jacques, S. R. (2001). Preferences for instructional activities and motivation: A comparison of student and teacher perspectives. In Z. Dörnyei & R. Schmidt (Eds.), *Motivation and second language acquisition* (Technical Report #23, pp. 185–211). Honolulu: University of Hawai'i, Second Language Teaching and Curriculum Center.

pervasive use of the battery of tests (the Attitude/Motivation Test Battery) developed to measure it.

Building on these theoretical underpinnings, Crookes and Schmidt (1991), Oxford and Shearin (1994), Dörnyei (1994a, 1994b), and others focused their attention outward. Crookes and Schmidt (1991) proposed four major motivational factors to describe second language classroom learning: interest, relevance, expectancy, and satisfaction. *Interest* refers to a student's desire to know (intrinsic motivation); *relevance*, to the connection between the student's personal goals, needs, and values and the course instruction; *expectancy*, to the student's perceived likelihood of success; and *satisfaction*, to a combination of extrinsic rewards such as praise or grades and intrinsic rewards such as pride and fulfillment. To these factors Dörnyei (1994a) adds teacher-specific and group-specific components. The teacher-specific components are: an *affiliative drive* (the desire to please one's teacher); *authority type* (whether the teacher is controlling or sharing in terms of decision-making in the classroom); *socialization of student motivation* (*modeling*, in terms of effort and interest in the subject); *task presentation* (raising students' awareness of the purpose of the activity); and *feedback* (informational feedback which comments on competence versus controlling feedback which judges performance against external factors). The group-specific components are: *goal-orientedness* (the extent to which the group is attuned to pursuing the goal); *norm and reward system* (group standards which the group enforces); *group cohesion* (the strength of the relationships linking the group members); and *classroom goal structures* (competitive, cooperative, or individualistic).

What is emerging is a broad conception of motivation resulting in models like that used in Schmidt, Boraie, and Kassabgy (1996) which "...fall generally within the broad category of value-expectancy theories of motivation. Such models assume that motivation is a multiplicative function of values and expectations. People will approach activities that they consider valuable and relevant to their personal goals and that they expect to succeed at" (p. 9).

Inherent in such an assumption is the fact that students will have decided preferences for certain instructional activities based upon their personal goals, instructional and cultural backgrounds, perceived value and difficulty of the tasks, and divergent personalities. "Learning style refers to the characteristic ways each individual collects, organizes, and transforms information into useful knowledge and action. It influences such things as the setting in which people wish to learn, the kinds of things they want to learn about, and how they will approach learning situations" (Henak, 1992, p. 24). Melton (1990) in a study of Chinese learners of English in the People's Republic of China discovered that contrary to the prevailing belief in the homogeneity of Chinese as learners, they expressed a preference for numerous different major and minor learning styles.

Additionally, it is important to acknowledge that teachers also have preferred teaching styles, based either on their experiences as learners or an acceptance of and adherence to the prominent pedagogical theories of the time, which may or may not agree with those of their students. In a study of migrant education programs in Australia, Nunan (1989) found that teachers were much more positive about communicative activities such as pair work, peer and self-correction of errors, and use of multi-media than were their students, who preferred vocabulary and pronunciation exercises and teacher correction of errors. Melton (1990) reported that the one learning style rated negatively by the Chinese learners was group learning. Stafford (1995), in a study of Japanese learners of English in Hawai'i, found that the least popular class in the students' program of study was the one based on a communicative approach, which included pair work, group work, and information-gap tasks. The students preferred the more structured, teacher-fronted grammar and pronunciation classes to such an extent that some concluded that the "communicative class" was not necessary.

The final factor to be considered in the present study is the often-overlooked issue of teacher motivation. Anecdotal evidence supporting the existence of motivated versus unmotivated teachers abounds. It is not uncommon to encounter teachers who say, "I feel burnt out and tired. I have no desire to move upward or stay in the classroom" (McKnight, 1992, cited in Pennington & Ho, 1995, p. 44) or to enter a classroom and know immediately that the teacher would rather be doing anything but teaching. With regard to language teaching, the situation may be even more pronounced. Richards and Lockhart (1994) seem to think that this is not unexpected given societal attitudes toward language teaching: "Language teaching is not universally regarded as a profession — that is, as having unique characteristics, as requiring specialized skills and training, as being a lifelong and valued career choice, and as offering a high level of job satisfaction" (p. 40). Pennington and Ho (1995) report that "teachers typically express moderate or high job satisfaction in categories having to do with the nature of teaching work and its intrinsic values, while registering low job satisfaction in categories having to do with pay and particularly with opportunities for advancement. Thus, teachers are generally satisfied with the *intrinsic rewards* of teaching but not with its *extrinsic rewards*" (p. 42).

Barnabe and Burns (1994), in a study involving Quebec teachers, attempted to describe the factors affecting teacher motivation by employing a tool developed by Hackman and Oldham (1980) for use in business settings. This model sets forth three conditions which promote high motivation and satisfaction at work: experiencing the work as meaningful, generally valuable, and worthwhile; experiencing responsibility for the results of the work; and understanding how effectively they are performing the job. Barnabe and Burns concluded that the results of their study favorably matched Hackman and Oldham's results in business settings.

Ames and Ames (1984) identified three systems of teacher motivation corresponding to ability, task mastery, and moral responsibility orientations. The ability system posits the protection of self-esteem and self-concept of ability as the most important concerns. The moral responsibility system refers to a teacher's concern for student welfare, as well as teacher values including cooperation, dependability, and duty. The task mastery system focuses on the primary concern of teachers for students' accomplishment of important learning objectives.

In the present study, both teacher and student questionnaires were constructed to investigate motivation in both language learning and language teaching and its relationship to preferences for instructional activities, as well as the areas of match and mismatch between student and teacher responses with regard to preferences for instructional activities.

The following research questions were framed for this study:

- Is there a relationship between student and teacher preferences for instructional activities?

- Are teachers' preferences for instructional activities related to motivation?

- Are students' preferences for instructional activities related to motivation?

METHOD

SUBJECTS

The subjects in this study were teachers ($N=21$) and students ($N=828$) in Spanish (levels 101, 102, 201, 202), French (level 102), and Portuguese (levels 102, 202) classes at the University of Hawai'i at Mānoa. The number of students in each teacher's classes ranged from 9 to 96 (teachers in the sample taught from one to five classes). According to the languages taught, the number of teachers and students was as follows:

Table 1: Distribution of subjects by language and status

language	# of teachers	# of students
French	4	68
Portuguese	1	20*
Spanish	16	740*

* One teacher who taught both Spanish and Portuguese classes returned questionnaires which were intermixed.

Unfortunately, several teachers administering the questionnaires misunderstood the instructions resulting in some classes believing that the questionnaires were to be anonymous. Consequently, the following statistics relating to numbers of males/females, previous language study, and so forth are incomplete:

Table 2: Distribution of subjects by gender, previous language study in college, and previous language study in foreign country

gender	# of students
female	334
male	296
missing	198

Previous study of this language in college (in semesters)

0	147
1	266
2	163
3	118
4	61
5+	19
missing	54

Previous language study in foreign country (in weeks)

0	439
1–4	121
5–8	25
9+	45
missing	198

MATERIALS

A student questionnaire, initially consisting of 123 items, was developed based on the instrument used by Schmidt, Boraie, and Kassabgy (1996) in their study of Egyptian learners of English. In consultation with the principal researcher of that study and numerous instructors in the Department of Languages and Literatures of Europe and the Americas at the University of Hawai'i at Mānoa, the questionnaire was revised to exclude questions particular to Egyptian learners and to include additional items based upon current research and instructor concerns. The subscales within the questionnaire, while initially based upon Schmidt et al.'s categorizations, were also revised with respect to said research and concerns, as well as results of factor analysis (see discussion section for explanation). After the instrument was piloted, 22 items were dropped, resulting in an instrument containing 101 items.

Part A of the student questionnaire (see Appendix A) consisted of 52 items concerning motivation, grouped into 13 subscales: Integrative Orientation (4 items), Interest in Foreign Language and Cultures (4 items), Foreign Language Requirement (1 item), Heritage Language (2 items), Instrumental Orientation (4 items), Intrinsic Motivation (8 items), Task Value (3 items), Expectancy (3 items), Anxiety (7 items), (perceived) Language Aptitude (4 items), Motivational Strength (6 items), Competitiveness (4 items), and Cooperativeness (2 items).

Part B   consisted of 23 items concerning preferences for instructional activities that were grouped into four subscales following the factor analysis (see discussion section): Practical Proficiency Orientation (9 items), Challenging Approaches (5 items), Cooperative Learning (3 items), Innovative Approaches (4 items), and Traditional Approach (2 items).

Part C   consisted of 26 items concerning learning strategies, data collected for another study and not reported here.

The 54-item teacher questionnaire (see Appendix B) was developed after administration of the student questionnaire and included two parts. Part A consisted of 33 items concerning motivation grouped into five subscales based on the literature concerning teacher motivation and job satisfaction: Job Satisfaction (11 items), Career Orientation (7 items), Perseverance (5 items), Perceived Teaching Ability (4 items), and Cultural Dissonance (6 items). Part B consisted of 21 items concerning preferences for instructional activities, which were identical to those on the student questionnaire except for slight wording changes to reflect the perspective of the teacher of the class rather than a student in the class (three items specifically referred to student preferences without a clear parallel question for the teacher of the class and were therefore deleted). These were grouped into five subscales: Practical Proficiency Orientation (9 items), Challenging Approaches (4 items), Cooperative Learning (3 items), Innovative Approaches (3 items), and Traditional Approach (2 items). Table 4, below, indicates the means, standard deviations and reliability statistics for sections A and B.

On both questionnaires, respondents indicated their level of agreement or disagreement with various statements. Unlike the Schmidt et al. (1996) Egyptian study, which employed a 6-point Likert scale, a practical decision to use a 5-point Likert scale was reached in this case, based upon the Scantron equipment available at the University of Hawai'i. Initially, there was some discussion concerning the presence of a neutral response available with a 5-point scale, which may encourage a clustering of scores on that response, rather than requiring a positive or negative decision. However, O'Bryen (1995), in a comprehensive review of methodological processes in motivation questionnaires, determined that 5-point scales are typically used for the quantitative measurement of motivation and, at present, this concern about clustering remains unresolved. Therefore, it was decided that, in such a large study, the advantages of using the available facilities outweighed possible score distribution problems.

PROCEDURES

The student questionnaires were administered in class during the first month of Spring semester 1996. The students were allowed 30 minutes to complete them, but teachers reported that some students finished in 15 to 20 minutes. The teachers were asked to complete the teacher questionnaires on their own time during the last month of Spring semester 1996. All answer sheets were then scanned at the University of Hawai'i's computing center and the results were fed into a StatView 4.5 (1994) spreadsheet for statistical computation.

StatView 4.5 software was used to compute descriptive statistics, correlations, and factor analyses. SuperANOVA v1.11 software (1995) was used to compute MANOVA statistics. Correlations were run on the subscales of both the teacher and student questionnaires and subscale scores were computed. Factor analyses were run on Part A and Part B of the student questionnaire but not on the teacher questionnaire since a factor analysis requires "…not less than 100 individuals for any analysis" (Gorsuch 1983, p. 332), and there were only 21 teachers involved in this study. A one-way MANOVA was conducted on Part B of both questionnaires with teacher and student status as the two levels of independent variable and the scores of the five subscales (Traditional, Practical Proficiency, Challenging, Innovative, and Cooperative) as the dependent variables.

RESULTS

STUDENT QUESTIONNAIRE

Table 3 indicates the means, standard deviations, and reliability statistics for the subscales in sections A and B. (The means and standard deviations of the individual items appear in Appendix A.)

Table 3: Student questionnaire subscales

Part A: Motivation (*alpha*=.89)				
	# of items	*alpha*	means	SD
Integrative Orientation	4	.80	12.222	3.778
Interest in Foreign Languages and Cultures	4	.65	14.097	3.249
Language Requirement	1	**	3.588	1.339
Heritage Language	2	.79	4.227	2.089
Instrumental Orientation	4	.62	11.015	3.208
Intrinsic Motivation	8	.89	26.091	6.674
Task Value	3	.62	7.613	1.498
Expectancy	3	.60	9.934	2.464
Language Aptitude	4	.70	12.348	2.881
Motivational Strength	6	.71	21.310	4.088
Competitiveness	4	.55	13.412	2.638
Cooperativeness	2	.44	7.609	1.364

continued…

Table 3: Student questionnaire subscales (cont.)

Part B: Preferences for instructional activities (*alpha=.82*)				
Practical Prof. Orientation	9	.79	37.002	4.259
Challenging Approaches	5	.62	15.786	3.112
Cooperative Learning	3	.62	11.219	2.219
Innovative Approaches	4	.45	13.598	2.244
Traditional Approaches	2	.60	7.530	1.543

It is important to remember that the variations in means scores of the subscales above correspond to the number of items contained therein. With regard to individual items, Table 4, below, lists the students most preferred and least preferred learning activities and their mean scores.

Table 4: Preferences for instructional activities (Part B)

most preferred

4.39	Students should ask questions whenever they have not understood a point in class.
4.29	It is important that the teacher give immediate feedback in class so that students know if they are correct.
4.24	Activities in this class should be designed to help the students improve their abilities to communicate in this language.
4.15	Language instruction should focus on the general language of everyday situations.
4.12	Vocabulary should be an important focus in this class.
4.11	Listening and speaking should be an important focus in this class.

least preferred

2.19	During this class I would like to have no English spoken.
2.96	I like language classes which use computer-assisted instruction.

It is interesting to note that since a 5-point Likert scale was used, the responses that are above 4 or below 2 indicate distinct agreement or disagreement with the statement. Whereas there were six statements that received means higher than 4, indicating an agreed preference, none received a means of 2 or less. Only two statements even registered in the 2-range, as indicated above. Of the six agreed-with statements all of them are Practical Proficiency Orientation items. Of the two most disagreed-with statements, one reflects Challenging Approaches and the other reflects Innovative Approaches.

In Table 5, below, the most-agreed-with and least-agreed-with statements concerning motivation are listed with their mean scores.

Table 5: Statements about motivation (Part A)

most agreed with

4.05	I enjoy meeting and interacting with people from many cultures.
4.04	It is most important to me to do my best in this class.
3.98	I learn best in a cooperative environment.
3.89	It is important to me to learn the course material in this class.

least agreed with

1.99	This language is important to me because it is part of my cultural heritage.
2.30	I have a personal attachment to this language as part of my identity.
2.41	I am afraid that my teacher is ready to correct every mistake I make.
2.44	I feel more tense and nervous in this class than in my other classes.
2.46	I am learning this language to understand films, videos, or music.
2.51	When I take a test, I think about how poorly I am doing.
2.60	I want to learn this language because it is important to show my ability to others.

The means of statements which sought to measure motivation were even less dispersed. Only two statements scored above 4, and only barely. Of them, two relate to Motivational Strength, one to Cooperative Learning and one to Interest in Foreign Languages. Due to the locale of the study, it is possible that the statement "I enjoy meeting and interacting with people from many cultures" is more a reflection of Hawaiʻi's unique multiculturalism than a strong conviction of all students who study foreign languages. The two statements receiving the strongest disagreement are concerned with heritage languages. While these items are the least agreed with in the context of Spanish, French, and Portuguese learning in Hawaiʻi, they were included for future research under the assumption that motivation for learning certain languages (such as Japanese or Hawaiian in the Hawaiʻi context) would be strongly influenced by heritage issues. The other responses, while scoring above 2.0, may indicate a leaning towards disagreement.

FACTOR ANALYSIS OF INSTRUCTIONAL PREFERENCES (PART B)

A varimax rotation of the five factors having an Eigen value of 1.00 or higher indicated that they account for 49.7% of the total variance in this sub-test with the following loadings:

Factor 1 — Practical Proficiency Orientation (9 items)

.76 It is important that the teacher give immediate feedback in class so that students know if they are correct.

.71 Students should ask a question when they have not understood a point in class.

.69 Activities in this class should be designed to help the students improve their abilities to communicate in this language.

.66 Language instruction should focus on the general language of everyday situations.

.61 Listening and speaking should be an important focus in this class.

.50 Vocabulary should be an important focus in this class.

.43 I like to have the goals and objectives of a course clearly set out for me.

.42 Language lessons should be relevant to the students' learning goals.

.41 Pronunciation should be an important focus in this class.

This factor was labeled Practical Proficiency Orientation because it contains items relating to communicative functions such as listening and speaking skills, vocabulary, general everyday language, and communication activities. It also stresses student responsibility, immediate teacher feedback, goal setting, and pronunciation skills.

Factor 2 — Challenging Approaches (5 items)

.74 I prefer to sit and listen and don't like being forced to speak in language class. (reverse coded)

.58 I prefer a language class in which there are lots of activities that allow me to participate actively.

.55 During this class, I would like to have no English spoken.

.54 In a class like this, I prefer activities and material that really challenge me to learn more.

.49 I prefer language classes in which the teacher sticks closely to the textbook. (reverse coded)

The items that load on Factor 2 indicate a desire to challenge oneself in the classroom with both materials and activities that promote participation.

Factor 3 — Cooperative Learning (3 items)

.88 I prefer to work by myself in this language class, not with other students. (reverse coded)

.81 I like language learning activities in which students work together in pairs or small groups.

.48 I prefer a language class in which the students feel they are a cohesive group.

Factor 3 emphasizes both group and pair work in the classroom as well as a desire to feel that the students learn as a group.

Factor 4 — Innovative Approaches (4 items)

.69 I like language classes that use lots of authentic materials.

.60 Culture should be an important focus in this class.

.53 I like language classes which use computer-assisted instruction.

.45 I like to set my own goals for language learning.

The items loading on Factor 4 have been labeled Innovative because they seem to be inclusive of approaches which have been recently introduced in the field such as computer-assisted instruction, individual goal-setting, and the use of authentic materials.

Factor 5 — Traditional Approach (2 items)

.81 Grammar should be an important focus in this class.

.74 Reading and writing should be an important focus in this class.

Factor 5, which stresses grammar, reading, and writing, is easily interpretable as a preference for traditional approaches to language learning.

FACTOR ANALYSIS OF MOTIVATIONAL FACTORS (PART A)

A varimax rotation of the six factors having an Eigen value of 1.00 or higher indicated that they account for 47.9% of the total variance in this sub-test with the following loadings:

Factor 1 — Value Components (20 items)

Integrative orientation (4 items)

.82 I am learning this language to be able to communicate with relatives who speak it.

.80 Studying this language is important because it will allow me to interact with people who speak it.

.69 I want to be more a part of the cultural group that speaks this language.

.59 I am learning this language to be able to communicate with friends who speak it.

Interest in Foreign Languages and Cultures (4 items)

.75 Studying foreign languages is an important part of education.

.72 I would like to learn several foreign languages.

.68 This language is important to me because it will broaden my world view.

.44 I enjoy meeting and interacting with people from many cultures.

Instrumental Orientation (4 items)

−.72 I mainly study this language to satisfy the university language requirement.

.68 Increasing my proficiency in this language will have financial benefits for me.

.62 Being able to speak this language will add to my social status.

.61 I am learning this language to understand films, videos, or music.

Intrinsic Motivation (6 items)

.75 I would take this class even if it were not required.

.61 I really enjoy learning this language.

.60 I don't like language learning. (reverse coded)

.54 I enjoy using this language outside of class whenever I have a chance.

.47 My language class is a challenge that I enjoy.

.44 When class ends, I often wish that we would continue.

Task Value (2 items)

.62 What I learn in this course will help me in other courses.

.52 I like the subject matter of this course.

The 20 items which load on the first factor are divided into five categories: Integrative Orientation, Interest in Foreign Language and Cultures, Instrumental Orientation, Intrinsic Motivation, and Task Value. Although these different orientations have often emerged as independent factors in past research, it is interesting to note that with the present subjects they load on one factor. That is, those who are integratively motivated also tend to see the instrumental value of language learning and are generally interested in foreign languages and cultures, and so forth. The exception is that students who report that they are mainly taking a language course to fulfill university requirements do not otherwise attribute value to language learning (studying to satisfy the requirement loads strongly negatively on this factor).

Factor 2 — Expectancy Components (14 items)

Expectancy (3 items)

.74 I am worried about my ability to do well in this class. (reverse coded)

−.47 I'm certain I can master the skills being taught in this class.

−.47 I believe I will receive an excellent grade in this class.

Anxiety (7 items)

.70 I have an uneasy, upset feeling when I take an exam.

.67 When I take a test, I think about how poorly I am doing.

.66 I feel more tense and nervous in this class than in my other classes.

.61 I feel uncomfortable when I have to speak in this class.

.57 I am afraid that the teacher is going to correct every mistake I make.

.54 I don't worry about making mistakes when speaking in front of this class. (reverse coded)

.36 I rarely have difficulty concentrating in this class. (reverse coded)

Language Aptitude (4 items)

−.38 I am good at grammar.

−.37 In general, I am an exceptionally good language learner.

−.32 I can imitate the sounds of this language very well.

−.26 I can guess the meanings of new vocabulary words very well.

This second factor also encompasses categories that have in some cases loaded separately. Students scoring high on this factor perceive their language aptitude as low, indicate a high degree of anxiety, and have low expectations of success. Those scoring low on the factor report low anxiety, high aptitude, and high expectancy.

Factor 3 — Motivational Strength (10 items)

.76 I work hard in this class even when I don't like what we are doing.

.73 I can truly put my best effort into learning this language.

.73 Even when the course materials are dull and uninteresting, I always finish my work.

.58 It is most important to me to do my best in this class.

.51 I often feel lazy or bored when I study for this class. (reverse coded)

.51 It is important to me to learn the course material in this class.

.50 When course work is difficult, I either give up or only study the easy parts. (reverse coded)

.39 When I am in class, I often think that I would rather be doing something else. (reverse coded)

.39 I find my language class boring. (reverse coded)

All of the items that load on Factor 3 are concerned with effort exerted to succeed in the language class. The three reverse coded items are concerned with not expending effort.

Factor 4 — Competitiveness (4 items)

.60 I learn best when I am competing with other students.

.60 I want to do better than the other students in this class.

.54 Getting a good grade in this class is the most important thing for me right now.

.43 I want to learn this language because it is important to show my ability to others.

The fourth factor is easily labeled Competitiveness since the items refer to the need to compete against other students and garner good grades.

Factor 5 — Heritage Language (2 items)

.73 This language is important to me because it is part of my cultural heritage.

.63 I have a personal attachment to this language as part of my identity.

This factor is labeled Heritage Language since the two items that load on it are concerned with the language/culture as personally attached to the student's self-identity.

Factor 6 — Cooperativeness (2 items)

.60 My relationship with the other students in this class is important to me.

.41 I learn best in a cooperative environment.

Cooperation is the basic element of the two items loading on Factor 6.

CORRELATIONS BETWEEN PART A & B

Several correlations among the subscales of parts A and B are both statistically significant ($p<.0001$) and potentially meaningful:

IM*CH   Learners who are intrinsically motivated to study a language favor challenging classroom activities ($r=.578$)

VA*CL   Learners who place a high value upon cooperativeness in learning favor group work in class ($r=.556$)

IN*CH   Learners who have a strong interest in foreign languages and cultures favor challenging classroom activities ($r=.506$)

IT*CH   Learners who are highly interested in integration into the target culture favor challenging classroom activities ($r=.464$)

VA*CH Learners who place high value on language learning favor challenging classroom activities ($r=.407$)

AX*CH Learners with high anxiety do not favor challenging classroom activities ($r=-.405$)

EX*CH   Learners who expect to do well in the class favor challenging classroom activities ($r=.364$)

IS*CH   Learners who are instrumentally motivated favor challenging classroom activities ($r=.360$)

AP*CH Learners who perceive themselves as good language learners favor challenging classroom activities ($r=.358$)

IN*IV   Learners who have a high interest in foreign languages and cultures favor innovative classroom activities ($r=.344$)

IN*PP   Learners who have a high interest in foreign languages and cultures favor classroom activities based upon practical proficiency orientation ($r=.338$)

VA*PP   Learners who place a high value on language learning favor classroom activities based upon practical proficiency orientation ($r=.320$)

FLR*CH Learners who are studying mainly to satisfy the university foreign language requirement do not favor challenging classroom activities ($r=-.416$)

FLR	Foreign Language Requirement	IT	Integrative Motivation
IV	Innovative Approaches	CL	Cooperative Learning Orientation
IM	Intrinsic Motivation	VA	Value
PP	Practical Proficiency Orientation	EX	Expectancy
IS	Instrumental Motivation	AX	Anxiety
CH	Challenging Approaches	AP	Aptitude (perceived)

TEACHER QUESTIONNAIRE

Table 6, below, reports the means, standard deviations, and reliability statistics for the subscales in sections A and B of the teacher questionnaire. (Means and standard deviations of the individual items appear in Appendix B.)

Table 6: Teacher questionnaire subscales

Part A: Motivation ($alpha=.68$)				
	# of items	alpha	means	SD
Job Satisfaction	11	.84	41.000	7.503
Career Orientation	7	.28	11.600	4.650
Perseverance	3	.14	11.161	2.594
Perceived Teaching Ability	4	.65	15.333	2.517
Cultural Dissonance	5	.63	9.809	3.276
Part B: Preferences for instructional activities ($alpha=.68$)				
Practical Profic. Orientation	9	.68	39.476	3.250
Challenging Approaches	4	.10	15.476	1.778
Cooperative Learning	2	.13	12.095	1.895
Innovative Approaches	3	.34	11.762	1.729
Traditional Approaches	2	.59	7.667	1.798

With regard to individual items, Table 7, below, lists the teachers' most and least preferred learning activities and their mean scores.

Table 7: Teachers' preferences for instructional activities (Part B)

	most preferred
4.71	I prefer a language class in which there are lots of activities that allow students to participate actively.
4.67	Activities in this class should be designed to help the students improve their abilities to communicate in this language.
4.67	Listening and speaking should be an important focus in this class.
4.48	Students should ask questions whenever they have not understood a point in class.
4.48	I like to clearly set out the goals and objectives for a course.
4.48	I prefer language activities and materials that really challenge students to learn more.

least preferred
no activities with means under 3.00

It is interesting to note that, unlike the student responses, the mean ratings for all instructional activities were above 3.0, indicating that the teachers either preferred or were neutral to all of them. This contrasts with the two most negative responses of the students, namely a dislike of no English in the classroom and, to a lesser degree, computer-assisted instruction. Similar to the student situation, however, was the fact that the items measuring Practical Proficiency Orientation were dominant in the list of most preferred instructional activities.

Table 8, below, lists the most agreed with and least agreed with statements regarding motivation with their mean scores.

Table 8: Teachers' statements about motivation (Part A)

	most agreed with
4.90	I don't like language teaching. (reverse coded)
4.90	It is most important for me to do my best when teaching this class.
4.81	I feel a very high degree of responsibility for the work I do.
4.57	I would like to acquire more knowledge about the language I teach.
4.52	I enjoy teaching this class.
4.52	Teaching allows me chances to use my personal initiative or judgment.
4.48	Teaching this class is a challenge that I enjoy.
4.24	I work hard at all aspects of language teaching, even though not all of them are equally pleasurable.
4.19	I am good at teaching grammar.
4.14	My job is not very significant in the broader scheme of things. (reverse coded)

4.10	A lot of other people are affected by how well I do my job.
4.10	I like the subject matter of this course.
4.10	Teaching requires me to use many high-level skills.
4.05	Teaching this course is important to my career development.
4.00	The amount of challenge in my job is very satisfying.

least agreed with

1.71	Most of the things I do in this job seem useless or trivial.
2.05	I often think of quitting this job.
2.81	I am satisfied with the salary I receive for this job.

It is also interesting to note that unlike the student responses to the motivation segment of the questionnaire, the teachers responded with many strongly positive and a few strongly negative answers. Of the 15 most agreed with statements, those which received the highest mean scores tend to describe intrinsic motivation, such as enjoying teaching in general and this course in particular, doing one's best while teaching, and so forth. Job satisfaction items tend to have somewhat lower mean scores.

CORRELATIONS BETWEEN PART A & B OF TEACHER QUESTIONNAIRES

The following correlations among the subscales of parts A and B on the teacher questionnaire were significant at $p<.05$:

P*IA	Teachers high in perseverance do not favor innovative approaches to teaching ($r=-.483$)
JS*TR	Teachers who are satisfied with their job situations favor traditional approaches to teaching ($r=.452$)
P	Perseverance
IV	Innovative Approaches
JS	Job Satisfaction
TR	Traditional Approaches

STUDENT VS. TEACHER

A MANOVA was conducted on Part B of both questionnaires with teacher and student status as the two levels of independent variable and the scores of the five subscales (Traditional, Practical Proficiency, Challenging, Innovative, and Cooperative) as five dependent variables. Upon checking the assumptions underlying this statistical procedure, there arose two concerns: the impossibility of random assignment to groups and the small N size of the teacher subjects. The first is less problematic since no causal claims are being made from the results. The second, however, should be avoided in future research by having a larger sample of teachers to ensure that the sample distributions are not skewed.

The Wilks Lambda test indicated that there was a significant multivariate difference ($p<.05$) between the student and teacher subjects with regard to preferences for instructional activities somewhere in the dependent variable. As a result, the five scales could be analyzed individually using univariate F-tests. The Innovative Approaches scale and the Practical Proficiency scale both yielded significant results ($p<.01$, adjusted because of the five dependent variables).

Table 9: Innovative approaches scale

Type III Sums of squares

source	df	sum of squares	mean square	F-value	P-value
subject class	1	69.503	69.503	14.124	.0002
residual	814	4005.789	4.921		

Table 10: Practical proficiency scale

Type III Sums of squares

source	df	sum of squares	mean square	F-value	P-value
subject class	1	125.321	125.321	6.997	.0083
residual	814	14580.237	17.912		

In contrast to the MANOVA results indicated above which depict the significant differences between students and teachers with respect to the subscales of Part B, Table 11 provides an item-by-item comparison of teacher and student means for the eight instructional activities in which the difference between the means of the two groups was more than .5.

Table 11: Comparison of teacher and student means for specific instructional activities

teachers	students	difference	item
4.476	3.463	1.013	In a class like this, I prefer activities and material that really challenge me (my students) to learn more.
4.714	3.848	.866	I prefer a language class in which there are lots of activities that allow me (my students) to participate actively.
3.000	2.187	.813	During this class, I would like to have no English spoken.
4.238	3.559	.679	I like language classes that use lots of authentic materials.
4.286	3.638	.648	Culture should be an important focus in this class.
4.286	3.663	.623	I like language learning activities in which students work together in pairs or small groups.

4.476	3.868	.608	I like to have the goals and objectives for a course clearly set out for me/I like to clearly set out the goals and objectives for a course.
4.667	4.106	.561	Listening and speaking should be an important focus in this class.

Note that of these activities, the only item registering more than a one-point difference concerns teachers having a very high opinion of challenging activities and materials, whereas students seem to have less of an opinion on the matter. Of the remaining items showing a substantial difference in approval by teachers and students, there are two more items form the subscale dealing with challenging approaches (dealing with class participation and use of English), two items each from the Practical Proficiency Orientation and Innovative Approaches subscales and one from the Cooperative Learning subscale.

DISCUSSION

At the outset of this study, three research questions were posed in order to direct the investigation. They will be repeated here to organize the discussion.

ARE STUDENTS' PREFERENCES FOR INSTRUCTIONAL ACTIVITIES RELATED TO MOTIVATION?

As Brown, Robson, and Rosenkjar (this volume) point out, "The issue of validity has to do with the degree to which an instrument is measuring what it claims to be measuring. One way to study the validity of a measure is to use factor analysis to study the convergence and divergence of a group of measures." The results of the factor analysis conducted on the student questionnaire indicate that it is reasonable to conclude that the subscales of Part A are adequately measuring the constructs of value (which includes integrative orientation, interest, intrinsic motivation, instrumental motivation, and task value), expectancy (which includes anxiety and language aptitude), motivational strength, competitiveness, heritage language, and cooperativeness. The subscales of Part B are likewise seen to be adequately measuring the constructs of a practical proficiency orientation and attitudes towards challenging approaches, cooperative learning, innovative approaches, and traditional approaches. The correlations between pairs of these same variables indicated that there are numerous relationships between certain motivational subscales and certain preferences for instructional activities subscales in the student responses. While it is important to refrain from claiming any causation in this type of relationship, it is safe to say that with this sizable subject pool, some variables are related. The strongest of these seems to be that students who study a language solely as a university requirement do not value language learning in and of itself. Less strong relationships were apparent between those same learners and a preference for challenging activities. Additionally, challenge was a positive element for those students who place a high value on language learning, but not so for anxious students.

ARE TEACHERS' PREFERENCES FOR INSTRUCTIONAL ACTIVITIES RELATED TO MOTIVATION?

Although more difficult to substantiate due to the inability to use factor analysis as corroboration, the subscales of the teacher questionnaire (especially Part B, which closely reflects the composition of Part B of the student questionnaire) seemed to be measuring what they claim to be, motivation and preferences for instructional activities. There is some concern about certain subscales of the teacher questionnaire being truly reliable. The Cronbach alpha scores reported for the Career Orientation (.28) and Perseverance (.14) subscales of Part A and for Cooperative Learning (.13), Challenge (.10), and Innovative Approaches (.34) in Part B are alarmingly low. There are several possible reasons for this outcome, among them the small number of subjects and the fact that most of these subscales were made up of only two or three items. Bearing in mind that any relationships may be due to random effects, it is still worth noting that some motivation-activities correlations may warrant further investigation, such as the apparent fact that teachers who are satisfied with their job situations favor traditional approaches to teaching.

IS THERE A RELATIONSHIP BETWEEN STUDENT AND TEACHER PREFERENCES FOR INSTRUCTIONAL ACTIVITIES?

Finally, the issue of perspective and preference with regard to instructional activities between teachers and students is considered. From a pedagogical standpoint, this question was the most compelling to the researcher of this study. As Nunan (1989), Stafford (1995), and Melton (1990) have commented, classroom practitioners often discover that some activities just don't seem to "hit the mark" with some language students. Finding a solution to this problem, however, poses many difficulties, not the least of which is the fact that every classroom situation is different. In the present study, the problem with subscale reliability and hence validity, especially with regard to the teacher questionnaire, causes the results of the MANOVA to be interpreted cautiously. However, the MANOVA indicated that the teachers and students responded in a significantly different manner with regard to both Innovative Approaches and Practical Proficiency Orientation questions. As shown in Table 11, the teachers indicated stronger agreement than the students on items concerning challenging activities, authentic materials, pair and group work, goal setting, and a focus on listening and speaking with active student participation. It is important to note, however, that the divergence between all these means is not enormous.

CONCLUSIONS

Motivation, both in terms of the student studying a second or foreign language and the teacher teaching it, may not only help us understand the reasons why we are doing what we are doing, but may also have a relationship to how we perceive and react to what is going on within the classroom. This study begins to look at the interplay between those two elements and how they may or may not be different depending upon one's perspective. The data seem to indicate that certain types of students and teachers engage in foreign languages for different purposes and prefer to learn or teach via certain classroom activities. It may not be realistic to assume that there could ever be perfect matches between student and teacher preferences in a classroom, but an understanding of what both sides need and expect would be a significant first step towards success. Stafford (1995) commented that in his study, "the absence of teacher-student communication about the learning process was clearly evident. Such dialogue was most likely absent because neither teachers nor students realized that there could in fact be cross-cultural communication on different views about language learning which they bring into the classroom" (p. 31).

In terms of future research, it will be important to include a larger sampling of teachers in order to create a more reliable and valid instrument for testing both motivational factors and preferences for instructional activities. Qualitative research, including interviews with students and teachers, classroom observations, and longitudinal research would also significantly facilitate this exploration and provide further layers for analysis.

REFERENCES

Ames, C., & Ames, R. (1984). Systems of student and teacher motivation: Toward a qualitative definition. *Journal of Educational Psychology, 76*, 535–556.

Barnabe, C., & Burns, M. (1994). Teacher's job characteristics and motivation. *Educational Research, 36*, 171–185.

Brown, J. D., Robson, G, & Rosenkjar, P. R. (2001). Personality, motivation, anxiety, strategies, and language proficiency of Japanese students. In Z. Dörnyei & R. Schmidt (Eds.), *Motivation and second language acquisition* (Technical Report #23, pp. 361–398). Honolulu: University of Hawai'i, Second Language Teaching and Curriculum Center.

Crookes, G., & Schmidt, R. (1991). Motivation: Reopening the research agenda. *Language Learning, 41*, 469–512.

Dörnyei, Z. (1994a). Motivation and motivating in the foreign language classroom. *The Modern Language Journal, 78*, 273–284.

Dörnyei, Z. (1994b). Understanding L2 motivation: On with the challenge! *The Modern Language Journal, 78*, 515–523.

Gardner, R. C., & Lambert, W. E. (1959). Motivational variables in second language acquisition. *Canadian Journal of Psychology, 13*, 266–272.

Gardner, R. C., & Tremblay, P. F. (1994). On motivation: Measurement and conceptual considerations. *The Modern Language Journal, 78*, 524–527.

Gorsuch, R. L. (1983). *Factor analysis.* Hillsdale, NJ: Lawrence Erlbaum Associates, Inc.

Hackman, J. R., & Oldham, G. R. (1980). *Work redesign.* Reading, MA.: Addison-Wesley.

Henak, R. (1992). Addressing learning styles. *The Technology Teacher, 52,* 23–28.

McKnight, A. (1992). 'I loved the course, but …': Career aspirations and realities in adult TESOL. *Prospect, 7.3,* 20–31.

Melton, C. D. (1990). Bridging the cultural gap: A study of Chinese students' learning style preferences. *RELC Journal, 21,* 29–47.

Nunan, D. (1989). Hidden agendas: The role of the learner in programme implementation. In R. K. Johnson (Ed.), *The second language curriculum* (pp. 176–186). Cambridge, UK: Cambridge University Press.

O'Bryen, P. (1995). *Methodological processes in motivation questionnaire development.* Unpublished manuscript, University of Hawai'i at Mānoa, Honolulu.

Oxford, R., & Shearin, J. (1994). Language learning motivation: Expanding the theoretical framework. *The Modern Language Journal, 78,* 12–28.

Pennington, M., & Ho, B. (1995). Do ESL educators suffer from burnout? *Prospect, 10,* 41–53.

Richards, J. C., & Lockhart, C. (1994). *Reflective teaching in second language classrooms.* Melbourne, Australia: Cambridge University Press.

Schmidt, R., Boraie, D., & Kassabgy, O. (1996). Foreign language motivation: Internal structure and external connections. In R. Oxford (Ed.), *Language learning motivation: Pathways to the new century* (Technical Report No. 11, pp. 9–70). Honolulu: University of Hawai'i, Second Language Teaching & Curriculum Center.

Stafford, M. (1995). *Views on English language teaching.* Unpublished manuscript, University of Hawai'i at Mānoa, Honolulu.

StatView v4.5 [Computer software]. (1994). Berkeley, CA: Abacus Concepts, Inc.

SuperANOVA v1.11 [Computer software]. (1995). Cary, NC: SAS Institute, Inc.

Tremblay, P. F., & Gardner, R. C. (1994). Expanding the motivation construct in language learning. *The Modern Language Journal, 79,* 505–518.

STUDENT QUESTIONNAIRE (*alpha=.94*)

5	4	3	2	1
strongly agree	agree	no opinion	disagree	strongly disagree

mean	SD	PART A: MOTIVATION (*alpha=.89*)

VALUE COMPONENTS

Integrative Orientation (4 items, alpha=.80)

3.537	1.183	Studying this language is important because it will allow me to interact with people who speak it.
3.021	1.312	I am learning this language to be able to communicate with relatives who speak it.
2.620	1.215	I am learning this language to be able to communicate with friends who speak it.
3.085	1.046	I want to be more a part of the cultural group that speaks this language.

Interest in Foreign Languages and Cultures (4 items, alpha=.65)

3.556	1.174	Studying foreign languages is an important part of education.
3.089	1.390	I would like to learn several foreign languages.
3.452	1.005	This language is important to me because it will broaden my world view.
4.048	.851	I enjoy meeting and interacting with people from many cultures.

Language Requirement (1 item)

3.588	1.339	I mainly study this language to satisfy the university language requirement.

Heritage Language (2 items, alpha=.79)

1.998	1.204	This language is important to me because it is part of my cultural heritage.
2.297	1.178	I have a personal attachment to this language as part of my identity.

Instrumental Orientation (4 items, alpha=.62)

3.095	1.191	Increasing my proficiency in this language will have financial benefits for me.
2.819	1.121	Being able to speak this language will add to my social status.
2.456	1.141	I am learning this language to understand films, videos, or music.
2.598	1.079	I want to learn this language because it is important to show my ability to others.

Intrinsic Motivation (8 items, alpha=.89)

2.767	1.421	I would take this class even if it were not required.
3.484	1.104	I really enjoy learning this language.
3.494	1.226	I don't like language learning. (reverse coded)
3.293	1.075	I enjoy using this language outside of class whenever I have a chance.
3.429	1.037	My language class is a challenge that I enjoy.
2.713	1.015	When class ends, I often wish that we would continue.

3.223	1.178	When I am in class, I often think that I would rather be doing something else. (reverse coded)
3.767	.983	I find my language class boring. (reverse coded)

Task Value (3 items, alpha=.62)

2.801	1.093	What I learn in this course will help me in other courses.
3.707	.913	I like the subject matter of this course.
3.893	.865	It is important to me to learn the course material in this class.

EXPECTANCY COMPONENTS
Expectancy (3 items, alpha=.60)

2.833	1.272	I am worried about my ability to do well in this class. (reverse coded)
3.591	.968	I'm certain I can master the skills being taught in this class.
3.457	.993	I believe I will receive an excellent grade in this class.

Anxiety (7 items, alpha=.65)

2.967	1.132	I have an uneasy, upset feeling when I take an exam.
2.514	1.149	When I take a test, I think about how poorly I am doing.
2.442	1.249	I feel more tense and nervous in this class than in my other classes.
2.710	1.177	I feel uncomfortable when I have to speak in this class.
2.768	1.083	I rarely have difficulty concentrating in this class. (reverse coded)
2.413	.941	I am afraid that the teacher is going to correct every mistake I make.
3.079	1.161	I don't worry about making mistakes when speaking in front of this class. (reverse coded)

Language Aptitude (4 items, alpha=.70)

2.914	1.135	I am good at grammar.
2.821	1.077	In general, I am an exceptionally good language learner.
3.313	1.051	I can imitate the sounds of this language very well.
3.267	.925	I can guess the meanings of new vocabulary words very well.

Motivational Strength (6 items, alpha=.71)

3.387	1.059	I can truly put my best effort into learning this language.
3.372	1.001	I work hard in this class even when I don't like what we are doing.
3.513	1.099	Even when the course materials are dull and uninteresting, I always finish my work.
3.246	1.078	I often feel lazy or bored when I study for this class. (reverse coded)
3.592	1.020	When course work is difficult, I either give up or only study the easy parts. (reverse coded)
4.037	.978	It is most important to me to do my best in this class.

COMPETITIVE VERSUS COOPERATIVE
Competitiveness (4 items, alpha=.55)

2.678	1.066	I learn best when I am competing with other students.
3.545	.999	I want to do better than the other students in this class.
3.397	1.186	Getting a good grade in this class is the most important thing for me right now.
3.734	.933	My teacher's opinion of me in this class is very important.

Cooperativeness (2 items, alpha=.44)

| 3.571 | .895 | My relationship with the other students in this class is important to me. |
| 3.981 | .836 | I learn best in a cooperative environment. |

mean	SD	PART B: PREFERENCES FOR INSTRUCTIONAL ACTIVITIES (*alpha*=.82)

Practical Proficiency Orientation (9 items, alpha=.79)

4.288	.721	It is important that the teacher give immediate feedback in class so that students know if they are correct.
4.391	.696	Students should ask a question when they have not understood a point in class.
4.243	.714	Activities in this class should be designed to help the students improve their abilities to communicate in this language.
4.150	.740	Language instruction should focus on the general language of everyday situations.
4.106	.765	Listening and speaking should be an important focus in this class.
3.868	.831	I like to have the goals and objectives of a course clearly set out for me.
4.115	.773	Vocabulary should be an important focus in this class.
3.855	.778	Language lessons should be relevant to the students' learning goals.
3.929	.902	Pronunciation should be an important focus in this class.

Challenging Approaches (5 items, alpha=.62)

4.243	.714	I prefer to sit and listen, and don't like being forced to speak in language class. (reverse coded)
2.187	1.065	During this class, I would like to have no English spoken.
3.055	1.036	I prefer language classes in which the teacher sticks closely to the textbook. (reverse coded)
3.463	.959	In a class like this, I prefer activities and material that really challenge me to learn more.
3.848	.913	I prefer a language class in which there are lots of activities that allow me to participate actively.

Cooperative Learning (3 items, alpha=.62)

3.569	1.051	I prefer to work by myself in this language class, not with other students. (reverse coded)
3.663	1.091	I like language learning activities in which students work together in pairs or small groups.
3.888	.806	I prefer a language class in which the students feel they are a cohesive group.

Innovative Approaches (4 items, alpha=.45)

3.559	.819	I like language classes that use lots of authentic materials.
2.958	.961	I like language classes which use computer-assisted instruction.
3.638	.919	Culture should be an important focus in this class.
3.477	.898	I like to set my own goals for language learning.

Traditional Approaches (2 items, alpha=.60)

| 3.725 | .929 | Grammar should be an important focus in this class. |
| 3.771 | .936 | Reading and writing should be an important focus in this class. |

APPENDIX B

TEACHER QUESTIONNAIRE (*alpha*=.78)

5	4	3	2	1
strongly agree	agree	no opinion	disagree	strongly disagree

mean	SD	PART A: MOTIVATION (*alpha*=. 68)

Job Satisfaction (11 items, alpha=.84)

mean	SD	
3.238	1.300	I am satisfied with the fringe benefits available to me in this position.
3.667	1.197	I am satisfied with the degree of respect and fair treatment I receive from this organization.
2.810	1.078	I am satisfied with the salary I receive for this job.
2.095	1.044	There are adequate opportunities for advancement in my job.
2.952	1.161	I am satisfied with the job security I have.
4.000	1.000	The amount of challenge in my job is very satisfying.
4.476	.680	Teaching this class is a challenge that I enjoy.
4.095	.700	Teaching requires me to use many high-level skills
4.524	.680	Teaching allows me chances to use my personal initiative or judgment.
3.857	1.276	I would want to teach first and second level language classes even if I didn't have to.
3.095	1.221	I feel I should personally take credit or blame for how well my students learn.
3.714	.956	The amount of support I receive from my supervisors is adequate.
3.857	1.153	Interaction with my co-workers is a very positive aspect of this job.
3.286	1.419	My supervisors and co-workers almost never give me any feedback about how well I am doing. (reverse coded)

Career Orientation (7 items, alpha=.28)

mean	SD	
4.571	.746	I would like to acquire more knowledge about the language I teach.
4.048	1.284	Teaching this course is important to my career development.
3.900	1.373	Teaching this course is important for future job prospects.
4.905	.301	I don't like language teaching. (reverse coded)
4.095	1.091	I like the subject matter of this course.
4.524	.981	I enjoy teaching this class.
3.524	1.030	When class ends, I often wish that we would continue.

Perseverance (3 items, alpha=.14)

mean	SD	
4.905	.301	It is most important for me to do my best when teaching this class.
4.238	.889	I work hard at all aspects of language teaching, even though not all of them are equally pleasurable.
2.048	1.203	I often think of quitting this job.

Perceived Teaching Ability (4 items, alpha=.65)

mean	SD	
4.190	.680	I am good at teaching grammar.
3.905	.768	Generally speaking, I think I am an excellent language teacher.

3.714	.956	I am good at teaching pronunciation.
3.571	.811	I am good at teaching reading and writing.

Cultural Dissonance (5 items, alpha=.63)

3.143	1.459	The importance of this language as part of my cultural heritage is reflected in my teaching.
4.810	.402	I feel a very high degree of responsibility for the work I do. (neg.)
4.095	.768	A lot of other people are affected by how well I do my job. (neg.)
4.143	1.108	My job is not very significant in the broader scheme of things. (reverse coded)
1.714	.845	Most of the things I have to do on this job seem useless or trivial. (neg.)

mean	SD	PART B: PREFERENCES FOR INSTRUCTIONAL ACTIVITIES (*alpha*=.68)

Practical Proficiency Orientation (9 items, alpha=.68)

4.333	.796	It is important that the teacher give immediate feedback in class so that students know if they are correct.
4.476	.814	Students should ask a question when they have not understood a point in class.
4.667	.577	Activities in this class should be designed to help the students improve their abilities to communicate in this language.
4.190	.750	Language instruction should focus on the general language of everyday situations.
4.667	.577	Listening and speaking should be an important focus in this class.
4.476	.602	I like to clearly set out the goals and objectives of a course.
4.333	.577	Vocabulary should be an important focus in this class.
4.190	.750	Language lessons should be relevant to the students' learning goals.
4.143	.727	Pronunciation should be an important focus in this class.

Challenging Approaches (4 items, alpha=.10)

3.000	1.265	During this class, I would like to have no English spoken.
3.286	.902	I prefer language classes in which the teacher sticks closely to the textbook. (reverse coded)
4.476	.602	I prefer activities and material that really challenge students to learn more.
4.714	.463	I prefer a language class in which there are lots of activities that allow students to participate actively.

Cooperative Learning (2 items, alpha=.13)

4.286	1.007	I like language learning activities in which students work together in pairs or small groups.
4.333	.730	I prefer a language class in which the students feel they are a cohesive group.

Innovative Approaches (3 items, alpha=.34)

4.238	.831	I like language classes that use lots of authentic materials.
3.238	1.136	I like language classes which use computer-assisted instruction.
4.286	.717	Culture should be an important focus in this class.

Traditional Approaches (2 items, alpha=.59)

3.762	1.044	Grammar should be an important focus in this class.
3.905	1.091	Reading and writing should be an important focus in this class.

Omneya Kassabgy
Career Development Center, Cairo
Deena Boraie
The American University in Cairo
Richard Schmidt
The University of Hawai'i at Mānoa

VALUES, REWARDS, AND
JOB SATISFACTION IN ESL/EFL

Abstract

When asked what aspects of work are most important to them personally, 107 experienced ESL/EFL teachers in Egypt and Hawai'i emphasized values and goals directly associated with teaching, including helping students to learn, having a job in which one can perform to the best of one's ability, and having good relationships with others. Extrinsic aspects of work such as salary, title, and opportunities for promotion were rated as less important. When asked to think about their current jobs and the rewards that they gain from them, job internal rewards were also stressed over extrinsic rewards, indicating a generally good (but not perfect) fit between what ESL teachers think is important at work and what they get. A factor analysis of responses to question items concerning work values suggests that there are five distinct sets of basic wants or needs: a relationship orientation (what is important is relationships with students, other teachers, supervisors, etc.), extrinsic motivation (what is important is security, salary, fringe benefits, etc.), autonomy needs (what is important is freedom, independence, encouragement of initiative, etc.), a self-realization factor (what is important is to be able to develop one's ability, have sufficient challenge, etc.), and institutional support needs (what is important is to have clear rules and procedures, a supervisor who gives clear guidance, flexible working hours, etc.). Factor analysis of job rewards indicates four factors, which partially overlap with these values factors. There seem to be four variants of "a good job": the job in a well managed institution, the job that provides professional status (extrinsic rewards plus an emphasis on creativity, independence, and initiative), the job where the primary rewards come from students and the classroom itself, and the challenging job that provides scope to learn and develop in a stimulating atmosphere. From the data reported here, it appears that job and career satisfaction are mostly influenced by job rewards rather than what teachers say they think is important (values). No support was found for either the "fit" hypothesis (the idea that what is important is the match between what one values and what one gets) or the "dual source" hypothesis (the idea that different factors contribute to satisfaction and dissatisfaction).

INTRODUCTION

The research described in this chapter evolved from an initial concern with learner motivation, specifically the motivation of learners of English in a foreign language environment. As we pursued this research over several studies (Schmidt, Boraie, & Kassabgy, 1996), it became increasingly clear to us that teachers have a very important influence on the motivation of language learners (see also Nikolov, this volume), and we know very little about the motivation of teachers themselves. The motivation of language teachers has been researched much less than the motivation

Kassabgy, O., Boraie, D., & Schmidt, R. (2001). Values, rewards, and job satisfaction in ESL/EFL. In Z. Dörnyei & R. Schmidt (Eds.), *Motivation and second language acquisition* (Technical Report #23, pp. 213–237). Honolulu: University of Hawai'i, Second Language Teaching and Curriculum Center.

of language learners, and few studies have been reported in the applied linguistics literature.

Jacques (this volume) compared the sources of motivation of foreign language learners and language teachers in a US university sample and reported that teacher motivations grouped generally into clusters including a job satisfaction component (subsuming both extrinsic and intrinsic rewards); a career orientation (e.g., "teaching this course is important to my career development"); a perseverance orientation (e.g., "I work hard at all aspects of language teaching, even though not all of them are equally pleasant"); and an ability cluster (e.g., "I am good at teaching grammar, pronunciation, reading and writing, etc."). However, the number of subjects in this study (21 teachers of Spanish, French, and Portuguese) was too small to allow the use of factor analysis or other techniques to uncover the underlying structure of teacher motivation in a more definitive way.

The most relevant work in the applied linguistics field has been that of Pennington and her students (Pennington, 1991, 1995; Pennington & Ho, 1995; Pennington & Riley, 1991; Wong & Pennington, 1993), who have approached the topic of teacher motivation through the perspective of job satisfaction in ESL, with a view to deriving implications for both program management and the development of English language teaching as a profession. Pennington and Riley (1991) found that ESL practitioners (a sample of TESOL members) were moderately satisfied with their jobs as a whole but expressed varying degrees of satisfaction with individual job facets. The areas of compensation, opportunities for advancement, and some aspects of administrative oversight were given generally lower ratings, while the most positive responses concerned the areas of human relations and the inherent rewards of teaching. Pennington and Ho (1995) used the Maslach Burnout Inventory with a sample of randomly selected members of TESOL, finding no indication of career burnout. Ratings on key variables were lower than for other groups surveyed using the same instrument, including K–12 teachers, social service workers, attorneys, and police, although the ESL group scored somewhat higher on an emotional exhaustion scale than several other groups. Pennington (1991) concluded that "For those who choose to go into ESL, there appears to be a reasonable match between their characteristics and aspirations and the inherent characteristics and requirements of ESL work" (p. 81). However, Pennington did not attempt to measure this relationship directly.

Although there have been relatively few studies of language teacher motivation, the motivation of teachers in other fields has been more extensively researched, and workplace motivation and job satisfaction have been the subject of a great deal of research in the human resource field (Pennington, 1995, provides a detailed review of the literature). Several studies of teacher motivation are relevant to the present study. Although the traditional view is that the structure of the teaching occupation favors the distribution of intrinsic (psychic) rewards that come from working with students rather than extrinsic (material) ones (Lortie, 1975), Ames and Ames (1984) identified three systems of teacher motivation, which they called an ability system (related to self-esteem), a task mastery system (focused on the accomplishment of objectives), and a moral responsibility system (concern for student welfare). Barnabe and Burns (1994) studied Québec teachers (not specifically language teachers), using a model positing three conditions for work satisfaction: experiencing the work as worthwhile, experiencing responsibility for results, and understanding how effectively they are performing.

Conley and Levinson (1993) examined interrelationships between work redesign (e.g., the establishment of career ladders), work rewards, values, and teacher job satisfaction. Conley and Levinson found differences between more and less experienced teachers in whether work redesign led to more satisfaction. A finding relevant to the study reported here is that Conley and Levinson looked at relationships between work values (what is "important" to individuals) and work satisfaction, as well as between work rewards (what one actually gets from a job) and satisfaction. Values were found to be unrelated to satisfaction, while rewards were highly correlated.

This is an interesting finding with respect to a number of theories of motivation in the workplace that can generally be labeled as process theories. Process theories, which are currently predominant in the organizational behavior literature, describe the ways in which motivation arises in the workplace and how people go about satisfying their needs (Moorhead & Griffin, 1995). Job satisfaction in these theories is viewed as contingent upon the interaction of work experiences and personal values (Hackman & Lawler, 1971; Kalleberg, 1977; Loscocco, 1989; Martin & Shehan, 1989; Mortimer, 1979; Mortimer & Lorence, 1979; Mottaz, 1987). These theories suggest that the essence of job satisfaction lies in the fit or congruence between the person and the job. The point seems obvious enough. People work for different reasons. Some want money, some, security. Some find their life's meaning in their jobs, while others want a job that is not too demanding and allows time for family and other concerns. The fit hypothesis posits that those who attach the most importance to specific rewards will be happiest if they get them and unhappiest if they do not. The fit hypothesis is assumed in many studies of job satisfaction. For example, Pennington (1991), writing about ESL teachers, commented that "The perception of the fit between these underlying values and expectations, on the one hand, and the reality of the work situation, on the other, gives rise to the complex emotional response, or affective reaction, that is here referred to as work satisfaction" (p. 60). However, Conley and Levinson's (1993) finding that rewards but not values predicted teacher job satisfaction casts some doubt on this hypothesis.

Another hypothesis investigated in this study is Herzberg's dual-structure hypothesis, which holds that different sets of factors lead to satisfaction and dissatisfaction. Herzberg (1968; Herzberg, Mausner, & Snyderman, 1959) has argued that motivational factors intrinsic to the work itself (such as achievement and recognition) determine satisfaction; when absent, the result is not dissatisfaction but merely lack of satisfaction. Dissatisfaction, on the other hand, is held to be affected by factors that are extrinsic to the work itself, such as job security, pay, and fringe benefits. According to this theory, low pay and lack of security lead to dissatisfaction; good pay and security lead not to satisfaction, however, but merely to the absence of dissatisfaction. Does this apply to ESL/EFL teachers as well?

The following research questions were addressed in this study:

1. What aspects of work are most important to ESL/EFL teachers?

2. What sorts of rewards do these teachers get from their current jobs?

3. How satisfied are ESL/EFL teachers with their jobs and their careers?

4. Do values or rewards (or the interaction between them) predict job and career satisfaction better?

5. Are the aspects contributing to job/career satisfaction the same or different from those leading to dissatisfaction?

METHOD

Subjects of the study were 107 experienced ESL/EFL teachers, 70 from Egypt and 37 from Hawai'i, who completed a questionnaire. Only teachers currently providing direct English language instruction to learners in the classroom were included (administrators, supervisors, former teachers, etc., were excluded). Subjects were approached in a variety of educational settings known to the researchers. Participation was voluntary in all cases.

The instrument used consisted of a questionnaire requesting the following information:

- Biographical data, including gender, age, qualifications, teaching situation (full or part-time, one or more employers), years of teaching experience, and level/stage of students taught

- Responses to four open-ended questions:
  1. Think of the educational organization where you work and list the major factors that have a positive influence on your job.
  2. List the major factors that have a negative influence on your job.
  3. Think of a time when, in your relationship with your supervisor (principal, department head, or another title), something very favorable and positive happened that made you feel good about your teaching and your relationship with your supervisor.
  4. Think of a time when, in your relationship with your supervisor (principal, department head, or another title), something very unfavorable and negative happened that did not make you feel good about your teaching and your relationship with your supervisor.

- Responses to a series of 36 statements concerning pay/working conditions, recognition and prestige, the need for power/autonomy, self-esteem/self-actualization/growth needs, achievement needs, affiliation needs, and needs for intrinsic satisfaction. Subjects were asked to rate each statement on a 5-point Likert scale according to "how important this aspect of work is to you personally."

- Responses to a series of 36 statements, matched to those in the previous section except that subjects were asked to indicate (again on a 5-point Likert scale) their agreement or disagreement concerning how each relates to their current job. For example, in the "values" section, subjects were asked to indicate the importance of "having a superior who gives clear guidance," and in the following "rewards" section, they agreed or disagreed with the statement "My supervisor gives clear guidance."

- Responses to a final set of four questions dealing with job and career satisfaction, two phrased positively ("I am truly satisfied with my present job/my profession as a teacher") and two phrased negatively ("I will change my career/job if I have the opportunity to do so").

A copy of the survey instrument appears in Appendix A.

RESULTS

PARTICIPANT DEMOGRAPHICS

As indicated above, two thirds (70/107) of our respondents were Egyptian EFL teachers; one third were ESL teachers in Hawai'i. In both samples, approximately 70% were female and two thirds were currently employed in programs teaching adults (i.e., university students or older), while one third taught at lower levels. About half of our teachers were full time, with the remainder split almost equally between holders of one part-time job and holders of two or more part-time jobs. As noted above, our sample of respondents represents experienced teachers. The mean number of years of experience was 10 for the Hawai'i ESL teachers and 15 for the Egyptian EFL teachers. Virtually all were "qualified," with credentials ranging from undergraduate qualifications (in ESL/EFL or education) to RSA certificates, MA degrees, and a few doctoral degrees. Given the small numbers of respondents in many of these categories, these demographic data were not used as variables in the analysis.

TEACHER VALUES AND TEACHING REWARDS

Our subjects think that most of the characteristics of employment mentioned in the survey instrument are important, and as indicated in Table 1, 15 items received overall means of 4.5 or higher, where 4 meant *somewhat important*, and 5 meant *very important*, while only 5 items were rated lower than the 3.0 neutral or *no opinion* point. These responses also confirm the stereotype that teachers as a group are altruistic and more concerned with the intrinsic, classroom based aspects of their profession than with its extrinsic aspects. Teachers in both Egypt and Hawai'i ranked "Really helping my students to learn English," "Having a job in which I can perform to the best of my ability," and "Being treated fairly in my organization" among the top five in importance. Having good relationships with students, colleagues, and supervisors was considered very important, as were student and supervisor evaluations.

Table 1: Teacher values

What's most important to ESL/EFL teachers? (means>4.5)	
Having a job in which I can perform to the best of my ability	4.883
Really helping my students to learn English	4.864
Having a job that is enjoyable and stimulating	4.814
Being fairly treated in my organization	4.806
Having the freedom to do what is necessary in my teaching to do a good job	4.767
Having a job in which I can learn and develop my abilities to my full potential	4.738
Being allowed to deal creatively with students' problems	4.699
Having a supervisor who is responsive to suggestions and grievances	4.650
Having a manageable work load	4.592
Having a supervisor who gives clear guidance	4.578
Having a friendly relationship with my students	4.670
Being evaluated positively by my supervisors	4.670
Having good relationships with colleagues	4.641
Having a good relationship with my supervisor(s)	4.563
Being evaluated positively by my students	4.553
What's least important to ESL/EFL teachers? (means<4.0)	
Fringe benefits	3.98
Having a profession that is prestigious	3.932
Being promoted to a senior supervisory job at some point in my career	3.476
Having a prestigious job title	3.369
Having a good relationship with my students' parents	3.08

In contrast, teachers in both Egypt and Hawai'i ranked having a prestigious career and job title and being promoted to a senior supervisory position among the five least important aspects of work to them personally. The fact that "Having a good relationship with my students' parents" was ranked last in importance by teachers in both locations probably reflects the high percentage of teachers of adult language learners in our sample.

It is probably a good thing that teachers value the intrinsic aspects of work over extrinsic factors, because —as shown in Table 2— ESL/EFL teaching provides more intrinsic than extrinsic rewards. Teachers in both locations identified job security, fringe benefits, and prospects for promotion as the three things that they most definitely do not have in their current jobs.

What rewards do ESL/EFL teachers get from their jobs? (means>4.0)	
I have good relationships with colleagues	4.495
I know that I am really helping my students to learn English	4.485
I work for a reputable educational organization	4.447
My students evaluate me positively	4.402
I have a good relationship with my supervisor(s)	4.388
My work is enjoyable and stimulating	4.257
My supervisor evaluates me positively	4.225
My job is challenging	4.188
I am allowed sufficient freedom to do what is necessary in my teaching in order to do a good job	4.165
My supervisor is responsive to suggestions and grievances	4.097
I have a manageable work load	4.07
My job provides scope to learn and develop my abilities to my full potential	4.01
My supervisor gives clear guidance	4.00
My job provides sufficient variety in tasks/type of activity	4.00
What rewards do ESL/EFL teachers *not* get from their jobs? (means<3.5)	
I am included in my organization's goal-setting process	3.267
I have a good relationship with my students' parents	3.237
Independence and initiative are rewarded	3.223
I am able to introduce changes without going through a lot of red tape	3.176
I have a good salary	3.167
I have good job security	2.647
I have good fringe benefits	2.663
I have prospects for promotion	2.696

Teachers do receive lots of rewards from their current jobs, though we note that none of the items in this section received group means higher than 4.5. The rewards that teachers get in their current jobs are in most cases congruent with what teachers say is important. Teachers agree with the statement that "I know that I am really helping my students to learn English" (which was also ranked as very important by teachers in both locations), and teachers in both locations strongly agree that they have friendly relationships with their students, also considered very important. There are some discrepancies between the ratings for importance and those for rewards received, however. Fair treatment and the ability to perform to the best of one's ability (both identified as very high in importance), for example, do not emerge as the most common rewards of ESL/EFL teaching jobs. On the other hand, teachers strongly agree that they work for reputable educational organizations and that their jobs are challenging, factors which were not ranked especially high in importance.

FACTOR ANALYSES

As implied above, the rankings of what teachers consider important and what teachers say they get from their jobs in terms of rewards showed no major discrepancies between EFL teachers in Egypt and ESL teachers in Hawai'i. This was somewhat surprising to us but suggests that quite a bit of what it means to be a teacher, perhaps particularly a language teacher, is common across national boundaries and cultural institutions. Considering this fact, the fact that both native and non-native speaking teachers of English were known to be represented in both groups (although we did not elicit this information) and the fact that factor analysis is licensed only with samples of 100 or more, we did not factor analyze the responses from the Egypt and Hawai'i-based teachers separately but treated them as a single group.

Questionnaire results were factor analyzed using principle components analysis and varimax rotation (oblique). In factor analyzing the responses, we considered factor analyses with as few as two and as many as six factors. Conley & Levinson (1993) found that both teacher values and teaching rewards could be reasonably accounted for by a factor analysis with a simple two-factor solution: extrinsic versus intrinsic. With this in mind, the first analysis we carried out was to see whether a similarly clean explicit/intrinsic split would emerge in this study for both values and rewards. However, a two-factor solution proved unsatisfactory for our data, accounting for only 32% of the variance in value questions and resulting in uninterpretable factors for work rewards. After examination of Scree plots and considering only factors contributing 5% or more of variance, a five-factor solution was chosen for work values that accounts for 50% of variance. For work rewards, a four-factor solution was chosen that accounted for 51% of the variance.

Factor analysis of values

The following items from that part of the questionnaire asking respondents to rate the importance of various factors in their work situation load on Factor 1:

.754	Being treated fairly in my organization
.738	Working with other teachers as a team
.686	Having a supervisor who is responsive to suggestions and grievances
.615	Having good relationships with colleagues
.609	Having a friendly relationship with my students
.581	Having a good relationship with my students' parents
.550	Having contact with professionals in the field of English language teaching
.518	Being able to introduce changes without going through a lot of red tape
.506	Really helping my students to learn English
.470	Having sufficient variety in tasks/type of activity
.450	Having a good relationship with my supervisor(s)
.430	Being included in the goal setting process

Factor 1 seems to represent the need for affiliation, or a Relationship Orientation. The items loading on this factor are primarily social in nature, concerning relationships with other teachers, supervisors, students, and professionals. Concerns for fair treatment and being included in goal setting can also be viewed as social relationship variables.

The following items load on Factor 2:

.722	Fringe benefits
.663	Having a profession that is prestigious
.618	Job security
.622	Earning a good salary
.581	Being promoted to a senior supervisory job at some point in my career
.667	Having a prestigious job title

Factor 2 clearly represents Extrinsic Motivation. All of the items that load on this factor are external to the classroom.

The following items load on Factor 3, which represents the need for autonomy and self-determination in one's work setting:

.762	Having the freedom to do what is necessary in my teaching to do a good job
.685	Being allowed to deal creatively with students' problems
.708	Being able to work independently and use my own initiative
.499	Being recognized for my teaching accomplishments
.427	Having a job that is fun

Four items load on Factor 4. They seem to represent Self-realization and personal growth. These are all directed at internal satisfaction needs, and none of the items mention other people:

.801	Having a job in which I can learn and develop my abilities to my full potential
.698	Having a challenging job
.665	Having a job in which I can perform to the best of my ability
.557	Having a job that is enjoyable and stimulating

The items loading on Factor 5 primarily represent needs that are satisfied through Institutional Support:

.694	Having a supervisor who gives clear guidance
.666	Being evaluated positively by my supervisors
.612	Having a job in which I am relaxed and have peace of mind
.642	Having clear rules and procedures
.554	Having a prestigious job title

.541	Having flexible working hours
.451	Having a profession that is prestigious
.440	Working for a reputable educational organization
.424	Having flexible working hours

Respondents who score high on this factor emphasize the need for institutional support from a reputable institution, including guidance, clear rules and procedures, and (favorable) evaluations by supervisors. People scoring high on this factor might be characterized as somewhat dependent and not concerned with internal growth. Feeling relaxed and having peace of mind are viewed as more important. This factor shares a certain similarity with Factor 2 (extrinsic rewards), though the rewards in this case have more to do with prestige than money.

Factor analysis of rewards (characteristics of current job)

Of the questionnaire items dealing with the rewards of English teaching, the following items loaded on Factor 1:

.826	My supervisor is responsive to suggestions and grievances
.853	I have a good relationship with my supervisor(s)
.738	I am fairly treated in the organization
.713	My supervisor gives clear guidance
.648	My supervisor evaluates me positively
.643	I have a manageable work load
.603	There are clear rules and procedures at work
.533	I'm relaxed and have peace of mind in my job

The items loading on this factor suggest that one way in which a job can be good (or not) depends on the administration of the school or program, including having clear guidance, rules and procedures, and flexible working hours, with a very strong emphasis on the role of the supervisor. Working within a well organized program and having a good boss are linked to having peace of mind in one's job. We label this factor of job rewards Good Management.

The following items load on Factor 2:

.723	I have prospects for promotion
.712	I have good fringe benefits
.620	Teaching accomplishments are recognized
.575	The emphasis is on team work
.560	I have good job security
.542	Teaching English is a prestigious profession
.536	I have a good relationship with my students' parents
.511	I am included in my organization's goal-setting process

| .502 | Independence and initiative are rewarded |
| .438 | Creativity is emphasized and rewarded |

We have labeled this factor of job rewards as a Professional Position. The items loading on it include extrinsic rewards (recognition, security, fringe benefits, opportunities for promotion) but are not limited to that, since this factor also includes an emphasis on creativity, independence and initiative, a team work orientation, and inclusion in goal-setting. While Factor 1 represents one way in which an institution can exhibit quality management (through support and supervision), this represents another (by encouraging staff development and participation).

Factor 3 includes the following items:

.774	I have a friendly relationship with my students
.745	I know that I am really helping my students to learn English
.705	I have good relationships with colleagues
.489	Teaching English is a prestigious profession
.443	My students evaluate me positively
.423	I work for a reputable educational organization

This factor indicates that another major source of job rewards is one's Students. A good job can be characterized according to this factor as working for a reputable organization with good students.

Factor 4 includes the following items:

.834	My job is challenging
.795	I have sufficient opportunities for contact with professionals in the field of English teaching
.766	My job provides scope to learn and develop my abilities to my full potential
.681	I am allowed sufficient freedom to do what is necessary in my teaching in order to do a good job.
.666	My job provides sufficient variety in tasks/type of activity
.622	My work is enjoyable and stimulating
.602	My job is fun
.496	I have a job in which I can perform to the best of my ability
.421	I receive frequent enough feedback about the effectiveness of my performance

This factor indicates that in addition to working for a well-managed institution or program, the benefits of a professional position, and rewards gained from one's students, another source of rewards in English teaching can come from having a Challenging Job. Such jobs encourage creativity, provide scope to learn, and allow one to perform to the best of one's ability. Such jobs are enjoyable, stimulating, and fun.

CAREER AND JOB SATISFACTION

In general, ESL/EFL teachers assign higher ratings when they are asked to rate some aspect of work in importance (the overall mean for all value items was 4.397, where 4=*somewhat important* and 5=*very important*) than when they are asked to agree with a statement that they get such a reward from their work (the overall mean for all reward items was 3.804, where 3=*no opinion or neutral* and 4=*agree*). This may be merely human nature — perhaps it is natural to be more enthusiastic about what one would like than what one has — but it may indicate discrepancy between values and rewards as perceived by teachers.

The teachers in our sample also seem to be somewhat more satisfied with their career choice than with the specific jobs they now have. We created a Career Happiness index by averaging ratings on the statement "I am truly satisfied with my profession as a teacher" with the ratings (reverse scored) on the statement "I will change my career if I have the opportunity to do so." By this measure, teachers seem reasonably happy with their careers as teachers (mean=3.948), compared to average scores for a similarly constructed measure of Job Happiness (mean=3.481).

Which of the different aspects of work related values and rewards discussed above influence job and career happiness most strongly? Recall that the "fit" hypothesis predicts that individual ratings of both values and perceived rewards — and especially the interaction between them — should determine job satisfaction, while more traditional theories emphasize the importance of rewards alone. In order to address this issue, we carried out Pearson product-moment correlations between job and career happiness scores and several possible predictor variables,[1] including subjects' average ratings on all "importance" items, their ratings of rewards associated with their current jobs, and what we call a Discrepancy Index, consisting of the ratings of importance of specific job attributes minus the ratings for whether one's current job provides those rewards. For example, if an individual rated "earning a good salary" as *very important* and strongly disagreed with the statement "I have a good salary," that person would have a value score of 5 for this variable, a reward score of 1, and a discrepancy score of 4. Another individual might rate having a good salary as *somewhat unimportant* and also strongly disagree with the statement "I have a good salary;" that person would be assigned a value score of 2, a reward score of 1 for this variable, and a discrepancy score of 1. We reasoned that, if the fit hypothesis is correct, there should be a stronger (negative) correlation between job/career happiness and the Discrepancy Index than between happiness and the various reward measures alone. The results of this analysis are shown in Table 3.

---

[1] It may be noted that we did not use the outputs from the factor analyses reported in the previous section as inputs for these analyses. Since those factor analyses produced a five-factor solution for values and a four-factor solution for rewards, it was not possible to compute a measure of discrepancy by subtracting one set of measures from the other.

Table 3: Predictors of job and career happiness

	career happiness	job happiness
career happiness	1.000	.732*
job happiness	.732*	1.000
values	.192 (NS)	.188 (NS)
rewards	.505*	.548*
discrepancy	−.402*	−.452*

* $p<.01$

Correlations between career and job happiness and average ratings for all value items, average ratings for all reward items, and a discrepancy measure (value/importance rating minus reward rating)

As shown in Table 3, for this sample of ESL/EFL teachers, it appears as though values (importance ratings) have relatively little effect on Job or Career Happiness compared to both rewards and the discrepancy between values and rewards. The average importance ratings for all 36 value items correlated with Career Happiness at only .192 (p=.0715, n.s.) and with Job Happiness at only .188 (p=.0779, n.s.), whereas the average ratings on reward items correlated with Career Happiness with meaningful and significant coefficients of .505 and .548 respectively. It should also be noted that Career and Job Happiness were highly correlated (.732) with each other.

We also looked at all correlations between individual item scores (both values and rewards) and the scores for Career and Job Happiness, once again finding that rewards have a strong relationship to happiness, values a minor one. Because this analysis involved a large number of correlations, we set a relatively stringent value of alpha at $p<.01$. By this criterion, only two value items ("having flexible working hours" and "having contacts with professionals in the field") were significantly related to Career Happiness, and only four value items ("having flexible working hours," "having clear procedures," "having a supervisor who gives clear guidance," and "working for a reputable educational organization") were significantly related to Job Happiness. In contrast, 21 of 36 reward items were meaningfully and significantly correlated with Career Happiness, and 18 of 36 reward items were significantly correlated with Job Happiness. Rewards correlating with both Career and Job Happiness include items from each of the four clusters of items identified in the factor analysis for rewards, although it is very interesting to note that the most consistently high correlations are with items that load on rewards Factor 4 (challenge and growth), including "My job provides scope to learn and develop my abilities to my full potential" (.601 correlation with Career Happiness and .476 with Job Happiness), "I have a job in which I can perform to the best of my ability" (.510 correlation with Career Happiness and .593 with Job Happiness), "My work is enjoyable and stimulating" (.433 correlation with Career Happiness and .496 with Job Happiness), and "My job provides sufficient variety" (.427 correlation with Career Happiness and .408 with Job Happiness).

Since our earlier analysis of values indicated that internal rewards such as having a job in which one can perform to the best of one's ability and developing one's full potential are very important to these teachers and since we have just indicated that whether or not these rewards are obtained from one's job predicts Job and Career Happiness, this might suggest some support for the fit hypothesis, as does the fact that (as shown in Table 3), there are significant correlations between the overall Discrepancy Index and both Career and Job Happiness. On the other hand, several variables that were rated as much less important by teachers, for example, having a profession that is prestigious and having a prestigious job title, also correlate significantly with both Job and Career Happiness. Recalling our reasoning that if the fit hypothesis is correct, then correlations between the Discrepancy Index and Job and Career Happiness than the comparable correlations using rewards alone, this is clearly not the case. The average of reward ratings correlates .505 with Career Happiness and .548 with Job Happiness, while the Discrepancy Index correlates lower at −.402 and −.452, respectively. Moreover, the overall average for rewards and the Discrepancy Index correlate highly with each other (−.759). These averages are not independent, and it is doubtful that there is any effect for the discrepancy between a value and a reward beyond the effect of the reward alone. The same picture emerges when we look at individual items to see the effects of rewards and the discrepancy measure. For 8 of 36 items, there is a significant (negative) correlation between the Discrepancy Index and Career Happiness, and for 11 items there is a significant correlation with Job Happiness. However, these items are a subset of those for which a significant correlation was found for rewards and Career/Job Happiness, and in every case the correlation is lower. We conclude, therefore, that the fit hypothesis is not supported by our data.

Our data also fail to support Herzberg's dual structure hypothesis, which claims that the factors contributing to satisfaction are different from those contributing to dissatisfaction. It is true, as we have noted, that these teachers are most satisfied with the more intrinsic rewards of teaching in their jobs and least satisfied (most dissatisfied) with the extrinsic rewards they receive, but this seems to reflect the rewards that teaching does and does not offer, rather than an inherent link between lower-level needs and the range between dissatisfied and neutral and between higher-level needs and the range neutral to satisfied. Because our satisfaction scales are continuous, from satisfied (*strongly agree* that I am truly satisfied with my current job) to dissatisfied (*strongly disagree* that I am truly satisfied with my current job), the fact that we have quite robust correlations with a large number of job-related rewards suggests that those rewards do not relate to just one end of the satisfaction-dissatisfaction continuum.

In order to pursue this question in a different way, we looked at the answers to the open-ended questions on our questionnaire. Recall that we asked our informants to list separately those factors that have positive and negative influences on their jobs, as well as to describe critical incidents that made them feel good or bad about their teaching and their relationship with a supervisor. The question we considered was whether different aspects of job and career were mentioned frequently only in connection with happiness or unhappiness rather than both.

For the most part, the answer to this question is "no." Of course, individual teachers cited different reasons for satisfaction and dissatisfaction with their particular jobs. For example, one teacher might mention having supportive colleagues and enthusiastic students as positive factors and lots of paperwork and large classes as negatives. But another teacher might mention small classes as a positive aspect of their job while reporting dissatisfaction with colleagues and unmotivated students. Students, colleagues, school or program administrative support, resources, and job conditions were all mentioned frequently as sources of both satisfaction and dissatisfaction. It also seems that most of the items on our questionnaire were related to things that informants bring up when asked more open-ended questions, although there were exceptions to this. None of our informants mentioned task variety as an important job attribute (either positive or negative) or, surprisingly, really helping students to learn. This might be because teachers simply assumed that they are in the language classroom to help their students learn and therefore neglected to mention it. There was also one variable that was not included in our questionnaire that did show up repeatedly in the responses to the open-ended questions: respect. Our questionnaire asked about prestige (a sociological variable), but many of our informants mentioned respect (a more interpersonal variable), especially in connection with their recounting of critical incidents. Incidents showing that a supervisor listens to, appreciates, and validates the opinions of teachers were often reported, and many respondents related stories in which their supervisor responded to a request, asked them for advice, took a suggestion seriously and implemented it, or otherwise showed respect and trust towards the teacher. Being treated without respect, as expendable, or being subjected to public embarrassment were equally often mentioned as causes of deep dissatisfaction.

CONCLUSIONS

Given the general lack of information in the applied linguistics literature concerning what makes English language teachers tick —their motivations, their goals, and their views on what teaching does and should offer to people who make a career of it— we view this study as exploratory and think that we have only brushed the surface of understanding what it means to be a teacher. However, we do think that we have established several basic findings for a limited sample of experienced teachers in two locations. First, not all teachers want the same things from their teaching jobs and careers. As a group, teachers emphasize the importance of intrinsic over extrinsic rewards, but there is considerable variation. One cluster of teacher values or needs concerns relationships of all kinds. Another concerns the extrinsic values of salary, security, fringe benefits, and so on. Other clusters of values relate to autonomy and self-realization (separate factors in our analysis), and teachers also vary in the extent to which they profess a need for institutional support. Second, ESL/EFL teaching jobs vary and provide different rewards, which also cluster into identifiable factors. One job may be better because it represents good management, another because it brings all the trappings of a professional position (including salary, recognition, and an emphasis on creativity); other jobs may lack these rewards but provide room for personal growth or the rewards of working with enthusiastic students.

Although the factors that indicate what (different) teachers think is important overlap considerably with the rewards that (different) jobs have to offer, values and rewards do not match precisely. The most interesting difference we found was that there is a value cluster associated with relationships of all kinds, but there do not appear to be jobs that provide all the elements of that cluster. Instead, relationships with one's students appears as part of a cluster that is all about students, while relationships with one's supervisor is more commonly related to the overall management of an institution or program.

We have also explored relationships between our variables of values and rewards, together with a Discrepancy Index that we created, and career and job satisfaction. Somewhat to our surprise, we found that while job rewards were highly correlated with job and career satisfaction, work values were not so correlated, and the correlations between happiness and our Discrepancy Index seemed to be spurious, attributable to the influence of rewards alone. That is, we cannot say much as a result of this study about whether a particular person will be happy as an English teacher by considering what aspects of work they value most highly, but we can predict their job and career happiness reasonably well by considering the rewards of a particular job. We think that there is a positive way to look at this finding. English language teachers are idealistic. However, just like anyone else, they will not be happy with a job or career that only fulfills their most idealistic needs. They also expect and demand respect, fairness, reasonable extrinsic rewards, and good management.

One methodological limitation of this study derives from the fact that we factor analyzed the results from teachers in Hawai'i and in Egypt as one group. Future research should certainly consider a much larger sample of English language teachers and might be more concerned with differences among teachers in different locations (to that end, readers should feel free to use the scales we created as instruments for additional studies), but our major concern here has been with the construct of English language teacher, not Egyptian or American teachers. On the other hand, our sample represents experienced career teachers with impressive qualifications. Quite a different picture might emerge from a study focusing on mostly young, untrained, and short term teachers such as the British EFL teachers surveyed in Blackie (1990). Another limitation, we think, is related to the quantitative methodology used in this study. Although we have not found support for either the fit hypothesis or Herzberg's dual source hypothesis, this could be attributable to the fact that we have looked at the interplay of variables across a fairly large number of subjects. We suspect that longitudinal qualitative case studies or studies of a small number of individuals might find closer relationships between values and career and job satisfaction than we have found, since our methodology has necessarily eliminated life histories and idiosyncratic patterns in favor of general trends. Finally, we have not even begun to approach the interesting question of how the worlds of teachers and students intersect with respect to motivation, goals, values, and rewards. In addition to the various things that teachers can do to motivate learners (see, for example, Noels, this volume), it is widely believed that teachers who are themselves highly motivated inspire their students to be motivated as well. Is this so, or do students respond more to personality traits than to perceptions of teacher motivation that might not be accurate in any case? We have only begun to look at what motivates teachers and have not yet turned to the possible impact of these influences on learners.

REFERENCES

Ames, C., & Ames, R. (1984). Systems of student and teacher motivation: Toward a qualitative definition. *Journal of Educational Psychology, 76,* 535–556.

Barnabe, C., & Burns, M. (1994). Teacher's job characteristics and motivation. *Educational Research, 36,* 171–185.

Blackie, D. (1990). *English language teacher supply: A pilot report.* London: British Council EFL Services.

Conley, S., & Levinson, R. (1993). Teacher work redesign and job satisfaction. *Educational Administration Quarterly, 29,* 453–478.

Hackman, J. R., & Lawler, E. E. (1971). Employee reactions to job characteristics. *Journal of Applied Psychology Monographs, 55,* 259–86.

Herzberg, F. (1968). One more time: How do you motivate employees? *Harvard Business Review,* January-February, 53–62.

Herzberg, F., Mausner, B., & Synderman, B. (1959). *The motivation to work.* New York: Wiley.

Jacques, S. R. (2001). Preferences for instructional activities and motivation: A comparison of student and teacher perspectives. In Z. Dörnyei & R. Schmidt (Eds.), *Motivation and second language acquisition* (Technical Report #23, pp. 185–211). Honolulu: University of Hawai'i, Second Language Teaching and Curriculum Center.

Kalleberg, A. L. (1977). Work values and job rewards: A theory of job satisfaction. *American Sociological Review, 42,* 124–43.

Lortie, D. (1975). *Schoolteacher: A sociological study.* Chicago: University of Chicago Press.

Loscocco, K. A. (1989). The instrumentally oriented factory worker: Myth or reality? *Sociology of Work and Occupations, 16,* 3–25.

Martin, J. K., & Shehan, C. L. (1989). Education and job satisfaction: The influences of gender, wage-earning status, and job values. *Sociology of Work and Occupations, 16,* 184–99.

Moorhead, G., & Griffin, R. W. (1995). *Organizational behavior: Managing people and organizations.* Boston: Houghton Mifflin.

Mortimer, J. T. (1979). *Changing attitudes toward work.* Scarsdale, NY: Work in America Institute.

Mortimer, J. T., & Lorence, J. (1979). Work experience and occupational value socialization: A longitudinal study. *American Journal of Sociology, 84,* 1361–1385.

Mottaz, C. J. (1987). Age and work satisfaction. *Sociology of Work and Occupations, 14*, 387–409.

Nikolov, R. C. (2001). A study of unsuccessful language learners. In Z. Dörnyei & R. Schmidt (Eds.), *Motivation and second language acquisition* (Technical Report #23, pp. 149–169). Honolulu: University of Hawai'i, Second Language Teaching and Curriculum Center.

Noels, K. (2001). New orientations in language learning motivation: Towards a model of intrinsic, extrinsic, and integrative orientations and motivation. In Z. Dörnyei & R. Schmidt (Eds.), *Motivation and second language acquisition* (Technical Report #23, pp. 43–68). Honolulu: University of Hawai'i, Second Language Teaching and Curriculum Center.

Pennington, M. C. (1991). Work satisfaction and the ESL profession. *Language, Culture and Curriculum, 4*, 59–86.

Pennington, M. C. (1995). Work satisfaction, motivation, and commitment in teaching English as a second language. Unpublished manuscript, University of Luton, UK. (ERIC Document Reproduction Service No. Ed 404 850)

Pennington, M. C., & Ho, B. (1995). Do ESL educators suffer from burnout? *Prospect, 10*, 41–53.

Pennington, M. C., & Riley, P. V. (1991). A survey of job satisfaction in ESL: ESL educators respond to the Minnesota Satisfaction Questionnaire. *University of Hawai'i Working Papers in ESL, 10*(1), 37–56.

Schmidt, R., Boraie, D., & Kassabgy, O. (1996). Foreign language motivation: Internal structure and external connections. In R. Oxford (Ed.), *Language learning motivation: Pathways to the new century* (Technical Report #11, pp. 9–70). Honolulu: University of Hawai'i, Second Language Teaching & Curriculum Center.

Wong, M., & Pennington, M. C. (1993). *Are resource class English teachers satisfied with their work?* (Research Report No. 31). Hong Kong: City Polytechnic of Hong Kong, English Department.

THE TEACHER'S WORLD SURVEY

The purpose of this survey is to identify some of the factors that influence, motivate, and empower English language teachers in EFL and ESL settings. The questionnaire concerns both job satisfaction and career satisfaction. There is no known risk associated with participation in this research. Participation is entirely voluntary. Data from the questionnaires that follow will be anonymous. Names of participants will not be connected to questionnaire information. This is not an evaluation of any language teaching program, and the identity of the program in which you work will not be connected to the data.

At the present time, we are asking that this questionnaire be completed *only* by individuals who are *currently teaching English*. You are eligible to participate if you are currently providing direct instruction to learners of English as a second or foreign language, either full or part time, at any institution or in any language program.

The survey consists of three sections. Section One consists of four open-ended questions, for which you are invited to respond in as much detail as you wish. Section Two consists of 36 statements each followed by a five-point scale on which you are requested to indicate the *extent of importance* that each statement has for you. Section Three consists of 40 statements specifically related to the organization or program in which you currently work. If you work for more than one organization or program, please *focus on one only*.

We greatly appreciate your contribution. If you are interested in finding out the results of this survey, you may do so by sending an email message to Richard Schmidt at schmidt@hawaii.edu.

BIODATA

Gender: male _____ female _____

Age: _____

Academic degrees, diplomas, certificates: _____

_____

Qualifications for teaching English: _____

_____

Please indicate which situation applies to you:

_____ I am employed full time in one educational organization

_____ I am employed part time in one educational organization

_____ I am employed part time in two or more educational organization

_____ I am employed both full time in one educational organization plus part-time at one or more additional organizations

Total number of years of teaching experience: _____

Level/stage of the students you teach:

_____ primary/elementary school

_____ preparatory or middle school

_____ secondary/high school

_____ university students

_____ adult learners not currently in school

SECTION ONE

Think of the educational organization where you work and list the major factors that have a positive influence on your job.

_____

_____

_____

List the major factors that have a negative influence on your job.

_____

_____

_____

Think of a time when, in your relationship with your supervisor (principal, department head, or another title), something very favorable and positive happened that made you feel good about your teaching and your relationship with your supervisor.

_____

_____

_____

Think of a time when, in your relationship with your supervisor (principal, department head, or another title), something very unfavorable and negative happened that did not make you feel good about your teaching and your relationship with your supervisor.

_____

_____

_____

SECTION TWO

Rate each of the following according to _how important this aspect of work_ is to you personally. Indicate your response by circling a number on the scale below each item. The numbers on the scale correspond to the following:

5=very important
4=somewhat important
3=no opinion
2=somewhat unimportant
1=not important at all

1. Earning a good salary

    1   2   3   4   5

2. Having flexible working hours

    1   2   3   4   5

3. Job security

    1   2   3   4   5

4. Fringe benefits

    1   2   3   4   5

5. Having clear rules and procedures

    1   2   3   4   5

6. Having a manageable work load

    1   2   3   4   5

7. Being fairly treated in my organization

    1   2   3   4   5

8. Having a supervisor who is responsive to suggestions and grievances

    1   2   3   4   5

9. Having a supervisor who gives clear guidance

    1   2   3   4   5

10. Having sufficient variety in tasks/type of activity

    1   2   3   4   5

11. Working for a reputable educational organization

    1   2   3   4   5

12. Having a profession that is prestigious

    1   2   3   4   5

13. Having a prestigious job title

    1   2   3   4   5

14. Having the freedom to do what is necessary in my teaching to do a good job

    1   2   3   4   5

15. Being allowed to deal creatively with students' problems

    1   2   3   4   5

16. Being included in the goal setting process

    1   2   3   4   5

17. Being able to introduce changes without going through a lot of red tape
    1   2   3   4   5
18. Having a job in which I can perform to the best of my ability
    1   2   3   4   5
19. Being promoted to a senior supervisory job at some point in my career
    1   2   3   4   5
20. Having a challenging job
    1   2   3   4   5
21. Having a job in which I can learn and develop my abilities to my full potential
    1   2   3   4   5
22. Having contact with professionals in the field of English language teaching
    1   2   3   4   5
23. Frequent feedback about the effectiveness of my performance
    1   2   3   4   5
24. Being able to work independently and use my own initiative
    1   2   3   4   5
25. Being evaluated positively by my students
    1   2   3   4   5
26. Being evaluated positively by my supervisors
    1   2   3   4   5
27. Being recognized for my teaching accomplishment
    1   2   3   4   5
28. Really helping my students to learn English
    1   2   3   4   5
29. Having good relationships with colleagues
    1   2   3   4   5
30. Having a friendly relationship with my students
    1   2   3   4   5
31. Having a good relationship with my supervisor(s)
    1   2   3   4   5
32. Having a good relationship with my students' parents
    1   2   3   4   5
33. Working with other teachers as a team
    1   2   3   4   5
34. Having a job that is enjoyable and stimulating
    1   2   3   4   5

35. Having a job that is fun

    1   2   3   4   5

36. Having a job in which I am relaxed and have peace of mind

    1   2   3   4   5

SECTION THREE

Read the following statements and think about each in relation to your current job. The numbers on the scale correspond to the following:

> 5=strongly agree
> 4=agree
> 3=no opinion
> 2=disagree
> 1=strongly disagree

1. I have a good salary.

    1   2   3   4   5

2. I have flexible working hours.

    1   2   3   4   5

3. I have good job security.

    1   2   3   4   5

4. I have good fringe benefits.

    1   2   3   4   5

5. There are clear rules and procedures at work.

    1   2   3   4   5

6. I have a manageable work load.

    1   2   3   4   5

7. I am fairly treated in the organization.

    1   2   3   4   5

8. My supervisor is responsive to suggestions and grievances.

    1   2   3   4   5

9. My supervisor gives clear guidance.

    1   2   3   4   5

10. My job provides sufficient variety in tasks/type of activity.

    1   2   3   4   5

11. I work for a reputable educational organization.

    1   2   3   4   5

12. Teaching English is a prestigious profession.

    1   2   3   4   5

13. My job title is satisfactory.

    1   2   3   4   5

14. I am allowed sufficient freedom to do what is necessary in my teaching in order to do a good job.

    1   2   3   4   5

15. Creativity is emphasized and rewarded.

    1   2   3   4   5

16. I am included in my organization's goal-setting process.

    1   2   3   4   5

17. I am able to introduce changes without going through a lot of red tape.

    1   2   3   4   5

18. I have a job in which I can perform to the best of my ability.

    1   2   3   4   5

19. I have prospects for promotion.

    1   2   3   4   5

20. My job is challenging.

    1   2   3   4   5

21. My job provides scope to learn and develop my abilities to my full potential.

    1   2   3   4   5

22. I have sufficient opportunities for contact with professionals in the field of English teaching.

    1   2   3   4   5

23. I receive frequent enough feedback about the effectiveness of my performance.

    1   2   3   4   5

24. Independence and initiative are rewarded.

    1   2   3   4   5

25. My students evaluate me positively.

    1   2   3   4   5

26. My supervisor evaluates me positively.

    1   2   3   4   5

27. Teaching accomplishments are recognized.

    1   2   3   4   5

28. I know that I am really helping my students to learn English.

    1   2   3   4   5

29. I have good relationships with colleagues.

    1   2   3   4   5

30. I have a friendly relationship with my students.
   1   2   3   4   5

31. I have a good relationship with my supervisor(s).
   1   2   3   4   5

32. I have a good relationship with my students' parents.
   1   2   3   4   5

33. The emphasis is on team work.
   1   2   3   4   5

34. My work is enjoyable and stimulating.
   1   2   3   4   5

35. My job is fun.
   1   2   3   4   5

36. I'm relaxed and have peace of mind in my job.
   1   2   3   4   5

37. I am truly satisfied with my profession as a teacher.
   1   2   3   4   5

38. I am truly satisfied with my present job.
   1   2   3   4   5

39. I will change my career if I have the opportunity to do so.
   1   2   3   4   5

40. I will change my job if I have the opportunity to do so.
   1   2   3   4   5

Paul F. Tremblay
Research Psychologists Press, London, Ontario, Canada

RESEARCH IN SECOND LANGUAGE LEARNING MOTIVATION: PSYCHOMETRIC AND RESEARCH DESIGN CONSIDERATIONS

Author's note

I would like to thank R. C. Gardner for his review and comments on this paper.

INTRODUCTION

There has been considerable progress in the field of second language learning (SLL) motivation. Research in that area has identified a number of motivation components and suggested how these may fit together. Among these are orientations or reasons for learning a second language, variables that describe the intensity and persistence of motivational behavior, classroom factors that may impact on student motivation, and variables related to the expectancy to achieve a desired goal such as self-efficacy and self-confidence. Several researchers, many of whom are authors in this book, have focused their research on trying to determine how these variables are interconnected. Some of them have postulated conceptual models; others have gone further and tested their models using statistical techniques such as structural equation modeling.

A number of review papers have also identified a number of motivation constructs from various areas of psychology such as social, educational, developmental, and organizational psychology that could be incorporated into the SLL area (e.g., Crookes & Schmidt, 1991; Dörnyei 1990; Oxford & Shearin, 1994; and Tremblay & Gardner, 1995). These reviews clearly indicate that there is a wide variety of variables that could be investigated to determine whether they can add to our understanding of motivation and provide additional predictive power in SLL. These include not only individual difference variables such as self-efficacy, perceived control, and causal attributions of success and failure, but also situational variables such as goal setting and feedback and classroom practices (e.g., competitive vs. cooperative goal structures; Ames & Archer, 1988). After reading these reviews, researchers may still be left with a fundamental question: How do we incorporate them into the SLL area?

The purpose of this chapter is to present a number of psychometric and research design considerations that relate to the above question. One fundamental problem that permeates the SLL research area or any area that studies individual difference variables is the lack of support for unequivocal causal statements. In a recent paper, Gardner (2000) has tackled this problem and suggested four ways to improve the

Tremblay, P. F. (2001). Research in second language learning motivation: Psychometric and research design considerations. In Z. Dörnyei & R. Schmidt (Eds.), *Motivation and second language acquisition* (Technical Report #23, pp. 239–255). Honolulu: University of Hawai'i, Second Language Teaching and Curriculum Center.

viability of causal models. These are a) construct measures, of the variables of interest, that have good measurement properties, b) assess the relationships of the variables with the major criteria using a variety of analytic procedures such as bivariate correlation, factor analysis, and structural equation modeling, c) assess the relationships of the variables with other variables that could be considered secondary criteria in the overall causal model, and d) make use of other procedures such as laboratory research to investigate aspects of the process believed to underlie the basic causal model. In the present chapter, I will explain how each of these recommendations provide some guidance for deciding how to aggregate the large set of motivational variables. Although these four recommendations do not solve the "causality problem," they do provide indirect ways of gathering incremental support for causal statements. The present chapter is structured around these four recommendations and presents a number of psychometric and research design considerations to deal with the challenge of incorporating "new" motivational variables into our current models.

MEASURES WITH GOOD PSYCHOMETRIC PROPERTIES

If we accept the call to incorporate various concepts of motivation into the SLL area, then one important task will be the development of measures of motivation concepts in the context of SLL. This task is not as easy as it may seem. As Gardner (2000) states, measures should have high internal consistency and, where applicable, test-retest reliability. A high level of reliability in a scale is a necessary condition if valid inferences about the concept underlying the scale are to be made.

RELIABILITY OF THE MEASURES

The importance of reliable measures rests on the fact that reliability places a ceiling on validity. This means that a measure with low reliability cannot have a high validity coefficient. For example, consider an example of a measure with a criterion validity coefficient of .40. More specifically let us assume that there is a correlation of .40 in the population between a measure of motivational intensity to learn a second language and final grade in a second language course. A researcher does not know the population value and conducts a study to evaluate the relationship with a sample of 100 students. If the researcher's measure of motivational intensity has a high level of reliability (e.g., .80), then there is a good chance that she will find a correlation near .40, assuming that there are no other problems. Note that there is always a certain level of attenuation of the validity coefficient unless the variables are perfectly reliable. If the measure were largely unreliable in the above example, then the maximum that the correlation can reach will be much less than .40.

INTERNAL CONSISTENCY RELIABILITY

A measure is said to be internally consistent when each of its components (i.e., the items) tap the same underlying concept. The standard measure of internal consistency reliability for measures with multi-point items (such as Likert items) is

Cronbach's coefficient alpha. This coefficient varies from 0 to 1 with high values indicating high internal consistency. Values above .80 are usually indicative of high internal consistency, while values below .50 are indicative of low internal consistency. There are at least three factors that will affect internal consistency: a) the similarity of the content of the items, b) the number of items, and c) the number of dimensions underlying the measure.

The similarity of the items

One way of increasing internal consistency reliability is to write items that are very similar to each other. For example consider the following items written for an effort scale: "I always complete my second language homework" and "I do all my second language assignments." These items are very similar and will therefore tend to correlate highly and help produce a high alpha coefficient. The problem, however, is that there is redundancy between the items. The second item adds little information. Scales with items that are highly redundant tend to have low criterion validity since they can only predict a very narrow range of behaviors. In order to increase the amount of information obtained from a scale, we may consider changing the second item to "I do extra work on my own to practice my second language." In order to obtain a set of items that are not too similar, the researcher could consider examples of different behaviors in different situations.

The number of items

With respect to the number of items, one well known classical test theory principle is that internal consistency reliability increases as the number of items increases assuming that all items assess the same construct. Internal consistency increases because each item adds a new piece of information about the underlying dimension, and peculiarities in the individual items are averaged out when combined into a scale. In some cases 10 items per scale may provide respectable levels of internal consistency.

When deciding how many items to include in a scale, the researcher is faced with a bandwidth-fidelity dilemma (Cronbach, 1990). The dilemma exists because only limited time is available for testing. Often one will design a questionnaire for a study and will be faced with the decision of how many items to include and how many concepts to assess. Questionnaires should usually require less than an hour of administration time. Bandwidth in this context would refer to the number of constructs being assessed and would be wider for inventories assessing several constructs. Fidelity refers to the precision or the reliability of a measure and would increase as the number of items increased. In situations of limited testing time, the question we are faced with is whether to measure several motivational concepts with limited fidelity or few dimensions with high fidelity. For example, a researcher may want to develop an inventory that assesses a number of motivational characteristics. The researcher calculates that he can ask approximately 200 brief questions (e.g., Likert-type test items) in a 45-minute session. The researcher can think of 20 different constructs to assess but he is also concerned about reliability. Some purposes in testing require higher reliability than others. Others require high bandwidth. Exploration analyses, such as a study trying to identify various dimensions of motivation may go for more bandwidth at the cost of lower reliability (with one-item scales, for example). On the other hand, if the scores are going to be used to make classification decisions about the respondents, then reliability should be a priority. In this case one should limit the number of scales in an inventory or a study and maximize the number of items. Twenty to 30 items per scale may be required in this latter case.

The number of dimensions in a scale

The number of dimensions underlying a scale also influences internal consistency. There should be only one dimension underlying a scale. For example, if the intent is to develop a scale to measure effort expended in learning a second language, that scale should not contain any items measuring anxiety, attitudes, or so forth. It is important that the scale assess only one dimension; otherwise, the score on that measure becomes ambiguous. This does not mean, of course, that there cannot be more than one scale in an inventory of measures.

Multidimensionality also tends to reduce internal consistency. The number of dimensions in a measure is not always clear. Consider the example of a second language learning anxiety measure. Imagine that some of the items deal with physiological responses such as "My heartbeat increases when I have to speak in a second language" and other items deal with cognitive-emotional responses "I get all worried when I speak a second language." Obviously, the two sample items measure SLL anxiety, and a case could be made that there is only one dimension. One could also argue that there are two dimensions: a physiological dimension and a cognitive-emotional dimension. In this case both solutions are probably acceptable. It may be advisable to treat the two components as separate scales if the correlation between the two was very low (e.g., lower than r=.50) suggesting that there is little commonality between the two.

One way to detect multidimensionality is to conduct an exploratory factor analysis of the items forming a measure. To the extent that more than one factor is detected, then there is some evidence of multidimensionality. A factor analysis of test items warrants caution however. Sometimes the analysis will result in dubious factors due to peculiarities of the items. For example, consider the example of a factor analysis of a ten item motivational intensity scale in which five of the items have been worded in a positive manner (e.g., I practice my second language every day) and five items have been worded in a negative manner (e.g., I often do not complete my second language homework). The researcher may anticipate that she has a one dimension scale but the factor analysis may reveal two factors: one for the positively worded items and one for the negatively worded items. She may be tempted to name the factors motivational intensity and lack of motivation. This is probably not the best way to proceed. Interpretation of factor analyses requires some judgement on the part of the researcher. In the above case, the researcher may conclude that even if two dimensions were detected, all the items measure motivational intensity, and the factors do not reveal any conceptually different concepts. One piece of evidence that would add support to this second view is the pattern of correlations between the items and the total scale score. If all these correlations were substantial then there would be additional evidence that they form one concept.

TEST-RETEST RELIABILITY

Test-retest reliability is also important and measures whether the scores are repeatable. If a student's motivational intensity to learn a second language is measured at Time 1 and at Time 2, the scores should be similar assuming that no changes in the individual have taken place. The test-retest coefficient is simply the correlation between individuals responses at Time 1 and at Time 2. Although the correlation coefficient can vary from −1 to +1 the test-retest reliability coefficient typically varies from 0 to 1. A high value suggests that individuals who obtain a high score at Time 1 also obtain a high score at Time 2 in relation to the other individuals in the sample. Low test-retest reliability may occur if there are ambiguities in the items. Items should be clearly stated and should ask only one thing. The item "I like to study French and English" is ambiguous because it has two objects: studying French and studying English. Low test-retest reliability may also occur if the respondents do not understand the instructions or the items in a questionnaire. In the second language learning area, test-retest reliability of measures may be difficult to evaluate due to individual changes in learning and second language experiences. Assuming that students have different learning experiences between the pre and post test, their scores may well fluctuate over time.

SCALE DEVELOPMENT USING THE CONSTRUCT-ORIENTED APPROACH

There are a number of ways to develop a scale. One is the factor analytic approach. This strategy would be useful if a researcher had a large set of items but was unclear about the underlying construct. Another approach is empirical-keying. This strategy focuses on maximizing prediction of a specific criterion without concern about the underlying concept in the scale. This approach could be used if one wanted to develop a scale to differentiate between successful and unsuccessful language learners without concern about the nature of the items. A third way is the construct-oriented approach as described by Jackson (1970). This is the most useful approach for the objectives stated in this chapter since it is founded on the idea that one should start with a well defined construct. This approach will be summarized here in terms of four principles.

The first principle calls for a clear theoretically-based definition of the constructs to be measured. This is in contrast to a factor analytic method where the researcher uses the factor structure to aid in defining the construct underlying the items. The definition should include a statement describing the difference between the concept in question and other similar concepts.

The second principle calls for suppression of variance that is due to sources other than the construct of interest. Such sources include socially desirable responding and acquiescence. Socially desirable responding involves a tendency to respond to scale items in a socially desirable direction no matter the targeted content of the items. One way to reduce the chance of socially desirable responding is to select only items that have low correlations with a scale designed specifically to measure socially desirable responding (e.g., Jackson, 1989). Another way to reduce the influence of socially desirable responding is to instruct participants that their responses will remain anonymous and that there are no correct or incorrect answers. Acquiescence is the tendency to agree with all items no matter the content, or to disagree with all the items no matter the content. One way to reduce the effect of acquiescence is to include positively worded and negatively worded items in a scale.

The third principle calls for scale homogeneity while simultaneously ensuring an adequate level of generalizability of the construct. Some researchers try to maximize the internal consistency of their instruments by writing highly homogeneous items. If the items are little more than paraphrases of each other, their intercorrelations will probably be high, and so will the coefficient of internal consistency. The scale will be very narrow, however, in the sense that it may not adequately sample the content domain of the construct. This may in turn lead to low criterion validity as discussed previously.

The fourth principle calls for discriminant validity at all stages of the test construction procedure. At the scale level, discriminant validity exists if the items in a scale correlate more highly with the total scale score than they do with other scales. For example if one is developing a battery of related scales such as effort, persistence, and goal setting, there may be a tendency for some of the items in the effort scale to correlate highly with the persistence scale. If the items from the effort scale correlate more highly with the persistence scale, they should be replaced.

One may consider conducting a sequential item analysis in which an initial pool of items is developed for a scale and administered to a first sample of respondents. An item analysis is then conducted and the item-total scale correlations and the correlations between items and other scales are inspected. The researcher may start with a set of 20 items and intend to keep only 10 in the final set. The items that have the highest item-total correlations and the lowest correlations with other scales would be retained. These items would then be administered to a second sample of respondents, and a second item analysis would be conducted to evaluate whether the properties of the final set of items remained similar to those of the previous analysis.

USING DIFFERENT ASSESSMENT PROCEDURES

Gardner (2000) suggested that different measurement strategies should be used. Although self-report measures are convenient in several ways, one disadvantage with using only one type of instrument is that respondents may answer items in a socially desirable manner. When one investigates the correlations between two self report measures (e.g., a measure of motivational intensity and attitude toward the language teacher), the results may be affected by response bias. Individuals who tend to answer in a socially desirable manner on one measure will in many cases do the same on the other measure. This will tend to artificially elevate the correlation between the two measures. Instead, if one used a laboratory measure of motivation such as time spent studying English-French pairs of words and a self-report measure of attitude toward the language teacher, the problem of response bias may be reduced.

When it is only possible to administer self-report measures, one can use various formats such as Likert, semantic differential, and multiple choice items. This may help reduce spurious relationships due to method variance which occurs when respondents tend to answer items in a similar way irrespective of the content. For example, some respondents may have a tendency to use the middle point of a Likert scale and not to use the extreme points. Consistent patterns of responding such as the above can affect the correlation coefficient in a spurious way. By having two methods, such as a Likert scale for one construct and a semantic differential for another construct, there is less chance of inflation of the relationship due to method variance. This is assuming that the tendency to use the middle point and not the extreme points on Likert items does not exist when answering semantic differential items.

INCREMENTAL VALIDITY

The topic of test validity is a vast one. In the past, validity was defined by some as following: A test or questionnaire is valid if it measures what it purports to measure (e.g., Drever, 1952). The problem with this definition is that validity of a measure depends on the context and on the particular application of the measure in a given situation. When considering validity what is really at issue is ensuring that the inferences that are made based on a measure are credible.

Of particular relevance to this chapter is the issue of incremental validity. A new measure can be said to have incremental validity if it adds something to the measure(s) in use. Consider the following example. Imagine a researcher who finds that her measure of self-confidence to learn a second language is related to final grade in a second language learning course. She reports a correlation of .40. Another researcher decides that perhaps Bandura's (1977) concept of self-efficacy should be incorporated into the SLL area because of its conceptual ties to motivation. He develops a self-efficacy measure to learn a second language and conducts a study correlating his measure with final grade in a second language learning course. He also finds a correlation of .40. Both the self-confidence and the self-efficacy measure seem to predict final grades with the same level of accuracy. Let us now try to improve predictability by combining the two predictors into a multiple regression. Assume that we find a multiple R of .42. This suggests that the second measure of self-efficacy did not add much to the prediction of grades and therefore does not reveal much evidence of incremental validity. The most likely reason why the multiple R was not any higher is because the two predictors were highly correlated. This begs the question: Is the self-efficacy concept redundant? How is it different from self-confidence?

The above potential scenario points to another challenge facing SLL motivation researchers. This challenge involves the scrutiny of potentially redundant concepts. Dörnyei (1996) states that "only by conceptualizing constructs in concrete terms can we hope to integrate the various factors in one coherent framework" (p. 78). This is an important methodological recommendation for two reasons. First, several constructs are conceptually very similar and potentially redundant. If we are going to incorporate new concepts of motivation into the SLL area, then we should ask ourselves how the new concepts differ from existing ones. Are we tapping new phenomena or only introducing new labels for already established concepts? The author's view in this matter is that many of the concepts are related by a common motivational phenomenon but a number of new concepts may explain some additional unique components of motivational behavior.

USING A VARIETY OF ANALYTIC PROCEDURES

Gardner's (2000) second recommendation for developing a viable model is to assess the relationships between variables and criteria using various procedures such as bivariate correlation, factor analysis, and structural equation modeling. These analytical strategies would serve particular purposes in relation to our goal of studying the large set of motivational variables. It should be noted, however, that any causal statement does not depend on the technique used. The key prerequisite in making a causal statement is random assignment of research participants before an experimental manipulation. The following section describes the usefulness of a number of statistical applications in relation to motivation research in the SLL area.

BIVARIATE CORRELATIONS

Simple bivariate correlations provide the most basic piece of information. They allow us to identify whether a variable such as motivational intensity correlates with criterion variables such as various performance and learning measures. They also allow us to detect redundant variables. If two variables are highly correlated, this may be an indication that they are measuring very similar phenomena, or perhaps the same phenomenon. For example, consider the earlier example of self-confidence and self-efficacy measures that were used to predict final grades in a second language learning course. In that example, both predictor variables had a correlation of .40 with grades. Thus both predictors were equally effective in predicting the criterion. However, assume that the two predictors have a correlation of .80 with each other. The squared value of the correlation indicates the proportion of variance in a variable that can be predicted from another variable. In this case, this proportion is 64% and thus suggests that there is considerable overlap between the two predictors.

MULTIPLE REGRESSION

A related technique, multiple regression, allows one to combine predictors in the most mathematically efficient way to predict a criterion. If the goal is to increase prediction, then the most effective predictor variables are those that correlate highly with the criterion variable but have low correlations among themselves. The lower the correlation among the predictors, the less the redundancy between them. In the above example, there is considerable redundancy between the two measures and therefore, one would not gain much by adding the second predictor to the equation. One misapplication of multiple regression is its use to identify the "best predictors." It is not uncommon to see some researchers report the best predictors in order of magnitude by referring to the regression weights (either standardized or raw). The problem with this strategy is that the predictive power of a particular variable is affected by the other variables in the equation. The unequivocal way of evaluating the best predictors is simply to compare their bivariate correlations with the criterion of interest.

The discussion of the above two techniques is not meant to suggest that predictor variables that correlate highly should be discarded. A researcher may argue that his new measure of self-efficacy is not exactly identical to a measure of self-confidence. In this case, a clear definition of the similarities and distinctions between the two measures are in order. This issue should in fact be considered prior to developing a new measure. As discussed previously, one of the first stages of the construct-oriented approach to test construction is to clearly define the construct of interest and to indicate how it is similar and distinct from other constructs. The author of this chapter was faced with this issue in developing very similar concepts of effort, attention, and persistence in academic studies. For example in delineating the similarities and the distinctions between persistence and attention, Tremblay (1998) stated

> Persistence is similar to attention in that both constructs refer to whether or not the student can stay focused on the task. The differences between the two, however, are the period of time involved in achieving the goal (e.g., completing the course successfully) and the type of distractions. Attention refers mainly to a short period of time and is affected by short-term factors such as noise in the classroom. Persistence refers to the long-run focus on the course and is affected by such factors as competing goals and other interests" (p. 34).

EXPLORATORY FACTOR ANALYSIS

Factor analysis is particularly useful in identifying how many unique concepts underlie a large set of variables. (For the purpose of this chapter, no distinction is made between factor analysis and principal components analysis. See Fabrigar, Wegener, MacCallum, & Strahan [1999] for a description of these two analytical procedures.) Recall that one application of factor analysis was the identification of dimensions in a set of items but that caution was in order due to the large proportion of measurement error associated with items. Another application of factor analysis is the identification of a set of factors (or latent variables or concepts) among a set of measures. In the early stages of a research program, the researcher may have a vague idea of the concepts underlying a set of variables. For example, consider the researcher who wants to incorporate the concept of causal attributions of success and failure in the context of learning a second language. He develops a questionnaire and creates the following scales to measure various causes of success and failure: ability/lack of ability, effort/lack of effort, aspiration/lack of interest, course easiness/difficulty, teacher effectiveness/ineffectiveness, personal condition, and luck/misfortune. There are several ways in which these variables may form factors and it may not be apparent at first. Tremblay (1998) developed such a questionnaire in the context of academic studies in general and found the following five dimensions: maladaptive attributions of failure, attributions of failure to the academic environment, attributions of success to motivation, attributions of success to a positive environment, and attributions of success to ability.

CONFIRMATORY FACTOR ANALYSIS

Exploratory factor analysis was described as a technique that can be used to explore the factor structure of a group of variables. Confirmatory factor analysis would be used when a researcher has a particular structure that she would like to test. The researcher proposes a particular structure and tests the fit or viability of this structure. That is, the researcher decides on the number of factors and the variables that identify each of them. In the study including causal attributions, Tremblay (1998) followed-up of the exploratory factor analysis of the attribution measures by conducting a confirmatory factor analysis using a new sample of individuals and proposed a structure consistent with what had been revealed in the exploratory factor analysis.

STRUCTURAL EQUATION MODELING

Structural equation modeling usually consists of two parts: the measurement model and the structural model. The measurement model is that part of a model that describes the latent variables (factors) and the indicator variables which define them. The measurement model does not specify how the latent variables are related. The structural model is the part of a model that specifies the relationships between the latent variables. Relationships that are allowed among the latent variables depend on the type of latent variables. There are two types of latent variables in a structural equation model: exogenous and endogenous variables. Exogenous variables are latent variables that are not influenced or "caused" by other variables. They are in a sense "the first variables in the chain of events" as proposed in the model. Only correlations can be proposed between these variables. Endogenous variables are influenced or "caused" by other endogenous or exogenous variables in the model. The causal links are known as regression coefficients and are identical to regression coefficients in multiple regression.

In constructing a model, one must specify the latent variables and the indicator variables that identify them. In the early stages of a research program, the researcher may have little information about the latent variables and may therefore conduct exploratory factor analyses to determine how to define them. One must then specify how the variables are interconnected. The model is then tested using estimation procedures such as maximum likelihood. There are several SEM software programs that exist. These programs provide fit indices and allow one to test the significance of the links in the model. The viability of a model depends on the model fit and on the statistical significance of the links. Links that are not significant suggest that modifications of the model may be in order. Lack of fit also suggest that the proposed model does not effectively reproduce the original set of relationships among the variables.

SEM has gained considerable popularity in psychology (Tremblay & Gardner, 1996) and in other disciplines. In SLL, a number of researchers have tested models using SEM (e.g., Clément & Kruidenier, 1985; Gardner, 1985; Kraemer, 1993; MacIntyre, 1994). It should be noted that SEM, also known as "causal modeling", does not usually allow one to make unequivocal causal statements. Recall that causal statements are dependent on random assignment. Bollen (1989) discusses three conditions that would have to be met before one could make causal statements between two variables, and he labels these *association, direction,* and *isolation. Association* refers to the fact that there must be a relationship between two variables. For example,, if one wants to make the causal statement that levels of self-reported effort in learning a second language causes performance in a second language course, then the first condition would entail a correlation between the two variables. *Direction* is the condition specifying that the predictor (in this case effort) must precede in time the criterion (in this case performance). In our example this condition would be met if we assessed effort sometime during the second language course and then gave a performance test sometime after the assessment of effort. *Isolation* is the condition that is most difficult to satisfy. Bollen (1989) actually suggests that this condition can not be fully satisfied. Full isolation would exist when two variables are in a vacuum. In our example, the researcher would have to identify all other variables that may account for the effort-performance relationship. This is sometimes referred to as the third variable problem. Of course, it is impossible to identify all the other variables that may be linked to the effort-performance relationship. However a model acquires more support as some of these third variables are identified. (This is a simplified presentation of the conditions described by Bollen [1989]).

Consider the example of a researcher who hypothesizes that self-efficacy to learn a second language "causes" performance in a second language test. The researcher assesses self-efficacy prior to the test and finds a significant correlation measure between the two variables. Another researcher suggests to him that the link between self-efficacy and test performance can simply be explained by second language ability level. The first researcher therefore tests a model in which both ability and self-efficacy predict test performance. To the extent that the second researcher is correct, only the ability- test performance link should be significant. To the extent that the first researcher is correct, both links should be significant. Research on self-efficacy (e.g., Collins, 1982; Wood & Locke, 1987) would seem to support the first researcher's claim. That is, once ability level has been accounted for, individual differences in self-efficacy would have a significant relationship with performance.

INCLUDE SECONDARY CRITERION VARIABLES IN THE MODEL

Gardner's third recommendation for making a model more viable is to include secondary criterion variables into a research program and to determine how they are linked to other variables. He uses the example of the link between integrative motivation and second language achievement. In order to strengthen the support for the idea that integrative motivation "'causes'" second language achievement, he suggested the investigation of other variables related to integrative motivation and achievement such as behavior in the classroom, perseverence in studying a language, and participation of second language field activities. Gardner's recommendation is essentially an exercise in construct validation. Cronbach and Meehl (1955) indicated in a classic paper on construct validity that learning more about a theoretical construct involves an elaboration of the nomological network in which the concept is found. Often, research projects begin with fuzzy concepts. One discovers more about the concept by linking it to other variables, especially if these other variables are directly observable. For example, by discovering a relationship between a self-report measure of motivation and grades in a SLL course (an observable measure of performance), we learn something about the nature of motivation.

MEDIATOR VARIABLES

In the above example, one could propose a model suggesting that individual differences in integrative motivation influence level of participation in the classroom which in turn influences achievement in the second language. In this example, level of participation in the classroom would be considered a mediating variable since it mediates or explains the relationship between integrative motivation and achievement.

Consider a second example of the potential relationships among goal setting, effort, and achievement to learn a second language. Goal setting theory postulates that difficult and specific goals lead to higher levels of performance through their effect on effort, persistence and direction (Locke & Latham, 1990). Tremblay and Gardner (1995) developed a goal salience measure as part of a study of motivation in language learning. The measure contained items assessing the specificity of students' goals and the frequency with which students used goal strategies such as planning. They found support for a structural equation model specifying that goal salience had a direct influence on a motivational variable defined in terms of motivational intensity, attention and persistence. Tremblay (1998) found a similar relationship in a study of academic motivation among university students. The value of mediators (in this case the motivational variable defined as motivational intensity, attention and persistence) is that they provide an explanation for other links such as the relationship between goal setting and achievement and thus make the link theoretically stronger. This is not to say that an unequivocal causal statement can be made. However, one can argue that by adding links to a model and by finding that the model has a good fit, one provides accumulative evidence of hypothesized relationships.

MODERATOR VARIABLES

Another type of variable that should be considered in a research program is moderators. These are variables that moderate the relationship between two other variables. Moderation in this case means an increase, a decrease, a presence, or an absence of the relationship. Stated in a different way, a moderator variable affects the strength and/or direction of the relationship between two other variables. Consider the example of the researcher who intends to incorporate individual difference variables of motivation and a classroom intervention measure such as teaching style and determine their role in second language performance. This is an example of a person by situation model. In this case, the individual difference variables refer to the person and the classroom intervention refers to the situation. In this study, we can investigate the effect of the individual difference variables and the classroom intervention on achievement. We will also be able to determine if there exists an interaction between the effects of the individual difference variables and the effects of the classroom intervention on second language performance. If we do detect an interaction, then moderation exists. Consider a number of potential outcomes of this study. First, the researcher might hypothesize that both the individual difference variables and the classroom intervention will have an effect on achievement. In the presence of main effects but the absence of an interaction, the researcher could conclude that the classroom intervention influenced every participant. Consider the outcome of a statistically significant interaction. There are several forms that this interaction could take but let us examine two possibilities. First, we find that the classroom intervention had an effect only on students who had high levels of self-reported motivation. Another possibility is that the classroom intervention had an effect on only the students who had a low level of self-reported motivation. In this case there is moderation; we can state that individual differences in motivation moderate the relationship between the classroom intervention and achievement. This type of study is valuable since it can identify whether a treatment intervention will have a positive impact on everyone or on a particular subset of individuals.

PROCEDURES SUCH AS LABORATORY RESEARCH TO INVESTIGATE UNDERLYING PROCESSES

Gardner's fourth recommendation for strengthening the viability of a model is to use procedures such as laboratory research to investigate aspects of the process believed to underlie the links in motivational models. Gardner described laboratory studies in which participants were presented with pairs of English-French words over a number of trials, and the task was to provide the correct French translations to the English words. This experiment made use of what is known as the *paired-associates learning paradigm.* In this type of experiment, it is possible to compare the learning curves over a number of trials of groups of participants. Groups can be formed based on individual difference variables such as integrative motivation. Thus, one could compare the learning curve of participants with high levels of integrative motivation with those who have low levels of integrative motivation. The words are presented on a computer and therefore permit the recording of several measures such as length of time the respondents spent studying the translations. Results have indicated that respondents with a high level of integrative motivation learn at a faster rate than those with a low level (Gardner & MacIntyre, 1991; Gardner, Day, & MacIntyre, 1992). Note that because integrative motivation in those studies was an individual difference variable, an unequivocal causal statement regarding the effect of integrative motivation on performance cannot be made.

If one wanted to make a stronger causal statement about the effect of integrative motivation on learning, it would be necessary to come up with a way to manipulate integrative motivation. This may appear like an impractical solution. Some individual difference variables are easier to model as experimental manipulations than others. Whereas integrative motivation may pose a considerable challenge, instrumental motivation may provide easier avenues. In fact, Gardner and MacIntyre (1991) studied the effect of instrumental motivation on performance by providing an incentive of $10 to members of one group for learning at least 23 of the 26 paired associates and providing no incentive to another group. Note that in Gardner and MacIntyre's study, participants were randomly assigned to the incentive or no incentive group, permitting a stronger statement about the effect of instrumental motivation on performance. What is particularly interesting about this study is the fact that the results mirrored the results of the effect of integrative motivation on performance. That is, in both studies, the rate of learning was steeper for the high motivation/incentive group than it was for the low motivation/no incentive group. One may go as far as suggesting that, since the results were similar for the two types of motivation, there is indirect support for the statement that integrative motivation "causes" achievement even though integrative motivation was presented as an individual difference variable.

One criticism of laboratory studies is that they do not capture the totality of the language learning experience. Classroom studies would provide a much more realistic picture of the language learning experience. In some cases, however, it would be difficult to introduce certain types of manipulations in natural environments and maintain the integrity of the experiment. Laboratory studies such as those using computers permit a more careful presentation of the manipulations without contamination. For example, consider the following research design to investigate the effects of goal setting on a second language learning task. The experimenter creates four experimental groups consisting of no goal, easy goal, moderate goal, and difficult goal by telling respondents that they should aim to learn a specific number of paired-associates. One could at the same time assess how much effort participants are applying by recording how much time they spend studying the translations. In addition, one could investigate the interaction between goal setting and individual differences in integrative motivation to identify whether goal setting has different effects on participants with high motivation than on participants with low motivation. With advancements in multimedia technology, there are several language learning variables such as speech accuracy that could supplement the basic paired-associates learning paradigm.

FINAL RECOMMENDATIONS

The intention of this chapter was to present a number of psychometric and research design recommendations in the context of the new motivational agenda in SLL. A number of challenges to the research program have been pointed out. These do not present road blocks but strategic directions. As described here, one of the great challenges will be to tap new motivational phenomena rather than duplicate already established concepts. This may be facilitated by a collaboration among researchers such as the collection of chapters in this book. We can learn from other areas that have been faced with similar problems. In the area of research on the structure of personality, for example, there has been considerable debate on the number of "core" personality dimensions. One dominant view is that there are five. Researchers are also attempting to determine if this structure is cross-cultural. Part of the problem is that researchers are factor analyzing different inventories, making it difficult to reach a consensus. One solution is to work from the same inventory or from similar measures. L. R. Goldberg at the Oregon Research Institute has developed an international pool of 1,412 personality items and made it publicly accessible (Goldberg, 1999). The same strategy could be adopted in the area of motivation in second language learning. This would be especially useful for documenting a number of orientations to learn a second language as well as other core motivational variables and to specify the cultural contexts in which they would be applicable.

The second challenge is to deal with the fact that in a large proportion of our research, we are dealing with individual difference variables, and therefore, unequivocal causal statements cannot be made. The paper by Gardner (2000) has suggested a number of ways to overcome this problem. Through careful modeling of all important variables and supportive experimental research to test links in the models, we can accumulate stronger support for our theories.

REFERENCES

Ames, C., & Archer, J. (1988). Achievement goals in the classroom: Students' learning strategies and motivation process. *Journal of Educational Psychology, 80,* 260–267.

Bandura, A. (1977). Self-efficacy: Toward a unifying theory of behavioral change. *Psychological Review, 84,* 191–215.

Bollen, K. A. (1989). *Structural equations with latent variables.* New York: John Wiley.

Clément, R., & Kruidenier, B. A. (1985). Aptitude, attitude and motivation in second language proficiency: A test of Clément's model. *Journal of Language and Social Psychology, 4,* 21–37.

Collins, J. L. (1982, March). *Self-efficacy and ability in achievement behavior.* Paper presented at the annual meeting of the American Educational Research Association, New York.

Cronbach, L. J. (1990). *Essentials of Psychological Testing. Fifth Edition.* New York: Harper Collins Publishers.

Cronbach, L. J., & Meehl, P. E. (1955). Construct validity in psychological tests. *Psychological Bulletin, 52,* 281–302.

Crookes, G., & Schmidt, R. W. (1991). Motivation: Reopening the research agenda. *Language Learning, 41,* 469–512.

Dörnyei, Z. (1990). Conceptualizing motivation in foreign language learning. *Language Learning, 40,* 45–78.

Dörnyei, Z. (1996). Moving language learning motivation to a larger platform for theory and practice. In R. L. Oxford (Ed.), *Language learning motivation: Pathways to the new century* (Technical Report #11, pp. 71–80). Honolulu: University of Hawai'i, Second Language Teaching & Curriculum Center.

Drever, J. (1952). *A dictionary of psychology.* Baltimore: Penguin.

Fabrigar, L. R., Wegener, D. T., MacCallum, R. C., & Strahan, E. J. (1999). Evaluating the use of exploratory factor analysis in psychological research. *Psychological Methods, 4,* 272–299.

Gardner, R. C. (1985). *Social psychology and second language learning: The role of attitudes and motivation.* London: Edward Arnold Publishers.

Gardner, R. C. (2000). Correlation, causation, motivation, and second language acquisition. *Canadian Psychology, 41,* 10–24.

Gardner, R. C., Day, J. B., & MacIntyre, P. D. (1992). Integrative motivation, induced anxiety, and language learning in a controlled environment. *Studies in Second Language Learning, 14,* 197–214.

Gardner, R. C., & MacIntyre, P. D. (1991). An instrumental motivation in language study: Who says it isn't effective? *Studies in Second Language Acquisition, 13,* 57–72.

Goldberg, L.R., (1999). A broad-bandwidth, public-domain, personality inventory measuring the lower level facets of several five-factor models. In I. Medvielde, I. J. Deary, F. DeFruyt, & F. Ostendorf (Eds.), *Psychology in Europe, Vol. 7* (pp. 7–28). Tilburg, The Netherlands: Tilburg University Press.

Jackson, D. N. (1970). A sequential system for personality scale development. In C. D. Spielberger (Ed.), *Current topics in clinical and community psychology, Vol. 2* (pp. 61–96). New York: Academic Press.

Jackson, D. N. (1989). *Personality Research Form manual. 3rd edition.* London, Ontario, Canada: Research Psychologists Press, Inc.

Kraemer, R. (1993). Social psychological factors related to the study of Arabic among Israeli high school students. *Studies in Second Language Acquisition, 15,* 83–105.

Locke, E. A., & Latham, G. P. (1990). *A theory of goal setting & task performance.* Upper Saddle Ridge, NJ: Prentice Hall.

MacIntyre, P. D. (1994). Variables underlying willingness to communicate: A causal analysis. *Communication Research Reports, 11*, 135–142.

Oxford, R. L., & Shearin, J. (1994). Language learning motivation: Expanding the theoretical framework. *Modern Language Journal, 78*, 12–28.

Tremblay, P. F. (1998). *Development and construct validation of the academic motivation inventory.* Unpublished doctoral dissertation, The University of Western Ontario, London, Ontario, Canada.

Tremblay, P. F., & Gardner, R. C. (1995). Expanding the motivation construct in language learning. *Modern Language Journal, 79*, 505–520.

Tremblay P. F., & Gardner, R. C. (1996). On the growth of structural equation modeling in psychological journals. *Structural Equation Modeling: A Multidisciplinary Journal, 3*, 93–104.

Wood, R. E., & Locke, E. A. (1987). The relation of self-efficacy and grade goals to academic performance. *Educational and Psychological Measurement, 47*, 1013–1024.

James Dean Brown
University of Hawai'i at Mānoa
Maria Isabel Azevedo Cunha
Sylvia de Fatima Nagem Frota
Anna Beatriz Fernandes Ferreira
Pontifícia Universidade Católica do Rio de Janeiro

THE DEVELOPMENT AND VALIDATION OF A PORTUGUESE VERSION OF THE MOTIVATED STRATEGIES FOR LEARNING QUESTIONNAIRE

Authors' note

This project was partially funded by a grant from the Pontifícia Universidade Católica do Rio de Janeiro.

Abstract

The purpose of this project was to create a Portuguese language version of the *Motivated Strategies for Learning Questionnaire* (MSLQ) for use by researchers in Brazil and other Portuguese speaking countries. A secondary purpose was to use the new version of the MSLQ (called the QEMA) to investigate differences between private and public school students at two institutions in Brazil on the characteristics measured by this instrument. The new QEMA version of the questionnaire was administered to 89 university students in Rio de Janeiro, and the data were analyzed statistically as follows: Cronbach alpha analyses were used to investigate the reliability of the subscales, especially in relation to the numbers of items involved in each subscale. The content and construct validity (using factor analysis) of the new instrument for use with students like those in this study were also explored. Finally, statistically significant differences were found between private and public school students on three characteristics measured by this instrument. The results are discussed in terms of the reliability, validity, and utility of the QEMA for use in Brazil and other Portuguese speaking countries.

INTRODUCTION

The *Motivated Strategies for Learning Questionnaire* (MSLQ) is a self-report questionnaire originally developed in English to measure university level students' "motivational orientations and their use of different learning strategies for a college course" (Pintrich, Smith, & McKeachie, 1989b, p. 2). While the manual does not make clear how the original version was administered and analyzed statistically, there is some discussion of these issues in Pintrich (1989; also see Pintrich, Smith, & McKeachie, 1989a, 1989b).

In this project, the MSLQ was translated into Portuguese for use by researchers in Brazil and other Portuguese speaking countries. First, the English directions and individual items were translated directly into Portuguese to create the *Questionário de Estratégias Motivacionais para Aprendizagem* (QEMA). Then, the translation was

Brown, J. D., Cunha, M. I. A., Frota, S. de F. N., & Ferreira, A. B. F. (2001). The development and validation of a Portuguese version of the Motivated Strategies for Learning Questionnaire. In Z. Dörnyei & R. Schmidt (Eds.), *Motivation and second language acquisition* (Technical Report #23, pp. 257–280). Honolulu: University of Hawai'i, Second Language Teaching and Curriculum Center.

checked for accuracy by two bilingual English-Portuguese language professors. The resulting QEMA is a self-report questionnaire, which may prove useful in studying university level Portuguese speaking students' motivational orientations and learning strategies. The final version of the QEMA is shown in Appendix A.

ORGANIZATION

The structure of the QEMA was purposely kept exactly like that of the original MSLQ. Thus the QEMA has 85 items which are organized into two sections that correspond to motivational orientations and learning strategies. The motivation section contains three major subscales with a total of 35 items: value components (14 items), expectancy components (16 items), and affective components (5 items). The learning strategies section is divided into two subscales with a total of 50 items: cognitive strategies (31 items) and resource management strategies (19 items). A further breakdown of the design of the instrument is as shown in Table 1:

Table 1: Scales and subscales of the QEMA

Motivation section	# of items
value components	
intrinsic goal orientation	4
extrinsic goal orientation	4
task value	6
expectancy components	
control beliefs	8
self-efficacy	5
expectancy for success	3
affective components	
test anxiety	5
total	35
Learning Strategies section value components	
cognitive strategies	
rehearsal strategies	4
elaboration strategies	6
organization strategies	4
critical thinking strategies	5
metacognitive strategies	12
resource management strategies	
time and study management	8
effort management	4
peer learning	3
help-seeking	4
total	50

The different sections and subscales of the QEMA were designed to be used as a single unit or separately. If administered together, it should take the students 20–30 minutes to finish filling out the entire questionnaire. When using the individual subscales of 3 to 12 items, it is important to recognize that they may be considerably less reliable than the total questionnaire (see discussion under the heading "Reliability" below).

PURPOSE

The primary purpose of this project was to create and validate the *QEMA* by (a) translating the *MSLQ*, (b) administering the instrument to students at Brazilian universities, and (c) analyzing the results statistically for descriptive statistics, reliability estimates, and validity indicators.

A secondary purpose was to use the *QEMA* to investigate differences between private and public school students at two institutions in Brazil in the characteristics measured by the instrument.

The results of this project will be reported here by addressing the following four research questions:

1. Are the scales on the *QEMA* appropriate (i.e., normally distributed) when the questionnaire is administered to university students in Brazil?

2. To what degree are the subscales on the *QEMA* reliable?

3. In terms of validity, how are the subscales on the *QEMA* related to each other?

4. What subscales on the *QEMA* differentiate between the private and public university students in this study?

The alpha level for all statistical decisions was set at the outset at (α=.05).

METHOD

PARTICIPANTS

The 89 participants in this project were all studying languages at the undergraduate level in Rio de Janeiro, Brazil. Forty-four (or 49.4%) were studying at the Pontifícia Universidade Católica do Rio de Janeiro (PUC/RJ), a private religiously affiliated university. Forty-five (50.6%) were studying at the Universidade Federal do Rio de Janeiro (UFRJ), a publicly funded university. In all, 90.7% were full-time day students, while 7% were taking mostly day courses with some night classes, and 2.3% were exclusively night students. It was not surprising that only 10.1% of the participants were male and 89.9% were female since language majors are predominantly female in Brazil.

Nearly 73% of the students had been taking supplementary language courses at private institutions outside of the university for two or more years while 18.1% had taken such courses for one to two years, and 1.1% for less than one semester. Only 8% had never taken such outside courses.

PROCEDURES

Administration

The QEMA was administered under typical classroom conditions. It was administered in tandem with a socio-cultural questionnaire (developed in Brazil for other research purposes) and a cloze passage. In this project, the socio-cultural questionnaire was the source of some of the biodata information reported in the "Participants" section above. The cloze test was used as a measure of overall English language proficiency. Brown (1980) reports that this particular cloze passage was reliable at .90 using the same exact-answer scoring used in this project and that the criterion-related (concurrent) validity was .88 between the cloze test scores and the overall three hour English as a Second Language Placement Examination at the University of California at Los Angeles.

The students filled out the QEMA by responding to each of a series of statements on a 1 to 7 Likert scale where *1* represented "not at all true of me" and *7* represented "very true of me." They were allowed 30 minutes to complete the task.

Scoring

The items in the QEMA were not presented to the students in clearly labeled sections corresponding to those listed above. On the contrary, the items were mixed together throughout the instrument with the result that the following items represent each of the subscales (Table 2):

Table 2: QEMA items on each of the subscales

Motivation section	item #s
value components	
intrinsic goal orientation	1, 18, 24, 26
extrinsic goal orientation	8, 12, 14, 34
task value	5, 11, 19, 25, 28, 29
expectancy components	
control beliefs	2, 4, 10, 15, 20, 27, 30, 33
self-efficacy	7, 13, 17, 22, 32
expectancy for success	6, 23, 35
affective components	
test anxiety	3, 9, 16, 21, 31

Learning strategies section	item #s
cognitive strategies	
rehearsal strategies	43, 50, 63, 76
elaboration strategies	57, 66, 68, 71, 73, 85
organization strategies	36, 46, 53, 67
critical thinking strategies	42, 51, 55, 70, 75
metacognitive strategies	37, 40, 45, 48, 58, 59, 60, 61, 65, 80, 82, 83
resource management strategies	
time and study management	39, 47, 56, 69, 74, 77, 81, 84
effort management	41, 52, 64, 78
peer learning	38, 49, 54
help-seeking	44, 62, 72, 79

Thus, researchers who want to administer individual subscales selectively will have to separate out the appropriate items for each subscale. (Note that, in the original *MSLQ*, there were further subdivisions of the scales into sections as small as two items. However, since the instrument was not used or analyzed in that much detail in this project, only the results for the groupings given immediately above are reported here.)

The scale score for any particular subscale is obtained by calculating the average of the 1 to 7 responses for the items involved in that subscale. Thus each student's score on the *intrinsic goal orientation* subscale would be obtained by averaging the student's 1 to 7 responses on items 1, 18, 24, 26.

In addition, it is important to recognize that four of the subscales (Metacognitive strategies, Time and study management, Effort management, and Help-seeking) have items that must be reverse coded. That is to say, these items are negatively worded such that they must be scored in reverse. Thus a student response of *1* becomes a *7*, 2 becomes 6, 3 becomes 5, 4 stays 4, 5 becomes 3, 6 becomes 2, and 7 becomes *1*. There are eight such items (numbers 37, 41, 44, 56, 61, 64, 81, 84). This reverse coding must be done before taking the averages that represent each student's scale scores. If this reverse coding is not done correctly, the scores for the four subscales involved will not be reliable.

RESULTS

The data were analyzed using the *QuattroPro*[tm] (1991) spreadsheet program and the *SPSS/PC+*[tm] (1991) statistical program on an IBM compatible personal computer. The data were entered and organized in the spreadsheet program. Then to answer the research questions posed at the outset of this project, descriptive, reliability, and validity statistics were calculated using the statistics program. The results of these analyses will be reported in the three sections that follow.

DESCRIPTIVE STATISTICS

Descriptive statistics are numerical representations which describe how participants performed on a test or questionnaire. The descriptive statistics in Table 4 are presented such that each statistic has its own column and each subscale has a row. These descriptive statistics are for the subscale scores, which are themselves averages for each student of all of the items in the corresponding subscales. The statistics include the number of participants (N), number of items (k), mean (M), standard deviation (SD), minimum (MIN) and maximum (MAX), median (MDN), mode ($MODE$), and skewness ($SKEW$). Table 4 shows the descriptive statistics for the total group ($N=89$) who took the QEMA. Notice that the number of items for each subscale (shown in the third column) varies from a low of 3 for EXPT to a high of 12 for META.

The variable labels represent each of the subscales as follows (Table 3):

Table 3: Variable labels

Motivation section	variable labels
value components	
intrinsic goal orientation	INTR
extrinsic goal orientation	EXTR
task value	TASK
expectancy components	
control beliefs	CONT
self-efficacy	SELF
expectancy for success	EXPT
affective components	
test anxiety	TEST
Learning strategies section	**variable labels**
cognitive strategies	
rehearsal strategies	REHR
elaboration strategies	ELAB
organization strategies	ORGS
critical thinking strategies	CRIT
metacognitive strategies	META
resource management strategies	
time and study management	TIME
effort management	EFFT
peer learning	PEER
help-seeking	HELP

The cloze test that was administered along with the QEMA as a measure of overall English language proficiency is also shown in the variable list.

Looking more closely at the descriptive statistics, the mean is an indicator of the central tendency, or typical performance of the group. In this case, it is exactly the same as the arithmetic average of the scores. Notice in Table 4 that the means for the various subscales show considerable variation ranging from a low of 3.01 for PEER to a high of 6.16 for TASK. Note that the median (the score that separates the students 50/50) and mode (the score most commonly received), found in columns 8 and 9, are two other indicators of the central tendency of the scores.

Table 4: Descriptive statistics

	N	k	M	SD	min	max	Mdn	mode	skew
INTR	89	4	5.41	1.04	2.25	7.00	5.50	6.00	-0.78
EXTR	89	4	3.86	1.37	1.00	6.75	4.00	4.25	-0.22
TASK	89	6	6.16	0.90	2.50	7.00	6.50	7.00	-1.86
CONT	89	8	4.09	0.70	2.50	6.25	4.00	4.00	-0.06
SELF	89	5	5.57	1.05	1.40	7.00	5.80	6.20	-1.15
EXPT	89	3	5.61	0.92	3.00	7.00	5.67	6.00	-1.04
TEST	89	5	3.27	1.15	1.00	6.20	3.20	3.80	-0.03
REHR	89	4	4.99	1.34	1.75	7.00	5.25	4.25	-0.45
ELAB	89	6	5.38	1.07	2.00	6.83	5.50	6.67	-0.95
ORGS	89	4	5.49	1.24	1.50	7.00	5.75	7.00	-0.97
CRIT	89	5	5.08	1.19	1.60	7.00	5.20	5.00	-0.56
META	89	12	4.58	0.89	2.25	6.33	4.75	3.17	-0.47
TIME	89	8	4.89	0.68	2.88	6.25	5.00	5.25	-0.75
EFFT	89	4	3.51	0.88	1.50	5.50	3.75	3.75	-0.37
PEER	89	3	3.01	1.41	1.00	6.00	3.00	1.00	0.17
HELP	89	4	4.98	1.07	2.00	7.00	5.25	5.50	-0.62
CLOZE	89	50	16.31	5.80	1.00	31.00	17.00	14.00	-0.08

The standard deviation, as well as the minimum and maximum scores, are indicators of the dispersion of scores around the mean. Inspection of Table 4 indicates that there was some variation among subscales in how broadly the scores were dispersed. However, an F_{max} test comparing the high and low standard deviations within Table 4 shows that there were no significant differences in dispersion among the subscales.

One key question in examining descriptive statistics is the degree to which the distributions are normal. The last column of Table 4 gives a skewness statistic. If the distribution of scores is skewed, that is, is non-normal because of a high number of high or low scores, the skewness statistic will vary markedly away from 0.00. This is true of the TASK subscale, which had a skewness statistic of -1.86 in Table 4. Thus, the distribution of scores for the TASK subscale appear to be negatively skewed and not normal in shape. Examination of the mean and standard deviation involved will reveal that the mean is high (6.16) on a scale of 1 to 7, and there is not room above the mean for even one standard deviation. This is typical of a negatively skewed distribution. Note that this comment is not a criticism of the subscale but rather a simple observation of the fact that, for the Brazilian students involved here, the distribution for TASK was not normal. It should also be noted that this subscale turned out to be one of the more reliable subscales. Four other scales, SELF, EXPT, ELAB, and ORGS, appear to be somewhat negatively skewed because they have skewness statistics close to or higher than 1.00 in absolute magnitude and relatively high means (with room for less than two standard deviations between that mean and the top possible score of seven). The other scales all appear to be approximately normal.

RELIABILITY

Reliability coefficients, as used here, indicate the degree to which a subscale is internally consistent, or reliable. The Cronbach alpha index was used to analyze this questionnaire. This coefficient can range from .00 to 1.00 and, by moving the decimal point two places to the right, can be directly interpreted as the percent of consistent variance in the scores. Thus if a subscale has a reliability of .82, that scale can be said to be 82% consistent, or reliable (and, by extension, 18% inconsistent, or unreliable).

Table 5: Subscale and cloze reliabilities

variable	k	MSLQ alpha	QEMA alpha	S-B (k=12)	S-B (k=50)	SEM
INTR	4	0.71	0.55	0.79	0.94	0.70
EXTR	4	NG	0.59	0.81	0.95	0.76
TASK	6	0.91	0.79	0.88	0.97	0.44
CONT	8	NG	0.38	0.48	0.79	0.53
SELF	5	0.89	0.82	0.92	0.98	0.45
EXPT	3	NG	0.67	0.89	0.95	0.53
TEST	5	0.82	0.45	0.67	0.89	0.86
REHR	4	0.65	0.61	0.82	0.95	0.86
ELAB	6	0.75	0.68	0.81	0.95	0.63
ORGS	4	0.73	0.66	0.85	0.96	0.74
CRIT	5	0.83	0.78	0.90	0.97	0.63
META	12	0.83	0.79	0.79	0.94	0.47
TIME	8	0.82	0.58	0.67	0.90	0.60
EFFT	4	0.70	0.43	0.70	0.91	0.93
PEER	3	NG	0.60	0.86	0.96	0.91
HELP	4	0.70	0.42	0.68	0.90	0.97
CLOZE	50	—	0.79	0.35	0.79	2.67

NG=not given in the manual for the original MSLQ

Reliability statistics, based on Cronbach's alpha, are presented in Table 5. Once again, the subscale row labels are given in the first column, and the different reliability statistics are labeled across the top. The number of items (k) for each subscale is given in the second column of Table 5 because of the known relationship between reliability and instrument length (discussed below).

Next, the reliability estimates are given for the original MSLQ (i.e., the original English language version that was used to create the QEMA). Notice that the reported values for the original MSLQ range from .65 to .91. No reliability coefficients were reported for six of the subscales in the manual for the MSLQ apparently because new items had been added in that most recent revision and the results had not been piloted and analyzed with those new items present. The Cronbach alpha reliability coefficients for the QEMA are reported in the fourth column of Table 5. Notice that the subscale reliabilities for the QEMA range from a low of .38 to a high of .82 and that, in all cases, they are lower than the equivalent values reported for the MSLQ. This difference may be due to restrictions in the range of motivational orientations and learning strategies found in the particular sample of Brazilian students used in this study. However, such a restriction seems unlikely given the normality of distributions on all but one scale and the relatively high degree of variation found in overall English language proficiency as measured by the cloze test.

Another issue related to reliability is the predictable relationship between the number of items on an instrument and the reliability of that instrument. Given that many of the subscales on the QEMA are very short, the subscale reliability values found here are probably acceptable. To illustrate the relationship between the number of items and reliability, columns five and six of Table 5 give estimates of what the reliability would be if the subscales were all 12 items in length and 50 items in length, respectively. These adjustments were calculated using the Spearman-Brown prophecy formula (S-B). Notice that the reliabilities for each of the subscales are predictably higher for all of the subscales when adjusted to 12 items and are even very high when adjusted to 50 items. However, since such long subscales are clearly impractical, the demonstration here is simply meant to be illustrative and is not meant to suggest that the subscales actually be lengthened to 12 or 50 items.

The last column of Table 5 presents the standard error of measurement (SEM). The SEM is an alternative way of looking at the reliability of an instrument in terms of the amount of random fluctuation that can be expected in scores on the instrument. The SEM can be interpreted as a band of scores around a students' true scores within which they would be expected to fall repeatedly (within certain probability limits) if they were to fill out the instrument time and again. For example, the SEM of .70 for the INTR indicates that a student who has a total score of 5 on that subscale can be expected to score (±1 SEM) 68% of the time, which means that the student would be expected to score between 4.30 (5−.70=4.30) and 5.70 (5+.70=5.70) 68% of the time.

In general, the reliability of the QEMA subscales can be said to be acceptable for some research purposes given the small number of items involved in those subscales.

However, some subscales, particularly TEST, EFFT, and HELP, which produced low reliability estimates and had very few items, would probably benefit from the additional items. The CONT subscale also produced a low reliability estimate, but since it already has eight items, this subscale would appear to have consistency problems not clearly related to the number of items.

VALIDITY

Validity is defined here as the degree to which an instrument measures what it claims to be measuring. Two strategies were used here to investigate the validity of the QEMA: the content validity strategy and the construct validity strategy.

Content validity

In defending the content validity of an instrument, the validity is supported when the content of the instrument can be shown to be a representative sample of the types of items that represent motivational orientations and learning strategies. Essentially, this is the argument presented by Pintrich (1989). That argument applies to the Portuguese QEMA version insofar as it applies to the original English MSLQ version.

Construct validity

Another strategy for examining the validity of an instrument is called construct validity. Basically, this strategy involves demonstrating experimentally that the instrument is measuring what it claims to be measuring. To that end, the correlation coefficients among the various subscales were calculated as shown in Table 6. Since the degree of relationship between any two variables may sometimes be masked by the unreliability of one or both of the measures (called attenuation), the correlation coefficients corrected for attenuation are also presented (in Table 7).

While individual correlation coefficients like those presented in Tables 6 and 7 may be of interest, any existing patterns among those coefficients are often difficult to discern. To help in that regard, factor analysis was used to explore the underlying variance structure within the set of QEMA subscale correlations. The Eigen value was set at 1.00 and a scree plot was examined. These steps indicated that a four factor solution fit these data. A VARIMAX rotation was then performed. The results of that rotation for the four factor solution are presented in Table 8.

The clearest results in Table 8 are those for the COGNITIVE section where all five of its component subscales load well above .30 on Factor 1. One variation in this picture is found in the REHR subscale which also loads at .52 on Factor 3.

Table 6: Intercorrelations of all subscales and cloze

	INTR	EXTR	TASK	CONT	SELF	EXPT	TEST	REHR	ELAB	ORGS	CRIT	META	TIME	EFFT	PEER	HELP
INTR	1.00															
EXTR	0.22*	1.00														
TASK	0.52*	0.40*	1.00													
CONT	0.35*	0.16	0.01	1.00												
SELF	0.25*	0.19	0.32*	0.08	1.00											
EXPT	0.39*	0.32*	0.45*	0.23*	0.65*	1.00										
TEST	-0.10	0.14	-0.20	0.08	-0.23*	-0.22*	1.00									
REHR	0.12	0.25*	0.16	0.14	-0.02	-0.07	0.16	1.00								
ELAB	0.34*	0.14	0.39*	-0.02	0.36*	0.28	0.01	0.36*	1.00							
ORGS	0.34*	0.19	0.33*	0.06	0.15	0.10	0.08	0.49*	0.64*	1.00						
CRIT	0.48*	0.07	0.23*	0.10	0.27*	0.34*	-0.11	0.31*	0.65*	0.59*	1.00					
META	0.53*	0.25*	0.37*	0.18	0.22*	0.19	-0.06	0.53*	0.63*	0.58*	0.72*	1.00				
TIME	0.37*	0.14	0.33*	0.09	0.12	0.32*	-0.08	0.41*	0.43*	0.42*	0.36*	0.51*	1.00			
EFFT	0.25*	0.35*	0.40*	0.09	0.23*	-0.12	0.05	0.28*	0.43*	0.49*	0.31*	0.43*	0.51*	1.00		
PEER	0.07	0.30*	-0.01	0.16	-0.13	0.12	0.16	0.35*	0.08	0.19	0.14	0.33*	0.04	0.10	1.00	
HELP	0.19	0.22*	0.13	0.12	0.07	0.19	0.23*	0.37*	0.32*	0.31*	0.31*	0.39*	0.20*	0.26*	0.44*	1.00
CLOZE	0.30*	0.05	0.23*	0.11	0.19	0.22*	-0.15	0.07	0.29*	0.20	0.20	0.34*	0.31*	0.15	-0.04	-0.10

* $p < .05$

Table 7: Intercorrelations of all subscales and cloze (corrected for attenuation)

	INTR	EXTR	TASK	CONT	SELF	EXPT	TEST	REHR	ELAB	ORGS	CRIT	META	TIME	EFFT	PEER	HELP
INTR	1.00															
EXTR	0.38	1.00														
TASK	0.79	0.59	1.00													
CONT	0.77	0.34	0.01	1.00												
SELF	0.37	0.28	0.40	0.15	1.00											
EXPT	0.64	0.51	0.62	0.45	0.87	1.00										
TEST	-0.21	0.28	-0.34	0.20	-0.38	-0.39	1.00									
REHR	0.20	0.41	0.23	0.30	-0.02	-0.11	0.30	1.00								
ELAB	0.56	0.22	0.53	-0.04	0.48	0.41	0.01	0.56	1.00							
ORGS	0.57	0.30	0.45	0.12	0.20	0.15	0.14	0.78	0.96	1.00						
CRIT	0.72	0.10	0.30	0.18	0.33	0.47	-0.19	0.45	0.89	0.82	1.00					
META	0.80	0.36	0.47	0.34	0.28	0.27	-0.10	0.76	0.87	0.80	0.91	1.00				
TIME	0.65	0.24	0.49	0.19	0.17	0.51	-0.15	0.69	0.68	0.67	0.53	0.76	1.00			
EFFT	0.52	0.69	0.69	0.23	0.39	-0.23	0.11	0.55	0.79	0.93	0.53	0.74	0.99	1.00		
PEER	0.12	0.50	-0.01	0.34	-0.19	0.19	0.31	0.58	0.13	0.31	0.21	0.48	0.07	0.20	1.00	
HELP	0.39	0.43	0.23	0.31	0.12	0.35	0.53	0.73	0.60	0.59	0.54	0.68	0.40	0.62	0.88	1.00
CLOZE	0.46	0.08	0.29	0.20	0.23	0.30	-0.26	0.10	0.39	0.28	0.25	0.43	0.46	0.25	-0.06	-0.17

Table 8: VARIMAX rotation of the four factor solution

	factor				
variable	1	2	3	4	h^2
Motivation					
INTR	.47*	.39*	−.09	.51*	.64
EXTR	−.00	.64*	.57*	.01	.73
TASK	.31*	.73*	−.00	−.09	.64
CONT	.00	.06	.19	.87*	.80
SELF	.12	.69*	−.27	.05	.57
EXPT	.12	.77*	−.14	.33	.74
TEST	−.07	−.22	.59*	−.04	.40
Cognitive					
REHR	.55*	−.06	.52*	−.03	.58
ELAB	.79*	.27	.00	−.15	.72
ORGS	.78*	.11	.23	−.11	.69
CRIT	.82*	.13	−.10	.18	.73
META	.82*	.03	.22	.25	.78
Management					
TIME	.62*	.22	−.20	.12	.49
EFFT	−.10	−.14	.54*	.02	.32
PEER	.18	.00	.61*	.26	.47
HELP	.40*	.31*	.62*	.04	.64
Proportion of Variance	.24	.16	.14	.08	.62

* loadings above .30

Almost as clear is the pattern which emerges for the MANAGEMENT section, for which three of the component subscales load most highly on Factor 3. However, the TIME subscale, which is loading most highly on Factor 1, appears to be more closely related to whatever Factor 1 is measuring (i.e., apparently something related to the COGNITIVE section) than are the other subscales of MANAGEMENT. In addition, since the HELP subscale is loading more generally above .30 on factors 1, 2, and 3, it may not be as unique and discrete a category as was thought when the instrument was designed.

Though five out of the seven component subscales of the MOTIVATION section load above .30 on Factor 2, it is clear that one of these component subscales (TEST) is loading most heavily on Factor 3 and thus may be more highly related to the MANAGEMENT section than to the MOTIVATION section. In addition, the INTR and CONT subscales are loading most heavily on another entirely different fourth factor. Finally, the INTR and TASK load above .30 on Factor 1, which probably indicates that these two scales of MOTIVATION are also related to the scales of the COGNITIVE section. In short, five of the seven subscales of the MOTIVATION section load on Factor 2, but the patterns of additional loadings above .30 make the pattern for the MOTIVATION section more difficult to interpret than the other two sections of the QEMA version of the MSLQ.

In general, however, it can be said that the loadings for MOTIVATION are predominantly on factor 2, the loadings for the COGNITIVE section are almost exclusively on factor 1, and the loadings for MANAGEMENT are predominantly on factor 3. Thus these analyses support the validity of these subscales to some degree but also point to subscales which might profitably be modified to better fit the model implied by the organization of the test.

Table 9: Univariate follow–up statistics for MANOVA

variable	hyp. SS	error SS	hyp. MS	error MS	F	p
INTR	.23258	88.60555	.23258	1.03030	.22574	.636
EXTR	2.76468	121.95200	2.76468	1.41805	1.94964	.166
TASK	1.89926	74.10205	1.89926	.86165	2.20420	.141
CONT	1.11615	38.51258	1.11615	.44782	2.49241	.118
SELF	2.70282	91.89621	2.70282	1.06856	2.52940	.115
EXPT	5.99190	66.38620	5.99190	.77193	7.76220	.007*
TEST	.99557	114.53626	.99557	1.33182	.74753	.390
REHR	7.73980	157.35970	7.73980	1.82976	4.22995	.043*
ELAB	.17073	99.05020	.17073	1.15175	.14824	.701
ORGS	11.42550	125.74873	11.42550	1.46219	7.81394	.006*
CRIT	5.61909	149.42037	5.61909	1.73745	3.23411	.076
META	1.04720	68.31140	1.04720	.79432	1.31836	.254
TIME	.06954	46.72361	.06954	.54330	.12799	.721
EFFT	2.66776	68.25288	2.66776	.79364	3.36143	.070
PEER	2.24564	180.71332	2.24564	2.10132	1.06868	.304
HELP	1.75538	103.93482	1.75538	1.20854	1.45248	.231

* $p<.05$

DIFFERENCES BETWEEN PRIVATE AND PUBLIC UNIVERSITIES

To investigate the degree to which the private university (PUC/RJ, $N=44$) and public university (UFRJ, $N=45$) means were significantly different, multivariate analysis of covariance (MANCOVA) was performed with subscale scores as 16 dependent variables and the two universities as two levels of a single independent variable. The cloze test scores were used as a covariate in order to control for differences between the two universities in overall English language proficiency. The MANCOVA analysis indicated that there were overall significant mean differences between the two universities on at least some of the subscales (Hotelling=.48325; Approximate $F=2.14$; $df=16$, 71; $p<.015$). As shown in Table 9, follow-up univariate F tests further indicated three particular subscales as potential sources for that overall difference between the two universities:

EXPT with an unadjusted mean of 5.52 for PUC/RJ and 5.70 for UFRJ ($F=7.76$; $p<.01$)
REHR with an unadjusted mean of 5.24 for PUC/RJ and 4.66 for UFRJ ($F=4.23$; $p<.04$)
ORGS with an unadjusted mean of 5.90 for PUC/RJ and 5.02 for UHRJ ($F=7.81$; $p<.01$)

In these results, the students at the private university (PUC/RJ) were significantly higher in rehearsal strategies (REHR) by .18 points and organization strategies (ORGS) by .58 points than the public university (UFRJ) students, while the reverse was true in expectancy for success (EXPT) by .88 points.

DISCUSSION

This discussion section will provide direct answers to the research questions posed at the outset of this study. To help guide the reader, those research questions will be used as headings to organize the discussion.

1. Are the scales on the QEMA appropriate (i.e., normally distributed) when the questionnaire is administered to university students in Brazil?

The descriptive statistics in this study indicate that the means for the various 7-point subscales vary considerably from a low of 2.99 for PEER to a high of 6.15 for TASK. The standard deviations indicate that there was also some variation among subscales in how broadly their scores were dispersed, though an F_{max} test showed that these differences were not statistically significant. In direct answer to the first research question, all of the scales except one were found to be approximately normal. The one clear exception was the TASK subscale, which definitely seemed to be negatively skewed. Four other scales also appear to be somewhat negatively skewed: SELF, EXPT, ELAB, and ORGS. The other nine scales appear to be approximately normal in distribution.

2. To what degree are the subscales on the QEMA reliable?

Recall that the Cronbach alpha reliability coefficients reported in this study indicate the degree to which each of the subscales was internally consistent, or reliable. The alpha coefficients for the QEMA subtests ranged from .38 to .82, all of which were lower than the equivalent estimates reported for the original MSLQ. In addition, the expected direct relationship between subscale length and reliability was shown to be a relevant factor in interpreting the reliability of the QEMA subscales. Finally, the standard error of measurement was discussed as an alternative way of interpreting the reliability of the various subscales. In short, the reliability of the QEMA subscales was found to vary considerably (possibly because of differences in subscale length), but most of the subscales can be said to be acceptably reliable for some research purposes, especially in view of the small number of items involved.

3. In terms of validity, how are the subscales on the QEMA related to each other?

Recall that validity is defined as the degree to which an instrument measures what it claims to be measuring. Demonstrating the content validity of an instrument involves establishing the degree to which the instrument is a representative sample of the types of items that, according to theory, should be on the instrument. The content validity of the original MSLQ was argued in Pintrich (1989) and those arguments apply to the Portuguese QEMA version, too. Demonstrating the construct validity of an instrument involves showing experimentally that the instrument is measuring what it claims to be measuring. The correlation coefficients among the various subscales showed some very strong relationships among scales that were theoretically related and weaker relationships between subscales that were theoretically unrelated. These patterns became clearer when a factor analysis with VARIMAX rotation showed that a four factor solution fit these data. The patterns of loadings indicated that, generally speaking, the MOTIVATION subscales load predominantly on factor 2, the COGNITIVE subscales load almost exclusively on factor 1, and the MANAGEMENT subscales load predominantly on factor 3. Thus to some degree, the analyses support the construct validity of these subscales.

4. What subscales on the QEMA differentiate between the private and public university students in this study?

MANCOVA analysis indicated overall significant mean differences between the two universities on at least some of the subscales when overall proficiency was controlled by using the cloze scores as a covariate. Follow-up univariate analyses indicated three possible sources of that overall significant difference: the students at the private university (PUC/RJ) were significantly higher in rehearsal strategies (REHR) and organization strategies (ORGS) than the public university (UFRJ) students, while the reverse was true in expectancy for success (EXPT). Thus students at the private university on average appear to use two of the cognitive learning strategies (rehearsal and organization) more than students at the public university, while students at the public university on average appear to be motivated by expectancy of success more than students at the public university.

CONCLUSION

On the whole, the QEMA was found to produce subscale scores and total scores that are (with one exception) normally distributed. Most of the subscales were also found to be reasonably reliable, though that reliability was found to be related to subscale length to a greater degree on some subscales than others. We conclude that some subscales of the QEMA, particularly TEST, EFFT, and HELP, had low reliability and relatively few items, so they would probably benefit from the addition of more items. The CONT subscale also showed low reliability but it already has eight items, and may therefore have other consistency problems not strictly related to subscale length.

Arguments were also presented here for the validity of the QEMA offering some support for the construct validity of the subscales. However, the results also indicate that some subscales should probably be revised to better fit the model implied in the original organization of the test, particularly the TIME subscale in the MANAGE- MENT section as well as the CONT and TEST subscales in the MOTIVATION section.

Finally, private university students were found on average to use two cognitive learning strategies (rehearsal and organization) significantly more than public university students. At the same time, public university students were found on average to be motivated by expectancy of success significantly more than public university students. Teachers in Brazilian private university language classrooms might benefit from realizing that their students may be more likely to use rehearsal and organization learning strategies; based on this knowledge, they could either tailor some activities to those learning strategies or train the students to strengthen other strategies. Conversely, teachers in the Brazilian public university language classrooms might benefit from knowing that their students may be less likely to use rehearsal and organization learning strategies either by avoiding activities that require those strategies or providing students with training in those strategies.

Teachers in public university language classrooms might further benefit from realizing that their students are more likely to have relatively high expectancies for success by capitalizing on that expectancy with classroom activities that build around it and at the same time training the students to draw on other motivations as well. Conversely, teachers at the Brazilian private university language classrooms might benefit from knowing that their students are slightly lower in expectancy for success by providing students with training that will bolster that expectation of success.

We hope that the Portuguese version of this instrument will prove useful to researchers in Brazil and other Portuguese speaking countries. It is further hoped that the analyses presented in this paper will inform and temper such use of the instrument.

SUGGESTIONS FOR FUTURE RESEARCH

As in most research, many questions were raised in the process of doing this study. In the hope that other researchers will be interested in following this line of research on the QEMA, we pose some of those questions here:

> Would the QEMA be reliable and valid if replicated at other institutions? In other Portuguese speaking countries?

> Would a revised version of the QEMA prove to be more reliable and valid than the version investigated in this study?

> What differences in motivation would be found by using the QEMA subscales to compare other groups (e.g., private/public universities again, low/high proficiency, males/females, science/humanities majors, etc.)?

What relationships would be found in comparisons between the QEMA and other measures of learner characteristics (e.g., personality, anxiety, study strategies, proficiency measures, etc.)?

Any feedback that future researchers can provide will be gratefully accepted.

REFERENCES

Brown, J. D. (1980). Relative merits of four methods for scoring cloze tests. *Modern Language Journal, 64*(3), 311–317.

Pintrich, P. R. (1989). The dynamic interplay of students motivation and cognition in the college classroom. In M. Mathr & C. Ames (Eds.) *Advances in motivation and achievement: Motivation enhancing environments,* Volume 6 (pp. 117–160). New York: JAI Press.

Pintrich, P. R., Smith, D. A. F., & McKeachie, W. J. (1989a). *Motivated Strategies for Learning Questionnaire (MSLQ).* Unpublished manuscript, National Center for Research to Improve Postsecondary Teaching and Learning, University of Michigan, Ann Arbor.

Pintrich, P. R., Smith, D. A. F., & McKeachie, W. J. (1989b). *A manual for the use of the Motivated Strategies for Learning Questionnaire (MSLQ).* Unpublished manuscript, National Center for Research to Improve Postsecondary Teaching and Learning, University of Michigan, Ann Arbor.

QuattroPro[tm]. (1991). Scotts Valley, CA: Borland International.

SPSS/PC+[tm]. (1991). Chicago, IL: SPSS Incorporated.

QUESTIONÁRIO DE ESTRATÉGIAS MOTIVACIONAIS PARA APRENDIZAGEM (QEMA)

Seu professor está participando de um estudo sobre ensino e aprendizagem em 3º grau. Gostaríamos de contar com a sua participação na pesquisa. Como parte do estudo, solicitaremos que você preencha alguns questionários relacionados à sua motivação e aprendizagem neste curso. Se você participar, receberá feedback com relação a suas habilidades de aprendizagem e motivação que poderão lhe ser úteis na sua carreira universitária. SUA PARTICIPAÇÃO É VOLUNTÁRIA E NÃO ESTÁ RELACIONADA DE FORMA ALGUMA COM SUA AVALIAÇÃO NO CURSO. Você pode decidir participar agora mas pode desistir de participar em qualquer momento durante o semestre, sem penalidade. Todas as suas respostas serão estritamente confidenciais e apenas os pesquisadores terão acesso a elas.

O questionário anexo lista afirmativas sobre seus hábitos de estudo, suas habilidades de aprendizagem e sua motivação para o trabalho neste curso: NÃO HÁ RESPOSTAS CERTAS OU ERRADAS AO QUESTIONÁRIO. ISTO NÃO É UM TESTE. Solicitamos que você responda ao questionário da forma mais precisa, refletindo sobre suas próprias atitudes e comportamentos neste curso. Suas respostas ao questionário serão analisadas pelo computador e você receberá, posteriormente, um relatório individual. Esse relatório individual irá ajudá-lo a identificar motivação e habilidades de aprendizagem que você poderá aprimorar durante o semestre. Por favor, preencha os espaços abaixo se você quiser participar deste estudo. Obrigado pela sua cooperação.

NOME (em letra de forma) _____

NOME DO PROFESSOR _____

CURSO _____

DISCIPLINA – HORÁRIO _____

DATA _____

Parte A . Motivação

As perguntas abaixo estão relacionadas à sua motivação e atitudes neste curso. Lembre-se de que não há respostas certas ou erradas, responda com a maior precisão possível. Use a escala abaixo para responder às perguntas. Se você considerar uma afirmativa definitivamente verdadeira, marque o número 7; se uma afirmativa for absolutamente falsa, marque o número 1. Se a afirmativa for mais ou menos verdadeira, encontre o número entre 1 e 7 que melhor se enquadre à sua análise.

| 1 | 2 | 3 | 4 | 5 | 6 | 7 |

Absolutamente falsa ←------------------------------→ Definitivamente verdadeira

1. Num curso como este, dou preferência a um tipo de material didático que apresente desafios para que me permitam aprender coisas novas. 1 2 3 4 5 6 7

2. Se eu estudar de forma apropriada, serei capaz de assimilar o conteúdo deste curso. 1 2 3 4 5 6 7

3. Ao fazer um teste, penso no quanto estou me saindo mal comparado com outros alunos. 1 2 3 4 5 6 7

4. Se eu não assimilo o conteúdo do curso, é porque ele é difícil demais. 1 2 3 4 5 6 7

5. Acredito que serei capaz de aplicar o que aprender neste curso em outros. 1 2 3 4 5 6 7

6. Acredito que vou tirar uma nota excelente neste curso 1 2 3 4 5 6 7

7. Estou certo que sou capaz de assimilar o conteúdo mais difícil apresentado na bibliografia deste curso. 1 2 3 4 5 6 7

8. Tirar uma boa nota neste curso é o maior prêmio para mim neste momento. 1 2 3 4 5 6 7

9. Quando faço uma prova, penso sobre questões que não sei responder em outras partes do teste. 1 2 3 4 5 6 7

10. A culpa é toda minha se não assimilar o conteúdo neste curso. 1 2 3 4 5 6 7

11. É importante para mim aprender o conteúdo ensinado neste curso. 1 2 3 4 5 6 7

12. A coisa mais importante para mim no momento é melhorar minha média geral; portanto, minha preocupação neste curso é tirar uma boa nota. 1 2 3 4 5 6 7

13. Tenho certeza que posso aprender os conceitos básicos ensinados neste curso. 1 2 3 4 5 6 7

14. Se depender de mim, vou tirar notas melhores do que a maioria dos outros alunos. 1 2 3 4 5 6 7

15. Se eu assimilar o conteúdo deste curso, é basicamente devido ao professor. 1 2 3 4 5 6 7

16. Quando faço provas, penso nas consequências de ser reprovado. 1 2 3 4 5 6 7

17. Tenho certeza de que posso assimilar o conteúdo mais complexo apresentado pelo professor neste curso. 1 2 3 4 5 6 7

18. Num curso como este, prefiro material didático que desperte minha curiosidade, mesmo que seja difícil de assimilar. 1 2 3 4 5 6 7

19. Estou muito interessado no conteúdo deste curso   1 2 3 4 5 6 7

20. Se eu me esforçar o suficiente, vou assimilar o conteúdo deste curso.   1 2 3 4 5 6 7

21. Tenho uma sensação negativa e desagradável quando faço uma prova.   1 2 3 4 5 6 7

22. Tenho certeza que posso ter um ótimo desempenho nos trabalhos e provas neste curso.   1 2 3 4 5 6 7

23. Espero ter um bom desempenho neste curso.   1 2 3 4 5 6 7

24. O que me traz maior satisfação neste curso é tentar assimilar o conteúdo da maneira mais detalhada possível.   1 2 3 4 5 6 7

25. Acho que o material deste curso é útil para o meu aprendizado.   1 2 3 4 5 6 7

26. Quando tenho oportunidade, escolho os trabalhos que possam me trazer conhecimento, mesmo que não me garantam uma boa nota.   1 2 3 4 5 6 7

27. Quando não assimilo o conteúdo do curso, é porque não me esforcei o suficiente.   1 2 3 4 5 6 ?

28. Gosto do assunto deste curso.   1 2 3 4 5 6 7

29. É muito importante para mim compreender o programa deste curso.   1 2 3 4 5 6 7

30. Quando não assimilo o conteúdo deste curso, é por causa do professor.   1 2 3 4 5 6 7

31. Sinto o meu coração bater forte quando estou fazendo uma prova.   1 2 3 4 5 6 7

32. Tenho certeza que posso dominar as habilidades desenvolvidas neste curso.   1 2 3 4 5 6 7

33. Se assimilo o conteúdo deste curso é porque ele é fácil.   1 2 3 4 5 6 7

34. Quero ser bem sucedido neste curso porque é importante mostrar meu potencial para a minha família, amigos, patrão, etc.   1 2 3 4 5 6 7

35. Tendo em vista o nível de dificuldade deste curso, o professor e o meu potencial, acho que serei bem sucedido neste curso.   1 2 3 4 5 6 7

Parte B. Estratégias de aprendizagem

As perguntas abaixo estão relacionadas às suas estratégias de aprendizagem e às habilidades de estudo. Mais uma vez, não há respostas certas ou erradas. Responda as perguntas sobre os seus hábitos de estudo com a maior precisão possível. Use a mesma escala para responder as perguntas que se seguem.

1	2	3	4	5	6	7

Absolutamente falsa ←--------------------------------→ Definitivamente verdadeira

36. Quando estudo os textos para este curso, esquematizo o material a fim de organizar meus pensamentos.   1 2 3 4 5 6 7

37. Durante a aula, frequentemente não percebo pontos importantes por estar pensando em outras coisas.   1 2 3 4 5 6 7

38. Ao estudar para este curso, frequentemente tento explicar a matéria a um colega.   1 2 3 4 5 6 7

39. Geralmente estudo num local onde posso me concentrar no meu trabalho.   1 2 3 4 5 6 7

40. Ao fazer as leituras para este curso, formulo perguntas que me orientem as leituras.   1 2 3 4 5 6 7

41. Frequentemente sinto tanta preguiça ou falta de motivação quando estou estudando para este curso que abandono antes de terminar o que havia planejado fazer.   1 2 3 4 5 6 7

42. Frequentemente me questiono sobre coisas que leio e ouço neste curso para decidir se concordo com elas.   1 2 3 4 5 6 7

43. Quando estudo para este curso, tenho o hábito de ler, reler (em voz alta) a matéria.   1 2 3 4 5 6 7

44. Mesmo que tenha problemas para assimilar o conteúdo deste curso, tento fazer o trabalho sozinho, sem nenhuma ajuda externa.   1 2 3 4 5 6 7

45. Quando fico confuso sobre alguma coisa que estou lendo para este curso, volto e tento solucionar a dúvida.   1 2 3 4 5 6 7

46. Quando estou estudando para este curso, leio os textos e minhas anotações e tento localizar as idéias mais importantes.   1 2 3 4 5 6 7

47. Faço bom uso do meu tempo para estudar para este curso.   1 2 3 4 5 6 7

48. Se tenho dificuldades em entender os textos deste curso, reformulo meu método de estudo.   1 2 3 4 5 6 7

49. Tento trabalhar com os outros alunos da turma para fazer os trabalhos.   1 2 3 4 5 6 7

50. Quando estudo para este curso, leio e releio minhas anotações e os textos do curso.   1 2 3 4 5 6 7

51. Quando uma teoria, uma interpretação ou uma conclusão é apresentada em sala de aula ou em textos, tento verificar se há boa fundamentação.   1 2 3 4 5 6 7

52. Tento me esforçar para ser bem sucedido neste curso, mêsmo não gostando do que estou fazendo.   1 2 3 4 5 6 7

53. Faço quadros, diagramas e tabelas bem simples que me ajudam a organizar o material deste curso.   1 2 3 4 5 6 7

54. Quando estudo para este curso, frequentemente reservo algum tempo para a discussão do conteúdo com um grupo de alunos da turma.   1 2 3 4 5 6 7

55. Trato o material do curso como um ponto de partida e tento desenvolver minhas próprias idéias.   1 2 3 4 5 6 7

56. Acho difícil seguir um horário de estudos.   1 2 3 4 5 6 7

57. Quando estudo para este curso, reuno informações de diferentes fontes, tais como palestras, textos e debates.   1 2 3 4 5 6 7

58. Antes de estudar um conteúdo novo detalhadamente, frequentemente o analiso para ver como ele é organizado.   1 2 3 4 5 6 7

59. Faço perguntas a mim mesmo para ter certeza de que assimilei o conteúdo que estou estudando.   1 2 3 4 5 6 7

60. Tento mudar a forma de estudar para me adaptar melhor às exigências do curso e ao estilo do professor.   1 2 3 4 5 6 7

61. Frequentemente, constato que faço leitura para este curso mas não consigo entender do que se trata.   1 2 3 4 5 6 7

62. Peço ao professor que esclareça conceitos que eu não compreendo bem.   1 2 3 4 5 6 7

63. Memorizo palavras chaves para me lembrar de conceitos importantes.   1 2 3 4 5 6 7

64. Quando um trabalho é difícil, desisto ou só estudo as partes fáceis.   1 2 3 4 5 6 7

65. Quando estudo para este curso, tento refletir sobre um tema para saber o que devo aprender ao invés de apenas ler e reler a matéria.   1 2 3 4 5 6 7

66. Tento relacionar idéias de um curso com idéias de outros cursos, quando possível.   1 2 3 4 5 6 7

67. Quando estudo para este curso, examino minhas anotações e faço um esquema dos conceitos importantes.   1 2 3 4 5 6 7

68. Quando leio para este curso, tento relacionar o conteúdo ao que já sei.   1 2 3 4 5 6 7

69. Tenho um local regular apropriado para estudar.   1 2 3 4 5 6 7

70. Tento lidar com minhas próprias idéias relacionando-as com o que estou aprendendo.   1 2 3 4 5 6 7

1	2	3	4	5	6	7

Absolutamente falsa ←--------------------------------→ Definitivamente verdadeira

71. Quando estudo para este curso, escrevo resumos das idéias centrais dos textos e de minhas anotações.   1 2 3 4 5 6 7

72. Quando não consigo assimilar o conteúdo deste curso, peço ajuda a outros colegas.   1 2 3 4 5 6 7

73. Tento assimilar o conteúdo fazendo ligações entre os textos e os conceitos expostos em aula.   1 2 3 4 5 6 7

74. Faço questão de me manter em dia com as leituras semanais e com os trabalhos.   1 2 3 4 5 6 7

75. Sempre que leio ou ouço uma afirmativa ou conclusão neste curso, penso sobre possíveis alternativas.   1 2 3 4 5 6 7

76. Listo a terminologia importante para este curso e memorizo-a.   1 2 3 4 5 6 7

77. Assisto as aulas regularmente.   1 2 3 4 5 6 7

78. Mesmo quando o material didático é chato ou pouco interessante, me mantenho envolvido até o fim.   1 2 3 4 5 6 7

79. Tento identificar os alunos da turma aos quais posso pedir ajuda se necessário.   1 2 3 4 5 6 7

80. Quando estudo para este curso, tento localizar os conceitos que não compreendo bem.   1 2 3 4 5 6 7

81. Frequentemente, acho que não dedico muito tempo a este curso por causa de outras atividades.   1 2 3 4 5 6 7

82. Quando estudo para este curso, estabeleço objetivos para mim mesmo a fim de direcionar as minhas atividades em cada período de estudo.   1 2 3 4 5 6 7

83. Quando eu me sinto confusa com as anotações feitas em sala, não deixo de organizá-las posteriormente.   1 2 3 4 5 6 7

84. Raramente tenho tempo para rever minhas anotações e textos antes de uma prova.   1 2 3 4 5 6 7

85. Tento aplicar as idéias dos textos a outras atividades tais como aulas e debates.   1 2 3 4 5 6 7

Anne-Marie Masgoret
University of Western Ontario

Mercè Bernaus
Universitat Autònoma de Barcelona

Robert C. Gardner
University of Western Ontario

EXAMINING THE ROLE OF ATTITUDES AND MOTIVATION OUTSIDE OF THE FORMAL CLASSROOM: A TEST OF THE MINI-AMTB FOR CHILDREN

Authors' note

Preparation of this chapter was facilitated by a scholarship (DOGC núm. 2625 de 23.4.1998, Ref. BCC98–01) awarded to the first author from the Comissionat per a Universitats i Recerca del Departament de la Presidència de la Generalitat de Catalunya [Presidency of the Catalan Government (Generalitat de Catalunya), Department of Higher Education and Research], and a doctoral fellowship (752–2000–1207) to the first author from the Social Sciences and Humanities Research Council of Canada, as well as a research grant (410–99–0147) to the last author.

INTRODUCTION

Extensive empirical research has demonstrated that attitudes and motivation are related to how well individuals learn a second/foreign language (Clément & Kruidenier, 1983; Dörnyei, 1994; Gardner, 1985). Until relatively recently, much of this research has been based on the Socio-Educational Model of Second Language Acquisition (Gardner, 1985). This model proposes that a number of attitudinal characteristics such as Integrativeness and Attitudes Toward the Learning Situation influence the students' level of motivation to learn another language and that high levels of motivation promote success in learning the language. A considerable number of research studies have supported this model (see, for example, Gardner, Tremblay, & Masgoret, 1997), and motivation has been widely accepted by both educators (Spolsky, 1989) and researchers (Clément, Dörnyei, & Noels, 1994; Dörnyei, 1998) as one of the key factors that influence the rate and success of second language learning in the classroom.

Relatively little research, however, has been directed to the language learning that occurs when individuals take part in foreign language activities outside of the formal classroom context, such as at summer language camps, excursion programs to the other language community, and so forth. The present study is unique in that it

Masgoret, A-M., Bernaus, M., & Gardner, R. C. (2001). Examining the role of attitudes and motivation outside of the formal classroom: A test of the mini-AMTB for children. In Z. Dörnyei & R. Schmidt (Eds.), *Motivation and second language acquisition* (Technical Report #23, pp. 281–295). Honolulu: University of Hawai'i, Second Language Teaching and Curriculum Center.

examines the relationships among attitudes, motivation, anxiety, and self-perceptions of foreign language achievement in children participating in a "native-like" summer language program.

This research involves a short-term intensive English as a foreign language program, known as "Enjoy English," that takes place in Spain each summer. The program is activity-based and involves British university students who are recruited to work as language instructors for groups of Spanish elementary students. Summer language camps such as Enjoy English have been developed to offer children the opportunity to learn a foreign language in a "native-like" environment by participating in a number of daily recreational activities that are led by native speakers. Like many exchange or immersion programs, Enjoy English attempts to foster inter-ethnic contact and is based on the premise that such contact promotes favorable intergroup relations that are conducive to second language acquisition.

Students' attitudes toward the second language group have consistently been shown to be related to their motivation to learn the second language, which in turn, is associated with their achievement in that language. This study examines how motivational determinants associated with learning a second language such as attitudes toward the learning situation, attitudes toward the language and second language group, and anxiety relate to English achievement in Spanish children participating in the Enjoy English summer language program.

THE RESEARCH CONTEXT: THE ENJOY ENGLISH PROGRAM

The setting for this investigation was the Enjoy English program, which has been operating in Spain since 1995. This program involves students from 5 to 15 years of age (with an average of 10 students per group, depending on their age) and takes place in a number of schools across Catalonia, the Basque Country, and the Balearic Islands. Enjoy English is a 4-week intensive, activity-based program that is conducted during the month of July (4 hours a day, 5 days a week). Each year this program involves approximately 1,500 students, 150 language monitors (i.e., English instructors), and 50 Spanish teachers of English.

The activities are lead by language monitors (students carefully selected from different universities in Great Britain and Ireland) and supervised by Spanish teachers of English. Both groups receive some training prior to the beginning of the program and are introduced to the materials that they will use for the language activities. During the course of the program, the monitors and the teachers hold daily meetings to discuss the activities already performed as well as the ones that will be performed the following day. If there are any questions or comments, they are discussed during the daily meeting. The monitors live with host Spanish families during the program. This exposure to members of the host community allows the monitors to learn more about the community, language, and culture of Spain. Similarly, the children are exposed to the Irish and/or British language and culture through their monitors.

The main objective of the program is to improve the children's oral and aural English skills. Secondary objectives include: (a) having the monitors become acquainted with the culture and the language of the community, and (b) having the children become acquainted with the British or the Irish culture through their monitors. These aims are achieved mainly through a set of structured activities that are designed differently for each age group. These activities include interactive stories followed by conversations, sports and games, songs, arts and crafts, and drama. Some of these activities are presented in a "show" each week for the rest of the participants, and families are invited to attend a final show during the last week of the program.

ATTITUDES AND MOTIVATION

Considerable research has demonstrated that attitudinal and motivational variables are related to how well individuals learn second languages in a classroom situation (Clément et al., 1994; Dörnyei, 1994; Gardner, 1985). Much of the research concerned with the role of attitudes and motivation in second language learning has assessed these variables using the Attitude/Motivation Test Battery (AMTB) (Gardner, 1985) or tests derived from it. The AMTB was designed to assess various individual difference variables proposed in Gardner's (1985) Socio-Educational Model of Second Language Acquisition. This model has developed over more than 40 years of research and is concerned with the role of various individual difference characteristics of the student in the learning of a second language.

The majority of the subtests in the AMTB are designed to measure three primary concepts: *Motivation, Integrativeness*, and *Attitudes toward the Learning Situation*. Motivation refers to a combination of the learner's attitudes, aspirations, and effort with respect to learning the second language. The subtests assessing it include Motivational Intensity, Desire to Learn the Language, and Attitudes Toward Learning the Language. Integrativeness reflects the individual's willingness and interest in social interaction with members of other groups and is measured using three subscales: Degree of Integrative Orientation, Attitudes Toward the Target Language Group, and Interest in Foreign Languages. The third component, Attitudes Toward the Learning Situation, refers to the student's reaction to formal instruction and includes two measures: Evaluation of the Language Instructor and Evaluation of the Language Course. Additional variables are often included in the AMTB based on the context of the study and the research questions being addressed. For example, *Language Anxiety*, which refers to apprehension experienced by the individual in the language class or any situation in which the language is used, is assessed using the measures of Language Class Anxiety, and Language Use Anxiety. Other measures have also included Degree of Instrumental Orientation and Parental Encouragement (to learn the language).

Research investigating the role of attitudes and motivation in second language learning has reported consistent relationships among these variables as well as their relation to indices of achievement. Generally, research using the AMTB has demonstrated that a primary determinant of achievement in the second language is

---

motivation and that other classes of variables such as Integrativeness, and Attitudes Toward the Learning Situation are important largely because they serve as foundations for this motivation.

In an alternative model of second language learning, Clément (1980) includes a *Self-Confidence* construct that is viewed as a combination of perceived proficiency in the language and an absence of language anxiety. According to this view, second language students develop self-confidence based on the frequency and quality of their contact with members of the host community. This contact plays a primary role in the development of the motivational processes that are major determinants of second language achievement (Clément, 1986; Clément, Gardner, & Smythe, 1980). Although Clément's (1980) Social Context Model is most applicable to bilingual contexts where students have a greater opportunity to interact with members of the second language community, recent studies have suggested that, in some cases, self-confidence may play a role in second language achievement even in unilingual contexts if the relative status of the second language is high and there is at least some exposure to the other language (Clément et al., 1994). One example of this could be the increasing status of English as a new European language of trade or as the lingua franca of international communication.

Since the majority of studies in this area have focussed on the role of the above variables within the context of the formal classroom situation, one purpose of the present study is to examine how measures assessing these variables relate to each other and to second language achievement in the context of an informal activity-based language program.

MEASURING ATTITUDES AND MOTIVATION IN CHILDREN USING THE MINI-AMTB

Another aim of this study is to introduce a new instrument which was designed to help researchers as well as teachers test hypotheses concerning the relationship between attitudinal/motivational variables and learning outcomes in samples of young school-aged children. Gardner's (1985) Attitude/Motivation Test Battery (AMTB) has shown its reliability and validity in numerous investigations. Recently, a shorter version of this questionnaire (the mini-AMTB) has been introduced to reduce the administration time while maintaining the basic conceptual structure of the original version. This instrument has the potential to allow researchers and instructors to gather data for research as well as curriculum evaluation purposes, while imposing as little as possible on class time.

Two studies (Gardner, Lalonde, & Moorcroft, 1985; Gardner & MacIntyre, 1993) have assessed the psychometric properties of the AMTB by using the Campbell and Fiske (1959) multitrait/multimethod approach to investigate the relationship between different measures of each of the various attributes. In both of these studies, one of the measures has been the mini-AMTB. Gardner and MacIntyre (1993) compared three different measures of the 11 attributes measured by the AMTB with a sample of 92 university students in the introductory French course. One measure

---

was based on a Likert (1932) format, the second was based on a semantic differential format, and the third on a Guilford (1954) single-item format (i.e., the mini-AMTB). Since the Likert AMTB format is the most frequently used, examining its relationship to the mini-AMTB provides a measure of the convergent validity of the single-item measures (i.e., the mini-AMTB). Overall, the correlations between the two measures of the same variables were significant and reasonably high given that each variable is measured with only one item in the mini-AMTB. The correlations between the Likert assessment of a variable and the mini-AMTB assessment of the same variable ranged from .46 (Degree of Instrumental Orientation) to .92 (French Teacher Evaluation). The median correlation was .72. Moreover, the two different measurement procedures demonstrated comparable correlations with measures of achievement in French. When attention is directed toward the correlation of an aggregate Integrative Motive Score (Integrativeness + Attitudes Toward the Learning Situation + Motivation) with five objective measures of French achievement, the correlations were comparable. They ranged from .17(ns) to .40 ($p<.01$, median=.30) for the Likert format and .17(ns) to .38 ($p<.01$, median=.30) for the mini-AMTB.

Similar findings were reported by Gardner et al. (1985) who also compared the Likert and the Guilford formats of the AMTB. Participants in this study were 168 student volunteers from the introductory psychology course. The correlations between the two different measures of the same attribute varied from .35 (Degree of Instrumental Orientation) to .70 (for both Attitudes Toward Learning French and Desire to Learn French). These correlations are slightly lower than those reported by Gardner and MacIntyre (1993) but this is to be expected. Research participants in the Gardner et al. study were not students of French, and it is reasonable to conclude that the constructs were not as meaningful to them as for the participants in the Gardner and MacIntyre study. This is reflected in the measures of internal consistency-reliability for the Likert scales in the two studies. The median internal consistency-reliability coefficient in the Gardner and MacIntyre (1993) study was .82, while that in the Gardner et al. (1985) study was only .71. Since the participants in the Gardner et al. study were not studying French, there were, of course, no correlations of the measures with indices of French achievement.

Overall, these analyses using the multitrait/multimethod approach among these two ways of measuring the variables normally assessed using the AMTB provides substantial support for the validity of these constructs using the mini-AMTB.

A more recent study (Tennant & Gardner, 1999) assessed the construct validity of the mini-AMTB by comparing the relationships among the aggregate measures of Motivation, Integrativeness, and Attitudes Toward the Learning Situation to those found in numerous studies that used the larger AMTB. In this study, 65 students, enrolled in a first year university level French language course, completed a computerized version of the mini-AMTB during the 5th and 10th sessions in their multimedia laboratory (measures were administered within a 5-week interval). This study found significant correlations between the measure of Motivation and both those of Integrativeness (pre-test, $r=.50$, $p<.01$; post-test, $r=.54$, $p<.01$) and

Attitudes Toward the Learning Situation (pre-test, $r=.70$, $p<.01$; post-test, $r=.67$, $p<.01$). Furthermore, a strong relationship was found between Integrativeness and Attitudes Toward the Learning Situation (pre-test, $r=.53$, $p<.01$; post-test, $r=.49$, $p<.01$). Finally, French Achievement on the post-test was significantly related to Integrativeness ($r=.28$, $p<.05$), Motivation ($r=.39$, $p<.01$), and Attitudes Toward the Learning Situation ($r=.30$, $p<.01$) assessed during the pre-test, while Achievement on the post-test was significantly correlated with both Integrativeness ($r=.30$, $p<.05$) and Motivation ($r=.40$, $p<.01$) assessed on the post-test. The high correlation between Achievement and Motivation is consistent with previous research using the AMTB which demonstrates that Motivation is a direct determinant of second language learning and should therefore be the most relevant variable of the three composite measures (Gardner, 1985). Thus, the relationships among Motivation, Integrativeness, Attitudes Toward the Learning Situation, and Achievement provide support for the construct validity of the mini-AMTB since studies carried out using the complete scales of the AMTB have repeatedly shown this same pattern of relationships among these variables. In addition to evidence of construct validity, Tennant and Gardner (1999) provided support for the reliability of the aggregate measures in their study by reporting relatively high test-retest correlations ranging from .75 for Integrativeness to .89 for Motivation, and .83 and .85 for Attitude toward the Learning Situation and Anxiety, respectively.

Both the AMTB and the mini-AMTB were originally developed to be used with older school-aged children and adults. These measures, however, are not as appropriate for younger children due to their item difficulty as well as the long administration time required to complete the larger AMTB. Since the present study deals primarily with younger children, a children's version of the mini-AMTB was developed. The mini-AMTB for children, which maintains the same conceptual structure of the original version, is more suitable for young children since the items are less difficult to process, and the entire test can be completed in a short period of time.

In sum, the purpose of the present study is twofold: a) to examine whether the consistent relationships found between a number of motivational determinants of second language achievement in formal classroom situations will generalize to children participating in an intensive activity-based program, and b) to investigate the conceptual structure and validity of the mini-AMTB for Children.

METHOD

PARTICIPANTS

The sample comprised 499 Spanish children (ranging from ages 10–15) participating in a 4-week English summer language program. Demographic information collected from the participants indicated that, of the children ranging from ages 10 to 15, 196 were 10 years of age, 131 were 11, 49 were 13, and 15 were older.

During the last week of the program, the children completed a questionnaire in Spanish containing two sections. Part I dealt with language learning attitudes and motivation, along with a number of items relevant to the language program, and Part II dealt with their self-perceptions of English proficiency. In addition, the monitors involved in the program completed evaluations for each of their students in terms of his or her English proficiency.

MEASURES COMPLETED BY THE CHILDREN

The following 16 measures were developed to provide single-item Spanish versions of the attributes measured by the Attitude/Motivation Test Battery (mini-AMTB; Gardner & MacIntyre, 1993). Although the mini-AMTB consists of 11 items, it was found necessary to develop 16 items to be used with young children in this context. These extra items are marked with an asterisk (*) in the listing below. All measures presented participants with a single item followed by a 7-point rating scale ranging from a *negative* to *positive* option. The following measures are grouped according to the subtests that are often aggregated to form higher order constructs using the full version of the AMTB.

Attitudes toward the learning situation

The following three measures were developed by the authors to assess various attitudes that are relevant to participation in the Enjoy English program:

Attitudes Toward the Enjoy English program. This item assesses the individual's attitude toward the activities in the Enjoy English program.

Attitudes Toward the Monitor. This measure was presented to assess one's attitude toward the language monitor.

*Desire to Return to the Program.** This item assesses the individual's desire to participate in the program again.

Motivation

Motivation was measured with the following five single-item measures:

Attitudes Toward Learning English. This item assesses the participant's feelings about learning English.

*Persistence.** This item refers to the amount of effort expended by the participant to learn English.

Motivational Intensity. This measure assesses the degree to which a child actively seeks assistance during the program when he or she encounters language difficulties.

Desire to Learn English. This item assesses the degree to which an individual wants to learn English.

*Participation in the Program.** This measure assesses the degree to which an individual actively participates during the Enjoy English activities.

Integrativeness

This measures the degree to which respondents were learning English for the purpose of interacting and communicating with English speakers. This aggregate measure was composed of single-item measures of the following four constructs:

Integrative Orientation. This item assesses the extent to which individuals seek to learn English for integrative reasons.

Attitudes Toward English Speakers. This item measures one's attitude about English-speaking people.

Interest in Foreign Languages. This item was presented to assess one's interest in foreign languages.

*Desire to Live in an English-speaking Country.** This item assesses one's feelings toward living in an English-speaking place.

Language Anxiety

This was assessed by two items:

English Use Anxiety. This measure assesses feelings of concern when faced with speaking English outside of class.

English Class Anxiety. This measure assesses one's level of apprehension when called upon to use English during the English activities.

Additional variables

Instrumental Orientation. This item assesses the degree to which participants adopt pragmatic reasons for learning English.

*Parental Encouragement.** This measure assesses the degree to which individuals are encouraged by their parents to learn and study English.

In addition to the mini-AMTB for children, the participants were asked to assess themselves in terms of their perceived English proficiency using the following two measures.

Self-perceptions of English achievement

Self-rated Oral Assessment. This measure requires participants to rate their English proficiency on a 4-point scale, in terms of their speaking skills.

Self-rated Comprehension Assessment. This measure requires participants to rate their English proficiency on a 4-point scale in terms of oral comprehension.

OBJECTIVE MEASURES OF ENGLISH ACHEIVEMENT

The following three evaluation measures were completed by the language monitors at the end of the last week of the Enjoy English program.

Relative Performance. This measure requires the language monitors to place each child in their group on a number line ranging from 0 to 10 based on his/her relative language performance within the group.

Oral Proficiency Assessment. This measure requires monitors to rate the English proficiency of each child in their group, on a 7-point scale in terms of his/her speaking skills.

Comprehension Assessment. This measure requires monitors to rate the English proficiency of each child, on a 7-point scale in terms of oral comprehension.

RESULTS AND DISCUSSION

In order to study the relations among the 18 measures, accounting for the variation attributable to age differences, the correlations involving the 19 measures were factor analyzed by means of a principal components analysis. Examination of the scree plot (Cattell, 1966) suggested that five factors accounted for 53.3% of the common variance. The factors were rotated by means of the varimax procedure, and the rotated factor matrix is presented in Table 1.

Factor I obtains appreciable loadings from 11 variables. Considering the four variables with the highest loadings, the pattern of loadings suggests that children with favorable Attitudes Toward the Monitor hold favorable Attitudes Toward the Enjoy English Program, favorable Attitudes Toward English Speakers, and a Desire to Return to the Program. Clearly, these variables suggest that this dimension is defined primarily by favorable attitudes toward learning and using English in the context of this program. It is thus best identified as an *Attitudes Toward English* factor. Other variables with loadings greater than .40 indicate that children with favorable attitudes toward English evaluate their oral and aural proficiency highly, express a strong desire to learn English, participate actively in classes, express favorable attitudes toward learning English, and a desire to live in an English-speaking country. Slightly lower loadings (greater than .30) were obtained by the measures of Persistence and Motivational Intensity. These results suggest that children with favorable attitudes toward English are highly motivated to learn English and feel that they are, in fact, quite proficient in English.

Table 1: Rotated factor matrix of children's mini-AMTB items

variables	FACTORS				
	I	II	III	IV	V
Age	−.132	.043	.045	.798	−.034
Attitudes toward the Enjoy English program	.724	.141	.110	−.217	.067
Attitudes toward the monitor	.759	−.044	−.021	.005	.086
Desire to return to the program*	.633	.229	.010	−.216	.190
Attitudes toward learning English	.467	.411	.159	−.503	−.102
Persistence*	.368	.360	.077	.010	.121
Motivational intensity	.386	.152	.541	−.071	−.089
Desire to learn English	.517	.255	.094	−.154	.241
Participation in the program*	.494	.125	.019	−.068	−.210
Integrative orientation	.021	.724	.095	.016	.045
Attitudes toward English speakers	.690	.142	.001	−.048	.166
Interest in foreign languages	.285	.601	.148	−.411	.045
Desire to live in an English-speaking country*	.431	.438	−.116	−.037	.094
English use anxiety	−.106	−.046	−.150	.322	−.615
English class anxiety	.149	.029	−.757	.121	−.179
Instrumental orientation	.135	.743	.021	.032	.019
Parental encouragement*	.223	.118	−.124	.231	.714
Self-perceptions of English achievement	.631	.099	.269	−.017	.091
Objective measure of English achievement	.150	.101	.743	.118	−.088

Factor II is defined by five variables. Loadings greater than .40 were obtained by the measures of Integrative Orientation, Instrumental Orientation, Interest in Foreign Languages, Desire to Live in an English-speaking Country, and Attitudes Toward Learning English. In addition, the Motivational Intensity measure had a loading greater than .30. This factor obviously reflects *Orientation to Learn English* and indicates that those children who perceive both integrative and instrumental orientations as important are those who are interested in all foreign languages, motivated to learn English, and interested in experiencing life in an English community.

Three variables define Factor III. Children who are evaluated very positively on English proficiency by the language monitors at the end of the program, score highly on the Motivational Intensity measure and demonstrate low levels of English Class Anxiety. It seems most meaningful, therefore, to define this factor as *English*

Proficiency, and to point out that such proficiency is associated with high levels of motivation and low levels of English Class Anxiety.

Factor IV obtains loadings greater than ±.40 from three measures. The pattern of the loadings suggest that children who are older tend to have less favorable attitudes toward learning English and less interest in foreign languages than younger children. Clearly, the major characteristic of this factor is *Age* and reflects the relationships of some of the variables to age. Moreover, the measure of English Use Anxiety has a loading greater than .30 suggesting that there is a tendency for older children to be somewhat anxious about using their English outside of the classroom situation.

Two variables define Factor V. Children who report high levels of encouragement from their parents tend to exhibit low levels of English Use Anxiety. This factor is tentatively defined as *Parental Encouragement*. This factor suggests that children receiving parental support tend to be less anxious about using English outside of the classroom situation.

One observation that can be made from the results of the factor analysis is that the various items of the mini-AMTB for children show different patterns of relationships than those frequently found in previous studies. This could be due to the nature of the setting, the age of the children, the wording of the items (they had to be much more specific than in the forms of the mini-AMTB used with university students), or even the additional five items. Whatever the reason, there is no clear indication of independent clusters reflecting Integrativeness, Attitudes Toward the Learning Situation, Motivation, or Language Anxiety. This is not surprising, however, considering the unique learning context of the present study.

There is evidence of some consistency among the items if one attempts to form the clusters by calculating the internal consistency reliability for these clusters. Aggregating the items as suggested by their groupings in the method section yielded the following Cronbach alpha reliability coefficients: Integrativeness (α=.62), Attitudes Toward the Learning Situation (α=.75), Motivation (α=.63), and Language Anxiety (α=.11). These internal consistency reliability coefficients are slightly lower than those obtained in other studies using the mini-AMTB. Gardner and MacIntyre (1993) reported a median internal consistency-reliability coefficient of .82, while that in the Gardner et al. (1985) study was .71. The low coefficient for Language Anxiety was due primarily to the English Use Anxiety item. This item was not considered meaningful to the majority of children, probably because they have little or no opportunity to use English outside of the program.

In addition to investigating the relationships among the variables, we can also direct attention toward the correlations of these measures with the objective measure of achievement as well as the children's self-perceptions of English achievement. Table 2 presents these correlations.

Table 2: Correlations of children's scores with English achievement

variables	Objective measure of English achievement	Self-evaluation of English achievement
Age	.013	−.142*
Attitudes toward the Enjoy English program	.156**	.450***
Attitudes toward the monitor	.107	.344***
Desire to return to the program*	.076	.441***
Attitudes toward learning English	.187***	.354***
Persistence*	.126*	.280***
Motivational intensity	.298***	.300***
Desire to learn English	.143*	.351***
Participation in the program*	.093	.253***
Integrative orientation	.132*	.156**
Attitudes toward English speakers	.086	.383***
Interest in foreign languages	.161**	.251***
Desire to live in an English-speaking country*	.046	.320***
English use anxiety	−.084	−.148*
English class anxiety	−.290***	−.120*
Instrumental orientation	.095	.182***
Parental encouragement*	−.041	.150**
Self-perceptions of English achievement	.215***	—

*$r=p<.01$ **$r=p<.001$ ***$r=p<.0001$

The two achievement scores are composed of various indices of achievement. The Objective Measure of English Achievement was obtained by summing the scores for Relative Performance, Oral Proficiency Assessment, and Comprehension Assessment. The score for the children's Self-perceptions of English Achievement is an aggregate of the children's Self-rated Oral Assessment and Self-rated Comprehension Assessment measures. These two measures were then correlated with the 16 measures assessed by the mini-AMTB, age, and each other.

Inspection of Table 2 will reveal that six of the correlations with the Objective Measure of English Achievement are significant at the .001 level (two-tailed). In order of absolute magnitude, these correlations suggest that the students who are evaluated as being more knowledgeable about English at the end of the program evidence higher levels of Motivational Intensity, lower levels of English Class Anxiety, perceive themselves as relatively proficient in English, express favorable

Attitudes Toward Learning English and a greater Interest in Foreign Languages, and have favorable Attitudes Toward the Enjoy English Program. As indicated, some of the other correlations with the Objective Measure of English Achievement are significant at the .01 or .05 levels, but given the large sample size, it seems meaningful to focus only on those correlations that are significant at the .001 level.

Inspection of Table 2 will also show that the majority of the variables are significantly (p<.001) correlated with the children's Self-perceptions of English Achievement. Only three variables fail to be significant at the .001 level: English Class Anxiety, English Use Anxiety, and Age (and even these are significant at the .01 level). Focusing attention on those correlations greater than .30 in magnitude, they suggest that children who evaluate their English skills highly are those who have favorable Attitudes Toward the Enjoy English Program, Attitudes Toward English Speakers, and Attitudes Toward Learning English. Moreover, they express a stronger Desire to Learn English, a favorable Attitude Toward the Monitor, a stronger Desire to Live in an English-speaking Country, and a higher level of Motivational Intensity to learn English.

Earlier it was indicated that the aggregate variables, Integrativeness, Attitudes Toward the Learning Situation, and Motivation, have reasonable levels of internal consistency reliability. Consequently, we investigated the correlations of these aggregates with each other and with the two measures of English Achievement. The correlations were comparable to those obtained in studies using the mini-AMTB. Similar to the findings reported by Tennant and Gardner (1999), this study found significant correlations between the measure of Motivation and both those of Integrativeness (r=.61, p<.0001) and Attitudes Toward the Learning Situation (r=.59, p<.0001). Furthermore, a significant relationship was found between Integrativeness and Attitudes Toward the Learning Situation (r=.54, p<.0001). Finally, the Objective Measure of English Achievement was significantly correlated with Integrativeness (r=.13, p<.01), Motivation (r=.25, p<.0001), and Attitudes Toward the Learning Situation (r=.13, p<.01), and Language Anxiety (r=−.28, p<.0001). Although the children's Self-perceptions of English Proficiency was significantly related to all of the aggregate measures, the highest correlations were found between Self-perceptions of English Achievement and Attitudes Toward the Learning Situation (r=.50, p<.0001), followed by Motivation (r=.47, p<.0001), Integrative Orientation (r=.41, p<.0001), and Language Anxiety (r=.18, p<.0001). The high correlation between achievement and motivation is consistent with previous research using the mini-AMTB in formal classroom contexts.

The relationships among Motivation, Integrativeness, Attitudes Toward the Learning Situation, and Achievement provide some support for the construct validity of the mini-AMTB, as studies carried out using the complete scales of the AMTB have repeatedly shown this same pattern of relationships. The factor analysis nonetheless does indicate an alternate structure in the relationships among the items, and future research should focus on the dimensions identified here.

SUMMARY AND CONCLUSIONS

This study made use of a series of single item measures of concepts assessed by the AMTB (Gardner, 1985). As indicated in the introduction, single item measures have been used with university level students, but this study is unique in that the items were written for use with children varying in age from 10 to 15 years of age. The study is further unique because participants were Spanish children in the Enjoy English program, held each summer in Spain to give them practice in using English for communication and to meet with teachers (monitors) who are university students from Great Britain and Ireland.

The study investigated the factor structure of 16 items, 15 of which were designed to measure the 11 attributes typically assessed by the AMTB, as well as the age of the children, self-ratings of English achievement and monitor ratings of the English achievement of the children (both assessed at the end of the program). The results indicated that five factors accounted for the relations among these 19 measures, *Attitudes Toward English*, *Orientation to Learn English*, *English Proficiency*, *Age*. and *Parental Encouragement*.

Further analyses indicated that many of the individual items correlated significantly with the two measures of English achievement. Also, in keeping with the research by Gardner (1985), aggregate scores were formed to compute scores on Integrativeness, Attitudes Toward the Learning Situation, and Motivation. The internal consistency reliability of these aggregates was low but acceptable. Moreover, the aggregates correlated meaningfully with each other and with the two indices of English achievement.

These results are informative because they demonstrate that it is possible to use single item indices of the components of the major attitude and motivation variables that have been shown to relate to achievement in formal language contexts and to develop a mini-AMTB for young children. Furthermore, it was also demonstrated that these measures can be used in informal language acquisition contexts and obtain results that are comparable to those found in more formal contexts. Further research is needed to demonstrate the generalizability of the findings reported here.

REFERENCES

Campbell, D. T., & Fiske, D. W. (1959). Convergent and discriminant validation by the multi-trait multi-method matrix. *Psychological Bulletin, 56*, 81–105.

Cattell, R. B. (1966). The scree test for the number of factors. *Multivariate Behavioral Research, 1*, 245–276.

Clément, R. (1980). Ethnicity, contact, and communicative competence in a second language. In W. Giles, P. Robinson, & P. M. Smith (Eds.), *Language: Social psychological perspectives* (pp. 147–154). Oxford, UK: Pergamon.

Clément, R. (1986). Second language proficiency and acculturation: An investigation of the effects of language status and individual characteristics. *Journal of Language and Social Psychology, 5*, 271–290.

Clément, R., Dörnyei, Z., & Noels, K. (1994). Motivation, self-confidence, and group cohesion in the foreign language classroom. *Language Learning, 44*, 417–448.

Clément, R., Gardner, R. C., & Smythe, P. C. (1980). Social and individual factors in second language acquisition. *Canadian Journal of Behavioural Science, 12*, 293–302.

Clément, R., & Kruidenier, B. G. (1983). Aptitude, attitude and motivation in second language proficiency: A test of Clément's model. *Journal of Language and Social Psychology, 4*, 21–37.

Dörnyei, Z. (1994). Motivation and motivating in the foreign language classroom. *Modern Language Journal, 78*, 273–284.

Dörnyei, Z. (1998). Motivation in second and foreign language learning. *Language Teaching, 31*, 117–135.

Gardner, R. C. (1985). *Social psychology and second language learning: The role of attitudes and motivation.* London, UK: Edward Arnold.

Gardner, R. C., Lalonde, R. N., & Moorcroft, R. (1985). The role of attitudes and motivation in second language learning: Correlational and experimental considerations. *Language Learning, 35*, 207–227.

Gardner, R. C., & MacIntyre, P. D. (1993). On the measurement of affective variables in second language learning. *Language Learning, 43*, 157–194.

Gardner, R. C., Tremblay, P. F., & Masgoret, A.M. (1997). Towards a full model of second language learning: An empirical investigation. *The Modern Language Journal, 81*, 344–362.

Guilford, J. P. (1954). *Psychometric methods.* New York: McGraw Hill.

Likert, R. (1932). *A technique for the measurement of attitudes.* Archives of Psychology, No. 140, 1–55.

Spolsky, B. (1989). *Conditions for second language learning.* Oxford, UK: Oxford University Press.

Tennant, J., & Gardner, R. C. (1999, June). *A quick computerized measure of attitudes, motivation and anxiety to learn French.* Paper presented at the 30th annual conference of the Canadian Association of Applied Linguistics, Sherbrooke, Quebec, Canada.

Ofra Inbar
Smadar Donitsa-Schmidt
Elana Shohamy
Tel Aviv University, Israel

STUDENTS' MOTIVATION AS A FUNCTION OF LANGUAGE LEARNING: THE TEACHING OF ARABIC IN ISRAEL

INTRODUCTION

Demotivation or low motivation among foreign and second language learners has been the center of attention of numerous research studies (e.g., Meng-Ching, 1998). Over the years attempts to motivate students to study foreign languages have been supported by reasons such as improved understanding of foreign cultures, the ability to understand one's own culture, and better insights into one's own language. An additional reason often cited is that the study of a foreign language fosters higher motivation and positive attitudes towards the community of speakers whose language is being studied. After all, learning languages is not an isolated event, as language is situated in a cultural, social, and political milieu.

Developing high motivation to learn about target cultures and language speakers as a result of foreign language study is of special relevance in situations of social and political conflict and group hostility. If learning foreign languages in such situations can increase the motivation of one group to know about the culture and people of the other, then it can be claimed that learning a foreign language has an additive value beyond knowing the language. The main question that this paper addresses is whether the study of a foreign language in a situation of political conflict can promote higher motivation on the part of the learner towards understanding the culture, communicating with the speakers of the language, as well as wishing to study the language in the future.

MOTIVATION AND LEARNING FOREIGN LANGUAGES

Despite disputes as to whether motivation predicts success or achievements predict motivation (Gardner, 1985; Gardner & Lambert, 1972), motivation is still often considered one of the main determinants of second and foreign language learning achievement. However, the connection between learning foreign languages and developing high motivation to learn is not really clear. Most studies that have examined the question have focussed on the relationship between language learning and language proficiency using correlational techniques, thus precluding any causal relationship between the two variables (Oller, 1981).

Inbar, O., Donitsa-Schmidt, S., & Shohamy, E. (2001). Students' motivation as a function of language learning: The teaching of Arabic in Israel. In Z. Dörnyei & R. Schmidt (Eds.), *Motivation and second language acquisition* (Technical Report #23, pp. 297–311). Honolulu: University of Hawai'i, Second Language Teaching and Curriculum Center.

Another problem with such studies is that it is not known whether students chose to study the languages and may therefore have had high motivation towards studying the language and its culture to begin with. It is therefore not known whether it is, in fact, the high motivations that made people choose to study the language, or the study of the language that created motivations. Thus, the question of interest is what the study of foreign language does to motivation in situations that are not the result of pure choice, that is, when students are required to study the language. What kinds of motivation will emerge as a result of language study in such no-choice situations? This question is especially interesting when students are required to study a language that represents a culture the learners are in political conflict with, as it may bear relevance to language policy decisions. Specifically, if the study of a foreign language is found to create positive high motivations to learn about the culture, should students be encouraged to study a foreign language?

THE ISRAELI CONTEXT

Israel offers a unique and interesting context to study such a question with regard to the study of Arabic. Due to political conflict with the Arab world, it is no surprise that the teaching of Arabic to Hebrew speaking students in Israel is characterized by low motivation, negative attitudes, limited achievement, and a high dropout rate. In fact, only 4% of the students choose to study Arabic in high school, where an additional foreign language apart from English is no longer required. Yet, the teaching of Arabic, which is an official language in Israel besides Hebrew, is a major goal of the recently introduced language policy (1996) for a number of reasons, such as the geo-political situation in the Middle East, viewing languages as a bridge to peace, facilitating communication with Israeli Arabs, as well as Arabic being a heritage language for many Jews.

The importance of Arabic on the one hand, and students' low motivation on the other, has created a contradictory situation. Although it is clearly stated in the language policy that Arabic is a compulsory language for three years (in grades 7 to 9), it is also mentioned that another foreign language can be studied instead. The current state is that in approximately 60% of Israeli schools Arabic is a compulsory subject, in 30% students are given the choice between Arabic or another foreign language, and in the remainder students are randomly assigned by the school to study either Arabic or another language (10%). Thus, in some schools students are *given a choice* between Arabic and another language (most commonly French), while in others they are *assigned* by the school to study either Arabic or another foreign language. Such a situation offers a suitable context for examining the question of the effect of the study of a foreign language on motivations of students towards various aspects of the language and culture.

An additional aspect characterizing the teaching of Arabic in Israel is that Modern Standard Arabic (MSA) is taught to most students in grade 7 onwards. Yet, grassroots movements including parents, teachers, principles, and municipal officials have taken initiatives in the past few years to promote the study of spoken Palestinian dialect at an early age. The goal is to make the language more meaningful and communicative for the learners and to improve motivation and attitudes towards the Arabic language and culture. The most comprehensive project was initiated in the city of Tel-Aviv in 1996, where 4,000 students in 38 schools (65% of the schools) are participating in a program of learning Palestinian dialect in grades 4 to 6 (9–12 year-olds).

In a study conducted by Inbar, Shohamy, and Donitsa-Schmidt (1999), it was found that elementary school students studying the spoken Palestinian variety of Arabic had more positive attitudes towards the Arab language and culture than their peers who did not study Arabic. They were also shown to have higher motivation towards studying the Arab language and culture than students who did not study Arabic. An important question that needs to be raised is whether these improved attitudes and higher motivation will be evident in higher grades as well, especially in situations where students switch to studying MSA. Thus, the issue questioned is the long-range effect of previous study of spoken Arabic on students' motivation.

The purpose of this study is to examine how the study of Arabic is related to motivation towards learning the Arabic language and culture. A further question relates to the extent to which the previous study of spoken Arabic affect students' motivation over time.

RESEARCH QUESTIONS

Three research questions are posed in this study:

1. Are there differences in motivation between students who studied Arabic and those who did not when

    a. the students have the *choice* of studying Arabic or another language?

    b. the students are *assigned* (i.e., have no choice) by the school to study either Arabic or another language?

2. Are there differences in motivation between students who had previously studied (spoken) Arabic and those who had not?

3. Which variables best predict students' motivation to study Arabic in the future?

METHOD

SAMPLE

The sample included 1,690 seventh grade students (12 years old, 872 boys and 818 girls) from nine heterogeneous junior high schools that are representative of the Tel-Aviv metropolitan population. Of these, 1,132 (67%) studied Arabic in junior high school while 558 (33%) did not (see Table 1). Each group was then divided into two conditions. Among those who study Arabic, 285 students chose to study

Arabic while 847 were assigned by their schools to study Arabic. Among those who did not study Arabic, 382 chose not to study (they chose another foreign language instead), and 172 were assigned by the school to study another foreign language instead of Arabic. Within each of these four groups, about half of the students had previously studied (spoken) Arabic in elementary school.

Table 1: Sample groups

study Arabic in junior high:	study (N=1132)				no study (N=558)			
condition:	chose* (N=285)		assigned** (N=847)		chose (N=382)		assigned (N=172)	
	yes	no	yes	no	yes	no	yes	no
	N=145	N=140	N=400	N=447	N=191	N=195	N=89	N=83

* chose: Students chose whether to enroll in Arabic or another language.

** assigned: Students are assigned by the school to study either Arabic or another language.

INSTRUMENT AND PROCEDURE

The research instrument was a questionnaire administered to students twice in a pre-test/treatment/post-test design. Administration of the questionnaire at the pre-treatment stage took place during the first week of the school year; administration of the post-test stage took place after 5 months of study. The questionnaire consisted of four parts, of which the first three parts were identical for the pre- and the post-test administrations, while the fourth part varied slightly in the two administrations.

Part 1 contained 17 demographic and background items, including previous study of Arabic, exposure and use of Arabic outside the school, as well as parents' knowledge and use of Arabic. Part 2 asked students to self-assess their Arabic language proficiency using nine "can-do" items. All items were rated on a 4-point Likert scale ranging from "no ability at all" (1) to "perform very well" (4). An exploratory factor analysis using orthogonal rotation conducted on the language proficiency items for both pre-test and post-test, yielded a one-factor solution for both times. Eigen values and cumulative percent of variance were 5.03 and 60% for the pre-test; 5.52 and 61.3% for the post-test. Cronbach's alpha reliability coefficients were 0.92 and 0.93.

Part 3 included 23 items that tapped different motives or reasons for studying Arabic, as well as items related to the desire to study Arabic in the future. Responses to items were on a 4-point Likert scale ranging from *strongly agree* to *strongly disagree*. Higher scores represented higher degrees of motivation. This section was validated using an explanatory factor analysis with orthogonal rotation. A five-factor solution was found to be the optimal structure both for the pre- and the post-test responses for motivational dimensions (three items were omitted during this procedure). The only factor loadings included were those greater than or equal to 0.35. The percentage of the total variance was 65.2% for the pre-test and 67.7% for the post-test. The five factors extracted from the factor analysis with their internal consistency coefficients, using Cronbach's alpha reliability, are presented in Table 2. As illustrated in Table 2 by sample items, *Instrumental Motivation* refers to the learning of Arabic due to its importance in achieving various future goals. *Cultural* taps the desire to understand and learn about the Arab culture and people. *Political* is related to the idea that the study of Arabic will help lead to peace in the Middle East. *Parental* refers to students' perceptions of their parents' attitudes and support of Arabic studies. *Future Studies* concerns motivation toward continuing to study Arabic in high school.

Table 2: Number of items, reliability coefficients, and sample items for all factors

motivational factors	# items	pre	post	sample item
instrumental	7	.84	.86	Arabic studies will help me in the future.
cultural	5	.82	.84	Knowledge of Arabic will help me understand Arab culture.
political (peace)	2	.80	.82	Knowledge of Arabic will help achieve peace with our neighbors.
parental	2	.86	.85	My parents think it is important that I study Arabic.
future studies	4	.81	.83	I want to study Arabic in high school.

The fourth and last part of the questionnaire contained six items related to degree of satisfaction with Arabic classes. In the pre-treatment administration, students who had studied Arabic in elementary school were asked to rate their level of satisfaction with their previous Arabic study. In the post-test administration, students currently studying Arabic in junior high were asked to rate their level of satisfaction with that study. An exploratory factor analysis conducted on this section yielded a one-factor solution for pre- and post-tests explaining 61.8 and 60.5% of variance respectively. Reliability coefficients were 0.88 for the pre-test responses and 0.89 for the post-test results.

RESULTS

EFFECTS OF ARABIC STUDIES ON STUDENTS' MOTIVATION

In order to answer the first research question as to the effects of Arabic studies and condition (choice vs. assigned) on students' motivation, a 2 (study) x 2 (condition) multivariate analysis of variance was performed twice, once for the pre-test results and once for the post-test administration. Means and standard deviations (in parentheses) are displayed in Table 3a. Table 3b presents the F values.

Table 3a: Motivational factors among the different groups (study x condition)

study		study		no study		
condition		chose (N=285)	assigned (N=847)	assigned (N=172)	chose (N=386)	F(p) time
instrument	pre	3.04 ⇒	2.90 ⇒	2.69	2.52	
		(.69)	(.65)	(.69)	(.70)	
F(p)		⇓	⇓ 92.02***	⇓	⇓	29.84***
	post	2.91 ⇒	2.76 ⇒	2.62	2.43	
		(.68)	(.73)	(.73)	(.64)	
F(p)			s			
cultural	pre	2.49	2.44 ⇒	2.14 ⇒	1.90	
		(.68)	(.73)	(.78)	(.60)	
F(p)		⇓	⇓ 103.80***	⇓	⇓	36.92***
	post	2.33	2.30 ⇒	2.08 ⇒	1.79	
		(.72)	(.75)	(.76)	(.62)	
F(p)			73.66**			
political	pre	2.99	2.99 ⇒	2.70	2.65	
		(.92)	(.90)	(.92)	(.94)	
F(p)		⇓	⇓ 29.76**	⇓	⇓	28.47***
	post	2.85	2.81 ⇒	2.53	2.46	
		(.93)	(.94)	(.94)	(.94)	
F(p)			35.55**			
parental	pre	3.09	2.98 ⇒	2.30	2.13	
		(.85)	(.91)	(.99)	(.87)	
F(p)		⇓	⇓ 208.90***	⇓	⇓	11.98***
	post	2.94	2.90 ⇒	2.23	2.05	
		(.95)	(.96)	(.99)	(.83)	
F(p)			188.04***			
future std	pre	2.46 ⇒	2.18 ⇒	1.83 ⇒	1.49	
		(.79)	(.79)	(.81)	(.56)	
F(p)		⇓	⇓ 198.20***	⇓	=	69.63***
	post	2.20 ⇒	1.96 ⇒	1.65 =	1.46	
		(.85)	(.79)	(.74)	(.53)	
F(p)			133.25***			

* $p<.05$; ** $p<.01$; *** $p<.001$

Table 3b: MANOVA effects (study x condition) in F values

time	pre			post		
effects	study[a]	cond	std x cond	study[a]	cond	std x cond
instrumental	92.02***	.18	14.22***	53.37***	.34	16.72***
cultural	103.80***	.77	10.89**	73.66***	.94	14.53***
political (peace)	29.76**	.01	.14	35.55***	.15	.89
parental	208.90***	.36	6.42*	188.94***	.25	2.36*
future studies	198.20***	.33	42.54***	133.25***	.31	23.46***
multivariate effect	56.14***	1.24	9.29***	47.42***	.65	6.62***

[a] these F values are also inserted in Table 3a
* $p<.05$; ** $p<.01$; *** $p<.001$

multivariate effect	$F(p)$ – pre	$F(p)$ – post
previous	1.81	1.25
study x previous	1.73	1.83
condition x previous	1.01	0.93
study x condition x previous	0.57	0.55

⇒ indicates significant differences between the means
= indicates no significant differences between the means

As noted in Tables 3a and 3b, the largest effect is for *study*, indicating that students who study Arabic have higher motivations, in all dimensions, than those who do not. This finding emerged in the pre-test and was sustained in the post-test as well. The differences between the groups vary slightly in their effect size, the most noticeable difference being the "parental" and "future studies" dimensions and the smallest being the "political" dimension.

There was no significant effect for *condition*, but a number of small-sized significant interactions were found for *study* x *condition*. In other words, in general, within the *study* and *no-study* groups there are few differences between those who chose versus those who were assigned. Nonetheless, within the *study* group, students who chose to study are found to be more motivated, both instrumentally and in their desire to continue studying Arabic in the future. Within the *no-study* group those who were assigned to study are more culturally motivated and express more desire to study Arabic in the future (only in the pre-test).

Thus, it could be concluded with regards to the first research question that it is the fact of studying the language and not the condition (choice vs. assigned) that affects students' motivation.

In addition, differences between the pre- and post-test for all motivational factors were examined using a multivariate analysis with repeated measures (*time* x *study* x *condition*). Results (presented in Table 3a and 3c) show that there was a consistent and significant small drop in motivation in the post-test for all groups in all motivational dimensions. No significant effects were found for either *study* or *condition* except for "future studies," where a significant interaction of *time* x *study* was found (F(df)=5.45; $p<.05$) since there was no motivational drop between the pre- and the post-treatments in the group that chose not to study Arabic.

Table 3c: MANOVA effects (time x study x condition) in F values

	instrument	cultural	political	parental	future std
time[a]	29.84***	36.92***	28.47***	11.98***	69.63***
time x study	2.09	2.86	.04	.14	5.45*
time x cond	.38	1.14	.08	.49	.96
time x std x cond	.12	.12	.43	.50	1.69

these F values are also inserted in Table 3a

* $p<.05$; *** $p<.001$

EFFECT OF PREVIOUS ARABIC STUDIES ON STUDENTS' MOTIVATION

In order to answer the second research question as to the effect of previous studies of Arabic in the elementary school, a 2 (previous) x 2 (study) x 2 (condition) multivariate analysis of variance was performed twice, for both the pre- and the post-test administrations. Means, standard deviations, and F values are displayed in Table 4.

Table 4: Differences in motivation between students who had previously studied Arabic versus those who had not

		study				no study			
		chose		assigned		assigned		chose	
previous studies		yes (145)	no (140)	yes (400)	no (447)	yes (89)	no (83)	yes (191)	no (195)
instrument	pre	(.60) =	(.71)	(.65) =	(.66)	(.66) =	(.74)	(.64) =	(.73)
		3.14 =	3.01	2.91 =	2.90	2.63 =	2.69	2.56 =	2.48
	post	(.67) =	(.67)	(.72) =	(.75)	(.71) =	(.78)	(.66) =	(.64)
		2.91 =	2.91	2.77 =	2.75	2.72 =	2.52	2.43 =	2.42
cultural	pre	(.62) =	(.76)	(.71) =	(.74)	(.74) =	(.83)	(.60) =	(.58)
		2.52 =	2.44	2.45 =	2.44	2.21 =	2.07	1.93 =	1.86
	post	(.71) =	(.74)	(.72) =	(.79)	(.78) =	(.81)	(.63) =	(.64)
		2.32 =	2.34	2.33 =	2.27	2.19 =	2.00	1.79 =	1.79

political	pre	(.92)	= (.91)	(.90)	= (.90)	(.94)	= (.91)	(.96)	= (.94)		
		3.03	= 2.97	2.97	= 3.00	2.59	= 2.82	2.65	= 2.69		
	post	(.91)	= (.93)	(.91)	= (.95)	(.95)	= (.97)	(.93)	= (.93)		
		2.87	= 2.83	2.85	= 2.79	2.60	= 2.47	2.44	= 2.48		
parental	pre	(.86)	= (.87)	(.91)	= (.92)	(.99)	= (.99)	(.93)	= (.84)		
		3.06	= 3.12	2.96	= 2.99	2.30	= 2.31	2.19	= 2.06		
	post	(.96)	= (.96)	(.94)	= (.98)	(.99)	⇒ (.96)	(.84)	= (.85)		
		2.95	= 2.93	2.94	= 2.86	2.42	⇒ 2.01	2.08	= 2.04		
future std	pre	(.75)	= (.87)	(.79)	= (.79)	(.74)	= (.84)	(.56)	= (.58)		
		2.46	= 2.44	2.15	= 2.19	1.74	= 1.91	1.48	= 1.51		
	post	(.81)	= (.85)	(.80)	= (.79)	(.70)	= (.74)	(.57)	= (.57)		
		2.23	= 2.17	2.01	= 1.90	1.67	= 1.64	1.45	= 1.47		

As noted in Table 4, no significant differences were found between students who had previously studied (spoken) Arabic versus those who had not. This finding is consistent across all groups regardless of (a) whether students are currently studying Arabic, and (b) whether students chose or were assigned to study Arabic, as indicated by the non significant interactions. In other words, no long-range effect was found for previous study of Arabic on students' motivation.

PREDICTION OF STUDENTS' MOTIVATION TO STUDY ARABIC IN THE FUTURE

In order to answer the third research question as to which variables best predict students' desire to study Arabic in the future, six multiple regression analyses were performed, with desire to study Arabic in the future as the dependent variable and 13 predictor variables. The method employed in all six regression equations was the "enter" method which enters all predictor variables simultaneously into the regression, regardless of whether their contribution to the prediction and total variance is significant or not.

Table 5a: Predicting motivation to study Arabic in the future (pre)

	all students		study in elementary		study in junior high	
	β	$t(p)$	β	$t(p)$	β	$t(p)$
instrumental	.22	7.65***	.22	5.65***	.18	6.03***
cultural	.33	12.29***	.20	4.97***	.30	8.33***
political	.05	2.05*	.03	ns	.04	ns
parental	.14	5.46***	.11	3.03*	.10	2.83**
previous studies	.06	2.66*	–	–	.03	ns

continued...

Table 5a: Predicting motivation to study Arabic in the future (pre) (cont.)

	all students		study in elementary		study in junior high	
	β	t(p)	β	t(p)	β	t(p)
study in jr high	.16	6.74***	.22	6.72***	–	–
choice	.04	ns	.03	ns	.11	3.80***
satisfaction: elem	–	–	.26	7.84***	–	–
satisfaction: jr high	–	–	–	–	.24	6.30***
language prof.	.03	ns	.00	ns	.01	ns
Arabic: home lang	.02	ns	.04	ns	.00	ns
Arabic: home use	.03	ns	.03	ns	.02	ns
Arabic: exposure	.04	ns	.03	ns	.05	ns
R^2		46%		53%		43%
$F(p)$		112.87***		71.29***		56.55***

* $p<.05$; ** $p<.01$; *** $p<.001$

Table 5b: Predicting motivation to study Arabic in the future (post)

	all students		study in elementary		study in junior high	
	β	t(p)	β	t(p)	β	t(p)
instrumental	.24	7.70***	.24	5.34***	.23	6.09***
cultural	.34	12.06***	.34	8.05***	.13	3.59***
political	.06	2.54*	.05	ns	.06	ns
parental	.17	5.99***	.13	3.39*	.08	2.62**
previous studies	.00		–	–	.04	ns
study in jr high	.10	4.33***	.17	6.00***	–	–
choice	.08	3.84***	.09	2.99**	.09	3.95***
satisfaction: elem	–	–	.12	4.01***	–	–
satisfaction: jr high	–	–	–	–	.46	13.73***
language prof.	.06	2.30*	.04	ns	.06	2.21*
Arabic: home lang	.03	ns	.02	ns	.04	ns
Arabic: home use	.04	ns	.01	ns	.03	ns
Arabic: exposure	.04	ns	.03	ns	.04	ns
R^2		47%		52%		54%
$F(p)$		120.25***		64.45***		94.87***

underlined figures represent values which are significantly different from the pre-stage
* $p<.05$; ** $p<.01$; *** $p<.001$

The results of the multiple regression analyses predicting motivation to study Arabic in the future both in the pre-test (Table 5a) and in the post-test (Table 5b) were all found to be significant, explaining between 43 and 54% of the total variance. The particular explanatory power of the 13 predictor variables in each regression, as indicated by the standardized beta coefficients and t-ratios suggest that the variables that significantly predict motivation to study Arabic in the future for all students in the pre-test are Cultural Motivation (β=.33), Instrumental Motivation (β=22), whether the student currently studies Arabic or not (β=.16), Parental Motivation (β=.14), previous Arabic studies in elementary school (β=.06), and Political Motivation (β=.05). In the post-test, all motivational factors as well as current Arabic studies remain as significant predictors of future Arabic studies. Yet, previous studies in elementary school are no longer significant, while two new significant variables enter the equation, that is, students' choice (β=.08) and level of language proficiency (β=.06).

When the regressions are conducted only for sub-samples, that is, for students who studied Arabic in elementary school and for students who study Arabic in junior high school, there is a new significant variable that best predicts future motivation, namely, the degree of satisfaction with Arabic classes. The degree of satisfaction is a significant predictor both at the pre (β=.26 for elementary school; β=24 for junior high) and the post-test (β=.12 for elementary school; β=.46 for junior high).

DISCUSSION AND IMPLICATIONS

The findings of this study indicate that learning a foreign language in a school context enhances students' motivations towards the culture and the language being studied. The two groups that studied Arabic were found to have higher motivations for instrumental, cultural, political, and parental reasons and higher motivation to study Arabic in the future in comparison to the two groups that did not study. This finding is especially important in the case of studying Arabic in Israel, a language associated with and representing the political conflict between Jews and Arabs.

In examining the differences between those who chose to study and those who were assigned to study, no significant differences were found in most dimensions. Thus, the main factor that affects students' motivations is the study of Arabic. It is worth noting that these findings were already observed in the initial phase of studying Arabic and were sustained even after 6 months of studying the language, in spite of the small drop in the means, found to be consistent in all groups.

What is it that causes students who were assigned to study a language that is unpopular and disliked to exhibit such high motivations, as high as the group that chose to study the language? The answer may be found in theories of cognitive psychology that focus on issues of forced-compliance constructs (Bem, 1972; Festinger & Carlsmith, 1959). In various experiments, it has been shown that subjects who were forced to behave in a way that was in a conflict with their initial stand changed their position as a result of the dissonance situation in which they found themselves. In other words, to reduce the resulting pressure of complying to study an undesired school subject, students changed their motivation (cognition) about it in a way that was consistent with their overt behavior. According to self-perception theories, students implicitly ask themselves, "What must my attitude be if I am willing to behave in such a way?" They infer that they must actually like to study Arabic and that it must be an important language to study if they are willing to comply with school requirements. Similarly, students who were assigned not to study Arabic also experience a need to over-justify their forced behavior and hence exemplify negative motivations towards Arabic, as low as those students who chose not to study Arabic.

Although one could interpret the findings related to the "choice" groups as obvious, that is, high/low motivations according to the students' choice, there may be an additional explanation that stems from the same phenomenon as above. As noted in the free-choice studies (Brehm & Cohen, 1962), when an individual is permitted to make a selection from a set of objects or courses of action, dissonance theory reasons that any unfavorable aspects of the chosen alternative provide cognitions that are dissonant with the initial cognition of the individual which led him/her to choose the way s/he did. To reduce the resulting dissonance pressure, the individual exaggerates the favorable features of the chosen alternative and plays down its unfavorable aspects. In the case of the students who chose to study Arabic, this may account for their high motivations as they feel the need to over-justify their choice. Similarly, students who chose not to study Arabic portray negative attitudes and low motivation that adhere to their initial choice.

As noted above, there was a decrease in motivation over time in all groups. The drop among students who have studied a language for some time is a well-known phenomenon in school contexts, since complex learning situations tend to reduce the role of the initial motivational influences and highlight the importance of motivational influences that affect action during the goal implementation itself (Dörnyei & Ottó, 1998). Yet, the fact that the drop was also evident among those who did not study may be accounted for by variables external to the school setting, especially in situation where political events external to the school contexts may be associated with motivations; after all, attitudes and motivations do not occur in a vacuum.

The results of the study also showed no significant effect of previous studies of spoken Arabic on current motivations toward the language and culture, not even in the pre-test phase. This finding might indicate that effects of studying a foreign language have immediate impact but do not seem to hold over time. This finding indicates that motivation is in fact a dynamic and unstable construct that tends to fluctuate and change over time depending on the present context and is influenced by immediate factors. It is therefore important to cultivate students' motivations on an on going basis within the educational context and invest in continuous "motivational maintenance" (Dörnyei & Ottó, 1998, p. 46).

In light of the positive motivations created by the enrollment and study of a foreign language, on the one hand, and the lack of effect of past studies, on the other, it is worthwhile to examine its plausible policy implications. The question that arises is whether in situations where there is a need to create high motivations towards an unpopular language, students should be required to study a foreign language for a certain period of time. In other words, is there a basis to make foreign language compulsory for students, particularly in conflict situation?

With regards to the variables that best predict motivation for future study of Arabic, the results showed that Cultural Motivation had the highest predictive power in both the pre- and post-test phases, followed by Instrumental, Parental, and Political motivations and current study of Arabic. The fact that all motivational factors significantly added to the prediction of desire for future studies shows that each dimension adds a unique perspective to comprehending the nature of students' motivation to study languages and implies that motivation is indeed a multifaceted construct (Dörnyei & Ottó, 1998). This supports a comprehensive rather than a reductionist approach to the motivation construct and verifies the assumption that relevant motivational influences have a cumulative effect. It is also interesting to note that the motivational factors found in this study highly correspond to Dörnyei and Ottó's (1998) model in which there are a number of motivational influences that are assumed to influence the stage of goal setting. More specifically, the *Instrumental* factor in this study corresponds with "incentive value of goal-related action, outcomes, and consequences (instrumental);" *Cultural* coincides with "language/language-learning-related attitudes (integrativeness);" *Political* conforms to "subjective values and norms;" and *Parental* matches the "environmental stimuli and family expectations" (p. 52). It should be noted that the motivational factor that can be seen to represent norms and values in Israeli society (i.e., the political dimension) emerged as having the lowest explanatory power (and also the lowest difference among the groups). This may indicate a growing consensus within the Israeli society as to the "peace" issue and the role of Arabic in obtaining it.

An additional important finding related to the variables that best predict students' motivation for future Arabic studies was the major contribution of the degree of satisfaction with Arabic classes to the prediction. This finding clearly implies that it is not the mere teaching that counts, but rather the way in which the language is taught which makes a difference, that is, the quality of the learning experience. This result corroborates previous findings (Inbar, Shohamy, & Donitsa-Schmidt, 1999) and bears important implications for pedagogical considerations such as syllabus design, teacher training, and material selection. It also highlights again the limited importance of initial goal-setting or "choice" motivation and the need to focus on "executive motivation" that operates during task-engagement.

Finally, with regard to the predictor variables, it is important to note that while students' language proficiency did not significantly predict motivation for future studies at the pre-test stage, it did become a significant factor at the post-test stage. Although this finding may hint at the ongoing debate as to whether it is success that motivates students, or motivation that affects language proficiency, there is a need for further investigation in order to reach more conclusive evidence.

Despite the importance of the findings of this study, a number of issues and questions still remain to be investigated with relation to the present results, and caution should therefore be exercised in interpreting it and generalizing from it. First, similar studies of this kind conducted on the motivations that students hold towards the other language alternative, that is, French, are unavailable. It would be interesting and important to compare students' attitudes and motivations towards these two languages. Such a comparison would lead to better understanding of the impact that foreign language studies bear on attitudes and motivations, especially when there is a major difference between the popularity and desirability of the alternative languages.

A second issue has to do with the question of what has really happened within the schools and specific classes during the period in which students were asked to choose between Arabic and French and during the first week of the school year (pre-stage). One remains puzzled as to the activities that took place in the schools and specific classes that may have had a major influence on students' motivations beyond the learning itself, for example, schools' culture and educational philosophy, teachers' ideology with regards to Arabic, and behavior of certain teachers. Studies suggest that the psychological environment of the school as a whole may also have a strong influence on students' motivation (Maehr & Midgley, 1991).

Third, the question as to whether the results of this study are typical only of the specific Israeli context or would be replicated in studies conducted on students of different ages, other languages, and other contexts is unknown.

Yet overall, the results of the present study are encouraging and provide information as to a major concern in the field of foreign language education regarding the effect of foreign language teaching on students' motivations towards cultures and people whose language are being studied.

REFERENCES

Bem, D. J. (1972). Self-perception theory. In L. Berkowitz (Ed.), *Advances in Experimental Psychology*, Vol. 6. (pp. 1–62). New York: Academic Press.

Brehm, J. W., & Cohen, A. R. (1962). *Explorations in cognitive dissonance.* New York: Wiley.

Dörnyei, Z., & Ottó, I. (1998). Motivation in action: A process model of L2 motivation. *Working Papers in Applied Linguistics, 4*, 43–69. London: Thames Valley University.

Festinger, L., & Carlsmith, J. M. (1959). Cognitive consequences of forced compliance. *Journal of Abnormal and Social Psychology, 58*, 203–210.

Gardner, R. C. (1985). *Social psychology and second language learning: The role of attitudes and motivation.* London: Edward Arnold.

Gardner, R. C., & Lambert, W. E. (1972). *Attitudes and motivation in second language learning.* Rowley, MA: Newbury House.

Inbar, O., Shohamy, E., & Donitsa-Schmidt, S. (1999, March). *The effect of teaching spoken Arabic dialect on students' attitudes, motivation and communicative competence in Israel.* Paper presented at the meeting of The American Association for Applied Linguistics (AAAL), Stamford, CT.

Maehr, M. L., & Midgley, C. (1991). Enhancing students motivation: A school-wide approach. *Educational Psychologist, 26,* 399–427.

Meng-Ching, H. (1998). Culture studies and motivation in foreign and second language learning in Taiwan. *Language, Culture and Curriculum, 11*(2), 165–182.

Oller, J. (1981). Research on the measurement of affective variables. Some remaining questions. In R. Anderson (Ed.), *New dimensions in second language acquisition research* (pp. 14–27). Rowley, MA: Newbury House.

Richard Schmidt
University of Hawai'i at Mānoa

Yuichi Watanabe
Kanda University of International Studies

MOTIVATION, STRATEGY USE, AND PEDAGOGICAL PREFERENCES IN FOREIGN LANGUAGE LEARNING

Abstract

This chapter reports the results of a survey of motivation, reported use of language learning strategies, and learner preferences for various kinds of pedagogical activities carried out with 2,089 learners of five different foreign languages (Mandarin Chinese, Filipino [Tagalog], French, Japanese, and Spanish) at the University of Hawai'i. Questionnaire responses were factor analyzed, and a common factor structure was found for the sample as a whole, consisting of the factors of Value (a belief that studying the language is worthwhile for a wide variety of reasons), Expectancy (a combination of self-confidence, self-assessed aptitude for language learning, and lack of anxiety), Motivational Strength, Competitiveness, and Cooperativeness. The fact that many of these students are studying the language of their ethnic heritage also emerged as a distinct motivational factor. Scales based on the factor analyses were used to analyze similarities and differences among groups of students learning the different target languages, as well as relationships between the various components of motivation and those related to learning strategy use and pedagogical preferences. It was found that motivation does indeed affect strategy use and preferences for different types of classroom activities, but some associations are much stronger than others. The motivational factors of Value, Motivational Strength, and Cooperativeness affect strategy use and pedagogical preferences most strongly, while the Heritage Language factor appears to have little or no influence on these variables. Of the different types of learning strategies, the use of cognitive and metacognitive strategies is most affected by motivation, and among the types of pedagogical preferences that we investigated, approval of challenging activities was most affected by motivation.

INTRODUCTION

The research reported in this chapter attempts to be integrative, bringing together a number of interests within the field of foreign language learning and teaching that have usually been investigated independently: the structure of foreign language learning motivation in a university setting, the kinds of learning strategies that foreign language learners use, and the kinds of classroom structures and types of activities to which foreign language students react positively. The research was stimulated by both practical and theoretical concerns.

Schmidt, R., & Watanabe, Y. (2001). Motivation, strategy use, and pedagogical preferences in foreign language learning. In Z. Dörnyei & R. Schmidt (Eds.), *Motivation and second language acquisition* (Technical Report #23, pp. 313–359). Honolulu: University of Hawai'i, Second Language Teaching and Curriculum Center.

On the practical level, most teachers of second and foreign languages recognize the importance of student motivation, want to know more about it, and want to enhance their students' motivation in whatever ways are possible. In particular, they hope that curriculum development (including textbook selection) both fosters learning and appeals to students sufficiently. Other issues in the particular learning and teaching context investigated in this study may be unusual but are by no means unique among American universities. The University of Hawaiʻi is a large multi-campus university, of which the University of Hawaiʻi at Mānoa is the flagship campus. One of its major strengths is the diversity and depth of its language offerings. Over 30 languages are regularly offered, including not only the major European languages and the major East Asian ones (Chinese, Japanese, and Korean), but also a large number of languages that are offered at few other institutions in the United States, including Vietnamese, Indonesian, Thai, Filipino (Tagalog), Ilokano, and Khmer among the languages of Southeast Asia, and Hawaiian (an official language of the State of Hawaiʻi, together with English), Samoan, Tahitian, Maori, and Chomorro among the languages of the Pacific. The offering of these specific clusters of languages is unique to this university, as is the fact that the three "biggest" languages (in terms of student enrollment) are Hawaiian, Japanese, and Spanish (instead of the usual trio of French, German, and Spanish), but some of the issues are not. A striking characteristic of the student population is that about half of all students are studying the language of their ethnic heritage,[1] with this rising to close to 100% for some languages. This is true across the United States for the less commonly taught languages (normally defined as every language except French, German, and Spanish), and the only reason that most languages are taught at all in the U.S. is that there are students of those particular ethnicities anxious to study them. As described in other chapters of this volume (Kondo-Brown, Syed), the heritage factor is an extremely important source of language learning motivation, affecting both language choice and persistence in second language learning. A second salient issue at the University of Hawaiʻi during the time of this research, not uncommon at U.S. universities, was the existence of a graduation requirement of two years of study of Hawaiian or a foreign language for all undergraduates.

With respect to theoretical issues, the research-based literature on motivation for foreign language learning has concentrated almost exclusively on learning second and foreign languages in the more traditional sense, that is, learning a language associated with someone else's culture rather than one associated with your own or one that you claim as part of your ethnic background. Integrative motivation, for example, has been viewed as an interest and willingness to get to know about

---

[1]   The term "heritage learner" has two definitions in current circulation. Some use it to refer to students who are studying their own first language in a school setting. Spanish classes for Spanish speakers fall within this definition. Others use the term more broadly, as we are using it here, to refer to members of ethnic groups who are studying that ethnic language. Some of the students we call heritage learners do speak that language as their mother tongue (with English as their second language), but many more in our sample are second, third, or fourth generation immigrants who in the Hawaiʻi context still colloquially refer to their "nationality" (i.e., ethnicity) as Japanese, Chinese, etc.

someone else's culture and to interact with members of that group, coupled with a willingness to learn a language to do so. However, the attitudes, orientations, and learning goals of heritage learners, who are learning a language of "inheritance" rather than "affiliation" in Rampton's (1990) terms might be different.

A second theoretical issue concerns the components of motivation in tertiary foreign language education and how these relate to theoretical models in the field. The immediate precursor to this study was a study of foreign language learners of English in Egypt (Schmidt, Boraie, & Kassabgy, 1996) in which application of multidimensional scaling to responses to an extensive questionnaire found three basic dimensions to EFL motivation, labeled *Goal Orientation*, *Expectancy*, and *Affect*. *Goal Orientation* in that study incorporated items related to a number of different traditionally recognized components of motivation, including both instrumental and integrative orientations. For that population, it did not seem to matter whether learners held integrative or instrumental orientations towards English. What mattered was that some learners were highly oriented towards the goal of learning English for both types of reasons (and others besides), while others attributed little value of any kind to the study of English. The dimension of *Expectancy* also included a number of factors often considered conceptually distinct, including self-confidence, positive thinking, and determination. *Affect* was a dimension that included intrinsic motivation for language learning (enjoyment of the activity itself), anxiety (reverse correlated), and a liking for challenge.

The major theoretical motivation for this study, however, was not to examine motivation in isolation but to see what links could be discovered between motivation on the one hand and learning strategies on the other. Looking for links between motivation and learning strategies is motivated by a concern with how motivation works. Although some view motivation as part of a general "affective filter" (Krashen, 1985), which if high keeps target language input from reaching the language acquisition device and if low allows input to simply "go in," we follow Gardner (1985, 1988) in believing that motivated learners achieve higher levels of proficiency because they put more of themselves into learning. Our basic assumption is that motivated learners learn more because they seek out input, interaction, and instruction, and when they encounter target language input they pay attention to it and actively process it however they can (Crookes & Schmidt, 1991; Schmidt, in press; Tremblay & Gardner, 1995). In other words, they use learning strategies.

Several previous studies have found links between motivation for language learning and reported strategy use. Oxford and Nyikos (1989) found that motivation was the best predictor of strategy use in a large-scale study of university students. More motivated students used learning strategies of all kinds more often than did less motivated students. In a study of 138 students in first year Italian and Spanish courses, MacIntyre and Noels (1996) found that three variables from the Gardner socio-educational model (Attitudes Toward the Learning Situation, Integrativeness, and Language Anxiety) correlated with three types of strategies: Cognitive, Metacognitive, and Social. A composite variable labeled *Motivation* correlated with the same three types of strategies, plus memory, compensation, and affective strategies. Schmidt et al. (1996) found that Egyptian EFL learners with high Expectancy (determination), those with strong Instrumental Motivation, and those high in Sociability all reported using active cognitive strategies and organizing strategies. One recent study of learners of French (Gardner, Tremblay, & Masgoret, 1997) found somewhat more perplexing results. While motivation and the use of learning strategies were associated with each other, reported strategy use was not significantly correlated with L2 achievement, and a path analysis suggested that the use of strategies was related to lower levels of achievement. Gardner et al. (1997) suggest that since most of these learners had at least 9 years of prior study of French, successful learners may have adopted a fairly narrow range of effective strategies, while less successful learners may continue to attempt to use a broader range of strategies.

Links between motivation and students' attitudes towards different aspects of language pedagogy have been left largely unresearched. It seems intuitively likely that depending on one's motivation for learning a language one might prefer different types of pedagogical activities. For example, if one is integratively oriented towards language learning one might prefer communicatively oriented classes over traditional ones. Schmidt et al. (1996) reported that students who scored high on the affect dimension of motivation welcomed communicative classes while those low on that dimension tended to reject the communicative classroom and that determined learners preferred classes in which there was a balance among different skill emphases and between teacher control and learner centeredness. We are not aware of any other research that addresses possible links between motivational factors and how students react to specific aspects of foreign language pedagogy.

In light of these concerns, the objectives of the research reported here were to identify the combinations of factors (intrinsic/integrative/instrumental orientations, expectations, anxiety, perceived language aptitude, etc.) that define "motivation" for a university population with many heritage learners and to identify relationships among these motivational factors, reported use of language learning strategies, and preferences for particular types of classroom activities. Because of our desire to gather data from a reasonably large number of students studying a number of foreign languages, survey instruments were developed and used for the research.

METHOD

PARTICIPANTS

A total of 2,089 participants completed our survey questionnaire, representing students of five different foreign languages: Chinese (Mandarin), Filipino (Tagalog), French, Japanese, and Spanish. In each case, the survey instrument was distributed by instructors who were interested in the project and willing to give up some class time and was completed by students on a voluntary basis. Students were promised confidentiality and assured that their grades would not by affected in any way because of their participation or non-participation. Partly because not all instructors participated, and partly because enrollment in these languages varies greatly, there were larger numbers of responses from students of Japanese and Spanish and fewer from Chinese and Filipino. Table 1 shows the distribution of participants by language and year of study at the university level.

Table 1: Number of subjects in each language sample

language	language/level	n	total
European	Spanish, 1st year	326	
	Spanish, 2nd year	315	
	French, 1st year	187	828
Japanese	1st year	466	
	2nd year	394	
	beyond	169	1029
Filipino	1st year	69	
	2nd year	45	114
Chinese	1st year	45	
	2nd year	60	
	beyond	13	118
			2089

Additional demographic data were gathered concerning these participants but are not being reported here because each participating language department collected different kinds of data as part of the survey. Some requested information concerning student ethnicity and some did not; some wanted to know if the language being studied was spoken by anyone in the student's immediate family and some did not; some wanted details on learning at the primary and secondary levels and some did not.

INSTRUMENTS

In a study carried out in Egypt by Schmidt et al. (1996), data were collected from 1,464 adult learners of EFL using a 97-item questionnaire that asked about the students' motivation, learning strategies, and preferences for classroom instructional activities. That instrument was used as the basis for the one used in this study, with some significant modifications. Items clearly relevant to Egyptian learners of English but not to American learners of other foreign languages were eliminated and additional items were added based on discussions with foreign language teachers at the University of Hawai'i concerning what they thought were the primary issues concerning the motivation of their students. This resulted in a 123-item questionnaire with questions on motivation, preferences for instructional activities, and learning strategies. The questions concerning motivation were grouped into 11 subcategories, with different scales addressing such aspects of motivation as intrinsic motivation, integrative orientation, anxiety, and perceived language aptitude. The questions in the second two parts were not initially grouped into subcategories.

In the first administration, the questionnaire was administered to students in first and second year Spanish and French courses. After correlational analyses and factor analyses were carried out, 22 items were judged to be ineffective and were removed from the questionnaire. After these analyses, the items concerning motivation were reorganized into separate scales and the questions concerning learning strategies and pedagogical preferences were also grouped into subcategories. In the next administration, the revised 101-item questionnaire was administered to students in all levels of Japanese courses and to students in first semester and third semester Filipino courses. Again, correlational analyses and factor analyses were conducted and 10 items were judged to be ineffective and removed. In the final administration, the revised 91-item questionnaire was administered to 118 second semester, fourth semester, and third year students of Mandarin Chinese. To enable comparisons of the data from different administrations, all the analyses to be reported here are based on the final version of the questionnaire, which consists of 91 items in three parts: Part A, Motivation, 47 items; Part B, Preferences for Instructional Activities, 20 items; and Part C, Learning Strategies, 24 items.

Part A contains a single item concerning the language requirement ("I mainly study this language to satisfy the university language requirement") and questions grouped into 12 scales. For each item participants were asked to indicate their degree of agreement with the statement on a five point scale (1=*strongly disagree*, 2=*disagree*, 3=*neutral or no opinion*, 4=*agree*, 5=*strongly agree*):

- *Intrinsic motivation*, statements expressing enjoyment of language learning

- *Instrumental orientation*, statements concerning the financial, social, or other benefits of learning a language

- *Integrative orientation*, statements about being able to interact with members of another cultural group

- *Heritage language orientation*, statements concerning the students' attachment to the language as part of their own identity and cultural heritage

- *Interest in foreign languages and cultures*, in general (not a specific language)

- *Task value*, that is, the value of the language course

- *Expectancy*, statements concerning a student's belief that s/he will do well and receive a good grade in the course

- *Anxiety*, statements concerning test and speaking anxiety

- *Language aptitude*, the student's own perception of her/his aptitude for grammar, pronunciation, and so forth

- *Competitiveness*, statements about doing better than other students and getting good grades

- *Cooperativeness*, statements concerning relationships with other students and the teacher and learning in a cooperative environment

- *Motivational strength*, statements concerning one's intention to put one's best effort into learning the language, keep up with the course, etc.

Part B contains 20 items related to the pedagogical preferences of language learners, also rated using a 5-point scale from *strongly disagree* to *strongly agree*, grouped into five categories (to be discussed in the results section). Part C contains 24 items concerning the use of learning strategies, also rated on a 5-point scale, grouped into four categories (to be discussed under results). The questionnaire items appear in Appendix A, together with the names of the scales to which they belong and brief labels used for easy reference in the tables that follow.

Data were collected by the teachers of the many different language course sections that participated in this study over a period of 2 years, for one target language group at a time, always between the second and fourth weeks of a given 14 week semester, that is, after class procedures had been established and students were beginning to get to know one another but before pressures started building in preparation for mid-term examinations. The data were machine scored, and negatively worded items were re-coded positively by the two authors of this paper. Factor analyses, correlational analyses, and ANOVAs were performed using SAS 6.11 (1989). and StatView 4.5 (1994). in order to address the research questions.

RESULTS

DIMENSIONS IN THE DATA

Responses to each of the three parts of the questionnaire were factor analyzed to determine relevant dimensions in the data. Because factor analysis requires a large sample size, the data from French and Spanish classes were combined into a category of European languages (n=828). The data from students of Japanese (n=1029) were factor analyzed separately. Factor analysis was not conducted with the data from students of Chinese or Filipino because of their relatively small sample size (n=114 and n=118 respectively). Instead a final factor analysis on the data from all five language groups (n=2089) was conducted. All the factor analyses described below were based on a common factor analysis called Iterated Principle Factor Analysis used in SAS (version 6.11) with varimax rotation. Common factor analysis, unlike principal component analysis, uses only the common variance between items. It excludes the variance that is unique to each item, or error variance. Common factor analysis was used because we were interested in finding or validating psychological traits that are manifested in multiple items in our questionnaire. Both oblique rotations (by promax) and orthogonal rotations (by varimax) were carried out. Oblique rotations allow correlation between factors, which usually produces more easily interpretable results, a "simple structure." However, orthogonal rotations have an advantage of obtaining "clean" factors uncontaminated by the overlap between factors. Since the results were practically identical between the two rotation methods in terms of extracted factors, results from varimax rotations will be reported. The number of factors was determined by the eigenvalue (minimum of one), the scree plot, and the interpretability of rotated factors.

In order for the dimensions in the data (i.e., categories) to be deemed valid, they need to demonstrate certain properties:

- *Convergent validity.* All the items in each category need to measure one and the same construct. Therefore, the category needs to be internally consistent. We can check this by Cronbach alpha, which is a way of measuring the correlations between items.

- *Divergent validity.* Each category needs to be distinct from other categories. Categories need to be distinct enough from each other to be called separate categories. Factor analysis addresses this problem.

- *Content validity.* Meeting the above criteria by statistical analysis is not enough. The naming of each category depends on judgments as to what it represents. Item selection and writing need to be based on theory. This is also necessary to obtain categories that are more likely to meet the criteria of convergent and divergent validity.

The selection of items and preliminary categories for Part A, Motivation, were based on relevant theories and past research findings, addressing the content validity criterion. The results of factor analyses and reliability estimates determine the extent to which the questionnaire satisfies the requirements of convergent validity and divergent validity. For Part A, factor solutions were very similar across European, Japanese, and the combined data sets. Tables 2, 3 and 4 summarize factor solutions obtained and the total variance accounted for. In each case, two solutions are presented with different numbers of factors specified. The number of subjects indicated are those remaining after list-wise deletions for missing data.

Table 2: Factors for Part A – European languages (N=790)

number of factors=6 (total variance accounted for=41%)	number of factors=5 (total variance accounted for=39%)
f1. Value components	f1. Value components
f2. Expectancy, Anxiety	f2. Expectancy components
f3. Motivational strength	f3. Motivational strength
f4. Aptitude, Competitiveness	f4. Competitiveness
f5. Heritage	f5. Heritage
f6. Cooperativeness	

Table 3: Factors for Part A – Japanese (N=1,007)

number of factors=7 (total variance accounted for=40%)	number of factors=5 (total variance accounted for=37%)
f1. Value components	f1. Value components
f2. Expectancy, Anxiety	f2. Expectancy, Anxiety, (Aptitude)
f3. Aptitude	f3. Motivational strength, Cooperativeness
f4. Motivational strength	f4. Competitiveness, (Aptitude)
f5. Competitiveness	f5. Heritage
f6. Heritage	
f7. Cooperativeness	

Table 4: Factors for Part A – All language groups (N=2,023)

number of factors=7 (total variance accounted for=41%)	number of factors=5 (total variance accounted for=38%)
f1. Value components	f1. Value components
f2. Anxiety	f2. Expectancy components
f3. Expectancy, Aptitude	f3. Motivational strength
f4. Motivational strength	f4. Competitiveness
f5. Heritage	f5. Heritage
f6. Competitiveness	
f7. Cooperativeness	

Table 5 shows the factor solution for the entire sample when five factors are specified for motivation. The most striking fact about Table 5 is that a large number of items that are conceptually rather different (such as instrumental orientation and integrative orientation) do not constitute separate factors but emerge as part of a single factor which we have labeled *Value*. A total of 20 questionnaire items load on this factor, including all items from our scales for intrinsic motivation, instrumental orientation, integrative orientation, task value, and interest in foreign languages and cultures. That is, it is not the case that some of the learners in our sample are instrumentally oriented towards language study while others are integratively oriented, others have a general interest in languages and cultures, and yet others just enjoy language learning. Instead, we find that our learners either see value in learning the foreign language they are studying for all of those reasons or for none of them.

Table 5: Factor solution for Part A — All language groups (N=2,023)

| | f1 | f2 | f3 | f4 | f5 |
	Value	Expectancy	Mot str	Competitive	Heritage
intrinsic 1	68*	31	25	8	11
intrinsic 1	58*	36	34	6	3
intrinsic 3	46*	20	19	3	4
intrinsic 4	55*	19	14	18	9
intrinsic 5	63*	37	17	1	3
intrinsic 6	73*	21	10	−10	14
lang req	−68*	−23	−6	16	−13
instrumental 1	43*	2	2	30	12
instrumental 2	49*	−3	8	14	10
instrumental 3	49*	6	−3	14	21
integrative 1	70*	6	13	12	13
integrative 2	57*	9	2	18	24
integrative 3	58*	5	9	14	19
interest 1	57*	15	5	9	−9
interest 2	36	5	17	9	−13
interest 3	69*	17	13	2	4
interest 4	62*	5	17	18	0
task value 1	59*	26	30	3	5
task value 2	46*	2	48*	6	2
task value 3	54*	10	8	8	−4
heritage 1	20	−5	10	2	82*
heritage 2	38	6	10	14	74*
expectancy 1	24	53*	16	20	2
expectancy 2	8	59*	20	29	−1
expectancy 3	2	72*	−7	−1	2
anxiety 1	−14	−45*	−2	−1	−2
anxiety 2	−6	−64*	−15	8	1
anxiety 3	−8	−63*	5	7	0
anxiety 4	−11	−44*	−1	−2	−8
anxiety 5	−8	−47*	−3	15	6
anxiety 6	−15	−56*	−3	2	6
aptitude 1	18	37	6	24	8

aptitude 2	11	39	0	29	–8
aptitude 3	7	40*	3	21	–6
aptitude 4	27	46*	10	32	2
compete 1	–1	–19	30	38	6
compete 2	32	6	3	43*	11
compete 3	7	21	–6	42*	4
compete 4	10	10	19	45*	0
cooperate 1	17	–1	29	11	–1
cooperate 2	15	–15	25	32	–4
cooperate 3	16	–5	24	20	6
motiv'l str 1	28	21	43*	–12	6
motiv'l str 2	0	–7	52*	7	2
motiv'l str 3	15	29	40*	–7	–2
motiv'l str 4	4	14	54*	11	4
motiv'l str 5	29	24	58*	10	12

note: Lines denote divisions between major categories. Values are multiplied by 100 and rounded to the nearest integer. Values greater than 0.4 have been flagged by an "*." Variance explained by each factor:

factor1	factor2	factor3	factor4	factor5
7.507308	4.567245	2.419648	1.721466	1.558590

A factor labeled Value shows up in each of the analyses shown in tables 3, 4, and 5, and the specific items that load on this factor are stable across all the analyses. The same is true of Factor 5, which we have labeled the *Heritage* factor and which consists of only the two items on our heritage language learning scale. That is, although an integrative orientation towards a language associated with another social group and culture did not emerge as a distinct motivational factor for this population, an orientation towards learning the language of one's own cultural heritage did. In each analysis, factors that we have labeled *Expectancy*, *Motivational Strength*, and *Competitiveness* also emerged, but there are some differences in which items load on these factors, depending on the target language sample and how many factors are specified for a solution. For example, items concerning anxiety appear to constitute a separate factor if a seven factor solution is chosen for the whole sample, but items related to anxiety load (negatively) on the Expectancy factor in all other solutions. A separate factor of *Cooperativeness* was formed only when the number of factors was specified as seven (for Japanese and all languages combined) or six (for pooled French and Spanish data).

For Part B (pedagogical preferences), unlike for Part A, no predetermined categories were established, and all of the categories were derived from factor analysis. Factor solutions were almost identical across the three data sets, as shown in tables 6, 7, and 8. Table 9 shows the factor solution for the entire sample when five factors are specified for pedagogical preferences.

Table 6: Part B – All language groups (N=2023)

number of factors=5 (total variance accounted for=40%)
f1. Practical
f2. Cooperative
f3. Challenging
f4. Traditional
f5. Innovative

Table 7: Part B – Japanese (N=1007)

number of factors=5 (total variance accounted for=41%)
f1. Practical
f2. Cooperative
f3. Challenging
f4. Traditional
f5. Innovative

Table 8: Part B – European (N=790)

number of factors=5 (total variance accounted for=40%)
f1. Practical
f2. Challenging
f3. Cooperative
f4. Innovative
f5. Traditional

Table 9: Factor solution for Part B — All language groups (N=2023)

	f1 Practical	f2 Cooperative	f3 Challenge	f4 Innovative	f5 Traditional
grammar	23	6	16	9	69*
read/write	26	6	7	16	52*
vocabulary	43*	4	7	12	38
relevant	39	7	−2	30	22
ask Q's	58*	15	10	5	13
pronunciation	37	2	22	25	21

listen/speak	53*	6	38	21	16
communicate	59*	12	22	21	14
feedback	64*	12	1	5	16
everyday lg	51*	9	–2	22	9
no English	–7	–14	41*	19	12
challenge	23	6	46*	32	26
active partic	21	39	48*	27	1
must speak	12	14	67*	–8	2
pairs/group	13	72*	–3	15	10
not alone	6	73*	12	–7	–1
cohesiveness	26	44*	1	32	8
culture	11	11	7	49*	13
goal-setting	22	2	3	35	3
authentic	10	3	17	53*	8

note: Lines denote divisions between major categories. Values are multiplied by 100 and rounded to the nearest integer. Values greater than 0.4 have been flagged by an "*". Variance explained by each factor:

factor1	factor2	factor3	factor4	factor5
2.489048	1.532095	1.392704	1.326841	1.194866

Five factors related to learner preferences for different aspects of foreign language pedagogy were extracted. The largest number of our questionnaire items load on Factor 1, which we have labeled a *Practical* approach because of the focus in these items on everyday, communicatively relevant language, feedback from the teacher, and the belief that students should ask questions when they do not understand something. Factor 2 consists of three items concerning group and pair work, not working alone, and a desire for cohesiveness in the language class. We have labeled this a preference for *Cooperative Learning*. Factor 3 clearly represents the dimension of *Challenge* and has been so labeled. Factors 4 and 5 are somewhat harder to label. Factor 4 consists of only three items, a focus on culture in the language classroom, the use of authentic materials, and an endorsement of goal-setting by language learners. We have labeled this *Innovative* for lack of a better term. Factor 5, which we have labeled *Traditional*, is made up of two core items concerning a focus on grammar and reading and writing. However, in the Japanese data the item concerning vocabulary also loaded on this factor, while in the data from learners of European languages this item loaded most highly on Factor 1, while also loading relatively highly on Factor 5. This makes some sense in terms of what vocabulary learning likely means for students of these languages. For Americans learning a European language that uses the same script as English, learning new vocabulary means primarily matching new phonological forms with familiar meanings and is likely to be viewed primarily as an important factor in becoming communicatively competent. For Americans learning Japanese, however, learning vocabulary is often viewed primarily as a matter of learning new kanji (Chinese characters used in written Japanese) and would therefore be associated with reading and writing and other aspects of traditional pedagogy. In the end, we decided to retain this item within our measure of a preference for a traditional approach, mainly to increase the number of items in this category and thereby increase its internal consistency.

For Part C (learning strategies), all the categories were also derived from factor analysis. The factor solutions were very similar across the three data sets. Tables 10, 11, and 12 summarize the factor solutions obtained for three different samples and the total variance accounted for. Table 13 presents a factor solution for the combined data, specifying four factors.

Table 10: Part C – All language groups (N=2023)

number of factors=4 (total variance accounted for=31%)
f1. Study skills
f2. Cognitive
f3. Coping
f4. Social

Table 11: Part C – Japanese (N=1007)

number of factors=4 (total variance accounted for=31%)
f1. Study skills
f2. Coping
f3. Cognitive
f4. Social

Table 12: Part C – European (N=790)

number of factors=4 (total variance accounted for=33%)
f1. Study skills
f2. Cognitive
f3. Social
f4. Coping

Table 13: Factor solution for Part C — All language groups (N=2023)

	f1 Study skills	f2 Cognitive	f3 Coping	f4 Social
relate vocab	20	50*	20	3
compare lgs	–2	51*	5	6
guess meaning	3	50*	–1	4
patterns	20	53*	9	–5
evaluate progress	33	35	23	4
preview	24	32	23	12
clarification	21	35	16	14
work with others	15	8	8	70*
classmates	11	10	10	72*
ask other's help	2	0	24	61*
organize study	39	20	31	18
review after test	38	22	22	11
place for study	33	18	17	3
time to prepare	47*	20	18	6
re-read materials	38	14	34	4
review early	74*	4	10	11
not last minute	72*	–10	–13	3
periodic study	41*	17	5	5
repeat words	23	27	34	6
find gaps	17	20	47*	14
see words first	4	12	35	10
look words up	30	19	31	2
try to keep up	13	–2	41*	7
what's on test?	–4	–8	45*	8

note: Lines denote divisions between major categories. Values are multiplied by 100 and rounded to the nearest integer. Values greater than 0.4 have been flagged by an "*". Variance explained by each factor:

factor1	factor2	factor3	factor4
2.521515	1.807837	1.538342	1.533918

As can be seen from Table 13, of the factors extracted for learning strategies, some are more easily interpretable than others. Factor 4, with high loadings from just three questionnaire items concerning working with others and seeking help from classmates, clearly represents social learning strategies. Factor 1, which we have labeled *Study Skills*, includes a coherent set of items concerning the methodical allocation of resources to getting the job of studying a language accomplished. We have labeled Factor 2 *Cognitive*, although we note that some of the items loading on this factor would be considered metacognitive strategies in a theoretically oriented scheme. Factor 3 is hardest to interpret, since some items loading on it do so weakly, but the high loading of items such as wanting to know what is on an upcoming test and trying to keep up with the course suggests that these are coping strategies.

INTERNAL CONSISTENCY

Internal consistency estimates, by Cronbach's coefficient alpha, of the three parts and of categories within each part for four language samples are reported in Table 14. Coefficient alpha ranged from .92 to .88 for Part A (47 items), from .84 to .81 for Part B (22 items), and from .83 to .79 for Part C (24 items). These estimates are acceptably high. However, coefficient alpha for categories and subcategories within each part varied greatly. Generally, the more items a category contains, the higher the reliability estimate was. This was true for value components (22 items, coefficient alpha=.93 to .86) and for expectancy components (13 items, coefficient alpha=.86 to .84) on one end, as well as for competitiveness (4 items, alpha=.55 to.39) and cooperativeness (3 items, alpha=.51 to .35) on the other. This is not surprising since internal consistency estimate is a function of the number of items and inter-correlations within a category. The more items a category contains and the more they are correlated with each other, the internal consistency estimate goes up. Due to the small number of items, the internal consistency estimates for some categories are only marginally acceptable.

Table 14: Cronbach's coefficient alpha reliability estimates

categories	# of items	Japanese	European	Filipino	Chinese
Part A	47	.91	.92	.88	.91
Value components	22	.91	.93	.86	.90
Intrinsic motivation	6	.84	.86	.74	.80
Instrumental orientation	3	.42	.64	.44	.51
Integrative orientation	3	.69	.73	.64	.68
Interest	4	.69	.71	.57	.69
Task value	3	.59	.64	.50	.68
Expectancy components	13	.84	.84	.86	.84
Expectancy	3	.69	.66	.66	.73
Anxiety	6	.76	.73	.76	.75
Perceived aptitude	4	.67	.64	.57	.64
Heritage language	2	.80	.78	.72	.79
Motivational strength	5	.65	.74	.44	.64
Competitiveness	4	.54	.55	.39	.42
Cooperativeness	3	.50	.51	.36	.35
Part B	20	.82	.83	.81	.84
Traditional approach	5	.65	.64	.70	.73
Practical proficiency orientation	7	.77	.78	.66	.84
Challenging approaches	4	.63	.62	.49	.51
Cooperative learning	3	.70	.65	.69	.53
Innovative approaches	3	.49	.53	.38	.38

Part C	24	.82	.83	.80	.79
Cognitive strategies	7	.69	.69	.63	.60
Social strategies	3	.73	.73	.72	.71
Study skills	8	.75	.74	.62	.72
Coping strategies	6	.52	.64	.50	.63

Overall, this questionnaire, with only 91 items, attempts to tap into three different aspects of individual differences among foreign language learners: motivation, preferences for instructional activities, and strategy use. Considering the small number of items, particularly within categories in each of the three parts, this instrument seems to serve its purpose fairly well. Factor analyses and internal consistency estimates indicate that the following categories meet the divergent and convergent validity criteria: for Part A—Value, Expectancy, Heritage Language, Motivational Strength, Competitiveness, and Cooperativeness; for Part B—Traditional Approach, Practical Proficiency Orientation, Challenging Approaches, Cooperative Learning, and Innovative Approaches; and for Part C—Cognitive Strategies, Social Strategies, Study Skills Strategies, and Coping Strategies. In order to be able to use these factors in further analyses, we have computed composite scores for each them, by summing the scores of the items loading on each factor. In the case of the expectancy scale, the scores for anxiety items were reversed to indicate a lack of anxiety. In addition, we include in our following analyses the responses to the single item concerning the subjective importance of the language requirement, since this is of interest to the participants and their instructors. Appendix B lists the scales and the items that have been summed to arrive at a scores for further analysis.

COMPARISONS AMONG STUDENTS STUDYING DIFFERENT LANGUAGES

Although not the major focus of this study, one question of interest is whether students studying different languages in a single institution are all more or less alike or whether the students of each language present a particular motivational profile. We also wondered whether students studying different languages might use different learning strategies or have preferences for different styles of foreign language pedagogy. It is often argued by foreign language teachers that learning their particular language requires a specific pedagogical approach or even that specific strategies may be especially useful for specific languages. To cite only one example, teachers of Japanese and Chinese as foreign languages often argue that because of the importance of learning large numbers of characters (kanji) for these languages, memorization strategies are crucial. The question we are asking here is whether students of these languages subscribe to similar beliefs or modify their strategies and preferences depending on the language they are learning.

Tables 15–18 display the results of each of the target language groups on each of these variables. In each case, an ANOVA procedure was used to determine whether there are statistically significant differences among the groups, followed by a post-hoc comparison of means (using the Scheffé test) to identify precisely where the differences lie. Because of the large number of statistical tests reported in this and the following sections, alpha was set at .001.

Table 15 shows the results of the analysis of variance on the scores on parts A (motivation), B (pedagogical preferences), and C (learning strategies) by target language group. As can be seen in the table, there are group differences on each of these measures, but Scheffé's test indicates that only a few of the pair-wise differences in means are significant. Learners of Spanish in our sample are, on the whole, less motivated than the learners of Chinese, Japanese, or Filipino. The students of Filipino have, overall, a higher level of appreciation for all aspects of language pedagogy than students of either French or Spanish, and Japanese learners also have a higher level of appreciation of pedagogical techniques (in general) than the learners of Spanish. Learners of Filipino report the highest use of strategies (all types combined) and their means on this part of our instrument are significantly higher than those of the learners of both Chinese and Japanese.

Table 15: Analysis of variance of scores on Parts A, B, and C by target language group

	French		Spanish		Japanese		Chinese		Filipino			
	mean	SD	mean	SD	mean	SD	mean	SD	mean	SD	F-value	p-value
Part A	3.300	.530	3.181	.503	3.421	.469	3.494	.456	3.538	.425	32.783	<.0001
Part B	3.773	.479	3.762	.401	3.884	.395	3.884	.437	3.989	.404	14.119	<.0001
Part C	3.526	.442	3.562	.419	3.532	.430	3.386	.400	3.716	.405	9.162	<.0001

Scheffé for Part A
effect: LANGUAGE
significance level: .1%

	mean diff.	crit. diff.	p-value	
Chinese, Filipino	−.044	.273	.9750	
Chinese, French	.194	.244	.0201	
Chinese, Japanese	.073	.202	.6628	
Chinese, Spanish	.313	.208	<.0001	S
Filipino, French	.238	.247	.0018	
Filipino, Japanese	.117	.205	.1991	
Filipino, Spanish	.357	.211	<.0001	S
French, Japanese	−.121	.165	.0410	
French, Spanish	.119	.173	.0650	
Japanese, Spanish	.241	.105	<.0001	S

Scheffé for Part B
  effect: LANGUAGE
  significance level: .1%

	mean diff.	crit. diff.	p-value	
Chinese, Filipino	−.105	.231	.4257	
Chinese, French	.110	.207	.2594	
Chinese, Japanese	.000	.171	>.9999	
Chinese, Spanish	.122	.176	.0650	
Filipino, French	.216	.209	.0006	S
Filipino, Japanese	.105	.173	.1446	
Filipino, Spanish	.227	.179	<.0001	S
French, Japanese	−.110	.140	.0214	
French, Spanish	.011	.146	.9984	
Japanese, Spanish	.122	.089	<.0001	S

Scheffé for Part C
  effect: LANGUAGE
  significance level: .1%

	mean diff.	crit. diff.	p-value	
Chinese, Filipino	−.330	.242	<.0001	S
Chinese, French	−.140	.219	.1076	
Chinese, Japanese	−.147	.180	.0154	
Chinese, Spanish	−.177	.187	.0024	
Filipino, French	.190	.220	.0080	
Filipino, Japanese	.184	.181	.0008	S
Filipino, Spanish	.154	.188	.0147	
French, Japanese	−.006	.149	.9999	
French, Spanish	−.036	.157	.9094	
Japanese, Spanish	−.030	.095	.7612	

Table 16 shows the ANOVA results on motivational scales by target language group and identifies both similarities and differences. Within each of the five target language groups, these university students agree most with statements suggesting a social, cooperative motivation and least with the statements on our Competitive scale, including a concern for grades, perhaps indicating the effect of a social desirability factor. As for the differences, the results for a number of these variables tend to break our students into two groups: learners of French and Spanish in one group; learners of Chinese, Japanese, and Filipino in the other. As can be seen, this is not only a contrast between European and Asian languages, but (in this context) between non-heritage and heritage languages. As shown by results of the Scheffé test for the Heritage scale, the group means are significantly different for all pairs of languages represented in our sample except for the comparison between French and

Spanish (neither of which is a heritage language for very many of these students) and the comparisons among Chinese, Filipino, and Japanese (all of which are heritage languages for large numbers of students). Besides being a non-heritage language for most students, Spanish occupies a distinctive position among these five target languages in several ways. The students in this sample who are studying Spanish are least likely to see the value of studying the language (a composite variable on which learners of Spanish report agreement at significantly lower levels than learners of each of the other four languages) and are significantly more likely than learners of any of the other languages to agree with the statement "I mainly study this language to satisfy the university language requirement."

Table 16: Analysis of variance of scores on motivation scales by target language group

	French		Spanish		Japanese		Chinese		Filipino			
	mean	SD	mean	SD	mean	SD	mean	SD	mean	SD	F-value	p-value
value	3.366	.757	3.124	.725	3.554	.632	3.645	.604	3.619	.537	47.973	<.0001
heritage	2.329	.960	2.178	.919	3.041	1.024	3.258	.976	3.636	.893	117.533	<.0001
expt	3.315	.681	3.179	.666	3.126	.678	3.384	.699	3.245	.755	6.343	<.0001
mot str	3.406	.762	3.447	.717	3.685	.622	3.429	.672	3.649	.551	17.710	<.0001
compet	2.950	.796	2.948	.745	3.044	.739	3.048	.639	3.126	.762	2.725	ns
coop	3.756	.654	3.790	.617	3.747	.639	3.554	.645	4.018	.605	8.436	<.0001
req	3.091	1.451	3.736	1.246	2.657	1.339	2.496	1.277	3.044	1.379	71.051	<.0001

Scheffé for Value scale
  effect: LANGUAGE
  significance level: .1%

	mean diff.	crit. diff.	p-value	
Chinese, Filipino	.026	.378	.9990	
Chinese, French	.279	.338	.0133	
Chinese, Japanese	.091	.279	.7419	
Chinese, Spanish	.521	.288	<.0001	S
Filipino, French	.253	.342	.0378	
Filipino, Japanese	.065	.284	.9143	
Filipino, Spanish	.495	.292	<.0001	S
French, Japanese	−.188	.229	.0137	
French, Spanish	.242	.239	.0008	S
Japanese, Spanish	.430	.145	<.0001	S

Scheffé for Heritage scale
    effect: LANGUAGE
    significance level: .1%

	mean diff.	crit. diff.	p-value	
Chinese, Filipino	−.377	.553	.0710	
Chinese, French	.930	.495	<.0001	S
Chinese, Japanese	.218	.409	.2633	
Chinese, Spanish	1.080	.422	<.0001	S
Filipino, French	1.307	.500	<.0001	S
Filipino, Japanese	.595	.416	<.0001	S
Filipino, Spanish	1.458	.428	<.0001	S
French, Japanese	−.712	.335	<.0001	S
French, Spanish	.151	.350	.4871	
Japanese, Spanish	.863	.212	<.0001	S

Scheffé for Expectancy scale
    effect: LANGUAGE
    significance level: .1%

	mean diff.	crit. diff.	p-value
Chinese, Filipino	.139	.385	.6600
Chinese, French	.069	.344	.9467
Chinese, Japanese	.257	.285	.0045
Chinese, Spanish	.205	.293	.0607
Filipino, French	−.070	.348	.9445
Filipino, Japanese	.118	.289	.5394
Filipino, Spanish	.066	.298	.9231
French, Japanese	.189	.233	.0163
French, Spanish	.136	.243	.2151
Japanese, Spanish	−.053	.147	.6714

Scheffé for Motivational Strength
effect: LANGUAGE
significance level: .1%

	mean diff.	crit. diff.	*p*-value	
Chinese, Filipino	−.220	.376	.1743	
Chinese, French	.022	.337	.9992	
Chinese, Japanese	−.256	.278	.0036	
Chinese, Spanish	−.018	.287	.9994	
Filipino, French	.243	.340	.0516	
Filipino, Japanese	−.036	.283	.9902	
Filipino, Spanish	.202	.291	.0627	
French, Japanese	−.278	.228	<.0001	S
French, Spanish	−.040	.238	.9701	
Japanese, Spanish	.238	.144	<.0001	S

Scheffé for Competiveness
effect: LANGUAGE
significance level: .1%

	mean diff.	crit. diff.	*p*-value
Chinese, Filipino	−.078	.420	.9590
Chinese, French	.098	.376	.8681
Chinese, Japanese	.004	.311	>.9999
Chinese, Spanish	.100	.320	.7705
Filipino, French	.176	.380	.4107
Filipino, Japanese	.082	.315	.8692
Filipino, Spanish	.178	.325	.2356
French, Japanese	−.094	.254	.6412
French, Spanish	.002	.266	>.9999
Japanese, Spanish	.096	.161	.1607

Scheffé for Cooperativeness
    effect: LANGUAGE
    significance level: .1%

	mean diff.	crit. diff.	p-value	
Chinese, Filipino	−.464	.355	<.0001	S
Chinese, French	−.202	.318	.1120	
Chinese, Japanese	−.193	.263	.0403	
Chinese, Spanish	−.236	.271	.0071	
Filipino, French	.262	.321	.0153	
Filipino, Japanese	.271	.267	.0008	S
Filipino, Spanish	.228	.275	.0129	
French, Japanese	.009	.215	.9999	
French, Spanish	−.034	.225	.9801	
Japanese, Spanish	−.043	.136	.7615	

Scheffé for Language Requirement
    effect: LANGUAGE
    significance level: .1%

	mean diff.	crit. diff.	p-value	
Chinese, Filipino	−.548	.748	.0416	
Chinese, French	−.596	.671	.0057	
Chinese, Japanese	−.162	.555	.8139	
Chinese, Spanish	−1.240	.572	<.0001	S
Filipino, French	−.048	.676	.9990	
Filipino, Japanese	.387	.561	.0668	
Filipino, Spanish	−.692	.578	<.0001	S
French, Japanese	.434	.453	.0020	
French, Spanish	−.645	.474	<.0001	S
Japanese, Spanish	−1.079	.286	<.0001	S

Students of Filipino agree most enthusiastically with the items contained in our motivational scale of Cooperativeness; the differences between students of Filipino and students of Chinese and Japanese are highly significant and the differences when compared to students of French and Spanish almost reach criterion. Learners of Japanese, on the other hand, are characterized by having high motivational strength (significantly higher than learners of French and Spanish), coupled with relatively low expectations of success (although none of the pair-wise comparisons on this scale reach the .001 level of confidence).

Table 17: Analysis of variance of scores on pedagogy scales by target language group

| | French | | Spanish | | Japanese | | Chinese | | Filipino | | | |
	mean	SD	mean	SD	mean	SD	mean	SD	mean	SD	F-value	p-value
traditional	3.868	.704	3.886	.643	4.070	.589	4.124	.596	4.102	.674	12.656	<.0001
practical	4.146	.585	4.145	.468	4.217	.464	4.220	.560	4.296	.432	4.055	ns
challenge	3.335	.723	3.141	.664	3.350	.677	3.444	.660	3.428	.668	12.631	<.0001
cooperative	3.604	.781	3.785	.724	3.864	.700	3.649	.674	4.061	.732	10.487	<.0001
innovative	3.561	.638	3.549	.626	3.650	.583	3.681	.607	3.836	.573	7.224	<.0001

Scheffé for Traditional
effect: LANGUAGE
significance level: .1%

	mean diff.	crit. diff.	p-value	
Chinese, Filipino	.022	.352	.9994	
Chinese, French	.256	.315	.0156	
Chinese, Japanese	.054	.260	.9387	
Chinese, Spanish	.238	.268	.0058	
Filipino, French	.234	.318	.0400	
Filipino, Japanese	.032	.264	.9915	
Filipino, Spanish	.216	.272	.0202	
French, Japanese	−.202	.213	.0022	
French, Spanish	−.018	.223	.9982	
Japanese, Spanish	.184	.135	<.0001	S

Scheffé for Practical Proficiency
effect: LANGUAGE
significance level: .1%

	mean diff.	crit. diff.	p-value
Chinese, Filipino	−.076	.272	.8388
Chinese, French	.074	.244	.7869
Chinese, Japanese	.004	.201	>.9999
Chinese, Spanish	.075	.208	.6547
Filipino, French	.150	.246	.1437
Filipino, Japanese	.079	.205	.5955
Filipino, Spanish	.151	.211	.0497
French, Japanese	−.071	.165	.4923
French, Spanish	.001	.172	>.9999
Japanese, Spanish	.072	.105	.0680

Scheffé for Challenge
  effect: LANGUAGE
  significance level: .1%

	mean diff.	crit. diff.	p-value	
Chinese, Filipino	.017	.383	.9998	
Chinese, French	.109	.343	.7575	
Chinese, Japanese	.094	.284	.7280	
Chinese, Spanish	.303	.293	.0005	S
Filipino, French	.093	.346	.8569	
Filipino, Japanese	.077	.287	.8533	
Filipino, Spanish	.287	.296	.0017	
French, Japanese	−.015	.231	.9992	
French, Spanish	.194	.242	.0183	
Japanese, Spanish	.209	.147	<.0001	S

Scheffé for Cooperative Learning
  effect: LANGUAGE
  significance level: .1%

	mean diff.	crit. diff.	p-value	
Chinese, Filipino	−.412	.407	.0008	S
Chinese, French	.045	.365	.9909	
Chinese, Japanese	−.215	.303	.0533	
Chinese, Spanish	−.136	.312	.4790	
Filipino, French	.457	.366	<.0001	S
Filipino, Japanese	.197	.304	.1000	
Filipino, Spanish	.277	.313	.0061	
French, Japanese	−.260	.245	.0003	S
French, Spanish	−.181	.256	.0568	
Japanese, Spanish	.080	.156	.3049	

Scheffé for Innovative
   effect: LANGUAGE
   significance level: .1%

	mean diff.	crit. diff.	p-value	
Chinese, Filipino	−.155	.341	.4284	
Chinese, French	.119	.306	.5871	
Chinese, Japanese	.031	.253	.9912	
Chinese, Spanish	.132	.261	.3165	
Filipino, French	.275	.308	.0054	
Filipino, Japanese	.186	.256	.0440	
Filipino, Spanish	.287	.264	.0002	S
French, Japanese	−.088	.206	.4915	
French, Spanish	.012	.216	.9995	
Japanese, Spanish	.101	.131	.0270	

As shown in Table 17, students studying all five languages reserve their highest agreement for aspects of foreign language pedagogy related to a practical proficiency approach, approve next most highly of a traditional approach, and are least likely to agree with statements concerning active participation and a desire to be challenged. There are also significant differences by target language group for all of the scales except Practical Proficiency, although only a few of the pair-wise comparisons using the Scheffé test produce statistically significant results. Learners of Japanese have significantly higher appreciation for the traditional approach (emphasis on grammar, vocabulary, reading, and writing) than do learners of Spanish. Learners of Spanish, while agreeing that practical proficiency should be the goal of pedagogy, do not agree strongly with the statements in our Challenge scale and are significantly different from learners of Chinese and Japanese in that regard. Learners of Filipino are significantly more likely than learners of Spanish to approve of innovative approaches (i.e., authentic materials, learner goal-setting, and a focus on culture) and score highest of the five groups on the Cooperative Learning scale (significantly higher than learners of Chinese, French, and Japanese).

Table 18: Analysis of variance of scores on strategy scales
by target language group

	French		Spanish		Japanese		Chinese		Filipino		F-value	p-value
	mean	SD	mean	SD	mean	SD	mean	SD	mean	SD		
Cognitive	3.608	.549	3.514	.536	3.409	.564	3.507	.494	3.578	.523	8.162	<.0001
Social	3.228	.828	3.347	.809	3.295	.805	3.132	.864	3.792	.783	11.982	<.0001
Study skills	3.243	.646	3.293	.629	3.355	.628	3.026	.614	3.521	.544	11.053	<.0001
Coping	3.957	.566	4.083	.426	4.034	.441	3.852	.505	4.109	.441	8.483	<.0001

Scheffé for Cognitive strategies
    effect: LANGUAGE
    significance level: .1%

	mean diff.	crit. diff.	p-value	
Chinese, Filipino	−.071	.313	.9151	
Chinese, French	−.101	.283	.6693	
Chinese, Japanese	.098	.232	.5081	
Chinese, Spanish	−.007	.241	>.9999	
Filipino, French	−.030	.284	.9953	
Filipino, Japanese	.169	.234	.0459	
Filipino, Spanish	.064	.243	.8613	
French, Japanese	.199	.192	.0005	S
French, Spanish	.094	.202	.4070	
Japanese, Spanish	−.105	.122	.0083	

Scheffé for Social strategies
    effect: LANGUAGE
    significance level: .1%

	mean diff.	crit. diff.	p-value	
Chinese, Filipino	−.660	.464	<.0001	S
Chinese, French	−.096	.419	.9130	
Chinese, Japanese	−.164	.345	.3826	
Chinese, Spanish	−.215	.357	.1518	
Filipino, French	.564	.421	<.0001	S
Filipino, Japanese	.496	.347	<.0001	S
Filipino, Spanish	.445	.360	<.0001	S
French, Japanese	−.067	.284	.9035	
French, Spanish	−.119	.299	.5713	
Japanese, Spanish	−.051	.181	.8260	

Scheffé for Study Skills strategies
    effect: LANGUAGE
    significance level: .1%

	mean diff.	crit. diff.	p-value	
Chinese, Filipino	−.495	.356	<.0001	S
Chinese, French	−.217	.322	.0773	
Chinese, Japanese	−.329	.265	<.0001	S
Chinese, Spanish	−.267	.274	.0016	
Filipino, French	.278	.323	.0084	
Filipino, Japanese	.166	.267	.1255	
Filipino, Spanish	.228	.276	.0131	
French, Japanese	−.112	.218	.3011	
French, Spanish	−.050	.230	.9292	
Japanese, Spanish	.062	.139	.4472	

Scheffé for Coping strategies
    effect: LANGUAGE
    significance level: .1%

	mean diff.	crit. diff.	p-value	
Chinese, Filipino	−.258	.258	.0010	
Chinese, French	−.105	.233	.4356	
Chinese, Japanese	−.183	.192	.0021	
Chinese, Spanish	−.232	.199	<.0001	S
Filipino, French	.152	.234	.0995	
Filipino, Japanese	.075	.193	.5970	
Filipino, Spanish	.026	.200	.9895	
French, Japanese	−.077	.158	.3508	
French, Spanish	−.126	.167	.0309	
Japanese, Spanish	−.049	.101	.3568	

As displayed in Table 18, although students of all five languages report using coping strategies more frequently than those in other categories, there are again some differences by target language. Cognitive strategies are used most often by students of French (only the pair-wise comparison with learners of Japanese is significant). Social strategies are used more often by learners of Filipino than learners of any other language (comparisons with learners of Chinese, French, Japanese, and Spanish are all significant). Learners of Chinese report using both coping strategies and strategies associated with study skills less frequently than other language learners (for study skills, the comparisons with Filipino and Japanese are significant; for coping strategies, only the comparison with Spanish is significant).

Tables 19–23 present the significant correlations (alpha again set at .001) between Part A (motivation) and Part C (learning strategies) and between each of the scales of motivation and the scales for learning strategies, separately for each target language group. Table 24 summarizes these results by presenting only those correlations for the entire learner sample that are significant at the .0001 level and that were also found to be significant for at least four of the five target language groups when these were analyzed separately.

Table 19: Correlations between the motivational scales and strategy scales for learners of Chinese

	Part C	Cognitive	Social	Study skills	Coping
Part A	.497*	.573*			.435*
Value	.508*	.406*			.359*
Heritage			.432*		
Expectancy		.390*			
Motiv'l Strength	.436*	.341*		.320	.390*
Competitiveness		.301			
Cooperativeness	.409*		.369		
Requirement					

*p<.0001

Table 20: Correlations between the motivational scales and strategy scales for learners of Filipino

	Part C	Cognitive	Social	Study skills	Coping
Part A	.488*	.456*		.437*	
Value	.392*	.453*		.344*	
Heritage					
Expectancy		.257		.246	
Motiv'l Strength	.406*	.243		.462*	.233
Competitiveness	.353	.273	.393*		.274
Cooperativeness	.391*		.334	.337*	.310
Requirement					

*p<.0001

Table 21: Correlations between the motivational scales and strategy scales for learners of French

	Part C	Cognitive	Social	Study skills	Coping
Part A	.575*	.588*		.536*	.268
Value	.553*	.534*		.500*	.279
Heritage					
Expectancy		.348*			
Motiv'l Strength	.500*	.390*		.532*	.310*
Competitiveness		.264			
Cooperativeness	.488*	.378*	.336*	.271	.443*
Requirement				−.300*	

*p<.0001

Table 22: Correlations between the motivational scales and strategy scales for learners of Japanese

	Part C	Cognitive	Social	Study skills	Coping
Part A	.447*	.498*		.373*	.238*
Value	.403*	.408*		.325*	.208*
Heritage	.111				
Expectancy	.172*	.264*			
Motiv'l Strength	.493*	.370*		.493*	.365*
Competitiveness	.214*	.241*		.190*	.253*
Cooperativeness	.394*	.240*	.328*	.250*	.408*
Requirement	−.140*	−.249*		−.141	

*p<.0001

Table 23: Correlations between the motivational scales and strategy scales for learners of Spanish

	Part C	Cognitive	Social	Study skills	Coping
Part A	.403*	.433*		.372*	
Value	.323*	.386*		.267*	
Heritage	.213*	.228*		.209*	
Expectancy		.266*		.141	
Motiv'l Strength	.485*	.312*	.138	.565*	.218*
Competitiveness	.232*	.247*		.177*	.152
Cooperativeness	.376*	.201*	.386*	.263*	.290*
Requirement	−.146	−.219*			

*p<.0001

Table 24: Summary of meaningful correlations between the motivational scales and strategy scales across all target language groups

	Part C	Cognitive	Social	Study skills	Coping
Part A	.430*	.456*		.378*	
Value	.369*	.419*		.315	
Heritage					
Expectancy		.298*			
Motiv'l Strength	.474*	.318*		.509*	.306*
Competitiveness		.243*			
Cooperativeness	.409*	.242*	.359*		.373*
Requirement					

*p<.0001

As can be seen in tables 19–24, the overall use of learning strategies (Part C) is significantly correlated both with Part A (motivation) and with three of our motivational scales Value, Motivational Strength, and Cooperativeness across and within all five target language groups, with correlation coefficients ranging from a low of .323 (Value∗Strategy Use for learners of Spanish) to a high of .508 (Value∗Strategy Use for learners of Chinese). Competitiveness can perhaps be considered an influence on strategy use also, since scores on this measure correlated with Part C at .232 for learners of Japanese, .232 for learners of Spanish, and a respectable .353 for learners of Filipino, but did not correlate significantly with Part C for learners of French or Chinese. Scores on the other three motivational scales appear to have much less of an effect on the use of learning strategies. The highest correlation between the Expectancy scale and Part C was .172 for learners of Japanese, significant only because of the large size of the sample and clearly not very meaningful. The Heritage scale correlated with reported overall strategy use only for learners of Japanese and Spanish, and again the correlations were low (.111 and .213, respectively). Finally, although responses to the Language Requirement correlated negatively with strategy use in the case of two groups (learners of Japanese and Spanish), these correlations are also low and cannot be considered meaningful.

This general pattern is confirmed when looking at correlations between specific scales for motivation and specific scales for learning strategies. Reported use of Cognitive strategies correlates with (in descending order of magnitude) scores on the Value, Motivational Strength, Expectancy, Competitiveness, and Cooperativeness scales. Study Skills strategies are correlated most highly with Motivational Strength; secondarily with Value. Coping strategies are significantly associated with Motivational Strength and Cooperativeness for all groups, with only some groups showing significant correlations with Value (Chinese and Japanese) and Competitiveness (Filipino and Spanish).

The results shown in Table 24 make it clear that not all aspects of motivation affect strategy use equally, and not all strategies are equally affected by motivational factors. The strongest predictor of strategy use among the motivational scales is Motivational Strength, closely followed by Value and Cooperativeness. Expectancy and Competitiveness predict some (but fewer) aspects of strategy use. The Heritage scale does not correlate significantly with any of the strategy scales for any target language group except for Cognitive and Study Skills strategies for learners of Spanish (.228 and .209, respectively) and Social strategies for learners of Chinese (.432). Although there are a few significant (negative) correlations between Language Requirement and Studies Skills (French, Japanese) and Cognitive Strategies (learners of Spanish), none of these relationships hold across the groups. It is also clear from tables 19–24 that the strategies most affected by motivation are those in our Cognitive scale, which contains items associated with both cognitive and metacognitive strategies, followed by Study Skills and Coping Strategies. The use of Social strategies appears largely unaffected by most aspects of motivation; the only exception is the significant correlation in all groups with the Cooperativeness scale from the motivation questionnaire.

MOTIVATION AND PEDAGOGY

Tables 25–29 display the significant correlations between Part A (motivation) and Part B (pedagogical preferences) and between each of the scales of motivation and the scales for pedagogy, separately for each target language group. Table 30 summarizes these results, displaying only those correlations for the entire learner sample that were consistently found to be significant when analyzing each group separately. As can be seen from these tables, motivation has an even greater effect on students' attitudes towards classroom pedagogy than it does towards their use of learning strategies. For each target language group, the correlation between Part A (motivation) and Part B (agreement with statements concerning pedagogy) is .50 or higher and highly significant. For learners of Japanese and Spanish, all seven motivational scales correlate significantly with Part B, and for learners of all target languages, Value, Motivational Strength, and Cooperativeness do. These three aspects of motivation, which (as shown above) have the strongest influence on learning strategies also have the strongest link with an overall appreciation of different aspects of foreign language pedagogy.

Table 25: Correlations between the motivational scales and pedagogy scales for learners of Chinese

	Part B	Traditional	Practical	Challenge	Cooperative	Innovative
Part A	.490*	.347*	.377*	.601*		.336
Value	.546*	.413*	.423	.634*		
Heritage						
Expectancy				.453*		
Motiv'l Strength	.289			.320		
Competitiveness						
Cooperativeness	.430*	.338	.354*		.343	.335
Requirement				−.385*		

*$p<.0001$

Table 26: Correlations between the motivational scales and pedagogy scales for learners of Filipino

	Part B	Traditional	Practical	Challenge	Cooperative	Innovative
Part A	.506*	.302	.329	.628*	.265	
Value	.421*			.556*		
Heritage						
Expectancy	.277			.474*		
Motiv'l Strength	.240					
Competitiveness	.307		.325	.279		
Cooperativeness	.442*	.408*		.310*	.475*	
Requirement				−.306		

*$p<.0001$

Table 27: Correlations between the motivational scales and pedagogy scales for learners of French

	Part B	Traditional	Practical	Challenge	Cooperative	Innovative
Part A	.564*	.277	.387*	.657*	.230	.416*
Value	.534*		.362	.600*		.490*
Heritage						.239
Expectancy				.453*		
Motiv'l Strength	.341*	.284*	.321*	.323*		
Competitiveness	.286*			.343*		
Cooperativeness	.617*	.385*	.507*	.353*	.521*	.414*
Requirement				−.326		

*$p<.0001$

Table 28: Correlations between the motivational scales and pedagogy scales for learners of Japanese

	Part B	Traditional	Practical	Challenge	Cooperative	Innovative
Part A	.529*	.378*	.347*	.587*		.327*
Value	.518*	.376*	.341*	.554*		.352*
Heritage	.108	.113				.186*
Expectancy	.233*	.184*	.128*	.428*		
Motiv'l Strength	.351*	.236*	.265*	.317*	.160*	.170*
Competitiveness	.271*	.204*	.214*	.253*		.174*
Cooperativeness	.457*	.224*	.352*	.252*	.469*	.232*
Requirement	−.261*	−.220*	−.130*	−.388*		−.140*

*p<.0001

Table 29: Correlations between the motivational scales and pedagogy scales for learners of Spanish

	Part B	Traditional	Practical	Challenge	Cooperative	Innovative
Part A	.501*	.299*	.321*	.604*		.294*
Value	.465*	.255*	.299*	.543*		.308*
Heritage	.217*	.148		.319*		.204*
Expectancy	.257*	.149	.199*	.406*		
Motiv'l Strength	.322*	.244*	.220*	.324*		.166*
Competitiveness	.229*	.159*	.136*	.282*		
Cooperativeness	.476*	.272*	.314*	.280*	.511*	.219*
Requirement	−.224*			−.375		−.175*

*p<.0001

Table 30: Summary of meaningful correlations between the motivational scales and pedagogy scales across all target language groups

	Part B	Traditional	Practical	Challenge	Cooperative	Innovative
Part A	.536*	.356*	.353*	.613*		
Value	.514*	.336*	.337*	.570*		.352*
Heritage						
Expectancy				.422*		
Motiv'l Strength	.345*			.321*		
Competitiveness				.272*		
Cooperativeness	.470*		.351*	.262*	.483*	
Requirement				−.394*		

*p<.0001

The correlations between the specific motivation scales and the specific scales for pedagogical preferences also show the strong influence of Value (the belief that learning the language will be valuable for a variety of reasons), Cooperativeness, and Motivational Strength. For all five target language groups, Value correlates with approval of both traditional pedagogy and a more practically oriented proficiency approach, innovative approaches, and challenging approaches to language teaching; in other words, it correlates with all of our pedagogy scales except for Cooperative Learning. Motivational Strength and Expectancy, on the other hand, correlate most highly (and consistently across the language groups) with approval of challenging activities in the language class. Looking at the issue from the other direction, asking which types of language class activities are most liked or disliked depending on the level of students' motivation, gives an especially clear answer: challenging activities, including those that require students to participate actively. Challenge is viewed positively by students who see value in learning the language, by those who expect to succeed, by those with high motivational strength, and by those who score high on both the Cooperativeness and Competitiveness scales. However, challenging activities are not liked by students who say that they are mainly studying to fulfill the language requirement. Reminiscent of the results for strategies, the pedagogical preference for Cooperative Learning was consistently and significantly associated with just one of our motivational scales, that of Cooperativeness.

DISCUSSION

One of the major findings of this study has been that, for this population of students studying foreign languages in a U.S. university setting, one of the main components of motivation is Value, a factor that includes a large number of items that we originally assigned to separate categories labeled intrinsic motivation, instrumental orientation, integrative orientation, task value, and a general interest in foreign languages and cultures. It does not appear to be the case that some of the learners in our sample are instrumentally oriented towards language study, others have a general interest in languages and cultures, and yet others just enjoy language learning. Instead, we find that our learners either see value in learning the foreign language they are studying for *all of these reasons* or for none of them. On the other hand, for this population we clearly identified a distinct heritage language learning component. While an integrative orientation towards languages associated other social groups and cultures did not emerge as a separate factor, an orientation towards learning the language of one's own cultural heritage did emerge as a distinctive component of motivation. In each of our analyses, factors also emerged that we have labeled Expectancy, Motivational Strength, and Competitiveness, with an additional factor of Cooperativeness apparently playing a role as well.

As shown in several previous studies, motivation does affect the use of learning strategies, but the research reported here allows us to be more specific about that influence. This study shows that not all aspects of motivation affect strategy use equally, and not all strategies are equally affected by motivational factors. The strongest predictor of strategy use among our motivational scales is Motivational

Strength, closely followed by Value and Cooperativeness. Expectancy and Competitiveness predict fewer aspects of strategy use, and there are no significant correlations that hold across the target language samples for either the Heritage scale or agreement with the statement that one is studying the language primarily to pass the language requirement. The strategies that are most affected by motivation are cognitive and metacognitive strategies. Those least affected are social strategies, which are consistently associated only with what we have called a Cooperativeness component of motivation, an orientation towards relationships with classmates and the teacher.

Not all aspects of motivation affect student preferences for pedagogical practices equally either, and the picture is very similar. Value, Motivational Strength, and Cooperativeness are consistently associated with scores indicating approval of various classroom practices, Expectancy and Competitiveness less consistently so, and the Heritage factor not at all. A liking for challenging activities in the foreign language classroom stood out among our pedagogy scales as the one most associated with various aspects of motivation, positively with Value, Expectancy, Motivational Strength, Competitiveness, and Cooperativeness but negatively with agreement with the statement that one is taking a language course primarily to fulfill the university language requirement.

Several of these findings merit some further comment: the fact that the use of cognitive strategies and a liking for challenge in the classroom are highly associated with motivation, whereas other strategies and other types of classroom activities are less so; the generally low association of Expectancy with either strategies or preferences compared with the influence of Value, Motivational Strength, and cooperativeness; the lack of influence of the heritage factor in general; the association of cooperativeness with the use of social strategies and a preference for cooperative learning; and the influence of the language requirement on motivation, reported strategy use, and classroom preferences.

- It makes sense that the use of cognitive strategies and a liking for challenge in foreign language classes are strongly associated with motivation, especially with the Value and Motivational Strength scales. If one believes that learning a language is worthwhile (for either instrumental or integrative reasons or simply because one enjoys language learning) one would reasonably be expected to use a variety of cognitive, metacognitive, and study skills strategies in order to achieve that valued goal. The same is true for those who demonstrate high motivational strength, which involves drive, determination, and a willingness to exert effort in support of the goal of language learning. An expectation of success based on self-confidence, low anxiety, and belief in one's language learning aptitude (internal, relatively stable factors) would perhaps not be linked as closely to the exercise of learning strategies, and was not in this study. However, an expectation of success ought to be (and was) linked to approval of challenging activities in the language classroom.

- The lack of consistently significant associations between the Heritage factor and either strategies or pedagogical preferences is surprising, since we had expected this factor (clearly a distinct component of motivation for this population) to play a strong role in both domains. We thought, for example, that ethnic Chinese and Japanese students studying their heritage language might have a higher level of appreciation for a more traditional approach, whereas those who did not share that ethnic heritage might prefer a more practical, proficiency-oriented approach. This was not the case. Most of our students appreciate both traditional and more contemporary approaches, and heritage and non-heritage students do not differ in this regard. We have no firm opinion as to why this is so, but speculate that both heritage and non-heritage students who commit to learning Japanese (for example) also make a commitment both to Japanese culture and to the culture of the Japanese language classroom. We know from other research such as that of Kondo-Brown (this volume) and Syed (this volume) that the heritage factor is enormously important in language choice and persistence, but it seems that heritage and non-heritage students are not different in either learning strategy use or the kinds of classrooms and class activities they prefer.

- The associations among our Cooperativeness scale for motivation, reported use of social strategies, and a preference for cooperative learning come as no surprise. It makes sense that a concern for relationships with classmates and the teacher, a liking for group and pair activities, and a preference for learning with others should go together. We believe that there is probably a broad, personality-based dimension of sociability that cuts across the tripartite division into motivation, strategies, and pedagogical preferences in our questionnaire.

- The fact that students who agree with the statement that they are studying a language mainly to fulfill the language requirement are less likely to score high on other measures of motivation, report less use of some learning strategies (for some target language groups), and consistently exhibit a dislike for challenging activities in the foreign language classroom, is not surprising in the light of many studies showing that (in education in general) students who are truly interested in learning tend to use cognitive and meta-cognitive strategies, while students who are concerned more with grades and the fulfillment of requirements (performance goal orientations) are more likely to engage in measuring the difficulty of the task to see if they can perform it well enough (Dweck & Elliot, 1984). However, we caution that no important policy decisions should be based on this finding. Although there are a few significant (negative) correlations between responses concerning the language requirement and reported use of some learning strategies (study skills strategies in the case of learners of French and Japanese and cognitive and metacognitive strategies in the case of learners of Spanish), none of these relationships hold across the groups. More importantly, we have not contrasted students who are studying in order to fulfill the language requirement with those who are not, since over

90% of the students in our sample were first and second year students who were, in fact, fulfilling the language requirement. This study does not show that having a language requirement lowers motivation or fosters poor learning habits. It shows that if students believe that the requirement is the only or primary reason to study the language then it has those negative effects.

We have also found differences among learners of different languages. Students of Spanish at this university are the most likely of any of our groups to report that they are studying the language mainly to satisfy the language requirement and least likely to claim the language as part of their heritage. They generally score lower than other groups on other measures of motivation, especially those items related to intrinsic motivation, both instrumental and integrative orientation, and interest in foreign language and culture that form our Value scale. Learners of Spanish, while agreeing that practical proficiency should be the goal of pedagogy, are less likely to agree strongly with the statements concerning active participation and challenge. Students of French share many of these characteristics to a certain degree, but usually not at levels that reach statistical significance in comparison with other groups. Although they score highest on our Cognitive learning strategy scale, they report the lowest frequency of strategy use overall. On no other scales do they have either the highest or lowest means.

Learners of Japanese at this university are characterized by their self-reports as having a high level of Motivational Strength (significantly higher than learners of French and Spanish), coupled with relatively low expectations of success compared to learners of other languages. It appears that learners of Japanese know that Japanese is a difficult language, and they are prepared to put in a great deal of effort for what they expect will be modest rewards. Appreciation of the importance and difficulty of learning kanji is perhaps why the learners of Japanese in our sample showed the highest agreement with a traditional pedagogical focus on grammar, vocabulary, reading, and writing.

Learners of Mandarin Chinese are similar to learners of Japanese and Filipino in scoring high on the heritage language factor and the motivational scale of Value. They score highest of any group on our Expectancy scale (which includes items related to self-confidence, self-related aptitude and lack of anxiety), although none of the pair-wise statistical comparisons were significant. They are somewhat less likely than students of other languages to indicate agreement that they are studying mainly to fulfill the language requirement. Learners of Chinese report using both coping strategies and strategies associated with study skills less frequently than other groups.

Learners of Filipino (Tagalog) in this population are mostly heritage learners. They are, in general, highly motivated and have especially high social motivation: They strongly agree that the teacher's opinion of them and their relationships with other students in the class are important. Learners of Filipino are especially likely to approve of innovative approaches (i.e., authentic materials, learner goal-setting, and a focus on culture) and score highest of the five groups on the Cooperative Learning scale. They also report using social language learning strategies more often than learners of all the other language.

These are all interesting group differences, which in many cases correspond to what teachers of these languages say about their students, but we admit to some unease about them. The problem we see is that most of our students of Japanese, Chinese, and Filipino are heritage learners, that is, ethnically Japanese, Chinese, or Filipino, and that these group differences are very similar to the ethnic stereotypes of hardworking and self-effacing Japanese, smart and confident Chinese, and gregarious Filipinos. The fact that these generalizations arise from analysis of self-report questionnaires may indicate that the stereotypes are partly true, or just that they have been internalized by members of those groups. The question of whether non-heritage learners also present themselves in ways similar to the ethnic stereotypes associated with the languages they are studying is intriguing and suggests the potential fruitfulness of studies of language socialization in foreign language classes, but is not something on which our data can shed any clear light.

REFERENCES

Crookes, G., & Schmidt, R. (1991). Motivation: Reopening the research agenda. *Language Learning, 41*, 469–512.

Dweck, C. S., & Elliot, E. S. (1984). Achievement motivation. In P. Mussen & E. M. Hetherington (Eds.), *Handbook of child psychology* (Vol. 4, pp. 643–691). New York: Wiley.

Gardner, R. C. (1985). *Social psychology and language learning: The role of attitudes and motivation*. London, Ontario, Canada: Edward Arnold.

Gardner, R. C. (1988). The socio-educational model of second-language learning: Assumptions, findings, and issues. *Language Learning, 38*, 101–126.

Gardner, R. C., Tremblay, P. F., & Masgoret, A.-M. (1997). Toward a full model of second language learning: An empirical investigation. *The Modern Language Journal, 81*, 344–362.

Kondo-Brown, K. (2001). Bilingual heritage students' language contact and motivation. In Z. Dörnyei & R. Schmidt (Eds.), *Motivation and second language acquisition* (Technical Report #23, pp. 433–459). Honolulu: University of Hawai'i, Second Language Teaching and Curriculum Center.

Krashen, S. D. (1985). *The input hypothesis*. New York: Longman.

MacIntyre, P. D., & Noels, K. A. (1996). Using social-psychological variables to predict the use of language learning strategies. *Foreign Language Annals, 29*, 373–386.

Oxford, R., & Nyikos, M. (1989). Variables affecting choice of language learning strategies by university students. *The Modern Language Journal, 73*, 291–300.

Rampton, M. B. H. (1990). Displacing the 'native speaker': Expertise, affiliation, and inheritance. *ELT Journal, 44*, 97–101.

SAS v6.11 [Computer software]. (1989). Cary, NC: SAS Institute, Inc.

Schmidt, R. (in press). Attention. In P. Robinson (Ed.), *Cognition and second language instruction*. Cambridge, UK: University Press.

Schmidt, R., Boraie, D., & Kassabgy, O. (1996). Foreign language motivation: Internal structure and external connections. In R. Oxford (Ed.), *Language learning motivation: Pathways to the new century* (Technical Report #11, pp. 9–70). Honolulu: University of Hawai'i, Second Language Teaching & Curriculum Center.

StatView v4.5 [Computer software]. (1994). Berkeley, CA: Abacus Concepts, Inc.

Syed, Z. (2001). Notions of self in foreign language learning: A qualitative analysis. In Z. Dörnyei & R. Schmidt (Eds.), *Motivation and second language acquisition* (Technical Report #23, pp. 127–148). Honolulu: University of Hawai'i, Second Language Teaching and Curriculum Center.

Tremblay, P. F., & Gardner, R. C. (1995). Expanding the motivation construct in language learning. *The Modern Language Journal, 79*, 505–520.

Part A: Motivation, 47 items

Intrinsic motivation

intrinsic 1	I really enjoy learning this language.
intrinsic 2	My language class is a challenge that I enjoy.
intrinsic 3	When class ends, I often wish that we could continue.
intrinsic 4	I enjoy using this language outside of class whenever I have a chance.
intrinsic 5	I don't like language learning. *(reverse coded)*
intrinsic 6	I would take this class even if it were not required.

Language requirement (1 item)

langreq 1	I mainly study this language to satisfy the university language requirement.

Instrumental orientation (3 items)

instr 1	Being able to speak this language will add to my social status.
instr 2	Increasing my proficiency in this language will have financial benefits for me.
instr 3	I am learning this language to understand films, videos, or music.

Heritage language (2 items)

heritage 1	This language is important to me because it is part of my cultural heritage.
heritage 2	I have a personal attachment to this language as part of my identity.

Integrative orientation (3 items)

integrative 1	Studying this language is important because it will allow me to interact with people who speak it.
integrative 2	I am learning this language to be able to communicate with friends who speak it.
integrative 3	I want to be more a part of the cultural group that speaks this language.

Interest in foreign languages and cultures (4 items)

interest 1	I would like to learn several foreign languages.
interest 2	I enjoy meeting and interacting with people from many cultures.
interest 3	Studying foreign languages is an important part of education.
interest 4	This language is important to me because it will broaden my world view.

Task value (3 items)

task val 1	I like the subject matter of this course.
task val 2	It is important to me to learn the course material in this class.
task val 3	What I learn in this course will help me in other courses.

Expectancy (3 items)

expectancy 1	I'm certain I can master the skills being taught in this class.
expectancy 2	I believe I will receive an excellent grade in this class.
expectancy 3	I am worried about my ability to do well in this class. *(reverse coded)*

Anxiety (6 items)

anxiety 1	I feel uncomfortable when I have to speak in this class.
anxiety 2	When I take a test I think about how poorly I am doing.
anxiety 3	I have an uneasy, upset feeling when I take an exam.
anxiety 4	I don't worry about making mistakes when speaking in front of this class. (RC)
anxiety 5	I am afraid that my teacher is ready to correct every mistake I make.
anxiety 6	I feel more tense and nervous in this class than in my other classes.

Language aptitude (4 items)

aptitude 1	I can imitate the sounds of this language very well.
aptitude 2	I can guess the meaning of new vocabulary words very well.
aptitude 3	I am good at grammar.
aptitude 4	In general, I am an exceptionally good language learner.

Competitiveness (4 items)

competitive 1	Getting a good grade in this class is the most important thing for me right now.
competitive 2	I want to learn this language because it is important to show my ability to others.
competitive 2	I learn best when I am competing with other students.
competitive 2	I want to do better than the other students in this class.

Cooperativeness (3 items)

cooperative 1	I learn best in a cooperative environment.
cooperative 2	My teacher's opinion of me in this class is very important.
cooperative 3	My relationship with the other students in this class is important to me.

Motivational strength (5 items)

mt strength 1	I often feel lazy or bored when I study for this class. *(reverse coded)*
mt strength 2	I work hard in this class even when I don't like what we are doing.
mt strength 3	When course work is difficult, I either give up or only study the easy parts. (RC)
mt strength 4	Even when course materials are dull and uninteresting, I always finish my work.
mt strength 5	I can truly say that I put my best effort into learning this language.

Part B: Preferences for instructional activities, 20 items

Traditional approach (3 items)

grammar	Grammar should be an important focus in this class.
read/write	Reading and writing should be an important focus in this class.
vocabulary	Vocabulary should be an important focus in this class.

Practical proficiency orientation (7 items)

relevant	Language lessons should be relevant to the students' learning goals.
ask Q's	Students should ask questions whenever they have not understood a point in class.
pronunciation	Pronunciation should be an important focus in this class.
listen/speak	Listening and speaking should be an important focus in this class.
communicate	Activities in this class should be designed to help the students improve their abilities to communicate in this language.
feedback	It is important that the teacher give immediate feedback in class so that students know if they are correct.
everyday lg	Language instruction should focus on the general language of everyday situations.

Challenging approaches (4 items)

no English	During this class, I would like to have no English spoken.
challenge	In a class like this, I prefer activities and material that really challenge me to learn more.
active part.	I prefer a language class in which there are lots of activities that allow me to participate actively.
must speak	I prefer to sit and listen, and don't like being forced to speak in language class. (reverse coded)

Cooperative learning (3 items)

pairs/group	I like language learning activities in which students work together in pairs or small groups.
not alone	I prefer to work by myself in this language class, not with other students. (reverse coded)
cohesiveness	I prefer a language class in which the students feel they are a cohesive group.

Innovative approaches (3 items)

culture	Culture should be an important focus in this class.
goal-setting	I like to set my own goals for language learning.
authentic	I like language classes that use lots of authentic materials.

Part C: Learning strategies, 24 items

Cognitive strategies (7 items)

relate vocab	I try to relate new vocabulary words to other words I know.
compare lgs	I always compare this language with other languages I know.
guess	I try to guess the meaning of new vocabulary words from context.
patterns	I look for patterns in this language on my own.
eval prog	I always evaluate my progress in learning this language.
preview	When studying, I think through a topic and decide what I need to learn about it.
clarify	I ask the instructor to clarify concepts I don't understand well.

Social strategies (3 items)

work w/ others	I try to work with other students from this class on assignments.
classmates	When studying, I often discuss the course material with my classmates.
ask other's help	When I can't understand the material, I ask another student in this class for help.

Study skills: time, place, & effort management (8 items)

organize study	When I study, I carefully organize what I have learned in this class.
review test	After a test I always review difficult material to be sure I understand it all.
place for study	I have a regular place set aside for studying.
time to prepare	I always arrange time to prepare before every language class.
re-read	When studying, I reread all the course material.
review early	In preparing for tests, I usually review the material a few days ahead of time.
not last minute	I usually wait until the night before to study for a quiz or a major test. (*reverse coded*)
periodic study	I usually study vocabulary periodically rather than in one long session.

Coping strategies (6 items)

repeat words	I repeat new vocabulary words to memorize them.
find gaps	When studying for a test, I try to determine which concepts I don't understand well.
see words first	I like to see words before I pronounce them.
look words up	When I get to a word that I don't know, I usually look it up.
try to keep up	I am mostly concerned in this class with keeping up with the materials and activities that we have to do.
what's on test?	I really like to know what will be on a test so that I can study for it.

SCALES USED IN ANOVA AND CORRELATIONAL ANALYSES

Part A: Motivation

Value

I really enjoy learning this language.
My language class is a challenge that I enjoy.
When class ends, I often wish that we could continue.
I enjoy using this language outside of class whenever I have a chance.
I don't like language learning. (*reverse coded*)
I would take this class even if it were not required.
Being able to speak this language will add to my social status.
Increasing my proficiency in this language will have financial benefits for me.
I am learning this language to understand films, videos, or music.
Studying this language is important because it will allow me to interact with people who speak it.
I am learning this language to be able to communicate with friends who speak it.
I want to be more a part of the cultural group that speaks this language.
I would like to learn several foreign languages.
I enjoy meeting and interacting with people from many cultures.
Studying foreign languages is an important part of education.
This language is important to me because it will broaden my world view.
I like the subject matter of this course.
It is important to me to learn the course material in this class.

Heritage

This language is important to me because it is part of my cultural heritage.
I have a personal attachment to this language as part of my identity.

Expectancy

I'm certain I can master the skills being taught in this class.
I believe I will receive an excellent grade in this class.
I am worried about my ability to do well in this class. (*reverse coded*)
I feel uncomfortable when I have to speak in this class. (*reverse coded*)
When I take a test I think about how poorly I am doing. (*reverse coded*)
I have an uneasy, upset feeling when I take an exam. (*reverse coded*)
I don't worry about making mistakes when speaking in front of this class.
I am afraid that my teacher is ready to correct every mistake I make. (*reverse coded*)
I feel more tense and nervous in this class than in my other classes. (*reverse coded*)
I can imitate the sounds of this language very well.
I can guess the meaning of new vocabulary words very well.
I am good at grammar.
In general, I am an exceptionally good language learner.

Motivational strength

I often feel lazy or bored when I study for this class. *(reverse coded)*
I work hard in this class even when I don't like what we are doing.
When course work is difficult, I either give up or only study the easy parts. (RC)
Even when course materials are dull and uninteresting, I always finish my work.
I can truly say that I put my best effort into learning this language.

Competitiveness

Getting a good grade in this class is the most important thing for me right now.
I want to learn this language because it is important to show my ability to others.
I learn best when I am competing with other students.
I want to do better than the other students in this class.

Cooperativeness

I learn best in a cooperative environment.
My teacher's opinion of me in this class is very important.
My relationship with the other students in this class is important to me.

Language requirement

I mainly study this language to satisfy the university language requirement.

Part B: Pedagogical preferences

Traditional approach

Grammar should be an important focus in this class.
Reading and writing should be an important focus in this class.
Vocabulary should be an important focus in this class.

Practical proficiency

Language lessons should be relevant to the students' learning goals.
Students should ask questions whenever they have not understood a point in class.
Pronunciation should be an important focus in this class.
Listening and speaking should be an important focus in this class.
Activities in this class should be designed to help the students improve their abilities to communicate in this language.
It is important that the teacher give immediate feedback in class so that students know if they are correct.
Language instruction should focus on the general language of everyday situations.

Challenge

During this class, I would like to have no English spoken.
In a class like this, I prefer activities and material that really challenge me to learn more.
I prefer a language class in which there are lots of activities that allow me to participate actively.
I prefer to sit and listen, and don't like being forced to speak in language class. *(reverse coded)*

Cooperative learning

I like language learning activities in which students work together in pairs or small groups.
I prefer to work by myself in this language class, not with other students. *(reverse coded)*
I prefer a language class in which the students feel they are a cohesive group.

Innovative approaches

Culture should be an important focus in this class.
I like to set my own goals for language learning.
I like language classes that use lots of authentic materials.

Part C: Learning strategies

Cognitive and metacognitive strategies

I try to relate new vocabulary words to other words I know.
I always compare this language with other languages I know.
I try to guess the meaning of new vocabulary words from context.
I look for patterns in this language on my own.
I always evaluate my progress in learning this language.
When studying, I think through a topic and decide what I need to learn about it.
I ask the instructor to clarify concepts I don't understand well.

Social strategies

I try to work with other students from this class on assignments.
When studying, I often discuss the course material with my classmates.
When I can't understand the material, I ask another student in this class for help.

Study skills strategies

When I study, I carefully organize what I have learned in this class.
After a test I always review difficult material to be sure I understand it all.
I have a regular place set aside for studying.
I always arrange time to prepare before every language class.
When studying, I reread all the course material.
In preparing for tests, I usually review the material a few days ahead of time.
I usually wait until the night before to study for a quiz or a major test. (*reverse coded*)
I usually study vocabulary periodically rather than in one long session.

Coping strategies

I repeat new vocabulary words to memorize them.
When studying for a test, I try to determine which concepts I don't understand well.
I like to see words before I pronounce them.
When I get to a word that I don't know, I usually look it up.
I am mostly concerned in this class with keeping up with the materials and activities that we have to do.
I really like to know what will be on a test so that I can study for it.

James Dean Brown
University of Hawai'i at Mānoa

Gordon Robson
Showa Women's University

Patrick R. Rosenkjar
Temple University Japan

PERSONALITY, MOTIVATION, ANXIETY, STRATEGIES, AND LANGUAGE PROFICIENCY OF JAPANESE STUDENTS

Authors' note

We would like to thank all of the individual teachers at Temple University Japan who helped us gather the data for this study: Elisabeth M. Brown, Ivy Cele, Desiderio Cubas, Rolph Fachtmann, Steven Fountaine, Ronald Grove, Barbara Hoshino, Dean Jensen, Loy Soo Kiak, Rosalie Kolesar, Elizabeth Lange, Nancy Lee, Keith Mallaburn, Sae Matsuda, Ruth McCutcheon, Eugenia Medrano-Endo, Annyce Meiners, Andrew Merzenich, Sonia Millett, Satsuki Nakai, Will Palmer, Mary Richards, Sharon Sargent, Richard Starin, Kay Summers, David Tsugawa, Jack Witt, and Joseph Zanghi. We would also like to thank Daniel Clapper, Susan Johnston, and Kathleen Schmitz for their administrative cooperation and assistance. Without the help of all these ESL professionals, this study would not exist.

Abstract

This study is the first to simultaneously examine the relationships among five language learning variables (*personality, motivation, anxiety, learning strategies,* and *language proficiency*) as they co-occur in a group of students with a single language background. The 320 students in this study are all Japanese nationals enrolled in the Intensive English Language Program at Temple University Japan in Tokyo. Six instruments are used: the *Yatabe-Guilford Personality Inventory* (including 12 subscales), the *Attitude/Motivation Test Battery* (with 13 subscales), the *Foreign Language Classroom Anxiety Scale*, the *Strategy Inventory for Language Learning* (containing six subscales), a cloze test, and the structure subtest of the *Michigan Placement Test* for a total of 34 variables.

Descriptive statistics characterize these Japanese students in terms of the 34 variables being studied. Cronbach alpha analysis shows that the personality, motivation, anxiety, and learning strategies instruments are all reasonably reliable in this situation. Factor analysis (with varimax rotation), used to study the validity of the instruments, indicates (with one exception) a reasonably high degree of convergence of subscales within the instruments and divergence between instruments. Discriminant function analysis reveals that five of the variables help reliably predict high, middle, and low proficiency group membership (as determined by the cloze test). Patterns in the intercorrelations of the subscales are also interpreted and discussed in detail.

Brown, J. D., Robson, G., & Rosenkjar, P. R. (2001). Personality, motivation, anxiety, strategies, and language proficiency of Japanese students. In Z. Dörnyei & R. Schmidt (Eds.), *Motivation and second language acquisition* (Technical Report #23, pp. 361–398). Honolulu: University of Hawai'i, Second Language Teaching and Curriculum Center.

INTRODUCTION

Five key psychological constructs are investigated in this study: personality, motivation, anxiety, learning strategies, and overall English language proficiency. We will begin by defining and reviewing each of these constructs in turn.

PERSONALITY

The personality construct investigated in this study is based mostly on the work of Guilford. Guilford's operationalizations of personality were based on studies of the correlations found between typical items on extraversion-introversion neuroticism-stable tests like those on the *Eysenck Personality Questionnaire* (Eysenck, 1970) and *Bernreuter Personality Inventory* (Bernreuter, 1931). Guilford analyzed two general personality types, extraversion and neuroticism, into their component traits. While Guilford's approach did not rest on a specific and clearly articulated theoretical foundation, his work was based on the trait theories set forth by Allport (1937), Eysenck (1959, 1970, 1978), and Cattell (1956). Trait theories defined the structure of personality as being made up of traits or predispositions, and assumed regularity and pattern to behavior over time and across situations (Pervin, 1989, p. 304). Guilford devised three tests in the 1940s with Martin: the *Guilford Personality Inventory for Factors STDCR*, the *Guilford and Martin Personality Inventory for Factors GAMIN*, and the *Guilford and Martin Personnel Inventory* (Vernon, 1953, p. 133). These three tests were combined and revised in a Japanese version with the help of Yatabe and other Japanese psychologists in 1952. After more than a decade of piloting and revising, the final test was published in Japanese as the *Yatabe-Guilford Personality Inventory* (Guilford & Yatabe, 1957).

Strong (1983) and Ely (1986) investigated personality traits in language learning situations. Strong's 1983 study looked at the relationship between personality factors and the acquisition of specific communicative language skills in a group of Spanish native-speaking kindergarten students. Ely (1986) operationalized personality as risktaking and language-class sociability through a self-report questionnaire. His results found risktaking to be a positive predictor of classroom participation.

Other studies (Busch, 1982; Chapelle & Roberts, 1986; Chastain, 1975; Naiman, Froehlich, Stern, & Todesco, 1978; Rossier, 1975) investigated correlations between measures of personality and overall language proficiency. A typical example of these studies is the one by Busch (1982), which looked for a relationship between extraversion and higher levels of proficiency. Though Busch had hypothesized that extraverts would be more proficient language learners than introverts, her results showed that introverts were in fact more proficient. To summarize briefly, a number of investigations in second language acquisition accept extraversion-introversion and neuroticism-stability as traits of human behavior. The results of various studies in educational psychology (Leith, 1969; Leith & Trown, 1970; Leith & Wisdom, 1970; Shadbolt, 1978) have also been somewhat mixed, but in general, extraverts have been shown to prefer unstructured classroom activities and to be active participants in language learning situations. Students scoring high on neuroticism and introversion appear to prefer more structured activities and are less active in their participation.

MOTIVATION

The view of motivation taken in this study is based on the work of Gardner and Lambert (1972), who investigated integrative and instrumental language learning orientations and, in the process, created the *Attitude/Motivation Test Battery* (A/MTB). This test battery depended on the theoretical model developed by Lambert, which in turn was based on the premise that successful language acquisition depended on the internalization of the "behavioral and cognitive attributes of another cultural community" (Gardner & Smythe, 1981, p. 511). Thus, the degree of proficiency attained was felt to rest on how closely learners identified with their own ethnic group and their attitudes toward the target community. Two key orientations toward learning were also identified: an integrative orientation which defined the goal of language learning as a genuine desire to meet and associate with members of the target language and cultural group, and an instrumental orientation which described the drive for knowledge of a foreign language as a desire for social recognition or economic advantage.

In a further elaboration of the theoretical background for the A/MTB (Gardner, 1985), motivation was viewed as being the sum of effort plus the desire to achieve a language learning goal plus attitudes or the degree of integrative orientation. Effort was described as being derived from several sources such as "compulsiveness, desire to please a teacher or parent, a high need to achieve, good study habits, social pressures, including examinations or external rewards" (Skehan, 1989, p. 55). The degree of desire to achieve a particular language learning goal was viewed as being related to the learner's attitudes.

The majority of Gardner's studies on motivation were concerned with finding correlations between high scores on the A/MTB and high levels of proficiency (for example, Gardner & Lambert, 1972). Many of these studies showed that integratively motivated students, regardless of language aptitude, were more likely to succeed in acquiring a second language than those less motivated, and that such students tended to stay with their language programs longer. However, as Au (1988) pointed out, a number of studies have also revealed zero or negative relationships between scores on the A/MTB and proficiency (Clément, Gardner, & Smythe, 1980; Gardner & Lambert, 1972).

Three articles examined the relationships between motivation and students' classroom characteristics. Gliksman, Gardner, and Smythe (1982) focused on whether integratively motivated students had greater levels of classroom participation, produced better quality responses, and had more positive attitudes toward the class. Berwick and Ross (1989) looked at motivation and proficiency in a Japanese context, and attempted to describe variables that may have an effect on changing motivation over time. Ely (1986) showed that, generally, strength of motivation did not have a predictive relationship to participation.

ANXIETY

The operationalization of anxiety used in this study is based on an instrument developed by Horwitz, Horwitz, and Cope (1986). This instrument was designed to measure what MacIntyre and Gardner (1991) identified as situational anxiety, or more specifically, anxiety related to language learning. Anxiety was characterized as a "subjective feeling of tension, apprehension, nervousness, and worry" (Horwitz et al., 1986, p. 125), as well as having difficulty concentrating, becoming forgetful, sweating, and having palpitations. More discrete problems caused by anxiety in the language learning classroom were identified as being particularly related to listening and speaking, such as difficulties discriminating sounds in the target language or difficulties with free speaking tasks. Horwitz et al. (1986) claimed three interrelated processes as the basis for their theory: "(1) communication apprehension; (2) test anxiety; and (3) fear of negative evaluation" (p. 127). Drawing from these processes, they developed a self-report questionnaire, called the *Foreign Language Classroom Anxiety Scale* (FLCAS), made up of 33 items that require respondents to identify particular "self-perceptions, beliefs, feelings and behaviors related to classroom language learning" (p. 128).

MacIntyre and Gardner in a survey article (1991) cited several studies (Horwitz et al., 1986; MacIntyre & Gardner, 1989; Muchnick & Wolfe, 1982) that provided support for claims that foreign language anxiety is separate from other forms of anxiety, and that language learning can be more anxiety provoking than learning in other subjects. Several other studies have examined anxiety and the production of certain grammatical patterns (Kleinmann, 1977), anxiety and story telling (Steinberg & Horwitz, 1986), and the relationships among anxiety, vocabulary learning, and recall (MacIntyre & Gardner, 1989). Still other studies examined the relationships between anxiety and proficiency (Gardner, Smythe, Clément, & Gliksman, 1976; Lalonde & Gardner, 1984), relationships between anxiety and language classroom performance (Kleinmann, 1977; Steinberg & Horwitz, 1986), relationships among language class discomfort, risktaking, and sociability (Ely, 1986), and relationships among communicative anxiety, vocabulary learning, and learning in both oral and written production (MacIntyre & Gardner, 1989).

LEARNING STRATEGIES

A large number of strategy training manuals for language teachers and learners have recently appeared. Oxford (1990), Brown (1991), and Wenden (1991) are typical examples. Such documents typically present strategy research findings as the springboard from which to develop student awareness of their own language learning strategies. The success of such a program must ultimately rest on the knowledge we have of how learners learn, that is, on learning strategy research. Much has been written about the strategy use of second language learners. These writings fall largely into four main categories.

First are those, as exemplified by Rubin (1975) and Stern (1975), in which authors relied on intuition, logic, and experience to enumerate behaviors thought to characterize successful language learning. Such articles may be thought of as early attempts to brainstorm a taxonomy of strategies for investigation.

Second, a number of researchers elicited strategy data from learners (for a review of these studies, see Oxford, 1989). The common methodology in these studies was some form of retrospection. For example, Naiman et al. (1978) interviewed successful language learners and identified five major learning strategies. Rubin (1981) similarly used directed self-report to compile a list of six strategies. Utilizing the taxonomies arising out of these two studies and their own intuitions, Politzer and McGroarty (1985) devised a questionnaire to discover the characteristics of the "good language learner." Chamot (1987) interviewed high school ESL students in the United States about their strategy use and was able to classify all the strategies into metacognitive, cognitive, and social-affective categories. Oxford and Nyikos (1989), working from a strategy taxonomy devised by Oxford, identified five major strategy categories in their data and investigated the relationship among these categories and a number of learner variables. (Note that the present study uses Oxford's strategy inventory.) More recently, O'Malley and Chamot (1990) furnished one possible theoretical model for strategies by placing second language learning within the wider context of general cognitive learning theory.

Third, introspective methods also offer a promising new perspective for second language research. A few studies (see Abraham & Vann, 1987; Faerch & Kasper, 1987; Hosenfeld, 1984; Rosenkjar, 1992; Vann & Abraham, 1990) investigated strategy use within the context of tasks through introspective self-revelation (also known as "think-aloud" and "concurrent verbal reports"). Vann and Abraham (1990) expanded the usefulness of think-aloud protocols in tasks by combining this method with analysis of task demands and subject performance.

A fourth category of strategy research consists of studies which examined the training of students in strategy use. O'Malley (1987), building on the work of Chamot (1987), compared posttest results for a group trained in metacognitive, cognitive, and social-affective strategies with results for a group trained solely in cognitive and social-affective strategies, as well as with results for a control group.

PURPOSE

The research cited above included a variety of studies of various pairings of five variables: personality, motivation, anxiety, learning strategies, and language proficiency. These studies mostly examined native English speakers learning foreign languages (at various ages) or ESL learners (of various nationalities) learning English. However, no published research has included all five variables in one study with a focus on a single nationality and age group. The purpose of this study was to simultaneously examine the relationships among personality, motivation, anxiety, learning strategies, and language proficiency for a reasonably large number of

Japanese university students. To that end, the following research questions were posed:

1. Are self-report scales on personality, motivation, anxiety, and learning strategies reliable when applied to Japanese university students?

2. Are self-report scales on personality, motivation, anxiety, and learning strategies valid when applied to Japanese university students?

3. What do personality, motivation, anxiety, and learning strategy scales tell us about Japanese university students in terms of descriptive statistics?

4. Which personality, motivation, anxiety, and learning strategy subscales significantly and reliably predict differences between the high, middle, and low proficiency Japanese students, and which most reliably predict those differences? How adequately are the resulting predictions classified?

5. How are subscales on each of these instruments related to subscales on the other instruments when they are administered to Japanese university students?

The alpha level for all statistical decisions was set at .05.

METHOD

SUBJECTS

The 320 students in this study were all Japanese nationals enrolled in the Intensive English Language Program (IELP) at Temple University Japan (TUJ) in Tokyo. The IELP is an academic English program designed to prepare non-native speakers to undertake college-level work in an English-medium university. There were 158 (49.4%) females, and 162 (50.6%) males. They ranged in age from 18 to 25 with a mean of 20.1 years. The six levels of study at TUJ ranged from the lowest course labeled level 20 to the highest course which was level 70. Of these students, fifty-two (16.3%) were in level 20, 74 (23.1%) were in level 30, 58 (18.1%) were in level 40, 91 (28.4%) were in level 50, 40 (12.5%) were in level 60, and 5 (1.6%) were in level 70. The average TOEFL score was 435 with scores ranging from 303 to 547 and a standard deviation of 39.7 for those 267 students who had a score on record in the IELP data base. In no case was that score more than one year old.

We must caution readers that, even though the group of students studied here was reasonably large, we do not and cannot claim that this sample represents all university students in Japan. The types of students who choose to attend American universities in Japan (like TUJ) may be very different from those who choose to go to the first-rate Japanese universities like Keio, Tokyo, Waseda, and so forth. The students in this study may even be different from students at any Japanese university because they have chosen to do something quite out of the mainstream of Japanese culture. We have made a start by studying this group of students. Other groups within Japan should also be examined, as well as groups in other countries.

MATERIALS

A total of five different constructs were operationalized in this study: personality, motivation, anxiety, learning strategies, and overall English language proficiency. Each operationalization is explained under a separate heading.

Personality

Personality was measured with the *Y/G Personality Inventory* (Guilford & Yatabe, 1957). This instrument was translated into Japanese and adapted to the Japanese situation by a group of Japanese psychologists. It is self-administered and comes with complete instructions and background information in Japanese. The inventory has been shown elsewhere to have reasonably high internal consistently reliability (ranging from .60 to .80) for such short subtests with ten items per trait (Robson, 1992).

The *Y/G Personality Inventory* assesses 12 traits: social extraversion, ascendance, thinking extraversion, rhathymia, general activity, lack of agreeableness, lack of cooperativeness, lack of objectivity, nervousness, inferiority feelings, cyclic tendencies, and depression. The 12 traits in this inventory have been shown (see Robson, 1992) to consistently fall into two categories: neuroticism and extraversion (in the list above, the first six represent extraversion and the next six represent neuroticism). In Robson (1992), the *Y/G Personality Inventory* was also shown to have a good level of concurrent validity with the *Maudsley Personality Inventory* (MPI, Eysenck, 1959, 1990). Generally, the six extraversion and six neuroticism traits had correlations from .60 to .80 with MPI extraversion and neuroticism and factored into the same two groups. Scores derived from this instrument can thus be said to have exhibited a high degree of construct and criterion-related validity in at least two situations. Furthermore, despite its age, the *Y/G Personality Inventory* is still regarded as an appropriate measure by leading researchers in the field (see Angleitner, 1991).

Each trait has 10 questions that require a *yes, no,* or *?* answer. *Yes* and *no* answers are marked with a circle and *?* answers are marked with a triangle. Circles receive two points and triangles one point for a possible 20 points per trait. Scores of zero are also possible. When a question is negatively worded, the *no* circle will register on the scoring sheet and when a question is positively worded, the *yes* circle will register. The test provides a method for combining the scores on each trait and classifying the examinees into one of five personality types; however, for this study only the raw scores on each trait were used for comparative analysis.

Motivation

Motivation was measured with the *Attitude/Motivation Test Battery* (A/MTB). Gardner and Smythe (1981, p. 511) put together a list of constructs that attempted to measure all of the attitudinal factors related to second language acquisition of French in Canada. They later developed the 11 sections of the *Attitudes/Motivation Test Battery* from that list (Skehan, 1989, p. 55). The assessment format for most of the constructs was a Likert scale, although a short section measuring *Motivational intensity* and desire to learn French used a multiple-choice format, and the evaluative reactions to French courses and French teachers employed a semantic differential technique.

The version of the A/MTB used in this study was adapted to the Japanese situation by Robson. Questions dealing with attitudes toward French Canadians and attitudes toward European French in particular were changed to ones asking for attitudes toward English-speaking Americans in Japan and English-speaking Americans in the United States, respectively, because these groups were identified as the target culture for these particular students.

The first section contained 64 items and asked for information about the following topics: attitudes toward English-speaking Americans in Japan (10 items); interest in foreign languages (10 items); attitudes toward English-speaking Americans in the United States (10 items); attitudes toward learning English (5 positively worded items and 5 negatively worded items); integrative orientation (4 items); instrumental orientation (4 items), English class anxiety (5 items); and parental encouragement (10 items). Each item was scored using a 7-point Likert scale with a score of 1 for strongly disagree, a score of 4 for neutral and a score of 7 for strongly agree, unless the question was negatively worded resulting in reverse scoring.

The second section contained 20 multiple-choice questions dealing with motivational intensity (10 items) and desire to learn English (10 items). Very little adaptation was necessary in this section. Negatively worded choices are scored 1, more neutral items are scored 2, and positively worded choices are scored 3. An additional item called an orientation index has two integrative orientation choices scored 2 points and two instrumental orientation choices scored 1 point for responses to the question "I am studying English because..."

The third and final section had two semantic differential assessments. Under the headings *My English Teacher* and *My English Course*, two rows of 25 descriptors each were provided with seven blanks in between. A mark next to a positively worded descriptor was scored 7 and a mark next to a negatively worded descriptor was scored 1 with a score of 4 for a mark in the middle. No adaptation was necessary in this section except for changing the word French to English wherever it occurred.

Following the adaptation, the A/MTB was translated into Japanese by two native-speaking Japanese instructors of EFL. The two translators cross-checked each other's work, after which the questionnaire was piloted, producing Cronbach alpha coefficients ranging from a low of .82 to a high of .85. The questionnaire was then re-checked by three other Japanese native speakers (also EFL instructors) resulting in the correction of several Kanji errors and the re-wording of a few items. The final questionnaire had a total of 134 items for a total possible score of 853.

Anxiety

Anxiety was measured by the *Foreign Language Classroom Anxiety Scale* (FLCAS) developed by Horwitz, Horwitz, and Cope (1986). No adaptation was required for the Japanese situation, but the scale was translated following the same method described above for the A/MTB. The questionnaire itself has 33 items scored on a 5-point Likert scale. Twenty-four of the items are negatively worded and the remaining nine items are positively worded. A typical example from the questionnaire would be, "I start to panic when I have to speak without preparation in language class." After piloting, an item analysis revealed Cronbach alpha coefficients ranging from .92 to .93. In recent studies conducted in Japan, the FLCAS produced scores that were reliable and valid for measuring situational anxiety in at least three situations (Castagnaro, 1992; Robson, 1992; Tanaka, 1992). Concurrent validity was demonstrated by Castagnaro (1992) and was also reported in Horwitz (1986). Moreover, MacIntyre and Gardner (1991) provide some support for the content and construct validity of the FLCAS (p. 105).

Language learning strategies

Oxford and Nyikos (1989) briefly described their primary data-gathering instrument, the *Strategy Inventory for Language Learning* (SILL), which was originally developed by Oxford. The SILL is a questionnaire containing 121 items, based on a 5-point Likert scale, which asks subjects to rate the frequency of use of various strategies. The theoretical justification for the inclusion of items is said to rest on a "comprehensive taxonomy of language learning strategies that systematically covers the four language skill areas" (Oxford & Nyikos, 1989, p. 292). The six strategies assessed by this instrument are as follows: remembering more effectively, using all your mental processes, compensating for missing knowledge, organizing and evaluating your learning, managing your emotions, and learning with others. The form of the SILL used in this study was a Japanese translation of Oxford's *Strategy Inventory for Language Learning*, Version 7.0, for ESL/EFL (Oxford, 1989). LoCastro (1994) criticizes the SILL for being potentially insensitive to Japanese learners' concerns and lacking clear theoretical bases. Nonetheless, the SILL is the most reliable of the available strategy questionnaires.

Using Cronbach alpha, the reliability of the SILL was found to be .96 for the 1,200-subject sample in the Oxford and Nyikos (1989) study and .95 for a 483-subject sample in an earlier study. Various validity arguments include a) a correlation of .95 between two raters who matched SILL items with strategies in the taxonomy on which it was based, b) the strong relationships between SILL items and self-reports of proficiency and motivation in the Oxford and Nyikos (1989) study, and c) a previous study in which the SILL was administered to more highly trained and less highly trained linguists, with the more highly trained subjects reporting "more frequent and more wide-ranging" strategy use (Oxford & Nyikos, 1989, p. 292). Furthermore, the researchers compared SILL results with interview data obtained from the earlier 483-subject test and sampled their SILL data to determine if they exhibited a halo effect. Finally, Green and Oxford (1995) explored the relationships between the SILL, L2 proficiency, and gender based on a sample of 374 students in Puerto Rico.

Overall English language proficiency

The English proficiency construct was operationalized by using two different types of scores: scores on a cloze test and scores on the structure subtest of the *Michigan Placement Test*. Two different instruments were used because we wanted to explore any differences in the ways an overall integrative test of English language proficiency and a discrete-point grammar test would measure proficiency in this Japanese sample.

The exact-answer cloze test used in this study was based on a 399 word passage taken from Kurilesz (1969, p. 58–59). Fifty words were deleted for an every-seventh-word deletion pattern. Brown (1980) found that this cloze test produced a K-R20 reliability coefficient of .90 and a criterion-related validity coefficient of .88 with the English as a Second Language Placement Examination at UCLA.

A portion of the *Michigan Placement Test* (Michigan, 1968) was also used to measure English proficiency in a more traditional manner. The grammar section of Form H was used. This section has forty discrete-point grammar items. Michigan (1977) reported Form H to be reliable (using the K-R21 formula) at .92 and presented general arguments for the validity of Michigan placement tests in general.

PROCEDURES

Teachers in the Intensive English Language Program (IELP) at Temple University Japan were asked to volunteer 2 days of class time during the last week of classes (which is after the testing, so it tends to be a "quiet" week). The result was that 27 sections of students participated in this study. All instruments were administered in comfortable, well-lit classrooms, and they were administered in the same order in all classes.

Only data from students who participated in both days of the data gathering were included in this study. Only 23 students out of a total of 343, or fewer than 7%, were missing on either the first or second day. These missing students were excluded from the analysis.

DESCRIPTIVE STATISTICS AND RELIABILITY

Table 1 shows the descriptive statistics for each of the instruments in this study (in capital bold-faced letters) and each of the subscales of those instruments. In each case, the number of subjects (*N*), mean (*M*), and standard deviation (*SD*) are given. Since the instruments and subscales use different scales, the total possible score (*k*) in each case is also given in order to make interpretation of these results easier.

Table 1: Descriptive statistics for all dependent variables

MEASURE Subscale	N	mean	SD	poss.	rel.	k
Y/GPI (personality)	**320**	**131.61**	**22.78**	**240**	**.84**	**120**
Social extraversion	320	14.74	4.65	20	.81	10
Ascendance	320	11.69	4.68	20	.76	10
Thinking extraversion	320	9.97	3.56	20	.42	10
Rhathymia	320	13.55	4.26	20	.69	10
General activity	320	12.35	4.53	20	.76	10
Agreeableness (lack)	320	13.11	3.91	20	.62	10
Cooperation (lack)	320	8.18	4.13	20	.68	10
Objectivity (lack)	320	9.69	4.07	20	.63	10
Nervousness	320	9.22	5.28	20	.80	10
Inferiority feelings	320	7.72	5.29	20	.81	10
Cyclic tendencies	320	10.81	4.56	20	.69	10
Depression	320	10.57	6.09	20	.85	10
A/MTB (motivation)	**320**	**679.52**	**60.47**	**853**	**.95**	**134**
Att Amer in Japan	320	54.08	7.56	70	.75	10
Interest foreign lang	320	64.51	5.30	70	.68	10
Att Amer in general	320	50.91	8.77	70	.87	10
Att learning English	320	61.12	7.02	70	.77	10
Integrative orient'n	320	25.42	3.05	28	.66	4
Instrumental orient'n	320	20.17	4.78	28	.60	4
English class anxiety	320	20.42	6.15	35	.73	5
Parent encouragement	320	54.51	10.31	70	.84	10
Motivat'l intensity	320	23.19	2.75	30	.58	10
Desire to lrn English	320	25.92	2.59	30	.66	10
Orientation	320	1.74	.44	2	na	1
Att English teacher	320	136.20	22.83	175	.95	25
Att English class	320	131.71	20.68	175	.94	25

continued...

Table 1: Descriptive statistics for all dependent variables (cont.)

| MEASURE | TOTAL | | | | | |
Subscale	N	mean	SD	poss.	rel.	k
FLCAS (anxiety)	320	107.05	15.85	165	.89	33
SILL (strategies)	320	3.29	.47	5	.94	50
Remembering	320	3.62	.54	5	.74	9
Mental processes	320	3.90	.54	5	.84	14
Compensating	320	4.11	.57	5	.69	6
Organizing & eval	320	4.25	.61	5	.88	9
Managing emotions	320	3.57	.63	5	.63	6
Learning with others	320	4.07	.59	5	.73	6
Michigan	320	17.45	4.73	40	.64	40
cloze	320	7.21	4.06	50	.71	50

Table 1 also gives reliability estimates for each of the instruments. All of these reliability estimates are Cronbach alphas. If the decimal is moved two places to the right, Cronbach alpha can be interpreted as the percent of reliable or consistent variance in each instrument. For instance, according to Table 1, the Social Extraversion scale of the Y/GPI has a Cronbach alpha of .81 in this study. This means that the instrument can be viewed as 81% reliable, and by extension 19% unreliable. Because reliability is often related to instrument length, the number of items (k) is given in the column furthest to the right. Notice that the reliability estimate for each of the instruments taken as a whole (in bold type in Table 1) is reasonably high in all cases. The reliability estimates for the Y/GPI, A/MTB, FLCAS, and SILL were .84, .95, .89, and .94, respectively. Note that the high reliability estimates for the Y/GPI, A/MTB, and SILL may not necessarily be good news. Recall that each of these instruments is made up of subscales that were designed to measure different psychological traits. Yet, we are finding a relatively high degree of reliability/consistency across all subscales, which may indicate that the scales are not as distinctly different as the original designers intended.

The subscale reliabilities were lower in most cases than the full test reliabilities, which makes sense because shorter instruments tend to be less reliable than longer instruments if all other factors are held constant. The scales fluctuated considerably from a low of .42 to a high of .88. Notice also that the proficiency measures were somewhat less reliable than the self-report instruments, with the reliability of the Michigan structure test estimated at .64 and the Cloze test estimated at .71 despite the fact that both of these tests have been shown to have high reliability elsewhere (Brown, 1980; Michigan, 1977). The lower reliability found in this study may be due to a relatively restricted range of student proficiency levels (as compared to the populations involved in the original norming).

Table 2 presents the results of a factor analysis using varimax rotation. Eight factors had Eigen values over 1.00. Examination of the scree plot confirmed that an eight factor solution was appropriate. These eight factors accounted for 66.2% of the variance. The loadings for each of the variables in this study on the eight factors are shown in Table 2. The asterisks indicate loadings of .30 or higher, and the bold-faced type indicates the highest loading for each variable. Furthest to the right, a column of communalities (h^2) is presented in italics. These communalitities indicate the total proportion of variance that the eight factors account for in each variable. For instance, for Social Extraversion h^2 is .679, so the eight factors can be said to account for 67.9% of the variance in that variable. In similar manner, Table 2 shows that 67.1% of the variance in Ascendance is accounted for by the eight factors, but only 46.6% of the variance in Thinking Extraversion, and so forth. At the bottom of the table, a row is provided in italics which shows the proportion of variance in the overall solution accounted for by each factor. For example, the proportion of variance accounted for by the first factor is .132, which represents 13.2% of the variance in the overall solution.

Table 2: Factor loadings after Varimax rotation

INSTRUMENT Subscale	FACTOR								
	1	2	3	4	5	6	7	8	h^2
Y/GPI (personality)									
Social extraversion	−.369*	.216	.121	**.580***	.295	.139	−.197	−.018	.679
Ascendance	−.381*	.146	.077	**.591***	.350	.143	−.082	−.016	.671
Thinking extraversion	**−.567***	−.203	−.001	.164	−.243	−.060	−.063	.100	.466
Rhathymia	.064	.070	.170	**.823***	−.042	−.033	−.082	.010	.724
General activity	−.370*	.248	.157	**.592***	.128	.136	−.003	−.144	.629
Agreeableness (lack)	.211	.158	.038	**.750***	.152	−.082	.034	.081	.670
Cooperation (lack)	**.685***	−.021	−.102	.051	−.043	−.106	−.043	−.132	.515
Objectivity (lack)	**.738***	.049	−.054	.243	−.149	.081	−.129	.088	.662
Nervousness	**.826***	−.062	−.076	−.160	−.083	−.034	.018	.037	.727
Inferiority feelings	**.697***	−.070	−.037	−.366*	−.358*	−.020	−.126	.060	.774
Cyclic tendencies	**.769***	−.127	.052	.196	−.099	−.033	−.042	.014	.661
Depression	**.828***	−.033	−.054	−.173	−.186	−.049	−.106	.084	.775
A/MTB (motivation)									
Att Amer in Japan	−.020	.076	**.755***	−.005	−.134	.251	−.067	−.141	.681
Interest foreign lang	−.047	.189	**.720***	.071	.107	−.044	.128	.244	.651
Att Amer in general	−.130	.085	**.667***	−.022	−.070	.329*	−.101	−.093	.602
Att learning English	−.118	.148	**.671***	.102	.225	.063	.054	.153	.578
Integrative orient'n	.023	.115	**.775***	.159	−.062	.061	.019	−.049	.651
Instrumental orient'n	.005	−.001	**.483***	.127	−.015	−.232	−.043	-.558*	.616
English class anxiety	−.178	.023	−.080	.118	**.824***	.011	.022	.013	.732
Parent encouragement	−.011	.147	**.527***	.105	−.080	.153	−.211	−.087	.392
Motivat'l intensity	−.023	.359*	.226	.073	**.554***	.135	−.036	.105	.523

continued...

Table 2: Factor loadings after Varimax rotation (cont.)

INSTRUMENT Subscale	FACTOR								
	1	2	3	4	5	6	7	8	h^2
Desire to lrn English	−.065	.296	.585*	.039	.338*	−.013	.034	.221	.599
Orientation	.024	−.071	.140	.048	−.003	−.026	.027	.812*	.688
Att English teacher	.018	−.003	.249	−.030	.082	.842*	.068	.053	.787
Att English class	−.107	.036	.215	.096	.011	.829*	.107	.021	.768
FLCAS (anxiety)	−.335*	.129	−.044	.248	.690*	−.037	.073	−.092	.683
SILL (strategies)									
Remembering	−.049	.755*	.075	.099	.033	.033	−.022	−.061	.595
Mental processes	.001	.872*	.139	.102	.127	−.003	.049	.054	.811
Compensating	−.024	.764*	.125	.033	.096	−.079	.010	−.005	.616
Organizing & eval	−.060	.842*	.242	.034	.100	.023	.065	.029	.788
Managing emotions	.094	.743*	.065	.136	−.098	.054	−.233	−.125	.666
Learning with others	−.076	.782*	.136	.157	.133	.059	.051	.004	.685
Michigan	−.117	.031	−.013	−.155	.032	.079	.809*	−.049	.703
cloze	−.082	−.047	−.064	.030	.005	.073	.837*	.095	.728
proportion of variance	.132	.128	.113	.084	.066	.053	.048	.037	.662

[bold] highest loading for each variable
* loadings of .300 or higher

Notice that all of the subscales of the SILL load most heavily on factor two, that the FLCAS loads most heavily on factor five, and that the proficiency measures (Michigan structure and Cloze) load heaviest on factor seven. Two other instruments, the A/MTB and the Y/GPI, present more complex patterns of loadings.

Eight of the subscales of the A/MTB load fairly heavily on factor three, and two subscales, English Class Anxiety and *Motivational intensity*, load most heavily on factor five with the FLCAS. This pattern makes sense because all three of the variables loading on factor five can be viewed as being related to anxiety. This is obvious for the FLCAS and the English class Anxiety scale, but Motivational Intensity may be related to anxiety because of the types of items in this scale (that is, many of its items deal with classroom behaviors such as speaking out, volunteering, or asking for assistance that could be negatively affected by foreign language specific anxiety in this sample of Japanese students). Attitude toward English Teacher and Attitude toward English Class both load most heavily on factor six and therefore appear to be similar to each other but different from the rest of the A/MTB subscales. In addition, the Orientation and Instrumental Orientation subscales both load most heavily on factor eight and appear to be related to a common factor that is different from the other scales in this study.

As for the Y/GPI, five of the first six subscales (which measure extraversion) load most heavily together on factor four, and all of the remaining six neuroticism subscales load most heavily on factor one. In addition, in this particular Japanese setting, the Thinking Extraversion subscale appears to be more highly related to neuroticism than to extraversion, a different result from Guilford's original findings. Guilford initially described this trait as *thinking extraversion* and later renamed it *thoughtfulness*, defining it with such adjectives as reflectiveness and meditativeness versus mental disconcertedness. Yatabe's subsequent renaming and rewriting of the items on this trait may be partly responsible for its loading with neuroticism.

One reader of an earlier version of this paper pointed out that we might be finding such clear patterns in our factor analysis results simply because we are using factor analysis on such highly diverse instruments. To ensure that our results were not a statistical relic of the diversity of our instruments, we ran additional factor analyses on those individual instruments that had multiple subscales. The factor analysis shown in Table 3 shows that all six subscales of the SILL load together on a single factor very much like it did in Table 2. Note that no VARIMAX rotation is performed on single factor solutions, yet still this factor analysis accounted for 66.9% of the variance with only one factor. Table 4 indicates that the subscales of the A/MTB load at .300 or over (after VARIMAX rotation) on four factors, thereby accounting for a total of 64.2%. This is very much the same pattern as the loadings on factors 3, 5, 6, and 7 in Table 2, with the sole exception that the single loading over .300 for Motivational Intensity on factor 2 in the Table 2 solution does not appear in Table 4. Finally, the factor analysis (with VARIMAX rotation) shown in Table 5 indicates that the subscales of the Y/GPI produce almost exactly the same pattern of loadings on two factors (both for those above .300 with an asterisk and the highest loadings in bold) that was found on factors 1 and 4 in Table 2, and account for 61.9% of the variance in the process of doing so. Since very similar patterns of loadings were found in factor analyses of the instruments with multiple subscales alone and together, we feel confident that the clear patterns shown in Table 2 are not just a statistical relic of using factor analysis on highly diverse instruments, but rather are a reflection of the variance structure of these instruments.

Table 3: Factors for SILL – Varimax rotation not performed on single factor solutions

INSTRUMENT	FACTOR	
Subscale	1	h^2
SILL (strategies)		
Remembering	.766*	.587
Mental processes	.899*	.808
Compensating	.786*	.618
Organizing & eval	.876*	.767
Managing emotions	.743*	.552
Learning with others	.826*	.682
proportion of variance	.669	.669

[bold] highest loading for each variable
*   loadings of .300 or higher

Table 4: Factor loadings for A/MTB subscales after Varimax rotation

INSTRUMENT Susbscale	FACTOR 1	2	3	4	H²
A/MTB (motivation)					
Att Amer in Japan	.795*	−.084	.250	−.064	.706
Interest foreign lang	.679*	.335*	−.013	.238	.630
Att Amer in general	.692*	−.016	.341*	−.032	.596
Att learning English	.600*	.442*	.107	.102	.577
Integrative orient'n	.793*	.074	.087	−.019	.642
Instrumental orient'n	.480*	.019	−.170	−.553*	.565
English class anxiety	−.215	.734*	.045	−.047	.589
Parent encouragement	.606*	−.027	.109	−.086	.387
Motivat'l intensity	.148	.761*	.129	−.026	.618
Desire to lrn English	.520*	.596*	−.006	.146	.647
Orientation	.118	.006	−.019	.874*	.778
Att English teacher	.187	.090	.873*	.058	.809
Att English class	.178	.108	.868*	.015	.797
proportion of variance	.275	.140	.136	.091	.642

[bold] highest loading for each variable
*   loadings of .300 or higher

Table 5: Factor loadings for Y/GPI subscales after Varimax rotation

INSTRUMENT Susbscale	FACTOR 1	2	H²
Y/GPI (personality)			
Social extraversion	−.316*	.755*	.670
Ascendance	−.344*	.741*	.667
Thinking extraversion	−.476*	.047	.229
Rhathymia	.186	.778*	.640
General activity	−.313*	.718*	.613
Agreeableness (lack)	.281	.735*	.619
Cooperation (lack)	.691*	−.049	.480
Objectivity (lack)	.790*	.145	.645
Nervousness	.804*	−.266	.717
Inferiority feelings	.699*	−.505*	.744
Cyclic tendencies	.792*	.044	.629
Depression	.832*	−.284	.773
proportion of variance	.351	.268	.619

[bold] highest loading for each variable
*   loadings of .300 or higher

PREDICTING PROFICIENCY GROUP MEMBERSHIP

Discriminant function analysis is designed to help researchers predict group membership from a set of predictors. On the basis of students' cloze test scores, the high proficiency group was created by combining the top 107 students, the middle group was similarly made to include 106 students, and the low proficiency group included 107 students. The proficiency groupings were based on the cloze test rather than on the Michigan structure test because the cloze test was found to be more reliable in this study and because the cloze is generally held in the literature to measure more highly integrated language skills (certainly as compared to the multiple-choice Michigan structure test).

Discriminant function analysis was then used to predict high, middle, and low proficiency group membership from all of the 32 subscales in the Y/GPI (Personality), A/MTB (Motivation), FLCAS (Anxiety), and SILL (Strategies). Discriminant function analysis is related to multivariate analysis of variance (MANOVA) procedures. In fact, mathematically, they are the same. But, they are two ways of viewing the issues involved. In MANOVA, a set of procedures familiar to many second language researchers, the multiple interval scales are the dependent variables and the grouping variable is the independent variable. The goal of MANOVA is to analyze the significance of differences in groups' performances on the various dependent variables. In contrast, in discriminant function analysis, the multiple interval scales are viewed as the independent variables and the grouping variable as the dependent variable, and the goal is to analyze the degree to which the set of predictor (or independent) variables reliably predict group membership (or the dependent variable). Unlike multiple regression analysis, which is limited to a single linear dimension, discriminant function analysis can investigate predictions along more than one dimension. This is the primary reason we selected discriminant analysis instead of regression analysis even though some precision was lost by converting interval scale cloze scores to nominal groups of high, middle, and low proficiency. In short, we chose discriminant function analysis because it could help us examine patterns of differences among predictor variables in order to better understand the dimensions along which the groups differ from each other. The stepwise method (using the Wilks' lambda criterion) was appropriately used here because: "When the researcher has no reasons for assigning some predictors higher priority than others, statistical criteria can be used to determine order of entry" (Tabachnick & Fidell, 1989, p. 528). Standard classification procedures were used instead of the jackknifing method because the latter was not available in the SPSS program.

Assumptions

As in MANOVA, data screening is particularly important before conducting a discriminant function analysis. Certain design conditions and assumptions must be met for the analyses to be correctly performed and the results to be reasonably accurate. To those ends, the following steps were taken in the data screening stage of this research.

- Univariate outliers were checked using the SPSS EXAMINE command. Box plots for all cells in the design for each of the independent variables indicated that there were some extreme cases or outliers. Eleven variables were found to have extreme values (defined here as cases that were more than 3.67 standard deviations above or below the mean, after Tabachnick & Fidell, 1989, p. 96). Twelve participants were producing these extreme values (in some cases on 2 of the 11 variables). These 12 participants were eliminated from the discriminant function analysis, leaving a total of 308 cases (with 101, 104, and 103 participants in the low, middle, and high groups, respectively). (Note that all of the other analyses in this study are based on the 320 participants described in the *Participants* section.)

- The remaining data were then checked for multivariate outliers using Mahalanobis distance in SPSS REGRESSION. None were found.

- Normality was checked with the SPSS EXAMINE command. Out of the 96 distributions in the cells of this design (3 proficiency groups∗32 predictor variables=96), only four had skewedness statistics slightly higher than 1.00 in magnitude (positive or negative). Tabachnick and Fidell (1989) said that:

> The central limit theorem proves that, with large sample sizes, sampling distributions of means are normally distributed regardless of the shapes of the distributions of variables. For example, if there are at least 20 degrees of freedom for error in a univariate ANOVA, the *F* test is said to be robust to violations of normality of variables (provided that there are no outliers). The degree to which robustness extends to multivariate analyses is not yet clear, but the larger the sample size the less effect nonnormality of variables is likely to have on your conclusion. (p. 71)

While the sample in this study is not huge, 308 far surpasses the 20 degrees of freedom mentioned above by Tabachnick and Fidell (1989). Hence, the slight violations of the assumption of normality found here were not felt to be problematic.

- Homogeneity of variance-covariance matrices was tested using the Box M statistics in SPSS MANOVA. The Box M statistic was not significant, indicating that there was no serious problem in this study with homogeneity of variance-covariance matrices.

- The linearity of relationships among all pairs of independent variables was examined using SPSS PLOT for each pair. While some relationships were somewhat weak, none appeared to be markedly non-linear.

- Multicollinearity was checked by examining the Pearson product-moment correlation matrix of all independent variables with each other. The vast majority of those correlations were very low. However, even the highest was .765 (considerably higher than all the others), which is below the .80 that Tabachnick and Fidell (1989) set as the problematic level of collinearity. Therefore, multicollinearity does not appear to be a major problem in this study.

In sum, after 12 cases with univariate extreme outliers were eliminated, no worrisome violations of the assumptions of discriminant function analysis remained in this study.

Significance and number of discriminant functions

The reliabilities of two discriminant functions were found to be statistically significant in this analysis. Chi-squared analysis indicated reliable association between proficiency group membership (high, middle, and low) and the 15 predictor variables that survived the stepwise analysis, $\chi^2(30)=77.67$, $p<.0001$. After the first function was removed, significant reliable association between groups and predictors remained in the second function, $\chi^2(14)=25.72$, $p<.028$. The first function accounted for 67.88% of the between-groups variance in discriminating among the three groups, and the second function accounted for 32.12%.

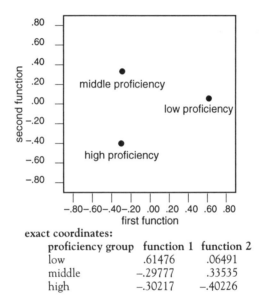

exact coordinates:

proficiency group	function 1	function 2
low	.61476	.06491
middle	–.29777	.33535
high	–.30217	–.40226

Figure 1: Plot of the three group centroids on two discriminant functions derived from 15 of the independent variables

The plot shown in Figure 1 illustrates how both discriminant functions are related to each other in predicting group membership. The first discriminant function (on the X axis) separates the low proficiency group from the other two groups, with the middle and high groups are fairly close together on that function. The second discriminant function (on the Y axis) separates the high proficiency group from the other two groups, with the low and middle proficiency groups reasonably close on that second function.

Importance of predictor variables

The 15 steps in the discriminant function analysis along with their associated Wilks' lambdas and probabilities of significance are shown in Table 6. These statistics were used to determine how many and which variables would add significantly to the effectiveness of the prediction of proficiency group membership. The standardized canonical discriminant function coefficients are also shown in Table 6. These statistics were used to calculate each subject's predicted group membership.

Table 6: Summary of stepwise discriminant function analysis

step entered		Wilks' lambda	p	standardized canonical discriminant function coeff.	
				function 1	function 2
1	Instrumental orient'n	.96030	.0021	.55435	−.11141
2	Inferiority feelings	.92965	.0002	.12363	.91305
3	Social extraversion	.90537	.0000	.51864	−.08418
4	Desire to lrn English	.88868	.0000	−.27936	.25636
5	Managing emotions	.87412	.0000	.44908	.06919
6	Remembering	.85889	.0000	−.17382	.45211
7	Learning with others	.84265	.0000	−.36142	−.58112
8	Att English class	.83263	.0000	−.25614	−.20092
9	Agreeableness (lack)	.82292	.0000	−.26997	.45765
10	Objectivity (lack)	.80600	.0000	.32152	−.37743
11	Compensating	.79717	.0000	.30658	.13477
12	Nervousness	.78970	.0000	−.42352	−.02545
13	Parent encouragement	.78230	.0000	.16799	.27962
14	Depression	.77633	.0000	.40818	−.23683
15	Thinking extraversion	.77055	.0000	.13214	−.28859

The loading matrix of correlations between the predictor variables and the two discriminant functions is shown in Table 7. Note that loadings over .300 are presented in bold-faced type; values lower than that are traditionally not interpreted. To help in interpreting the results of the discriminant function analysis, the means and standard deviations for the high, middle, and low proficiency groups are shown in Table 8 for all of the predictor variables. The results in Tables 7 and 8 suggest that the most reliable predictors for distinguishing between the low proficiency group and the other two groups (the first function) are Instrumental Orientation as measured on the A/MTB (with a loading of .46565) and Managing Emotions as measured by the SILL (with a loading of .36242). High and middle proficiency students appear to have less Instrumental Orientation on average (with means of 19.52 and 19.79, respectively) than the low proficiency students (M=21.62). In addition, the high and middle groups appear to be slightly less prone to Managing Emotions (with means of 3.49 and 3.56, respectively) than the low proficiency group (M=3.72).

At the same time, Table 7 indicates that the most reliable predictors for distinguishing between the high proficiency students and the other two groups (the second function) are Inferiority Feelings (with a loading of .55289), Nervousness (loading at .38502), and Thinking Extraversion (with a .38293 loading), all three of which were measured on the Y/GPI (Personality) scale. High proficiency students appear to have considerably less Inferiority Feelings on average (M=6.45) than the middle proficiency group (M=8.65) or low proficiency group (M=7.94). High proficiency students also appear to experience less Nervousness on average (M=8.54) than the middle proficiency group (M=9.97) or low proficiency group (M=8.86). High proficiency students also score higher on average on Thinking Extraversion (M=10.29) than the middle proficiency group (M=9.36) and only slightly more than the low proficiency group (M=10.18). These differences, which are not great, indicate that the high proficiency group tends to be somewhat slower on average to make decisions when compared with the low proficiency group but somewhat faster than the middle group. However, on average, the means indicate that all three groups are fairly well-balanced because they fall approximately in the middle of the 20-point range, being neither too contemplative nor too quick in their thinking styles.

Table 7: Loadings for predictor variables on discriminant functions

variable	function 1	function 2	univariate F(2,305)
Y/GPI (personality)			
Social extraversion	.24518	−.21148	2.36
Ascendance	.08794	−.27785	.96
Thinking extraversion	.07173	**−.38293***	2.17
Rhathymia	.20878	−.00517	1.93
General activity	.09949	−.27512	.51
Agreeableness (lack)	−.04776	.16301	.43
Cooperation (lack)	.10212	.22724	2.62
Objectivity (lack)	.25309	.07181	1.93
Nervousness	−.04312	**.38502***	2.09
Inferiority feelings	.13668	**.55289***	4.74
Cyclic tendencies	.11802	.26245	1.66
Depression	.21708	.29934	2.60
A/MTB (motivation)			
Att Amer in Japan	.13068	.06407	.69
Interest foreign lang	−.02574	.03750	.20
Att Amer in general	.06269	−.01620	1.34
Att learning English	.01914	.02278	.38
Integrative orient'n	.13520	.06948	.24

continued...

Table 7: Loadings for predictor variables on discriminant functions (cont.)

variable	function 1	function 2	univariate F(2,305)
Instrumental orient'n	.46565*	−.02111	6.30
English class anxiety	−.10571	−.19511	1.34
Parent encouragement	.27675	.18754	2.71
Motivat'l intensity	−.17681	−.02077	.50
Desire to lrn English	−.16962	.12087	1.04
Orientation	−.18690	.05900	.03
Att English teacher	−.18234	−.14699	.29
Att English class	−.21414	−.19049	1.83
FLCAS (anxiety)	−.06339	−.23294	2.96
SILL (strategies)			
Remembering	−.02116	.25567	.91
Mental processes	.07856	.07500	.02
Compensating	.20139	.11082	1.35
Organizing & eval	.06713	.00203	.24
Managing emotions	**.36242***	.09574	3.94
Learning with others	−.02847	−.23895	.81
canonical R	.4000	.2875	
Eigen value	.1905	.0901	

* loadings of .300 or higher

Table 8: Descriptive statistics for low, middle, and high proficiency groups for discriminant function analysis (N=308)

instrument subscale	low (N=101) mean	SD	middle (N=104) mean	SD	high (N=103) mean	SD	function
Y/GPI (personality)							
Social extraversion	15.56	4.42	14.18	4.51	14.71	4.84	
Ascendance	11.82	4.88	11.22	4.59	12.10	4.61	
Thinking extraversion	**10.18**	**3.15**	**9.36**	**3.65**	**9.94**	**3.80**	function 2
Rhathymia	14.25	4.36	13.45	4.01	13.11	4.37	
General activity	12.44	4.62	12.04	4.52	12.67	4.39	
Agreeableness (lack)	13.00	3.62	13.44	4.11	13.01	3.99	
Cooperation (lack)	8.49	4.08	8.53	4.04	7.39	4.06	
Objectivity (lack)	10.27	3.58	9.54	4.34	9.17	4.19	
Nervousness	**8.86**	**5.41**	**9.97**	**5.21**	**8.54**	**5.17**	function 2
Inferiority feelings	**9.94**	**5.20**	**8.65**	**5.65**	**6.45**	**4.77**	function 2
Cyclic tendencies	10.89	4.31	11.29	4.68	10.16	4.62	
Depression	11.24	5.69	10.96	6.54	9.44	5.95	
A/MTB (motivation)							
Att Amer in Japan	55.06	7.09	54.34	7.19	53.93	6.79	
Interest foreign lang	64.79	4.47	65.12	5.60	64.75	4.90	
Att Amer in general	52.39	8.14	50.58	8.21	51.06	8.21	
Att learning English	61.40	6.77	61.04	6.92	61.85	6.42	

Integrative orient'n	25.62	2.49	25.74	2.35	25.49	2.88	
Instrumental orient'n	**21.62**	**4.51**	**19.79**	**4.52**	**19.52**	**4.75**	function 1
English class anxiety	19.60	5.95	20.36	6.14	21.01	6.36	
Parent encouragement	56.54	9.86	55.11	9.34	53.39	9.84	
Motivat'l intensity	23.10	2.53	23.47	2.60	23.21	2.93	
Desire to lrn English	25.85	2.40	26.31	2.46	26.16	2.16	
Orientation	1.74	0.43	1.74	0.43	1.75	0.43	
Att English teacher	136.22	21.47	136.27	20.04	138.27	24.36	
Att English class	129.62	19.42	131.51	21.94	134.99	19.63	
FLCAS (anxiety)	105.64	13.37	105.35	17.59	110.10	15.72	
SILL (strategies)							
Remembering	3.63	0.50	3.70	0.46	3.60	0.58	
Mental processes	3.94	0.53	3.93	0.44	3.94	0.51	
Compensating	4.20	0.53	4.14	0.55	4.08	0.54	
Organizing & eval	4.31	0.54	4.33	0.50	4.28	0.53	
Managing emotions	**3.72**	**0.65**	**3.56**	**0.54**	**3.49**	**0.58**	function 1
Learning with others	4.09	0.63	4.04	0.53	4.14	0.56	

Adequacy of classification

For the classification analysis, sample sizes were taken into account in estimating prior probabilities of group membership. The classification procedure indicated that, overall, 170 (or 55.19%) were correctly classified as shown in Table 9. However, the accuracy of the classifications varied for the three levels. The analysis was more likely to correctly classify low proficiency students than the other two groups. Low proficiency students were classified correctly with 66.3% accuracy, while middle proficiency students were classified with 48.1% accuracy, and high proficiency students were classified correctly with 51.5% accuracy.

Table 9: Classification results

		predicted group membership		
actual group	N	low	middle	high
low proficiency group	101	**67**	21	13
		66.3%	20.8%	12.9%
middle proficiency group	104	23	**50**	31
		22.1%	**48.1%**	29.8%
high proficiency group	103	25	25	**53**
		24.3%	24.3%	**51.5%**

[bold] correct predictions

Table 10: Intercorrelations of all variables with correlation coefficents above the diagonal [in bold] and coefficients adjusted for attenuation in both variables below the diagonal

variables	1	2	3	4	5	6	7	8	9	10	11	12	13	14	15	16	17
1 Social extraversion	1.00	0.73	0.10	0.46	0.59	0.30	-0.26	-0.14	-0.41	-0.51	-0.24	-0.43	0.12	0.19	0.16	0.28	0.20
2 Ascendance	0.93	1.00	0.18	0.38	0.56	0.34	-0.28	-0.14	-0.39	-0.58	-0.23	-0.45	0.10	0.19	0.13	0.27	0.14
3 Thinking extraversion	0.18	0.32	1.00	0.10	0.12	-0.09	-0.27	-0.28	-0.42	-0.26	-0.24	-0.39	0.00	-0.03	0.07	0.03	-0.04
4 Rhathymia	0.61	0.53	0.18	1.00	0.43	0.56	0.03	0.19	-0.09	-0.18	0.20	-0.08	0.13	0.16	0.11	0.19	0.23
5 General activity	0.76	0.73	0.21	0.59	1.00	0.33	-0.21	-0.12	-0.40	-0.55	-0.28	-0.42	0.20	0.21	0.24	0.25	0.20
6 Agreeableness (lack)	0.43	0.50	-0.18	0.85	0.49	1.00	0.14	0.23	0.00	-0.25	0.25	-0.03	-0.01	0.14	-0.02	0.12	0.15
7 Cooperation (lack)	-0.35	-0.39	-0.51	0.04	-0.29	0.22	1.00	0.49	0.49	0.46	0.42	0.50	-0.06	-0.14	-0.14	-0.19	-0.08
8 Objectivity (lack)	-0.20	-0.21	-0.55	0.29	-0.17	0.38	0.76	1.00	0.54	0.43	0.53	0.62	0.00	-0.05	-0.06	-0.10	0.01
9 Nervousness	-0.50	-0.50	-0.72	-0.13	-0.52	0.00	0.66	0.76	1.00	0.70	0.57	0.72	-0.06	-0.13	-0.13	-0.19	-0.10
10 Inferiority feelings	-0.62	-0.74	-0.44	-0.25	-0.70	-0.35	0.61	0.60	0.86	1.00	0.53	0.73	-0.03	-0.14	-0.10	-0.22	-0.08
11 Cyclic tendencies	-0.32	-0.31	-0.44	0.29	-0.39	0.38	0.62	0.80	0.77	0.71	1.00	0.60	-0.01	-0.04	-0.11	-0.05	0.10
12 Depression	-0.51	-0.56	-0.65	-0.10	-0.52	-0.04	0.66	0.85	0.87	0.88	0.78	1.00	-0.02	-0.09	-0.12	-0.20	-0.07
13 Att Amer in Japan	0.15	0.13	0.00	0.18	0.26	-0.01	-0.08	0.01	-0.07	-0.04	-0.01	-0.03	1.00	0.44	0.77	0.38	0.55
14 Interest foreign lang	0.25	0.27	-0.05	0.24	0.29	0.22	-0.21	-0.08	-0.07	-0.04	-0.06	-0.12	0.62	1.00	0.37	0.55	0.55
15 Att Amer in general	0.19	0.16	0.11	0.14	0.30	-0.02	-0.18	-0.08	-0.16	-0.12	-0.14	-0.14	0.95	0.48	1.00	0.38	0.45
16 Att learning English	0.35	0.35	0.06	0.25	0.33	0.17	-0.27	-0.14	-0.24	-0.28	-0.07	-0.24	0.49	0.76	0.46	1.00	0.45
17 Integrative orient'n	0.27	0.19	-0.08	0.34	0.28	0.23	-0.12	0.02	-0.14	-0.10	0.15	-0.09	0.78	0.82	0.59	0.63	1.00
18 Istrumental orient'n	0.12	0.09	0.06	0.29	0.23	0.15	0.08	-0.11	-0.11	-0.10	0.09	-0.13	0.37	0.26	0.29	0.34	0.57
19 English class anxiety	0.41	0.50	0.06	0.13	0.27	0.22	-0.27	-0.28	-0.30	-0.56	-0.23	-0.38	-0.15	0.05	-0.04	0.21	-0.09
20 Parent encouragement	0.27	0.19	-0.07	0.24	0.23	0.08	-0.10	0.07	-0.06	-0.03	0.00	-0.05	0.56	0.34	0.39	0.39	0.61
21 Motivat'l intensity	0.45	0.44	-0.22	0.20	0.40	0.43	-0.13	-0.11	-0.23	-0.39	-0.19	-0.25	0.20	0.46	0.25	0.42	0.30
22 Desire to lrn English	0.41	0.35	-0.04	0.21	0.36	0.20	-0.18	-0.09	-0.20	-0.26	-0.13	-0.22	0.49	0.77	0.42	0.74	0.57
23 Orientation	-0.01	-0.03	0.02	0.05	-0.08	0.12	-0.02	0.06	0.05	0.02	0.03	0.05	0.01	0.19	0.06	0.13	0.10
24 Att English teacher	0.08	0.14	-0.08	0.02	0.13	-0.05	-0.16	0.03	-0.05	-0.05	-0.01	-0.08	0.35	0.25	0.38	0.31	0.30
25 Att English class	0.24	0.20	0.09	0.09	0.23	0.05	-0.17	-0.10	-0.22	-0.16	-0.07	-0.22	0.32	0.23	0.34	0.32	0.34
26 FLCAS	0.52	0.58	0.19	0.20	0.45	0.26	-0.25	-0.40	-0.42	-0.65	-0.35	-0.50	-0.06	0.09	0.03	0.19	0.00

variables	1	2	3	4	5	6	7	8	9	10	11	12	13	14	15	16	17
27 Remembering	0.30	0.24	-0.23	0.20	0.34	0.32	-0.08	0.01	-0.15	-0.19	-0.16	-0.15	0.19	0.22	0.18	0.25	0.29
28 Mental processes	0.36	0.29	-0.26	0.23	0.37	0.29	-0.02	0.05	-0.10	-0.18	-0.11	-0.08	0.20	0.39	0.18	0.31	0.31
29 Compensating	0.26	0.28	-0.27	0.17	0.31	0.27	-0.03	-0.04	-0.12	-0.16	-0.13	-0.09	0.16	0.31	0.14	0.34	0.29
30 Organizing and eval	0.33	0.25	-0.22	0.15	0.35	0.27	-0.14	-0.03	-0.17	-0.19	-0.16	-0.14	0.26	0.47	0.25	0.41	0.33
31 Managing emotions	0.35	0.21	-0.23	0.29	0.28	0.32	0.08	0.28	0.00	0.02	0.09	0.07	0.26	0.23	0.23	0.20	0.25
32 Learning with others	0.40	0.40	-0.14	0.26	0.51	0.30	-0.14	-0.02	-0.18	-0.28	-0.13	-0.19	0.20	0.41	0.22	0.35	0.31
33 Michigan	-0.11	-0.08	-0.07	-0.28	-0.07	-0.22	-0.16	-0.30	-0.08	-0.20	-0.27	-0.21	-0.01	0.09	-0.01	0.00	-0.06
34 cloze	-0.16	0.02	0.09	-0.12	0.04	-0.05	-0.19	-0.20	-0.04	-0.16	-0.14	-0.17	-0.09	0.03	-0.10	0.06	-0.08
alpha	0.81	0.76	0.42	0.69	0.76	0.62	0.68	0.63	0.80	0.81	0.69	0.85	0.75	0.68	0.87	0.77	0.66

variables	18	19	20	21	22	23	24	25	26	27	28	29	30	31	32	33	34
1 Social extraversion	0.08	0.32	0.23	0.31	0.30	-0.01	0.07	0.21	0.44	0.23	0.30	0.19	0.28	0.25	0.31	-0.08	-0.12
2 Ascendance	0.06	0.37	0.15	0.29	0.25	-0.03	0.12	0.17	0.48	0.18	0.23	0.20	0.21	0.15	0.30	-0.06	0.01
3 Thinking extraversion	0.03	0.03	-0.04	-0.11	-0.02	0.01	-0.05	0.06	0.12	-0.13	-0.15	-0.14	-0.13	-0.12	-0.08	-0.04	0.05
4 Rhathymia	0.19	0.09	0.18	0.12	0.14	0.04	0.01	0.07	0.16	0.14	0.18	0.12	0.12	0.19	0.19	-0.18	-0.08
5 General activity	0.16	0.20	0.19	0.27	0.26	-0.07	0.11	0.20	0.37	0.26	0.29	0.23	0.29	0.19	0.38	-0.05	0.03
6 Agreeableness (lack)	0.09	0.15	0.06	0.26	0.13	0.09	-0.04	0.04	0.20	0.22	0.21	0.17	0.20	0.20	0.20	-0.14	-0.03
7 Cooperation (lack)	0.05	-0.19	-0.08	-0.08	-0.12	-0.02	-0.13	-0.14	-0.20	-0.05	-0.02	-0.02	-0.11	0.05	-0.10	-0.11	-0.13
8 Objectivity (lack)	-0.07	-0.19	0.05	-0.07	-0.06	0.05	0.02	-0.08	-0.30	0.01	0.04	-0.03	-0.03	0.17	-0.01	-0.19	-0.13
9 Nervousness	-0.07	-0.23	-0.05	-0.16	-0.15	0.05	-0.05	-0.19	-0.35	-0.11	-0.09	-0.09	-0.15	0.00	-0.14	-0.06	-0.03
10 Inferiority feelings	-0.07	-0.43	-0.02	-0.27	-0.19	0.02	-0.05	-0.14	-0.55	-0.15	-0.15	-0.12	-0.16	0.02	-0.22	-0.15	-0.12
11 Cyclic tendencies	0.06	-0.16	0.00	-0.12	-0.09	0.03	-0.01	-0.06	-0.27	-0.12	-0.09	-0.09	-0.12	0.06	-0.09	-0.18	-0.09
12 Depression	-0.09	-0.30	-0.05	-0.17	-0.16	0.05	-0.07	-0.19	-0.43	-0.12	-0.07	-0.07	-0.12	0.05	-0.15	-0.15	-0.13
13 Att Amer in Japan	0.25	-0.11	0.44	0.13	0.34	0.01	0.29	0.27	-0.05	0.14	0.16	0.11	0.21	0.18	0.15	-0.01	-0.07
14 Interest foreign lang	0.17	0.04	0.25	0.29	0.52	0.16	0.20	0.18	0.07	0.16	0.29	0.21	0.37	0.15	0.29	0.06	0.02
15 Att Amer in general	0.21	-0.03	0.34	0.18	0.32	0.05	0.35	0.30	0.03	0.15	0.16	0.11	0.22	0.17	0.17	-0.01	-0.08
16 Att learning English	0.23	0.16	0.31	0.28	0.53	0.11	0.26	0.27	0.15	0.19	0.25	0.24	0.34	0.14	0.26	0.00	0.04
17 Integrative orient'n	0.36	-0.06	0.46	0.19	0.38	0.08	0.24	0.27	0.00	0.20	0.23	0.19	0.26	0.16	0.21	-0.04	-0.05
18 Istrumental orient'n	1.00	-0.06	0.21	0.05	0.15	-0.17	0.01	0.01	0.03	0.11	0.06	0.11	0.12	0.09	0.09	-0.08	-0.17

continued....

Table 10: Intercorrelations of all variables with correlation coefficents above the diagonal [in bold] and coefficients adjusted for attenuation in both variables below the diagonal (cont.)

	18	19	20	21	22	23	24	25	26	27	28	29	30	31	32	33	34
19 English class anxiety	-0.09	**1.00**	-0.05	0.33	0.17	0.03	0.04	0.02	0.66	0.08	0.15	0.10	0.11	-0.02	0.17	0.06	0.07
20 Parent encouragement	0.30	-0.06	**1.00**	0.12	0.25	0.03	0.18	0.19	0.00	0.13	0.20	0.17	0.24	0.21	0.19	-0.11	-0.13
21 Motivat'l intensity	0.08	0.50	0.18	**1.00**	0.46	0.03	0.17	0.19	0.28	0.32	0.38	0.28	0.41	0.22	0.39	0.00	-0.01
22 Desire to lrn English	0.25	0.24	0.33	0.75	**1.00**	0.12	0.17	0.18	0.20	0.26	0.39	0.28	0.41	0.21	0.34	0.02	0.03
23 Orientation	-0.22	0.03	0.03	0.04	0.15	**1.00**	0.08	0.04	-0.01	-0.04	0.02	-0.01	-0.01	-0.14	-0.02	0.02	0.05
24 Att English teacher	0.02	0.05	0.20	0.23	0.21	0.09	**1.00**	0.68	0.00	0.04	0.04	0.03	0.11	-0.01	0.11	0.08	0.07
25 Att English class	0.01	0.03	0.21	0.26	0.23	0.04	0.72	**1.00**	0.04	0.09	0.09	0.02	0.13	0.06	0.11	0.11	0.11
26 FLCAS	0.04	0.82	0.00	0.38	0.26	-0.01	0.00	0.04	**1.00**	0.17	0.26	0.19	0.19	0.06	0.27	0.08	0.11
27 Remembering	0.17	0.11	0.16	0.48	0.38	-0.04	0.05	0.11	0.22	**1.00**	0.68	0.49	0.57	0.52	0.52	-0.02	-0.05
28 Mental processes	0.08	0.19	0.23	0.55	0.52	0.02	0.05	0.10	0.30	0.86	**1.00**	0.67	0.76	0.60	0.67	0.03	0.01
29 Compensating	0.17	0.15	0.22	0.45	0.42	-0.02	0.04	0.02	0.24	0.68	0.88	**1.00**	0.66	0.45	0.58	0.01	-0.06
30 Organizing and eval	0.17	0.13	0.28	0.58	0.54	-0.01	0.12	0.15	0.21	0.71	0.89	0.85	**1.00**	0.56	0.71	0.09	-0.03
31 Managing emotions	0.15	-0.03	0.29	0.36	0.33	-0.18	-0.01	0.08	0.07	0.77	0.82	0.68	0.75	**1.00**	0.56	-0.15	-0.19
32 Learning with others	0.13	0.24	0.24	0.59	0.49	-0.02	0.14	0.13	0.33	0.71	0.85	0.81	0.88	0.83	**1.00**	0.03	0.02
33 Michigan	-0.13	0.09	-0.15	0.00	0.03	0.03	0.11	0.15	0.10	-0.02	0.04	0.01	0.12	-0.24	0.04	**1.00**	0.48
34 cloze	-0.25	0.10	-0.17	-0.01	0.04	0.06	0.09	0.13	0.14	-0.08	0.02	-0.08	-0.04	-0.29	0.03	0.71	**1.00**
alpha	0.60	0.73	0.84	0.58	0.66	1.00	0.95	0.94	0.89	0.74	0.84	0.69	0.88	0.63	0.73	0.64	0.71

* $r = .15$ significant at .05

Relationships among predictor variables

Pearson product-moment correlations were calculated for all possible combinations of the 32 independent variables in this study. Many of those would reach statistical significance at the .01 level (all $r<.2540$, two-tailed) if they were tested a priori. The full correlation matrix is presented in Table 10 with the correlation coefficients shown above the diagonal and the coefficients after being adjusted for attenuation in both variables below the diagonal. We cannot discuss each and every coefficient in prose, however, we do present them all in Table 10 and we will discuss the highlights of these correlational analyses.

Earlier in the discussion of Tables 2 through 5, we explored the relationships of subscales in terms of convergence and divergence within and between the instruments involved. Here, we will discuss relationships of the subscales in each instrument to the subscales in other instruments. In other words, we will not examine the correlations of subscales to other subscales within the same instrument. In addition, only correlation coefficients of .30 or higher will be considered, so the relationships we are discussing can all be said to represent at least 9% overlapping variance ($r^2=.30^2=.09$, or 9%).

First, correlations between the personality subscales (on the Y/GPI) and motivation subscales (on the A/TMB) were examined. The Motivational Intensity subscale and the Desire to learn English subscale were both found to be positively correlated with Social Extraversion (.31 and .30, respectively). Apparently, outgoing, socially active individuals tend to also have a greater desire to learn English and to be more highly motivated. Positive correlations were also found for English Class Anxiety with Social Extraversion (.32) and with Ascendance (.37), and negative correlations were found for English Class Anxiety with Inferiority Feelings (−.43) and Depression (−.30). This pattern of results seems to indicate that, contrary to previous findings, English Class Anxiety is somewhat related to outgoingness and leadership tendencies, and negatively related to some aspects of neuroticism in this population. In short, to some degree, this anxiety scale seems to be an indicator of facilitating anxiety for these Japanese students. This issue will be revisited below.

Second, correlations between the anxiety subscales (on the FLCAS) and personality subscales (on the Y/GPI) were inspected. The FLCAS positively correlated with Social Extraversion (.44), Ascendance (.48), and General Activity (.37), and negatively correlated with Lack of Objectivity (−.30), Nervousness (−.35), Inferiority Feelings (−.55), and Depression (−.43). Moreover, the FLCAS was found to be correlated at .66 with the motivation subscale Classroom Anxiety (on the A/MTB). These results further support the notion that anxiety can be beneficial, at least in this population. Note also that the group means shown in Table 8 indicate that the high proficiency group was more anxious on average than either the middle or low groups (110.10, 105.35, 105.64, respectively, on the FLCAS, and 21.01, 20.36, 19.60, respectively, on the English Class Anxiety scale). These correlations and mean differences must be interpreted in light of personality theory, which typically places anxiety in scales measuring neuroticism—a conclusion quite different from the results found here.

Third, correlations between the learning strategies subscales (on the SILL) and motivation subscales (on the A/MTB) were evaluated. Mental Processes correlated positively with Motivational Intensity (.38). Positive correlations were also found between Organizing and Evaluation Strategies with Interest in Foreign Languages (.37), Attitudes toward learning English (.34), Motivational Intensity (.41), and Desire to learn English (.41). Learning with Others correlated positively with Motivational Intensity (.39). Notice that three of the SILL subscales correlated above .30 with Motivational Intensity. However, also note that none of these three SILL subscales was found to significantly differentiate among the three proficiency groups in the discriminant function analysis. So, though the use of these learning strategies does not appear to be related to proficiency, they may be somewhat related to motivation and attitudes towards language learning.

Finally, correlations between the learning strategies subscales (on the SILL) and personality subscales (on the Y/GPI) were inspected. Mental Processes positively correlated with Social Extraversion (.30). Learning with Others with Social Extraversion (.31) and Ascendance (.30). Note that all correlations between personality variables and language learning strategies were with traits that are classified as Extraversion traits on the Y/GPI.

DISCUSSION

The purpose of this section is to provide direct answers to the research questions posed at the beginning of the study. To help orient readers, those original research questions are repeatedbelow to organize the discussion.

1. Are self-report scales on personality, motivation, anxiety, and learning strategies reliable when applied to Japanese university students?

The reliability of any instrument has to do with the degree to which it is measuring consistently. Recall that the results for the total scales on the self-report instruments were all fairly reliable, ranging from .84 to .95 (which may not be good news given that the subscales were originally designed to measure different traits). The proficiency measures were found to be less reliable (cloze=.71; Michigan=.64). Most of the subscales were generally found to be even lower in reliability; they also varied considerably in the magnitude (ranging from .42 to .88). Subscale reliabilities naturally tend to be lower than the overall reliabilities of instruments because the subscale estimates are based on scales that are shorter. If all other factors are held constant, shorter subscales will tend to be less reliable than longer ones.

In fact, these reliability estimates are generally much higher than we expected before doing this study. Based on the individual differences literature and our own teaching and research experiences in Japan, we expected Japanese students to be relatively homogeneous with regard to personality, motivation, anxiety, and learning strategies. However, a homogeneous population would have produced little variance (and this would have been reflected in relatively low reliability estimates). Yet, the standard deviations reported in Table 1 indicate that these students do vary considerably in terms of personality, motivation, anxiety, and learning strategies, and the reliability estimates are relatively high. The students in this study are in fact far from being homogeneous with regard to these variables, and the instruments are reasonably reliable in measuring those variables.

2.   Are self-report scales on personality, motivation, anxiety, and learning strategies valid when applied to Japanese university students?

The issue of validity has to do with the degree to which an instrument is measuring what it claims to be measuring. One way to study the validity of an instrument is to use factor analysis to study the convergence and divergence of a group of instruments. The results in Table 2 indicate that all of the subtests on the SILL converge on one factor and diverge from all other instruments in this analysis. Thus, the six subscales in this instrument appear to be fairly uniformly measuring a single construct which is different from the other scales in this study.

Similarly, the Y/GPI loads on only two factors, one of which appears to be related to extraversion and the other to neuroticism. Thus the Y/GPI seems to be measuring two constructs (with only one subscale not conforming to that two-way classification). Thus, for the most part, the Y/GPI appears to be measuring two constructs—constructs that are not measured on the other scales—just as it was designed to do.

The A/MTB presents a more complex picture because it loads on four different factors—factors that are divergent in the sense that they are different from all of the other instruments. Eight of the subscales load on one factor thus showing considerable convergence, while two load on a second factor apparently related to anxiety (because the FLCAS also loads on that factor), two (Attitudes Toward English Teachers and Classes) load on a third factor, and two (Instrumental Orientation and Orientation) load on a fourth factor. Thus for Japanese students, the A/MTB seems to measure at least four different things—though the majority of subscales are on one factor. Hence there is some question about the validity of this instrument at least in terms of measuring a unitary construct. However, recall that the A/MTB included three distinct item types. This fact combined with the fact that the FLCAS was included in the analysis may go a long way toward explaining why the subscales of the A/MTB loaded on four factors. Clearly, further study of the construct validity of the A/MTB is warranted, especially when it is applied to this population.

Lastly, there are no subscales on the FLCAS to help in exploring convergence. However, in terms of divergence, this scale appears to be quite different from all of the other scales in this study except two subscales (English class anxiety and Motivational Intensity) on the A/MTB, which, as we explained above, may logically be related to anxiety. Thus, this pattern of loadings supports the validity of the FLCAS as a measure of anxiety.

3. What do personality, motivation, anxiety, and learning strategy scales tell us about Japanese university students in terms of descriptive statistics?

Beginning first with personality, we can see that on average these students tend to be more extraverted than either introverted or neurotic. In particular, the scores on Social Extraversion, Rhathymia (carefreeness), General Activity (physical activity), and lack of Agreeableness (argumentativeness) were rather high. These findings seem to contradict teachers' expectations about Japanese students' classroom behavior as well as findings of some studies (see Sato, 1982). However, Robson (1992, 1994) found relationships between students' oral classroom participation and high levels of extraversion and noted in general that the Japanese students in that study tended to be extraverted. In fact, the reticent classroom behavior of many Japanese students may be conditioned by factors other than personality—factors like cultural expectations (for more on this topic, see Anderson, 1993).

The descriptive statistics for motivation show that these students generally have a high degree of interest in learning foreign languages and a good attitude toward learning English as well as a desire to do so. Moreover, these students are somewhat more integratively motivated as shown in both the Integrative Orientation and Orientation subscales. Oddly, given that they are more integratively oriented, the students' attitudes toward Americans (in Japan and in general) are not particularly high. English Class Anxiety is not particularly high either, nor are the scores on the attitude scales related to English teachers and English classes. These students may thus be characterized as being well motivated to learn and to integrate, but with mixed feelings toward Americans, their teachers, and their classes.

The mean of the FLCAS shows these students to be relatively anxious, though not extremely so. In Robson (1992, 1994), those students found to score high on this instrument tended to participate orally less often. Thus, given the relatively high anxiety score, it would be reasonable to expect some of these students to be fairly quiet in class when speaking English, which is a condition that is often noted by English teachers in Japan.

Three subscales of the SILL—Compensating (for missing knowledge), Organizing and Evaluating, and Learning with Others—have rather high scores. What might account for this? The subjects under investigation here were all studying intensive English with a view to undertaking college-level work through the medium of English. Perhaps in the process, they were exposed to larger amounts of English input than they could comfortably handle. If this were the case, they might be compelled to adopt strategies for survival in a language learning environment which severely taxed their abilities to cope. One way to do this would be to organize one's life in order to maximize potential learning opportunities. Another way would be to rely on communication strategies which assist in dealing with missing linguistic knowledge. In addition, they might grow to depend on help from other people, such as fellow students. Finally, in such an intense foreign language learning environment, the students might need to stretch in order to use all available mental processes. Remember, all of these possibilities are just speculation.

4. Which personality, motivation, anxiety, and learning strategy subscales significantly and reliably predict differences between the high, middle, and low proficiency Japanese students, and which most reliably predict those differences? How adequately are the resulting predictions classified?

The results of this study indicate that Instrumental Motivation in the A/MTB (Motivation) and Managing Emotions in the SILL (Strategies) were the most reliable predictors for distinguishing between the low proficiency group and the other two groups (the first discriminant function). High and middle proficiency students appear to have less instrumental motivation on average than the low proficiency students and are slightly less prone to managing emotions than the low proficiency group (M=3.72). At the same time, Inferiority Feelings, Nervousness, and Thinking Extraversion, all on the Y/GPI (Personality) scale seem to be the most reliable predictors for distinguishing between the high proficiency students and the other two groups (the second discriminant second function). High proficiency students seem to be different from the middle and low proficiency groups in three ways: (a) high proficiency students have considerably less Inferiority Feelings on average than the other two groups, (b) high proficiency students appear to be less nervous on average than the other groups, and (c) high proficiency students tend to be somewhat slower on average to make decisions than the low proficiency group but somewhat higher than the middle group (though on average all three groups should be viewed as fairly well-balanced in their thinking styles).

When all is said and done, the classification procedure indicated that over 55%, were correctly classified (as shown in Table 9) with the accuracy varying somewhat for the three levels. Low proficiency predictions had 66.3% accuracy; middle proficiency classifications were 48.1% accurate, and high proficiency students were classified correctly with 51.5% accuracy. These rates of accuracy in the predictions, while far from perfect, are well above chance fluctuations and could provide useful information for identifying students likely to be low in proficiency, who could benefit from supplementary help in one way or another.

5. How are subscales on each of these instruments related to subscales on the other instruments when they are administered to Japanese university students?

Generally, the relationships found among the subscales on the A/TMB and the Y/GPI seem to indicate that extraverted or socially active students tend to be more motivated and have a greater desire to learn English. These results would seem similar to those found by Gardner and his associates. However, the positive relationship between Anxiety (in the A/TMB) and Extraversion (in the Y/GPI) and the negative relationship between Anxiety and Neuroticism are somewhat odd. The positive relationship found between Anxiety and Extraversion is unexpected because it indicates that what would typically be labeled as detrimental anxiety is beneficial or facilitating in this setting (if we view extraversion as a positive classroom behavior). In other words, where we found a positive relationship between Anxiety and Extraversion, personality theory would predict that Anxiety would be a neurotic trait and would be negatively related to Extraversion. At the same time, the negative relationship found between Anxiety and Neuroticism is unexpected because, in personality theory, anxiety is considered a neurotic trait and should be positively associated with neuroticism.

Similarly, a positive relationship was found between Anxiety as measured by the FLCAS and the Y/GPI Extraversion, and a negative one was found between FLCAS Anxiety and Y/GPI Neuroticism. This is again the reverse of what would typically be expected both theoretically and based on previous studies (see Robson, 1994 in particular). As the high proficiency group was the most anxious, we must interpret these findings as indicating beneficial anxiety, or anxiety that pushes students to perform better. Such results may be limited to this population alone and may have a relationship to their unique status among Japanese university students.

The relationships found between Learning Strategies (SILL) and Motivation (A/MTB) may indicate that strategies necessary to survive in an intensive English language program impact on the students' level of motivation by pushing it higher. There also seems to be an important relationship between such survival strategies and Extraversion (Y/GPI), which would seem to indicate that socially active students are more prone to employing such strategies. In addition, the positive relationship between Extraversion and Mental Processes strategies is similar to those found elsewhere in this study between Anxiety and Extraversion because this subscale also deals with anxiety. Thus again, we see a beneficial side to anxiety.

CONCLUSIONS

In theoretical terms, this study was the first to examine personality, motivation, anxiety, strategies, and multiple measures of language proficiency all at the same time. The results indicate that the instruments are effective for doing research on Japanese students in that they turned out to be reasonably reliable. All of the instruments, except the A/MTB, were fairly clearly shown to be valid in the sense that subtests on the different instruments tended to converge on the same factors; at the same time, the various instruments were apparently tapping into distinctly different traits, as indicated by the fact that they were loading most heavily on different factors. Even with a single nationality, as in this study, sufficient variance was produced by these self-report instruments for us to learn a great deal about the students. In a practical sense, however, future researchers should realize that two of the instruments, the Y/GPI and A/MTB were both somewhat cumbersome to administer and score because they have 120 and 134 items, respectively. The FLCAS and the SILL are shorter and considerably easier to administer.

The main point of this study, and of many of the studies looking at individual differences, has been the desire to determine what constitutes a good or proficient language learner. Although a far from complete profile has been provided by this study, certain generalizations can be made. We see that learners in the high proficiency group can be categorized as being a) well-balanced in their thinking styles—neither too quick nor too indecisive—given their medium range of scores for Thinking Extraversion, b) emotionally stable due to the low scores on Inferiority Feelings and Nervousness, c) less instrumentally motivated (and thus more integratively motivated, M=25.5 on a 28-point scale), and d) less anxious as measured by the Managing Emotions scale of the SILL.

Some of the findings here seem to support a relationship between Cognitive Academic Language Proficiency (CALP) (or general second language proficiency as measured by the cloze test) and emotionally stable personality types; these results are somewhat unexpected because previous studies in general have been unable to establish such relationships (see Ellis, 1994 for a summary of this research, and Robson, 1994 for an example of such null findings). The additional findings of a predictive relationship between individuals with personalities prone to well-balanced thinking styles and CALP are also unique.

The fact that the high and middle proficiency groups were found to be less instrumentally motivated on average than the low proficiency group (discriminant function one) seems to contradict the theory underlying the A/MTB, which is generally taken to be that instrumentally oriented students have a drive for knowledge of a foreign language due to desires for social recognition or economic advantage. In such a view, the students in the Temple University (TUJ) EFL program would be seeking English language proficiency for economic advantage, which is typically believed to be the reason for higher education in Japan. However, the high proficiency group was found to be more integratively motivated on average. Perhaps on average, these students are not studying at TUJ to become economically or socially successful, but rather to become closer to the target (that is, American) community, a tendency which may be reflected in the desire of many students to study at the main Temple University campus in Philadelphia. However, note that the majority of studies using the A/MTB do not precisely indicate how scores on the battery were compared with whatever measure of language learning was being used. Were the different components of the battery simply added together or were certain sections selected? This ambiguity makes it difficult to compare our results with the earlier studies.

Finally, a close examination of the individual items in Part E (Managing Emotions) of the SILL revealed that this subtest is basically a sort of anxiety questionnaire with items such as, "I try to relax whenever I feel afraid of using English." It is curious that scores on the FLCAS, which has been shown to have moderately high (and significant) relationships with both language learning proficiency and classroom participation (Robson, 1994) were higher on average for the high proficiency group, while scores on Part E were low for this group. Perhaps the difference in results is due to instability in the Managing Emotions subscale as reflected in its relatively low reliability (.63) which could be due in part to the scale's relatively short length.

To sum up a bit, one of the most important things we learned from this study is that it is useful to examine specific populations of students, like the Japanese in this case. In so doing, their characteristics can be explored in terms of personality, motivation, anxiety, and learning strategies variables. Perhaps we should also consider the possibility that simple linear explanations of those characteristics as they relate to even a well-defined population like that in this study (using for example, multiple regression analysis or multivariate analysis of variance approaches to analyze the results) may be inadequate. Subpopulations may exist as defined by proficiency levels. More precisely, the variables that separate low, middle, and high proficiency students from one another may be different at different levels. Put another way, the three groups may vary from each other along two or more dimensions.

SUGGESTIONS FOR FURTHER RESEARCH

This study has broken new ground by simultaneously investigating a number of affective and strategic instruments in Japanese translation in an EFL setting in Japan and by using discriminant function analysis to do so. Nonetheless, further research would be useful on the personality, motivation, anxiety, and learning strategies of Japanese students of English. To that end, the following suggestions for future research are offered:

- Would similar results be obtained if this study were replicated with students at different levels of study?

- Would similar results be obtained if this study were replicated at universities in other countries? Or would there be interesting, systematic differences between language groups and/or cultures?

- Would similar results be obtained if this study were replicated with Japanese students studying at Japanese (as opposed to American) universities?

- Would the self-report instruments prove as reliable and valid elsewhere as they did in this study?

- What other psychological tests and observation techniques could be used to validate these self-report instruments?

- Could other techniques be used which would be more reliable and valid than the self-report instruments?

- What other psychological constructs might usefully be used to characterize Japanese learners of English?

- How might information like that found in the discriminant function analysis in this study be used to develop strategies to help potentially low proficiency students become better language learners?

REFERENCES

Abraham, R. G., & Vann, R. J. (1987). Strategies of two language learners: A case study. In A. Wenden & J. Rubin (Eds.), *Learner strategies in language learning* (pp. 85–102). Englewood Cliffs, NJ: Prentice-Hall.

Allport, G. W. (1937). *Personality: A psychological interpretation.* New York: Holt, Rinehart, & Wilson.

Anderson, F. (1993). The enigma of the college classroom: Nails that don't stick up. In P. Wadden (Ed.), *A handbook for teaching English at Japanese colleges and universities* (pp. 101–110). Oxford, UK: Oxford University.

Angleitner, A. (1991). Personality psychology: Trends and developments. *European Journal of Personality, 5,* 185–197.

Au, S. Y. (1988). A critical appraisal of Gardner's social-psychological theory of second-language (L2) learning. *Language Learning, 38,* 75–100.

Bernreuter, R. G. (1931). *Bernreuter personality inventory.* Stanford, CA: Stanford University.

Berwick, R., & Ross. S. (1989). Motivation after matriculation: Are Japanese learners of English still alive after exam hell? *JALT Journal, 11,* 193–210.

Brown, H. D. (1991). *Breaking the language barrier: Creating your own pathway to success.* Yarmouth, ME: Intercultural Press.

Brown, J. D. (1980). Relative merits of four methods for scoring cloze tests. *Modern Language Journal, 64,* 311–317.

Busch, D. (1982). Introversion-extraversion and the EFL proficiency of Japanese students. *Language Learning, 32,* 109–132.

Castagnaro, P. (1992). Introduction of physiological measures in locating aversive stimulation related to second language learning among Japanese university students. Unpublished manuscript, Temple University Japan, Tokyo.

Cattell, R. B. (1956) Personality and motivation theory based on structural measurement. In J. L. McCary (Ed.), *Psychology of personality* (pp. 63–120). New York: Logos.

Chamot, A. U. (1987). The learning strategies of ESL students. In A. Wenden & J. Rubin (Eds.), *Learner strategies in language learning* (pp. 71–84). Englewood Cliffs, NJ: Prentice-Hall.

Chapelle, C., & Roberts, C. (1986). Ambiguity tolerance and field independence as predictors of proficiency in English as a second language. *Language Learning, 36,* 27–45.

Chastain, K. (1975). Affective and ability factors in second language acquisition. *Language Learning, 25,* 153–161.

Clément, R., Gardner, R. C., & Smythe, P. C. (1980). Social and individual factors in second language acquisition. *Canadian Journal of Behavioural Science, 12*, 293–302.

Ellis, R. (1994). *The study of second language acquisition*. Oxford, UK: Oxford University.

Ely, C. M. (1986). An analysis of discomfort, risktaking, sociability, and motivation in the L2 classroom. *Language Learning, 36*, 1–25.

Eysenck, H. J. (1959). *Maudsley personality inventory*. London: University of London.

Eysenck, H. J. (1970). *The structure of human personality* (3rd ed.). London: Methuen.

Eysenck, H. J. (1978). The development of personality and its relation to learning. In V. Sarris & S. Parducci (Eds.), *Perspectives in psychological experimentation: Towards the year 2000* (pp. 179–195). Hillsdale, NJ: Erlbaum.

Eysenck, H. J. (1990). *Maudsley personality inventory* (6th ed.). Tokyo: MPI Kenkyū-kai.

Faerch, C., & Kasper, G. (1987). *Introspection in second language research*. Clevedon, UK: Multilingual Matters.

Gardner, R. C. (1985). *Social psychology and second language learning*. Rowley, MA: Newbury House.

Gardner, R. C., & Lambert, W. E. (1972). *Attitudes and motivation in second-language learning*. Rowley, MA: Newbury House.

Gardner, R. C., & Smythe, P. C. (1981). On the development of the Attitude/Motivation Test Battery. *The Canadian Modern Language Review, 37*, 510–525.

Gardner, R. C., Smythe, P. C., Clément, R., & Gliksman, L. (1976). Second language acquisition: A social psychological perspective. *The Canadian Modern Language Review, 32*, 198–213.

Gliksman, L., Gardner, R. C., & Smythe, P. C. (1982). The role of the integrative motive on students' participation in the French classroom. *The Canadian Modern Language Review, 38*, 625–647.

Green, J. M., & Oxford, R. (1995). A closer look at learning strategies, L2 proficiency, and gender. *TESOL Quarterly, 29*, 261–297.

Guilford, J. P., & Yatabe, T. (1957). *Yatabe-Guilford personality inventory*. Osaka, Japan: Institute for Psychological Testing.

Horwitz, E. K. (1986). Preliminary evidence for the reliability and validity of a foreign language anxiety scale. *TESOL Quarterly, 20*, 559–562.

Horwitz, E. K., Horwitz, M. B., & Cope, J. (1986). Foreign language classroom anxiety. *Modern Language Journal, 70*, 125–132.

Hosenfeld, C. (1984). Case studies of ninth grade readers. In J. C. Alderson & A. H. Urquhart (Eds.), *Reading in a foreign language* (pp. 231–249). London: Longman.

Kleinmann, H. H. (1977). Avoidance behavior in adult second language acquisition. *Language Learning, 27*, 93–107.

Kurilesz, M. (1969). *Man and his world: A structured reader.* New York: Crowell.

Lalonde, R. N., & Gardner, R. C. (1984). Investigating a causal model of second language acquisition: Where does personality fit? *Canadian Journal of Behavioural Science, 16*, 224–237.

Leith, G. O. (1969). Learning and personality. In W. R. Dunn & C. Holroyd (Eds.), *Aspects of educational technology* (pp. 101–110). London: Methuen.

Leith, G. O., & Trown, E. A. (1970). The influence of personality and task conditions on learning and transfer. *Programmed Learning, 7*, 181–188.

Leith, G. O., & Wisdom, B. (1970). An investigation of the effects of error making and personality on learning. *Programmed Learning, 7*, 120–126.

LoCastro, V. (1994). Learning strategies and learning environments. *TESOL Quarterly, 28*, 409–414.

MacIntyre, P. D., & Gardner, R. C. (1989). Anxiety and second language learning: Toward a theoretical understanding. *Language Learning, 39*, 251–275.

MacIntyre, P. D., & Gardner, R. C. (1991). Methods and results in the study of anxiety and language learning: A review of the literature. *Language Learning, 41*, 85–117.

Michigan (1968). *Michigan placement test–Form H.* Ann Arbor, MI: University of Michigan.

Michigan (1977). *Michigan placement test–Technical manual.* Ann Arbor, MI: University of Michigan.

Muchnick, A. G., & Wolfe, D. E. (1982). Attitudes and motivation of American students of Spanish. *Canadian Modern Language Review, 38*, 262–281.

Naiman, N., Froehlich M., Stern, D., & Todesco, A. (1978). *The good language learner.* Toronto, Canada: Ontario Institute for Studies in Education.

O'Malley, J. M. (1987). The effects of training in the use of learning strategies on learning English as a second language. In A. Wenden & J. Rubin (Eds.), *Learner strategies in language learning* (pp. 133–144). Englewood Cliffs, NJ: Prentice-Hall.

O'Malley, J. M., & Chamot, A. U. (1990). *Learning strategies in second language acquisition.* Cambridge, UK: Cambridge University.

Oxford, R. (1989). Use of language learning strategies: A synthesis of studies with implications for strategy training. *System, 17*, 235–247.

Oxford, R. (1990). *Language learning strategies: What every teacher should know.* New York: Newbury House.

Oxford, R., & Nyikos, M. (1989). Variables affecting choice of language learning strategies by university students. *The Modern Language Journal, 73*, 291–300.

Pervin, L. A. (1989). *Personality, theory and research* (5th ed.). Toronto: John Wiley.

Politzer, R., & McGroarty, M. (1985). An exploratory study of learning behaviors and their relationship to gains in linguistic and communicative competence. *TESOL Quarterly, 19*, 103–123.

Robson, G. (1992). *Individual learner differences*. Unpublished manuscript, Temple University Japan, Tokyo.

Robson, G. (1994). *Relationships between personality, anxiety, proficiency, and participation*. Unpublished doctoral dissertation, Temple University Japan, Tokyo.

Rosenkjar, P. R. (1992). The use of strategies in task-based language production: Case study of a Japanese learner. In K. Yoshioka, B. Murdoch, J. Smith, & Y. Kato (Eds.), *Proceedings of the 4th conference on second language research in Japan* (pp. 79–93). Niigata, Japan: The International University of Japan.

Rossier, J. C. (1975). *Extraversion-introversion as a significant variable in the learning of English as a second language*. Unpublished doctoral dissertation, University of Southern California, Los Angeles.

Rubin, J. (1975). What the "good language learner" can teach us. *TESOL Quarterly, 9*, 41–51.

Rubin, J. (1981). Study of cognitive processes in second language learning. *Applied Linguistics, 11*, 110–131.

Sato, C. J. (1982). Ethnic styles in classroom discourse. In M. Hines & W. Rutherford (Eds.), *On TESOL '81* (pp. 11–34). Washington, DC: TESOL.

Shadbolt, D. R. (1978). Interactive relationships between measured personality and teaching strategy variables. *British Journal of Educational Psychology, 48*, 227–231.

Skehan, P. (1989). *Individual differences in second-language learning*. London: Edward Arnold.

Steinberg, F. A., & Horwitz, E. K. (1986). The effect of induced anxiety on the denotative and interpretive content of second language speech. *TESOL Quarterly, 20*, 131–136.

Stern, H. H. (1975). What can we learn from the good language learner? *The Canadian Modern Language Review, 31*, 304–318.

Strong, M. (1983). Social styles and the second language acquisition of Spanish-speaking kindergartners. *TESOL Quarterly, 17*, 241–258.

Tabachnick, B. G., & Fidell, L. S. (1989). *Using multivariate statistics* (2nd ed.). New York: Harper Collins.

Tanaka, Y. (1992). *Classroom participation and individual differences: An exploratory study*. Unpublished manuscript, Temple University Japan, Tokyo.

Vann, R. J., & Abraham, R. G. (1990). Strategies of unsuccessful language learners. *TESOL Quarterly, 24*, 177–198.

Vernon, P. (1953). *Personality tests and assessments*. London: Methuen.

Wenden, A. (1991). *Learner strategies for learner autonomy*. Englewood Cliffs, NJ: Prentice-Hall.

Zoltán Dörnyei
University of Nottingham
Richard Clément
University of Ottawa

MOTIVATIONAL CHARACTERISTICS OF LEARNING DIFFERENT TARGET LANGUAGES: RESULTS OF A NATIONWIDE SURVEY

Authors' note

Such a large-scale study could not have been carried out without the support and help of a number of organizations and individuals. We are particularly grateful to the Hungarian Scientific Research Foundation for providing the financial resources; to the Department of English Applied Linguistics, Eötvös University, Budapest, for providing a range of research facilities; and to Krisztina Kertész and Emese Nyilasi for their invaluable contribution as Research Assistants during the project.

Abstract

This study reports on the results of a large-scale attitude/motivation survey (N=4765) conducted in Hungary. The affective dispositions of school children aged 13–14 years old toward five different target languages (English, German, French, Italian, and Russian) were assessed, and the data were analyzed by means of a number of univariate and multivariate statistical procedures focusing on the underlying structure of the learners' motivation and the similarities/differences related to the different target languages. As well, variations linked to gender and to regional characteristics were examined. The emerging motivational components were also studied as they related to two criterion measures: the pupils' *language choice* for future language studies and the amount of *effort* they were planning to expend in learning the selected languages.

INTRODUCTION

Human motivation to learn is a complex phenomenon involving a number of diverse sources and conditions. Some of the motivational sources are situation-specific, that is, they are rooted in the student's immediate learning environment, whereas some others appear to be more stable and generalized, stemming from a succession of the student's past experiences in the social world (for recent overviews, see Dörnyei, 2000, 2001; Clément & Gardner, in press). This paper presents the results of a nationwide attitude/motivation survey carried out among 13- and 14-year-old teenagers in Hungary. The focus here was restricted to non-situation-specific motives for two reasons

1. Our study involved a substantial stratified national sample (with over 4,700 participants), and in order to obtain comparable measures we needed variables that were generalizable across various learning situations.

Dörnyei, Z., & Clément, R. (2001). Motivational characteristics of learning different target languages: Results of a nationwide survey. In Z. Dörnyei & R. Schmidt (Eds.), Motivation and second language acquisition (Technical Report #23, pp. 399–432). Honolulu: University of Hawai'i, Second Language Teaching and Curriculum Center.

2. One key aspect of our investigation concerned the participating students' *language choice* for future language studies after leaving primary school (which in Hungary took place at the time of the survey at the age of 14), and in this case —because the appraisal involves decision-making prior to actual engagement in the planned learning process— non-situation-specific motives are of particular importance.

Generalized (and usually socially grounded) motives that underlie the study of an L2 have been the subject of extensive research during the past decades. A number of different frameworks and models have been suggested to describe the multi-faceted nature of the L2 motivation construct, including Clément, Dörnyei and Noels (1994); Crookes and Schmidt (1991); Dörnyei (1994); Dörnyei and Ottó (1998); Gardner (1985); Schmidt, Boraie and Kassabgy (1996); Schumann (1998); Tremblay and Gardner (1995); Williams and Burden (1997). While these constructs have included some identical or very similar components, attesting to the existence of some broad, generalizable factors/dimensions that make up the motivational disposition of L2 learners, other constituents were specific to one or a few constructs only. In an attempt to identify the common dimensions, Dörnyei (1998) has presented a synthesis of 13 different constructs by tabulating the main motivational domains underlying them. It was found that almost all the motivational constituents of the selected models/frameworks could be classified into seven broad dimensions:

1. *Affective/integrative dimension*, referring to a general affective "core" of the L2 motivation complex related to attitudes, beliefs and values associated with the process, the target and the outcome of learning, including variables such as "integrativeness," "affective motive," "language attitudes," "intrinsic motivation," "attitudes toward L2 learning," "enjoyment" and "interest;"

2. *Instrumental/pragmatic dimension*, referring to extrinsic, largely utilitarian factors such as financial benefits;

3. *Macro-context-related dimension*, referring to broad, societal and sociocultural factors such as multicultural, intergroup and ethnolinguistic relations;

4. *Self-concept-related dimension*, referring to learner-specific variables such as self-confidence, self-esteem, anxiety and need for achievement;

5. *Goal-related dimension*, involving various goal characteristics;

6. *Educational context-related dimension*, referring to the characteristics and appraisal of the immediate learning environment (i.e., classroom) and the school context; and

7. *Significant others-related dimension*, referring to the motivational influence of parents, family, and friends.

Dörnyei concluded that the different L2 motivation models varied in the extent of emphasis they placed on each of the seven dimensions, in the actual ways they operationalized them, and in the way they linked the different factors to each other and to the general process of second language acquisition.

What causes the variation in the components of the different frameworks/models? Several reasons can be suggested. The observed differences can be the result of variation in

- the data gathering instruments and data processing techniques (in the case of empirical studies);

- the actual target language(s) studied;

- the particular language learning situations examined (e.g., the level and format of learning) and the characteristics of the learners (e.g., age, gender, and status);

- various aspects of the social milieu in which L2 learning took place (including social expectations and ethnolinguistic attitudes); and

- other geographical and geopolitical factors.

The systematic examination of these (and other) modifying factors has been an ongoing process in L2 motivation research; the current investigation sets out to contribute to this discussion in four ways.

COMPARING FIVE TARGET LANGUAGES

Most studies examining L2 motivation base their generalizations on the study of the motivational characteristics of one specific target language (typically English or French). Far fewer studies have compared the learning of different L2s (e.g., Clément & Kruidenier, 1983; Julkunen & Borzova, 1997; Laine, 1995; Tachibana, Matsukawa, & Zhong, 1996), and the vast majority of these comparative analyses have involved the study of different L2s in *different* learning communities (e.g., comparing Finns and Russians learning English in the Julkunen & Borzova study). Hardly any studies have focused on the motivational dispositions related to learning various L2s within the *same* community (for exceptions, see Clément & Kruidenier, 1983; Schmidt & Watanabe, this volume), even though it is only through such investigations that the learning population can be held constant and thus L2-related variation in the motivation construct can be reliably identified. Therefore, the question of to what extent motivational constructs generalized on the basis of studying one or two specific languages are valid is still a largely unresolved issue, particularly when comparing world languages (such as English), other major international languages traditionally taught in a particular region (such as Russian in Hungary), and less commonly taught languages (such as Italian). In the light of this hiatus, the first objective of our study is to compare L2-related attitudes/motivation associated with several target languages within the same speech community. For the purpose of our particular analysis, we have selected five languages:

- *English* and *German*, which are the dominant foreign languages in Hungary;

- *Russian*, which, for political reasons, was the compulsory first foreign language taught in Hungarian schools for four decades, until 1989;

- *French*, which has a long tradition in the country and, besides German, used to be the language of the Hungarian aristocracy;

- *Italian*, which, although usually associated with happy memories of summer holidays and a rich culture, is by no means viewed as a "world" or "international" language by Hungarians and can therefore be seen as a "control" with which to compare the other languages.

GENDER-BASED VARIATION

Recording gender differences in language attitudinal/motivational data has got a long history; studies have again and again evidenced that male and female learners show systematic difference in their disposition toward language studies (e.g., Burstall, Jamieson, Cohen, & Hargreaves, 1974; Clark & Trafford, 1995; Djigunović, 1993; Julkunen, 1994; Ludwig, 1983). However, the amount of systematic gender-specific research has been meager relative to the potential importance of the issue, which may be partly due to the fact that sample sizes often did not allow for confident gender-based generalizations. Because our sample is representative of the total population of a national speech community, it is particularly appropriate for the purpose of examining the motivational characteristics of the boys and the girls, and the multi-language design of the study allows us to investigate any gender-based biases toward the five target languages.

THE IMPORTANCE OF THE VARIOUS MOTIVATIONAL CLUSTERS

A particular strength of survey studies (such as ours) in general is their effectiveness in assessing a wide range of relevant variables, which can then be processed by means of various statistical procedures to distill broader underlying dimensions. This has been a standard procedure in L2 motivation research, going back to Gardner and Lambert's (1959) pioneering factor analytical study of L2 learners in Montreal. Dovetailing with the issue of the underlying structure is that of the procedural outcome of that structure. In the context of this study, students are presented with multiple potential L2s. Language choice and degree of involvement are not only questions with immediate pedagogical consequences but also decisions which risk altering the linguistic profile of the nation. In order to address this issue, we have included in our survey two criterion measures, *language choice* (i.e., the selection of certain L2s that the participants wished to study in the future) and *intended effort* (i.e., the amount of effort that the participants were planning to exert in their future language studies). Determining the extent of association between these criterion variables and the identified motivational dimensions can provide information about the relative importance of the various factors, which is the third objective of the study.

GEOGRAPHICAL VARIATION

It has been one of the main assumptions underlying L2 motivation research during the past four decades that the social milieu in which language learning takes place exerts a profound influence on L2 motivation; accordingly, there have been several studies investigating the motivational impact of macro-contextual variation (e.g., differences between foreign language learning and second language acquisition contexts, or between multicultural contexts characterized by different ethnolinguistic setup) (for reviews, see Clément & Gardner, in press; Dörnyei, in press; Gardner, 1985; Gardner & MacIntyre, 1993). An interesting question that has not been studied extensively before is whether the geographical location within a relatively homogeneous community has a motivational impact.

Although Hungary, the site of our survey, is a relatively small country, with the greatest distance within the country not exceeding 320 miles, it is located in a special position within Europe, along the latent borderline separating Eastern and Western Europe. This borderline has been in evidence for the past 2000 years, with the Roman Empire having its eastern border in Hungary, the Turkish Empire having its western border in Hungary, the Habsburg Empire having its eastern border in Hungary, and recently the Soviet Union having its western border (the "Iron Curtain") in Hungary. The country also lies at the dividing line between Western Christianity and Eastern (Orthodox) Christianity, which reflects the country's position being halfway between Rome and Byzantium (Istanbul), the two religious centers that determined Christian orientation in the early middle ages.

A further peculiarity of Hungary's geographical position is that the latent geopolitical/cultural border between Eastern and Western Europe appears to cut *through* the country, along the River Danube, which divides Hungary into two roughly equal parts. This dividing line can be acutely felt in the country even today: while the east of the country is largely rural, "traditional," and relatively poor, the west of the country (adjacent to Austria) is far more developed and westernized. The capital of Hungary, Budapest, situated along the Danube in the center of the country, is a modern metropolis, forming a "country within the country" with a quarter of the total population living there. It is by far the most developed area in the country, constituting the undisputed economic and cultural center. In view of these geopolitical considerations, the fourth objective of our study was to examine whether the marked regional division was reflected in the learners' L2-related affective dispositions as well. In order to answer this question, we have systematically sampled learners from different parts of Hungary, and also coded the type of the dwelling (i.e., village, town, or city) the data were collected in.

METHOD

PARTICIPANTS

The participants of the survey were 4,765 (2,377 males; 2,305 females; 83 with missing gender data) eighth grade primary school pupils (ages 13–14) living in various parts of Hungary (see Table 1). This population fitted the investigation best, because at the time of the survey this was the most mature age group in the Hungarian educational system which studied within a more or less homogenous curricular and organizational framework (i.e., the national primary school system). Therefore, by sampling students from this cohort, we did not need to be concerned with the modifying influences of various specialized secondary school types. At the same time, these learners were in the final year of their primary school studies and were just about to make the decision about which type of secondary education to choose for their further studies and which foreign language they wished to study during the consecutive years. This lent particular relevance and validity to our question concerning language choice.

Table 1: The sample investigated in the survey

| | number of | | | | |
| | schools | classes | pupils[a] | | |
			total	boys	girls
whole country	77	212	4765	2377	2305
capital	15	38	792	406	372
city	13	45	1083	538	514
town	32	94	2128	1048	1052
village	17	35	762	385	366

[a] Some questionnaires had missing gender data.

INSTRUMENTS

When designing the questionnaire we had to achieve a trade-off: On the one hand, L2 motivation is known to be a complex, multi-dimensional construct, and therefore in order to obtain a comprehensive motivation measure one needs to administer a rather elaborate (and therefore long) instrument with every variable assessed by multi-item scales. On the other hand, the practical constraints inherent to the survey (namely, that in order to get permission to administer the questionnaire in over 70 schools across the country we had to make sure that we disrupted the course of teaching as little as possible) imposed a significant limitation to the time we could have access to the students. Rather than narrowing down the scope of the instrument, we decided to cut down on the number of items focusing on each variable. In order to ensure that the instrument had appropriate psychometric properties, the items we used were adopted from established motivation questionnaires (some of which had been specifically developed to be used in Hungary), with sufficient validity and reliability coefficients (e.g., Clément et al., 1994; Dörnyei, 1990; Gardner, 1985).

The final version of the questionnaire used in the survey (see Appendix A) consisted of 37 items, assessing various student attitudes toward five target languages (English, German, French, Italian, and Russian) and toward six L2 communities (the United States, the United Kingdom, Germany, France, Italy, and Russia), and also asking about various aspects of the students' language learning environment and background. Because 21 of the 37 items focused on more than one L2 or L2 community (in a grid format), even this relatively short instrument yielded a total of 139 variables.

The main variable groups in the questionnaire were as follows (with the total number of items and the actual item numbers given in parentheses):

Items concerning the five target languages (5-point rating scales)

- *Orientations*, that is, the students' various reasons for learning a given language (5 items: Nos. 2, 4, 6, 7, & 10)
- *Attitudes toward the L2* (2 items: Nos. 1 & 3)
- *Intended effort*, that is, the amount of effort the student was willing to put into learning the given language (1 item: No. 5)
- *Parents' language proficiency* (2 items: Nos. 8 & 9)

Items concerning the six target language communities (5-point rating scales)

- *Attitudes toward the L2 community* that is, the extent to which students felt positively toward the particular countries and its citizens (2 items: Nos. 11 & 17), and the international importance they attached to these communities (2 items: Nos. 12 & 13). Britain and the US were mentioned separately to explore differences in the evaluations of the two communities, in spite of their common language (referred to in this study where relevant as English/UK and English/US).
- *Contact with the L2 and its speakers*; both the quantity (2 items: Nos. 18 & 20) and the quality (5 items: Nos. 14, 15, 16, 19, & 21) of the contact (e.g., watching L2 TV programs, meeting tourists) were assessed.

Non-language-specific Likert scales (5-point scales)

- *Attitudes toward L2 learning at school* (1 item: No. 25)
- *Contact with foreign languages* through watching satellite TV (1 item: No. 26)

- *Fear of assimilation*, that is, the extent to which students believed that learning and using the foreign language might lead to the loss of the native language and culture (1 item: No. 28)

- *Self-confidence* in L2 learning and use (3 items: Nos. 22, 23, & 29)

- *Language learning milieu*, that is, the extent of the parents' support (1 items: No. 27) and the friends' attitudes toward L2 learning (1 item: No. 24)

Background questions (open-ended and multiple-choice items)

- *Language choice*: Students were asked to name three languages they were intending to learn in the next school year (1 item: No. 30)

- *Personal variables*, such as the student's gender and language learning background (7 items: Nos. 31–37)

DATA COLLECTION AND ANALYSIS

Data collection was conducted by a research team consisting of the two principal researchers (Zoltán Dörnyei and Richard Clément), two graduate student research assistants (Krisztina Kertész and Emese Nyilasi), and a number of paid workers who helped to administer and to code the questionnaires (mostly recruited from English majors at Eötvös University, Budapest). First we approached the selected schools by an official letter from Eötvös University, Budapest (which hosted the project), providing information about the purpose of the survey and details of the actual administration of the questionnaires. Once permission was granted by the Principal of a school, we contacted the form-masters of the selected classes individually, asking for their cooperation. The questionnaires were filled in during class time (but not during language classes so as to avoid the students being influenced by the situation). A representative of the university was always present at the administration, providing the introduction and overseeing the procedure. Answering the questions took the students approximately 20 minutes on average.

The data obtained were computer-coded and negatively worded items were recoded positively. Following Gardner's (1985, pp. 78–79) recommendation, in order to form unitary groups from heterogeneous sources (as was the case in our study with students sampled from different schools and classes), before conducting any correlation-based analyses we computed standard scores within each class and used these rather than the raw scores in the computations (however, for the purpose of comparing subsample means —through ANOVA— we used the raw scores). Where the classes were not large enough (i.e., did not have more than 25 students), pooled data within the particular school with more parallel classes were standardized.

RESULTS

MAIN ATTITUDINAL/MOTIVATIONAL DIMENSIONS
(ANALYSIS OF ITEMS 1–21)

In order to reduce the number of variables in the student questionnaire by identifying broader underlying dimensions, we submitted the attitude items concerning the L2s and L2 communities to factor analyses (separate analyses were conducted for each language). A maximum likelihood extraction method was applied and, because the factors were assumed to be intercorrelated, we used subsequent oblique rotation. As is well known, it is not always an unambiguous task to decide how many factors should be extracted in factor analysis. The final solutions were arrived at after applying Cattell's (1966) scree test and making sure that the factor matrix had a "simple structure" (i.e., each variable had salient loadings only on one factor without any cross-loadings). The high ratio of cases to variables (approximately 300:1) ensured the stability of the solutions.

The final pattern matrices obtained in the factor analyses met our requirements and contained relatively easily interpretable clusters of variables determining each factor. A five-factor solution appeared to explain our data adequately in the case of all the target languages. The emerging factors in the different solutions were similar, though not identical. Table 2 presents a summary of the variable clusters for each factor for each L2 (the actual factor pattern matrices are included in Appendix B). In the table, we referred to the variables by short labels (and because the item numbers may be more useful for quick visual comparisons of factor contents, these are also listed); the complete list of questionnaire items are included in Appendix A.

English and German. As can be seen in Table 2, the factor matrices for English and German are very similar, the only real differences found in the matrix concerning English/US, which can be attributed to the fact that the mean scores for some US-related items were so high that the resulting insufficient variance depressed some of the correlations underlying the analysis. Looking at the English/UK and German matrices, Factor 1 is associated with Items 14, 17, and 11. These all concern direct contact with members of the L2 community, and therefore this factor is labeled *Direct contact with L2 speakers.*

Factor 2 has received salient loadings from four items (3, 2, 6, & 7). They are all associated with the pragmatic, instrumental values of knowing a world language and will therefore be labeled *Instrumentality.*

Factor 3 shows salient loadings from two variables (12 & 13), both concerning the perceived importance and wealth of the L2 communities; accordingly, this factor will be referred to as *Vitality of L2 community.*

Table 2: Results of the factor analyses of the attitudinal items:
Variable clusters determining each factor for each target language
(for the actual factor matrices, see Appendix A)

	factor 1	factor 2	factor 3	factor 4	factor 5
English (US)	12 country: developed	10 similar to L2 speakers 4 get to know culture 1 like L2	3 L2 important in world 2 become knowledgeable 6 useful for travel 7 useful for career 13 country: important	16 like TV programs 15 like films 19 like magazines 21 like pop music	14 meet L2 speakers 17 like L2 speakers 11 travel to country
English (UK)	14 meet L2 speakers 17 like L2 speakers (11 travel to country)	3 L2 important in world 2 become knowledgeable 6 useful for travel 7 useful for career	12 country: developed 13 country: important	16 like TV programs 15 like films 19 like magazines 21 like pop music	10 similar to L2 speakers 4 get to know culture 1 like L2
German	14 meet L2 speakers 17 like L2 speakers 11 travel to country	3 L2 important in world 6 useful for travel 2 become knowledgeable 7 useful for career	12 country: developed 13 country: important	15 like films 16 like TV programs 21 like pop music 19 like magazines	10 similar to L2 speakers 1 like L2 4 get to know culture
French	14 meet L2 speakers 1 like L2 17 like L2 speakers 10 similar to L2 speakers 11 travel to country 4 get to know culture (19 like magazines)	2 become knowledgeable 3 L2 important in world	16 like TV programs 15 like films 21 like pop music	12 country: developed 13 country: important	6 useful for travel 7 useful for career
Italian	14 meet L2 speakers 17 like L2 speakers 1 like L2 10 similar to L2 speakers 11 travel to country 4 get to know culture	2 become knowledgeable 3 L2 important in world	12 country: developed 13 country: important	16 like TV programs 15 like films 21 like pop music (19 like magazines)	6 useful for travel 7 useful for career
Russian	10 similar to L2 speakers 7 useful for career 1 like L2 4 get to know culture	16 like TV programs 15 like films 21 like pop music 19 like magazines	14 meet L2 speakers 17 like L2 speakers 11 travel to country	12 country: developed 13 country: important	3 L2 important in world 2 become knowledgeable 6 useful for travel

The four items loading onto Factor 4 (15, 16, 21, & 19) all have to do with the appreciation of cultural products (films, TV programs, magazines, and pop music) associated with the particular L2. These cultural products are conveyed through the media and therefore this factor will be termed *Media usage*.

The last factor, Factor 5, has salient loadings from three items,. 10, 1, and 4. These concern a general positive outlook on the L2 and its culture, to the extent that learners scoring high on this factor would like to become similar to the L2 speakers. Because of the strong resemblance with *Integrativeness* in Gardner's (1985) motivation theory, this factor will be labeled accordingly.

French and Italian. Two of the factors in the matrices obtained for French and Italian (Media Usage and Vitality of L2 Community) are similar to the corresponding factors for English and German, the only difference being that the media factor does not receive salient loading from "magazines," most probably because French and Italian magazines are not widely accessible in Hungary. With respect to the other three factors, an interesting variation can be observed. Integrativeness and Direct Contact with L2 Speakers merge into one factor and Instrumentality splits into two factors. The former change may be related to the fact that the number of French and Italian visitors coming to Hungary is very low compared to the other language communities, and therefore direct contact with them takes place primarily when visiting France and Italy, which have been traditional tourist targets for Hungarians. Therefore, the positive outlook on the community (as reflected by Integrativeness) is very closely associated with qualitative aspects of the time spent in these countries (as reflected by Direct Contact).

The split of Instrumentality into two constituents (determined by Items 2 & 3, and 6 & 7, respectively) reflects the specific nature of French and Italian. The first subcluster concerns the importance of these languages in the world and the contribution their proficiency makes to being an educated person. The second is related to the pragmatic values associated with competence in these languages. For English and German, the two subclusters formed one unified cluster, indicating that, for Hungarian learners, these languages represent at the same time rich cultural heritage as well as pragmatic values stemming from their being seen as world languages. In contrast, although Italian and French are associated with definite cultural values, they are not considered of primary importance for instrumental purposes, which resulted in the separation of the two subclusters.

Russian. The factor matrix obtained for Russian is similar to the ones describing English and German in every main respect except for one, but this difference is quite interesting. Item 7, concerning the capacity of the L2 in furthering one's career, is not associated with Instrumentality but with Integrativeness. This is likely to have a historical explanation: After the dramatic political changes in Eastern and Central Europe at the end of the 1980's, Hungary consciously opened up toward the western world, thereby replacing the traditional Russian orientation of the Communist times. Consequently, even though the knowledge of Russian has without any doubt major pragmatic potential in the region, only those learners are willing to recognize this who do not have a negative integrative predisposition toward the language.

Summary of factor analysis of language-related items. In terms of their underlying attitudinal/motivational structure, the five languages investigated in our study can be divided into three groups: (a) English and German, the two dominant international languages in the Central European region; (b) French and Italian, which are two important languages associated with a lively culture and rich historical heritage, but without playing the role of lingua francas; and (3) Russian, which functions like an "ex-colonial" language, with political and experiential considerations tainting the learners' perceptions.

We must, on the other hand, also notice that the differences are not very big, particularly in view of the fact that the all the factors —including the ones that display marked differences— show strong intercorrelations (e.g., in the case of French and Italian, the correlation between the two subclusters of *Instrumentality* is .59 and .61, respectively, whereas in the case of Russian, the correlation between Instrumentality and Integrativeness is .61).

Thus, we may conclude that Hungarian teenage language learners appraise different target languages through the same mental framework or schema, in terms of five broad and interrelated dimensions: Integrativeness, Instrumentality, Direct contact, Media usage (or "indirect contact") and Vitality. The boundaries between these dimensions are not rigid and, depending on the perceived ethnolinguistic significance of a particular L2, there can be overlaps between them.

FACTOR ANALYSIS OF THE NON-L2 SPECIFIC LIKERT-TYPE ITEMS

The student questionnaire contained eight items (22–29) which concerned the learners' generalized perceptions related to their milieu and linguistic self-confidence that were not linked to particular languages. To these we added the mean of the variables concerning the language proficiency of the learners' parents across the five languages (items 8 & 9) and conducted a factor analysis similar to the ones performed for the L2-specific items. The factor matrix in Table 3 presents a simple, two-factor solution. Factor 1 has salient loadings from items related to the general appreciation of foreign languages in the learners' immediate environment, like the school context and friends' and parents' views. This factor is labeled therefore *Milieu*. The items loading on Factor 2 are in accordance with Clément's (1980) conceptualization of Linguistic Self-confidence, and therefore this factor will be termed accordingly.

Table 3: Factor analysis of the non-language-specific Likert-type items: Maximum likelihood extraction, oblique rotation, pattern matrix*

	factor 1	factor 2
I don't think that foreign languages are important school subjects.	.65	
My parents do not consider foreign languages important school subjects.	.62	
People around me tend to think that it is a good thing to know foreign languages.	−.43	
Learning foreign languages makes me fear that I will feel less Hungarian because of it.	.35	
I think I am the type who would feel anxious and ill at ease if I had to speak to someone in a foreign language.		.47
Learning a foreign language is a difficult task.		.42
I am sure I will be able to learn a foreign language well.	−.30	−.34
Parents' mean language proficiency		

* loadings under .3 not shown

There are two interesting points concerning the factor matrix that are worth mentioning: (a) the lack or any appreciable loadings by the parents' mean L2 proficiency on either of the factors and (b) the crossloading by the variable concerning the learner's certainty about being able to learn a L2 well. In the first case, it is possible that the participants' perception of their parents' L2 competence was not reliable enough. Alternatively, the parents' proficiency may not directly be related to the milieu factor (where it was expected to belong) but is mediated by the parent's socializing behavior — in which case this indirect relationship would not show up in this analysis. Regarding the second point, the confidence item appeared to capture the communality between the two factors (which is also confirmed by the two factors' intercorrelation of .25). It would appear that both the milieu and personal confidence are related in the student's self-assurance in being able to learn a second language.

COMPUTING COMPOSITE MOTIVATIONAL VARIABLES

The factor matrices (and the subsequent discussion above) have highlighted seven broad dimensions underlying the learners' L2-related appraisals. In order to be able to use these factors in further analyses, we have computed composite factor scores for them by summing up the item scores related to each dimension. Table 4 presents the seven scales, the list of the variables they are made up of, descriptive statistics for each scale, and the Cronbach alpha internal consistency reliability coefficient for each scale. The table also contains t-test statistics comparing the boys' and the girls' scores. The mean reliability coefficient of the scales is .67, which is acceptable with such relatively short scales.

Table 4: Descriptive information about the seven main motivational dimensions, and t-test statistics comparing boys' and girls' scores

scale	question items	$\bar{x}$	SD	Cronbach alpha	$\bar{x}$ (boys)	$\bar{x}$ (girls)	t-value
Direct contact with L2 speakers	11, 14, 17						
English (US)		4.49	.67	.67	4.42	4.56	−7.33***
English (UK)		4.20	.76	.70	4.10	4.31	−9.69***
German		3.97	.86	.74	3.96	4.00	−1.56
French		3.97	.85	.72	3.77	4.17	−16.64***
Italian		4.01	.85	.73	3.83	4.19	−17.74***
Russian		2.42	1.02	.77	2.34	2.50	−5.48***
Instrumentality	2, 3, 6, 7						
English		4.65	.55	.73	4.61	4.70	−6.27***
German		4.41	.63	.75	4.37	4.46	−4.97***
French		3.58	.77	.73	3.48	3.68	−8.76***
Italian		3.19	.86	.77	3.07	3.31	−9.47***
Russian		2.52	1.00	.81	2.46	2.58	−4.12***
Integrativeness	1, 4, 10						
English		4.20	.80	.66	4.07	4.33	−11.32***
German		3.67	.94	.72	3.66	3.70	−1.52
French		3.39	.93	.70	3.12	3.67	−21.17***
Italian		3.32	1.00	.73	3.06	3.58	−18.18***
Russian		2.04	.86	.66	1.98	2.10	−4.79***
Vitality of L2 community	12, 13						
English (US)		4.84	.40	.56	4.86	4.83	3.09**
English (UK)		4.28	.62	.59	4.28	4.29	−.73
German		4.19	.62	.60	4.20	4.18	1.00
French		3.95	.62	.54	3.90	4.00	−5.13***
Italian		3.49	.70	.61	3.41	3.57	−8.09***
Russian		2.81	.85	.41	2.87	2.76	4.49***
Cultural interest	15, 16, 19, 21						
English (US)		4.56	.59	.66	4.52	4.61	−5.53***
English (UK)		3.90	.79	.70	3.79	4.02	−9.93***
German		3.74	.79	.67	3.72	3.77	−2.03*
French		3.42	.90	.68	3.28	3.57	−10.89***

Italian		3.44	.93	.71	3.30	3.58	−10.24***
Russian		1.74	.79	.78	1.70	1.77	−2.80**
Milieu	24, 25, 27, 28	4.43	.70	.61	4.31	4.56	−12.24***
Linguistic self-confidence	22, 23, 29	3.32	.75	.41	3.28	3.36	−3.83***

*=p<.05; **=p<.01; ***=p<.001

As we can see, all the variables show a very consistent rank order across the various languages, with English obtaining the top and Russian the bottom scores. English is indeed a very popular language in Hungary, with every aspect of it highly appraised, with an average rating of 4.39 on a 5-point scale. Interestingly, even though the dominant English variety in Hungary has traditionally been British English, in the items where the UK and the US have been separated, US-based attitudes are always higher (so that if we ignore the UK-based scores, the average rating is as high as 4.55!).

German appears to be still widely endorsed among Hungarian teenagers, although the distribution of ratings here shows an imbalance toward the instrumental aspects, reflecting the importance of German economic influence in the region. With respect to French, the third language in the rank scale, the figures in the Table indicate that its international importance is not recognized fully by the respondents. This is reflected by the facts that it is rated significantly lower than German (a mean of 3.66 vs. 4.00) and that the appraisal of Italian not only approaches the average French ratings (3.49 vs. 3.66), but in two scales (Cultural Interest and Direct Contact with L2 Speakers) actually exceeds them. Finally, the ratings of Russian are very low: Even the strongest aspect, its vitality, failed to reach 3.00 and the average rating across the dimensions was only 2.31, reflecting a general dislike.

GENDER DIFFERENCES

The gender-based results in Table 4 confirm the frequent observation in the motivation literature that there is a tendency for girls' scores to be significantly higher than boys'. Out of the 30 variables included in the table, this tendency is true for 24, with the mean differences sometimes exceeding .50. The only exceptions concern three of the five German-specific scales where the differences are not statistically significant, and the Vitality of L2 Community scale with regard to the Americans and the Russians, where the boys' scores are higher than the girls' (and with English/UK not reaching statistical significance). With every motivational dimension, the biggest gender differences in favor of girls occur with French and Italian.

Looking at the language choice measures in Table 5, we find certain gender-preferences: English appears to be gender-neutral, French and Italian tend to be preferred by females, whereas German and Russian can be seen preferred by males.

LANGUAGE CHOICE

Table 5 presents the foreign languages the students intended to learn in order of popularity. The scores were obtained the following way: If a language was marked as the student's first choice, it was assigned 3 points, if it was the second choice, 2 points, and if it was the third choice, 1 point. Non-ranked languages received a score of 0. The table confirms the rank order of the five target languages included in the survey presented in Table 4. English is indisputably the most popular foreign language among Hungarian primary school pupils. It is preferred to German, although proficiency in the latter language is still regarded as generally desirable. We find again that French does not have much general appeal in Hungary. Although it is the third most popular language, the fact that it is basically in the same preference range as Italian shows that Hungarian school children do not see its world significance. Although Russian is little endorsed relative to its historical significance, it has not completely lost its importance: it still precedes Spanish and Latin amongst others.

Table 5: Composite language choice measures for every L2 mentioned by the pupils and t-test statistics comparing boys' and girls' scores with regard to the five target languages in the survey

| language | score | $\bar{x}$ | | | t-value |
		total	boys	girls	
English	11352	2.39	2.39	2.39	.15
German	8466	1.78	1.94	1.62	10.49**
French	3921	.82	.70	.97	−10.93**
Italian	2485	.52	.41	.64	−9.33**
Russian	684	.14	.16	.12	2.85*
Spanish	369				
Latin	229				
Japanese	94				
Chinese	40				
Portuguese	21				
Dutch	17				
Greek	15				
Arabic	9				
Romanian	9				
Swedish	7				
Norwegian	5				
Esperanto	4				
Finnish	4				
Tibetan	4				

Turkish	4
Hindi	2
Hebrew	2
Polish	1

*=p<.01; **=p<.001

THE RELATIONSHIP BETWEEN THE MOTIVATIONAL SCALES AND LANGUAGE CHOICE

In order to evaluate the potency of the obtained motivational factors, let us now examine how they are related to the learners' language choice. Table 6 presents correlations between the seven motivational scales and the language choice measure for each of the six target language communities investigated. Three motivational dimensions show substantial positive correlations with language choice across all the six L2 communities: Integrativeness, Instrumentality, and Direct Contact with L2 Speakers. The table also presents multiple correlation coefficients between all the motivational scales and language choice. Except for Russian, the coefficients are fairly high, explaining between 19–24% of the variance. A closer look at these coefficients, however, reveals an intriguing phenomenon: the multiple correlation coefficients are only marginally higher than the correlations obtained with integrativeness alone. This would suggest that integrativeness represents a certain "core" of the learners' attitudinal/motivational disposition, subsuming, or mediating most other variables.

Table 6: Correlations between the attitudinal/motivational scales and language choice, computed for each target language community

Motivational scales	English (UK)	English (US)	German	French	Italian	Russian
Direct contact with L2 speakers	.23*	.17*	.33*	.31*	.32*	.12*
Instrumentality	.28*		.30*	.27*	.29*	.20*
Integrativeness	.43*		.47*	.42*	.43*	.25*
Vitality of the community	.12*	.12*	.11*	.13*	.16*	.07*
Cultural interest	.14*	.12*	.20*	.20*	.26*	.12*
Milieu	.12*		.01	.03	.01	−.05*
Linguistic self-confidence	.07*		−.00	.03	−.01	−.02
Multiple correlations	**.44***	**.44***	**.49***	**.44***	**.45***	**.27***

*=p<.001

In order to verify this claim, we have carried out a multiple regression analysis in which the seven motivational scales were entered as a block to predict language choice, the dependent variable, for each of the five languages (Table 7). As could be expected, all the equations were significant, and the results confirm the correlational findings, namely that Integrativeness is by far the most important predictor of language choice.

Table 7: Regression analysis of the motivational scales
with language choice as the dependent variable

Language choice	standardised beta	t	sig.	correlation		
				zero-ord.	partial	part
Direct contact with L2 speakers						
English (US)	−.01	−.84	.402	.17	−.01	−.01
English (UK)	.05	2.76	.006	.23	.04	.04
German	.10	5.90	.000	.33	.09	.08
French	.10	5.35	.000	.31	.08	.07
Italian	.08	4.29	.000	.32	.06	.06
Russian	−.04	−1.81	.070	.20	.07	.07
Instrumentality						
English	−.08	4.77	.000	.28	.07	.06
German	.08	5.08	.000	.30	.07	.06
French	.05	3.31	.001	.27	.05	.04
Italian	.03	1.90	.058	.29	.03	.03
Russian	.09	4.55	.000	.20	.07	.07
Integrativeness						
English	.39	22.83	.000	.43	.32	.30
German	.40	24.10	.000	.47	.33	.31
French	.35	19.47	.000	.42	.28	.26
Italian	.36	19.14	.000	.43	.27	.15
Russian	.21	10.69	.000	.25	.16	.16
Vitality of L2 community						
English (US)	.03	1.80	.072	.12	.03	.02
English (UK)	−.01	−.82	.411	.12	−.01	−.01
German	−.03	−2.41	.016	.11	−.04	−.03
French	−.01	−.74	.461	.13	−.01	−.01
Italian	−.02	−1.32	.188	.16	−.02	−.02
Russian	−.01	−.76	.449	.07	−.01	−.01

Media usage						
English (US)	−.02	−1.20	.230	.12	−.02	−.02
English (UK)	−.02	−.91	.363	.14	−.01	−.01
German	−.01	−.70	.481	.20	−.01	−.01
French	.01	.83	.000	.20	.01	.01
Italian	−.06	3.94	.000	.26	.06	.05
Russian	.03	1.86	.063	.12	.03	.03
Milieu						
English	−.02	−1.10	.270	.12	−.02	−.02
German	−.06	−4.44	.000	.01	−.07	−.06
French	−.07	−4.85	.000	−.03	−.07	−.06
Italian	−.05	−3.44	.001	.01	−.05	−.05
Russian	−.06	−4.13	.000	−.05	−.06	−.06
Linguistic self-confidence						
English	−.02	−1.38	.168	.07	−.02	−.02
German	−.06	−4.51	.000	−.00	−.07	−.06
French	−.01	−.77	.442	.03	−.01	−.01
Italian	−.05	−3.58	.000	.01	−.05	−.05
Russian	−.02	−1.04	.300	−.02	−.02	−.02

THE RELATIONSHIP BETWEEN THE MOTIVATIONAL SCALES AND INTENDED EFFORT

Table 8 presents the correlations between the seven motivational scales and intended effort. The coefficients in the table are generally higher than the ones in Table 6, which is partly due to the fact that "intended effort" was assessed in the same format as the independent variables. Again, Integrativeness, Instrumentality and Direct Contact with L2 Speakers show stronger associations with the criterion measure than the other scales, and again Integrativeness explains nearly as much variance as the multiple correlation coefficients. To illustrate the magnitude of the latter coefficients, they explain around half of the variance in intended effort, which is quite remarkable.

Table 8: Correlations between the attitudinal/motivational scales and intended effort, computed for each target language community*

Motivational scales	English (UK)	English (US)	German	French	Italian	Russian
Direct contact with L2 speakers	.38	.30	.46	.50	.51	.45
Instrumentality		.50	.49	.51	.54	.57

continued...

Table 8: Correlations between the attitudinal/motivational scales and intended effort, computed for each target language community* (cont.)

Motivational scales	English (UK)	English (US)	German	French	Italian	Russian
Integrativeness		.63	.66	.70	.71	.64
Vitality of L2 community	.23	.23	.22	.25	.27	.24
Cultural interest	.26	.25	.31	.32	.35	.30
Milieu		.29	.18	.17	.13	.07
Linguistic self-confidence		.26	.19	.17	.14	.08
Multiple correlation	.68	.68	.69	.72	.73	.68

* all the correlation coefficients are significant at the $p<.001$ level

We have conducted a multiple regression analysis (Table 9) in a similar way to the one presented in Table 7, and it confirmed that Integrativeness was the major predictor of intended effort. In this equation, however, there was also a second scale which played a significant (although far smaller) role: Instrumentality.

Table 9: Regression analysis of the motivational scales with intended effort as the dependent variable

Language choice	standardised beta	t	sig.	correlation		
				zero-ord.	partial	part
Direct contact with L2 speakers						
English (US)	.01	.50	.620	.30	.01	.01
English (UK)	.06	3.94	.000	.38	.06	.04
German	.08	5.77	.000	.46	.08	.06
French	.11	7.75	.000	.50	.11	.08
Italian	.11	8.04	.000	.51	.12	.08
Russian	.10	6.32	.000	.45	.10	.07
Instrumentality						
English	.19	14.12	.000	.50	.20	.15
German	.16	12.13	.000	.49	.17	.13
French	.17	13.81	.000	.51	.20	.14
Italian	.17	13.23	.000	.54	.19	.13
Russian	.26	17.26	.000	.57	.25	.19

Integrativeness						
English	.46	33.06	.000	.63	.44	.36
German	.51	36.91	.000	.66	.47	.39
French	.53	38.17	.000	.70	.49	.39
Italian	.54	37.79	.000	.71	.49	.38
Russian	.42	27.44	.000	.64	.38	.30
Vitality of L2 community						
English (US)	.04	3.19	.001	.23	.05	.03
English (UK)	−.01	−.54	.590	.23	−.01	−.01
German	−.00	−.27	.791	.22	−.00	−.00
French	−.01	−.45	.656	.25	−.01	−.01
Italian	−.02	−2.07	.039	.27	−.03	−.02
Russian	−.03	−2.53	.011	.24	−.04	−.03
Media usage						
English (US)	.01	.51	.612	.25	.01	.01
English (UK)	.00	.33	.743	.26	.01	.00
German	.01	1.10	.272	.31	.02	.01
French	.01	1.15	.249	.32	.02	.01
Italian	.01	.42	.676	.35	.01	.00
Russian	.04	2.82	.005	.30	.04	.03
Milieu						
English	.05	4.38	.000	.29	.06	.05
German	.04	3.34	.001	.18	.05	.04
French	.00	.38	.705	.17	.01	.00
Italian	.02	1.60	.110	.13	.02	.02
Russian	−.00	−.34	.735	.07	−.01	−.00
Linguistic self-confidence						
English	.11	9.79	.000	.26	.14	.11
German	.08	7.03	.000	.19	.10	.07
French	.08	7.24	.000	.17	.11	.07
Italian	.06	5.39	.000	.14	.08	.05
Russian	.04	3.65	.000	.08	.06	.04

These findings, together with the results obtained with language choice being the dependent variable, unambiguously confirm Gardner's (1985; this volume) repeated claim that the integrative motive plays a significant role in shaping L2 motivation.

GEOGRAPHICAL VARIATION IN THE LEARNERS' LANGUAGE ATTITUDES AND LANGUAGE CHOICE

As explained in the Introduction, participants in our study were systematically sampled from various regions in Hungary. We also argued that the country displays a historical capital/east/west division. In order to investigate the extent to which this regional division is reflected in the students' L2 attitudes, we have conducted analyses of variance of the two most important motivational scales, Integrativeness and Instrumentality, as well as the main criterion measure, Language Choice, according to a combined measure of regions and dwelling types (i.e., contrasting students from, say, an eastern village and a western city). Tables 10–12 present the results.

Table 10: Analysis of variance of *Integrativeness* across regions and dwelling types

	English	German	French	Italian	Russian
1. capital	4.22	3.81	3.29	3.49	2.14
2. Western town	4.15	3.78	3.34	3.27	1.86
3. Western village	4.11	3.65	3.35	3.19	1.98
4. Eastern town	4.24	3.62	3.43	3.26	2.08
5. Eastern village	4.20	3.67	3.48	3.23	2.22
F	3.316*	18.807***	4.29**	9.538***	20.319***
post-hoc comparison[a]: LSD (Least Significant Difference)	4, 1, 5	1	5, 4, 3, 2	1	5, 1
	1, 5, 2	2, 3	1	2, 4, 5, 3	1, 4
	5, 2, 3	5, 4			3
					2

[a] numbers refer to dwelling types; numbers in the same line indicate non-significant, in different lines significant, mean differences.

*=$p<.05$; **=$p<.01$; ***=$p<.001$

Table 11: Analysis of variance of *Instrumentality* across regions and dwelling types

	English	German	French	Italian	Russian
1. capital	4.81	4.47	3.65	3.37	2.77
2. Western town	4.61	4.51	3.47	3.10	2.27
3. Western village	4.50	4.40	3.51	3.20	2.33
4. Eastern town	4.63	4.32	3.60	3.14	2.61
5. Eastern village	4.55	4.29	3.69	3.14	2.58
F	29.430***	18.257***	10.360***	13.661***	39.286***

post-hoc comparison[a]: LSD (Least Significant Difference)	1	2, 1	5, 1, 4	1	1
	4, 2	1, 3	3, 2	3, 4, 5	4, 5
	2, 5, 3	4, 5		4, 5, 2	3, 2

[a] numbers refer to dwelling types; numbers in the same line indicate non-significant, in different lines significant, mean differences.

***=$p<.001$

Table 12: Analysis of variance of *Language choice* across regions and dwelling types

	English	German	French	Italian	Russian
1. capital	2.51	1.55	.65	.67	.14
2. Western town	2.27	2.06	.73	.53	.10
3. Western village	2.23	1.97	.84	.44	.11
4. Eastern town	2.44	1.68	.91	.46	.18
5. Eastern village	2.40	1.62	1.09	.44	.20
F	13.995***	41.127***	22.118***	10.455***	5.990***
post-hoc comparison[a]: LSD (Least Significant Difference)	1, 4, 5	2, 3	5	1	5, 4, 1
	2, 3	4, 5	4, 3	2	1, 3, 2
		5, 1	2	4, 3, 5	
			1		

[a] numbers refer to dwelling types; numbers in the same line indicate non-significant mean differences.

***=$p<.001$

Although the tables reveal a seemingly complex pattern, we can find some strong tendencies across the three measures. The cosmopolitan nature of Budapest is well reflected by the high scores on practically all the variables. The popularity of English is fairly even across the regions, with the west of the country falling slightly behind, which may be due to the importance attached to German there (see below). There is a marked preference for German in the west of the country, which is clearly related to the fact that Hungary's western neighbor is German-speaking Austria, and the number of German visitors in this part of the country is particularly high: Attracted by the lower prices, Austrians often come over to Western Hungary to do their shopping or even to go to the dentist. With regard to French, we can conclude that the more eastern and more rural a particular area is, the more marked the preference for French in it. This may be due to the prevalence of more traditional values in these communities. Italian is endorsed in the capital, which may be due to the fact that Budapest is the target of most Italian tourists and also that the city is the cultural center of Hungary. Finally, Russian is preferred (or rather, less disliked) in the east of the country, which is in accordance with the eastern influence there and the fact that Hungary's eastern neighbor used to be the Soviet Union and is currently Ukraine. Russian is also more tolerated in Budapest, which might be related to the increased awareness there about the pragmatic benefits that trade with Russia brings about.

In sum, even in a relatively small country such as Hungary, macro-contextual (geopolitical) factors actively shape language attitudes and language learning motivation. Hungary has traditionally been somewhere in the middle between Eastern and Western Europe, at the dividing line of Germanic and Russian dominance. This is clearly reflected in the preference for German in the west and Russian in the east of the country. French appears to be endorsed in more eastern and rural areas; we have proposed the explanation that this is due to the fact that in more traditional communities the past importance attached to the French language in Hungary has prevailed more than in other parts of the country.

CONCLUSION

The nationwide attitude/motivation survey described in this paper has produced a wealth of data, and the current study has provided the first systematic presentation of the results. Although some aspects of the data have not been processed yet (e.g., the impact of the participants' varying degree of contact with the L2 and L2 speakers), the findings reported above reveal some interesting patterns and trends. In this paper we have addressed four main issues: a) the comparison of the attitudinal/motivational basis of learning different target languages; b) the exploration of any systematic gender-based variation in the data; c) the assessment of the relative importance of the emerging motivational clusters by relating them to two criterion measures, language choice and intended effort; and d) the examination of geographical (macro-contextual) variation in the responses.

(a) Our analyses have indicated that Hungarian language learners' general motivational disposition toward different target languages is characterized by a similar structure, consisting of five broad dimensions: Integrativeness, Instrumentality, Direct Contact with L2 speakers, Media Usage (or "indirect contact"), and Vitality of L2 Community. The main language-specific effect that has emerged was the fact that with certain languages some of these components have merged together into a broader disposition or have split up into sub-dimensions, depending on the perceived ethnolinguistic vitality of the L2 in question. However, the emerging factors were strongly intercorrelated in the case of all the five target languages, indicating that the general disposition toward a particular target language and L2 community among Hungarian school children is fairly homogeneous. Only Russian was an exception to this tendency with the historical heritage of the communist era having a strong enough impact to divide the image of "Russia/Russian" into a power-related and a culture-related dimension.

(b) We found marked gender differences in terms of the boys' and girls' dispositions toward the different languages. Girls in general tended to score higher on most attitudinal/motivational measures, the only main exception being three factors related to the German language. A comparison of girls' and boys' language choice preferences confirmed that German —along with Russian— is indeed a more "masculine" language, whereas French and Italian are more "feminine;" this gender-bias is in accordance with Ludwig's (1983) findings in a markedly different language learning context: among college students of French and German in the US. It was interesting to note that English was largely gender-neutral amongst our participants.

(c) Our findings reveal a strong association between the motivational measures and the criterion variables, explaining as much as 20–50% of the variance. Our results also confirm the uncontested superiority of integrativeness as a predictor of language choice relative to the other motivational scales: The regression analyses revealed that the bulk of the variance in language choice explained by motivational factors was, in fact, due to the impact of the integrativeness factor. Furthermore, what is even more remarkable, we obtained exactly the same pattern when examining the association between the attitudinal/motivational measures and the other criterion measure in out study, intended effort. This suggests that integrativeness represents a certain "core" of the learners' generalized attitudinal/ motivational disposition, subsuming or mediating other variables, which is in complete accordance with Gardner's (1985) motivation theory.

(d) Comparing the data gathered in different regions of the country and in different dwelling types, a very straightforward picture emerged. Budapest, the most cosmopolitan part of Hungary produced the highest scores in most variables. In the west of the country (nearest to the Austrian border), German displayed a marked preference, whereas the generally unpopular Russian language was more endorsed in the east of the country (nearest to the ex-Soviet border). French was favored in more traditional (eastern and rural) communities, whereas Italian was particularly popular in the capital, which is the cultural and tourist center. These findings provide unambiguous support to the claim that macrocontextual, geopolitical factors significantly affect people's language attitudes.

In conclusion, the results of our survey have confirmed a number of assumptions and theories about L2 motivation and also revealed some important patterns and trends. Given the extensive size of our sample, these findings can be seen as fairly robust. We should note, however, that our results describe only one particular age group, 13/14-year-old teenagers, and with younger or older learners both the composition and the relative weighting of the L2 motivation construct may vary (e.g., instrumentality might have more of an impact, as was the case in the study by Dörnyei, 1990). Another special characteristic of our sample was that it included language learners for whom the L2 was primarily a school subject, and extracurricular contact with the L2 was rather limited. In contexts where L2 use is a regular practice, different motives might assume increasing importance. In order to explore the motivational characteristics of our sample in more detail, we are planning to conduct further in-depth analyses of our data set and have recently completed a follow-up survey study, involving over 3,800 participants, whose purpose was to explore the longitudinal changes in the motivation patterns of the investigated population.

REFERENCES

Burstall, C., Jamieson, M., Cohen, S., & Hargreaves, M. (1974). *Primary French in the balance*. Windsor, UK: NFER

Cattell, R. B. (1966). The scree test for the number of factors. *Multivariate Behavioral Research, 1*, 245–276.

Clark, A., & Trafford, J. (1995). Boys into modern languages: An investigation of the discrepancy in attitudes and performance between boys and girls in modern languages. *Gender and Education, 7*, 315–325.

Clément R. (1980). Ethnicity, contact and communicative competence in a second language. In H. Giles, W. P. Robinson, & P. M. Smith (Eds.), *Language: Social psychological perspectives* (pp. 147–154). Oxford, UK: Pergamon.

Clément, R., Dörnyei, Z., & Noels, K. (1994). Motivation, self-confidence and group cohesion in the foreign language classroom. *Language Learning, 44*, 417–448.

Clément, R., & Gardner, R. (in press). Second language mastery. In H. Giles & W. P. Robinson (Eds.), *The new handbook of language and social psychology* (2nd ed.). New York: John Wiley & Sons.

Clément, R., & Kruidenier, B. (1983). Orientations on second language acquisition: 1. The effects of ethnicity, milieu and their target language on their emergence. *Language Learning, 33*, 273–291.

Crookes, G., & Schmidt, R. W. (1991). Motivation: Reopening the research agenda. *Language Learning, 41*, 469–512.

Djigunoviç, M. J. (1993). Effects of gender on some learner-dependent variables in foreign language learning. *Studia Romanica et Anglica Zagrabiensia, 38*, 169–180.

Dörnyei, Z. (1990). Conceptualizing motivation in foreign language learning. *Language Learning, 40*, 46–78.

Dörnyei, Z. (1994). Motivation and motivating in the foreign language classroom. *Modern Language Journal, 78*, 273–284.

Dörnyei, Z. (1998). Motivation in second and foreign language learning. *Language Teaching, 31*, 117–135.

Dörnyei, Z. (2000). Motivation in action: Towards a process-oriented conceptualisation of student motivation. *British Journal of Educational Psychology, 70*, 519–538.

Dörnyei, Z. (2001). *Teaching and researching motivation*. Harlow: Longman.

Dörnyei, Z. (in press). Motivation. In J. Verschueren, J-O. Östmann, J. Blommaert, & C. Bulcaen (Eds.), *Handbook of pragmatics*. Amsterdam: John Benjamins.

Dörnyei, Z., & Ottó, I. (1998). Motivation in action: A process model of L2 motivation. *Working Papers in Applied Linguistics (Thames Valley University, London)*, *4*, 43–69.

Gardner, R. C. (1985). *Social psychology and second language learning: The role of attitudes and motivation*. London: Edward Arnold.

Gardner, R. C. (2001). Integrative motivation and second language acquisition. In Z. Dörnyei & R. Schmidt (Eds.), *Motivation and second language acquisition* (Technical Report #23, pp. 1–19). Honolulu: University of Hawai'i, Second Language Teaching and Curriculum Center.

Gardner, R. C., & Lambert, W. E. (1959). Motivational variables in second language acquisition. *Canadian Journal of Psychology*, *13*, 266–272.

Gardner, R. C., & MacIntyre, P. D. (1993). A student's contributions to second-language learning. Part II: Affective variables. *Language Teaching*, *26*, 1–11.

Julkunen, K. (1994). Gender differences in students' situation- and task-specific foreign language learning motivation. In S. Tella (Ed.), *Näytön paikka. Opetuksen kulttuurin arviointi* [Evaluating the culture of teaching] (pp. 171–180). Helsinki: University of Helsinki, Teacher Education Department.

Julkunen, K., & Borzova, H. (1997). *English language learning motivation in Joensuu and Petrozavodsk*. Joensuu, Finland: University of Joensuu.

Laine, E. J. (1995). *Learning second national languages: A research report*. Frankfurt, Germany: Peter Lang.

Ludwig, J. (1983). Attitudes and expectations: A profile of female and male students of college French, German and Spanish. *Modern Language Journal*, *67*, 216–227.

Schmidt, R., Boraie, D., & Kassabgy, O. (1996). Foreign language motivation: Internal structure and external connections. In R. Oxford (Ed.), *Language learning motivation: Pathways to the new century* (Technical Report No. 11, pp. 9–70). Honolulu: University of Hawai'i, Second Language Teaching & Curriculum Center.

Schmidt, R., & Watanabe, Y. (2001). Motivation, strategy use, and pedagogical preferences in foreign language learning. In Z. Dörnyei & R. Schmidt (Eds.), *Motivation and second language acquisition* (Technical Report #23, pp. 313–359). Honolulu: University of Hawai'i, Second Language Teaching and Curriculum Center.

Schumann, J. H. (1998). *The neurobiology of affect in language*. Oxford, UK: Blackwell.

Tachibana, Y., Matsukawa, R., & Zhong, Q. X. (1996). Attitudes and motivation for learning English: A cross-national comparison of Japanese and Chinese high school students. *Psychological Reports*, *79*, 691–700.

Tremblay, P. F., & Gardner, R. C. (1995). Expanding the motivation construct in language learning. *Modern Language Journal, 79*, 505–520.

Williams, M., & Burden, R. (1997). *Psychology for language teachers*. Cambridge, UK: Cambridge University Press.

ENGLISH TRANSLATION OF THE HUNGARIAN QUESTIONNAIRE
USED IN THE SURVEY

Language orientation questionnaire

We would like to ask you to help us by answering the following questions concerning foreign language learning. This is not a test so there are no "right" or "wrong" answers and you don't even have to write your name on it. We are interested in your personal opinion. Please give your answers sincerely as only this will guarantee the success of the investigation. Thank you very much for your help.

I. In the following section we would like you to answer some questions by simply giving marks from 1 to 5.

5 = very much, 4 = quite a lot, 3 = so-so, 2 = not really, 1 = not at all

For example, if you like "hamburgers" very much, "bean soup" not very much, and "spinach" not at all, write this:

	hamburgers	bean soup	spinach
How much do you like these foods?	5	2	1

Please put one (and only one) whole number in each box and don't leave out any of them. Thanks.

5 = very much, 4 = quite a lot, 3 = so-so, 2 = not really, 1 = not at all

	German	French	Russian	English	Italian
1. How much do you like these languages?					
2. How much do you think knowing these languages would help you to become a more knowledgeable person?					
3. How important do you think these languages are in the world these days?					
4. How important do you think learning these languages is in order to learn more about the culture and art of its speakers?					

	France	England	Russia	Germany	USA	Italy
5. How much effort are you prepared to expend in learning these languages?						
6. How much do you think knowing these languages would help you when travelling abroad in the future?						
7. How much do you think knowing these languages would help your future career?						
8. How well does your mother speak these languages?						
9. How well does your father speak these languages?						
10. How much would you like to become similar to the people who speak these languages?						

	France	England	Russia	Germany	USA	Italy
11. How much would you like to travel to these countries?						
12. How rich and developed do you think these countries are?						
13. How important a role do you think these countries play in the world?						
14. How much do you like meeting foreigners from these countries?						
15. How much do you like the films made in these countries? (Write 0 if you don't know them.)						
16. How much do you like the TV programs made in these countries? (Write 0 if you don't know them.)						
17. How much do you like the people who live in these countries?						
18. How often do you see films/TV programs made in these countries?						
19. How much do you like the magazines made in these countries? (Write 0 if you don't know them.)						
20. How often do you meet foreigners (e.g., in the street, restaurants, public places) coming from these countries?						
21. How much do you like the pop music of these countries? (Write 0 if you don't know it.)						

Have you put a number in each box? Thank you!

II. Now there are going to be statements some people agree with and some people don't. We would like to know to what extent they describe your own feelings or situation. After each statement you'll find five boxes. Please put an "X" in the box which best expresses how true the statement is about your feelings or situation. For example, if you like skiing very much, put an "X" in the last box:

	not at all true	not really true	partly true partly untrue	mostly true	abso-lutely true
I like skiing very much.					**X**

There are no good or bad answers — we are interested in your personal opinion.

	not at all true	not really true	partly true partly untrue	mostly true	abso-lutely true
22. I am sure I will be able to learn a foreign language well.					
23. I think I am the type who would feel anxious and ill at ease if I had to speak to someone in a foreign language.					
24. People around me tend to think that it is a good thing to know foreign languages.					
25. I don't think that foreign languages are important school subjects.					
26. I often watch satellite programs on TV.					
27. My parents do not consider foreign languages important school subjects.					
28. Learning foreign languages makes me fear that I will feel less Hungarian because of it.					
29. Learning a foreign language is a difficult task.					

III. Finally, please answer these few personal questions.

30. If you could choose, which foreign languages would you choose to learn next year at school (or work)? Please mark three languages in order of importance.
    1. _____
    2. _____
    3. _____

31. Underline which gender you are: boy   girl

32. What foreign language(s) are you learning at school? _____

33. Have you learnt any foreign languages outside school? _____

34. If yes, which ones? _____

35. At what age did you start learning a foreign language? _____

36. Have you ever been abroad for longer than six months (e.g., when your parents worked there)? _____

37. If yes, where? _____

FACTOR ANALYSIS OF THE ATTITUDINAL ITEMS: MAXIMUM LIKELIHOOD EXTRACTION, OBLIQUE ROTATION, PATTERN MATRICES*

English (US)						English (UK)					
	factor						factor				
item	1	2	3	4	5	item	1	2	3	4	5
12	1.03					14	.78				
10		.58				17	.40			.31	
4		.52				11	.34				
1		.47				3		.66			
3			.63			2		.61			
2			.56			6		.46			
6			.48			7		.37			
7			.36			12			.72		
13			.32			13			.44		
16				.58		16				.72	
15				.55		15				.61	
19				.54		19				.48	
21				.50		21				.46	
14					.75	10					.64
17					.48	4					.50
11					.43	1					.47

German						French					
	factor						factor				
item	1	2	3	4	5	item	1	2	3	4	5
14	.89					14	.60				
17	.34					1	.59				
11						17	.54				
3		.73				10	.50				
6		.59				11	.40				
2		.52				4	.39				
7		.39				19					
12			.82			2		.64			
13			.46			3		.41			
15				.63		16			.75		
16				.62		15			.61		
21				.53		21			.37		
19				.36		12				.55	
10					−.63	13				.52	
1					−.55	6					.64
4					−.52	7					.44

Italian						Russian					
	factor						factor				
item	1	2	3	4	5	item	1	2	3	4	5
14	.63					10	.52				
17	.58					7	.35				
1	.57					1	.33				
10	.52					4	.32				
11	.44					16		.76			
4	.37					15		.65			
2		.85				21		.51			
3		.41				19		.42			
12			.63			14			.70		
13			.59			17			.69		
16				.75		11			.39		
15				.70		12				.41	
21				.35		13				.39	
19						3					.83
6					.53	2					.66
7					.44	6					.35

* loadings under .3 not shown

Items submitted to the analyses

1. How much do you like these languages?
2. How much do you think knowing these languages would help you to become a more knowledgeable person?
3. How important do you think these languages are in the world these days?
4. How important do you think learning these languages is in order to learn more about the culture and art of its speakers?
6. How much do you think knowing these languages would help you when travelling abroad in the future?
7. How much do you think knowing these languages would help your future career?
10. How much would you like to become similar to the people who speak these languages?
11. How much would you like to travel to these countries?
12. How rich and developed do you think these countries are?
13. How important a role do you think these countries play in the world?
14. How much do you like meeting foreigners from these countries?
15. How much do you like the films made in these countries?
16. How much do you like the TV programs made in these countries?
17. How much do you like the people who live in these countries?
19. How much do you like the magazines made in these countries?
21. How much do you like the pop music of these countries?

Kimi Kondo-Brown
University of Hawai'i at Mānoa

BILINGUAL HERITAGE STUDENTS' LANGUAGE CONTACT AND MOTIVATION

Author's note

I am grateful that this research was conducted with support given by the University of Hawai'i Japan Studies Endowment. An earlier version of this article was presented at the 1997 Spring Annual Conference of Nihongo Kyooiku Gakkai (The Society for Teaching Japanese as a Foreign Language) in Tokyo.

Abstract

This study investigates the extent and frequency of language contacts and use as well as the attitudes of 145 bilingual heritage students enrolled in various levels of college Japanese. Findings include the fact that bilinguals in advanced Japanese classes, especially those in fourth year classes, had much more extensive Japanese language contacts and use in *informal* learning environments than those in first and second year classes. Second, among the various kinds of informal language resources available to these students, Japanese mothers' language choices were most critically associated with their language behavior. Third, there were both similarities and differences in motivation among bilingual heritage students in the various levels of Japanese: Most bilinguals in all classes studied Japanese to improve or maintain the language for work and for communication with Japanese people, although an equally high percentage of bilinguals in first and second year Japanese also studied Japanese to satisfy the language requirement; most bilinguals in all classes found learning Japanese challenging, interesting, and important, although more bilinguals in first and second year classes reported fewer rewards and higher frustration in learning Japanese; bilinguals in all classes unanimously saw the economic advantages of bilingualism, but more bilinguals in advanced Japanese saw personal advantages to bilingualism and supported societal bilingualism as well.

THEORETICAL BACKGROUND AND RESEARCH PURPOSE

A considerable number of researchers of second language (L2) acquisition have investigated social-psychological contexts as factors influencing individual language behavior, reporting that individual learners' achievement in the target language (TL) is associated with motivation (Clément, 1980; Clément & Kruidenier, 1985; Gardner, 1985, 1988; Gardner & Lambert, 1972; McGroarty, 1996; Oxford, 1996; Oxford & Shearin, 1994; Tremblay & Gardner, 1995; Warschauer, 1996), attitudes (Baker, 1992; Gardner, 1985; Spolsky, 1989), perceptions of ethnolinguistic vitality (Giles & Byrne, 1982), egocentric and exocentric beliefs (Allard & Landry, 1994), and investment (McKay & Wong, 1996; Norton Peirce, 1995).

The theoretical frameworks of these researchers vary considerably, but their arguments are commonly built on the following three grounds. First, extensive

Kondo-Brown, K. (2001). Bilingual heritage students' language contact and motivation. In Z. Dörnyei & R. Schmidt (Eds.), *Motivation and second language acquisition* (Technical Report #23, pp. 433–459). Honolulu: University of Hawai'i, Second Language Teaching and Curriculum Center.

contacts with the TL as well as the opportunities to use/practice the language are necessary conditions for the individual learner's achievement in the TL. Second, the quality and quantity of the learner's contacts in the TL are influenced by macro-sociological and/or micro-interactional environments, such as the vitality of ethnolinguistic groups and the individual's networks of linguistic contacts. Third, an inquiry into the learner's reactions to the opportunities for using/practicing the TL requires investigation of his or her cognitive and affective mechanisms (e.g., attitude, motivation, investment).

As a language teacher at the University of Hawai'i at Mānoa (UHM), I have met hundreds of bilingual heritage students whose oral and literacy skills in Japanese vary considerably.[1] They study Japanese in classes of various levels — from first to fourth year courses. The considerable variations in Japanese proficiency among these students suggest that some of them not only have had extensive contacts in Japanese but also have actively engaged in meaningful use/production of the language, while others have not for a variety of reasons (see Swain, 1985). The purpose of this study is to investigate the extent and frequency of language contacts and use as well as motivation among UHM bilingual heritage students of Japanese whose proficiency in Japanese varies considerably. This study will answer the following questions:

1. In what contexts have UHM bilingual heritage students in advanced Japanese classes made more frequent contacts and use in the language than those in beginning/intermediate Japanese?

2. Why do bilingual heritage students of Japanese study the language in college? Are there differences in motivation among bilinguals in various levels of Japanese classes?

3. What attitudes do bilingual heritage students have toward learning the language and bilingualism? Are there differences in attitudes among bilinguals in various levels of Japanese classes?

---

[1] There is little consensus on what it is meant by the term "heritage language" (Van Deusen-Scholl, 2000). In this study, "heritage students of Japanese" are defined as those who have chosen to study Japanese, their parental/home language, in a formal setting. There is no uniform opinion about the norms to define bilingualism, either (Baker, 1996; Grosjean, 1982; Hakuta, 1986; Romaine, 1995). Bilinguals in this study are not "balanced bilinguals" (see Baker, 1996) who demonstrate equal fluency in both languages. They have lived in Hawai'i all or almost all of their lives and speak English as their dominant language, but they fall within a definition that includes as bilinguals those who "develop a greater function ease in English for dealing with most contexts and domains outside of the home and immediate community" (Valdés & Figueroa, 1994, p. 17). They have developed various levels of Japanese language proficiency. Some speak Japanese effectively and fluently in most informal situations and speak it regularly. Others speak Japanese that is limited to small utterances or fragments. These students also have various degrees of Japanese literacy skills. Kondo (1998b) reviews present and past formal and nonformal Japanese language education programs available for heritage students of Japanese in Hawai'i and discusses the political and historical background of Japanese language education in Hawai'i.

I will review selected social-psychological models of L2 acquisition or bilingualism that help conceptualize the relationships among (a) macro-sociological and micro-interactional environments, (b) socio-psychological or motivational mechanisms, and (c) individual learners' language behavior. These models/theories are Clément's Social Context Model, Gardner's Socio-Educational Model, and Allard and Landry's Additive Subtractive Bilingualism Model.

Clément's social context model

Clément's model (1980) conceptualizes the influence of cultural/social settings on the individual learner's communicative competence in the TL in terms of two sets of social motivation factors, viewed as primary and secondary motivational processes. *Primary motivational process* refers to an interplay of two oppositional social-psychological forces, *integrativeness* (positive feelings towards the target language and community) and *fear of assimilation* (the fear that learning the L2 might lead to the loss of L1 language and culture; Clément & Kruidenier, 1985). *Secondary motivational process* refers to the individual learner's self-confidence in using the TL, defined in terms of low language use anxiety and high self-perceptions of one's L2 competence (Clément, Dörnyei, & Noels, 1994, p. 422). According to Clément, self-confidence influences communicative competence in the L2 "both directly and indirectly through attitude toward and effort expanded on learning" the TL (Clément et al., 1994, p. 441). The more confident the learner is, the more frequent engagement in practicing the language, therefore, the higher proficiency.

The 1980 model predicts that, in *unicultural contexts*, that is, social settings where "contact with members of the TL group is not available" (Clément & Kruidenier, 1985, p. 24), the primary motivational process directly determines the learner's motivation to learn the L2, which in turn determines his or her communicative competence in the L2. In the latest study, however, Clément et al., (1994) show that motivational processes in a unicultural social setting are more complex than described in the original model. Socially grounded factors such as appraisal of classroom environment are also closely associated with the learner's L2 learning behavior. On the other hand, in *multicultural contexts* where "contact (with members of the TL group) is possible" (Clément & Kruidenier, 1985, p. 24), self-confidence is the most important determinant of communicative competence in the L2. Clément and Kruidenier (1985) propose that self-confidence, which consists of high self-evaluation and low language use anxiety, is also a cause of achievement in the TL. The higher the level of confidence one has about one's own language skills, the more frequent contacts with the TL and higher achievement in the language are expected.[2]

---

[2]   The notions of primary and secondary motivational processes have been tested in both a multicultural context (Clément & Kruidenier, 1985) and a unicultural context (Clément et al., 1994), with results supporting the model. Although Clément's model is primarily concerned with motivational mechanisms, it is assumed that "language aptitude is also an

Gardner's socio-educational model

Gardner's (1985) socio-educational model primarily concerns the role that social factors play in L2 acquisition in classroom settings, although it also considers natural settings. The model has been revised over the years, but the central concept of Gardner's model continues to be motivation (Tremblay & Gardner, 1995). The following description mostly refers to the 1985 version. The 1985 version of the model conceptualizes the interrelations of four aspects of language learning: (a) the social/cultural milieu, (b) individual learner differences in motivation and aptitude, (c) formal and informal language learning contexts, and (d) linguistic and nonlinguistic outcomes.

One of the central predictions of Gardner's model is that L2 acquisition takes place in a particular social/cultural milieu; the individual learner grows up in a home and community in which cultural beliefs about the significance of learning the L2 or bilingualism are transmitted (Gardner, 1988; Gardner, Lalonde, & Pierson, 1983). Although Gardner has not clearly defined what constitutes the cultural beliefs generally held by a community or society (Au, 1988; Gardner, 1988), he suggests that they include beliefs about ethnolinguistic vitality (Giles & Byrne, 1982) and suggests that one way of assessing cultural beliefs held by a given community is to investigate the perceptions of its members (Gardner, 1988).

Another central prediction of Gardner's model is that the individual learner's social and cultural background influences *language attitude*, which consists of *integrativeness* and *attitudes toward the learning situation*. Language attitude affects motivation or "the extent to which the individual works or strives to learn the language because of a desire to do so and the satisfaction experienced in this activity" (Gardner, 1985, p. 10). In Gardner's model, motivation is seen as a cause of L2 achievement ("the causative hypothesis;" Au, 1988), but it is not clear if motivation is a cause or a result of achievement or both (Au, 1988; Crookes & Schmidt, 1991). Others have argued that motivation is, after all, an interactive process — it is both a cause and a result of success in L2 learning (e.g., Ellis, 1994). Gardner (1991) himself acknowledges the problem and takes a less assertive position, writing that "the process underlying the relationship (between motivation and L2 achievement) is certainly open to question" (p. 50).

At the final stage of the model, linguistic outcomes (e.g., mastery of communicative fluency in the target language) are closely bound with nonlinguistic outcomes such as attitudes, self-concepts, values, and beliefs. The model is not static but dynamic

---

influential determinant of competence" (Clément & Kruidenier, 1985, p. 23). Clément and Kruidenier (pp. 33–34) suggest that "contextualized performance" is more closely linked to motivation than to aptitude, whereas performance in standardized tests is more related to aptitude.

and cumulative. Learners' changes in attitudes, self-concepts, values, and beliefs influence subsequent language learning.[3]

Earlier, Gardner and Lambert (1972) made a distinction between integrative and instrumental motivation. Instrumental motivation refers to instrumental/occupational reasons for learning a language. Integrative motivation refers to "positive attitudes toward the target language group and the potential for integrating into that group, or at the very least an interest in meeting and interacting with members of the target language group" (Crookes & Schmidt, 1991, pp. 471–472). Most studies by Gardner and his associates have focused on integrative motivation (Gardner & Tremblay, 1994). Previous studies show that integratively motivated individuals are successful L2 learners because they are active learners (Gardner, 1988).

Allard and Landry's model of additive and subtractive bilingual development

Allard and Landry's model (1994) includes macro-sociostructural, micro-interactional, and psychological factors that contribute to the development of additive and subtractive bilingualism. Key concepts of the model are the *individual network of linguistic contact* (INLC) and subjective *ethnolinguistic vitality* (EV) as a belief system. Allard and Landry utilize Prujiner, Deshaies, Hamers, Blanc, Clément, & Landry's (1984) conception of EV, which expands and reconstructs Giles and Byrne's (1982) original notion of EV. In the model, the EV of a language group is determined by the group's demographic, economic, political, and cultural "capitals," that is, the group's population, its monetary, commercial, and industrial power, its representation in government, and its institutional support for education, religion, and culture.

One of the important predictions of the model is that the relative EV of L1 and L2 directly affects the structure and content of the learner's INLC, which consists of interpersonal contacts, contacts through the media, and educational support. Interpersonal contacts include communication with family members and friends, at work, or visiting the country where the TL is spoken. Contacts through the media include television, radio, newspapers, telecommunications, and so forth. Educational support includes the availability of formal and nonformal instruction in the TL (e.g., foreign language class, ethnic language school). Thus, linguistic experiences through one's INLC may be formal or informal, low or high cognitive demand, and interactive or non-interactive.

Another important prediction of the model is that one's INLC determines one's linguistic competence and "cognitive and affective disposition," a set of general and personal beliefs concerning group vitality and individual identity. These two factors

---

[3] In the Gardner model, the role of language aptitude is also considered: while motivation influences the learner's mastery of the L2 in both formal and informal learning contexts, aptitude is influential only in formal learning contexts.

—linguistic competence and cognitive-affective disposition— interactively determine one's language behavior.

The framework for cognitive-affective disposition is derived from the cognitive orientation theory originally developed by Kreitler and Kreitler (1972). According to Kreitler and Kreitler, there are four types of beliefs —general, normative, personal, and goal beliefs— which contribute significantly to better predictions of behavior. Drawing on Kreitler and Kreitler's conceptualization of beliefs, Allard and Landry (1994) identify two categories of beliefs that predict language behavior: *exocentric* beliefs and *egocentric* beliefs. Exocentric beliefs refer to perceptions of sociostructural factors and behavior of others that may affect a group's EV. Egocentric beliefs are related to one's feeling of belonging to an ethnolinguistic group (belongingness beliefs), the value one perceives in learning and using the language (valorization beliefs), confidence in one's ability to master the language (efficacy beliefs), and desire and aspiration to utilize the language (goal beliefs). The relationship between language behavior and the INLC in the model is dynamic; language behavior feeds back to the INLC. The end result is varying levels of bilingualism, and the process may be additive or subtractive.

METHODOLOGY

INFORMANTS

One hundred and forty five bilingual heritage students, enrolled in first through fourth year Japanese language classes at UHM, participated in the survey. The students' ethnic background and immigration status were identified by a background information sheet filled out at the beginning of each semester. I selected students with at least one parent who was a native speaker of Japanese. Participants were systematically classified into the following three groups by the Japanese course that they were taking at the time of the survey.[4]

Bilinguals in first/second year Japanese courses

These students were taking a first or second year Japanese course (Japanese 100, 101, 102, 201, 202) when the questionnaire was distributed. None of them reported that they speak Japanese fluently or very fluently. Over half (55%) of the students reported they understand Japanese TV programs "little," and the rest said they understand "half." About a third (32.5%) of the students said they can read and write basic Japanese *kana* fluently or very fluently, and the rest said either average (37.5%) or poor or very poor (30%).

---

[4] At UHM, incoming students of Japanese are normally placed into classes based on background information, placement test score, and performance on a short written essay. The placement test, developed by a group of faculty members in the Department of East Asian Languages and Literatures at UHM, consists of three sections (grammar, aural skills, and reading). Teachers also obtain information concerning the family backgrounds of their students and all Japanese language courses taken at educational institutions.

Bilinguals in special Japanese 307/308 courses

These students were all enrolled in special third year Japanese courses for bilingual students (Japanese 307 or 308) when the questionnaire was distributed.[5] Nearly half (46.7%) of the students reported that they speak Japanese fluently or very fluently and the rest reported their oral skill as average (38.6%) or poor (17.3%).[6] Most (74.7%) reported that they understand everything or almost everything when they watch Japanese TV programs. Half (50.7%) of the students said they can read and write basic Japanese *kana* fluently or very fluently, and the rest said either average (40%) or poor (9.3%). Just more than half (54.6%) of the students said they understand Japanese newspapers a little, and the rest said not at all.

Bilinguals in advanced fourth year Japanese

These students were all taking a 400-level Japanese course at the time the questionnaire was distributed. They were either directly placed in advanced 400-level Japanese class or had satisfactorily completed Japanese 307 and/or 308 before taking a 400-level class. Most (86.7%) reported that they speak Japanese fluently or very fluently, and the rest said average. Almost all (93.3%) reported that they understand everything or almost everything when they watch Japanese TV programs. Most (86.6%) said they can read and write basic Japanese *kana* fluently or very fluently, and the rest said average. Less than a third (26.8%) of the students said they understand Japanese newspapers well or very well and the rest said a little.

There were 40 first and second year students (M=18, F=22), 75 third year students (M=26, F=49), and 30 fourth year students (M=12, F=18). The mean age was 22.3. Fifty six participants (38.6%) have two Japanese parents (native speakers of Japanese). Eighty four participants (57.9%) have a Japanese mother and non-Japanese father. Among these, the father's ethnic background varies: 47 Japanese-Americans, 15 Caucasians, 5 African Americans, 5 Filipinos, 4 Chinese, 2 Indians, 2 mixed, and 4 unknown. The other 5 students (3.4%) have a Japanese father and a Japanese-American mother. Thus, it turned out that, while all participants but five have a Japanese mother from Japan, most have a father who is not a native speaker

---

[5] Since 1977, UHM has provided a special track of Japanese courses (Japanese 307 and 308) for English-Japanese bilingual students who demonstrate high levels of proficiency in spoken Japanese but who do not have enough literacy skills to be placed in advanced fourth year Japanese. Bilingual students on the Japanese 307/308 track are not allowed to take regular first, second, and third year Japanese.

[6] All third year students were my former students, and therefore I could compare their reported Japanese oral skills with the oral skills that I observed. Seven of these students evaluated their own Japanese oral skills as being poor, but in my judgment, they were not really "poor." Actually they were as fluent as those who reported their Japanese oral skills as being very fluent, fluent, or average. It seems that the way they reported their own Japanese language skills was partly affected by the gap between their perceived skills and expected skills; the wider the gap, the lower the self-evaluation. It is possible that cultural values such as modesty and taboos on self-assertion may influence self-reported proficiency. A recent study shows that attitudes toward one's minority culture and language affect self-reported proficiency (Hakuta & D'Andrea, 1993).

---

of Japanese and who comes from various ethnic backgrounds. The occupational backgrounds of the parents are shown in Table 1, from which it can be seen that parental socio-economic background was not associated with bilingual heritage students' Japanese proficiency. One hundred and eight (74.5%) informants still lived with their parents. Table 2 lists the participants' diverse majors. The most popular major was business (29.6%) — finance, accounting, management, international business, travel industry, and so forth. Japanese was the second most popular major (14.5%). An equal number of participants also responded either "liberal arts" or "undecided." Table 2 also indicates that business was the most popular among first and second year students (37.5%) and third year students (33.3%), while Japanese was the most popular among fourth year students (50%).

Table 1: Parental occupation

	1st/2nd-yr BL (N=40)	3rd-yr BL (N=75)	4rd-yr BL (N=30)	total
father				
accountant	1	0	1	2
business owner	4	4	2	10
chemist	0	1	0	1
cook/chef	2	2	1	5
construction worker	0	2	0	2
engineer	2	2	2	6
fisherman	1	2	0	3
gardener	0	1	0	1
journalist	0	1	0	1
plumber	0	1	0	1
professor	0	1	0	1
manager/supervisor	5	12	4	21
military employee	4	5	3	12
minister	0	4	1	5
music composer	0	0	1	1
sales person	2	6	0	8
security guard	0	1	1	2
technician/mechanic	8	5	3	16
missing/retired/ deceased	11	25	11	47
mother				
accountant	1	0	0	1
business owner			1	1
clerk/secretary	6	2	0	8

cook/chef	1	2	0	3
hostess	1	0	0	1
housewife/homemaker	5	18	8	31
journalist	0	0	1	1
lawyer	1	0	0	1
manager/supervisor	6	4	2	12
sales person	9	18	6	33
teacher	3	5	2	10
tour guide	0	3	1	4
waitress/cafe worker	3	5	2	10
missing/retired/ deceased	4	18	7	29

1st/2nd-yr BL   Bilinguals in first/second year Japanese courses
3rd-yr BL   Bilinguals in special Japanese 307/308 courses
4rd-yr BL   Bilinguals in advanced fourth year Japanese

Table 2: Majors among survey participants

	1st/2nd-yr BL (N=40)	3rd-yr BL (N=75)	4rd-yr BL (N=30)	total
business	15	25	3	43
Japanese	1	5	15	21
liberal arts/ undecided	5	14	2	21
engineering	2	9	2	13
journalism/ communication	2	4	0	6
fine arts	3	2	0	5
education	1	1	3	5
architect	2	2	0	4
pre-medicine/ pre-dental	2	2	0	4
English/ESL	0	2	0	2
political science	1	0	0	1
computer science	1	0	1	2
double (business & Japanese)	0	3	2	5
biology	1	1	0	2
physics	1	1	0	2
sociology	0	2	0	2

continued...

Table 2: Majors among survey participants (cont.)

	1st/2nd-yr BL (N=40)	3rd-yr BL (N=75)	4rd-yr BL (N=30)	total
psychology	0	2	0	2
nursing/pre-nursing	0	0	2	2
zoology	1	0	0	1
history	1	0	0	1
social work	1	0	0	1

1st/2nd-yr BL	Bilinguals in first/second year Japanese courses
3rd-yr BL	Bilinguals in special Japanese 307/308 courses
4rd-yr BL	Bilinguals in advanced fourth year Japanese

INSTRUMENTS AND PROCEDURES

The data were gathered as part of my wider, interdisciplinary doctoral dissertation research into UHM bilingual heritage students' Japanese language learning, academic achievement, and identity (Kondo, 1998a). In 1995 and 1996, a questionnaire and a letter of introduction were either mailed or directly given to 250 students. The letter explained the purpose of the research project and how the data would be used. They were assured of anonymity. The return rate of the questionnaire was 58%. The question items on the questionnaire were as follows (also see Appendix I for a questionnaire sample):

- *Background information.* Age, sex, name, address, phone number, class standing, major, parental ethnic background and occupation, attendance at *nihongo gakkoo* (Japanese language school) and secondary school, length of time spent in Japan, and frequency of visits to Japan.[7]

- *Language choice/use.* Students' use of Japanese with parents, siblings, friends, and at work; parental use of Japanese with the students; frequency of watching TV in Japanese.[8]

- *Self-evaluation of one's proficiency in Japanese.* Students evaluate their oral fluency in Japanese, fluency in reading and writing *hiragana* and *katakana*, comprehension of Japanese TV programs, ability to read Japanese newspapers, and relative ease in speaking Japanese/English.

- *Motives for studying Japanese.* Students were asked to select (all that apply) from two external motives (language requirement and pleasing parents) and six internal motives (language maintenance, communication, cultural understanding, occupational advantage, study abroad, and travel).

---

[7] I asked my informants to provide their names and phone numbers because I planned to interview the informants.

[8] Two TV channels —KIKU (Oceanic 21) and NGN (premium cable channel)— are broadcast in Japanese.

- *Attitudes towards learning Japanese.* Students were asked to select (all that apply) from eight positive choices (interesting, important, fun, nurturing, challenging, enjoyable, proud, and rewarding) and three negative choices (painful, frustrating, and time-consuming). Students were also asked if they became more interested in the Japanese language and their cultural roots after they became a college student.

- *Attitudes towards bilingualism and monolingualism.* Students were asked to select (all that apply) from five positively worded views of bilingual Nisei (second generation Japanese) students in comparison to monolingual Nisei students (job advantage, cultural understanding, closeness with Japanese parents, enrichment of life, and flexibility). Students were also asked if they think bilingualism should be a universal norm for all people in the U.S. or if it should be encouraged. Students were also asked to select (all that apply) from two positively worded views of monolingual Nisei students' adjustment advantages in comparison to bilingual Nisei students and one negatively worded view of monolingual Nisei students' assimilation (isolation from Japanese family and community).

- *A follow-up interview.* Students were asked if they would consent to a follow-up interview.

RESULTS

USE OF JAPANESE IN THE HOME

Table 3 shows the students' use of Japanese with their parents; Table 4 shows parental use of Japanese. Notable differences among bilinguals in various levels of Japanese classes were observed in the use of Japanese for communication with their mothers. Most third year (65.3%) and fourth year students (90%) use Japanese predominantly when they talk to their mothers, whereas none of the first and second year students do so. The great majority of the third year students' mothers (85.3%) and fourth year students' mothers (96.7%) use Japanese predominantly in communicating with the students, but only 15% of first and second year students' mothers do the same. Most students in all groups do not use Japanese regularly with their fathers, and as is the case with their mothers, first and second year students use Japanese the least with their fathers.

Table 3: Use of Japanese with parents (in %)

	with mother			with father		
	1st/2nd-yr BL (N=40)	3rd-yr BL (N=75)	4th-yr BL (N=30)	1st/2nd-yrBL (N=40)	3rd-yr BL (N=75)	4th-yr BL (N=30)
always/mostly	0	65.3	90.0	0	24.0	33.3
half	25.0	12.0	6.7	10.0	9.3	6.7
seldom/not at all	75.0	22.7	3.3	77.5	64.0	60.0
unknown	0	0	0	12.5	2.7	0

Table 4: Parental use of Japanese (in %)

	mother			father		
	1st/2nd-yr BL (N=40)	3rd-yr BL (N=75)	4th-yr BL (N=30)	1st/2nd-yrBL (N=40)	3rd-yr BL (N=75)	4th-yr BL (N=30)
always/mostly	15.0	85.3	96.7	12.5	25.3	36.7
half	40.0	12.0	3.3	0	10.7	3.3
seldom/not at all	45.0	2.7	0	75.0	60.0	60.0
unknown	0	0	0	12.5	4.0	0

The use of English dominates first and second year students' and third year students' communication with their siblings. All first and second year students use English with their siblings, and 88.1% of third year students do the same. As for the fourth year students, a little less than half (43.5%) use Japanese with their siblings. The majority in every group has some exposure to Japanese TV programs, although a higher percentage of fourth year students (40%) watches Japanese TV programs regularly compared to first and second year (5%) and third year students (24%; see Table 5).

Table 5: Exposure to Japanese TV programs

	1st/2nd-yr BL (N=40)	3rd-yr BL (N=75)	4rd-yr BL (N=30)
always/most of the time	2 (5%)	18 (24%)	12 (40%)
sometimes	27 (67.5%)	47 (62.7%)	16 (53.3%)
seldom/never	11 (27.5%)	10 (13.3%)	2 (6.7%)
1st/2nd-yr BL	Bilinguals in first/second year Japanese courses		
3rd-yr BL	Bilinguals in special Japanese 307/308 courses		
4rd-yr BL	Bilinguals in advanced fourth year Japanese		

FORMAL AND NONFORMAL EDUCATION IN JAPANESE

Table 6 shows students' attendance in formal and nonformal Japanese language programs. While the majority of the first and second year students (62.5%) and the third year students (70.7%) attended *nihongo gakkoo*, less than half of the fourth year students (43.3%) did so. However, among those who attended *nihongo gakkoo*, the fourth year students stayed in the school longer (average 6.5 years) than first and second year students (average 4.2 years) or third year students (average 5.1 years). As for formal Japanese language education, the majority in each group studied Japanese at secondary school for a little less than three years, although a higher percentage of fourth year students (80%) studied Japanese in high school than did third year students (62.5%) or first and second year students (64%).

Table 6: Formal and non-formal education in Japanese

	1st/2nd-yr BL (N=40)	3rd-yr BL (N=75)	4rd-yr BL (N=30)
nihongo gakkoo			
attended	25 (62.5%)	53 (70.7%)	13 (43.3%)
did not attend	15 (37.5%)	22 (29.3%)	17 (56.7%)
secondary school Japanese class			
enrolled	25 (62.5%)	48 (64%)	24 (80%)
did not enroll	15 (37.5%)	27 (36%)	6 (20%)

1st/2nd-yr BL	Bilinguals in first/second year Japanese courses
3rd-yr BL	Bilinguals in special Japanese 307/308 courses
4rd-yr BL	Bilinguals in advanced fourth year Japanese

LANGUAGE CONTACTS OUTSIDE HOME AND SCHOOL

Table 7 shows students' Japanese language contacts outside home and school. Fourth year students use Japanese at work much more than third year students or first and second year students: 60% of the fourth year students use Japanese predominantly at work, while 33.3% of third year students do the same, and none of the first and second year students use Japanese regularly at work. As for the use of language with friends, English dominates the communication regardless of the students' proficiency in Japanese: most fourth year (80%) and third year students (85.3%) do not use Japanese with their friends, and none of the first and second year students use Japanese with their friends. The majority in all groups reported that they have visited Japan at least a few times. All fourth year students have visited Japan at least a few times, as have the majority of third year (86.6%) and first and second year students (67.5%).

Table 7: Language contacts outside home and school

	1st/2nd-yr BL (N=40)	3rd-yr BL (N=75)	4rd-yr BL (N=30)
use of Japanese at work			
always/mostly	0	25 (33.3%)	18 (60%)
sometimes	14 (35%)	14 (18.7%)	3 (10%)
seldom/never	21 (52.5%)	21 (28%)	3 (10%)
NA (do not work)	5 (12.5%)	15 (20%)	6 (20%)
use of Japanese with friends			
use	0	11 (14.7%)	6 (20%)
do not use	40 (100%)	64 (85.3%)	24 (80%)
visits to Japan			
more than 5 times	8 (20%)	34 (45.3%)	19 (63.3%)
a few times	19 (47.5%)	31 (41.3%)	11 (36.7%)
once	5 (12.5%)	9 (12%)	0
never	8 (20%)	1 (1.3%)	0

1st/2nd-yr BL   Bilinguals in first/second year Japanese courses
3rd-yr BL   Bilinguals in special Japanese 307/308 courses
4rd-yr BL   Bilinguals in advanced fourth year Japanese

MOTIVES FOR STUDYING JAPANESE AT THE UNIVERSITY

Table 8 shows students' motives for studying Japanese at the university. Language maintenance was the most common internal motive for studying Japanese among the survey participants. As for first and second year students, an external motive —or language requirement— was the most common reason (80%), although this was the least common reason for fourth year students (13.3%). The next most common motives among the students were to use the language for a job and to communicate with Japanese. About 40% of the students in each group study Japanese for better cultural understanding. The least common motive in every group was to travel in Japan.

Table 8: Motivation for studying Japanese (in %)

	1st/2nd-yr BL (N=40)	3rd-yr BL (N=75)	4rd-yr BL (N=30)
language requirement	80.0	52.0	13.3
maintaining/improving skills	77.5	88.0	80.0
communication	70.0	66.7	60.0
job	62.5	65.3	63.3
cultural understanding	40.0	42.7	40.0
pleasing parents	35.0	22.7	16.7
study in Japan	15.0	22.7	20.0
travel in Japan	12.5	16.0	10.0
others	20.0	6.7	6.7

ATTITUDES TOWARD LEARNING JAPANESE

Table 9 shows students' attitudes towards learning Japanese. The majority in every group responded that learning Japanese is interesting, challenging, and important. Fewer students in each group reported that learning Japanese is fun and enjoyable. About 30% of the students from each group feel proud of studying Japanese. "Nurturing" and "painful" were the items that received the lowest number of responses from all groups. More fourth year students (63.3%) and third year students (56%) reported that learning Japanese is rewarding than first and second year students (40%). On the other hand, a higher percentage of first and second year students reported that learning Japanese is frustrating (62.5%) than third year students (29.8%) or fourth year students (13.3%). More first and second year students also reported that learning Japanese is time-consuming (56.7%) than third year students (40%) and fourth year students (33.3%).

Table 9: Attitudes toward learning Japanese (in %)

	1st/2nd-yr BL (N=40)	3rd-yr BL (N=75)	4rd-yr BL (N=30)
challenging	85.0	80.0	70.0
important	70.0	74.5	73.7
frustrating	62.5	29.8	13.3
interesting	62.5	70.7	73.7
time-consuming	57.5	40.0	33.3
enjoyable	42.5	42.5	33.3
rewarding	40.0	56.0	63.3

continued…

Table 9: Attitudes toward learning Japanese (in %) (cont.)

	1st/2nd-yr BL (N=40)	3rd-yr BL (N=75)	4rd-yr BL (N=30)
fun	37.5	38.2	36.7
proud	27.5	26.7	33.3
nurturing	12.5	21.3	23.3
painful	10.0	12.0	6.7
others	7.5	2.7	0

Table 10 indicates that the majority of the survey participants, especially fourth year students, agreed or strongly agreed that their interest in the Japanese language and their cultural roots increased after they became college students.

Table 10: Increased interest in Japanese language and heritage

	1st/2nd-yr BL (N=40)	3rd-yr BL (N=75)	4rd-yr BL (N=30)
strongly agree/ agree	20 (50%)	45 (60%)	21 (70%)
maybe	13 (32.5%)	23 (30.7%)	5 (16.7%)
disagree/ strongly disagree	7 (17.5%)	7 (9.3%)	4 (13.3%)

1st/2nd-yr BL Bilinguals in first/second year Japanese courses
3rd-yr BL   Bilinguals in special Japanese 307/308 courses
4rd-yr BL   Bilinguals in advanced fourth year Japanese

ATTITUDES TOWARD BILINGUALISM

Table 11 shows students' attitudes towards bilingualism. More than 90% in each group reported that bilingual Niseis have more advantages in the job market in Hawai'i. The majority in each group also reported that bilingual Niseis have better cultural understanding, although more fourth year (80%) and third year students (77.3%) than first and second year students (60%) reported so. In addition, the majority of the fourth year (66.7%) and third year students (70.7%) reported that bilingual Niseis have closer relationships with their Japanese parents and relatives. A much smaller number of first and second year students (37.5%) reported the same. Less than half of the students in each group reported that bilingual Niseis have a more enriched life and more flexibility. On the other hand, approximately half of the students in each group reported that monolingual Niseis are more isolated from the Japanese community than bilingual Niseis. In addition, a small number of students from each group reported that monolingual Niseis have a better command of English and are more adjusted to American society.

As for reactions to the statement that "bilingualism should be a universal norm for all people in the U.S. or that it should be encouraged," a majority of the students in each group reported that they agreed or strongly agreed, although more fourth year (70%) and third year students (64.9%) than first and second year students (55%) reported so. Less than 15% of the students in each group disagreed with the statement.

Table 11: Attitudes toward bilingualism (in %)

	1st/2nd-yr BL (N=40)	3rd-yr BL (N=75)	4rd-yr BL (N=30)
about monolingual Nisei			
more isolation from Japanese community	47.5	50.7	53.3
better adjustment to American society	30.0	22.7	30.0
better command of English	15.0	18.7	26.7
others	12.5	4.0	0
about bilingual Nisei			
more advantage in job market	92.5	97.3	90.0
better cultural understanding	60.0	77.3	80.0
more flexible	40.0	48.0	36.7
closer relationships with parents/relatives	37.5	70.7	66.7
more enriched life	17.5	29.3	20.0
others	7.5	5.3	3.3

DISCUSSION AND CONCLUSION

This survey study has investigated the extent and frequency of language contacts and use as well as the language learning motivation of 145 bilingual heritage students enrolled in various levels of Japanese courses at UHM. This study has only examined correlations among language behavior, language contact, and motivation; we still don't know which factors affect which. A limitation of this study is that students who volunteered to participate in the survey may have more positive views and attitudes toward learning Japanese than those who did not. In other words, a voluntary survey method can exclude students whose thoughts and feelings about Japanese language learning and maintenance are not as positive as those who participated in the survey. This study did not include students who chose not to take Japanese courses at college. This exclusion, too, may have brought some biases to the research results. Within these limitations, I will discuss my conclusions by answering the research questions posed earlier.

1. In what contexts have UHM bilingual heritage students in advanced Japanese classes made more frequent contacts and use in the language than those in beginning/intermediate Japanese?

My survey results suggest that UHM bilingual heritage students in advanced Japanese have had much more extensive Japanese language contacts and use in *informal* learning environments than those in beginning and intermediate Japanese, and within the various informal Japanese language contacts available to these students, the choice of language for communication with mothers seems most critically associated with their language behavior. Previous research has suggested that language shift begins with women, who prefer high-prestige language varieties (e.g., Gal, 1984; Paulston, 1994). My survey results suggest the central role of mothers in Japanese language maintenance in Hawai'i. Follow-up interviews with UHM students also confirm that, even in multicultural/multiethnic Hawai'i, there is a strong assimilative pull from the dominant culture. In this sociocultural milieu, Japanese mothers play a critical role in Japanese language maintenance, especially oral skills (Kondo, 1997). A much less significant role for fathers resulted partly because 58% of them were not native speakers of Japanese. Many of these non-Japanese fathers —by choice or necessity— do not seem to use Japanese with their children.

Second, my survey results suggest that the number of years of formal instruction in Japanese during the pre-college period is not a critical factor differentiating their language behavior. The majority of the bilinguals in all Japanese classes took several years of Japanese at secondary school and/or *nihongo gakkoo*. These students did not achieve advanced oral skills unless they spoke Japanese at home with their mothers. This finding supports the claim that formal instruction helps learners to learn the target language when the learners also have opportunities to practice the language in a natural setting (Ellis, 1994, pp. 615–616). However, this does not necessarily mean that formal instruction does not help students who have little opportunities to use the language outside the classroom. I have suggested elsewhere that one of the critical reasons that many heritage bilingual students fail to achieve advanced skills in spoken and or written Japanese during the pre-college period is inappropriate formal learning environments. I have observed problems with educational support for Japanese language maintenance in Hawai'i such as the dominant use of English at *nihongo gakkoo* and bilingual heritage students' socially isolating and academically unsatisfactory Japanese learning experiences in foreign language classes in secondary school (see Kondo, 1997).

2. Why do bilingual heritage students of Japanese study the language in college? Are there differences in motivation among bilinguals in various levels of Japanese classes?

There are few differences in internal motives for studying Japanese among bilinguals at various levels of Japanese study, except that the great majority of bilinguals in beginning and intermediate-level Japanese also study Japanese for an external reason, to fulfill a language requirement. Most bilinguals at all levels of Japanese have both instrumental and integrative motives: the most common motives are to maintain or improve Japanese language skills for work and for communication with Japanese people. On the other hand, they have little interest in learning Japanese for visiting or staying in Japan as a tourist or a student. There are many opportunities to use Japanese for work and communication in Hawai'i, and bilingual heritage students of Japanese seem to learn the language so that they can use it in their immediate environments rather than social settings remote to them.

3. What attitudes do bilingual heritage students have toward learning the language and bilingualism? Are there differences in attitudes among bilinguals in various levels of Japanese classes?

My survey results suggest that there are both similarities and differences in attitudes toward learning Japanese among bilinguals at various levels of Japanese. First, most students at all levels of Japanese reported that Japanese language learning is challenging, interesting, and important, although less than half reported that it is enjoyable, fun, proud, or nurturing. At the same time, more bilinguals in beginning/intermediate Japanese than those in advanced Japanese reported that Japanese language learning is unrewarding, frustrating, and time-consuming. Thus, overall, bilinguals in advanced Japanese have more positive attitudes toward learning Japanese than those in beginning/intermediate Japanese.

Second, the majority of bilinguals at all levels of Japanese, especially those who are in fourth year Japanese, responded that their interests in Japanese language and culture increased after they became college students. In other words, bilingual heritage students' attitudes towards their heritage language are not static. As they grew up, they have developed stronger interest in their heritage (see also Kondo, 1998a). It is not clear what has caused this change, although some studies emphasize the developmental nature of language attitude (e.g., Baker, 1992) and ethnic identity (e.g., Cross, 1991; Tse, 1998). The predominant L2 acquisition models of motivation generally do not pay attention to developmental changes (Oxford & Shearin, 1994; for an exception, see Baker, 1992), but this study suggests that developmental considerations are important in understanding students' motivation and attitudes.

Lastly, bilinguals at all levels of Japanese unanimously see the economic advantages of Nisei's bilingualism. In addition, most bilinguals at all levels of Japanese disagree that monolingual Niseis have linguistic/social advantages such as better command of English. At the same time, more bilinguals in advanced Japanese than those in beginning/intermediate Japanese see bilingual Niseis' other personal advantages such as closer relationship with parents/relatives and support societal bilingualism as well. Thus, bilingual heritage students of Japanese in my study generally have positive attitudes toward bilingualism, and they at least see its instrumental/economic advantages.[9]

---

[9] Follow-up interviews with the participants also confirm that motivation strongly influences their persistence in taking college Japanese and the intensity with which they use Japanese outside the classroom (Kondo, 1999).

REFERENCES

Allard, R., & Landry, R. (1994). Subjective ethnolinguistic vitality: A comparison of two measures. *International Journal of the Sociology of Language, 108*, 117–144.

Au, S. Y. (1988). A critical appraisal of Gardner's social-psychological theory of second language (L2) learning. *Language Learning, 38*, 75–100.

Baker, C. (1992). *Attitudes and language.* Clevedon, UK: Multilingual Matters.

Baker, C. (1996). *Foundations of bilingual education and bilingualism,* (2nd Ed.). Clevedon, UK: Multilingual Matters.

Clément, R. (1980). Ethnicity, contact and communicative competence in a second language. In H. Giles, W. P. Robinson, & P. M. Smith (Eds.), *Language: Social psychological perspectives* (pp. 147–54). Oxford, UK: Pergamon.

Clément, R., Dörnyei, Z., & Noels, K. A. (1994). Motivation, self-confidence, and group cohesion in the foreign language classroom. *Language Learning, 44,* 417–448.

Clément, R., & Kruidenier, B. G. (1985). Aptitude, attitude and motivation in second language proficiency: A test of Clément's model. *Journal of Multilingual and Multicultural Development, 4,* 21–37.

Crookes, G., & Schmidt, R. (1991). Motivation: Reopening the research agenda. *Language Learning, 41,* 469–512.

Cross, W. E. (1991). *Shades of Black: Diversity in African-American identity.* Philadelphia: Temple University Press.

Ellis, R. (1994). *The study of second language acquisition.* Oxford, UK: Oxford University Press.

Gal, S. (1984). Peasant men can't get wives: Language change and sex roles in a bilingual community. In J. Baugh & J. Sherzer (Eds.), *Language in use: Readings in sociolinguistics* (pp. 292–304). Englewood Cliffs, NJ: Prentice-Hall.

Gardner, R. C. (1985). *Social psychology and second language learning: The role of attitudes and motivation.* London: Edward Arnold.

Gardner, R. C. (1988). The socio-educational model of second language learning: Assumptions, findings, and issues. *Language Learning, 38*, 101–126.

Gardner, R. C. (1991). Attitudes and motivation in second language learning. In A. Reynolds (Ed.), *Bilingualism, multiculturalism, and second language learning* (pp. 43–64). Hillsdale, NJ: Lawrence Erlbaum.

Gardner, R. C., & Lambert, W. (1972). *Attitudes and motivation in second language learning.* Rowley, MA: Newbury House.

Gardner, R. C., Lalonde, R. N., & Pierson, R. (1983). The socio-educational model of second language acquisition: An investigation using LISREL causal modeling. *Journal of Language and Social Psychology, 2,* 1–15.

Gardner, R. C., & Tremblay, P. F. (1994). On motivation, research agendas, and theoretical frameworks. *Modern Language Journal, 78,* 359–368.

Giles, H., & Byrne, J. L. (1982). An intergroup approach to second language acquisition. *Journal of Multilingual and Multicultural Development, 3*, 17–40.

Grosjean, F. (1982). *Life with two languages.* Cambridge, MA: Harvard University Press.

Hakuta, K. (1986). *Mirror of language: The debate on bilingualism.* New York: Basic Books.

Hakuta, K., & D'Andrea, D. (1993). Some properties of bilingual maintenance and loss in Mexican background high-school students. *Applied Linguistics, 13*, 72–99.

Kondo, K. (1997). Social-psychological factors in language maintenance: Interviews with shin Nisei university students in Hawaiʻi. *Linguistics and Education, 9*, 396–408.

Kondo, K. (1998a). *Japanese language learning, academic achievement and identity: Voices of new second generation Japanese American university students in Hawaiʻi.* Unpublished doctoral dissertation, University of Hawaiʻi at Mānoa, Honolulu.

Kondo, K. (1998b). The paradox of US language policy and Japanese language education in Hawaiʻi. *International Journal of Bilingual Education and Bilingualism, 1*, 47–64.

Kondo, K. (1999). Motivating bilingual and semibilingual university students of Japanese: An analysis of language learning persistence and intensity among students from immigrant backgrounds. *Foreign Language Annals, 32*, 77–88.

Kreitler, H., & Kreitler, S. (1972). The model of cognitive orientation: Towards a theory of human behavior. *British Journal of Psychology, 63*, 9–30.

McGroarty, M. (1996). Language attitudes, motivation, and standards. In S. L. McKay & N. H. Hornberger (Eds.), *Sociolinguistics and language teaching* (pp. 3–46). New York: Cambridge University Press.

McKay, S. L., & Wong, S. C. (1996). Multiple discourses, multiple identities: Investment and agency in second language learning among Chinese adolescent immigrant students. *Harvard Educational Review, 66*, 577–608.

Norton Peirce, B. (1995). Social identity, investment, and language learning. *TESOL Quarterly, 29*, 9–31.

Oxford, R. (Ed.). (1996). *Language learning motivation: Pathways to the new century* (Technical Report #11). Honolulu: The University of Hawaiʻi at Mānoa, Second Language Teaching & Curriculum Center.

Oxford, R., & Shearin, J. (1994). Language learning motivation: Expanding the theoretical framework. *The Modern Language Journal, 78*, 12–28.

Paulston, C. B. (1994). *Linguistic minorities in multilingual settings.* Amsterdam: John Benjamins.

Prujiner, A., Deshaies, D., Hamers, J. F., Blanc, M., Clément, R., & Landry, R. (1984). *Variation du comportement langagier lorsque deux langues sont en contact.* [Variations in language behaviour when two languages are in contact] Quebec: Centre international de recherches sur le bilinguisme.

Romaine, S. (1995). *Bilingualism* (2nd ed.) Oxford, UK: Basil Blackwell.

Spolsky, B. (1989). *Conditions for second language learning.* Oxford, UK: Oxford University Press.

Swain, M. (1985). Communicative competence: Some roles of comprehensible input and comprehensible output in its development. In S. M. Gass & C. G. Madden (Eds.), *Input in second language acquisition* (pp. 235–253). Rowley, MA: Newbury House.

Tremblay, P. F., & Gardner, R. C. (1995). Expanding the motivation construct in language learning. *The Modern Language Journal, 79,* 505–518.

Tse, L. (1998). Ethnic identity formation and its implications for heritage language development. In S. D. Krashen, L. Tse, & J. McQuillan (Eds.), *Heritage language development* (pp. 15–30). Culver City, CA: Language Education Associates.

Valdés, G., & Figueroa, R. (1994). *Bilingualism and testing: A special case of bias.* Norwood, NJ: Ablex.

Van Deusen-Scholl, N. (2000, March). *Toward a definition of 'heritage language': Pedagogical and sociopolitical considerations.* Paper presented at the meeting of the American Association for Applied Linguistics.

Warschauer, M. (1996). Motivational aspects of using computers for writing and communication. In M. Warschauer (Ed.), *Telecollaboration in foreign language learning: Proceedings of the Hawai'i symposium.* (Technical Report #12, pp. 29–46). Honolulu: University of Hawai'i, Second Language Teaching & Curriculum Center.

APPENDIX I: SURVEY QUESTIONNAIRE FORM

LANGUAGE SURVEY OF SECOND GENERATION JAPANESE AMERICANS

name: _____ age: _____ sex: male/female

phone #: _____

nationality: _____ primary language: _____

class standing:
    a. freshman
    b. sophomore
    c. junior
    d. senior
    e. graduate

major: _____

your mother: _____

    ethnic background: _____ occupation: _____

your father: _____

    ethnic background: _____ occupation: _____

_____

1. Did you attend Japanese language school?
    a. yes   school: from 19_____ to 19_____
    b. no

2. Did you study Japanese in secondary school?
    a. yes   school: from 19_____ to 19_____
    b. no

3. Have you lived in Japan ?
    a. yes   where? _____ from 19____ to 19_____
    b. no

4. How many times have you visited Japan?
    a. never
    b. once
    c. a few times
    d. more than five times

5. Check if either of your parents is a *native speaker of Japanese*:
    a. mother
    b. father

6. How long did you live with your parent(s)?
   a. I still live with my parents
   b. until I graduated from high school
   c. other (please specify) _____

7. When you were a child, what were your *first* language(s) ? (circle all as apply)
   a. English
   b. Japanese
   c. Okinawan
   d. others (please specify) _____

8. How often do *you* use *Japanese* when you talk to your *mother*?
   a. always
   b. most of the time
   c. half
   d. seldom
   e. not at all
   f. not applicable

9. How often do *you* use *Japanese* when you talk to your *father*?
   a. always
   b. most of the time
   c. half
   d. seldom
   e. not at all
   f. not applicable

10. How often does your *mother* use Japanese when she talks to you?
    a. always
    b. most of the time
    c. half
    d. seldom
    e. not at all
    f. not applicable

11. How often does your father use Japanese when he talks to you?
    a. always
    b. most of the time
    c. half
    d. seldom
    e. not at all
    f. not applicable

12. What languages do you use most with your sibling(s)? (circle all as apply)
    a. English
    b. Japanese
    c. others (please specify) _____
    d. not applicable

13. What languages do you use most with your friends? (circle all as apply)
    a. English
    b. Japanese
    c. others (please specify) _____

14. Do you watch TV in Japanese?
    a. always
    b. most of the time
    c. sometimes
    d. seldom
    e. never
    f. not applicable

15. Do you use Japanese at work?
    a. always
    b. most of the time
    c. sometimes
    d. seldom
    e. never
    f. not applicable

16. Which is easier for you to speak, Japanese or English?
    a. Japanese
    b. English
    c. about the same

17. How do you evaluate your oral fluency in Japanese?
    a. very fluent
    b. fluent
    c. average
    d. poor
    e. very poor

18. How do you evaluate your fluency in reading and writing *hiragana* and *katakana*?
    a. very fluent
    b. fluent
    c. average
    d. poor
    e. very poor

19. How do you feel about your language skills in Japanese? (circle all as apply)
    a. happy
    b. proud
    c. good
    d. convenient
    e. depressed
    f. frustrated
    g. bad
    h. others (please specify)_____

20. How much do you understand Japanese TV programs?
    a. everything
    b. almost everything
    c. half
    d. little
    e. not at all

21. Can you read Japanese newspapers?
    a. very well
    b. well
    c. little
    d. not at all

22. After you became a college student, do you think that you became more interested in Japanese language and your cultural roots?
    a. strongly agree
    b. agree
    c. maybe
    d. disagree
    e. strongly disagree

23. Why do you study Japanese? (circle all as apply)
    a. to satisfy the foreign language requirement
    b. to please Japanese parent(s)
    c. to go to Japan for vacation
    d. to use Japanese for a job
    e. to go to Japan to study
    f. to maintain and/or improve language skills in Japanese
    g. to understand Japanese culture and people better
    h. to communicate with native speakers of Japanese
    i. other (please specify) _____

24. How do you feel about studying Japanese? (circle all as apply)
    a. interesting
    b. important
    c. fun
    d. nurturing
    d. challenging
    e enjoyable
    f. proud
    g. rewarding
    h. painful
    i. frustrating
    j. time-consuming
    k. other (please specify) _____

25. Compared to English monolingual Niseis, *Japanese-English bilingual Niseis*: (circle all as apply)
    a. have more advantages in the job market, especially in Hawaiʻi.
    b. have a better understanding of Japanese culture.
    c. have closer relationships with their Japanese parents and relatives.
    d. have more enriched lives.
    e. are more flexible.
    f. other (please specify) _____

26. Compared to Japanese-English bilingual Niseis, *English monolingual Niseis*: (circle all as apply)
    a. have a better command of English.
    b. are more adjusted to American society.
    c. feel more isolated from their Japanese family and community.
    d. other (please specify) _____

27. Do you think that bilingualism should be a universal norm for all people in the United States, or that it should be encouraged?
    a. strongly agree
    b. agree
    c. maybe
    d. disagree
    e. strongly disagree

28. I would like to know if I could interview you.
    a. Yes, I would consent to an interview.
    b. No, I would not consent to an interview at this time.

(THE END. THANK YOU VERY MUCH)

Peter D. MacIntyre
Keith MacMaster
Susan C. Baker
University College of Cape Breton

THE CONVERGENCE OF MULTIPLE MODELS OF MOTIVATION FOR SECOND LANGUAGE LEARNING: GARDNER, PINTRICH, KUHL, AND MCCROSKEY

Authors' note

This research was facilitated by a research grant from the Social Sciences and Humanities Research Council of Canada. We would like to thank the teachers, staff, and students of Breton Education Centre in New Waterford, Nova Scotia, Canada for participating in this study. We would like to acknowledge the assistance of Brenna Fraser and Roger Covin. Correspondence related to this research should be sent to Peter MacIntyre, University College of Cape Breton, Sydney, Nova Scotia, Canada B1P 6L2, e-mail pmacinty@uccb.ns.ca

Abstract

Gardner's socio-educational model of second language acquisition, which revolves around the integrative motive, has generated a great deal of research support. Recently, critics have challenged that the model excludes a number of variables identified as potentially relevant to second language learning. The present study empirically tests for the overlap among 10 concepts from Gardner's model, six concepts from an academic motivation model offered by Pintrich and associates, three concepts from an action control model proposed by Kuhl and associates, and three communication-related variables employed by McCroskey and associates. Factor analysis reveals a three-factor solution which accounts for 55% of the variance in the 22 scales employed. This high degree of empirically demonstrable similarity among concepts from four separate research paradigms indicates the breadth of the Gardner model and the value of testing empirically the theoretical distinctions among specific motivation constructs.

INTRODUCTION

In 1959, Gardner and Lambert highlighted the importance of two variables in language learning: aptitude and motivation. This has produced a research agenda that has been followed for decades. Over 40 years later, Clément and Gardner (in press) note that while research activity in the study of aptitude has lagged in recent years, research into the role and process of motivation for second language learning

MacIntyre, P. D., MacMaster, K., & Baker, S. C. (2001). The convergence of multiple models of motivation for second language learning: Gardner, Pintrich, Kuhl, and McCroskey. In Z. Dörnyei & R. Schmidt (Eds.), *Motivation and second language acquisition* (Technical Report #23, pp. 461–492). Honolulu: University of Hawai'i, Second Language Teaching and Curriculum Center.

is still vibrant. Motivation represents one of the most appealing, yet complex, variables used to explain individual differences in language learning.

The present study attempts to demonstrate links among four theoretical frameworks and their corresponding sets of variables that approach the topic of motivation from different directions. The first framework is Gardner's (1985) socio-educational (S-E) model, which proposes that motivation is based in large part on inter-group attitudes and an attraction to the target language and culture. The second set of variables, offered by Pintrich and associates (Pintrich, Smith, Garcia, & McKeachie, 1991), is focused primarily on variables taken from the broad social-learning literature on motivation (such as self-efficacy, task value, and intrinsic goal orientation) as applied to academic learning contexts. The third model emerges from psycho-physiological studies of motivation by Kuhl (1994a) who proposed a theory of action-control, which highlights the role of three interrelated processes: preoccupation with failure, hesitation in taking action after a decision has been made, and volatility or instability in performing enjoyable activities. The fourth collection of variables, studied by McCroskey and associates (McCroskey & Richmond, 1991), comes from the literature on native language communication. Variables such as willingness to communicate, communication apprehension, and communication competence are making their way into the second language literature. Each of these perspectives will be discussed, followed by a theoretical analysis of the links among them.

GARDNER'S SOCIO-EDUCATIONAL MODEL

Perhaps the most significant development in the study of language learning motivation was Gardner's S-E model. Dörnyei (1994) has commented on this model:

> I believe that the most important milestone in the history of L2 motivation research has been Gardner and Lambert's discovery that success is a function of the learner's attitude toward the linguistic-cultural community of the target language, thus adding a social dimension to the study of motivation to learn an L2... By combining motivation theory with social psychological theory, the model of L2 motivation that Gardner and Lambert developed was much more elaborate and advanced than many contemporary mainstream psychological models of motivation in that it was empirically testable and did indeed explain a considerable amount of variance in student motivation and achievement. (p. 519)

Gardner's model incorporates four basic sets of variables (Gardner & MacIntyre, 1993). The first is the socio-cultural milieu and the beliefs associated with the intergroup relations that exist between language communities. The second set of variables is based on individual differences among learners that lie at the heart of Gardner's theory and research. Integrative motivation is the centrepiece of the individual differences studied by Gardner and associates over the years. Acquisition contexts represent the third set of variables in the model and can be grouped into two broad classes, formal learning contexts and informal ones. Finally, language learning outcomes, both linguistic and non-linguistic, feed back into the rest of the model making it dynamic and its elements modifiable over the course of the language learning experience.

Motivation has been studied as an individual difference variable, but other variables have been implicated as well. The first group falls under the heading of *affect* and includes variables such as attitudes and motivation (Gardner, 1985), anxiety (Horwitz, Horwitz, & Cope, 1986) and self-confidence (Clément, 1980; Gardner, Tremblay, & Masgoret, 1997). The second group refers to *ability* and includes language aptitude (Carroll & Sapon, 1959), intelligence (Spolsky, 1989), and field independence (Chapelle & Greene, 1992). The final group is called *individual actions* and is concerned with language learning strategies (Oxford, 1990). According to Gardner (1996), when an individual has the opportunity to learn an L2, these variables will impact how much and how quickly he/she will learn. Obviously, motivation will be one of the most important factors during the learning process.

Gardner (1996) describes two distinct perspectives one might take on motivation. The first is motivation as a characteristic of the individual or an internal attribute. The second is motivation as an external attribute, meaning that motivation can be created by some external force or reward. A hybrid perspective, and one that the majority of researchers appear to endorse, is that motivation can be an internal attribute that is the result of an external force (Gardner, 1996). Gardner (1996), however, argues that motivation must be a characteristic of the individual and that it cannot be created, out of nothing, by an external force. An external force can *arouse* motivation, as when a teacher attempts to motivate a student. The potential to be motivated must already exist and be a property of the student in order for a particular pedagogical technique to be effective. As Gardner (1996) simply states, "you can't motivate a rock" (p. 25).

In the socio-educational model, motivation has most frequently been characterised as an *Integrative Motive*, which is comprised of integrativeness, attitudes toward the learning situation, and motivation (Gardner, 1985). Integrativeness refers to an individual's desire to interact with the L2 group and is measured by three scales: integrative orientation, attitudes toward the target language group, and interest in foreign languages in general. Attitudes toward the learning situation deal with the individual's evaluation of the course and the teacher. Finally, motivation assesses three components related to the L2: the individual's attitude toward learning, desire to learn, and the effort invested, which is referred to as motivational intensity. Thus, Gardner's concept of motivation provides for behavioural, cognitive, and affective components.

A widely misunderstood feature of the Gardner model is the distinction between orientations and motivation; motivation is not synonymous with orientations. On one hand, orientations are clusters of reasons for studying an L2. On the other hand, motivation is an attribute of the individual describing the psychological qualities underlying behavior with respect to a particular task. Motivation is clearly defined in Gardner's (1985) socio-educational model as the interplay among desire to achieve a goal, effort expended, and the pleasure associated with a task. Gardner (1996) asserts that all three components must be present for an individual to be motivated. Furthermore, it is possible to recognize the value of a language and to be oriented toward that language, but without activating effort and positive affect, the individual would be oriented but not motivated to learn the L2.

Positive affect also tends to indicate a lack of anxiety about the second language, though the role of anxiety in Gardner's model is not as explicit as the role of motivation. Gardner (1985) found that anxiety was situation-specific and was negatively related to L2 achievement. Research has shown that anxiety is also negatively related to attitudes and motivation (Gardner, Lalonde, & Moorcroft, 1985; Gardner, Day, & MacIntyre, 1992). There has been some question about whether anxiety should be seen as a cause of differences in proficiency or as a product of them (Young, 1986). MacIntyre and Gardner (1994) found experimental evidence that anxiety can lead to decrements in language learning, but Gardner, Tremblay, and Masgoret (1997) found support for a model in which self-confidence was a product of higher L2 proficiency. In Clément's (1980, 1986) model, self-confidence is essentially the feeling of proficiency in the L2 and is characterized by low levels of anxiety. Clément argues that self-confidence can be a secondary motivational process running in parallel to the sort of inter-group processes discussed by Gardner (1985).

Although there were bothersome issues, such as the role played by anxiety, as well as published criticisms (Au, 1988; Oller, 1981), Gardner's theory went virtually unchallenged until the mid-1990s. At that time, critics argued that motivation should be studied from different perspectives (see Dörnyei, 1990, 1994; Oxford & Shearin, 1994; Crookes & Schmidt, 1991). These authors claim that Gardner's theory put too much emphasis on the integrative and instrumental distinction and tended to ignore a list of variables from the broad psychological literature on motivation, including extrinsic rewards, self-efficacy, expectancy, attributions, locus of control, and so on. Gardner and Tremblay (1994) responded that the socio-educational model makes a distinction between instrumental and integrative *orientations* and not *motivations*. Instrumental motivation is actually discussed in very little detail and, whereas integrative motivation is a key concept in the model, it is not the foremost concept of Gardner's theory.

The critics have argued that an expansion of the socio-educational model seems to be necessary. However, caution must be exercised when proposing new motivational variables and frameworks. At a minimum, such variables should tap into processes not already covered in the socio-educational model. The socio-educational model has been shown to account for a significant amount of variance in language proficiency (Dörnyei, 1998; Gardner & MacIntyre, 1993). To suggest "new research directions" that cover the same conceptual ground would seem to be a wasteful exercise. Therefore, the purpose of the present study is to examine the level of empirical similarity between the variables represented by (1) Gardner socio-educational model, (2) Pintrich's MSLQ, (3) Kuhl's ASC–90, and (4) McCroskey's communication variables, using factor analysis.

PINTRICH'S PERSPECTIVE ON ACADEMIC MOTIVATION

The model offered by Pintrich and associates (Pintrich et al., 1991) examines general academic motivation from an expectancy-value perspective. Pintrich, Marx, & Boyle (1993) argue that the process of learning involves both the *assimilation* of new information, which is a relatively effortless process, and the more difficult process of changing the structure of internalized knowledge, called *accommodation*. Accommodation places heavy demands on the cognitive system requiring a great deal of effort. For this reason, the process of accommodation is seen as depending on student motivation to a large extent. If we consider language learning, especially at the early stages, a great deal of accommodation is necessary to acquire everything from grammar structure and syntax to cultural norms and idioms. For this reason, the types of motivational variables discussed by Pintrich are likely to apply to the language learning environment. The instrument developed by Pintrich et al., the Motivated Strategies for Learning Questionnaire (MSLQ) has two sections: the motivation subsection and the learning strategy subsection. Only the motivation subsection was used in the present study, in part, because strategies are viewed as an outcome of motivational patterns.

Expectancy-value theories have a long history in psychology (Reeve, 1992). In essence, expectancy refers to the anticipated outcomes of behavior and value refers to the desirability of those outcomes (Tolman, 1959). Six components of the MSLQ were used in the present investigation:

- *Value Component: Intrinsic Goal Orientation.* A student's goal orientation involves the perception of the reasons behind learning something new. An orientation is intrinsic if the reasons for taking the course include such things as challenge, curiosity, and developing expertise. Other researchers have referred to this as a mastery orientation (see Dörnyei, 1998) focused on developing competence in a task for its own sake, rather than for external rewards. Such an orientation would be manifested in a language course particularly in terms of communicative and possibly cultural goals, although these are not mentioned explicitly in the MSLQ items themselves.

- *Value Component: Extrinsic Goal Orientation.* This is often presented as "the opposite of" intrinsic reasons on taking a course. Extrinsic goals include good grades, higher pay, and comparing one's performance to that of others. There is no conceptual reason to consider intrinsic and extrinsic goals as mutually exclusive. Indeed, a student might have both intrinsic and extrinsic goals, just one of them, or neither. The extent to which these orientations correlate will be examined in the present data set.

- *Value Component: Task Value.* Task value represents the perception of how interesting, useful, and important the course is. It measures the extent to which the course is seen as valuable within the student's frame of reference. This differs from goal orientations, which refer to the reasons why a task is undertaken, not the importance of the task.

- *Expectancy Component: Control of Learning Beliefs.* This component refers to how much the student expects to be able to control the outcomes of the course. If outcomes are contingent upon their own behavior, students will have a high perception of control over learning and should study more effectively. Students with low perceived control over learning would believe that they would not have positive outcomes, no matter how much effort is put into learning.

- *Expectancy Component: Self-Efficacy for Learning and Performance.* This subscale is made up of two parts: the expectancy for success and self-efficacy. Expectancy for success is the amount of performance the person anticipates will arise from his/her behavior. Self-efficacy is the judgment made about one's ability to complete the course and master the material. Overall, the items in the scale reflect a perception of competence.

- *Affective Component: Test Anxiety.* The affective component in Pintrich et al.'s (1991) model is test anxiety. A great deal of research has been conducted into the origins and effects of test anxiety in general (see Sarason, 1986) and some work has been done in the language area as well (Horwitz et al., 1986; MacIntyre & Gardner, 1991). It is a fairly safe conclusion that academic performance is negatively correlated with anxiety. Anxiety has long been viewed as having two components (Leibert & Morris, 1967), a cognitive component (worry/negative thoughts) and an emotional component (affective/physiological arousal).

KUHL'S ACTION CONTROL MODEL

Kuhl (1994a) takes a different approach to the study of motivation. Kuhl's model focuses on a theory of action versus state orientation. It assesses the individual differences in the ability to initiate and maintain levels of behaviour versus a tendency toward hesitation and rumination. His measurement instrument, the action control scale (ACS–90), was an attempt to integrate the various state and action concepts into one coherent model. He postulated that if the motivation level was high enough, then there would be a tendency towards an action orientation. If motivation were low or moderate, then individual differences in action control would determine the level of action. On one hand, action oriented people tend to be active rather than passive, and unwilling or unable to sit back and do nothing. Those with a state orientation, on the other hand, are more likely to let things happen without intervention. State oriented people tend to contemplate past and present feelings rather than taking action to change their affective state.

Developed primarily to assess individual differences in personality affecting the ability to maintain arousal to start or complete a task, the ACS–90 scale (Kuhl, 1994b) can be extended to include the motivation necessary to learn a second language. Similar to the other scales used in the present study, the ACS–90 is a self-report measure. The items themselves present concrete situations where the respondent is forced to choose between an action alternative and a state alternative: for example, "When I know I must finish something soon…" The choices are (a) "I have to push myself to get started" or (b) "I find it easy to get it done and over with." Kuhl (1994b) argues that forced choice is preferable to Likert response scales because the "phenomenal concomitants of action/state orientation in a concrete situation may be easily retrievable from explicit (episodic) memory (c.f. Schacter, 1987), where information concerning the globality of the underlying trait may be represented on an implicit level only" (p. 48).

Kuhl uses the term action control to encompass all of the processes mediating intentions. State orientation is the inability to initiate an intended behavior because of a preoccupation or hesitation. These two key concepts are represented as subscales in Kuhl's model, along with a volatility scale that represents an excessively energetic action control system. The following three scales make up the ACS–90:

- *Action Orientation Subsequent to Failure versus Preoccupation (AOF)*. This scale measures the extent to which intrusive and enduring thoughts cause a person to fail to initiate or change a behavior. The focus on explicit references to past or future state reduces the individual's availability to engage in other necessary cognitive activities, which are needed to solve a given problem, such as when learning a language. The failure component involves unpleasant feelings associated with not being able to complete the tasks. The failure component occupies half of the AOF questions, but the AOF is not confined to achievement situations. Therefore, Kuhl claims that the preoccupation component is different from, and therefore should not correlate with, the worry component of test anxiety, which is confined to achievement related settings (e.g., the Pintrich Test Anxiety Scale). For example, a student who incorrectly answers a question might be so embarrassed and unable to "get over it" that he will not volunteer an answer again even if he is certain of the answer. Another student in the same situation, given the same reaction from her classmates, might have no difficulty at all attempting to answer a later question because she is low in preoccupation.

- *Prospective and Decision-related Action Orientation versus Hesitation (AOD)*. This scale describes difficulties associated with the initiation of an intended activity, without having reference to any decision related behavior. Hesitation involves the inability to translate decisions into action. The AOD is an intermediary between making the decision and actually carrying out the intended behavior. It occurs after the decision of intention to behavior has been made but before the action is actually carried out. It is at this time that people vacillate between continuing their current behavior and following through on the decision to initiate the action that they just contemplated. That is, after deciding on a course of action, people take different amounts of time to act on those decisions. For example, a language student might decide to take a tourist excursion to the target language community, having every intention to do so at some future time, but never actually do it.

- *Action Orientation During (successful) Performance of Activities (intrinsic orientation) versus Volatility (AOP)*. This scale contains items that assess the ability to stay within self-initiated and pleasant activities without shifting prematurely to alternative activities. It is how well one person can stay focused on a topic. Kuhl believes that volatility impairs the maintenance of activities by an *over functioning* of the action system. Pleasant activities are abandoned in favor of novel ones simply to satisfy a desire for change. For example, an Anglophone studying French might experience success but move on to a new language or other activity, therefore not gaining much French proficiency despite enjoying the language.

In arguing for the value of his model over existing formulations, Kuhl (1994a) states that "expectancy-value theories cannot account for the paradoxical behaviors [of human beings]" (p. 9). Expectancy-value theorists state that humans would likely engage in those activities that have the highest subjective reward. However, Kuhl states that these theories do not account for the seemingly contradictory behavior where humans continually engage in low beneficial behavior while knowing that there are more rewarding alternative activities that can be performed. This most directly contradicts Pintrich et al.'s (1991) notion of task value. Pintrich et al. state that the higher the task value, the more motivated the person will be, and we can infer this will lead to more emphasis on learning the language. Kuhl argues that motivation does not imply action. He states that placing a high value on a task will not necessarily mean a correspondingly high action level. Gardner (1996) has proposed that motivated behavior requires an intensity of effort, in addition to the presence of goals and positive affect, thereby bypassing the issue of action-taking that Kuhl seeks to address.

Perhaps the most significant action one can take in language learning is speaking the L2. In addition to the motivational processes raised thus far, a host of communication processes might impinge on L2 communication. It is certain that some of these processes will be motivational in nature, including those based on intergroup relations, attraction to the target language and culture, as well as interpersonal motives of affiliation and control. A recent model (MacIntyre, Clément, Dörnyei, & Noels, 1998) synthesizes these and other influences in proposing that communication in the L2 is most immediately preceded by an intention or Willingness to Communicate. This idea has been advanced at both the trait and state level (see MacIntyre, Babin, & Clément, 1999) to account for both enduring patterns of reactions as well as the desire to communicate with a specific person at a specific time.

Not all people communicate to the same degree as others. Some talk incessantly, some talk if an interlocutor initiates a conversation, and others will remain silent as often as possible. McCroskey and Baer (1985) employed the term "willingness to communicate" to describe an individual difference reflecting the general propensity to initiate communication when free to do so.

Founded upon Burgoon's (1976) work on unwillingness to communicate, and from McCroskey and Richmond's (1982) work on shyness, willingness to communicate (WTC) was first used to refer to L1 communication (McCroskey & Baer, 1985). Recently, WTC has been extended to L2 communication situations (Baker & MacIntyre, 2000; MacIntyre & Charos, 1996; MacIntyre et al., 1998). Willingness to communicate is a situation specific conception similar to Ajzen and Fishbein's (1980) concept of behavioural intentions.

The WTC scale is based upon the assumption that WTC is a personality-based, trait-like predisposition that is consistent across situations and types of receivers (McCroskey & Richmond, 1991). The WTC scale (McCroskey, 1992) has four communication contexts: public speaking, talking in meetings, talking in small groups, and talking in dyads. Each of these is applied to three types of receivers (strangers, acquaintances, and friends) yielding a total of 12 items.

The two most immediate influences on WTC are communication competence and communication apprehension. Self-perceived communication competence tends to be highly correlated with willingness to communicate (McCroskey & McCroskey, 1988). Communication competence represents an adequate ability to pass along or give information, through a verbal or written medium (McCroskey, 1984). In this study, a self-reported construct of perceived competence is used, because perceived competence may play a more significant role in WTC than does actual competence. McCroskey and McCroskey (1988) developed the Self-Perceived Communication Competence Scale (SPCC) using the same basic 12-item structure as employed for the WTC scale described above.

The second key antecedent of WTC is communication apprehension. Communication apprehension is defined as the level of fear associated with real or anticipated communicative outcomes with another person or group of people (McCroskey, 1984). In the present study, the Personal Report of Communication Apprehension (PRCA–24B; McCroskey, 1986) was used. Communication apprehension is consistently one of the best predictors of willingness to communicate and may also play a role in the motivation towards using a language (see Gardner, Day, & MacIntyre, 1992; MacIntyre & Charos, 1996). Communication apprehension can have a substantial, negative impact on communication competence (Rubin, 1990). Apprehensive speakers recall less information and have more negative, task irrelevant thoughts (Ayres, 1992), a point also made by Kuhl (1994b).

THE PRESENT STUDY

The present study was designed to examine the four models described above with specific reference to a language course. Gardner's socio-educational model (1985) was designed to apply to language learning contexts. The other three sets of variables have been studied in other contexts but can easily be applied to language learning. The central question is to what degree do the concepts represented in these four conceptual frameworks overlap? To address the research question, the various scales all will be administered to a group of language learners and the data subjected to factor analysis.

METHOD

PARTICIPANTS

One hundred and fifty-three high school students participated in the study. There were 44 males and 77 females (32 did not indicate their gender). The ages of the subjects ranged from 14 years to 19 years (32 did not indicate their age) and the average age was 16.6 years. All students spoke English as their first language and had between 4 and 15 years experience studying French (Mean=7.8 years).

MATERIALS

Materials in this experiment consisted of a questionnaire that included four different batteries with a total of 22 subscales. They included:

Attitude/Motivation Test Battery
(Gardner, Tremblay, & Masgoret, 1997)

Ten subscales on a 7-point Likert scale measured students' attitudes and motivation for learning French. Items were mixed at random.

1. *Attitudes toward French Canadians* $(\propto=.76)$. This scale consists of five positively and five negatively worded items. A high score indicates more positive attitudes. For example, "I would like to know more French Canadians."

2. *Attitudes toward Learning French* $(\propto=.89)$. This measure consists of five positively and five negatively worded items, with a high score indicating a positive attitude. For example, "French is really great."

3. *Desire to Learn French* $(\propto=.86)$. Five positive and five negative items comprise this measure. High scores reflect positive attitudes. For example, "I wish I were fluent in French."

4. *French Class Anxiety* $(\propto=.72)$. This measure consists of five positively and five negatively worded items. A high score represents a considerable level

of apprehension experienced when asked to speak French in the classroom. For example, "It embarrasses me to volunteer answers in our French class."

5. *French Use Anxiety* ($\propto=.76$). This measure consists of five positively and five negatively worded items. A high score reflects considerable apprehension when asked to use French. For example, "Speaking French bothers me."

6. *Interest in Foreign Languages* ($\propto=.80$). This measure consists of five positive and five negative items, with a high score indicating an interest in learning and using any L2. For example, "I really have no interest in foreign languages."

7. *Instrumental Orientation* ($\propto=.67$). This measure consists of four positively and four negatively worded items, which assess the degree to which students seek to learn French for pragmatic reasons. High scores indicate greater endorsement of instrumental reasons for learning French. For example, "Studying French is important because it will make me appear more cultured."

8. *Integrative Orientation* ($\propto=.80$). Four positively and four negatively worded items make up this measure to assess the extent to which students seek to learn French for integrative reasons such as meeting and communicating with Francophones. High scores indicate greater endorsement of integrative reasons for learning French. For example, "Studying French can be important for me because it will allow me to meet and converse with more and varied people."

9. *Motivational Intensity* ($\propto=.76$). This measure comprises five positively and five negatively worded items. A high score indicates considerable effort expended to learn French. For example, "I really work hard to learn French."

10. *Self-Confidence* ($\propto=.84$). This measure combines 11 items from the three self-confidence scales presented in Gardner et al. (1997). The first scale contains 10 positively worded items, 4 of which were used in the present study. For example, "I'm sure I could speak French well in almost any circumstances." The second scale is called "ability controlled" and contains six positively worded items, which distinguish self-confidence from achievement. Five of these items were used in the present study. For example, "Regardless of how much French I know, I feel confident about using it." The third scale is called "given ability" and contains three positively and three negatively worded items, which account for differences in self-confidence as well as differences in ability. Two positively worded items were used in the present study. For example, "I am as confident using French as other people who know as much French as I do."

Action Control Scale
(Kuhl, 1994a)

This measure consists of three subscales. Each scale consists of 12 dichotomous, forced-choice items, which describe a particular situation. The items were presented in mixed random order. The subscales include:

11. *Failure-related action orientation versus preoccupation (AOF)* *($\propto$=.69)*. The 12 items in this subscale describe situations in which thoughts concerning unpleasant experiences interfere with one's ability to change behavior. The sum of the answers ranges from 0–12. For example, "When I'm in a competition and have lost every time: (a) I can soon put losing out of my mind, (b) the thought that I lost keeps running through my mind."

12. *Decision-related action orientation versus hesitation (AOD)* *($\propto$=.74)*. The 12 items in this subscale describe difficulties associated with initiating an intended activity without referring to ruminating thoughts due to state orientation. The sum of the answers ranges form 0–12. For example, "When I know I must finish something soon: (a) I have to push myself to get started, (b) I find it easy to get it done and over with."

13. *Performance-related action orientation versus volatility (AOP)* *($\propto$=.60)*. The 12 items in this subscale describe one's ability to continue pleasant activities without a sudden shift to alternative activities. The sum of answers ranges from 0–12. For example, "When I have learned a new and interesting game: (a) I quickly get tired of it and do something else, (b) I can really get into it for a long time."

The Motivated Strategies for Learning Questionnaire (MSLQ)
(Pintrich et al., 1991)

This scale is composed of two subsections: the motivation subsection and the learning strategy subsection. Only the motivation subsection was used in the present study and it has six subscales. In each of the scales, students rate themselves on a 7-point Likert scale from 1–7 (*1*=not at all true of me; *7*=very true of me). Some items were reversed so that students could not simply read the first question and respond with the same answer to all of the questions.

14. *Value component: Intrinsic Goal Orientation* *($\propto$=.74)*. The scale has four positively worded items representing the perception of taking the language course for internal reasons, such as challenge, curiosity, and expertise. For example, "In a class like this, I prefer course material that really challenges me so I can learn new things."

15. *Value component: Extrinsic Goal Orientation* *($\propto$=.70)*. This scale consists of four items, all of which are positively worded. Items represent reasons for taking a course, including grades, rewards, and comparing their

performance to that of others. For example, "If I can, I want to get better grades in this class than most of the other students."

16. *Value component: Task Value* ($\propto=.88$). The scale consists of six positively worded items assessing how interesting or exciting the course seems to be. For example, "I am very interested in the content area of this course."

17. *Expectancy component: Control of Learning Beliefs* ($\propto=.70$). This four-item subscale refers to how much the student expects to be able to master the course, given enough effort is put into it. For example, "It is my own fault if I don't learn the material in this course."

18. *Expectancy component: Self-Efficacy for Learning and Performance* ($\propto=.89$). Eight positively worded items measure (1) the expectancy for success and (2) self-efficacy. Expectancy for success is the amount of performance the person anticipates will arise from his/her behavior. Self-Efficacy is the judgement made about one's ability to complete the course. For example, "I expect to do well in this class."

19. *Affective component: Test Anxiety* ($\propto=.66$). Academic performance is negatively related to anxiety, and the scale consists of four items. For example, "I feel my heart beating fast when I take an exam."

Communication measures

20. *Self-perceived Communication Competence* Scale (McCroskey & McCroskey, 1988) ($\propto=.91$). Twelve items assessed the average percentage of time, ranging from 0% to 100%, that students felt competent in using French to speak in 12 situations, for example, "talk in a small group of friends."

21. *Willingness to Communicate* (McCroskey & Baer, 1985) ($\propto=.97$). Twenty items assessed the average percentage of time, ranging from 0% to 100% that students would choose to communicate in French in a variety of situations, for example, "Talk in a large meeting of friends." In addition to the 12 speaking contexts noted in item number 1 above, 8 "filler" items were also included, for example, "Talk with a secretary."

22. *Language Anxiety* (McCroskey, Richmond, & McCroskey, 1987) ($\propto=.92$). Twelve items, taken from a scale assessing communication apprehension, assessed the average percentage of nervousness, ranging from 0% to 100%, that the students felt in communicating in French in 12 situations, for example, "When presenting a talk to a group of strangers."

PROCEDURE

The local school board and principal of the school were contacted and permission to conduct testing was obtained. Informed consent was obtained from the students for their voluntary, anonymous participation. Testing took approximately 45 minutes.

RESULTS

The objectives of the present study were to

- (RQ1) examine the correlations among the Gardner, Kuhl, Pintrich, and McCroskey test batteries,

- (RQ2) investigate the consistency of the proposed models in the present study with the models proposed by Gardner, Kuhl, Pintrich, and McCroskey, and

- (RQ3) test for the degree of overlap among the constructs of the test batteries using factor analysis.

Two hundred and thirty-one correlations were obtained among the 22 variables described above. The complete correlation matrices are provided in the appendix. Space does not permit a complete discussion of all theoretically or statistically significant correlations. There are some interesting correlations both within the test batteries and between them. For instance, Gardner's instrumental orientation significantly correlates with Pintrich's extrinsic goal orientation (r=.62). This is not surprising as instrumental and extrinsic orientations essentially measure one's desire to learn for pragmatic gains. It might be surprising that instrumental orientation also correlates significantly with both integrative orientation (r=.69) and intrinsic orientation (r=.47) despite the frequently cited theoretical distinctions among them. It is findings like these that lead us to further examine the relationships through factor analysis.

The second purpose of this study was to verify the consistency among the models proposed by Gardner, Kuhl, Pintrich, and McCroskey with the models proposed in the present study. Structural equation modeling allows testing of whether a hypothesized model can account for the relationships among the variables. The first causal model is from Gardner's socio-educational model. The model proposes specific correctional and causal relationships linking nine observed variables: attitudes toward French Canadians, interest in foreign languages, French class anxiety, French use anxiety, self-efficacy, desire to learn, motivational intensity, integrative orientation, and attitudes toward learning French.

The model was tested using AMOS 3.51, developed by Arbuckle (1995). For an evaluation of the fit indices reported below, see Hu and Bentler (1995). In the model, all paths were significant (t>2.0), except self-confidence to motivation (see Figure 1). The model shows excellent fit to the data. The goodness of fit index (GFI) was .900 and the adjusted goodness of fit index (AGFI) was .812. The Chi-square test was significant ($\chi^2(24)$=66.3, p<.05), but the Chi-square/degrees of freedom ratio was low (2.76). These indices indicate an adequate model. Both the Tucker-Lewis Index (TLI) and the Normed Fit Index (NFI) compare the hypothesized model's structure with the null model. The TLI (.889) and the NFI (.891) indicate a well-defined structure. In addition, the root mean square residual (RMR) (.064) was acceptable, and the RMSEA was only 0.128.

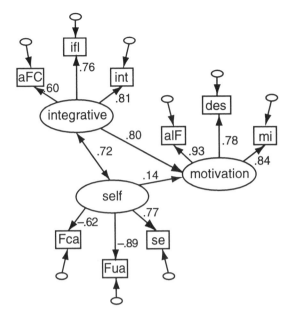

aFC = attitudes towards French Canadians
ifl = interest in foreign languages
int = integrative orientation
alF = attitudes towards learning French
des = desire to learn French
mi = motivational intensity
Fca = French class anxiety
Fua = French use anxiety
se = self-efficacy
self = self-confidence

Figure 1: Gardner's motivation model

The second model tested Kuhl's Action Control Scale (see Figure 2). The Chi-square was nonsignificant ($\chi^2(51)$=62.119, n.s.), and the Chi-square/degrees of freedom ratio (1.218) was well below 2.0, suggesting a very good model. The goodness of fit index (.929) and the adjusted goodness of fit index (.892) were quite high, as was the Normed Fit Index (.839) and the Tucker-Lewis Index (.955), all of which suggests a well defined model. The RMR (.057) and the RMSEA (.041) were also acceptable.

The third model was Pintrich's MSLQ (see Figure 3). The Chi-square was significant, ($\chi^2(237)$=817.082, p<.05), and the Chi-square/degrees of freedom (3.242) was well above 2.0, suggesting that there is variance still unaccounted for by the model. The RMR (.282) and the RMSEA (.132) support the hypothesis that there is a great deal of variance left unaccounted for by the proposed model structure. The goodness of fit index (.633), the adjusted goodness of fit index (.563), the Tucker-Lewis fit index (.576), and the Normed fit index (.526) all indicate that the model is not well defined, and substantial improvement should be made. While this model is not completely unacceptable, it is not as strong as the other models presented in the present study.

If the latent variables in the Pintrich model are allowed to correlate among themselves, then a much more acceptable solution is produced. In the revised model, the Chi-square still is significant (χ^2 (237)=440.032, p<.05), but the Chi-square/degrees of freedom drops to 1.857, which is below 2.0, suggesting a good model. The RMR (.081) and the RMSEA (.081) support the assertion that there is a little variability left unaccounted for by the present model. The goodness of fit index (.796), the adjusted goodness of fit index (.742), the Tucker-Lewis Index (.838), and the Normed Fit Index (.746) all indicate that the model is an adequate representation of the data in the correlation matrix.

Finally, McCroskey's WTC construct (see Figure 4) was analyzed using the structure proposed by MacIntyre (1990). The Chi-square was significant (χ^2(32)=49.998, p<.05), but the χ^2/df ratio was acceptable (1.56). In addition, the RMR (.035) and the RMSEA (.065) indicate that there was little variance left unaccounted for by the model. The goodness of fit index (.935), the adjusted goodness of fit (.890), the Tucker-Lewis Index (.980), and the Normed Fit Index (.962) all suggest a well-defined model.

Given evidence that each of the models, tested individually, shows adequate fit to the data, we pursued the third goal of the present study, to test for the degree of overlap among the constructs. All 22 variables were included in a principal components analysis with Kaiser normalization and oblique rotation. An application of the scree test suggested extracting three or four factors. After considering both solutions, a three-factor solution accounting for 56% of the variance in the correlation matrix was chosen.

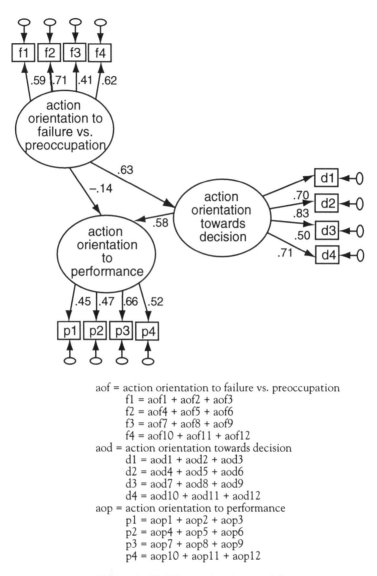

aof = action orientation to failure vs. preoccupation
    f1 = aof1 + aof2 + aof3
    f2 = aof4 + aof5 + aof6
    f3 = aof7 + aof8 + aof9
    f4 = aof10 + aof11 + aof12
aod = action orientation towards decision
    d1 = aod1 + aod2 + aod3
    d2 = aod4 + aod5 + aod6
    d3 = aod7 + aod8 + aod9
    d4 = aod10 + aod11 + aod12
aop = action orientation to performance
    p1 = aop1 + aop2 + aop3
    p2 = aop4 + aop5 + aop6
    p3 = aop7 + aop8 + aop9
    p4 = aop10 + aop11 + aop12

Figure 2: Kuhl's motivation model

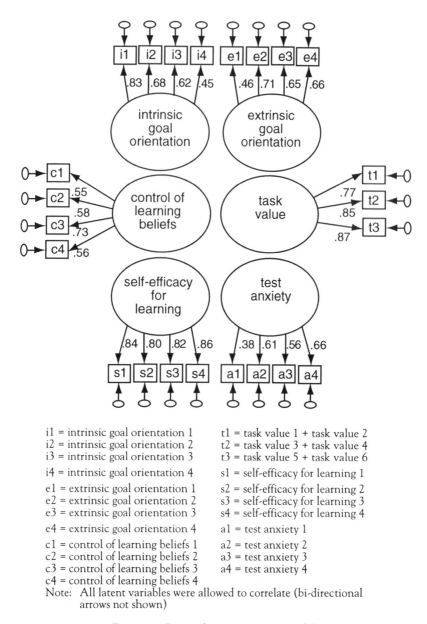

i1 = intrinsic goal orientation 1
i2 = intrinsic goal orientation 2
i3 = intrinsic goal orientation 3
i4 = intrinsic goal orientation 4

e1 = extrinsic goal orientation 1
e2 = extrinsic goal orientation 2
e3 = extrinsic goal orientation 3
e4 = extrinsic goal orientation 4

c1 = control of learning beliefs 1
c2 = control of learning beliefs 2
c3 = control of learning beliefs 3
c4 = control of learning beliefs 4

t1 = task value 1 + task value 2
t2 = task value 3 + task value 4
t3 = task value 5 + task value 6

s1 = self-efficacy for learning 1
s2 = self-efficacy for learning 2
s3 = self-efficacy for learning 3
s4 = self-efficacy for learning 4

a1 = test anxiety 1
a2 = test anxiety 2
a3 = test anxiety 3
a4 = test anxiety 4

Note: All latent variables were allowed to correlate (bi-directional arrows not shown)

Figure 3: Pintrich's motivation model

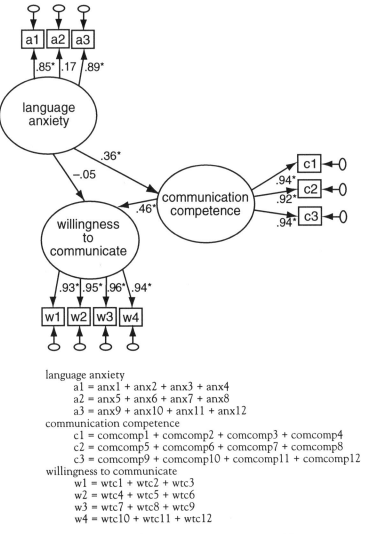

language anxiety
    a1 = anx1 + anx2 + anx3 + anx4
    a2 = anx5 + anx6 + anx7 + anx8
    a3 = anx9 + anx10 + anx11 + anx12
communication competence
    c1 = comcomp1 + comcomp2 + comcomp3 + comcomp4
    c2 = comcomp5 + comcomp6 + comcomp7 + comcomp8
    c3 = comcomp9 + comcomp10 + comcomp11 + comcomp12
willingness to communicate
    w1 = wtc1 + wtc2 + wtc3
    w2 = wtc4 + wtc5 + wtc6
    w3 = wtc7 + wtc8 + wtc9
    w4 = wtc10 + wtc11 + wtc12

Figure 4: McCroskey's communication variables

Factor one can be called *Attitudinal Motivation*. Examination of the structure matrix (see Table 1), which displays correlations between the variables and the factors, reveals that Attitudinal Motivation receives substantial (>.50) loadings from 14 variables, and significant (>.35) loadings from three variables. All of the Gardner AMTB variables load above .37 on this factor. All of the Pintrich MSLQ variables load above .59 on this factor, except for Test Anxiety. Two other variables load on this factor as well, Performance-Related Action Orientation and Willingness to Communicate. It is not surprising that attitudes towards learning and the desire to learn French both appear on this factor because of their extremely high correlation (r=.88). Nor is it surprising that motivational intensity also loads on this factor, as it has a very high correlation with attitudes towards learning (r=.79) and desire to learn (r=.71). Similarly, the correlations between task value and attitudes toward learning (r=.77) and desire to learn (r=.71) indicate that these variables converge on measuring the amount of worth placed on the second language. Task value also correlates highly with intrinsic goal orientation (r=.69). Given that the interrelations of these variables are reflected in the structure of Factor I, it is clearly related to the attitudes expressed by the respondents. For reference, the pattern matrix showing the coefficients used to construct the factor scores is presented in Table 2.

Table 1: Structure matrix

	attitudinal motivation	action motivation	self-confidence
Value	.877**	−.188	−.187
ALF	.845**	−.320	.069
Desire	.843**	−.280	−.010
Efficacy	.816**	−.221	−.244
Extrinsic	.815**	−.017	−.042
Integ	.751**	.051	−.127
Effort	.743**	−.462*	−.176
Inst	.727**	.143	−.166
Intrinsic	.722**	−.236	−.347*
Interest	.677**	−.329	.203
Confidence	.675**	−.134	−.538**
UseAnx	−.635**	.307	.568**
Control	.597**	−.006	−.118
AFC	.507**	−.219	.279
Hesitation	.196	−.680**	−.350*
Preoccupation	.193	−.618**	−.189
Competence	.105	−.605**	−.395*
Test Anxiety	.004	.557**	−.040
Volatility	.421*	−.454*	−.085
ClassAnx	−.374*	.295	.721**
LanguageAnx	.001	.270	.675**
WTC	.418*	−.377*	−.450*

Table 2: Pattern matrix

	attitudinal motivation	action motivation	self-confidence
Value	.866**	−.007	−.066
ALF	.837**	−.187	.213
Desire	.834**	−.135	.127
Efficacy	.789**	−.045	−.128
Extrinsic	.851**	.143	.054
Integ	.786**	.214	−.051
Effort	.674**	−.324	−.034
Inst	.774**	.312	−.106
Intrinsic	.675**	−.066	−.244
Interest	.674**	−.246	.334
Confidence	.623**	.059	−.460*
UseAnx	−.544**	.128	.473*
Control	.614**	.124	−.052
AFC	.526**	−.173	.378*
Hesitation	.036	−.635**	−.249
Preoccupation	.064	−.591**	−.090
Competence	−.050	−.567**	−.316
Test Anxiety	.139	.602**	−.112
Volatility	.347	−.389*	.022
ClassAnx	−.253	.144	.663**
LanguageAnx	.142	.197	.665**
WTC	.316	−.259	−.366*

*   loading>.35
**   loading>.5

key: Value   task value
ALF   attitudes toward learning French
Efficacy   self-efficacy
Extrinsic   extrinsic goal orientation
Integ   integrativeness
Effort   motivational intensity
Instr   instrumentality
Intrinsic   intrinsic goal orientation
Interest   interest in foreign languages
Confidence   self-confidence
UseAnx   french use anxiety
Control   control of learning beliefs
AFC   attitudes toward French Canadians
Hesititation failure-related action orientation
Preoccupation decision-related action orientation
Volatility   performance-related action orientation
ClassAnx   french class anxiety
LanguageAnx language anxiety
WTC   willingness to communicate

Factor II can be called *Motivated Action*. It contains substantial loadings from four variables, and significant results from three additional variables. Kuhl's test battery makes up the majority of this second factor. The negative factor loadings can be interpreted in the same way as negative correlations. The specific pattern of positive and negative loadings suggest that this particular factor is defined such that high scores indicate a lack of motivated action. This does not alter the interpretation of the factor but would affect the expected correlations involving factor scores obtained from the present analysis. Anxiety, communication competence, and WTC also load on this factor, which is not surprising because anxiety, competence, and WTC can essentially impact one's preoccupation with and decision to perform an activity like L2 communication. Also, intrinsic goal orientation was included in this factor, indicating that reasons for studying an L2 might help determine whether or not one takes action to learn the L2. The Action Motivation factor shows a surprisingly low correlation with the Attitudinal Motivation factor ($r=.197$).

Factor III can be called *Self-confidence*. It obtained four substantial loadings and four significant loadings. As with Factor II, the pattern of positive and negative loadings indicates that high scores on this factor would be indicative of low self-confidence. The highest loadings are obtained for measures of French class anxiety, communication apprehension, and French use anxiety. The factor is also defined by low ratings of self-confidence, perceived communicative competence, intrinsic goal orientation, and decision-related action. The final variable loading on this factor is Willingness to Communicate. Examining the key correlations underlying this factor, self-efficacy and self-confidence correlated at .68 suggesting that these are very similar variables that measure the beliefs one has concerning their abilities. They both involve the belief that one can control the outcome of the learning situation based upon the amount of effort expended. The self-confidence factor induces a conviction that one's ability is dependent upon the effort put into the language learning process. Thus, anxiety is a detriment to this process as it induces a state of self-doubt where uncertainty reigns supreme. However, similar to Gardner's model, this factor also contains communication competence, which creates the perception that one has the knowledge to perform in the L2. The Self-Confidence factor is relatively independent of both the Attitudinal Motivation factor ($r=.139$) and the Action Motivation factor ($r=.152$).

It is particularly interesting that WTC loads on all three factors, indicating a strong relationship with motivational processes. WTC is related to Attitudinal Motivation possibly because if a person is willing to communicate in the L2, it seems likely that she or he has a positive attitude toward it and a reason or motive for doing so. WTC can also be related to the Action Motivation factor as it involves a conscious decision to embark on a particular course of action. Finally, WTC can help to increase Self-confidence by increasing frequency of communication, which would allow an individual to be in more L2 communication situations where they could improve their L2 communication skills. With less novel L2 situations, the individual is likely to feel more competent when communicating.

DISCUSSION

The major purpose of this study (RQ3) was to examine the degree of overlap among four sets of variables. The three motivation models, as well as the communication variables, all are likely to be relevant to the language learning process. Clearly, the present data shows that there is substantial overlap among the various concepts addressed by the scales employed. The 22 variables tested can be reduced to three factors that account for over half of the variance in the correlations among the original variables.

The first factor accounts for the majority of the variables tested. Gardner's Integrative Motive and Pintrich's Expectancy-Value model defined the Attitudinal Motivation factor and appear to have much in common. It might be surprising that there is such a high degree of overlap, but it should be noted that the Gardner model has always covered a great deal of conceptual ground. Perhaps it is not surprising that the value students place on a language course and their expectancies for success in that course would be reflected in the same factor. Whereas the concepts clearly can be distinguished theoretically, the degree of empirical similarity is quite high in this sample. It remains an empirical question whether similar results would be obtained in different socio-cultural or educational environments.

The highest loadings on Attitudinal Motivation come from task value, attitudes toward learning French, and desire to learn French. These variables share the theme of seeing value in learning the language. Four of the orientation scales, representing goals for language learning, also load highly on this factor. The integrative and instrumental orientations load together on Attitudinal Motivation and are accompanied by both intrinsic and extrinsic goal orientations. It might be expected that integrative and intrinsic orientations should be closely related, both referring to the inherent usefulness of language learning for its own sake. Likewise, one might expect that instrumental and extrinsic orientations would load together because both emphasize the pragmatic gains from language learning. Furthermore, it might be assumed that all four orientations loading together on one factor would be anomalous or counter-intuitive. However, there is no theoretical reason to require that the variables will be uncorrelated despite the fact that they are conceptually distinct. Indeed, it is easy to imagine students who value the target language for both its communication and pragmatic gains and students who value neither. Prior research has shown that integrative and instrumental orientations correlate with each other in several samples (Gardner & MacIntyre, 1993; Gardner, Tremblay, &Masgoret, 1997). The correlations reported for the present study show that these orientations can be highly correlated.

As Gardner (1996) has noted, the correlations among the integrative, instrumental, intrinsic, and extrinsic orientations must not be mistaken for related concepts applied to motivation. By definition, motivation implies taking effortful action to achieve a goal (Gardner, 1985). In the present study, self-reported Action Motivation processes can be distinguished from the goals and attitudes themselves, as represented by Attitudinal Motivation. The Action Motivation factor includes scales tapping into the "energized" behavior typically associated with the motivated student (see also Crookes & Schmidt, 1991). Kuhl's (1994b) action control measures load together on Action Motivation; the strongest loading is for the Decision-related Action versus Hesitation scale. This is the measure most clearly associated with the initiation of behavior, or "crossing the rubicon" of action as Dörnyei and Ottó (1998) describe it. The rumination and volatility measures that complete the action control cluster load on this factor as well.

The separation of factors one and two raises an interesting question about their relative predictive validity. It is possible to assess language performance using a variety of measures, ranging from broad-based indices such as course grades to specific tests of learning or communication performance in a highly restricted area. The Gardner (1985) socio-educational model has been found to account for a significant amount of variance in several types of measures (e.g., Gardner & MacIntyre, 1993). The extent to which the Action Motivation factor might also predict cumulative and/or circumscribed indices of performance is an empirical question. Future research might employ measures of Action Motivation in predicting student participation in specific language activities, such as in an excursion program or initiating an assignment. The cumulative effects of the motivation to participate in such activities throughout a language course or program could also be assessed, and indeed might be fairly strong.

The largest loadings on the third factor, Self-Confidence, are for French class anxiety, communication apprehension, and French use anxiety. The self-confidence scale (Gardner, Tremblay, & Masgoret, 1997), self-efficacy and communication competence also load on Self-Confidence yielding the combination of anxiety and perceived competence that Clément (1986) describes. The hesitation measure and intrinsic goal orientations support this clustering of variables. It is interesting that hesitation, rather than rumination or volatility, appears on this factor. This might give some insight into the nature of language anxiety among the students in the present study. Language anxiety has been assumed to be based on previous experiences with poor performance. However, past failure might not be the primary support for the negative effect of anxiety among students at this level, but rather an inability to do what is necessary to engage with the language. Presumably students would have enough previous experience to have both success and failure experiences to contemplate. For these students, language anxiety might be manifest in procrastination over assignments, putting-off communication opportunities, and general dilly-dallying. According to the action control model (Kuhl, 1994a, 1994b), a student's personality might predispose him or her to the tendency to hesitate, and this might be associated with the development of language anxiety. The approach teachers might take to this variety of anxiety might be very different from that approach taken to ameliorate anxiety emanating from sources such as negative experiences. This suggestion is speculative at this point, and future research into language anxiety would be required to assess its applicability.

The other two research questions (RQ1 and RQ2) were addressed prior to examining the principal components analysis. Clearly, there are several interesting correlations among the scales reported in the appendix, some of which were pointed out in examining the factors that were extracted. Each of the four sets of variables, taken individually, showed the expected structure. The only exception was the model based on the Pintrich et al. (1991) variables. It should be noted that the Pintrich et al. (1991) manual reports fit indices similar to those obtained in the present sample. Making the relatively minor adjustment of allowing the latent variables to correlate with each other brought the structural fit indices to acceptable levels.

In summary, the finding that Attitudinal Motivation and Action Motivation might be separate, relatively uncorrelated factors suggests several potentially interesting avenues for future research. The results of the present study clearly demonstrate the necessity of doing empirical research to test theoretical distinctions and hypothesized relations because simply adding new conceptual terms, without mapping out new conceptual territory, seems like a wasteful exercise. It would seem that motivational variables in second language learning are still a vibrant area of research.

REFERENCES

Ajzen, I., & Fishbein, M. (1980). *Understanding attitudes and predicting social behavior.* Englewood Cliffs, NJ: Prentice Hall.

Arbuckle, J. L. (1995). *Amos user's guide.* Chicago: Smallwaters Corporation.

Au, S. Y. (1988). A critical appraisal of Gardner's socio-psychological theory of second-language (L2) learning. *Language Learning, 38,* 75–100.

Ayres, J. (1992). An examination of the impact of anticipated communication and communication apprehension on negative thinking, task irrelevant thinking, and recall. *Communication Research Reports, 9,* 3–11.

Baker, S. C., & MacIntyre, P. D. (2000). Effects of gender and immersion on communication and second language orientations. *Language Learning, 50,* 311–341.

Burgoon, J. K. (1976). The unwillingness-to-communicate scale: Development and validation. *Communication Monographs, 43,* 60–69.

Carroll, J. B., & Sapon, S. M. (1959). *Modern Language Aptitude Test (MLAT).* New York: Psychological Corporation.

Chapelle, C., & Greene, P. (1992). Field independence/dependence in second language acquisition research. *Language Learning, 42,* 47–83.

Clément, R. (1980). Ethnicity, contact and communicative competence in a second language. In H. Giles, W. P. Robinson, & P. Smith (Eds.), *Language: Social psychological perspectives* (pp. 147–154). Oxford, UK: Pergamon Press.

Clément, R. (1986). Second language proficiency and acculturation: An investigation of the effects of language status and individual characteristics. *Journal of Language and Social Psychology, 5,* 271–290.

Clément, R., & Gardner, R. C. (in press). Second language mastery. In H. Giles & W. P. Robinson (Eds.), *Handbook of language and social psychology* (2nd edition). London: Wiley.

Crookes, G., & Schmidt, R. W. (1991). Motivation: Reopening the research agenda. *Language Learning, 41*, 469–512.

Dörnyei, Z. (1990). Conceptualizing motivation in foreign-language learning. *Language Learning, 40*, 45–78.

Dörnyei, Z. (1994).Understanding L2 motivation: On with the challenge! *Modern Language Journal, 78*, 515–523.

Dörnyei, Z. (1998). Motivation in second and foreign language learning. *Language Teaching, 31*, 117–135.

Dörnyei, Z., & Ottó, I. (1998). Motivation in action: A process of L2 motivation. *Working Papers in Applied Linguistics* (Thames Valley University, London), *4*, 43–69.

Gardner, R. C., (1985). *Social psychology and second language learning: The role of attitudes and motivation*. London: Edward Arnold.

Gardner, R. C. (1996). Motivation and second language acquisition: Perspectives. *Journal of CAAL, 18*, 19–42.

Gardner, R. C., Day, B., & MacIntyre, P. D. (1992). Integrative motivation, induced anxiety, and language learning in a controlled environment. *Studies in Second Language Acquisition, 14*, 197–214.

Gardner, R. C., Lalonde, R. N., & Moorcroft, R. (1985). The role of attitudes and motivation in second language learning: Correlational and experimental considerations. *Language Learning, 35*, 207–227.

Gardner, R. C., & Lambert, W. E. (1959). Motivational variables in second language acquisition. *Canadian Journal of Psychology, 13*, 266–272.

Gardner, R. C., & MacIntyre, P. D. (1993). On the measurement of affective variables in second language learning. *Language Learning, 43*, 157–194.

Gardner, R. C., & Tremblay, P. F. (1994). On motivation, research agendas, and theoretical frameworks. *Modern Language Journal, 78*, 359–368.

Gardner, R. C., Tremblay, P. F., & Masgoret, A. M. (1997). Towards a full model of second language learning: An empirical investigation. *Modern Language Journal, 81*, 344–362.

Horwitz, E. K., Horwitz, M. B., & Cope, J. (1986). Foreign language classroom anxiety. *Modern Language Journal, 70*, 125–132.

Hu, L., & Bentler, P. M. (1995). Evaluating model fit. In R. H. Hoyle (Ed.), *Structural equation modelling: Concepts, issues, and applications* (pp. 76–99). Thousand Oaks, CA: Sage Publications.

Kuhl, J. (1994a). A theory of action and state orientations. In J. Kuhl & J. Beckmann (Eds.), *Volition and personality* (pp. 9–46). Gottingen: Hogrefe & Huber Publishers.

Kuhl, J. (1994b). Action vs. state orientation: Psychometric properties of the Action Control Scale (ACS–90). In J. Kuhl & J. Beckmann (Eds.), *Volition and personality* (pp. 47–59). Göttingen, Germany: Hogrefe & Huber Publishers.

Leibert, R. M., & Morris, L. W. (1967). Cognitive and emotional components of test anxiety: A distinction and some initial data. *Psychological Reports, 20,* 975–978.

MacIntyre, P. D. (1994). Variables underlying willingness to communicate: A causal analysis. *Communication Research Reports, 11*(2), 135–142.

MacIntyre, P. D., Babin, P. A., & Clément, R. (1999). Willingness to communicate: Antecedents and consequences. *Communication Quarterly, 47,* 215–229.

MacIntyre, P. D., & Charos, C. (1996). Personality, attitudes, and affect as predictors of second language communication. *Journal of Language and Social Psychology, 15,* 3–26.

MacIntyre, P. D., Clément, R., Dörnyei, Z., & Noels, K. A. (1998). Conceptualizing willingness to communicate in a L2: A situational model of L2 confidence and affiliation. *Modern Language Journal, 82,* 545–562.

MacIntyre, P. D., & Gardner, R. C. (1991). Methods and results in the study of anxiety in language learning: A review of the literature. *Language Learning, 41,* 85–117.

MacIntyre, P. D., & Gardner, R. C. (1994). The subtle effects of language anxiety on cognitive processing in the second language. *Language Learning, 44,* 283–305.

McCroskey, J. C., Richmond, V. P., & McCroskey, L. L. (1987). *Correlates of self-perceived communication competence.* Paper presented at the annual convention of the International Communication Association, Montreal, Canada.

McCroskey, J. C. (1984). The communication apprehension perspective. In J. A. Daly & J. C. McCroskey (Eds.), *Avoiding communication: Shyness, reticence, and communication apprehension.* Beverly Hills, CA: Sage.

McCroskey, J. C. (1986). *An introduction to rhetorical communication* (5th ed.). Englewood Cliffs, NJ: Prentice-Hall.

McCroskey, J. C. (1992). Reliability and validity of the willingness to communicate scale. *Communication Quarterly, 40,* 16–25.

McCroskey, J. C., & Baer, J. E., (1985, November). *Willingness to communicate: The construct and its measurement.* Paper presented at the meeting of the Speech Communication Association, Denver, CO.

McCroskey, J. C., & McCroskey, L. L. (1988). Self-report as an approach to measuring communication competence. *Communication Research Reports, 5,* 108–113.

McCroskey, J. C., & Richmond, V. P. (1982). Communication apprehension and shyness: Conceptual and operational distinctions. *Central States Speech Journal, 33,* 458–468.

McCroskey, J. C., & Richmond, V. P. (1991). Willingness to communicate: A cognitive perspective. In M. Booth-Butterfield (Ed.), *Communication, Cognition and anxiety* (pp. 19–37). Newbury Park, CA: Sage.

Oller, J. (1981). Research on the measurement of affective variables: Some remaining questions. In R. W. Andersen (Ed.), *New dimensions in second language acquisition research* (pp. 114–127). Rowley, MA: Newbury House.

Oxford, R. (1990). Styles, strategies, and aptitude: Connections for language learning. In T. S. Parry & C. W. Stansfield (Eds.), *Language aptitude reconsidered* (pp. 67–125). Englewood Cliffs, NJ: Prentice Hall Regents.

Oxford, R., & Shearin, J. (1994). Language learning motivation: Expanding the theoretical framework. *Modern Language Journal, 78,* 12–28.

Pintrich, P. R., Marx, R. W., & Boyle, R. A. (1993). Beyond cold conceptual change: The role of motivational beliefs and classroom contextual factors in the process of conceptual change. *Review of Educational Research, 63,* 167–199.

Pintrich, P. R., Smith, D. A., Garcia, T., & McKeachie, W. J. (1991). *A manual for the use of the Motivated Strategies for Learning Questionnaire (MSLQ).* Ann Arbor, MI: The Regents of the University of Michigan.

Reeve, J. (1992). *Understanding motivation and emotion.* Toronto: Harcourt Brace Jovanovich College Publishers.

Rubin, R. B. (1990). Communication competence. In G. M. Phillips & J. T. Woods (Eds.), *Speech communication: Essays to commemorate the 75th anniversary of the Speech Communication Association* (pp. 94–129). Carbondale, IL: Southern Illinois University Press.

Sarason, I. G. (1986). Test anxiety, worry, and cognitive interference. In R. Schwarzer (Ed.), *Self-regulated cognition in anxiety and motivation* (pp. 19–34). Hillsdale, NJ: Erlbaum.

Schacter, D. L. (1987). Implicit memory: History and current status. *Journal of Experimental Psychology: Learning, Memory, and Cognition, 14,* 501–518.

Spolsky, B. (1989). *Conditions for second language learning.* Toronto, Ontario: Oxford University Press.

Tolman, E. C. (1959). Principles of purposeful behavior. In S. Koch (Ed.), *Psychology: A study of a science, Vol. 2* (pp. 92–157). New York: McGraw-Hill.

Young, D. J. (1986). The relationship between anxiety and foreign language oral proficiency ratings. *Foreign Language Annals, 19,* 439–445.

Correlations between Kuhl's and Gardner's variables

	Preocc	Hesit	Volat	AFC	ALF	Desire	ClassAnx	UseAnx	Interest	Inst	Integ	Effort	Conf
Preocc	1.00												
Hesit	.444**	1.00											
Volat	.175	.261*	1.00										
AFC	.266**	.248*	.052	1.00									
ALF	.212*	.190	.326**	.459**	1.00								
Desire	.133	.167	.367**	.394**	.880**	1.00							
ClassAnx	-.318**	-.314**	-.134	-.085	-.288*	-.257*	1.00						
UseAnx	-.285**	-.350**	-.296**	-.220*	-.563**	-.601**	.574**	1.00					
Interest	.219*	.177	.313**	.476**	.631**	.672**	-.601**	-.081	1.00				
Inst	.148	.134	.164	.251*	.524**	.558**	-.177	-.498**	.497**	1.00			
Integ	.185	.194	.160	.460**	.605**	.601**	-.231*	-.512**	.523**	.693**	1.00		
Effort	.303**	.360**	.326**	.391**	.790**	.712**	-.327*	-.537**	.485**	.459**	.524**	1.00	
Conf	.288**	.245*	.241*	.251*	.525**	.512**	-.446**	-.563**	.390**	.515**	.558**	.554**	1.00

*   significant at 0.05 level (2 tailed)
**   significant at 0.01 level (2 tailed)
$N = 110$, pairwise deletion

key:
Preocc	failure-related action orientation
Hesit	decision-related action orientation
Volat	performance-related action orientation
AFC	attitudes toward French Canadians
ALF	attitudes toward learning French
Desire	desire to learn French
ClassAnx	French class anxiety
UseAnx	French use anxiety
Interest	interest in foreign languages
Inst	instrumentality
Integ	integrativeness
Effort	motivational intensity
Conf	self-confidence

Correlations between Pintrich's and Gardner's variables

	Intrins	Extrins	Value	Control	Efficacy	TAnx	AFC	ALF	Desire	ClassAnx	UseAnx	Interest	Inst	Intg	Effort	Conf
Intrins	1.00															
Extrins	.615**	1.00														
Value	.691**	.623**	1.00													
Control	.528**	.526**	.596**	1.00												
Efficacy	.652**	.659**	.741**	.521**	1.00											
TAnx	.046	.080	.006	-.054	-.154	1.00										
AFC	.369*	.317**	.239*	.392**	.654**	.073	1.00									
ALF	.551**	.627**	.414**	.659**	.659**	-.043	.537**	1.00								
Desire	.545**	.656**	.773**	.340**	.708**	.002	.465**	.877**	1.00							
ClassAnx	-.297**	-.180	-.155	-.422**	-.525**	.169	-.104	-.241**	-.252*	1.00						
UseAnx	-.549**	-.352**	-.262**	-.525**	-.422**	.105	-.205*	-.499**	-.601	.549**	1.00					
Interest	.414**	.566**	.536**	.476**	.553**	-.062	.493**	.643**	.667**	.048	-.446**	1.00				
Inst	.472**	.622**	.621**	.418**	.589**	.151	.334**	.526**	.551**	-.147	-.483**	.500*	1.00			
Integ	.536**	.563**	.647**	.346**	.605**	.126	.511**	.612**	.617**	-.217*	-.489**	.523**	.692**	1.00		
Effort	.524**	.507**	.655**	.356**	.677**	-.118	.458**	.760**	.685**	-.331**	-.521**	.470**	.443**	.502**	1.00	
Conf	.600**	.444**	.624**	.445**	.624**	-.025	.252*	.525**	.523**	-.419**	-.635**	.400**	.525	.554	.498	1.00

* significant at 0.05 level (2 tailed)
** significant at 0.01 level (2 tailed)
N = 110, pairwise deletion

key:
Preocc	failure-related action orientation
Intrins	intrinsic goal orientation
Extrins	extrinsic goal orientation
Value	task value
Control	control for learning beliefs
Efficacy	self-efficacy
TAnx	test anxiety
AFC	attitudes toward French Canadians
ALF	attitudes toward learning French
Desire	desire to learn French
ClassAnx	French class anxiety
UseAnx	French use anxiety
Inst	instrumentality
Integ	integrativeness
Effort	motivational Intensity
Conf	self-confidence

Correlations between Kuhl's and Pintrich's variables

	Preocc	Hesit	Volat	Intrins	Extrins	Value	Control	Efficacy	TAnx
Preocc	1.00								
Hesit	.447**	1.00							
Volat	.239*	.348**	1.00						
Intrins	.201*	.384**	.344**	1.00					
Extrins	-.052	.129	.303**	.594**	1.00				
Value	.187*	.257**	.308**	.693**	.637**	1.00			
Control	-.007	.024	.154	.483**	.504**	.548**	1.00		
Efficacy	.157	.286**	.348**	.676**	.648**	.722**	.537**	1.00	
TAnx	-.286**	-.277**	-.111	.072	.143	.074	.002	-.080	1.00

*	significant at 0.05 level
**	significant at 0.01 level
key: Preocc	failure-related action orientation
Hesit	decision-related action orientation
Volat	performance-related action orientation
Desire	desire to learn French
Intrins	intrinsic goal orientation
Extrins	extrinsic goal orientation
Value	task value
Control	control for learning beliefs
Efficacy	self-efficacy
TAnx	test anxiety

Correlations between McCroskey's and other scales

	WTC	COMPETENCE	ANXIETY
COMPETENCE	.555**	1.000	−.324**
WTC	1.00	.555**	−.190*
Hesit	.222*	.291**	−.222*
Preocc	.287**	.312**	−.299**
Volat	.158	.169	−.191*
ALF	.292**	.164	−.087
Desire	.281**	.169	−.105
ClassAnx	−.287**	−.182*	.296**
UseAnx	−.308**	−.203*	.306**
Interest	.276**	.193*	−.105
Instr	.194	.052	−.181*
Integr	.352**	.072	−.131
Effort	.371**	.199*	−.205*
Intrinsic	.297**	.184*	−.231*
Extrinsic	.174*	.124	−.054
Value	.316**	.196*	−.142
Control	.283**	.079	.089
Efficacy	.316**	.159	−.195*
TestAnx	−.039	−.129	.076

*	significant at 0.05 level	
**	significant at 0.01 level	
key:	Hesit	Action Orientation to Failure vs. Hesitation
	Preocc	Action Orientation for Decision vs. Preoccupation
	Volat	Action Orientation toward Performance vs. Volatility
	ALF	Attitudes toward Learning French
	Desire	Desire to Learn French
	ClassAnx	French Class Anxiety
	UseAnx	French Use Anxiety
	Interest	Interest in Foreign Languages
	Instr	Instrumental Orientation
	Integr	Integrativeness
	Effort	Motivational Intensity
	Intrinsic	Intrinsic Goal Orientation
	Extrinsic	Extrinsic Goal Orientation
	Value	Task Value
	Control	Control for Learning Beliefs
	Efficacy	Self-Efficacy
	TestAnx	Test Anxiety

ABOUT THE CONTIBUTORS

EDITORS

ZOLTÁN DÖRNYEI worked at Eötvös University, Budapest, where he was director of studies of the interdepartmental PhD programme in language pedagogy, before moving to the UK in 1998. Currently he is the Co-Director of the Centre for Research in Applied Linguistics within the School of English Studies at Nottingham University. He has published widely on various psychological aspects of second language acquisition; his most recent books include *Interpersonal Dynamics in Second Language Education* (with M. Ehrman; Sage, 1998) and *Teaching and Researching Motivation* (Longman, 2001).
E-mail: zoltan.dornyei@nottingham.ac.uk

RICHARD SCHMIDT is a professor in the Department of Second Language Studies (formerly English as a Second Language) at the University of Hawai'i at Mānoa, where he teaches in the MA program in ESL and the doctoral program in second language acquisition. He is also director of the National Foreign Language Resource Center at the University of Hawai'i. His academic interests are in the cognitive and social aspects of second and foreign language learning, including motivation.
E-mail: schmidt@hawaii.edu

AUTHORS

SAFIYA AL-BAHARNA is an English language teaching curriculum specialist with the Ministry of Education in Bahrain. She has been involved in teaching English as a foreign language and teacher education for a number of years. Safiya is currently studying for a Doctor of Education degree at the University of Exeter.

SUSAN C. BAKER graduated from Université Sainte-Anne in 1997 with a Baccalauréat ès Art français (BA French) and from the University College of Cape Breton in 1999 with a BA Honors Psychology degree. She is currently pursuing her doctoral studies at the University of Ottawa.

MERCÈ BERNAUS earned a first university degree in romance languages and defended her PhD in 1992 on "The Role of Motivation in the Learning of English as a Foreign Language." She has worked in the fields of education and foreign language teaching since 1968, teaching at the primary and secondary levels at well as at the Universitat Autònoma de Barcelona. She also worked for 13 years at the Ministry of Education of the Autonomous Government of Catalonia (Spain). Her main interest is the role of attitudes and motivation in the learning of foreign languages, about which she has written a number of articles.
E-mail: Merce.Bernaus@uab.es

DEENA BORAIE has a BS in solid state science and an MA in TEFL from the American University in Cairo. She has been the coordinator for testing and research in the Center for Adult and Continuing Education (CACE), the American University in Cairo, and is now head of the assessment unit of the CACE. She is a teacher trainer for the Royal Society of Arts certificate for overseas teachers and frequently conducts teacher training workshops in Egypt and Saudi Arabia. She has been involved in motivation research for the last 5 years.
E-mail: dboraie@aucegypt.edu

JAMES DEAN ("JD") BROWN, professor on the graduate faculty of the Department of Second Language Studies at the University of Hawai'i at Mānoa, has published numerous articles on language testing and curriculum development, as well as several books on reading statistical language studies (Cambridge University Press); language curriculum (Heinle & Heinle); language testing (Prentice-Hall; Japanese translation by Wada, Taishukan Shoten publishers); language testing in Japan (edited with S. Yamashita for the Japanese Association of Language Teachers); testing pragmatics (two books with T. Hudson and E. Detmer, technical reports number 2 and 7 in this series), two with J. M. Norris and T. Hudson on performance testing (technical reports number 18 and 22 in this series); and an edited collection of ideas for classroom testing (published by TESOL).
E-mail: brownj@hawaii.edu

ROBERT L. BURDEN is Professor of Applied Educational Psychology and Head of the School of Education at the University of Exeter. He has been a teacher educator for the past 30 years and is the author of numerous articles in the area of educational and school psychology, as well as the co-author of several publications with Marion Williams on the application of psychological research and theory to language teaching. He is a former president of the International School Psychology Association.
E-mail: R.L.Burden@exeter.ac.uk

RICHARD CLÉMENT is a professor of psychology at the University of Ottawa, Canada. His research interests cut across the fields of social psychology, cross-cultural psychology, education, and communication. They include issues related to the acquisition and use of second languages, inter-ethnic relations and communication, and the relevance of these for the adaptation of refugees and immigrants. He has been invited as a visiting scholar in French, British, and American universities and currently sits on the editorial boards of many journals. He is a fellow of the Canadian Psychological Association and his work has been recognized more recently by the Modern Language Association.
E-mail: rclement@uottawa.ca

MARIA ISABEL AZEVEDO CUNHA teaches English as a foreign language to students of the laboratory school of the Federal University of Rio de Janeiro (UFRJ).

She also coordinates a project for teachers and learners working with exploratory practice.
E-mail: belcunha@amcham.com.br

SMADAR DONITSA-SCHMIDT is a lecturer at the language education program at Tel-Aviv University School of Education. Her research interests include language maintenance and shift among immigrants, ethnolinguistic identities of minorities, attitudes, and stereotypes towards languages in multilingual societies.
E-mail: smadar@post.tau.ac.il

SYLVIA DE FATIMA NAGEM FROTA is Professor of English as a Foreign Language and Applied Linguistics at the Federal University of Rio de Janeiro. She has been specifically teaching second language acquisition theory and English language for the last 20 years. She is co-author (with Richard Schmidt) of the article "Developing Basic Conversational Ability in a Second Language: A case study of an adult learner of Portuguese" (1986, in R. R. Day, Ed., *Talking to Learn: Conversation in second language acquisition,* Newbury House) and has also published several article on teaching methodologies. She is currently writing a doctoral dissertation on advertising discourse, carrying out a comparative gender study of ads in American and Brazilian magazines.
E-mail: frota@plugue.com.br

ROBERT C. GARDNER obtained his PhD from McGill University in 1960, and joined the University of Western Ontario in 1961, where he is now Professor Emeritus in the Department of Psychology. He has published 150 articles on second language acquisition, ethnic stereotypes, language behaviour, and statistics. In addition, he is the author of two books (one on second language acquisition, and the other on statistical analysis), co-author of another (on second language acquisition), and co-editor of another (on ethnic relations). He has served as editor of the *Canadian Journal of Behavioural Science,* and is a Fellow of the Canadian Psychological Association. In 1999, he received the Canadian Psychological Association award for Distinguished Contributions to Education and Training.
E-mail: gardner@julian.uwo.ca

OFRA INBAR is a lecturer on language education at Tel-Aviv University and Beit Berl Teachers' College where she chairs the English Department. Her research interests include language policy and language assessment issues. She is also involved in the writing and implementation of a new national curriculum for English teaching in Israel.
E-mail: ofra_in@netvision.net.il

STEPHEN R. JACQUES is a faculty member in the Department of Second Language Studies (formerly English as a Second Language) at the University of Hawai'i at Mānoa where he received his MA in ESL. He currently teaches language skills to international and immigrant students in the university's English Language

Institute and as Assistant Undergraduate Program Director he advises undergraduate students and teaches upper division teacher training courses. He also coordinates a volunteer tutoring program, frequently presents workshops on professional development, and maintains a research interest in motivation and learner preferences.
E-mail: jacques@hawaii.edu

KYÖSTI JULKUNEN (MA, University of Helsinki; PhD, University of Joensuu) is Docent in Language Pedagogy at the University of Joensuu, Finland. His research interests include foreign language learning motivation, learning strategies, the teaching of content through foreign languages, and teacher education.
E-mail: kyosti.julkunen@joensuu.fi

OMNEYA-KARIMA FAYEK KASSABGY has been interested in the topic of foreign language motivation since she wrote her MA thesis in TEFL at the American University in Cairo in 1976 on attitudes and motivation in foreign language learning. She is currently executive vice president of the Career Development Center (CDC), Cairo, where she is responsible for coordinating the educational development division of the center, marketing programs locally and abroad, organizing conferences and seminars, training teachers, and designing a variety of teacher development activities. She is also President of EgypTESOL.
E-mail: cdc@gega.net

KIMI KONDO-BROWN is an assistant professor of Japanese at the University of Hawai'i at Mānoa. She earned an EdD from the University of Hawai'i in 1998. She has published articles on bilingualism and bilingual education, heritage language learning, and second language acquisition of Japanese. She has also conducted research on Japanese language curriculum development. Her current research interests are Japanese language testing and program evaluation.
E-mail: kondo@hawaii.edu

MARY MCGROARTY, Professor of Applied Linguistics in the English Department at Northern Arizona University, Flagstaff, teaches courses in sociolinguistics, language pedagogy, policy, and assessment, the areas of her principal research efforts. She has also been a faculty member at the University of California, Los Angeles. Publications include articles in *Applied Linguistics*, *Bilingual Review*, *Language Learning*, *TESOL Quarterly*, and several anthologies. President of the American Association for Applied Linguistics in 1997–98, she has served on the editorial boards of *Applied Linguistics*, *Second Language Instruction/Acquisition Abstracts*, and *TESOL Quarterly*, and is current editor of the *Annual Review of Applied Linguistics*.
E-mail: Mary.McGroarty@NAU.EDU

PETER D. MACINTYRE is currently an associate professor of psychology at the University College of Cape Breton in Sydney, Nova Scotia, Canada. Peter received his undergraduate degree from that institution before attending the

University of Western Ontario where he received his PhD in 1992. From 1992–1994 he held a position as a post doctoral research fellow at the University of Ottawa. In 1999, Peter received the UCCB alumni award for teaching excellence.

E-mail: pmacinty@uccb.ns.ca

KEITH MACMASTER graduated from the University College of Cape Breton with his Bachelor's of Science (Distinction) degree in psychology in May 2000. Keith is now pursuing his Bachelor of Laws degree at Dalhousie University in Halifax, Nova Scotia, Canada.

ANNE-MARIE MASGORET (MA, The University of Western Ontario) is a doctoral candidate in the psychology department at the University of Western Ontario, Canada. Her research interests include the role of attitudes and motivation in second language learning and the acculturation processes of immigrants. Recent work appears in the *Journal of Language and Social Psychology*, the *Journal of Multicultural and Multilingual Development*, and *Foreign Language Annals*.

E-mail: Amasgore@julian.uwo.ca

MARIANNE NIKOLOV teaches courses in applied linguistics at the Department of English Applied Linguistics, University of Pécs as an associate professor. Her research interests focus on learning and teaching issues, including early start foreign language programmes, motivation, classroom research, testing, and issues in teacher education and language policy. Her latest publications include two co-edited volumes on the international perspectives on young learners. Presently she is involved in a nation-wide survey of Hungarian students' performances in English and German in state education.

E-mail: nikolov@btk.jpte.hu

KIMBERLY A. NOELS (PhD, University of Ottawa) is an assistant professor in the Department of Psychology at the University of Alberta. Her research focuses on motivation for language learning and the role of communication in the process of cross-cultural adaptation. Her studies have been published in journals such as *The Modern Language Journal*, *Journal of Language and Social Psychology*, and *Language Learning*. In 1999, she was a co-recipient of the Mildenberger prize from the Modern Language Association.

E-mail: knoels@ualberta.ca

GORDON ROBSON (EdD, Temple University, Japan, 1994) is an associate professor in the English Language and Literature Department at Showa Women's University in Tokyo, Japan, where he coordinates the reading and writing program and teaches undergraduate courses in psycholinguistics and research methodology as well as graduate courses in phonology and pronunciation teaching. His current fields of interest continue to be research centering on individual learner differences, particularly personality and anxiety as well as reading strategies, in which areas he has presented and published several papers.

E-mail: robsongo@swu.ac.jp

PATRICK R. ROSENKJAR holds an MA in TESOL from San Francisco State University and an EdD in English education from Temple University. He is an assistant professor of English Education in the College of Liberal Arts of Temple University Japan in Tokyo where he teaches both graduate TESOL and undergraduate humanities courses. He established and designed a program of undergraduate EFL adjunct courses at Temple which were intended to introduce students to academic work while simultaneously building English skills. His research interests include foreign language reading and content-based EFL instruction.
E-mail: rosenkja@owls.tuj.ac.jp

JOHN H. SCHUMANN is the chair of the Department of Applied Linguistics and TESL at UCLA. His research includes the role of social and affective factors on SLA. Recently he has been working on neurobiology of learning and language. His interests also include evolutionary biology, evolutionary psychology, and the evolution of communication. He is the author of *The Neurobiology of Affect in Language* published by Blackwell.
E-mail: Schumann@humnet.ucla.edu

ELANA SHOHAMY is a professor and chair of the language education program at the Tel Aviv University School of Education, Israel. Her main research and writings are in the areas of language testing, language policy, and language acquisition. Together with Professor Bernard Spolsky, she was behind the introduction of a new multilingual policy in Israel. In the past year she completed two books — *The Languages of Israel: Policy, ideology, and practice* (with Bernard Spolsky, Multilingual Matters, 1999, and *The Power of Tests: A critical perspective of language tests* (Longman, in press).
E-mail: elana@post.tau.ac.il

ZAFAR SYED (PhD candidate, Aston University) has worked as a teacher educator for more than 10 years in Japan, Hawai'i, Canada, and the United Arab Emirates. He received his MA in ESL from the University of Hawai'i where he also served as a research assistant with the National Foreign Language Resource Center and the Center for Second Language Research. He has published in the areas of identity, instructional technology, and educational practice. His present research involves a longitudinal study of how instructional technology impacts what and how teachers teach. He is currently working as an educational consultant.
E-mail: zafar37@emirates.net.ae

PAUL F. TREMBLAY is director of test development at Research Psychologists Press. His current work involves the revision and development of personality, leadership, and motivation instruments. He received his PhD in psychological measurement in 1998 from the University of Western Ontario. He is the co-author of more than a dozen articles and book chapters mainly on SLL motivation-related issues. His research interests have focused on motivation in

SLL, academic motivation, and the assessment of individual differences.
E-mail: paul.tremblay4@sympatico.ca

EMA USHIODA is a research fellow in applied linguistics at the Centre for Language and Communication Studies, Trinity College Dublin, Ireland. Her principal research interest is the study of motivation in second/foreign language learning, with a particular focus on intrinsic motivation, motivational self-regulation, and learner autonomy, and their implications for classroom practice, learner development, and teacher development. She is also a strong advocate of longitudinal research designs and qualitative investigative approaches in the study of language learning motivation.
E-mail: eushioda@tcd.ie

YUICHI WATANABE is Assistant Professor of English at Kanda University of International Studies in Japan, where he teaches English and applied linguistics. He is also a doctorate candidate in second language acquisition at the University of Hawai'i at Mānoa. His research interests include language testing, second language acquisition, and second language reading and writing. He is the author of "Motivation, Reported Strategy Use, and Preferences for Activities in Foreign Language Classes at the University of Hawai'i at Mānoa: Reliability and validity of instruments" (NetWork #17)
http://www.lll.hawaii.edu/nflrc/NetWorks/NW17/
E-mail: yu-wata@kanda.kuis.ac.jp

MARION WILLIAMS is a reader in Applied Linguistics at the School of Education, University of Exeter, where she co-ordinates the postgraduate courses in TEFL. She has written extensively in the areas of psychology in language teaching and teacher education, and together with Bob Burden is the co-author of *Psychology for Language Teachers*, published by Cambridge University Press. Marion has been involved in language teacher education for the last 30 years in Nigeria, Hong Kong, Singapore, and UK.
E-mail: M.D.Williams@exeter.ac.uk

SLTCC
TECHNICAL REPORTS

*The Technical Reports of the Second Language Teaching and Curriculum Center
at the University of Hawai'i (SLTCC) report on ongoing curriculum projects,
provide the results of research related to second language learning and teaching,
and also include extensive related bibliographies. SLTCC Technical Reports are available
through University of Hawai'i Press.*

RESEARCH METHODS IN INTERLANGUAGE PRAGMATICS

GABRIELE KASPER
MERETE DAHL

This technical report reviews the methods of data collection employed in 39 studies of interlanguage pragmatics, defined narrowly as the investigation of nonnative speakers' comprehension and production of speech acts, and the acquisition of L2-related speech act knowledge. Data collection instruments are distinguished according to the degree to which they constrain informants' responses, and whether they tap speech act perception/comprehension or production. A main focus of discussion is the validity of different types of data, in particular their adequacy to approximate authentic performance of linguistic action. 51 pp.

(SLTCC Technical Report #1)   ISBN 0–8248–1419–3 $10.

A FRAMEWORK FOR TESTING CROSS-CULTURAL PRAGMATICS

THOM HUDSON
EMILY DETMER
J. D. BROWN

This technical report presents a framework for developing methods that assess cross-cultural pragmatic ability. Although the framework has been designed for Japanese and American cross-cultural contrasts, it can serve as a generic approach that can be applied to other language contrasts. The focus is on the variables of social distance, relative power, and the degree of imposition within the speech acts of requests, refusals, and apologies. Evaluation of performance is based on recognition of the speech act, amount of speech, forms or formulæ used, directness, formality, and politeness. 51 pp.

(SLTCC Technical Report #2)   ISBN 0–8248–1463–0 $10.

PRAGMATICS OF JAPANESE AS NATIVE & TARGET LANGUAGE GABRIELE KASPER (Editor)	This technical report includes three contributions to the study of the pragmatics of Japanese: • A bibliography on speech act performance, discourse management, and other pragmatic and sociolinguistic features of Japanese; • A study on introspective methods in examining Japanese learners' performance of refusals; and • A longitudinal investigation of the acquisition of the particle *ne* by nonnative speakers of Japanese. 125 pp. (SLTCC Technical Report #3) ISBN 0–8248–1462–2 $10.
A BIBLIOGRAPHY OF PEDAGOGY & RESEARCH IN INTERPRETATION & TRANSLATION ETILVIA ARJONA	This technical report includes four types of bibliographic information on translation and interpretation studies: • Research efforts across disciplinary boundaries—cognitive psychology, neurolinguistics, psycholinguistics, sociolinguistics, computational linguistics, measurement, aptitude testing, language policy, decision-making, theses, dissertations; • Training information covering—program design, curriculum studies, instruction, school administration; • Instruction information detailing—course syllabi, methodology, models, available textbooks; and • Testing information about aptitude, selection, diagnostic tests. 115 pp. (SLTCC Technical Report #4) ISBN 0–8248–1572–6 $10.
PRAGMATICS OF CHINESE AS NATIVE & TARGET LANGUAGE GABRIELE KASPER (Editor)	This technical report includes six contributions to the study of the pragmatics of Mandarin Chinese: • A report of an interview study conducted with nonnative speakers of Chinese; and • Five data-based studies on the performance of different speech acts by native speakers of Mandarin—requesting, refusing, complaining, giving bad news, disagreeing, and complimenting. 312 pp. (SLTCC Technical Report #5) ISBN 0–8248–1733–8 $15.
THE ROLE OF PHONOLOGICAL CODING IN READING *KANJI* SACHIKO MATSUNAGA	In this technical report the author reports the results of a study that she conducted on phonological coding in reading *kanji* using an eye-movement monitor and draws some pedagogical implications. In addition, she reviews current literature on the different schools of thought regarding instruction in reading *kanji* and its role in the teaching of non-alphabetic written languages like Japanese. 64 pp. (SLTCC Technical Report #6) ISBN 0–8248–1734–6 $10.

DEVELOPING PROTOTYPIC MEASURES OF CROSS-CULTURAL PRAGMATICS

THOM HUDSON
EMILY DETMER
J. D. BROWN

Although the study of cross-cultural pragmatics has gained importance in applied linguistics, there are no standard forms of assessment that might make research comparable across studies and languages. The present volume describes the process through which six forms of cross-cultural assessment were developed for second language learners of English. The models may be used for second language learners of other languages. The six forms of assessment involve two forms each of indirect discourse completion tests, oral language production, and self assessment. The procedures involve the assessment of requests, apologies, and refusals. 198 pp.

(SLTCC Technical Report #7)   ISBN 0–8248–1763–X $15.

VIRTUAL CONNECTIONS: ONLINE ACTIVITIES & PROJECTS FOR NETWORKING LANGUAGE LEARNERS

MARK WARSCHAUER
(Editor)

Computer networking has created dramatic new possibilities for connecting language learners in a single classroom or across the globe. This collection of activities and projects makes use of e-mail, the World Wide Web, computer conferencing, and other forms of computer-mediated communication for the foreign and second language classroom at any level of instruction. Teachers from around the world submitted the activities compiled in this volume — activities that they have used successfully in their own classrooms. 417 pp.

(SLTCC Technical Report #8) ISBN 0–8248–1793–1 $30.

ATTENTION & AWARENESS IN FOREIGN LANGUAGE LEARNING

RICHARD SCHMIDT
(Editor)

Issues related to the role of attention and awareness in learning lie at the heart of many theoretical and practical controversies in the foreign language field. This collection of papers presents research into the learning of Spanish, Japanese, Finnish, Hawaiian, and English as a second language (with additional comments and examples from French, German, and miniature artificial languages) that bear on these crucial questions for foreign language pedagogy. 394 pp.

(SLTCC Technical Report #9) ISBN 0–8248–1794–X $20.

LINGUISTICS &
LANGUAGE TEACHING:
PROCEEDINGS
OF THE
SIXTH JOINT
LSH-HATESL
CONFERENCE

C. REVES,
C. STEELE,
C. S. P. WONG
(*Editors*)

Technical Report #10 contains 18 articles revolving around the following three topics:

- Linguistic issues—These six papers discuss various linguistics issues: ideophones, syllabic nasals, linguistic areas, computation, tonal melody classification, and *wh*-words.
- Sociolinguistics—Sociolinguistic phenomena in Swahili, signing, Hawaiian, and Japanese are discussed in four of the papers.
- Language teaching and learning—These eight papers cover prosodic modification, note taking, planning in oral production, oral testing, language policy, L2 essay organization, access to dative alternation rules, and child noun phrase structure development. 364 pp.

(SLTCC Technical Report #10) ISBN 0–8248–1851–2 $20.

LANGUAGE LEARNING
MOTIVATION:
PATHWAYS
TO THE
NEW CENTURY

REBECCA L. OXFORD
(*Editor*)

This volume chronicles a revolution in our thinking about what makes students want to learn languages and what causes them to persist in that difficult and rewarding adventure. Topics in this book include the internal structures of and external connections with foreign language motivation; exploring adult language learning motivation, self-efficacy, and anxiety; comparing the motivations and learning strategies of students of Japanese and Spanish; and enhancing the theory of language learning motivation from many psychological and social perspectives. 218 pp.

(SLTCC Technical Report #11) ISBN 0–8248–1849–0 $20.

TELECOLLABORATION
IN FOREIGN
LANGUAGE
LEARNING:
PROCEEDINGS
OF THE
HAWAI'I SYMPOSIUM

MARK WARSCHAUER
(*Editor*)

The Symposium on Local & Global Electronic Networking in Foreign Language Learning & Research, part of the National Foreign Language Resource Center's *1995 Summer Institute on Technology & the Human Factor in Foreign Language Education*, included presentations of papers and hands-on workshops conducted by Symposium participants to facilitate the sharing of resources, ideas, and information about all aspects of electronic networking for foreign language teaching and research, including electronic discussion and conferencing, international cultural exchanges, real-time communication and simulations, research and resource retrieval via the Internet, and research using networks. This collection presents a sampling of those presentations. 252 pp.

(SLTCC Technical Report #12) ISBN 0–8248–1867–9 $20.

LANGUAGE LEARNING STRATEGIES AROUND THE WORLD: CROSS-CULTURAL PERSPECTIVES

REBECCA L. OXFORD
(Editor)

Language learning strategies are the specific steps students take to improve their progress in learning a second or foreign language. Optimizing learning strategies improves language performance. This ground-breaking book presents new information about cultural influences on the use of language learning strategies. It also shows innovative ways to assess students' strategy use and remarkable techniques for helping students improve their choice of strategies, with the goal of peak language learning. 166 pp.

(SLTCC Technical Report #13) ISBN 0–8248–1910–1 $20.

SIX MEASURES OF JSL PRAGMATICS

SAYOKO OKADA YAMASHITA

This book investigates differences among tests that can be used to measure the cross-cultural pragmatic ability of English-speaking learners of Japanese. Building on the work of Hudson, Detmer, and Brown (Technical Reports #2 and #7 in this series), the author modified six test types which she used to gather data from North American learners of Japanese. She found numerous problems with the multiple-choice discourse completion test but reported that the other five tests all proved highly reliable and reasonably valid. Practical issues involved in creating and using such language tests are discussed from a variety of perspectives. 213 pp.

(SLTCC Technical Report #14) ISBN 0–8248–1914–4 $15.

NEW TRENDS & ISSUES IN TEACHING JAPANESE LANGUAGE & CULTURE

HARUKO M. COOK, KYOKO HIJIRIDA, & MILDRED TAHARA
(Editors)

In recent years, Japanese has become the fourth most commonly taught foreign language at the college level in the United States. As the number of students who study Japanese has increased, the teaching of Japanese as a foreign language has been established as an important academic field of study. This technical report includes nine contributions to the advancement of this field, encompassing the following five important issues:

- Literature and literature teaching
- Technology in the language classroom
- Orthography
- Testing
- Grammatical versus pragmatic approaches to language teaching
  164 pp.

(SLTCC Technical Report #15) ISBN 0–8248–2067–3 $20.

THE DEVELOPMENT OF A LEXICAL TONE PHONOLOGY IN AMERICAN ADULT LEARNERS OF STANDARD MANDARIN CHINESE

SYLVIA HENEL SUN

The study reported is based on an assessment of three decades of research on the SLA of Mandarin tone. It investigates whether differences in learners' tone perception and production are related to differences in the effects of certain linguistic, task, and learner factors. The learners of focus are American students of Mandarin in Beijing, China. Their performances on two perception and three production tasks are analyzed through a host of variables and methods of quantification.

(SLTCC Technical Report #16) ISBN 0–8248–2068–1 $20.

SECOND LANGUAGE DEVELOPMENT IN WRITING: MEASURES OF FLUENCY, ACCURACY, & COMPLEXITY

KATE WOLFE-QUINTERO, SHUNJI INAGAKI, & HAE-YOUNG KIM

In this book, the authors analyze and compare the ways that fluency, accuracy, grammatical complexity, and lexical complexity have been measured in studies of language development in second language writing. More than 100 developmental measures are examined, with detailed comparisons of the results across the studies that have used each measure. The authors discuss the theoretical foundations for each type of developmental measure, and they consider the relationship between developmental measures and various types of proficiency measures. They also examine criteria for determining which developmental measures are the most successful, and they suggest which measures are the most promising for continuing work on language development.

(SLTCC Technical Report #17) ISBN 0–8248–2069–X $20.

DESIGNING SECOND LANGUAGE PERFORMANCE ASSESSMENTS

JOHN M. NORRIS, JAMES DEAN BROWN, THOM HUDSON, & JIM YOSHIOKA

This technical report focuses on the decision-making potential provided by second language performance assessments. The authors first situate performance assessment within a broader discussion of alternatives in language assessment and in educational assessment in general. They then discuss issues in performance assessment design, implementation, reliability, and validity. Finally, they present a prototype framework for second language performance assessment based on the integration of theoretical underpinnings and research findings from the task-based language teaching literature, the language testing literature, and the educational measurement literature. The authors outline test and item specifications, and they present numerous examples of prototypical language tasks. They also propose a research agenda focusing on the operationalization of second language performance assessments.

(SLTCC Technical Report #18) ISBN 0–8248–2109–2 $20.

FOREIGN LANGUAGE TEACHING & MINORITY LANGUAGE EDUCATION

KATHRYN A. DAVIS
(*Editor*)

This volume seeks to examine the potential for building relationships among foreign language, bilingual, and ESL programs towards fostering bilingualism. Part I of the volume examines the sociopolitical contexts for language partnerships, including:

- obstacles to developing bilingualism
- implications of acculturation, identity, and language issues for linguistic minorities.
- the potential for developing partnerships across primary, secondary, and tertiary institutions

Part II of the volume provides research findings on the *Foreign language partnership project* designed to capitalize on the resources of immigrant students to enhance foreign language learning.

(SLTCC Technical Report #19) ISBN 0–8248–2067–3 $20.

A COMMUNICATIVE FRAMEWORK FOR INTRODUCTORY JAPANESE LANGUAGE CURRICULA

WASHINGTON STATE JAPANESE LANGUAGE CURRICULUM GUIDELINES COMMITTEE

In recent years the number of schools offering Japanese nationwide has increased dramatically. Because of the tremendous popularity of Japanese language and the shortage of teachers, quite a few untrained, non-native and native teachers are in the classrooms and are expected to teach several levels of Japanese. These guidelines are intended to assist individual teachers and professional associations throughout the United States in designing Japanese language curricula. They are meant to serve as a framework from which language teaching can be expanded and are intended to allow teachers to enhance and strengthen the quality of Japanese language instruction.

(SLTCC Technical Report #20) ISBN 0–8248–2350–8 $20.

A FOCUS ON LANGUAGE TEST DEVELOPMENT: EXPANDING THE LANGUAGE PROFICIENCY CONSTRUCT ACROSS A VARIETY OF TESTS

THOM HUDSON & JAMES DEAN BROWN
(*Editors*)

This volume presents eight research studies that introduce a variety of novel, non-traditional forms of second and foreign language assessment. To the extent possible, the studies also show the entire test development process, warts and all. These language testing projects not only demonstrate many of the types of problems that test developers run into in the real world but also afford the reader unique insights into the language test development process.

(SLTCC Technical Report #21) ISBN 0–8248–2351–6 $20.

STUDIES ON
KOREAN IN
COMMUNITY
SCHOOLS

DONG-JAE LEE
SOOKEUN CHO
MISEON LEE
MINSUN SONG
WILLIAM O'GRADY
(Editors)

The papers in this volume focus on language teaching and learning in Korean community schools.   Drawing on innovative experimental work and research in linguistics, education, and psychology, the contributors address issues of importance to teachers, administrators, and parents. Topics covered include childhood bilingualism, Korean grammar, language acquisition, children's literature, and language teaching methodology.

[in Korean]

(SLTCC Technical Report #22) ISBN 0–8248–2352–4 $20.

MOTIVATION
AND
SECOND
LANGUAGE
ACQUISITION

ZOLTÁN DÖRNYEI
RICHARD SCHMIDT
(Editors)

This volume —the second in this series concerned with motivation and foreign language learning— includes papers presented in a state-of-the-art colloquium on L2 motivation at the American Association for Applied Linguistics (Vancouver, 2000) and a number of specially commissioned studies. The 20 chapters, written by some of the best known researchers in the field, cover a wide range of theoretical and research methodological issues, and also offer empirical results (both qualitative and quantitative) concerning the learning of many different languages (Arabic, Chinese, English, Filipino, French, German, Hindi, Italian, Japanese, Russian, and Spanish) in a broad range of learning contexts (Bahrain, Brazil, Canada, Egypt, Finland, Hungary, Ireland, Israel, Japan, Spain, and the US).

(SLTCC Technical Report #23) ISBN 0–8248–2458–X $25.